BILDER EINER
FLIESSENDEN WELT

IMAGES OF
A FLOATING WORLD

Die Ausstellung steht unter der Schirmherrschaft
von Bundespräsident Frank-Walter Steinmeier.

The exhibition is under the patronage of Federal
President Frank-Walter Steinmeier.

RENOIR—MONET—GAUGUIN

BILDER EINER FLIESSENDEN WELT

Die Sammlungen von Kōjirō Matsukata
und Karl Ernst Osthaus

IMAGES OF A FLOATING WORLD

The Collections of Kōjirō Matsukata
and Karl Ernst Osthaus

Museum Folkwang

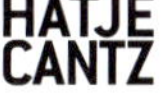

DANK | THANKS

'The founders […] will establish an association whose purpose it is, in conjunction with the city of Essen, to purchase, administer, expand the Folkwang Museum in Hagen and make it permanently usable as a public collection for the purposes of research and popular education and make it available to the population of the Rhine-Westphalian industrial region for their edification and instruction.' (Contract between the city of Essen and the founders concerning the purchase of the Museum Folkwang, 29 May 1922)

In 1902, Karl Ernst Osthaus, son of a banking and business family, opened the Museum Folkwang in his home town of Hagen. By the time of his early death in 1921, the private museum he founded had evolved into one of the leading museums in Germany. In his will, Osthaus insisted that the Folkwang collections should be preserved as a whole. To this end, an association of companies in Essen began to join forces in the same year, alongside mayor Hans Luther and the director of Kunstmuseum Essen, Ernst Gosebruch. This brought the city into competition with Hagen, Düsseldorf and Munich to bid for the opportunity to ensure the preservation of the Museum Folkwang for the Ruhr region. In spite of the difficult financial situation at the time, by March 1922 they had managed to raise the purchasing price of 15 million Marks – a sum strongly increased by inflation. The Rhenish-Westphalian Coal Syndicate alone put in 6 million Marks; its legal advisors played a considerable part in elaborating the fundamental agreement for the takeover of the Museum Folkwang, as well as the statutes of the Folkwang Museum Association, which was founded in June 1922. The syndicate's director, Albert Janus, and Mayor Luther signed the contract between the founders and the city of Essen. The Rhenish-Westphalian Electricity Works AG was also among the biggest donors from the very beginning. Its committee member, Ernst Henke, would accompany the fortunes of the Museum Folkwang until the period after the Second World War. Another of the driving forces behind the acquisition of the collection was the chemicals business run by Theo and Karl Goldschmidt, Th. Goldschmidt AG. With the endowment of their villas on Bismarckstrasse in 1917 and 1922, the brothers ensured the future location of the Museum Folkwang in Essen.

The connection between these three businesses with the Museum Folkwang remains unbroken 100 years after the transfer of the collections to Essen, and continues in the commitment of their successor institutions. For their generous support of the jubilee exhibition and 100 shared years dedicated to art and cultural education we would like to thank the RAG-Stiftung, the RWE AG and the Evonik Industries AG.

„Die Stifter […] werden einen Verein gründen, dessen Zweck es ist, gemeinsam mit der Stadt Essen das Folkwang-Museum in Hagen zu erwerben, zu verwalten, auszubauen und als öffentliche Sammlung den Zwecken der Forschung und Volksbildung dauernd nutzbar zu machen und der Bevölkerung des rheinisch-westfälischen Industriebezirks zur Erbauung und Belehrung zur Verfügung zu stellen." (Vertrag zwischen der Stadt Essen und den Stifter:innen über den Erwerb des Museum Folkwang, 29. Mai 1922)

1902 eröffnete der Bankiers- und Kaufmannssohn Karl Ernst Osthaus in seiner Heimatstadt Hagen das Museum Folkwang. Bis zum frühen Tod des Mäzens im Jahr 1921 hatte sich das Privatmuseum zu einem der führenden Häuser in der deutschen Museumslandschaft entwickelt. In seinem Testament verfügte Osthaus, dass die Folkwang-Sammlungen als Ganzes erhalten bleiben sollten. Zu diesem Zweck begann sich noch im gleichen Jahr an der Seite von Oberbürgermeister Hans Luther und dem Direktor des Kunstmuseum Essen Ernst Gosebruch ein Verbund von Unternehmen in Essen zusammenzuschließen. Die Stadt trat damit in Konkurrenz zu Hagen, Düsseldorf und München, um den Erhalt des Museum Folkwang für das Ruhrgebiet zu sichern. Trotz der schwierigen finanziellen Situation der damaligen Zeit gelang es, bis März 1922 die durch die Inflation stark angestiegene Kaufsumme von 15 Millionen Mark aufzubringen. Das Rheinisch-Westfälische Kohlen-

Syndikat stiftete allein 6 Millionen Mark; dessen Rechtsbeistände hatten maßgeblichen Anteil an der Ausarbeitung der grundlegenden Abkommen zur Übernahme des Museum Folkwang sowie der Satzung des Folkwang-Museumsvereins, der sich im Juni 1922 gründete. Syndikatsdirektor Albert Janus und Oberbürgermeister Luther unterzeichneten den Vertrag zwischen Stifter:innen und Stadt. Auch die Rheinisch-Westfälische Elektrizitätswerke AG engagierte sich von Beginn an unter den großen Spendern. Ihr Vorstandsmitglied Ernst Henke sollte die Geschicke des Museum Folkwang bis in die Zeit nach dem Zweiten Weltkrieg begleiten. Zu den treibenden Kräften beim Erwerb der Sammlung gehörte des Weiteren das von Theo und Karl Goldschmidt geführte Chemieunternehmen gleichen Namens, die Th. Goldschmidt AG. Mit der Stiftung ihrer Villen an der Bismarckstraße in den Jahren 1917 und 1922 sicherten die Brüder den zukünftigen Standort des Museum Folkwang in Essen.

Die Verbundenheit dieser drei Unternehmen mit dem Museum Folkwang ist einhundert Jahre nach der Überführung der Sammlungen nach Essen ungebrochen und setzt sich im Engagement ihrer Nachfolgeinstitutionen fort. Für die großzügige Unterstützung der Jubiläumsausstellung und hundert gemeinsame Jahre im Zeichen der Kunst und kulturellen Bildung bedanken wir uns bei der RAG-Stiftung, der RWE AG und der Evonik Industries AG.

Hauptförderer | Main Supporter

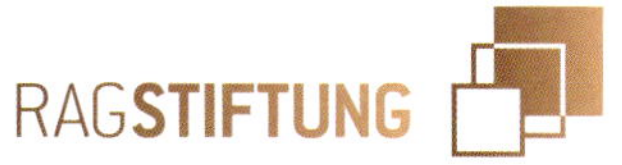

Hauptsponsoren | Main Sponsors

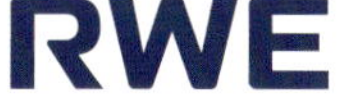

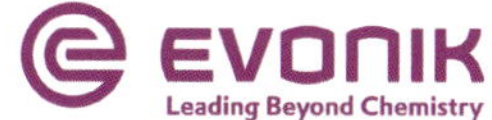

INHALT | CONTENTS

PREFACE

Peter Gorschlüter
Director of the Museum Folkwang, Essen

One hundred years ago on 29 October 1922, after Karl Ernst Osthaus's Hagen Folkwang collections had been transferred to the city of Essen, the Museum Folkwang opened its doors in its new location. In his ceremonial address as its first director in Essen, Ernst Gosebruch stressed the wish of the founders, who had previously come together to form the Folkwang Museum Association (Folkwang-Museumsverein e.V.), that the 'Folkwang in Essen might become a source of life for the citizens of our city, and beyond that for the population of our region'.[1] Apart from Theo and Karl Goldschmidt, who made their private villas available for the new museum, the outstanding former founders included the mining industry with the Rhenish-Westphalian Coal Syndicate at their head, as well as Rhenish-Westphalian Electricity Works (Rheinisch-Westfalische Elektrizitätswerke AG). Even today, a hundred years after the opening of the Museum Folkwang in Essen, they remain, with their successor companies and institutions – the RAG Foundation, RWE AG and Evonik Industries AG – important partners to us, whose generous support made the Jubilee exhibition *Renoir, Monet, Gauguin: Images of a Floating World. The Collections of Kōjirō Matsukata and Karl Ernst Osthaus* possible. In his opening speech, however, Gosebruch also emphasized the close connection with Osthaus and the support that the predecessor institution – the Kunstmuseum Essen, of which Gosebruch had previously been director – had received in many ways from the Hagen museum. 'Folkwang in Essen' was another step on the way to a museum of modern art, a new type of institution that was still much discussed in the German museum landscape at the time. The young generation of museum makers, of whom Gosebruch was one, saw the task of their institutions lay in

9

Peter Gorschlüter
Direktor des Museum Folkwang, Essen

Vor hundert Jahren, nachdem die Hagener Folkwang-Sammlungen von Karl Ernst Osthaus der Stadt Essen übergeben worden waren, öffnete das Museum Folkwang am 29. Oktober 1922 am neuen Standort seine Türen. Als dessen erster Essener Direktor betonte Ernst Gosebruch in seiner feierlichen Ansprache den Wunsch der Stifter, die sich zuvor zum Folkwang-Museumsverein e. V. zusammengeschlossen hatten, dass das „Folkwang in Essen ein Lebensbrunnen werden möchte für die Bürgerschaft unserer Stadt und darüber hinaus für die Bevölkerung unseres Bezirks".[1] Neben Theo und Karl Goldschmidt, die ihre Privatvillen für das neue Museum zur Verfügung stellten, zählten zu den herausragenden Stiftern von einst der Bergbau mit dem Rheinisch-Westfälischen Kohlen-Syndikat an seiner Spitze sowie die Rheinisch-Westfälische Elektrizitätswerke AG. Sie sind uns auch heute, hundert Jahre nach der Eröffnung des Museum Folkwang in Essen, mit ihren Nachfolgeunternehmen und -institutionen – der RAG-Stiftung, der RWE AG und der Evonik Industries AG – wichtige Partner, mit deren großzügiger Unterstützung die Jubiläumsausstellung *Renoir, Monet, Gauguin – Bilder einer fließenden Welt. Die Sammlungen von Kōjirō Matsukata und Karl Ernst Osthaus* ermöglicht wurde. Gosebruch hob in seiner Eröffnungsrede aber auch die enge Verbundenheit zu Osthaus und die Unterstützung hervor, die schon die Vorgängerinstitution – das Kunstmuseum Essen, das Gosebruch zuvor geleitet hatte – auf vielfältige Weise durch das Hagener Museum erfahren hatte. „Folkwang in Essen", das war ein weiterer Schritt auf dem Weg zu einem Museum moderner Kunst, einem neuen Typus von Institution, der in der deutschen Museumslandschaft zu jener Zeit noch diskutiert wurde. Die junge Generation von Museumsmacher:innen, zu

VORWORT

actively helping to shape the aesthetic standards of their time.[2] For them the museum was a symbol of the cultural identity of a society, both in terms of its history and its present.[3] They countered the rejection of the older generation by strategically cooperating, and thus forming a phalanx with power and influence. In addition to Osthaus in Hagen, Gosebruch also forged close contacts with progressive collectors in cities such as Berlin, Halle, Hanover, Cologne, Mannheim and Zurich; within this group the Essen art collections – first as the Kunstmuseum Essen and then as the Museum Folkwang Essen – played an active role in the establishment of the 'museum of the present' in the German-speaking world.[4]

Consequently, collaboration with similar institutions as well as the exchange with other collections at the Museum Folkwang has a long tradition, and over its hundred-year history in Essen this has found expression time and again in exhibitions. Within the field of modern art, for example, the substantial support of the newly founded Museum of Modern Art in New York for the 1931 exhibition *German Painting and Sculpture* should be mentioned, or the special exhibition devoted to the Russian collectors Morosov and Shchukin which was held in Essen in 1993. Out of this constant in the history of our museum arose the wish to collaborate with a major collection that had a comparable collecting focus and a similar genesis on the occasion of the anniversary year 2022. It made sense to focus on Impressionism and Post-Impressionism, since the Museum Folkwang has been viewed as a pioneer of modern art since the days of Karl Ernst Osthaus due to its rich holdings from these two styles. It was thanks to the kind mediation of Detmar Westhoff that our initial discussions with the National Museum of Western Art in Tokyo

quickly developed into a partnership. As one of the most important museums of modern art in Japan, since its foundation in 1959 it has preserved the core holding of the collection of the Japanese shipbuilding magnate Kōjirō Matsukata – a collection that is still not well enough known in Europe, and which was internationally unrivalled in terms of the size and quality of its holdings of French modern art at the time of its creation in the 1910s and 1920s. The exhibition history of the National Museum of Western Art, like that of the Museum Folkwang, is informed by its exchange with other institutions; its collaborative partners include such major institutions as the Barnes Foundation in Philadelphia, the National Gallery in London and the Musée d'Orsay in Paris. The Museum Folkwang now has the unique opportunity to be able to exhibit the Matsukata Collection on a larger scale in Europe for the first time since the 1950s. The building of the National Museum of Western Art in Tokyo, designed by Le Corbusier, which along with other buildings by the architect was declared a UNESCO World Heritage Site in 2016, is currently under renovation, which is why the museum's major works are able to travel. We are particularly delighted that the accord between our two collections is continuing in June 2022, when some forty masterpieces from the Folkwang Collections will enhance the exhibition celebrating the reopening of the museum in Tokyo.

The first person I should like to thank, therefore, is the acting Director of the National Museum of Western Art, Masayuki Tanaka, who has continued our joint exhibition plans after the departure of his predecessor Akiko Mabuchi with the same enthusiasm, just as the leading curator, Shinsuke Watanabe, followed on seamlessly from the commitment of his predecessor, Hiroya Murakami.

der Gosebruch zählte, sah die Aufgabe ihrer Institutionen darin, aktiv die ästhetischen Standards ihrer Zeit mitzugestalten.[2] Für sie war das Museum Symbol für die kulturelle Identität einer Gesellschaft und das sowohl in Hinblick auf deren Geschichte als auch auf deren Gegenwart.[3] Der Ablehnung der älteren Generation begegneten sie strategisch, indem sie kooperierten und so eine Phalanx mit Wirkmacht bildeten. Neben Osthaus in Hagen baute Gosebruch unter anderem enge Kontakte zu den progressiven Sammlungsleiter:innen in Berlin, Halle, Hannover, Köln, Mannheim oder Zürich auf; in diesem Verbund wirkten die Kunstsammlungen Essen – zunächst als Kunstmuseum Essen und dann als Museum Folkwang Essen – aktiv an der Etablierung des „Museum[s] der Gegenwart" im deutschsprachigen Raum mit.[4]

Die Zusammenarbeit mit vergleichbaren Institutionen sowie der Austausch mit anderen Sammlungen haben am Museum Folkwang folglich eine lange Tradition und in seiner nunmehr hundertjährigen Geschichte am Standort Essen immer wieder in Ausstellungen Niederschlag gefunden. Im Bereich der Moderne seien hier etwa die substanzielle Unterstützung des gerade gegründeten Museum of Modern Art in New York bei der Ausstellung *German Painting and Sculpture* von 1931 genannt oder die große Sonderausstellung zu den russischen Sammlern Morosow und Schtschukin, die 1993 in Essen stattfand. Aus dieser Konstante in der Geschichte unseres Museums entwickelte sich der Wunsch, anlässlich des Jubiläumsjahres 2022 mit einer bedeutenden Sammlung zu kooperieren, die einen vergleichbaren Sammlungsschwerpunkt und eine ähnliche Genese aufweist. Es lag nahe, dabei den Impressionismus und Post-Impressionismus in den Vordergrund zu stellen, da das Museum Folkwang aufgrund seiner

reichen Bestände aus diesen beiden Stilrichtungen bereits seit Karl Ernst Osthaus als Wegbereiter der Moderne rezipiert wird. Der freundlichen Vermittlung von Detmar Westhoff ist es zu verdanken, dass sich aus ersten Gesprächen mit dem National Museum of Western Art in Tokio schnell eine Partnerschaft entwickelte. Als eines der wichtigsten Museen moderner Kunst in Japan bewahrt es seit seiner Gründung im Jahr 1959 den Kernbestand der Sammlung des japanischen Schiffbauunternehmers Kōjirō Matsukata – eine in Europa noch viel zu wenig bekannte Sammlung, die zu ihrer Entstehungszeit in den 1910er- und 1920er-Jahren im Bereich der französischen Moderne in Größe und Qualität international ihresgleichen suchte. Auch die Ausstellungsgeschichte des National Museum of Western Art ist wie die des Museum Folkwang geprägt vom Austausch mit anderen Institutionen; zu den bisherigen Kooperationspartnern zählen solch bedeutende Häuser wie die Barnes Foundation in Philadelphia, die National Gallery in London oder das Musée d'Orsay in Paris. Das Museum Folkwang hat nun die einzigartige Möglichkeit, die Sammlung Matsukata erstmals seit den 1950er-Jahren wieder in größerem Umfang in Europa präsentieren zu können. Denn das von Le Corbusier entworfene Gebäude des National Museum of Western Art in Tokio, das 2016 mit weiteren Bauten des Architekten zum UNESCO-Weltkulturerbe erklärt worden ist, wird derzeit instand gesetzt, weshalb die Hauptwerke des Museums überhaupt erst auf Reisen gehen konnten. Wir freuen uns besonders, dass sich der Zusammenklang unserer beiden Sammlungen im Juni 2022 in Japan fortsetzt, wenn rund vierzig Meisterwerke aus den Folkwang-Sammlungen die Ausstellung zur Wiedereröffnung des Museums in Tokio bereichern werden.

The partnership of our two institutions would not have come about had it not been for the initiative of Detmar Westhoff. We should like to thank both him and Megumi Jingaoka, one of the most intimate connoisseurs of the Matsukata Collection, who has tirelessly accompanied both exhibition projects from the Japanese side with passion, care and an open ear to all requests.

I am also most grateful to the other lenders of the exhibition: the Musée d'Orsay in Paris, the Sumitomo Mitsui Banking Corporation and the Artizon Museum with the Ishibashi Foundation in Tokyo, the Wallraf-Richartz-Museum & Fondation Corboud in Cologne and particularly the Osthaus Museum in Hagen, with which we are connected through Osthaus's legacy. All of them made it possible to bring together works from the collections of Matsukata and Osthaus, some of which had been separated from one another for decades.

We are also very pleased that the two Japanese artists Chiharu Shiota and Tabaimo, as well as the prizewinning writer Sayaka Murata, responded to our invitation and are opening the exhibition and the catalogue up to the present with their contributions. Our warmest thanks to them and to the studio directors Julia Strebelow and Imoimo. We should not neglect to mention the kind mediation of Anvar Čukoski of Aufbau-Verlag, Julie Hottner of the König Galerie or Amie Stuart at the James Cohan Gallery.

Particular thanks to the designers of the exhibition Alicja Jelen, Clemens Müller and Antonia Gaida of the design studio please don't touch. In an extraordinary way they managed to capture not only the idea of floating on which the curatorial concept is based, and to allow visitors to experience the simultaneous contrast that distinguishes the art of Post-Impressionism amenable in spatial terms, but also to adapt the architecture to the needs of a major special exhibition.

With its wonderful layout, for which Martha Stutteregger from Vienna is responsible, the accompanying catalogue complements and extends the exhibition. This would not have been possible without the commitment of Hatje Cantz Verlag, for which we would like to express our thanks to Richard Viktor Hagemann. The authors of the catalogue, whom we also wish to thank, have opened new perspectives on the collections of Kōjirō Matsukata and Karl Ernst Osthaus in a great many ways. In terms of the rare and sometimes rather inaccessible English literature on these two patrons, this is particularly valuable, and is bound to resonate with the research community.

I would like to thank the whole team of the Museum Folkwang for having realized such a lavish project with the greatest possible commitment and insistence on quality. Every individual has enriched the project with their work. Particular credit, however, must go to the curator of the exhibition, Nadine Engel. She has set off on the trail of Osthaus and Matsukata and translated the various stages of the biographies of these collectors and their joint passion for French modern art into impressive combinations of works, hitherto unique in this form. She received considerable support from our freelance colleague Rebecca Herlemann, who not only familiarized herself with the task with great motivation and in a very short period of time, but also held all the threads together in the final phase of preparations for the exhibition. I would also like to thank Hans-Jürgen Lechtreck, Thomas Grimm and Tobias Burg, who supported Ms Herlemann during Ms Engel's parental leave from November 2021.

Mein erster Dank gilt daher dem amtierenden Direktor des National Museum of Western Art Masayuki Tanaka, der unsere gemeinsamen Ausstellungsvorhaben nach dem Ausscheiden seiner Vorgängerin Akiko Mabuchi mit gleichem Enthusiasmus fortgeführt hat, wie auch der leitende Kurator Shinsuke Watanabe nahtlos an das Engagement seines Vorgängers Hiroya Murakami anknüpfte. Die Partnerschaft unserer beiden Institutionen wäre ohne die Initiative von Detmar Westhoff nicht zustande gekommen. Ihm sei ebenso gedankt wie Megumi Jingaoka, einer der intimsten Kennerinnen der Sammlung Matsukata, die beide Ausstellungsprojekte von japanischer Seite unermüdlich mit Passion, Umsicht und einem offenen Ohr für jegliches Anliegen begleitete.

Mein großer Dank gilt darüber hinaus den weiteren Leihgeber:innen der Ausstellung: dem Musée d'Orsay in Paris, der Sumitomo Mitsui Banking Corporation sowie dem Artizon Museum mit der Ishibashi Foundation in Tokio, dem Wallraf-Richartz-Museum & Fondation Corboud in Köln und insbesondere dem Osthaus Museum in Hagen, mit dem uns das Osthaus'sche Erbe verbindet. Sie alle ermöglichten die Zusammenführung von Werken aus den Sammlungen von Matsukata und Osthaus, die zum Teil seit Jahrzehnten voneinander getrennt waren.

Begeistert sind wir darüber hinaus, dass die beiden japanischen Künstlerinnen Chiharu Shiota und Tabaimo sowie die preisgekrönte Literatin Sayaka Murata unserer Einladung gefolgt sind und mit ihren Beiträgen Ausstellung und Katalog in die Gegenwart öffnen. Ihnen und den Studioleiterinnen Julia Strebelow und Imoimo danken wir herzlich. Nicht unerwähnt soll die freundliche Vermittlungstätigkeit von Anvar Čukoski vom Aufbau-Verlag, Julie Hottner von der König Galerie sowie Amie Stuart von der James Cohan Gallery bleiben.

Ein besonderer Dank gilt den Gestalter:innen der Ausstellung Alicja Jelen, Clemens Müller und Antonia Gaida vom Büro please don't touch. Ihnen ist es auf einzigartige Weise gelungen, nicht nur die Idee des Fließens, auf der das kuratorische Konzept beruht, und den Simultankontrast, der die Kunst des Post-Impressionismus auszeichnet, räumlich erfahrbar zu machen, sondern darüber hinaus die Architektur den Bedürfnissen einer großen Sonderausstellung anzupassen.

Mit seinem wunderbaren Layout, für das Martha Stutteregger aus Wien verantwortlich zeichnet, ergänzt und erweitert der Begleitkatalog die Ausstellung. Dies wäre nicht möglich gewesen ohne das Engagement des Hatje Cantz Verlags, für das wir stellvertretend Richard Viktor Hagemann unseren Dank aussprechen. Die Autor:innen des Kataloges, denen wir ebenso herzlich danken möchten, haben mit ihren Beiträgen auf vielfältige Weise neue Perspektiven auf die Sammlungen von Kōjirō Matsukata und Karl Ernst Osthaus eröffnet. Im Hinblick auf die rare und teils schwer zugängliche englischsprachige Literatur zu den beiden Mäzenen ist dies besonders wertvoll und wird in der Forschungsgemeinschaft sicherlich Nachhall finden.

Dem gesamten Team des Museum Folkwang möchte ich dafür danken, ein derart aufwendiges Projekt mit größtem Engagement und Qualitätsanspruch umgesetzt zu haben. Jede und jeder einzelne hat das Projekt durch ihre/seine Tätigkeit bereichert. Im Besonderen aber ist es der Verdienst der Kuratorin der Ausstellung, Nadine Engel. Sie hat sich auf die Spuren von Osthaus und Matsukata begeben und die Stationen ihrer Sammlerbiografien und ihrer gemeinsamen

Our Jubilee exhibition is particularly honoured by the sponsorship of Federal President Frank-Walter Steinmeier and the support of the German Foreign Office. They are expressions of the fact that the Museum Folkwang has not only enriched the city and region – in line with the wishes of the founders at the time – but developed into an institution with a national and international standing.

1 Ernst Gosebruch, 'Folkwang in Essen. Ansprache des Museumsdirektors Gosebruch bei der Wiedereröffnung des Folkwangmuseums in Essen, [29.10.1922]' in *Die Heimat. Monatsschrift für Land, Volk und Kunst in Westfalen und am Niederrhein*, 5, January/December 1923, 21 f., here 22.

2 Kurt Winkler, *Museum und Avantgarde. Ludwig Justis Zeitschrif 'Museum der Gegenwart' und die Musealisierung des Expressionismus (Berliner Schriften zur Museumskunde*, 17), Opladen 2002, 43.

3 Ibid., 42.
4 Cf. Ibid., 13, Ill. 1.

Leidenschaft für die französische Moderne in
beeindruckende, in dieser Form bisher einzigartige Zusammenführungen von Werken übersetzt.
Unterstützt wurde sie maßgeblich durch unsere
freie Mitarbeiterin Rebecca Herlemann, die sich
nicht nur in kürzester Zeit hoch motiviert einge-
arbeitet hat, sondern auch in der Endphase der
Ausstellungsvorbereitungen alle Fäden zusammen-
hielt. Mein Dank gilt darüber hinaus Hans-Jürgen
Lechtreck, Thomas Grimm und Tobias Burg, die
Frau Herlemann während der Elternzeit von Frau
Engel ab November 2021 unterstützten.

Eine besondere Ehre wird unserer Jubiläums-
ausstellung durch die Schirmherrschaft von
Bundespräsident Frank-Walter Steinmeier und die
Unterstützung durch das Auswärtige Amt zuteil.
Sie sind Ausdruck dafür, dass das Museum Folk-
wang in seiner hundertjährigen Geschichte in
Essen nicht nur – wie es damals der Wunsch der
Stifter war – die Stadt und den Bezirk bereichert,
sondern sich zu einer Institution mit bundesweiter
und internationaler Strahlkraft entwickelt hat.

1 Ernst Gosebruch, „Folkwang in
Essen. Ansprache des Museumsdirektors Gosebruch bei der
Wiedereröffnung des Folkwang-
museums in Essen" [29.10.1922],
in: *Die Heimat. Monatsschrift für
Land, Volk und Kunst in Westfalen
und am Niederrhein*, 5, Januar/
Dezember 1923, S. 21 f., hier S. 22.

2 Kurt Winkler, *Museum und Avant-
garde. Ludwig Justis Zeitschrift
„Museum der Gegenwart" und
die Musealisierung des Expressionismus (Berliner Schriften zur
Museumskunde,* 17), Opladen
2002, S. 43.

3 Ebd., S. 42.
4 Vgl. ebd., S. 13, Abb. 1.

Masayuki Tanaka
Director of the National Museum
of Western Art, Tokyo

PREFACE

The National Museum of Western Art (NMWA) opened in 1959 in Ueno Park, the most important art district in Tokyo. Beloved by a wide range of people, it remains the only national museum in Asia dedicated to the art of the West and has welcomed countless visitors since its founding over sixty years ago. The core of the NMWA's holdings is the Matsukata Collection, acquired in Europe between 1916 and 1927 by the industrialist Kōjirō Matsukata. Matsukata purchased over 3000 works during this period, from paintings and sculptures to drawings, prints as well as decorative arts, and around 400 are stored at the museum today.

The energy with which Matsukata applied himself to collecting was partly motivated by the lack of opportunity to see Western art in person, even in Tokyo, the nation's capital. Interest in painting and other artworks from Europe was on the rise in Japan at the time, and there were already several Japanese collectors of modern French art and frequent exhibitions, but there was not yet a museum with a permanently displayed collection of Western art. Matsukata was determined to establish such a museum so that Japan's young artists could learn from these works directly and other visitors could deepen their understanding of them. In an interview in *American Art News* (21 January 1922), Matsukata stated that understanding Western art was vital if the Japanese people were to understand the spirit and psychology of the West. 'Art is the expression of the soul of a people,' he declared. He also believed that knowledge of Western art would help the Japanese understand Western manufacturing industry. In the interview he emphasized that he had no interest in controversies over different schools of art – 'I want examples of it all,' he said. This diversity would help provide a deeper, broader understanding of

17   Masayuki Tanaka
Direktor des National Museum of Western Art,
Tokio

Das National Museum of Western Art wurde 1959 im Ueno-Park in Tokio eröffnet, dem bedeutendsten Kunstviertel in der japanischen Hauptstadt. Im asiatischen Raum ist das National Museum of Western Art das einzige staatliche Museum, das ausschließlich der westlichen Kunst gewidmet ist. Seit seiner Eröffnung vor mehr als sechzig Jahren erfreut sich diese Einrichtung großer Beliebtheit und empfängt jedes Jahr zahlreiche Besucher:innen aus dem In- und Ausland. Das Herzstück des Museums bildet die Sammlung Matsukata: westliche Kunstwerke, die der Industrielle Kōjirō Matsukata in den Jahren 1916 bis 1927 in Europa gesammelt hat. Er erwarb mehr als 3000 Objekte, die außer Gemälden und Skulpturen auch Zeichnungen, Drucke und Kunsthandwerk umfassen. Ein Teil davon, etwa 400 Exponate, befindet sich derzeit im National Museum of Western Art.

Matsukatas Motiv für das Sammeln westlicher Kunst beruhte zum Teil darauf, dass es in Japan kaum Gelegenheit gab, diese Kunst zu Gesicht zu bekommen, nicht einmal in der Hauptstadt Tokio. Zu jener Zeit interessierten sich die Menschen in Japan zunehmend für europäische Kunst und es gab bereits einige Sammler:innen, die Kunstwerke der Moderne aus Frankreich besaßen. Gelegentlich wurden Ausstellungen veranstaltet, aber es gab noch kein Museum mit dauerhaft präsentierten Beständen westlicher Kunst.

Matsukata war entschlossen, ein solches Museum einzurichten, um jungen Künstler:innen für ihr Studium Anschauungsmaterial aus erster Hand zu bieten und in der japanischen Bevölkerung das Verständnis für westliche Kunst zu vertiefen. In einem Interview der amerikanischen Kunstzeitschrift *American Art News* erklärte Matsukata am 21. Januar 1922, dass die Kenntnis westlicher Kunst überaus wichtig sei, um den Geist und die Psychologie westlicher Kultur besser zu erfassen.

VORWORT

Western psychology. Thanks to his nonconformist approach, he created the first important collection of Impressionist and Post-Impressionist art in Japan.

While in Europe in 1921, Matsukata visited Berlin and Hamburg. There are stories that the true purpose for these trips was to secretly obtain blueprints for German submarines, and that Matsukata played the role of an ostentatious art buyer as cover. It is unclear whether there is any truth to the tale of Matsukata successfully obtaining the submarine plans, smuggling them to Paris hidden among the paintings he bought in Germany, and then carrying them back to Japan in a diplomatic bag, but it has all the thrill of a spy movie.

Matsukata's activities in Europe as an art collector soon became known in Germany: in 1921, articles about his collecting appeared in art magazines such as *Der Cicerone* and *Kunstchronik und Kunstmarkt*. In Berlin, Matsukata visited Paul Cassirer's gallery and the Galerie van Diemen where he also bought artworks, the majority of which was modern French art, but also included works by Scandinavian, Dutch and German artists, such as Edvard Munch and Adolph von Menzel. Coincidentally, on the following page after the report on Matsukata's collecting in the same 4 November 1921 edition of *Kunstchronik und Kunstmarkt*, there is an article about the Museum Folkwang in Hagen. The article discusses the future of the collection assembled for the museum by Karl Ernst Osthaus, who had died that year. It reports that while Hagen's city council had formally requested that the museum remain in the city, other cities such as Essen and Munich were eager to purchase the collection for themselves.

With the Museum Folkwang's move to Essen, Osthaus's collection had the good fortune to continue its development, but Matsukata's collec-tion was fated to chart an unhappier course. Japan's financial panic of 1927 left Matsukata's Kawasaki Dockyard with severe debts, the repayment of which required most of the collection to be dispersed through auction sales. On top of this, a fire in 1939 destroyed almost every one of the 950 pieces Matsukata had left in a warehouse in London due to difficulties sending them to Japan. A further 400 to 500 pieces had been left in France, and towards the end of the Second World War these were confiscated by the French government as enemy property.

In 1951, the Japanese government opened negotiations with France for the return of the Matsukata Collection. One of the conditions France imposed was the construction of a museum to house the collection, and this was the genesis of the NMWA. In the end, 372 works were returned to Japan by France, including some that were badly damaged. The collection was greatly diminished, but the museum of Western art that Matsukata had dreamed of finally opened in Tokyo. Since then, the museum has continued to purchase artworks once owned by Matsukata. Including items that are not part of the Matsukata Collection, its holdings now include over 6000 works in a range of media.

Any collection is stamped with its collector's dreams and ideals. This exhibition will shed new light on the dreams and ideals of two such collectors, one from Germany and one from Japan. The works in the Matsukata Collection were gathered together just as Osthaus's own collection was taking shape, and this combined exhibition at the Museum Folkwang is a valuable opportunity to increase the value of this collection even further. I would like to take this opportunity to offer my heartfelt gratitude to everyone who strove to make this exhibition a reality.

19

Matsukata begriff „Kunst als Ausdruck der Seele eines Volkes". Außerdem glaubte er, dass die Kenntnis westlicher Kunst zugleich mit dem Verständnis westlicher verarbeitender Industrie verknüpft sei. Im gleichen Interview betonte er, dass er nicht an Kontroversen über verschiedene Kunstströmungen interessiert sei, sondern exemplarisch Exponate aller Stilrichtungen sammeln wolle. Diese Vielfalt sollte dazu beitragen, ein tieferes und breit gefächertes Verständnis für den westlichen Geist zu vermitteln. Dank seines nonkonformistischen Ansatzes schuf Matsukata die erste bedeutende Sammlung impressionistischer und post-impressionistischer Kunst in Japan.

Während seines Europa-Aufenthalts 1921 besuchte Matsukata auch Berlin und Hamburg. Es heißt, dass der eigentliche Zweck der Reise darin bestand, sich heimlich Blaupausen für ein deutsches U-Boot-Fabrikat zu beschaffen, und er deshalb in auffälliger Weise Kunstwerke erwarb, um seine wahren Absichten zu vertuschen. Angeblich sei ihm die Beschaffung der U-Boot-Pläne dann auch gelungen und er habe sie, versteckt zwischen den in Deutschland gekauften Gemälden, nach Paris schmuggeln können, um sie anschließend in einer Diplomatentasche sicher nach Japan zu bringen. Ob die dramatisch klingende Geschichte der Wahrheit entspricht, sei dahingestellt, aber sie hat den Nervenkitzel eines Spionagefilms.

Matsukatas Sammlertätigkeit in Europa war auch in Deutschland bekannt und 1921 erschienen Artikel über ihn in den Kunstzeitschriften *Der Cicerone* sowie *Kunstchronik und Kunstmarkt*. Er besuchte die Galerien Paul Cassirer und Van Diemen in Berlin, wo er ebenfalls Werke kaufte. Bei den meisten handelte es sich um moderne französische Kunst, aber es fanden sich auch Arbeiten von skandinavischen, holländischen oder deutschen Malern wie Edvard Munch oder Adolph von Menzel darunter. Zufälligerweise befindet sich in der schon erwähnten Zeitschrift *Kunstchronik und Kunstmarkt*, die im November 1921 über Matsukatas Kunstsammlung berichtet, auf der Folgeseite ein Artikel über das Museum Folkwang in Hagen. Es ging dabei um die Zukunft der Sammlung von Karl Ernst Osthaus, der in jenem Jahr verstorben war: Der Stadtrat von Hagen hatte den Verbleib der Sammlung in der Stadt gefordert, während auch die Städte Essen und München Interesse an der Sammlung Osthaus bekundeten.

Der Umzug des Museum Folkwang nach Essen erwies sich als glückliche Fügung für die Osthaus-Sammlung, die dort erweitert wurde. Matsukatas Kollektion dagegen ereilte ein unglückliches Schicksal. Im Zusammenhang mit der Finanzkrise im Jahr 1927 war auch Matsukatas Kawasaki-Werft hoch verschuldet, und so wurde ein Großteil seiner Sammlung veräußert und in alle Winde zerstreut. Weitere 950 Werke, die nicht nach Japan verbracht, sondern in einem Lagerhaus in London deponiert worden waren, wurden 1939 durch einen Brand fast vollständig zerstört. Darüber hinaus befanden sich gegen Ende des Zweiten Weltkriegs 400 bis 500 Objekte in Frankreich, die von der französischen Regierung als Feindeseigentum beschlagnahmt wurden.

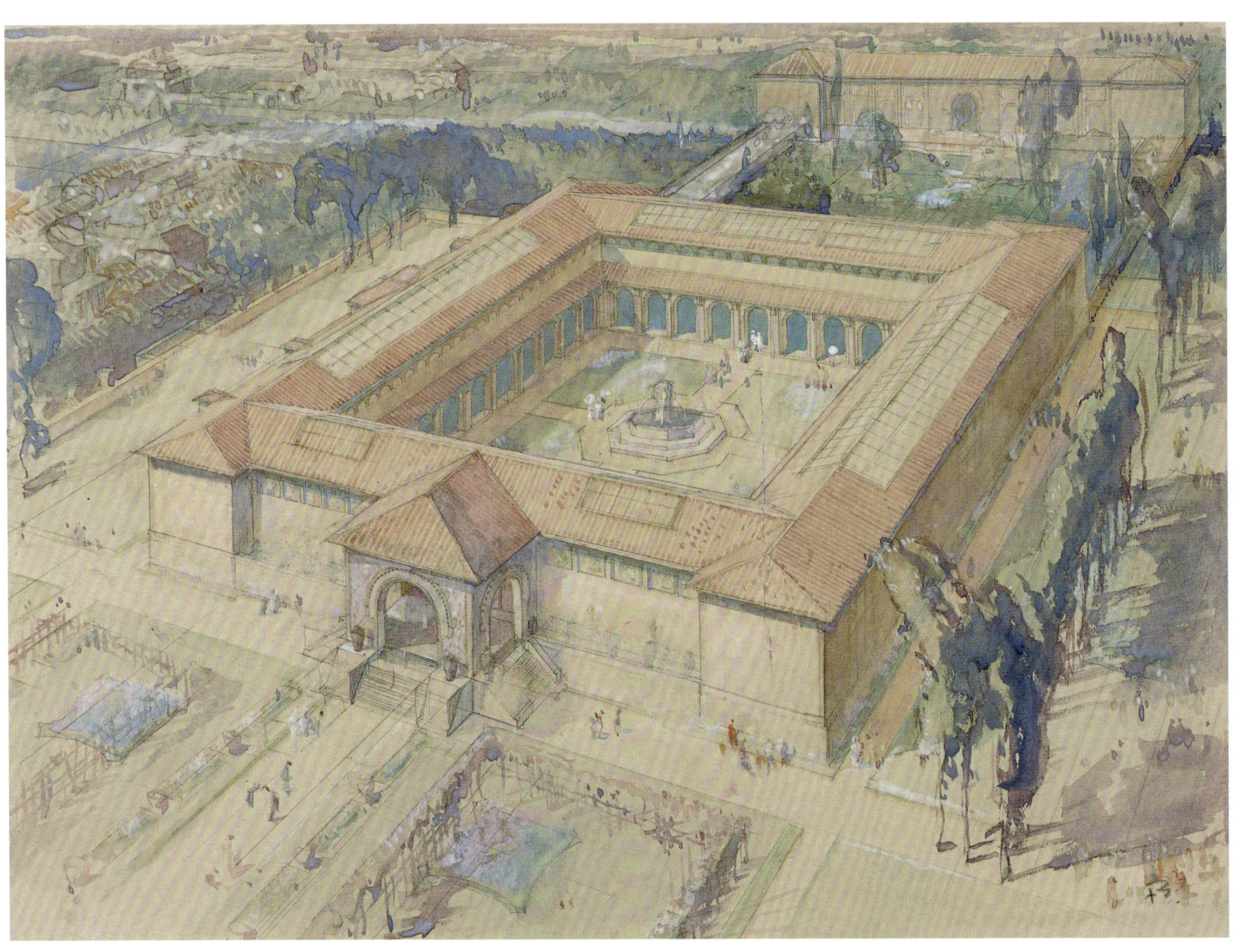

Frank Brangwyn
Aerial Perspective of Kyōraku Art Museum, Tokyo
The National Museum of Western Art, Tokyo

Nach 1951 verhandelten die japanische und die französische Regierung über die Rückgabe der Sammlung Matsukata. Frankreich stellte die Bedingung, dass eine Restitution der Bilder an Japan nur erfolgen könne, wenn dafür ein Kunstmuseum errichtet würde – und so entstand das National Museum of Western Art. Das Konvolut der zurückgeführten Werke aus der Sammlung Matsukata umfasste 372 Exponate, die teils stark beschädigt waren. Obgleich der ursprüngliche Umfang seiner Sammlung erheblich dezimiert war, wurde damit schließlich Matsukatas Traum eines Museums für westliche Kunst in Tokio verwirklicht. Seit der Eröffnung erwarb das Museum immer wieder Werke aus Matsukatas einstigem Besitz und heute beherbergt es mehr als 6000 Kunstwerke

unterschiedlichster Art, auch solche, die nicht zum ursprünglichen Sammlungsbestand Matsukatas gehören.

Jede Kunstsammlung ist von den Träumen und Idealen ihres Urhebers oder ihrer Urheberin geprägt. Diese Ausstellung wirft ein neues Licht auf die Träume und Ideale von zwei solchen Sammlern, einem aus Deutschland und einem aus Japan. Die Werke der Sammlung Matsukata wurden zusammengetragen, als Osthaus' eigene Kollektion Gestalt annahm, und die gemeinsame Ausstellung im Museum Folkwang ist eine wertvolle Gelegenheit, ihren Wert noch weiter zu steigern. Ich möchte allen Beteiligten, die sich für das Zustandekommen dieses Projekts eingesetzt haben, aus tiefstem Herzen danken.

21

FRENCH MODERNISM AT THE MUSEUM FOLKWANG AND ITS JUXTAPOSITION WITH THE MATSUKATA COLLECTION –

A KALEIDOSCOPE

Nadine Engel

Impressionism and Post-Impressionism
at the Museum Folkwang in Hagen

'MODERNE KUNST' was emblazoned in big
letters on the cover of the first catalogue of the
collection, published in 1912, ten years after Karl
Ernst Osthaus founded the Museum Folkwang
in Hagen in Westphalia.[1] Although a publication on
the 'historical collections'[2] of the museum was
planned, the small volume would remain the only
catalogue of its holdings to have been brought out
in Osthaus's lifetime.[3] It is telling that the artworks
of the nineteenth and twentieth century formed
the introduction to the planned series, since the
Museum Folkwang had not been conceived from
the outset exclusively as a museum of fine art.[4]
As Rainer Stamm relates in his contribution to this
catalogue, using the example of a collection
of paintings by the Düsseldorf School – Osthaus
acquired it in his first years as a collector, but it
is not mentioned in the 1912 inventory catalogue
although it was only sold off five years later – the
collector himself encouraged the perception
of the Museum Folkwang as the supposedly 'first
museum of modernism'[5] in Germany.[6] So, as he
wrote in his introduction to the 1912 catalogue: 'The
collection of modern paintings in the Folkwang
was created in order to produce artistic life. Only
a few works of the early nineteenth century establish a link with the older art commonly nurtured
in German museums. The most important works in
the collection, not least the early major work by
Renoir [p. 209], were acquired at a time when their
masters in Germany were still known little or not
at all. They helped to facilitate an understanding of
the great initiators of modern painting, Van Gogh,
Gauguin and Cézanne, in Germany. [...] the pointillistes did not find their place any earlier in any

„MODERNE KUNST" prangte in großen Lettern auf
dem Einband des ersten Sammlungskataloges, der
1912, zehn Jahre nachdem Karl Ernst Osthaus das
Museum Folkwang im westfälischen Hagen gegründet hatte, erschien.[1] Auch wenn in der Folge eine
Publikation zu den „historischen Sammlungen"[2]
des Museums beabsichtigt war, so sollte der kleine
Band doch der einzige Bestandskatalog bleiben,
der zu Osthaus' Lebzeiten herausgegeben wurde.[3]
Es ist bezeichnend, dass die Kunstwerke des 19.
und 20. Jahrhunderts den Auftakt der geplanten
Reihe bildeten, war das Museum Folkwang doch
nicht von Anfang an ausschließlich als Museum für
Bildende Kunst konzipiert worden.[4] Wie Rainer
Stamm in seinem Beitrag zu diesem Katalog am
Beispiel eines Gemäldekonvoluts der Düsseldorfer
Schule darstellt – Osthaus hatte es in seinen ersten Sammlerjahren erworben, im Bestandskatalog
von 1912 findet es jedoch keine Erwähnung, obwohl es erst fünf Jahre später abgestoßen wurde –,
beförderte der Sammler selbst die Wahrnehmung
des Museum Folkwang als vermeintlich „[e]rstes
Museum der Moderne"[5] in Deutschland.[6] So führte
er in seiner Einführung zum Katalog von 1912 aus:
„Die Sammlung moderner Gemälde im Folkwang
ist aus dem Bestreben entstanden, künstlerisches
Leben zu erzeugen. Nur wenige Werke des frühen
19. Jahrhunderts ermöglichen eine Anknüpfung an
die in deutschen Museen gemeinhin gepflegte
ältere Kunst. Die wichtigsten Werke der Sammlung,
nicht zum wenigsten das Hauptwerk des frühen

23   Nadine Engel

FRANZÖSISCHE MODERNE AM MUSEUM FOLKWANG UND IHRE GEGENÜBERSTELLUNG MIT DER SAMMLUNG MATSUKATA –

EIN KALEIDOSKOP

Abb. | Fig. 1
Pierre-August Renoir, *Lise,* 1867, in:
Ausst.-Kat. I exh. cat. Berliner Secession,
Berlin 1901, S. | p. 91

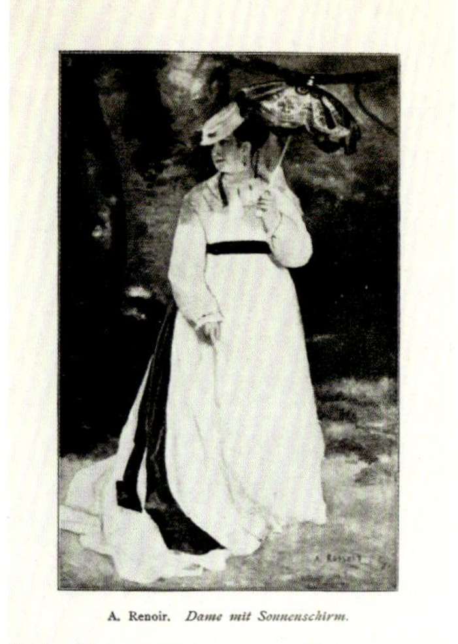

German museum.'[7] The deliberate distinction from other general museum collections that Osthaus was expressing here, the self-image of his own museum, developed out of modern art, and its desired reception by the public, must be seen in the context of the social status of the founder of the Folkwang: as Béatrice Joyeux-Prunel has documented, commitment to contemporary art, particularly from the French-speaking world, was able to grant German collectors such as Osthaus, Harry Graf Kesser and Eberhard von Bodenhausen cultural, social and even political status which would otherwise have been out of their reach as members of the new property-owning bourgeoisie.[8] Eva Rovers has observed the same thing about Helene Kröller-Müller, born near Essen, who made her collection of modern art that she had begun in 1905 accessible to a selected public from 1913 in exhibition spaces near the headquarters of the family business in The Hague.[9] A visit to Osthaus in Hagen arranged by the designer Peter Behrens in 1911 probably contributed to this decision.[10]

While the first acquisitions for the collection of the Museum Folkwang are documented from around 1897, French art became a focus of the painting department after the purchase of Pierre-Auguste Renoir's painting *Lise – La femme à l'ombrelle* (*Lise with a Parasol;* fig. 1; p. 209) at the *Dritte Kunstausstellung* of the Berliner Secession in 1901. The works entering the collection in the first years of the museum were particularly spectacular, as they were often among

the earliest and most progressive acquisitions of contemporary art in the German museum landscape. One frequently cited example is Vincent van Gogh's painting *La moisson* (*The Wheatfield behind Saint Paul's Hospital with a Reaper,* 1889; p. 315), created during the artist's highly productive phase in Arles, which was already exhibited at the opening of the Museum Folkwang (fig. 2). Vincent van Gogh, Paul Gauguin, Paul Cézanne and the Pointillistes (a group of painters who composed their images from juxtaposed dots [French: 'point'] or patches of pure colour): in Osthaus's list it becomes apparent that the main emphasis of the Museum Folkwang rested with the artists who followed on from Impressionism. While this movement had taken its name in 1874 from a painting by Claude Monet at the first exhibition of a group organized in deliberate distinction from the established Salon as a *société anonyme* around Renoir and Monet, Berthe Morisot, Edgar Degas, Alfred Sisley and Camille Pissarro,[11] in 1886, in reference to the cooperative's eighth and last exhibition, the journalist and author Félix Fénéon identified the style of younger artists like Georges Seurat as 'néo-impressioniste'.[12] The British art critic Roger Fry, writing in 1910 in the context of his pioneering exhibition *Manet and the Post-Impressionists* at the Grafton Galleries in London, confirmed that the boundaries between the two generations were entirely fluid: 'Cézanne, Gauguin and van Gogh all learnt in the Impressionist school.' His view was that they were less concerned with the depiction of what the eye perceives than on

25

Renoir [S. 209], sind zu einer Zeit erworben worden, als ihre Meister in Deutschland noch wenig oder gar nicht bekannt waren. Sie haben dazu beigetragen, das Verständnis für die großen Anreger moderner Malkunst, van Gogh, Gauguin und Cézanne in Deutschland zu erschließen. Auch […] die Pointillisten fanden in keinem deutschen Museum früher ihren Platz."[7] Die bewusste Abgrenzung zum landläufigen musealen Sammeln, der Osthaus damit Ausdruck verleiht, das aus der modernen Kunst heraus entwickelte Selbstverständnis seines eigenen Museums und dessen erwünschte Rezeption in der Öffentlichkeit muss in Zusammenhang mit dem sozialen Status des Folkwang-Gründers gesehen werden: Wie Béatrice Joyeux-Prunel belegt hat, vermochte das Engagement für die zeitgenössische Kunst, insbesondere für die aus dem französischen Sprachraum, deutschen Sammler:innen wie Osthaus, Harry Graf Kessler oder Eberhard von Bodenhausen kulturell, gesellschaftlich, ja sogar politisch Geltung zu verschaffen, welche ihnen als Angehörigen des neuen Besitzbürgertums anderweitig verwehrt geblieben wäre.[8] Gleiches hat Eva Rovers für die nahe Essen geborene Helene Kröller-Müller ausgeführt, die ihre seit 1905 angelegte Sammlung moderner Kunst ab 1913 in Ausstellungsräumen neben der Firmenzentrale des Familienunternehmens in Den Haag für ausgewähltes Publikum öffnete.[9] Ein Besuch bei Osthaus in Hagen, den der Gestalter Peter Behrens 1911 vermittelte, trug wohl zu diesem Entschluss bei.[10]

Sind erste Ankäufe für die Sammlung des Museum Folkwang ab etwa 1897 belegt, so entwickelte sich die französische Kunst seit dem Erwerb von Pierre-Auguste Renoirs erwähntem Gemälde *Lise – La femme à l'ombrelle (Lise mit dem Sonnenschirm*; Abb. 1; S. 209) auf der *Dritten Kunstausstellung* der Berliner Secession von 1901 zu einem Schwerpunkt der Gemäldeabteilung. Insbesondere die Sammlungszugänge in den ersten Jahren des Museums waren spektakulär, gehörten sie doch oftmals zu den frühesten und progressivsten Erwerbungen zeitgenössischer Kunst in der deutschen Museumslandschaft. Ein häufig zitiertes Beispiel ist Vincent van Goghs Gemälde *La moisson (Die Ernte, Kornfeld mit Schnitter*, 1889; S. 315), das während der hochproduktiven Phase des Künstlers in Arles entstand und bereits zur Eröffnung des Museum Folkwang gezeigt wurde (Abb. 2).

Vincent van Gogh, Paul Gauguin, Paul Cézanne und die Pointillist:innen – eine Gruppe von Maler:innen, die ihre Bilder aus nebeneinander gesetzten Punkten (franz. „point") bzw. Flecken reiner Farbe aufbauten – in Osthaus' Aufzählung manifestiert sich, dass das Hauptaugenmerk im Museum Folkwang auf den Künstler:innen lag, die an den Impressionismus anschlossen. Hatte Letzterer seinen Namen 1874 nach einem Gemälde von Claude Monet auf der ersten Ausstellung einer Gruppe erhalten, die sich in bewusster Abgrenzung vom etablierten Salon als *Société anonyme* um Renoir und Monet, Berthe Morisot, Edgar Degas, Alfred Sisley und Camille Pissarro organisiert hatte,[11] bezeichnete der Journalist und Literat Félix Fénéon 1886 anlässlich der achten und letzten Schau der Kooperative die Malweise beteiligter

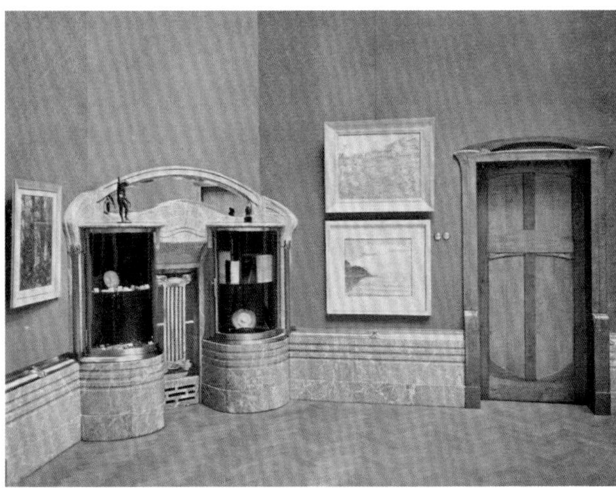

Abb.|Fig. 2
Museum Folkwang, Hagen, Eckwand
des Großen Bildersaales|corner of the
great picture hall, 1902

26

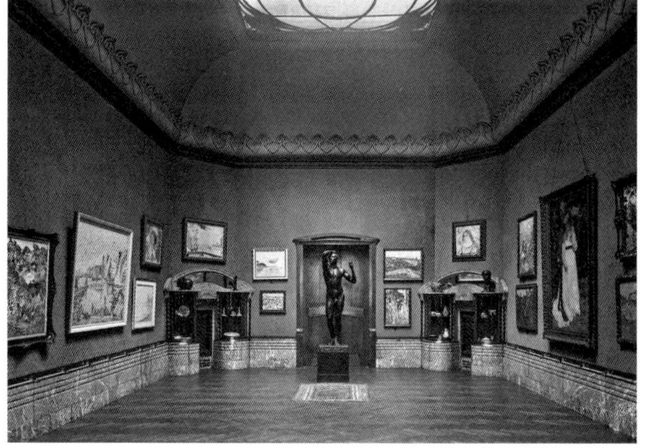

Abb. | Fig. 3
Museum Folkwang, Hagen, Großer
Bildersaal | great picture hall, 1920

'the emotional significance which lies in things'
(cf. p. 315). Tellingly, their works appeared 'disconcerting'. Their art was ultimately concerned
with painting 'a line round a mental conception
of the object'.[13] With this metaphor Fry is describ-
ing both the characteristic interplay between
line and colour of the largely flat conception of
the image with which the Post-Impressionists
distanced themselves from the style of the Impressionists (cf. pp. 325, 331). The term 'Post-Impressionism' established by Fry will be used as a stylistic
term in this publication. But as John Rewald noted
in his historical treatise on the generation in question, the term is only an aid to summarize French art
of the period from 1886 until around the beginnings
of Cubism in 1906.[14] Rewald quotes the Belgian
poet Emile Verhaeren: 'There is no single school, in
fact there are barely individual groups, as these are
constantly fragmenting. The diverse tendencies
remind me of agitated, kaleidoscopic geometri-
cal patterns that are juxtaposed in order to come
together a moment later, that now merge, part
once more and then fall apart, but which in spite of
everything move within an unchanging circle, that
of the new art.'[15] That very moment when artistic
trends were pluralizing, and individual styles were
beginning to form, was at the time seen as the
beginning of modern art. Osthaus was just as committed to this now-outdated model of history as
was the critic Julius Meier-Graefe, who published
his influential *Entwicklungsgeschichte der modernen Kunst* (History of the Development of Modern
Art) in 1904.[16]

Comparable with the exposed position that
Edouard Manet assumed in Fry's 1910 exhibition, the Museum Folkwang presented French
Impressionism and Realism as impulses behind
modern art. Works like *Lise* or Honoré Daumier's
Ecce Homo (1851) were shown as solitary paintings within the collection, even if, as in the case of
Auguste Rodin or indeed Renoir, there were
convolutions available (fig. 3).[17] Artists like Monet,
Pissarro and Eugène Delacroix were not represented in the Folkwang at all. After 1914, the profile
of French art from the first half of the nineteenth
century was further thrown into relief when, after
considerable financial burdens caused by the
First World War, Osthaus chose to divest himself
of several works including *Flock of Sheep* by
François Millet as well as *Stag* attributed to Gustave
Courbet (fig. 4).[18] Did he do this at random, or was
it deliberate, as we may assume of Osthaus?
Academic expertise at the Museum Folkwang was
far less pronounced in the field of older art than
it was in the contemporary field: Henri Matisse and
Paul Signac (p. 297), Cézanne, Rodin or Renoir –
wherever possible, personal contact was sought
with living artists so that Osthaus was very closely
familiar with many bodies of work from having
seen them in the flesh.[19] Even today questions of
authenticity in these cases do not arise. In contrast,
however, as early as 1916 Paul Cassirer doubted
the authorship of the aforementioned Courbet
work;[20] since the 1920s the attribution of the small
canvas *L'explosion* (*The Explosion*, 1871; p. 222),
which Osthaus bought in 1905 at the Galerie Arnold

27

jüngerer Künstler:innen wie Georges Seurat als „néo-impressionniste"[12]. Dass die Grenzen zwischen den beiden Generationen durchaus fließend waren, belegte 1910 auch der britische Kunstkritiker Roger Fry im Kontext seiner wegweisenden Ausstellung *Manet and the Post-Impressionists* in den Londoner Grafton Galleries: Cézanne, Gauguin und van Gogh seien alle impressionistisch ausgebildet; ihre Kunst jedoch ziele nicht mehr auf die Darstellung dessen, was das Auge wahrnehme, sondern vielmehr auf die emotionale Bedeutung ihrer Sujets (vgl. S. 315). Bezeichnenderweise würden ihre Werke beunruhigend [„disconcerting"] wirken. Ihre Malerei beruhe letztlich darauf, eine Kontur um das geistige Konzept eines Gegenstandes zu ziehen.[13] Mit dieser Metapher beschreibt Fry zugleich das charakteristische Zusammenspiel zwischen Linie und Farbe der betont flächigen Bildauffassung, mit der sich die Post-Impressionist:innen von der Malweise der Impressionist:innen absetzten (vgl. S. 325, 331). Die Bezeichnung Post-Impressionismus, die Fry etablierte, wird in dieser Publikation als Stilbegriff Verwendung finden. Wie jedoch schon John Rewald in seiner historischen Abhandlung der entsprechenden Generation bemerkt, ist die Bezeichnung nur ein Hilfsmittel, um die französische Kunst aus dem Zeitraum von 1886 bis etwa zur Entstehung des Kubismus im Jahr 1906 zusammenzufassen.[14] Rewald zitiert dazu den belgischen Poeten Emile Verhaeren: „Es gibt keine einzelne Schule, sogar kaum noch einzelne Gruppen, da diese sich dauernd zersplittern. Die vielfältigen Tendenzen erinnern mich an bewegliche, kaleidoskopartige geometrische Muster, die einander gegenüberstehen, um sich im nächsten Augenblick zu vereinen, die jetzt verschmelzen, sich wieder trennen und dann zerfallen, die sich aber trotz alledem innerhalb eines gleichbleibenden Kreises bewegen, dem der neuen Kunst."[15] Eben jener Zeitpunkt, an dem sich die Kunstströmungen pluralisierten und Individualstile herauszubilden begannen, galt seinerzeit als Beginn der modernen Kunst. Osthaus war diesem heute überholten Geschichtsmodell ebenso verpflichtet wie der Kritiker Julius Meier-Graefe, der 1904 seine einflussreiche *Entwicklungsgeschichte der modernen Kunst* publizierte.[16]

Vergleichbar zur exponierten Stellung, die Edouard Manet in Frys Ausstellung von 1910 einnahm, präsentierte das Museum Folkwang den französischen Impressionismus und Realismus als Impulsgeber für die Moderne. Werke wie *Lise* oder Honoré Daumiers *Ecce Homo* (1851) wurden als Solitäre innerhalb der Sammlung inszeniert, selbst wenn wie im Fall von Auguste Rodin oder auch Renoir Konvolute vorhanden waren (Abb. 3).[17] Künstler:innen wie Monet, Pissarro oder Eugène Delacroix waren erst gar nicht im Folkwang vertreten. Nach 1914 wurde das Profil der französischen Kunst aus der ersten Hälfte des 19. Jahrhunderts noch geschärft, als Osthaus infolge erheblicher finanzieller Belastungen durch den Ersten Weltkrieg unter anderem eine *Schafherde* von François Millet sowie einen Gustave Courbet zugeschriebenen *Rehbock* (Abb. 4) veräußerte.[18] Geschah dies willkürlich oder vielmehr gezielt, wie es für Osthaus zu vermuten ist? Auch die wissenschaftliche

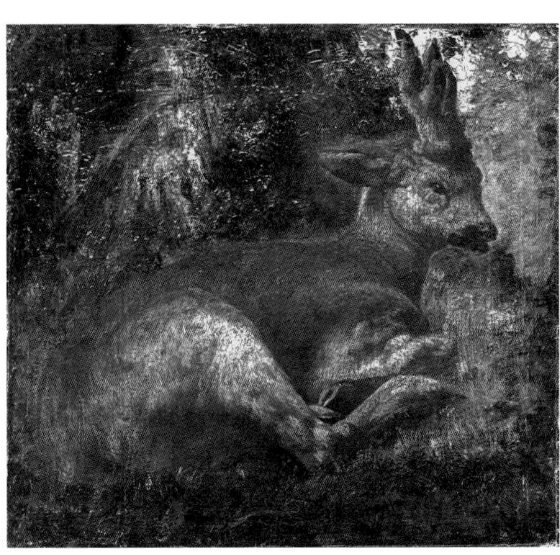

Abb. | Fig. 4
Gustave Courbet, *Rehbock*,
Verbleib unbekannt | location unknown

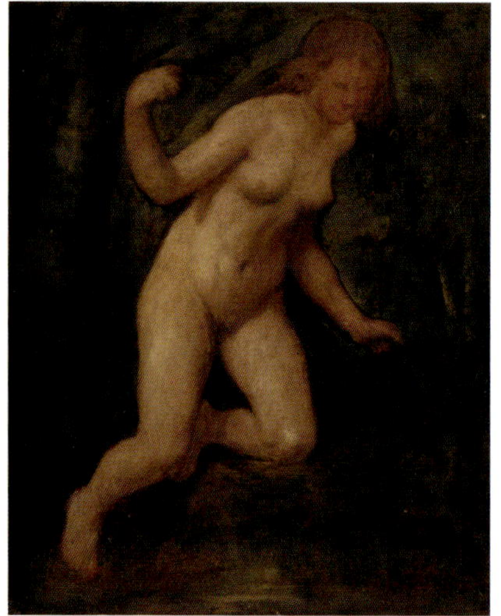

Abb. | Fig. 5
Nachahmer von | imitator of
Jean-Baptiste Camille Corot, *Nymphe,*
Museum Folkwang, Essen

in Dresden[21] as a 'Study for Fight at the Barricade'
by Manet has been the subject of debate;[22] and a
nude that still appears in the 1912 inventory catalogue as a Camille Corot (fig. 5)[23] turned out to be
the work of an imitator.

   Mario von Lüttichau pointed out that the Museum
Folkwang's concentration on Post-Impressionism
may have been considerably influenced by the
already considerably higher market values of the
artists of Impressionism.[24] The collector paid careful attention to the prices he paid; he tried where
possible to negotiate purchases without an intermediary like Cassirer, which often led to disagree-
ments.[25] For a long time insufficient attention was
paid to the fact that the art of Van Gogh, Gauguin
or the Pointillistes was much closer to the social
task of the Museum Folkwang, both symbolically
and in terms of content, than the paintings of
Monet, for example. At a conference of the Central
Office for Workers' Charitable Institutions, devoted
to *Museen als Volksbildungsstätten* (Museums as
Places of Popular Education) in 1903, Osthaus referred to the mission of the Folkwang: 'It is also my
ultimate goal to bring culture to everyone, and also
my firm conviction that the most important questions of social life are insoluble without the influence of art.'[26] Even if Osthaus finally attempted to
achieve change by primarily addressing 'affluent
manufacturers' and 'city administrations',[27] and was
hence thinking hierarchically from the top down-
wards, the focus of many Post-Impressionist works
in the Museum Folkwang was on the 'simple' population and the working classes, meaning the

physically active human being (pp. 205, 307, 331).
According to Robyn Roslack, against the background of French politics even the landscape
paintings of Signac or Henri Edmond Cross can
be seen as symbols of the desire for an upheaval
of society, in which Gothic monuments are cited
as a sign of a lost social cohesion (p. 288), or a
post-revolutionary paradise outlined (p. 289).[28]
In this context just the integration of a motif that
includes the battles at the barricades was key to
the Museum Folkwang – both in terms of French
and German history (p. 222).[29] In the circles
around Osthaus as early as the 1910s, Eberhard
von Bodenhausen, initiator of the journal *Pan* and
from 1907 active on the board of Krupp, spoke
of the 'dematerialization and symbolic transposi-
tion'[30] in Signac's landscapes. Thus, on the German
collecting scene the idea of a deeper meaning
to Pointilliste art was highly pervasive.

   By the time Henri Fauconnier's Cubist *Paysage*
(*Landscape*; fig. 6), and the Fauvist compositions
L'oliveraie (*Alpine Landscape with Goatherd,* 1912;
p. 291) by Pierre Bonnard and *La fenêtre bleue*
(*The Blue Window*; fig. 7) by Henri Matisse entered
the Folkwang collection in 1912 and 1913 as three
of the last works of French art, a substantial collection from the second half of the nineteenth century
and the first few years of the twentieth century
was already in place.[31] After the museum had since
1903 regularly shown contemporary French artists
in changing presentations, a last special exhibition with paintings and works on paper by Cross,
Signac, Théo van Rysselberghe and Maximilien

29

Expertise am Museum Folkwang war im Bereich der älteren Kunst weit weniger ausgeprägt als im Fall der zeitgenössischen: Henri Matisse und Paul Signac (S. 297), Cézanne, Rodin oder Renoir – wo immer möglich, wurde der persönliche Kontakt zu lebenden Künstler:innen gesucht, sodass Osthaus mit vielen Œuvres aus eigener Anschauung und aufs Engste vertraut war.[19] Fragen der Echtheit stellen sich in diesen Fällen bis heute nicht. Im Gegensatz dazu zweifelte 1916 schon Paul Cassirer die Autorschaft des oben genannten Courbet-Werkes an;[20] seit den 1920er-Jahren wird, wenn auch nie abschließend, immer wieder die Zuschreibung der kleinen Leinwand *L'explosion* (*Die Granate,* 1871; S. 222) diskutiert, die Osthaus 1905 in der Dresdner Galerie Arnold als „,Studie zum Barrikadenkampf' von Manet"[21] erwarb;[22] und eine Aktdarstellung, die im Bestandskatalog des Jahres 1912 noch als Camille Corot erscheint (Abb. 5),[23] stellte sich als Werk eines Epigonen heraus.

Mario von Lüttichau hat darauf aufmerksam gemacht, dass die Konzentration auf den Post-Impressionismus im Museum Folkwang durch die zu Osthaus' Zeiten bereits erheblich höheren Marktwerte der Künstler:innen des Impressionismus beeinflusst worden sein mag.[24] Der Sammler achtete stark auf die Preise, die er bezahlte; Ankäufe versuchte er möglichst ohne einen Zwischenhändler wie Cassirer abzuwickeln, was nicht selten zu Unstimmigkeiten führte.[25] Zu wenig betont wird dagegen bislang, dass die Kunst van Goghs, Gauguins oder der Pointillist:innen der sozialen Aufgabe des Museum Folkwang inhaltlich

und symbolisch weit näher stand als etwa die Gemälde Monets. Auf einer Konferenz der Centralstelle für Arbeiter-Wohlfahrtseinrichtungen, die sich den *Museen als Volksbildungsstätten* widmete, bezog Osthaus schon 1903 zur Aufgabe des Folkwang Stellung: „Es ist auch mein letztes Ziel, die Bildung allen zu bringen, auch meine feste Überzeugung, daß ohne die Mitwirkung der Kunst die wichtigsten Fragen des sozialen Lebens unlösbar sind."[26] Auch wenn Osthaus letztlich Veränderung zu erreichen suchte, indem er an erster Stelle „begüterte Fabrikanten" und „Stadtverwaltungen" adressierte,[27] hierarchisch also von oben nach unten dachte: Im Mittelpunkt vieler post-impressionistischer Werke im Museum Folkwang stand die „einfache" Bevölkerung und der arbeitende, das heißt der körperlich tätige Mensch (S. 205, 307, 331). Vor dem Hintergrund der französischen Politik lassen sich nach Robyn Roslack selbst die Landschaftsdarstellungen von Signac oder Henri Edmond Cross als Symbole für den Wunsch nach einem Umbruch der Gesellschaft verstehen, indem gotische Monumente als Zeichen eines verlorenen sozialen Zusammenhalts zitiert (S. 288) oder ein post-revolutionäres Paradies entworfen werden (S. 289).[28] In diesem Zusammenhang erscheint auch die Integration eines Motivs, das die Barrikadenkämpfe aufgreift, für das Museum Folkwang schlüssig – sowohl im Hinblick auf die französische wie auch auf die deutsche Geschichte (S. 222).[29] Im Umkreis von Osthaus sprach in den 1910er-Jahren schon Eberhard von Bodenhausen, Initiator der Zeitschrift *Pan* und seit 1907 im Vorstand von Krupp tätig, von der

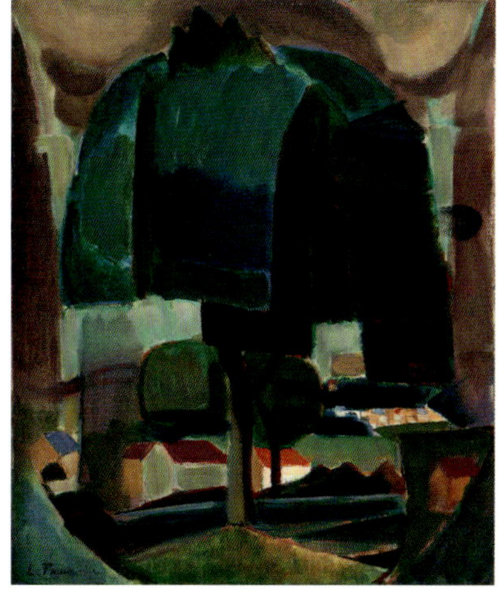

Abb. | Fig. 6
Henri Le Fauconnier, *Paysage,* 1912,
Museum Folkwang, Essen

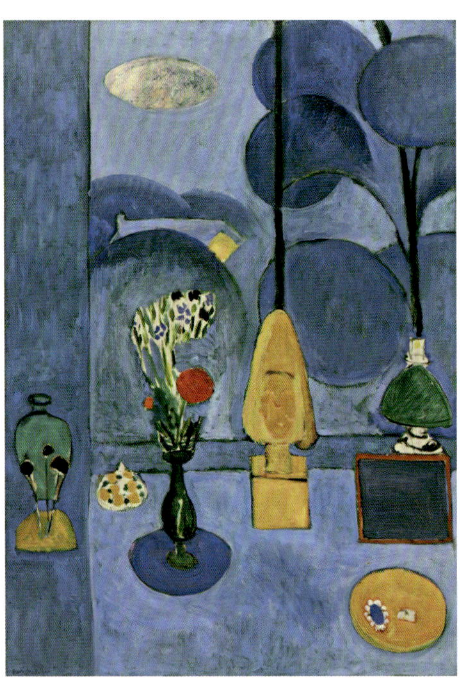

Abb. | Fig. 7
Henri Matisse, *La fenêtre bleue,* 1913,
The Museum of Modern Art, New York

Luce was held in 1913.[32] Over the subsequent few years Osthaus would devote himself increasingly to German Expressionism, various journalistic and critical projects and, along with his museum assistant Karl With, non-Western objects.[33] At this time the collection of French art at the Museum Folkwang was already held in high regard among collectors and artists, as well as in the younger scene around museums and critics: the first two editions of Meier-Graefe's *Entwicklungsgeschichte der modernen Kunst* even mentioned the paintings of Van Gogh, while Renoir's *Lise,* Paul Gauguin's *Contes barbares* (1902; p. 339) and Aristide Maillol's *Jeune fille debout* (*Young Girl Standing*; fig. 8) were even given full-page illustrations.[34] This would undoubtedly have been one of the reasons why Osthaus was often asked whether he would part with works like the Renoir painting, which he did occasionally, but entirely on his own initiative and preferably to collections with which he was familiar, like that of Helene Kröller-Müller (fig. 9).[35] At the same time other collectors offered the museum paintings for sale. The editor in chief of the journal *Kunst und Künstler* Emil Heilbut even allowed his painting *La maîtresse de Baudelaire* (*Baudelaire's Mistress [Jeanne Duval]*; fig. 10) by Manet to hang on view for a whole three years in the Museum Folkwang. In the end the sale fell through.[36] Osthaus himself was very well aware of the reputation of his collection: 'I think that of all the German galleries I run the one which, relatively speaking, contains the most French paintings,' he publicly observed in 1911 when the purchase of Vincent van Gogh's *Poppies in the Field* (1889) by the Kunsthalle Bremen led to a nationwide dispute over the 'flooding' of Germany with French art and the corresponding discrimination against German artists.[37] In this sense, Osthaus put the

„Entmaterialisierung und Versetzung ins Symbol"[30] in den Landschaften Signacs. In der deutschen Sammler:innenszene war der Gedanke an eine tiefere Bedeutung der pointillistischen Kunst also zu Osthaus' Zeiten durchaus virulent.

Bis mit Henri Le Fauconniers kubistischer *Paysage (Landschaft*; Abb. 6) sowie den fauvistischen Kompositionen *L'oliveraie (Alpenlandschaft mit Ziegenherde*, 1912; S. 291) von Pierre Bonnard und *La fenêtre bleue (Das blaue Fenster*; Abb. 7) von Henri Matisse in den Jahren 1912 und 1913 drei der letzten Werke französischer Kunst in die Folkwang-Sammlung kamen, war längst ein substanzieller Bestand aus der zweiten Hälfte des 19. Jahrhunderts und den ersten Jahren des 20. Jahrhunderts angelegt.[31] Nachdem das Museum seit 1903 regelmäßig in wechselnden Präsentationen aktuelle französische Positionen gezeigt hatte, fand 1913 eine letzte Sonderausstellung mit Gemälden und Papierarbeiten von Cross, Signac, Théo van Rysselberghe und Maximilien Luce statt.[32] In den kommenden Jahren sollte sich Osthaus verstärkt dem deutschen Expressionismus, vielfältigen publizistischen Projekten und, gemeinsam mit seinem Museumsassistenten Karl With, nichtwestlichen Objekten widmen.[33] Bei Sammler:innen und Künstler:innen sowie in der jüngeren Museums- und Kritikerszene genoss der Bestand an französischer Kunst im Museum Folkwang zu diesem Zeitpunkt bereits hohes Ansehen: Schon in den ersten zwei Auflagen von Meier-Graefes *Entwicklungsgeschichte der modernen Kunst* waren die Gemälde van Goghs aufgeführt, Renoirs *Lise,* Paul Gauguins *Contes barbares* (1902; S. 339) und Aristide Maillols

Jeune fille debout (Stehende junge Frau; Abb. 8) sogar ganzseitig abgebildet.[34] Sicherlich auch deshalb wurde Osthaus manches Mal gefragt, ob er sich von Werken wie dem Renoir-Gemälde trennen würde, was er vereinzelt, aber ausschließlich auf eigene Initiative und mit Vorliebe an ihm bekannte Sammlungen wie jene Helene Kröller-Müllers tat (Abb. 9).[35] Zugleich boten andere Sammler:innen dem Museum französische Gemälde zum Kauf an. Der Redaktionsleiter der Zeitschrift *Kunst und Künstler* Emil Heilbut nahm dabei sogar in Kauf, dass sein Bild *La maîtresse de Baudelaire (Baudelaires Geliebte (Jeanne Duval)*; Abb. 10) von Manet ganze drei Jahre lang zur Ansicht im Museum Folkwang hing. Letztlich zerschlug sich der Verkauf.[36] Osthaus selbst war sich der Reputation seiner Sammlung sehr bewusst: „Ich glaube diejenige von allen deutschen Galerien zu leiten, die relativ die meisten französischen Bilder besitzt", bezog er 1911 öffentlich Stellung, als anlässlich der Erwerbung von Vincent van Goghs *Mohnfeld* (1889) durch die Bremer Kunsthalle eine landesweiter Streit um die „Überflutung" Deutschlands mit französischer Kunst und eine entsprechende Benachteiligung deutscher Künstler:innen entbrannte.[37] In diesem Sinne relativierte Osthaus, er habe „für diese sämtlichen französischen Bilder, unter denen sich Meisterwerke von Daumier, Renoir, Cézanne, Gauguin und Matisse befinden, kaum soviel ausgegeben, wie für die zwei wichtigen deutschen Bilder des Museums allein."[38] Vor dem Hintergrund der Debatte um die Berechtigung französischer Kunst in den deutschen Museen und dem Ende der Ankaufstätigkeit für diesen Sammlungsbereich

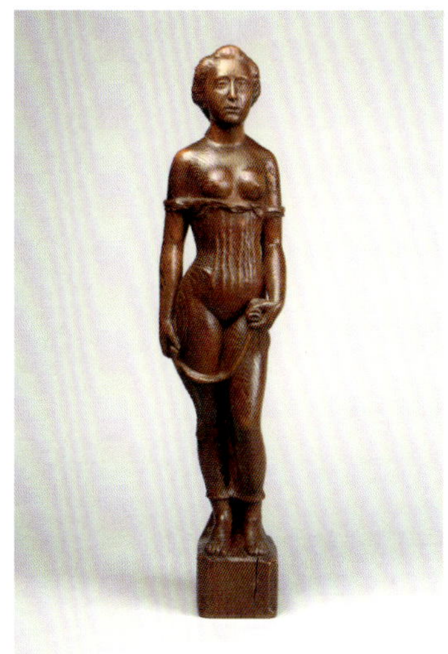

Abb. | Fig. 8
Aristide Maillol, *Jeune fille debout,* 1902,
Museum Folkwang, Essen

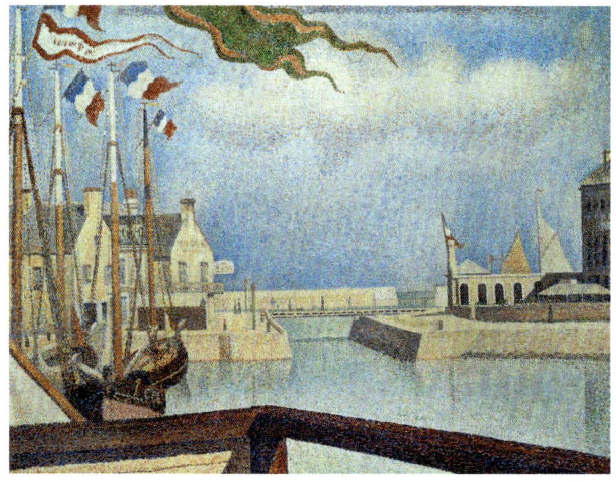

Abb. | Fig. 9
Georges Seurat, *Port-en-Bessin,
un dimanche*, 1888,
Kröller-Müller Museum, Otterlo

issue into perspective by saying that he had 'barely spent as much for all these French paintings, which include masterpieces by Daumier, Renoir, Cézanne, Gauguin and Matisse, as for the two important German paintings in the museum alone.'[38] Against the background of the debate concerning the justification of French art in German museums and the end of purchasing activity for this field of collecting in Hagen, the 1912 inventory catalogue has as much symbolic force as the participation of the Museum Folkwang in the *International Art Exhibition* organized in Cologne the same year by the 'Sonderbund', whose chair Osthaus was. This significant project, which was to become a model for the *Armory Show* in New York, derived the work of the German Expressionists from French Post-Impressionism. With Van Gogh, Cézanne, Gauguin, Cross and Signac, the canon of exhibited artists matched the profile of the Folkwang collections – or, conversely, a specific trend in collecting was manifested in the Folkwang. Accordingly, the museum loaned major works both for the so-called 'retrospective' section and for that of living artists (fig. 11; p. 319).[39]

The Collection of French Art in Essen

When the acquisition of works of French modern art at the Museum Folkwang in Hagen came to an end, Ernst Gosebruch at the Kunstmuseum Essen was just beginning to take this art into consideration with purchases. This was, without a doubt, on the one hand down to the museum's previous financial situation: it was only with the foundation of its own sponsorship association, the Essener Kunstverein (Art Association) and the present-day Kunstring Folkwang, that it was able to act independently of the other city collections and invest increasingly in contemporary art – albeit not to the extent that the new museum director imagined.[40] On the other hand, the still-young institution had since Gosebruch's provisional assumption of the post of director in 1910 attempted increasingly to position itself as a progressive establishment within the German museum landscape.[41] This is confirmed not only by the exhibition and talks programme, but among other things by the journal *Der Cicerone,* which was used as a regular publicity outlet by museums with a focus on modern art such as the Wallraf-Richartz, the Städel or indeed the Kunsthalle Mannheim. In 1912, the Kunstmuseum Essen joined this progressive line and was from then on listed just after the Museum Folkwang in Hagen under the heading 'Review – collections'.[42] 'Essen must ensure that it becomes a city of art,' the editor of the art section of the Essen *General-Anzeiger,* Max Hehemann, who was also a member of the Art Association, demanded in the same year: 'We have no money to buy Old Masters [...]. But we can set ourselves the task of showing the development of German painting in the last century, while at the same time not forgetting the connections with art abroad. [...] A modern gallery without Van Gogh is unthinkable [...]'.[43] With these words Hehemann was speaking up for the purchase of the painting *Les bateaux amarrés (Quay with*

in Hagen besitzt der Bestandskatalog von 1912 ebenso Symbolkraft wie die Beteiligung des Museum Folkwang an der im gleichen Jahr in Köln organisierten *Internationale[n] Kunstausstellung* des Sonderbundes, dem Osthaus vorstand. Das bedeutende Projekt, das zum Vorbild für die New Yorker *Armory Show* werden sollte, leitete das Schaffen der deutschen Expressionist:innen aus dem französischen Post-Impressionismus her. Mit van Gogh, Cézanne, Gauguin, Cross und Signac entsprach der gezeigte Kanon an Künstler:innen dem Profil der Folkwang-Sammlungen – oder umgekehrt manifestierte sich im Folkwang ein spezifischer Sammlungstrend. Entsprechend lieh das Museum sowohl für die sogenannte retrospektive Abteilung als auch für jene der lebenden Künstler:innen Hauptwerke (Abb. 11; S. 319).[39]

Die Sammlung französischer Kunst in Essen

Als der Erwerb von Werken der französischen Moderne am Museum Folkwang in Hagen beendet wurde, begann Ernst Gosebruch am Kunstmuseum Essen gerade, diese Kunst mit Ankäufen in den Blick zu nehmen. Geschuldet war das sicherlich zum einen der bisherigen finanziellen Situation des Museums: Erst mit der Gründung eines eigenen Fördervereins, dem Essener Kunstverein und heutigen Kunstring Folkwang, konnte es unabhängig von den übrigen städtischen Sammlungen agieren und vermehrt in zeitgenössische Kunst investieren – wenn auch nicht in dem Maße, wie es sich der neue Museumsleiter vorstellte.[40] Zum anderen war die noch junge Institution seit Gosebruchs

kommissarischer Übernahme des Direktorenpostens im Jahr 1910 verstärkt darum bemüht, sich als progressives Haus innerhalb der deutschen Museumslandschaft zu positionieren.[41] Dies belegt neben dem Ausstellungs- und Vortragsprogramm unter anderem die Zeitschrift *Der Cicerone*, die Museen mit Fokus auf der modernen Kunst wie das Wallraf-Richartz, das Städel oder auch die Kunsthalle Mannheim als ständiges Publikationsorgan nutzten. 1912 schloss sich das Kunstmuseum Essen dieser progressiven Reihe an und wurde in der Rubrik „Rundschau – Sammlungen" fortan direkt hinter dem Museum Folkwang in Hagen genannt.[42] „Essen muss sorgen, [...] eine Kunststadt zu werden", forderte im selben Jahr der Kunstschriftleiter des *Essener General-Anzeigers* Max Hehemann, der zugleich Mitglied im Kunstverein war: „Alte Meister zu kaufen, haben wir kein Geld [...]. Doch können wir uns als Aufgabe setzen, die Entwicklung der deutschen Malerei im letzten Jahrhundert zu zeigen, wobei wir die Zusammenhänge mit der Kunst des Auslands nicht vergessen dürfen. [...] Eine moderne Galerie ohne van Gogh ist undenkbar [...]".[43] Hehemann sprach sich damit zugleich für den Ankauf des Gemäldes *Les bateaux amarrés (Rhonebarken,* 1888; S. 320) aus, das Gosebruch zunächst als Leihgabe im Kunstmuseum zeigte und im Anschluss nach Rücksprache mit dem Vorstand des Kunstvereins erwarb.[44] Diese Ausweitung der Essener Sammlung passte nicht nur zum Hintergrund der allgemeinen Entwicklung in der Museums- und Ausstellungsszene, wie sie sich etwa in der Kölner Sonderbundausstellung manifestierte, sondern auch zur lokalen Situation: Schon zur Zeit,

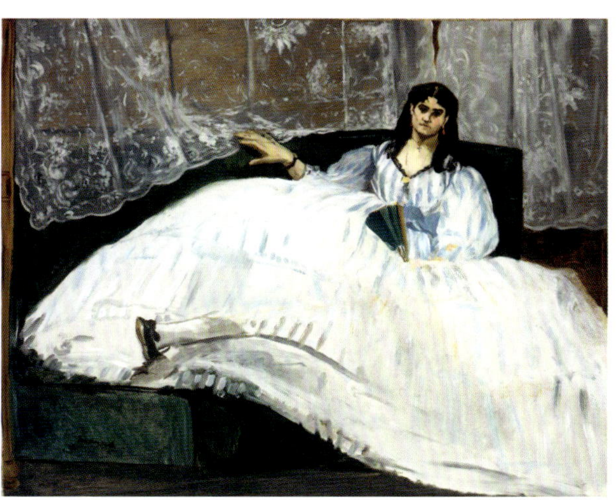

Abb. | Fig. 10
Edouard Manet, *La maîtresse de Baudelaire (Jeanne Duval),* 1862, Szépművészeti Muzeum, Budapest

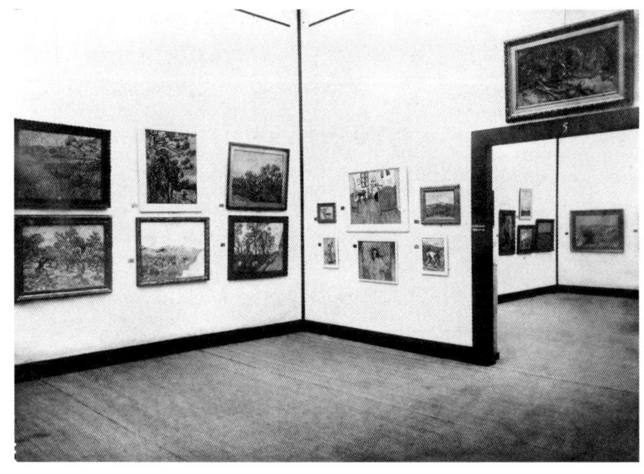

Abb. | Fig. 11
Vincent van Gogh, *Le parc de l'hôpital,
à Saint-Rémy*, 1889, Sonderbund-Ausstellung,
Köln 1912, Saal 5 | Sonderbund Exhibition,
Cologne 1912, room 5

Men Unloading Sand Barges, 1888; p. 320), which Gosebruch first showed as a loan in the Kunstmuseum and then purchased after a discussion with the chair of the Art Association.[44] This expansion of the Essen collection was in line not only with a general development in the museum and exhibition scene, as manifested, for example, in the Cologne Sonderbund exhibition, but also with the local situation: at the time when Gosebruch was still museum assistant, the focus of the art museum had shifted increasingly to German Impressionism and Post-Impressionism schooled by France. Purchases included paintings by Max Clarenbach, Fritz Erler, Albert Haueisen and Otto Modersohn, whose Worpsweder motif *Herbstabend im Moor* (*Autumn Evening in the Swamp*, ca. 1904; fig. 12) clearly shows the influence of the Barbizon School.[45] From 1910, Gosebruch further opened up the Kunstmuseum's exhibitions and acquisitions into the present and concentrated on German Expressionism, whose origins (as described above) can also be traced back to French modern art. We may take it as read that apart from establishments such as the Wallraf-Richartz-Museum under Alfred Hagelstange, the activities in the Museum Folkwang in Hagen influenced decisions in Essen: Osthaus and Gosebruch were already in close contact in 1912.[46] Van Gogh's painting *Quay with Men Unloading Sand Barges* was the first pioneering new acquisition by the Kunstmuseum Essen in the field of French modern art. Whether the funds to purchase it came from the Art Association or the Krupp Jubilee Foundation is unclear today.[47] But the price of 16,000 Marks for the painting, a high one for the institution, was still being discussed in public two years later, when Gosebruch showed his *Französische Kunstausstellung aus den letzten drei Jahrzehnten der franz. Malerei* (French Art Exhibition from the Last Three Decades of French Painting; fig 13), in connection with which the Art Association funded the purchase of a canvas by Signac at a value of 2,400 Marks – so it was investing 'only' a sixth of the sum that had been raised for the Van Gogh.[48]

With five galleries and the domed hall, the *French Art Exhibition* extended over large parts of the Grillohaus museum building on Burgplatz and gave a wide-ranging survey of developments since Impressionism. The younger generation of artists was represented to a marked degree: Pablo Picasso, Juan Gris and Georges Braque, André Derain, Maurice de Vlaminck and others represented Cubism and Fauvism; with Kees van Dongen and Marie Laurencin the exhibition opened itself up to avant-garde figure-painting.[49] In addition, Eberhard von Bodenhausen, who lived in the Bredeney district of Essen, made his significant Pointilliste collection available in its entirety.[50] As Ursula Bode has shown, the collector had for a long time appeared publicly only at the Cologne Sonderbund Exhibition in 1912 with paintings by Cézanne, Cross and Signac.[51] In the Kunstmuseum Essen the works of these artists from Bodenhausen's collection, amongst others, were prominently displayed in the domed hall; the collection thus formed one of the highlights of the exhibition.[52]

als Gosebruch noch Museumsassistent war, hatte sich der Fokus des Kunstmuseums zunehmend auf den an Frankreich geschulten deutschen Impressionismus und Post-Impressionismus verlagert. Erworben worden waren unter anderem Gemälde von Max Clarenbach, Fritz Erler, Albert Haueisen oder Otto Modersohn, dessen Worpsweder Motiv *Herbstabend im Moor* (Abb. 12) deutlich den Einfluss der Schule von Barbizon zeigt.[45] Seit 1910 öffnete Gosebruch Ausstellungen und Erwerbungen des Kunstmuseums weiter in die Gegenwart und konzentrierte sich auf den deutschen Expressionismus, dessen Ursprünge (wie oben beschrieben) historisch ebenfalls auf die französische Moderne zurückgeführt wurden. Dass neben Häusern wie dem Wallraf-Richartz-Museum unter Alfred Hagelstange die Aktivitäten am Museum Folkwang in Hagen die Entscheidungen in Essen beeinflussten, kann als gesichert gelten: Osthaus und Gosebruch pflegten 1912 bereits engen Kontakt.[46] Van Goghs Gemälde *Rhonebarken* war die erste wegweisende Neuerwerbung des Kunstmuseum Essen im Bereich der französischen Moderne. Ob die Mittel dazu aus den Erlösen des Kunstvereins oder der Krupp-Jubiläumsstiftung kamen, ist heute unklar.[47] Der für die Institution hohe Preis von 16.000 Mark aber wurde noch zwei Jahre später öffentlich diskutiert, als Gosebruch eine *Französische Kunstausstellung aus den letzten drei Jahrzehnten der franz. Malerei* (Abb. 13) zeigte, in deren Zusammenhang der Kunstverein dem Museum eine Leinwand von Signac im Wert von 2400 Mark stiftete – er investierte also „nur" rund

ein Sechstel der Summe, die für den van Gogh aufgebracht worden war.[48]

Mit fünf Sälen und der Kuppelhalle erstreckte sich die *Französische Kunstausstellung* über große Teile des Grillohauses und gab einen weitgefassten Überblick über die Entwicklungen seit dem Impressionismus. Insbesondere die jüngere Künstler:innengeneration war vertreten: Pablo Picasso, Juan Gris und Georges Braque, André Derain, Maurice de Vlaminck und andere repräsentierten Kubismus und Fauvismus; mit Kees van Dongen und Marie Laurencin öffnete sich die Schau hin zu avantgardistischen Figurenbildern.[49] Darüber hinaus stellte der im Essener Stadtteil Bredeney lebende Eberhard von Bodenhausen seine bedeutende Pointillist:innen-Sammlung vollständig zur Verfügung.[50] Wie Ursula Bode dargelegt hat, war der Sammler bislang ausschließlich auf der Kölner Sonderbundausstellung von 1912 mit Gemälden von Cézanne, Cross und Signac an die Öffentlichkeit getreten.[51] Im Kunstmuseum Essen waren die Werke dieser Künstler aus dem Besitz von Bodenhausen unter anderem prominent in der Kuppelhalle inszeniert; die Sammlung bildete damit einen der Höhepunkte der Präsentation.[52] Im gleichen Saal wurden auch Signacs *La Tour Rose, Marseille (Hafen von Marseille,* 1913; S. 301) und *Le Pont des Arts (Der Pont des Arts,* 1912/13; S. 300) gezeigt, das damals noch als *La cité* bezeichnet und als eines der schönsten Ausstellungsstücke beschrieben wurde.[53] Beide Gemälde gingen nach der Ausstellung in den Besitz des Kunstmuseum Essen über. Aus privaten Spenden gelang es Gosebruch zudem, eine Anzahlung von

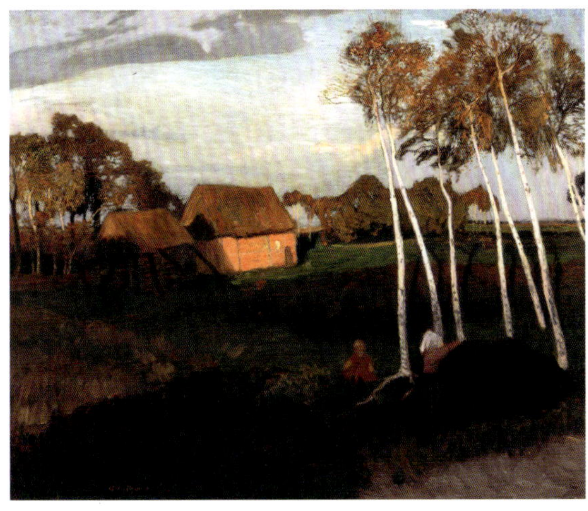

Abb. | Fig. 12
Otto Modersohn, *Herbstabend im Moor,* ca. 1904,
Museum Folkwang, Essen

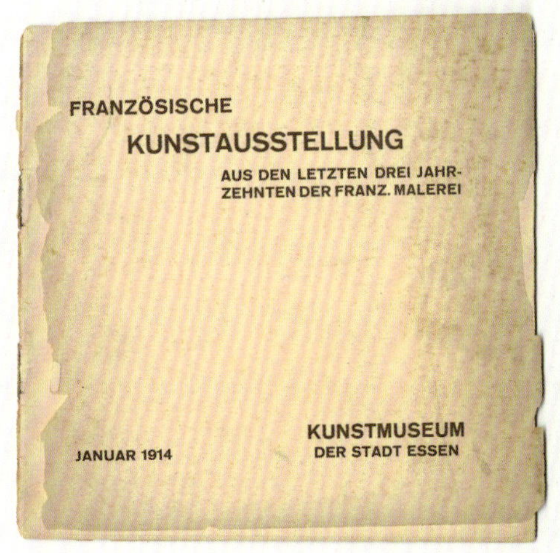

Abb. | Fig. 13
Ausst.-Kat. | exh. cat. Kunstmuseum Essen,
Januar | January 1914, Cover

Also on show in the same gallery were Signac's *La Tour Rose, Marseille* (*The Pink Tower, Marseille,* 1913; p. 301) and *Le Pont des Arts* (*The Pont des Arts,* 1912/13; p. 300), still identified at the time as *La cité,* and described as one of the most beautiful exhibits.[53] After the exhibition both paintings entered the collection of the Kunstmuseum Essen. From private subscriptions Gosebruch also managed to raise a payment of 10,000 Marks for a representative landscape by Claude Monet, which in contemporary sources is called *Bassin d'Argenteuil* (*The Basin at Argenteuil,* 1872).[54] By 1918, however, that the Kunstmuseum would not succeed in raising the balance of the total purchase price of 28,000 francs, which was why Gustav Krupp von Bohlen und Halbach agreed to make available funds from the Krupp Jubilee Foundation and incorporate the painting into its collection.[55] In 1922, after the transfer of the Hagen collections to Essen, Gosebruch would request the work as a loan.

In retrospect the *French Art Exhibition* is an important basis for the further development of the French holdings in Essen, particularly with reference to Cubism: we must assume that not only André Derain's *Les salins de Martigues* (*Salt Ponds in Martigues,* 1913) was bought after the exhibition;[56] by 1924, with *Vue de Cagnes* (*View of Cagnes;* fig. 14) Gosebruch transferred another work by the artist from the former possession of the Wallraf-Richartz-Museum.[57] In addition the collector Carl Hagemann, who was closely involved with the museum, gifted his home town with *La calanque, temps gris* (*The Cove, La Ciotat,*

1907, Bavarian State Painting Collections), by Georges Braque, along with André Derain's still life *Nature morte au calvaire* (*Still Life with Calvary,* 1912, Kunstmuseum Basel) and *Nature morte, pain et fruits,* (*Still Life,* 1913, National Gallery of Art, Washington) three more works by artists whose works had been introduced to the Essen public in 1914.[58]

By this point most of Osthaus's holdings had been part of the Essen collection for seven years, and the Museum Folkwang had reopened in its new location.[59] After the decision had been made, by 1925 at the latest, to erect a new building on Bismarckstrasse for the collections, which had grown significantly through the merger, Gosebruch strove, while this building work was still going on, to bring the Hagen and Essen collections together in a meaningful way through targeted purchases.[60] This seems all the more remarkable in the field of French art when we bear in mind that the occupation of the Ruhr had only just come to an end. With Marc Chagall's *Purim* (fig. 15), for example, Gosebruch was establishing a connection with works from the École de Paris such as Lasar Segall's *Veuve* (*The Widow,* 1919, destroyed) from Osthaus's collection.[61] Today, however, the most important acquisition in the field of French modern art under Gosebruch is held to be Manet's *Portrait de Faure dans le rôle d'Hamlet* (*Portrait of Faure as Hamlet,* 1877; p. 223), a suggestion actively supported by Georg Simon Hirschland, co-owner of the Simon Hirschland banking house, head of the Jewish community in Essen and founder

37

10.000 Mark auf eine repräsentative Landschaft von Claude Monet zu leisten, die in den zeitgenössischen Quellen *Bassin d'Argenteuil (Seinebecken von Argenteuil,* 1872) genannt wird.[54] Dem Kunstmuseum sollte es bis 1918 aber nicht gelingen, den Restbetrag der insgesamt 28.000 Francs umfassenden Kaufsumme aufzubringen, weshalb Gustav Krupp von Bohlen und Halbach einwilligte, Mittel der Krupp-Jubiläumsstiftung zur Verfügung zu stellen und das Gemälde in diese zu übernehmen.[55] 1922, nach der Überführung der Hagener Bestände nach Essen, sollte Gosebruch das Werk als Leihgabe erbitten.

Rückblickend bildete die *Französische Kunstausstellung* ein wichtiges Fundament für die weitere Entwicklung der französischen Bestände in Essen, insbesondere in Hinblick auf den Kubismus: Zu vermuten ist nicht nur, dass im Zuge der Ausstellung auch André Derains *Les salins de Martigues (Die Salzteiche von Martigues,* 1913) erworben wurde;[56] spätestens 1924 übernahm Gosebruch mit *Vue de Cagnes (Ansicht von Cagnes;* Abb. 14) ein weiteres Werk des Künstlers aus dem ehemaligen Besitz des Wallraf-Richartz-Museums.[57] Darüber hinaus schenkte der mit dem Haus eng verbundene Sammler Carl Hagemann seiner Heimatstadt mit *La calanque, temps gris (Bucht bei La Ciotat,* 1907, Bayerische Staatsgemäldesammlungen, München) von Georges Braque sowie André Derains Stillleben *Nature morte au calvaire (Stillleben mit Kalvarienberg,* 1912, Kunstmuseum Basel) und *Nature morte, pain et fruits (Stillleben, Brot und Früchte,* 1913, National Gallery of Art, Washington) ab 1929 drei weitere Werke

von Künstlern, deren Arbeiten dem Essener Publikum schon 1914 vorgestellt worden waren.[58]

Zu diesem Zeitpunkt war der Großteil der Osthaus'schen Bestände bereits seit sieben Jahren in Essener Besitz übergegangen und das Museum Folkwang am neuen Standort wiedereröffnet.[59] Nachdem spätestens 1925 die Entscheidung gefallen war, an der Bismarckstraße einen Neubau für die durch den Zukauf signifikant angewachsenen Sammlungen zu errichten, bemühte sich Gosebruch parallel zu den Bauarbeiten durch gezielte Erwerbungen um eine sinnvolle Zusammenführung der Hagener und Essener Bestände.[60] Im Bereich der französischen Kunst erscheint dies umso bemerkenswerter, bedenkt man, dass die Ruhrbesatzung gerade erst beendet war. Mit Marc Chagalls *Purim (Purimfest;* Abb. 15) knüpfte Gosebruch 1928 etwa an Werke der Ecole de Paris wie Lasar Segalls *Veuve (Die Witwe,* 1919, zerstört) aus der Osthaus'schen Sammlung an.[61] Als bedeutendster Zukauf im Bereich der französischen Moderne unter Gosebruch gilt heute aber Manets *Portrait de Faure dans le rôle d'Hamlet (Der Sänger Jean Baptiste Faure als Hamlet,* 1877; S. 223), ein Vorschlag, den Georg Simon Hirschland, Mitinhaber des Bankhauses Simon Hirschland, Vorsteher der jüdischen Gemeinde in Essen und Gründungsmitglied des Folkwang-Museumsvereins, aktiv unterstützte.[62] Die französische Kunst des Impressionismus und Post-Impressionismus bildete auch in den Privatsammlungen der Hirschland einen Schwerpunkt; Werke wie van Goghs *Les roses blanches (Weiße Rosen;* Abb. 16) sollten nach der Enteignung der Familie 1939 weit unterhalb ihres

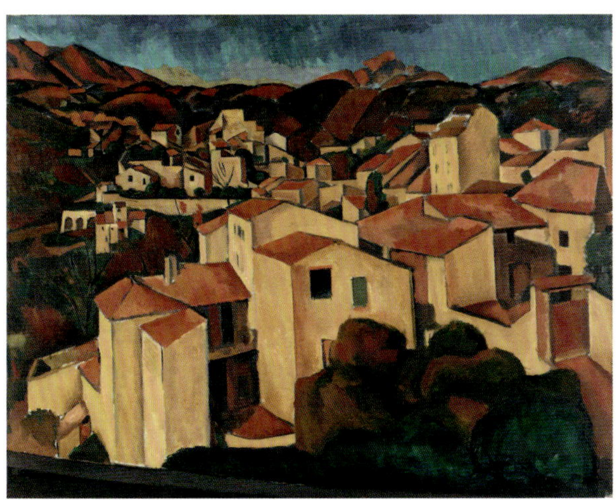

Abb. | Fig. 14
André Derain, *Vue de Cagnes,* 1910,
Museum Folkwang, Essen

member of the Folkwang Museum Association.[62] The French art of Impressionism and Post-Impressionism was also a focus in the Hirschlands' private collections; works like Van Gogh's *Les roses blanches* (*White Roses*; fig. 16) would be incorporated into the collection of the Museum Folkwang, far below their actual value, after the expropriation of the family's possessions in 1939. Similarly, from 1940, a large portfolio of French art of the eighteenth and nineteenth centuries was acquired at low prices from Germany's occupied neighbour (fig. 17).[63] These additions to the collection, viewed critically today, apparently encountered no resistance (Albert Bormann would even temporarily appropriate Hirschland's Van Gogh for the Reich Chancellery in Berlin),[64] while the acquisition in 1927 of Manet's painting from the Matthiesen Gallery in Berlin, which specialized in French Impressionism, had sparked another scandal. Spurred by the Berlin press a debate raged, not without reason, about the enormously high purchase price, and Essen's mayor felt forced to make an official statement on the subject: no city funds had been used for the purchase.[65] Not all details concerning the financing of the painting by the museum, 200,000 Marks in all, were revealed until well into the 1960s.[66] In spite of these adversities, and after Osthaus's failed efforts to buy *La maîtresse de Baudelaire,* a representative work by Manet finally complemented the Folkwang collections from 1927. Gosebruch stressed the importance of the painting, on a par with Daumier's *Ecce homo* and Renoir's *Lise,* and by the beginning of 1928, he pursued concrete plans for the ways in which he wanted to present French modern art in Essen: 'In the new building of the Folkwang Museum, which is due to open in six months, the French hall, which runs from Corot via Daumier,

Manet and Renoir to Van Gogh, Gauguin, Derain and Matisse, will be a great attraction.' [67] This 'French hall' was subsequently installed on the first floor of the so-called Körner building in Essen (fig. 18). With it, Gosebruch visualized the predominant theory of the evolution of modern art and complemented the presentation on the moving longitudinal walls of the gallery with works from German Expressionism. Over a period of almost twenty years, the hanging in the Museum Folkwang in Hagen had already tended towards a comparable dialogue between the generations. In the great picture hall on the upper floor, it had assumed its definitive form by 1920, when the iconic view of the installation in the painting gallery was published in Osthaus's monograph on Henry van de Velde (fig. 3).[68]

An Introduction to the Exhibition
and the Catalogue

As we have shown, the French art of the late nineteenth and early twentieth centuries developed into a focus of the collections of the Museum Folkwang in Hagen. From 1912, Ernst Gosebruch pursued a similar strategy at the Kunstmuseum Essen, and continued to develop it consistently from 1922 against the background of the amalgamation of the Hagen and Essen collections. With major acquisitions such as Claude Monet's *Le bassin aux nymphéas* (*The Water Lily Pond,* ca. 1916; p. 283) or Courbet's *La vague* (*The Wave,* 1870; p. 264) and reacquisitions such as Maillol's *Young Girl Standing* (fig. 8) the Museum Folkwang was able to follow this line of development through the prosperous post-war years until the present day in Essen. Ultimately the definition and reception of the Museum Folkwang as a

eigentlichen Wertes dem Bestand des Museum Folkwang einverleibt werden. Ebenso wurde ab 1940 ein größeres Konvolut an französischer Kunst des 18. und 19. Jahrhunderts aus dem von Deutschland besetzten Nachbarland zu niedrigsten Preisen erworben (Abb. 17).[63] Diese heute kritisch beurteilten Sammlungserweiterungen erregten anscheinend keinen Widerstand (Albert Bormann sollte Hirschlands van Gogh sogar zeitweise für die Berliner Reichskanzlei vereinnahmen)[64], während die Übernahme des Manet-Gemäldes aus der auf den französischen Impressionismus spezialisierten Berliner Galerie Matthiesen 1927 abermals einen Skandal ausgelöst hatte: Angestoßen von der Berliner Presse wurde in der Debatte nicht zu Unrecht über die enorme Höhe des Ankaufspreises spekuliert, woraufhin der Essener Oberbürgermeister sich zur öffentlichen Stellungnahme gezwungen sah: Für den Erwerb des Gemäldes würden keine städtischen Mittel verausgabt.[65] Noch bis weit in die 1960er-Jahre hinein wurde die Finanzierung des Gemäldes in Höhe von insgesamt 200.000 Mark von Seiten des Museums nicht in allen Details offengelegt.[66] Trotz dieser Widrigkeiten und nach Osthaus' gescheiterten Bemühungen um *Baudelaires Geliebte* ergänzte ab 1927 endlich ein repräsentatives Werk Manets die Folkwang-Sammlungen. Gosebruch betonte die Daumiers *Ecce homo* und Renoirs *Lise* ebenbürtige Bedeutung des Gemäldes und verfolgte spätestens seit Anfang 1929 konkrete Pläne, wie er die französische Moderne in Essen präsentieren wollte: „In dem Neubau des Folkwang-Museums, dessen Eröffnung in einem halben Jahr zu erwarten

ist, wird der Franzosensaal, der von Corot über Daumier, Manet, Renoir zu van Gogh, Gauguin, Derain und Matisse führt, eine große Sehenswürdigkeit sein."[67] Dieser „Franzosensaal" wurde in der Folge im ersten Obergeschoss des sogenannten Körnerbaus in Essen eingerichtet (Abb. 18). Mit ihm visualisierte Gosebruch die vorherrschende Entwicklungstheorie der modernen Kunst, ergänzte er die Präsentation auf den mobilen Längswänden des Raumes doch mit Werken des deutschen Expressionismus. Auf einen vergleichbaren Dialog zwischen den Generationen war über einen Zeitraum von fast zwanzig Jahren schon die Hängung im Museum Folkwang in Hagen zugespitzt worden. Im großen Bildersaal des Obergeschosses hatte sie ihre endgültige Form spätestens dann erreicht, als 1920 die heute ikonische Installationsansicht der Gemäldegalerie in Osthaus' Monografie zu Henry van de Velde publiziert wurde (Abb. 3).[68]

Zur Einführung in Ausstellung und Katalog

Wie gezeigt worden ist, entwickelte sich die französische Kunst des ausgehenden 19. und beginnenden 20. Jahrhunderts seit den ersten Jahren des Museum Folkwang in Hagen zu einem Schwerpunkt der Sammlungen. Ab 1912 verfolgte Ernst Gosebruch am Kunstmuseum Essen eine vergleichbare Strategie und dachte diese ab 1922 vor dem Hintergrund einer Zusammenführung der Hagener und Essener Bestände konsequent weiter. Mit kapitalen Erwerbungen wie Claude Monets *Le bassin aux nymphéas (Der Seerosenteich*, ca. 1916; S. 283)

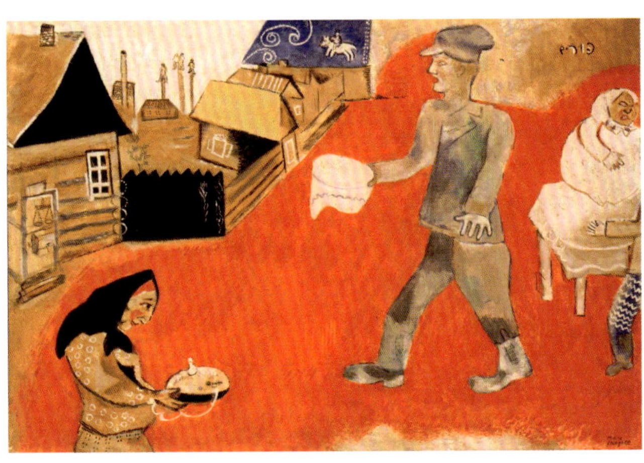

Abb. | Fig. 15
Marc Chagall, *Purim,* ca. 1916/17,
Philadelphia Museum of Art

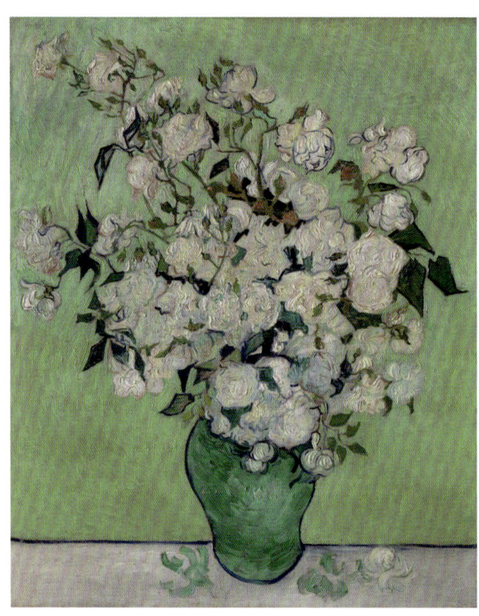

Abb. | Fig. 16
Vincent van Gogh, *Les roses blanches,* 1890,
The Metropolitan Museum of Art, New York

museum of modern art continues to maintain the
focus originally propagated by Karl Ernst Osthaus.
So it was natural to begin the celebrations for the
100-year Jubilee with an exhibition in Essen that
places French Impressionism and Post-Impressionism at the centre of consideration. The fascination
that has emanated from Osthaus from the 1920s at
the latest remains unbroken, although the popular
image of the man and his collections demands
to be put in perspective in many respects. When
Amy Gilman, director of the Chazen Museum of Art
in Wisconsin, recently called for the age of the
visionary museum director to be brought to an end
in the twenty-first century,[69] this can equally apply
to the romantic idea connected with the generation of directors at the beginning of the twentieth
century: it demonstrates clear parallels with the
cult around the male genius artist. Far from being
the creation of a single individual, the emergence
of the Folkwang collections can be traced back to
a network. The people 'in the shadow of Osthaus'
have long been named throughout the literature,
and the significance that an advisor like Henry van
de Velde had for the development of the collections has always been emphasized – interestingly,
quite in contrast with the role that someone like
the artist Ida Gerhardi played in establishing such
an important contact as that with Auguste Rodin in
Paris.[70] In his essay in this volume, for example,
Rainer Stamm introduces in Theodor Rocholl, Emil
Rudolf Weiss and Konrad Ferdinand von Freyhold,
three further intermediaries who influenced the
fate of the Folkwang collections at different times.
None the less, Karl Ernst Osthaus has never faded
into the background as the major player at the
Folkwang, while his contemporary Helene Kröller-
Müller still has her autonomy and expertise as a
collector denied in a publication from the 2000s

oder Courbets *La vague (Die Woge*, 1870; S. 264)
bis hin zu Rückkäufen wie Maillols *Stehender
junger Frau* (Abb. 8) konnte das Museum Folkwang
diese Entwicklungslinie über die prosperierenden
Nachkriegsjahre bis in unsere Gegenwart hinein
in Essen weiterverfolgen. Letztlich basiert die Definition und Rezeption des Museum Folkwang als
Museum für moderne Kunst bis heute maßgeblich
auf dem schon von Karl Ernst Osthaus propagierten Fokus. Es lag daher nahe, die Feierlichkeiten
zum hundertjährigen Jubiläum am Standort Essen
mit einer Ausstellung zu beginnen, die den französischen Impressionismus und Post-Impressionismus ins Zentrum der Betrachtung stellt. Die Faszination, die spätestens seit den 1920er-Jahren
von Osthaus ausgeht, ist weiterhin ungebrochen,
obwohl das landläufige Bild seiner Person wie
auch seiner Sammlungen längst in vielerlei Hinsicht
zu relativieren ist. Wenn Amy Gilman, Direktorin
des Chazen Museum of Art in Wisconsin, erst
jüngst gefordert hat, dass die Ära des visionären
Museumsleiters im 21. Jahrhundert beendet werden sollte,[69] so kann dies gleichermaßen für die
romantische Vorstellung gelten, die sich mit der
Direktorengeneration am Beginn des 20. Jahrhunderts verbindet; sie weist deutliche Parallelen zum
Kult um das männliche Künstlergenie auf. Weit
mehr als eine Kreation einer einzigen Person lässt
sich die Entstehung der Folkwang-Sammlungen
auf ein Netzwerk zurückführen. Die Personen „im
Schatten von Osthaus" sind in der Literatur längst
in weiten Teilen benannt, die Bedeutung, die
ein Berater wie Henry van de Velde für die Entwicklung der Sammlungen hatte, ist stets hervorgehoben worden – interessanterweise ganz im
Gegensatz zu der Rolle, die etwa die Künstlerin
Ida Gerhardi bei der Vermittlung eines so wichtigen Kontakts wie dem zu Auguste Rodin in Paris
spielte.[70] Rainer Stamm stellt in seinem Beitrag

zu diesem Band mit Theodor Rocholl, Emil Rudolf
Weiss und Konrad Ferdinand von Freyhold allein
drei weitere Vermittler vor, die auf das Geschick
der Folkwang-Sammlungen zu unterschiedlicher
Zeit Einfluss nahmen. Dessen ungeachtet ist Karl
Ernst Osthaus als handelnder Akteur des Folkwang
in der Rezeption nie in den Hintergrund getreten,
während seiner Zeitgenossin Helene Kröller-Müller
aufgrund ihres Rückgriffs auf (männliche) Berater
noch in einer Publikation aus den 2000er-Jahren
Autonomie und Expertise als Sammlerin abgespro-
chen werden.[71] Neben dem festlichen Begehen
des hundertjährigen Jubiläums mit einer Würdigung der reichen Bestände im Museum Folkwang
soll deshalb gerade auch auf Probleme hingewiesen werden, die die Ausstellung aufgeworfen hat,
und die Lösungen benannt werden, die – so weit
möglich – gefunden wurden. Aufgrund ihrer unterschiedlichen Medialität ergänzen sich Katalog
und Ausstellung dabei. Einige Fragen müssen jedoch weiterhin unbeantwortet bleiben, so etwa
die nach dem Beweggrund für Osthaus' relativ
schnellen Wandel zum Liebhaber und Verteidi-
ger der französischen Moderne, welcher seiner
deutsch-nationalen Gesinnung diametral gegen-
übersteht. Dass er diese Haltung um 1900 nicht
einfach hinter sich ließ, wie noch in den 1970er-
Jahren behauptet worden ist,[72] zeigt sich insbesondere in den Aktivitäten der 1910er-Jahre; und das
nicht nur aus dem Blickwinkel des heutigen post-
kolonialen Diskurses. Der Einfluss van de Veldes
mag zur Offenheit für die Kunst des Nachbarlandes
beigetragen haben, ihn aber als einzigen Impetus
zu interpretieren, erscheint unzureichend.

Erklärtes Ziel dieses Ausstellungsprojekts war es
von Beginn an, die Folkwang-Bestände nicht singulär
zu betrachten, sondern innerhalb der Sammlungs-
und Institutionsgeschichte des 20. Jahrhunderts
zu verorten, um sich so, frei nach Verhaeren, nicht

because of her reliance on (male) advisors.[71] For this reason, apart from the celebration of the 100-year Jubilee with an appreciation of the rich holdings of the Museum Folkwang, we should point out some problems thrown up by the exhibition and name the solutions which – as far as possible – were found for them. Because of their different media, the catalogue and the exhibition complement one another. Some questions, however, must remain unanswered, such as the motivation behind Osthaus's relatively swift transformation into a lover and defender of French modern art, which is diametrically opposed to his German-nationalist inclinations. The fact that he did not simply abandon this attitude around 1900, as was still being claimed in the 1970s,[72] is particularly apparent in the activities of the 1910s; and not only from the point of view of contemporary postcolonial discourse. Van de Velde's influence may have played a part in his openness to the art of his country's neighbour, but to see that as the sole impulse appears inadequate.

The stated goal of this exhibition project from the outset was not to view the Folkwang holdings in isolation, but rather to locate them within the history of collecting and institutions in the twentieth century, in order, to paraphrase Verhaeren, not to move in an 'unchanging circle', the risk sometimes inherent in a preoccupation with one's own collection. Through collaboration with the National Museum of Western Art in Tokyo, which houses the core holdings of the collection of Kōjirō Matsukata, a unique opportunity presented itself. Osthaus and Matsukata were separated by an age difference of less than eight years. They both began collecting in reaction to the specific cultural or business milieux that surrounded them: mining or shipbuilding (pp. 205, 198). From the beginning of their collecting activity both planned to generate added value, with the conception of two public museums, for the societies in which they were rooted. Even though they were separated by an ocean, and the younger Osthaus began making his acquisitions about twenty years before Matsukata, the two collectors were both led to the French art of Impressionism and Post-Impressionism by artistic and museum-based advisors. This collecting focus was powerfully consolidated within a short time, in the Folkwang between 1901 and 1913, in the case of Matsukata from about 1917 until the mid-1920s. While their interests in certain artists coincided, their attention, for example in the case of Rodin or Gauguin could concentrate completely on different phases of their work. While many positions in fin-de-siècle French art, such as the work of Van Gogh, had not yet gained widespread recognition, and at the time of the first phase of purchasing in Hagen were even viewed critically, by the time of Matsukata's involvement, Impressionism and Post-Impressionism had already developed into global phenomena. Finally, a piece of the history of twentieth-century taste can be understood from the stories of the collections of the Museum Folkwang and the National Museum of Western Art. Following on from her joint publication with Alexis Clark from 2020, in her contribution to this catalogue Frances Fowle shows that this development occurred not only among artists, but also within the international collecting body. Another thing that becomes clear is the immense influence that the economic situation of the individual collectors had on the art that they owned. On the one hand, the different financial forces among patrons influenced purchasing decisions, as can be read for example in the extensive collection of paintings by Monet in Matsukata's possession, while the

43

in dem „gleichbleibenden Kreis" zu bewegen, den die Beschäftigung mit den eigenen Werken als Gefahr bergen kann. Durch die Kooperation mit dem National Museum of Western Art in Tokio, das den Kernbestand der Sammlung von Kōjirō Matsukata bewahrt, bot sich dazu eine einzigartige Möglichkeit. Osthaus und Matsukata trennte ein Altersunterschied von nicht einmal acht Jahren. Beide begannen ihre Sammlertätigkeit in Reaktion auf das spezifische kulturelle bzw. unternehmerische Milieu, das sie umgab: den Berg- bzw. Schiffsbau (S. 205, 198). Beide beabsichtigten vom Anfang ihres Sammelns an mit der Konzeption zweier öffentlicher Museen Mehrwert für die Gesellschaften zu generieren, in denen sie verankert waren. Obwohl ein Ozean zwischen ihnen lag und der jüngere Osthaus etwa zwanzig Jahre vor Matsukata mit seinen Ankäufen begann, fanden die zwei Sammler angeregt durch künstlerische und museale Berater:innen zur französischen Kunst des Impressionismus und Post-Impressionismus. Dieser Sammlungsfokus wurde innerhalb von kurzer Zeit stark ausgebaut, im Folkwang zwischen 1901 und 1913, bei Matsukata von etwa 1917 bis in die Mitte der 1920er-Jahre. Überschnitten sich dabei die Interessen für bestimmte Künstler:innen, konnte sich die Aufmerksamkeit, beispielsweise im Fall von Rodin oder Gauguin, durchaus auf verschiedene Werkphasen konzentrieren. Während viele Positionen der französischen Kunst um die Jahrhundertwende, wie etwa das Schaffen van Goghs, noch keine breite Anerkennung gefunden hatten, sondern zur Zeit der ersten Ankaufsphase in Hagen sogar kritisch beurteilten wurden, hatten sich

Impressionismus und Post-Impressionismus während Matsukatas Engagement bereits zu globalen Phänomenen entwickelt. Letztlich lässt sich an den Geschichten der Sammlungen des Museum Folkwang und des National Museum of Western Art ein Stück Geschmackshistorie des 20. Jahrhunderts nachvollziehen. Anknüpfend an ihre gemeinsame Publikation mit Alexis Clark aus dem Jahr 2020 beleuchtet Frances Fowle in ihrem Beitrag zu diesem Katalog, dass sich diese Entwicklung nicht nur auf der Seite der Künstler:innen vollzog, sondern ebenso innerhalb der internationalen Sammler:innenschaft. Deutlich wird dabei auch, welchen immensen Einfluss die ökonomische Situation der einzelnen Sammler:innen auf ihren Kunstbesitz ausübte. Die unterschiedliche Finanzkraft von Mäzen:innen beeinflusste einerseits Kaufentscheidungen, abzulesen etwa am umfangreichen Konvolut von Bildern Monets im Besitz von Matsukata, während das Museum Folkwang, trotz der Bemühungen Gosebruchs, erst in den 1960er-Jahren Werke des Künstlers in seinen Bestand integrieren konnte. Dabei ist, wie Shingo Shimada in seinem Beitrag am Beispiel von Matsukata herausstellt, aus heutigem Blickwinkel durchaus kritisch zu betrachten, auf welche Weise das Vermögen zuvor erlangt worden war (oder, wenn man den Gedanken für die Osthaus'schen Bestände fortsetzt, in welche Objekte dieses zu welcher Zeit investiert wurde). Andererseits mussten sowohl die Sammlung Matsukata als auch die des Folkwang in finanziellen wie politischen Krisenzeiten wesentliche Einschnitte hinnehmen. Hinsichtlich der schieren Menge an Verlusten von

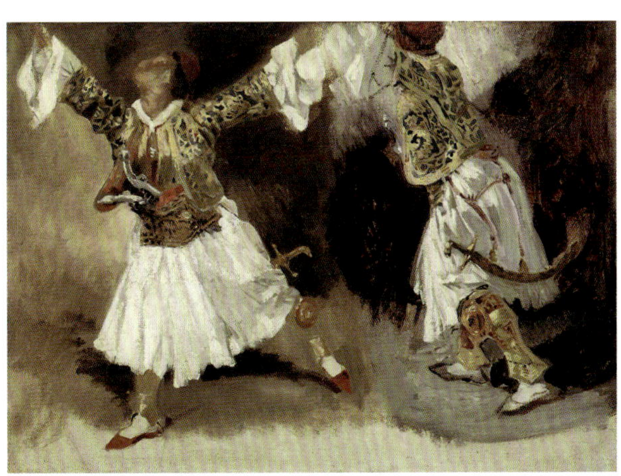

Abb. | Fig. 17
Eugène Delacroix, *Deux guerriers grecs dansant. Etude de costumes souliotes*, 1823–1826, Musée du Louvre, Paris

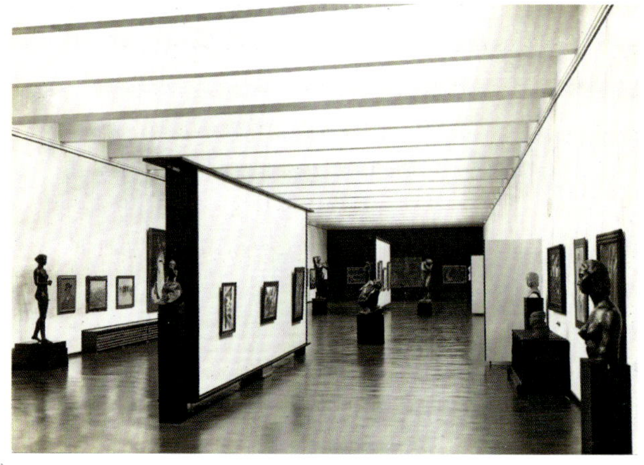

Museum Folkwang, in spite of Gosebruch's efforts, could not incorporate works by the artist into ts holdings until the 1960s. At the same time, as Shingo Shimada highlights in his essay using the example of Matsukata, from today's point of view we should take an entirely critical view of the way in which the assets had previously been acquired (or, if we extend the idea to Osthaus's holdings, which objects they were invested in and at what time). On the other hand, both the Matsukata and the Folkwang collections were subject to significant losses in times of financial and political crisis. In terms of the sheer quantity of works lost, these were probably more drastic for Matsukata, if we consider only the thirteen auctions across which large parts of the holdings were dispersed between 1928 and 1941, or indeed the London Pantechnicon fire of 1939, which destroyed over 900 works that were temporarily stored there.[73] Unlike collections such as that of Elizabeth Workman, however, the two collections were none the less fortunate in that a considerable holding of works was kept together because it either was or was due to be institutionalized. According to Léa Saint-Raymond and Maxime Georges Métraux's expositions in this volume, it can be argued that the very confiscation of Matsukata's collection by the French state during the Second World War was pursuing that precise purpose before the idea of a national museum of Western art even took shape. This continues to influence the reception of the collections of Matsukata and Osthaus even today, because their fame can be traced back to their institutionalization. David Challis speaks in another context about the 'economy of translocation',[74] the title of the exhibition, *Images of a Floating World*, refers to the movements of the art works shown in this catalogue between countries and continents; it also, however, refers to the historical upheavals and instabilities which led to fact that the Matsukata and Osthaus collections now exist neither in their original form nor in their original place. At the same time the title refers to the world of motifs of Impressionism and Post-Impressionism, in which water, in its various states, and the fluidity of the gaze play crucial parts (pp. 303, 317).

In view of the contemporary discourse around global modern art, from the start of the project it seemed imperative to break open deliberately the Eurocentric focus of the exhibition and not only to bring French art from Japan to Essen, particularly given – as Marie Yasunaga explains in her essay – both Kōjirō Matsukata and Karl Ernst Osthaus collected Japanese art and exhibited it, or planned to, in their museums alongside European works. After lengthy negotiations, the pandemic, together with other circumstances, unfortunately prevented a collection of *ukiyo-e* (woodblock prints) formerly owned by Matsukata from enriching the exhibition. Thanks to support from the Tokyo National Museum, however, this catalogue is able to illustrate a representative selection of valuable pieces (pp. 256–261). In the Museum Folkwang in Hagen, Japanese art was presented as an immediate precursor to and hence precondition for French modern art (p. 180, fig. 6).[75] The presentation of

45

Werken waren diese für Matsukata ohne Zweifel tiefgreifender, bedenkt man allein die 13 Auktionen, über die große Teile der Bestände zwischen 1928 und 1941 verstreut wurden, oder auch das Feuer im Londoner Pantechnicon-Haus, das 1939 über 900 dort zwischengelagerte Kunstwerke zerstörte.[73] Im Gegensatz zu Sammlungen wie jener von Elizabeth Workman aber war den beiden Sammlungen nichtsdestotrotz das Glück beschieden, dass ein maßgeblicher Bestand an Werken im Verbund erhalten blieb, weil er institutionalisiert war bzw. werden sollte. Nach Léa Saint-Raymonds und Maxime Georges Métraux' Ausführungen in diesem Band lässt sich argumentieren, dass schon die Beschlagnahmung der Sammlung Matsukata durch den französischen Staat während des Zweiten Weltkriegs eben jenen Zweck verfolgte, bevor die Idee eines Nationalmuseums für westliche Kunst überhaupt Gestalt annahm. Dies beeinflusst die Rezeption der Sammlungen von Matsukata und Osthaus noch heute nachhaltig, denn ihre Bekanntheit ist auf ihre Institutionalisierung zurückzuführen. Hat David Challis in anderem Zusammenhang von der „Ökonomie der Translokation" gesprochen,[74] dann knüpft der Titel der Ausstellung, *Bilder einer fließenden Welt,* zum einen an die Bewegungen der in diesem Katalog abgebildeten Kunstwerke zwischen Ländern und Kontinenten an; zum anderen spielt er aber auch auf die historischen Umbrüche und Instabilitäten an, die dazu führten, dass die Sammlungen Matsukata und Osthaus heute weder in ihrer ursprünglichen Form noch am ursprünglichen Ort fortbestehen. Zugleich nimmt der Titel Bezug auf die Motivwelt von Impressionismus und Post-Impressionismus, in dem das Wasser in seinen unterschiedlichen Aggregatzuständen sowie das Fluide des Blicks entscheidende Rollen spielen (S. 303, 317).

Angesichts des aktuellen Diskurses um eine globale Moderne erschien es von Beginn des

Projekts an zwingend, den eurozentristischen Fokus der Ausstellung gezielt aufzubrechen und nicht ausschließlich französische Kunst aus Japan nach Essen zu bringen, zumal – wie Marie Yasunaga in ihrem Beitrag darlegt – sowohl Kōjirō Matsukata als auch Karl Ernst Osthaus japanische Kunst sammelten und in ihren Museen gemeinsam mit europäischen Werken ausstellten bzw. zu zeigen beabsichtigten. Nach langen Verhandlungen hat die pandemische Lage im Zusammenspiel mit anderen Umständen unglücklicherweise verhindert, dass ein Konvolut von *ukiyo-e* (Holzschnitten) aus ehemaligem Matsukata-Besitz die Ausstellung bereichert. Dank der Unterstützung des Nationalmuseums in Tokio kann dieser Katalog aber eine repräsentative Auswahl der wertvollen Stücke abbilden (S. 256–261). Die japanische Kunst wurde im Museum Folkwang in Hagen als unmittelbarer Vorläufer, das heißt als Voraussetzung für die französische Moderne inszeniert (S. 180, Abb. 6).[75] Die Präsentation von ausgewählten japanischen Objekten aus dem Osthaus'schen Bestand in *Bilder einer fließenden Welt* knüpft an diese Vorstellung an (S. 253–255).

Darüber hinaus nehmen drei großformatige Werke von Chiharu Shiota (*1972) und Tabaimo (*1975) mit irisierend-roten Polyurethan-Netzen und immersiven Videoprojektionen an neuralgischen Punkten den Raum der Ausstellung für sich ein. Das Zusammenwirken von Geschichte und Gegenwart, der Austausch zwischen der älteren und der jüngeren Künstlergeneration, der sich dadurch sowohl inhaltlich als auch symbolisch eröffnet – diese Aspekte gehörten zu den Hauptbeweggründen, warum Matsukata und Osthaus für ihre Sammlungen Museen konzipierten. Daher ist es uns eine besondere Freude, dass Tabaimo in Auseinandersetzung mit der japanischen Sammlung des Museum Folkwang für die Ausstellung eine neue Arbeit geschaffen hat und die Bestseller-Autorin

selected Japanese objects from Osthaus's collection in *Images of a Floating World* derives from this idea (pp. 253–255).

Apart from this, three large-format works by Chiharu Shiota (b. 1972) and Tabaimo (b. 1975) with iridescent red polyurethane nets and immersive video projections at neuralgic points occupy the exhibition space. The interplay of history and the present, the exchange between the older and the younger generation of artists that is opened both symbolically and in terms of content were among the chief motivations for Matsukata and Osthaus in conceiving museums for their collections. So, we are particularly delighted that Tabaimo has made a new work for the exhibition in dialogue with the Japanese collection of the Museum Folkwang, and the bestselling author Sayaka Murata (b. 1979) has written a short story specially for the accompanying catalogue. At the same time, the three positions of contemporary women artists from the fields of visual art and literature are deliberate insertions within the male artistic canon propagated by the Matsukata and Osthaus collections. With only a few exceptions the role of women in these collections, aside from that of the relatively ignored intermediary, was not that of a creator of art, but was limited to being the object in the image, as strikingly displayed in Renoir's depiction of his companion Lise Tréhot as a lady of the harem (p. 219). In this con-text, Ida Gerhardi may once again be seen as an example of the fact that this discrepancy may be explained not only with reference to historical circumstances or the history of the collection. As early as 1902 the artist reported in a letter to her sister: 'On Wednesday afternoon Herr Osthaus was here with his charming young wife and, so to speak, "dumbstruck" about my exhibition, wants to have me as a professor at his painting school in Hagen, where he is already employing a quite famous Impressionist, Rohlfs [p. 212] – now what he was lacking was someone like me.'[76] Why then, given this enthusiasm, did only Gerhardi's commissioned portraits enter the collection of the Museum Folkwang in Hagen – works that enabled the painter to make a living – but not the progressive compositions from her time in Paris?

Over a century after the death of Émile Verhaeren, the author Elif Shafak has also described the present day as a time of fragmentation. Borrowing from a poem by Walt Whitman she describes our human nature as immeasurable, and as containing huge diversity.[77] In Whitman's original words: 'Do I contradict myself? / Very well then I contradict myself, (I am large, I contain multitudes.)'[78] In the kaleidoscope that this exhibition and the accompanying catalogue wish to open up in juxtaposing two significant collections from the first half of the twentieth century and their founders, contradictions also find their justification.

Sayaka Murata (*1979) für den begleitenden Katalog eigens eine Kurzgeschichte entwickelte. Zugleich handelt es sich bei den drei Positionen zeitgenössischer Künstlerinnen aus den Bereichen von Bildkunst und Literatur um bewusste Setzungen innerhalb des männlichen Künstlerkanons, den die Sammlungen Matsukata und Osthaus propagieren. Mit nur wenigen Ausnahmen war die Rolle der Frau in ihnen, neben jener der wenig beachteten Vermittlerin, nicht die einer Schöpferin von Kunst, sondern beschränkte sich auf das Objekt im Bild, markant zur Schau gestellt etwa in Renoirs Darstellung seiner Lebensgefährtin Lise Tréhot als Haremsdame (S. 219). Ida Gerhardi mag in dem Zusammenhang abermals als Beispiel gelten, dass diese Diskrepanz nicht allein mit den historischen Umständen oder der Sammlungsgeschichte zu erklären ist: Schon 1902 berichtet die Künstlerin in einem Brief ihrer Schwester: „[...] Mittwoch nachmittag war Herr Osthaus mit seiner reizenden jungen Frau hier u. sozusagen ‚baff‘ über meine Ausstellung, will mich als professeur an seine Malschule in Hagen haben, wo er schon einen

ganz famosen Impressionisten, Rohlfs [S. 212], angestellt – nun fehlte ihm gerade so jemand wie ich."[76] Warum gingen angesichts dieser Begeisterung ausschließlich Porträts von Gerhardi in die Sammlung des Museum Folkwang in Hagen ein, also Auftragsarbeiten, die den Lebenserwerb der Malerin sicherten, nicht aber die progressiven Kompositionen aus ihrer Zeit in Paris?

Mehr als ein Jahrhundert nach dem Tod von Emile Verhaeren hat die Literatin Elif Shafak auch unsere Gegenwart als Zeit der Zersplitterung beschrieben. In Anlehnung an ein Gedicht von Walt Whitman beschreibt sie unser menschliches Wesen als unermesslich und als Gefäß von Mannigfaltigkeiten.[77] Bei Whitman selbst heißt es im englischen Original: „Do I contradict myself? / Very well then I contradict myself, (I am large, I contain multitudes.)"[78] Im Kaleidoskop, das diese Ausstellung und der begleitende Katalog in der Gegenüberstellung zweier bedeutender Sammlungen aus der ersten Hälfte des 20. Jahrhunderts und ihrer Gründer eröffnen möchten, haben denn auch Widersprüche ihre Berechtigung.

47

1 Die Auslieferung erfolgte erst Anfang 1913; vgl. Christoph Dorsz, Karl Ernst Osthaus (1874–1921), www.osthausmuseum.de/web/media/files/keom/museum/Osthaus_Chronologie.pdf [zuletzt aufgerufen am 3.9.2021].

2 Karl Ernst Osthaus, „Vorwort", in: *Museum Folkwang*, Bd. 1, *Moderne Kunst. Plastik, Malerei, Graphik*, bearb. von Kurt Freyer, Hagen 1912 (Nachdruck 1983), S. 3–5, hier S. 4.

3 Vgl. Herta Hesse-Frielinghaus u. a., *Karl Ernst Osthaus. Leben und Werk*, Recklinghausen 1971, S. 519.

4 Dass damit die übrigen Sammlungsteile in den Hintergrund getreten seien, wie Rainer Stamm 2002 interpretiert, lässt sich etwa anhand von Osthaus' Hinwendung zu Objekten aus West- und Ostafrika sowie Deutsch-Neuguinea nach 1912 widerlegen; vgl. *Karl Ernst Osthaus. Reden und Schriften. Folkwang, Werkbund, Arbeitsrat (Kontext. Schriftenreihe für Kunst, Kunsterziehung und Kulturpädagogik*, 3), hrsg. und komm. von Rainer Stamm, Köln 2002, S. 45.

5 Vgl. *Gauguin, van Gogh bis Dalí. Folkwang: Erstes Museum der Moderne*, hrsg. von Johann Georg Prinz von Hohenzollern und Hubertus Gaßner, Ausst.-Kat. Kunsthalle der Hypo-Kulturstiftung, München, München 2004.

6 Dies ist durchaus zu relativieren, denkt man etwa an die Neue Pinakothek in München, die schon 1853 als weltweit erstes Museum für zeitgenössische Kunst eröffnete, wenngleich die Bestände des französischen Impressionismus und Post-Impressionismus erst mit der sogenannten Tschudi-Spende ab 1911 in ihren Besitz übergingen; vgl. Joachim Kaak, „Neue Pinakothek", in: *Die Pinakotheken in Bayern*, hrsg. von Bernhard Maaz, München 2015, S. 25–34, hier S. 25 ff.

7 Karl Ernst Osthaus, „Vorwort", S. 3 f.

8 Béatrice Joyeux-Prunel, „Graf Kessler und die Internationalisierung der modernen Kunst", in: *Harry Graf Kessler. Porträt eines europäischen Kulturvermittlers (Passagen*, 52), hrsg. von Julia Drost und Alexandre Kostka, Berlin und München 2015, S. 53–75, hier

S. 53 ff. Auf der gleichen Annahme basiert Inga Rossi-Schrimpf, „Kessler, Osthaus, Waerndorfer – Des animateurs d'art en quête d'identité: quelques réflexions à partir de trois exemples", in: *Animateur d'art. Marchand, collectionneur, critique, éditeur*, hrsg. von Ingrid Goddeeris und Noémie Goldman, Brüssel 2015, S. 83–97, hier S. 84 ff.

9 Eva Rovers, „Monument to an industrialist's wife. Helene Kröller-Müller's motives for collecting", in: *Journal of the History of Collections*, 21, 2, 2009, S. 241–252, hier S. 242 ff.

10 Ebd., S. 243 f., sowie Herta Hesse-Frielinghaus u. a., *Karl Ernst Osthaus*, S. 422.

11 Vgl. *Société anonyme des artistes peintres, sculpteurs, graveurs, etc. Première Exposition. 1874*, Ausst.-Kat. Paris 1874.

12 Félix Fénéon, „L'impressionnisme aux Tuileries", in: *L'art moderne*, 6, 38, 19.9.1886, S. 300–302, hier S. 302.

1 The delivery did not take place until early in 1913; see, Christoph Dorsz, Karl Ernst Osthaus (1874–1921), www.osthausmuseum.de/web/media/files/keom/museum/Osthaus_Chronologie.pdf [last accessed November 2021].

2 Karl Ernst Osthaus, 'Vorwort', in Kurt Freyer (ed.), *Museum Folkwang*, Vol. 1, *Moderne Kunst: Plastik, Malerei, Graphik* (Hagen 1912) [Reprint 1983], 3 ff, here 4.

3 See, Herta Hesse-Frielinghaus et al., *Karl Ernst Osthaus: Leben und Werk*, (Recklinghausen, 1971), 519.

4 The idea that the other parts of the collection faded into the background, as Rainer Stamm suggests in 2002, is contradicted by Osthaus's increasing interest in objects from West and East Africa as well as German New Guinea after 1912; see Rainer Stamm (ed.), *Reden und Schriften. Folkwang, Werkbund, Arbeitsrat*, Kontext. Schriftenreihe für Kunst, Kunsterziehung und Kulturpädagogik, 3, (Cologne, 2002), 45.

5 Cf. Johann Georg Prinz von Hohenzollern and Hubertus Gaßner (eds.), *Gauguin, van Gogh bis Dalí. Folkwang: Erstes Museum der Moderne*, exh. cat., Kunsthalle der Hypo-Kulturstiftung, (Munich, 2004).

6 This needs to be put into perspective if we think, for example, of the Neue Pinakothek in Munich, which opened as early as 1853 as the first museum of contemporary art in the world, even though the holdings of French Impressionism and Post-Impressionism only entered its possession with the so-called Tschudi donation in 1911; cf. Joachim Kaak, 'Neue Pinakothek', in Bernhard Maaz (ed.), *Die Pinakotheken in Bayern* (Munich, 2015) 25–34, here 25 ff.

7 Karl Ernst Osthaus, 'Vorwort', 3 f.

8 Béatrice Joyeux-Prunel, 'Graf Kessler und die Internationalisierung der modernen Kunst', in Julia Drost and Alexandre Kostka (eds.), *Harry Graf Kessler: Porträt eines europäischen Kulturvermittlers* (*Passagen*, vol. 52) (Berlin/Munich, 2015), 53–75, here 53 ff. Inga Rossi-Schrimpf makes the same assumption in 'Kessler, Osthaus, Waerndorfer – Des animateurs d'art en quête d'identité: quelques réflexions à partir de trois exemples', in Ingrid Goddeeris and Noémie Goldman (eds.), *Animateur d'art: Marchand, collectionneur, critique, éditeur* (Brussels, 2015), 83–97, here 84 ff.

9 Eva Rovers, 'Monument to an industrialist's wife: Helene Kröller-Müller's motives for collecting', in *Journal of the History of Collections*, 21, 2, (2009), 241–252, here 242 ff.

10 Ibid., 243 f.; see also Herta Hesse-Frielinghaus et al., *Karl Ernst Osthaus*, 422.

11 Cf. *Société anonyme des artistes peintres, sculpteurs, graveurs, etc. Première Exposition. 1874*, exh. cat. Paris, 1874.

12 Félix Fénéon, 'L'impressionnisme aux Tuileries', in *L'art moderne*, 6, 38, (19.9.1886), 300–302, here 302.

13 [Roger Fry], 'The Post-Impressionists', in *Manet and the Post-Impressionists*, exh. cat. Grafton Galleries, London, 1910, 7–13, here 7 ff.

14 John Rewald, 'Einleitung', in idem., *Von Van Gogh bis Gauguin: Die Geschichte des Nachimpressionismus* (*Das moderne Sachbuch*, vol. 65), (Cologne, 1967) 7–10, here 9.

15 Emile Verhaeren, quoted in: ibid., 7.

16 Contemporary discourse dates the beginning of modern art considerably earlier, recognizing the whole of artistic developments in the so-called long nineteenth century from 1780; see, e.g. www.global19c.com [last accessed November 2021].

17 According to Stamm, Gertrud Osthaus only convinced her husband about Renoir's late work on the occasion of a visit at the artist's studio in 1913; Rainer Stamm, 'Im "Strömen und Wollen unserer Zeit": Die Sammlerin Gertrud Osthaus', in Dorothee Wimmer, Christina Feilchenfeldt and Stephanie Tasch (eds.), *Kunstsammlerinnen: Peggy Guggenheim bis Ingvild Goetz*, (Berlin, 2009), 85–97, here 88.

18 *Moderne Gemälde aus dem Nachlass A. W. von Heymel. Sammlung M. Pickenpack et al*, Kunstsalon Paul Cassirer and [Galerie] Hugo Helbing, auc. cat. Berlin, 8.3.1917, [no pagination] No. 69; Herta Hesse-Frielinghaus et al., *Karl Ernst Osthaus*, 147. Neither painting is listed in the artists' catalogues raisonnés.

19 See for example, Stamm (ed.), *Karl Ernst Osthaus: Reden und Schriften*, 155 ff.

20 Herta Hesse-Frielinghaus et al., *Karl Ernst Osthaus*, 147. The work is not listed in Courbet's catalogue raisonné.

21 Invoice from the Galerie Ernst Arnold, Dresden, 10.4.1905, Osthaus Museum, Hagen, Archive, F2 903a/4.

22 Cf. the documentation in the files relating to the painting in the Museum Folkwang, Essen.

23 Kurt Freyer (ed.), *Museum Folkwang*, vol. 1, *Moderne Kunst. Plastik, Malerei, Graphik* (Hagen, 1912) [Reprint, 1983], 13, No. 116.

24 Mario von Lüttichau, 'Ein Haus für die Väter der Moderne. Zur frühen Sammlungsgeschichte des Museum Folkwang', in *Gauguin, van Gogh bis Dalí*, exh. cat, 43–51, here 46. See also the quotation from Konrad von Freyhold cited by Rainer Stamm in this volume, p. 103.

25 Cf. Walter Feilchenfeldt, *Vincent van Gogh & Paul Cassirer, Berlin: The reception of van Gogh in Germany from 1901 to 1914* (Zwolle, 1988), 21 ff.

26 Karl Ernst Osthaus, 'Der Folkwang in Hagen', lecture from 21.9.1903, 1904, reprinted in: Stamm (ed.), *Karl Ernst Osthaus. Reden und Schriften*, 40–42, here 40.

27 Ibid., 41.

28 Robyn Roslak, *Neo-Impressionsm and Anarchism in Fin-De-Siècle France: Painting, Politics and Landscape*, (London and New York, 2007), 174.

29 The Kunsthalle Mannheim bought the thematically related, monumental *L'exécution de l'empereur Maximilien* (*The Execution of Emperor Maximilian*, 1868/69) 1910, five years after Osthaus's purchase from Arnold; http://sammlung-online.kuma.art/node/627 [last accessed November 2021].

30 Eberhard von Bodenhausen to unknown recipient, letter of 23.1.1916, quoted from Felix Billeter, 'Zwischen Kunstgeschichte und Industriemanagement: Eberhard von Bodenhausen als Sammler neoimpressionistischer Malerei', in Andrea Pophanken and Felix Billeter (eds.), *Die Moderne und ihre Sammler. Französische Kunst in deutschem Privatbesitz vom Kaiserreich zur Weimarer Republik* (*Passagen*, vol. 3), (Berlin, 2001), 125–143, here 137.

13 [Roger Fry], „The Post-Impressionists", in: *Manet and the Post-Impressionists,* Ausst.-Kat. Grafton Galleries, London, London 1910, S. 7–13, hier S. 7 ff.

14 John Rewald, „Einleitung", in: ders., *Von Van Gogh bis Gauguin. Die Geschichte des Nachimpressionismus (Das moderne Sachbuch,* 65), Köln 1967, S. 7–10, hier S. 9.

15 Emile Verhaeren, zit. nach: ebd., S. 7.

16 Der aktuelle Diskurs datiert den Beginn der Moderne wesentlich früher, erkennt er doch die Gesamtheit der Kunstentwicklungen im sog. langen 19. Jahrhundert seit 1780 an; vgl. etwa www.global19c.com [zuletzt aufgerufen am 14.10.2021].

17 Nach Stamm überzeugte Gertrud Osthaus ihren Mann erst bei einem Besuch in Renoirs Atelier im Jahr 1913 von dessen Spätwerk; Rainer Stamm, „Im ‚Strömen und Wollen unserer Zeit'. Die Sammlerin Gertrud Osthaus", in: *Kunstsammlerinnen. Peggy Guggenheim bis Ingvild Goetz,* hrsg. von Dorothee Wimmer, Christina Feilchenfeldt und Stephanie Tasch, Berlin 2009, S. 85–97, hier S. 88.

18 *Moderne Gemälde aus dem Nachlass A. W. von Heymel. Sammlung M. Pickenpack u. a.,* hrsg. vom Kunstsalon Paul Cassirer und [Galerie] Hugo Helbing, Aukt.-Kat. Berlin, 8.3.1917, [o. S.], Nr. 69; Herta Hesse-Frielinghaus u. a., *Karl Ernst Osthaus,* S. 147. Beide Gemälde sind nicht in den Werkverzeichnissen der Künstler aufgeführt.

19 Vgl. etwa *Karl Ernst Osthaus. Reden und Schriften,* S. 155 ff.

20 Herta Hesse-Frielinghaus u. a., *Karl Ernst Osthaus,* S. 147. Im Werkverzeichnis von Courbet wird das Gemälde nicht gelistet.

21 Rechnung der Galerie Ernst Arnold, Dresden, vom 10.4.1905, Osthaus-Museum, Hagen, Archiv, F2 903a/4.

22 Vgl. die Dokumentation in der Werkakte des Gemäldes im Museum Folkwang, Essen.

23 *Museum Folkwang,* Bd. 1, *Moderne Kunst. Plastik, Malerei, Graphik,* bearb. von Kurt Freyer, Hagen 1912 (Nachdruck 1983), S. 13, Nr. 116.

24 Mario von Lüttichau, „Ein Haus für die Väter der Moderne. Zur frühen Sammlungsgeschichte des Museum Folkwang", in: *Gauguin, van Gogh bis Dalí,* Ausst.-Kat., S. 43–51, hier S. 46. Vgl. auch das von Rainer Stamm in diesem Band angeführte Zitat von Konrad von Freyhold, S. 103.

25 Vgl. Walter Feilchenfeldt, *Vincent van Gogh & Paul Cassirer, Berlin. The reception of van Gogh in Germany from 1901 to 1914,* Zwolle 1988, S. 21 ff.

26 Karl Ernst Osthaus, „Der Folkwang in Hagen", Vortrag vom 21.9.1903, 1904, wieder abgedruckt in: *Karl Ernst Osthaus. Reden und Schriften,* S. 40–42, hier S. 40.

27 Ebd., S. 41.

28 Robyn Roslak, *Neo-Impressionsm and Anarchism in Fin-De-Siècle France. Painting, Politics and Landscape,* London und New York 2007, S. 174.

29 Die Kunsthalle Mannheim erwarb die motivisch verwandte, monumentale *L'exécution de l'empereur Maximilien (Die Erschießung Kaiser Maximilians,* 1868/69) 1910, das heißt fünf Jahre nach Osthaus' Ankauf bei Arnold; http://sammlung-online.kuma.art/node/627 [zuletzt aufgerufen am 9.9.2021].

30 Eberhard von Bodenhausen an unbekannt, Brief vom 23.1.1916, zit. nach: Felix Billeter, „Zwischen Kunstgeschichte und Industriemanagement. Eberhard von Bodenhausen als Sammler neoimpressionistischer Malerei", in: *Die Moderne und ihre Sammler. Französische Kunst in deutschem Privatbesitz vom Kaiserreich zur Weimarer Republik (Passagen,* Bd. 3), hrsg. von Andrea Pophanken und Felix Billeter, Berlin 2001, S. 125–143, hier S. 137.

31 Hesse-Frielinghaus setzt den Abschluss des Sammlungsbereichs dagegen um 1905/06 an; Herta Hesse-Frielinghaus u. a., *Karl Ernst Osthaus,* S. 147.

32 Vgl. die bislang einzige Ausstellungsübersicht in ebd., S. 511, 514, die dringend überarbeitet werden müsste.

33 Vgl. die kommende Sonderausstellung *Expressionisten am Folkwang. Entdeckt – verfemt – gefeiert,* die ab August 2022 im Museum Folkwang stattfinden wird.

34 Vgl. Julius Meier-Graefe, *Entwicklungsgeschichte der modernen Kunst. Vergleichende Betrachtung der bildenden Künste als Beitrag zu einer neuen Ästhetik,* 3 Bde., Bd. 3, Stuttgart 1904, zit. nach: Walter Feilchenfeldt, *Vincent van Gogh. Die Gemälde 1886–1890. Händler, Sammler, Ausstellungen. Die frühen Provenienzen (Quellen-studien zur Kunst,* 3), Wädenswil 2009, S. 300, sowie 2. Aufl., München 1915, S. 442, 470, 526, 603.

35 Vgl. Herta Hesse-Frielinghaus u. a., *Karl Ernst Osthaus,* S. 142.

36 Hendrik Ziegler, „Emil Heilbut. Ein früher Apologet Claude Monets", in: *Die Moderne und ihre Sammler. Französische Kunst in deutschem Privatbesitz vom Kaiserreich zur Weimarer Republik (Passagen,* 3), hrsg. von Andrea Pophanken und Felix Billeter, Berlin 2001, S. 41–65, hier S. 50.

37 Karl Ernst Osthaus, in: *Kampf um die Kunst. Die Antwort auf den „Protest deutscher Künstler",* München 1911, S. 16–19, hier S. 17.

38 Ebd.

39 Vgl. *Internationale Kunstausstellung des Sonderbundes Westdeutscher Kunstfreunde und Künstler zu Cöln,* Ausst.-Kat. Städtische Ausstellungshalle am Aachener Tor, Köln, 1912, S. 14 f.; S. 28, Nr. 91; S. 34, Nr. 156. Interessanterweise werden in der Liste der Leihgeber:innen sowohl Osthaus selbst als auch das Museum Folkwang aufgeführt, während in der Exponatliste das Museum nicht in den Besitzangaben erscheint.

40 Vgl. Ernst Gosebruch an Gustav Krupp von Bohlen und Halbach, Brief vom 15.1.1911, Historisches Archiv Krupp, Essen, nach: Käthe Klein, „Ankäufe ausländischer Meisterwerke durch Ernst Gosebruch (1910–1914)", in: *Museum Folkwang Essen. Mitteilungen,* hrsg. vom Folkwangmuseumsverein [sic], Bd. 1, Essen 1967, S. 35–42, hier S. 35.

41 Vgl. Käthe Klein, „Fünfzig Jahre Kunstring Folkwang", Vortrag vom 26.9.1960, wieder abgedruckt in: *50 Jahre Kunstring Folkwang (Jahresgabe 1960/61),* hrsg. vom Kunstring Folkwang, Essen 1960, S. 9–48, hier S. 28.

42 *Der Cicerone. Halbmonatsschrift für die Interessen des Kunstforschers & Sammlers,* 4, 17, 1912, S. 19.

43 Max Hehemann, „Kunstpolitik", in: *Essener General-Anzeiger,* 15.11.1912, zit. nach: Käthe Klein, „Ankäufe ausländischer Meisterwerke durch Ernst Gosebruch (1910–1914)", S. 37.

44 Vgl. ebd., S. 35, 38.

45 Vgl. Günter Busch, „Otto Modersohn und die Maler von Barbizon", 1978, wieder abgedruckt in: *Barbizon und Otto Modersohn. Meisterwerke von Corot bis Rousseau aus einer Privat-

31 Hesse-Frielinghaus, on the other hand, dates the conclusion of the collecting activity to 1905/06; Herta Hesse-Frielinghaus et al., *Karl Ernst Osthaus,* 147.

32 See the so far only exhibition survey in ibid., 511, 514, which is in urgent need of revision.

33 Cf. the forthcoming exhibition, *Expressionists at Folkwang: Discovered – Defamed – Celebrated,* which will be held from August 2022 in the Museum Folkwang.

34 See, Julius Meier-Graefe, *Entwicklungsgeschichte der Modernen Kunst. Vergleichende Betrachtung der bildenden Künste als Beitrag zu einer neuen Ästhetik,* 3 vols, vol. 3 (Stuttgart, 1904), quoted from Walter Feilchenfeldt, *Vincent van Gogh. Die Gemälde 1886–1890. Händler, Sammler, Ausstellungen: Die frühen Provenienzen (Quellenstudien zur Kunst,* vol. 3), (Wädenswil 2009), p. 300, and see 2nd ed., (Munich, 1915), 442, 470, 526, 603.

35 Cf. Herta Hesse-Frielinghaus et al., *Karl Ernst Osthaus,* 142.

36 Hendrik Ziegler, 'Emil Heilbut: Ein früher Apologet Claude Monets', in Andrea Pophanken and Felix Billeter (eds.), *Die Moderne und ihre Sammler: Französische Kunst in deutschem Privatbesitz vom Kaiserreich zur Weimarer Republik (Passagen,* vol. 3), (Berlin 2001), 41–65, here 50.

37 Karl Ernst Osthaus, in *Kampf um die Kunst. Die Antwort auf den 'Protest deutscher Künstler'* (Munich, 1911), 16–19, here 17.

38 Ibid.

39 See, *Internationale Kunstausstellung des Sonderbundes Westdeutscher Kunstfreunde und Künstler zu Cöln,* exh. cat. Städtische Ausstellungshalle am Aachener Tor (Cologne, 1912), 14 f.; 28, no. 91; 34, no. 156. Interestingly, both Osthaus himself and the Museum Folkwang are included in the list of lenders, while in the list of exhibits the museum is not listed among the owners.

40 See, Ernst Gosebruch to Gustav Krupp von Bohlen und Halbach, letter of 15.1.1911, Historisches Archiv Krupp, Essen, quoted from Käthe Klein, 'Ankäufe ausländischer Meisterwerke durch Ernst Gosebruch (1910–1914)', in *Museum Folkwang Essen: Mitteilungen,* Folkwangmuseumsverein [sic], vol. 1, (Essen, 1967), 35–42, here 35.

41 See, Käthe Klein, 'Fünfzig Jahre Kunstring Folkwang', lecture from 26 September 1960, reprinted in *50 Jahre Kunstring Folkwang (Jahresgabe 1960/61),* ed. Kunstring Folkwang (Essen 1960), 9–48, here 28.

42 *Der Cicerone: Halbmonatsschrift für die Interessen des Kunstforschers & Sammlers,* 4, 17, (1912), 19.

43 Max Hehemann, 'Kunstpolitik', in *Essener General-Anzeiger,* 15.11.1912, quoted from Käthe Klein, 'Ankäufe ausländischer Meisterwerke durch Ernst Gosebruch (1910–1914)', 37.

44 See, ibid., 35, 38.

45 See, Günter Busch, 'Otto Modersohn und die Maler von Barbizon', 1978, reprinted in *Barbizon und Otto Modersohn: Meisterwerke von Corot bis Rousseau aus einer Privatsammlung,* exh. cat. Otto Modersohn Museum, (Tecklenburg, 2019), 4–12, here 6 ff.

46 Cf. Käthe Klein, 'Ankäufe ausländischer Meisterwerke durch Ernst Gosebruch (1910–1914)', 35.

47 In ibid., 38, Klein quotes Gosebruch's acquisition report in the annual report of the Essen Art Association for 1913/14: 'Raising this considerable sum in 1912 was only possible because very large sums were available to us from the year's big sales.' The annual reports, which were plainly still available in the 1960s, are sadly no longer in the archive of the Museum Folkwang today, and have not been located in any other place, even though there are indications that they have been sent to other museums.

48 Käthe Klein, 'Ankäufe ausländischer Meisterwerke durch Ernst Gosebruch (1910–1914)', 38, names *Le Pont des Arts (The Pont des Arts;* p. 300), while the 1929 collection catalogue names *La Tour Rose, Marseille (The Pink Tower, Marseille;* p. 301); cf. Agnes Waldstein, *Museum Folkwang,* Vol. I, *Moderne Kunst. Malerei, Plastik, Grafik,* Essen 1929 [Reprint 1983], 29, no. 299.

49 *Französische Kunstausstellung aus den letzten drei Jahrzehnten der franz. Malerei,* exh. cat., Kunstmuseum Essen (Essen, 1914), 15 ff.

50 Ibid., 3.

51 See, *Internationale Kunstausstellung des Sonderbundes Westdeutscher Kunstfreunde und Künstler zu Cöln,* exh. cat., 32, 36 ff.; Ursula Bode, 'Von kunstfreundlichen Bürgern: Sammler in Essen 1900–1945', in *'Das schönste Museum der Welt': Museum Folkwang bis 1933. Essays zur Geschichte des Museum Folkwang (Folkwang Texte,* vol. 1), Museum Folkwang (Göttingen, 2010), 141–156, here 146 f.

52 See, *Französische Kunstausstellung aus den letzten drei Jahrzehnten der franz. Malerei,* exh. cat., 15 f.

53 Ibid, 16, no. 10 (with spelling mistake in the title) and no. 11; See also, Käthe Klein, 'Ankäufe ausländischer Meisterwerke durch Ernst Gosebruch (1910–1914)', 38.

54 See, ibid., 40 and *Französische Kunstausstellung aus den letzten drei Jahrzehnten der franz. Malerei,* exh. cat., 18, no. 38.

55 Käthe Klein, 'Ankäufe ausländischer Meisterwerke durch Ernst Gosebruch (1910–1914)', 38. While in 1914 Bertha Krupp had bought a work by Monet from the *French Art Exhibition* for the family collection, Wildenstein's catalogue raisonné lists only *Vétheuil* (1880) with the appropriate provenance; surprisingly giving Gosebruch as the previous owner. How can this discrepancy be explained? See, Gustav Krupp von Bohlen und Halbach to Ernst Gosebruch, letter 23.2.1914, Historisches Archiv Krupp, Essen, quoted from Käthe Klein, 'Ankäufe ausländischer Meisterwerke durch Ernst Gosebruch (1910–1914)', 39; *Französische Kunstausstellung aus den letzten drei Jahrzehnten der franz. Malerei,* exh. cat., 17, no. 26; Daniel Wildenstein, *Monet or the Triumph of Impressionism: Catalogue Raisonné,* 4 vols. (Cologne, 1999), vol. 2, nos. 1–968, p. 233, no. 607.

56 *Französische Kunstausstellung aus den letzten drei Jahrzehnten der franz. Malerei,* exh. cat., 17, no. 24; the list of the painting in the collection catalogue from 1929 was previously the *terminus ante quem* for the acquisition, see, Agnes Waldstein, *Museum Folkwang,* 14, no. 122.

57 'Die Zeit und der Markt. Sammlungen', in *Der Cicerone: Halbmonatsschrift für die Interessen des Kunstforschers & Sammlers,* 16, 17, 1924, p. 825 f., here 825. With thanks to Christoph Dorsz for kindly directing the article to Mario von Lüttichau in March 2015.

51

sammlung, Ausst.-Kat. Otto Modersohn Museum, Tecklenburg, Tecklenburg 2019, S. 4–12, hier S. 6 ff.

46 Vgl. Käthe Klein, „Ankäufe ausländischer Meisterwerke durch Ernst Gosebruch (1910–1914)", S. 35.

47 Klein zitiert ebd., S. 38, Gosebruchs Ankaufsbericht im Jahresbericht des Essener Kunstvereins von 1913/14: „Diese beträchtliche Summe aufzubringen war 1912 nur dadurch möglich, daß uns aus den großen Verkäufen des Jahres sehr erhebliche Provisionen zur Verfügung standen." Die in den 1960er-Jahren offensichtlich noch vorhandenen Jahresberichte befinden sich heute bedauerlicherweise nicht mehr im Archiv des Museum Folkwang und sind bislang an keinem anderen Ort belegt, auch wenn es Hinweise gibt, dass sie an andere Museen verschickt wurden.

48 Käthe Klein, „Ankäufe ausländischer Meisterwerke durch Ernst Gosebruch (1910–1914)", S. 38, nennt hier *Le Pont des Arts (Der Pont des Arts;* S. 300), der Sammlungskatalog von 1929 dagegen *La Tour Rose, Marseille (Hafen von Marseille;* S. 301); vgl. Agnes Waldstein, *Museum Folkwang,* Bd. I, *Moderne Kunst. Malerei, Plastik, Grafik,* Essen 1929 (Nachdruck 1983), S. 29, Nr. 299.

49 *Französische Kunstausstellung aus den letzten drei Jahrzehnten der franz. Malerei,* Ausst.-Kat. Kunstmuseum Essen, Essen 1914, S. 15 ff.

50 Ebd., S. 3.

51 Vgl. *Internationale Kunstausstellung des Sonderbundes Westdeutscher Kunstfreunde und Künstler zu Cöln,* Ausst.-Kat., S. 32, 36 ff.; Ursula Bode, „Von kunstfreundlichen Bürgern. Sammler in Essen 1900–1945", in: *„Das schönste Museum der Welt". Museum Folkwang bis 1933. Essays zur Geschichte des Museum Folkwang (Folkwang Texte,* 1), hrsg. vom Museum Folkwang, Göttingen 2010, S. 141–156, hier S. 146 f.

52 Vgl. *Französische Kunstausstellung aus den letzten drei Jahrzehnten der franz. Malerei,* Ausst.-Kat., S. 15 f.

53 Ebd., S. 16, Nr. 10 (mit orthografischem Fehler im Titel) und Nr. 11; vgl. auch Käthe Klein, „Ankäufe ausländischer Meisterwerke durch Ernst Gosebruch (1910–1914)", S. 38.

54 Vgl. ebd., S. 40 sowie *Französische Kunstausstellung aus den letzten drei Jahrzehnten der franz. Malerei,* Ausst.-Kat., S. 18, Nr. 38.

55 Käthe Klein, „Ankäufe ausländischer Meisterwerke durch Ernst Gosebruch (1910–1914)", S. 38. Hatte 1914 schon Bertha Krupp für die Familiensammlung ein Werk Monets aus der *Französische[n] Kunstausstellung* erworben, listet das Werkverzeichnis von Wildenstein nur mehr *Vétheuil* (1880) mit der entsprechenden Provenienz; erstaunlicherweise wird hier Gosebruch als Vorbesitzer genannt. Wie ist diese Unstimmigkeit zu erklären? Vgl. Gustav Krupp von Bohlen und Halbach an Ernst Gosebruch, Brief vom 23.2.1914, Historisches Archiv Krupp, Essen, zit. nach: ebd., S. 39; *Französische Kunstausstellung aus den letzten drei Jahrzehnten der franz. Malerei,* Ausst.-Kat., S. 17, Nr. 26; Daniel Wildenstein, *Monet or the Triumph of Impressionism. Catalogue Raisonné,* 4 Bde., Köln 1999, Bd. 2, Nr. 1–968, S. 233, Nr. 607.

56 *Französische Kunstausstellung aus den letzten drei Jahrzehnten der franz. Malerei,* Ausst.-Kat., S. 17, Nr. 24; als *terminus ante quem* für die Erwerbung galt bislang die Listung des Gemäldes im Sammlungskatalog von 1929, vgl. Agnes Waldstein, *Museum Folkwang,* S. 14, Nr. 122.

57 „Die Zeit und der Markt. Sammlungen", in: *Der Cicerone. Halbmonatsschrift für die Interessen des Kunstforschers & Sammlers,* 16, 17, 1924, S. 825 f., hier S. 825. Mit Dank an Christoph Dorsz für seinen freundlichen Hinweis auf den Artikel an Mario von Lüttichau im März 2015.

58 Sowohl das Werk von Braque als auch drei der Derain-Gemälde wurden dem Museum Folkwang 1937 bei der Aktion *Entartete Kunst* entzogen.

59 Ausgenommen blieben die Objekte des Deutschen Museum für Kunst in Handel und Gewerbe, die das Kaiser Wilhelm Museum in Krefeld 1923 übernahm, wie auch Werke aus der Privatsammlung des Ehepaares, die Archivalien aus der Hagener Zeit inkl. der Osthaus'schen Korrespondenz (heute zu großen Teilen im Osthaus Museum Hagen) sowie der fotografische Nachlass (heute im Bildarchiv Foto Marburg).

60 Vgl. Paul Vogt, *Das Museum Folkwang Essen. Die Geschichte einer Sammlung junger Kunst im Ruhrgebiet,* Köln 1965, S. 56 ff.

61 Im Beschlagnahmeinventar des Reichsministeriums für Volksaufklärung und Propaganda von 1941/42 wird Segalls Bild ebenfalls unter dem Titel *Purimfest* geführt; „Entartete" Kunst [sog. Harry Fischer Liste], Digitalisat des maschinengeschriebenen Verzeichnisses des Reichsministeriums für Volksaufklärung und Propaganda, um 1941/42, Victoria & Albert Museum, National Art Library Fischer Collection, MSL/1996/7, Bd. I, Aachen-Görlitz, hier S. 194, Nr. 1124 (EK-Nr. 15958), http://www.vam.ac.uk/__data /assets/pdf_file/0020/240167/ Entartete_Kunst_Vol1.pdf [zuletzt aufgerufen am 27.9.2021].

62 Vgl. Paul Vogt, *Das Museum Folkwang Essen,* S. 62, sowie Ulrike Laufer, *Sammlerfleiß und Stiftungswille. 90 Jahre Folkwang-Museumsverein – 90 Jahre Museum Folkwang,* hrsg. vom Folkwang-Museumsverein e. V., Göttingen 2012, S. 86 ff.

63 Ebd., S. 166 ff., 185 ff. sowie Ursula Bode, *Von kunstfreundlichen Bürgern,* S. 151 ff. Die beiden Ereignisse können hier nur als Ausblick benannt werden. Es fehlt bislang an einer kritischen Institutionsgeschichte des Museum Folkwang in der Zeit zwischen 1934 und 1945.

64 Ursula Bode, *Von kunstfreundlichen Bürgern,* S. 154.

65 Vgl. Ulrike Laufer, *Sammlerfleiß und Stiftungswille,* S. 87.

66 Vgl. ebd., S. 88, sowie Paul Vogt, *Das Museum Folkwang Essen,* S. 62.

67 Ernst Gosebruch, [um 1929], zit. nach: Ulrike Laufer, *Sammlerfleiß und Stiftungswille,* S. 89.

68 Karl Ernst Osthaus, *Van de Velde. Leben und Schaffen des Künstlers (Die neue Baukunst,* 1), Hagen 1920, S. 24.

69 Amy Gillman, „The Era of the Visionary Museum Director Is Over … or It Should Be", 27.7.2021, 5https://hyperallergic.com/665251/ era-of-visionary-museum-director -is-over-or-it-should-be/ [zuletzt aufgerufen am 29.9.2021].

70 Vgl. Ida Gerhardi an Auguste Rodin, Briefe vom 30.12.1902 und 20.3.1903, in: *Ida Gerhardi 1862– 1927. Eine westfälische Malerin zwischen Paris und Berlin,* hrsg. von Annegret Rittmann, Münster

58 Both the work of Braque and three of the Derain paintings were withdrawn from the Museum Folkwang in 1937 in the Degenerate Art operation.

59 Excluded from this were the objects of the German Museum of Art in Trade and Craft that were taken over by the Kaiser Wilhelm Museum in Krefeld in 1923, as well as works from the couple's private collection, the archives from the Hagen period including Osthaus's correspondence (today mostly in the Osthaus Museum Hagen) as well as the photographic legacy (today in Bildarchiv Foto Marburg).

60 Cf. Paul Vogt, *Das Museum Folkwang Essen: Die Geschichte einer Sammlung junger Kunst im Ruhrgebiet* (Cologne, 1965), 56 ff.

61 In the confiscation inventory of the Reich Ministry of Public Enlightenment and Propaganda for 1941/42 Segall's painting is also listed under the title *Purimfest;* 'degenerate' art [so-called Harry Fischer list], digitalization of the typed list of the Reich Ministry of Public Enlightenment and Propaganda, ca. 1941/42, Victoria & Albert Museum, National Art Library Fischer Collection, MSL/1996/7, Vol. I, Aachen-Görlitz, here 194, No. 1124 (EK-No. 15958), http://www.vam.ac.uk/__data/assets/pdf_file/0020/240167/Entartete_Kunst_Vol1.pdf [last accessed November 2021].

62 See, Paul Vogt, *Das Museum Folkwang Essen,* 62, and Ulrike Laufer, *Sammlerfleiß und Stiftungswille: 90 Jahre Folkwang-Museumsverein – 90 Jahre Museum Folkwang,* ed. Folkwang Museumsverein e. V., (Göttingen, 2012), 86 ff.

63 Ibid., 166 ff., 185 ff. and Ursula Bode, *Von kunstfreundlichen Bürgern,* 151 ff. The two events can only be mentioned here as an outlook. There is as yet no critical institutional history of the Museum Folkwang in the period between 1934 and 1945.

64 Ursula Bode, *Von kunstfreundlichen Bürgern,* 154.

65 Cf. Ulrike Laufer, *Sammlerfleiß und Stiftungswille,* 87.

66 Cf. ibid., 88, as well as, Paul Vogt, *Das Museum Folkwang Essen,* 62.

67 Ernst Gosebruch, [ca. 1929], quoted from, Ulrike Laufer, *Sammlerfleiß und Stiftungswille,* 89.

68 Karl Ernst Osthaus, *Henry van de Velde: Leben und Schaffen des Künstlers* (*Die neue Baukunst,* vol. 1), (Hagen, 1920), 24.

69 Amy Gillman, 'The Era of the Visionary Museum Director Is Over … or It Should Be', 27.07.2021, https://hyperallergic.com/665251/era-of-visionary-museum-director-is-over-or-it-should-be/ [last accessed November 2021].

70 See, Ida Gerhardi to Auguste Rodin, letters of 30.12.1902 and 20.3.1903, in Annegret Rittmann (ed.), *Ida Gerhardi 1862–1927: Eine westfälische Malerin zwischen Paris und Berlin* (Münster, 1993), 209 and 213 f.; Nadine Engel, 'Im Schatten von Karl Ernst Osthaus: Personen hinter der Sammlung des Museum Folkwang'. Lecture on the occasion of the symposium 'Provenance and Collection History of the 20th Century' in the Franz Marc Museum, Kochel am See, 1 October 2021.

71 See, for example, Anneke Bokern, 'Zum ‚Nutzen und Genuss des Gemeinwesens': Die Sammlerin Helene Kröller-Müller', in Dorothee Wimmer, Christina Feilchenfeldt and Stephanie Tasch (eds.), *Kunstsammlerinnen: Peggy Guggenheim bis Ingvild Goetz* (Berlin, 2009, 59–72, here 59.

72 Herta Hesse-Frielinghaus et al., *Karl Ernst Osthaus,* 34.

73 See, Masako Kawaguchi and Megumi Jingaoka (eds.), *The Matsukata Collection: Complete Catalogue of the European Art,* Vol. 1, *Paintings* (Tokyo 2018), 369 ff., and 384 ff.

74 David Martin Challis, 'Rodin's Sculpture in Japan and the Economics of Translocation', in *Journal for Art Market Studies,* 2, 2, *Translocations and the Art Market* (2018), https://doi.org/10.23690/jams.v2i2.21 [last accessed November 2021].

75 See, Nadine Engel, 'Zwischen *objets sauvages* und Avantgarde: Zu den Anfängen der ostasiatischen Keramik im Museum Folkwang', in *Young-Jae Lee. Das Grün in den Schalen,* exh. cat., Folkwang, Essen (Stuttgart, 2020), 14 ff.

76 Ida Gerhardi to Lilli Gerhardi, letter of 21.9.1902, in *Ida Gerhardi 1862–1927: Eine westfälische Malerin zwischen Paris und Berlin,* 205 f., here 205.

77 Elif Shafak, *How to Stay Sane in an Age of Division* (London, 2020), 46: '[E]very human being is boundless and contains multitudes.'.

78 Walt Whitman, *Song of Myself,* section 51, https://iwp.uiowa.edu/whitmanweb/en/writings/song-of-myself/section-51 [last accessed November 2021].

52

1993, S. 209 und 213 f.; Nadine Engel, „Im Schatten von Karl Ernst Osthaus. Personen hinter der Sammlung des Museum Folkwang", Vortrag anlässlich des Symposiums *Provenienz und Sammlungsgeschichte des 20. Jahrhunderts* im Franz Marc Museum, Kochel am See, 1.10.2021.

71 Vgl. etwa Anneke Bokern, „Zum ‚Nutzen und Genuss des Gemeinwesens'. Die Sammlerin Helene Kröller-Müller", in: *Kunstsammlerinnen. Peggy Guggenheim bis Ingvild Goetz,* hrsg. von Dorothee Wimmer, Christina Feilchenfeldt und Stephanie Tasch, Berlin 2009, S. 59–72, hier S. 59.

72 Herta Hesse-Frielinghaus u. a., *Karl Ernst Osthaus,* S. 34.

73 Vgl. Masako Kawaguchi und Megumi Jingaoka (Hrsg.), *The Matsukata Collection. Complete Catalogue of the European Art,* Bd. 1, *Paintings,* Tokio 2018, S. 369 ff. sowie S. 384 ff.

74 David Martin Challis, „Rodin's Sculpture in Japan and the Economics of Translocation", in: *Journal for Art Market Studies,* 2, 2, *Translocations and the Art Market,* 2018, https://doi.org/10.23690/jams.v2i2.21 [zuletzt aufgerufen am 3.10.2021].

75 Vgl. Nadine Engel, „Zwischen *objets sauvages* und Avantgarde. Zu den Anfängen der ostasiatischen Keramik im Museum Folkwang", in: *Young-Jae Lee. Das Grün in den Schalen,* Ausst.-Kat. Museum Folkwang, Essen, Stuttgart 2020, S. 14 ff.

76 Ida Gerhardi an Lilli Gerhardi, Brief vom 21.9.1902, in: *Ida Gerhardi 1862–1927. Eine westfälische Malerin zwischen Paris und Berlin,* S. 205 f., hier S. 205.

77 Elif Shafak, *How to Stay Sane in an Age of Division,* London 2020, S. 46: „[E]very human being is boundless and contains multitudes." („Jedes menschliche Wesen ist grenzenlos und enthält Mannigfaltigkeiten", Übers. der Autorin).

78 Walt Whitman, *Song of Myself,* Sektion 51, https://iwp.uiowa.edu/whitmanweb/en/writings/song-of-myself/section-51 [zuletzt aufgerufen am 6.10.2021], in der deutschen Übersetzung der Universität von Iowa: „Widersprech ich mir selbst? / Nun gut, so widersprech ich mir selbst. (Ich bin weiträumig, enthalte Vielheit.)"

THE LAST EXHIBITION

Sayaka Murata

The planet below was black as pitch. On close inspection, however, K could make out shapes in an even darker black, which he knew meant oceans and islands. Avoiding the waters, he deftly guided his spaceship toward a landing on solid ground. Further scanning during his final approach confirmed his suspicions: the planet was all but devoid of life. He had hoped it would be the end of his long journey.

K disembarked from his spaceship and walked for a while. Just as he was about to turn back with a sigh, he found something square buried in the dark earth.

It was the head of a robot. It had what looked like eyes and a mouth, but it was buried from the neck down.

K activated his translation device. 'Are you from this planet?' he asked. 'Do you have speech functionality?'

After a brief pause, the robot's eyes glowed blue in response to K's greeting.

'I AM THE ROBOT MATSUKATA,' it said. 'I AM HERE.'[1]

K's translation device took a while to translate these words into the language of K's home planet, but it succeeded in the end, feeding the words into K's ears with a mechanical ring.

'I'm glad to hear that,' said K. 'There doesn't seem to be much life left on this planet. Are the beings that created you still around somewhere?'

'THEY ARE NOT. I AM HERE ALONE.'

K walked closer to the robot. He was no stranger to planets where only robots were left.

'I've been on a long journey,' he said. 'Does this planet have the concept 'Hyupopororahyun'?'

'I DO NOT UNDERSTAND THAT WORD,' the robot said. 'PLEASE REPEAT.'

'"Hyupopororahyun". It might be untranslatable. The word is originally from the planet Tokoronron, so I don't really understand it either. I've been travelling a long time to find a planet with the concept of "Hyupopororahyun".' K was not as young as he had been at the start of his journey. He took out a folding chair, set it up by the robot head, and then sat down, begging its pardon with a small bow.

Der Planet unter ihm war schwarz wie Pech. Bei genauerer Betrachtung konnte K jedoch auf seiner Oberfläche Konturen ausmachen, die, wie er wusste, Meere und Inseln voneinander unterschieden. Geschickt umflog er das Wasser und landete mit seinem Raumschiff auf festem Boden.

Wie er es sich beim Anblick der Oberfläche vom Raumschiff aus bereits vorgestellt hatte, war hier kaum Leben zu erwarten. K hatte gehofft, auf diesem Planeten seine Reise beenden zu können.

Er verließ das Raumschiff und lief eine Weile umher. Gerade als er mit einem Seufzer umkehren wollte, entdeckte er einen rechteckigen Gegenstand, der halb begraben in der schwarzen Erde steckte.

Es war der Kopf eines Roboters. Er sah aus, als hätte er Augen und Mund, und war vom Hals abwärts in der Erde eingegraben.

K aktivierte sein Übersetzungstool. „Bist du von diesem Planeten? Besitzt du eine Sprachfunktion?"

Es dauerte eine Weile, bis die Roboteraugen als Reaktion auf Ks Zuruf blau aufleuchteten.

„ICH BIN DER ROBOTER MATSUKATA", sagte er. „ICH BIN HIER."[1]

Bis Ks Übersetzungstool diese Worte in die Sprache seines eigenen Planeten übersetzt hatte, verging ein Moment, schließlich aber drangen sie mit mechanischem Klang in Ks Ohr ein.

„Das freut mich! Mir scheint, dass auf diesem Planeten kaum Leben existiert. Sind die Wesen, die dich erschaffen haben, vielleicht noch irgendwo in der Nähe?"

„NEIN. ICH BIN ALLEIN HIER."

K ging auf den Roboter zu. Er kannte solche Planeten, wo nur noch Roboter existierten.

„Ich habe eine lange Reise hinter mir. Ist dies ein Planet mit dem Konzept ‚Hyupopororahyun'?"

Der Roboter erwiderte:

„WORTLAUT NICHT VERSTÄNDLICH. NOCH EINMAL, BITTE!"

„‚Hyupopororahyun'. Man kann es wohl nicht übersetzen. Es stammt vom Planeten Tokoronron, deshalb weiß auch ich nicht genau, was es bedeutet. Ich bin schon eine Ewigkeit unterwegs auf der Suche nach einem Ort, wo es dieses Konzept gibt."

K war inzwischen erheblich älter als zu Beginn seiner Raumfahrt. Er holte einen Klappstuhl, stellte ihn neben dem Kopf des Roboters

55 Sayaka Murata

DIE LETZTE AUSSTELLUNG

Then he sighed. 'How can I explain this?' he asked.

'I AM HERE.'

'Thank you. All right—why don't I start by telling you about myself?'

K went and got a coffee-like beverage from his spaceship and sipped it slowly. He could hear waves on the shore. This was the first planet he'd visited in some time to have an ocean. It seemed that only the tiniest of insects still survived here, though. They flitted through his peripheral vision like little black shadows.

'I've always loved to travel,' K said at last. 'I was born on the planet Karkatta, and there were lots of other animals there, but only the Karkattans had language and technology. We Karkattans live for around a hundred million years, and once I was old enough to get my spaceship license, I did a lot of travelling. One day, I landed on a far-off planet called Tokoronron. It was a beautiful world. Its people were very kind, and quite devoted to "Hyupopororahyun". I made a friend there named Karl, and he showed me lots of examples of it. We don't use names on Karkatta, so Karl was the one who gave me my name, too.

'Then a giant meteor was spotted, headed directly for Tokoronron. The planet faced total destruction. I urged Karl and the others to escape on my spaceship, but they asked me to take examples of "Hyupopororahyun" instead, to carry them somewhere safe.'

'I did as they asked, loading up my spaceship with as much "Hyupopororahyun" as it could hold and leaving Tokoronron alone. I have roamed the universe ever since. I'm trying to find another planet with the concept of "Hyupopororahyun", you see, so I can entrust my cargo to the beings there. I've travelled for nearly a hundred million years—almost my entire life—but I haven't found a planet like that anywhere.'

MATSUKATA listened to K in silence. Its eyes flashed blue and white, apparently indicating that it was processing K's words in its slow-moving way.

auf und setze sich mit einer kurzen, um Erlaubnis bittenden
Verbeugung. „Wie soll ich es dir am besten erklären?", seufzte K.

„ICH BIN HIER."

„Danke. Also gut – vielleicht erzähle ich Dir erstmal etwas über
mich."

K holte sich ein kaffeeähnliches Getränk aus dem Raumschiff
und nahm bedächtig ein paar Schlucke. Er konnte das Rauschen der
Wellen hören. Wie lange hatte er keinen Planeten mehr mit einem Meer
erlebt. Hier hatten anscheinend nur noch die kleinsten Insekten über-
lebt. Manchmal huschten sie als winzige Schatten am Rande seines
Gesichtsfelds vorbei.

„Ich habe seit jeher das Reisen gemocht. Ich wurde auf dem Planeten Karkatta geboren, wo es eine Menge anderer Lebewesen gibt,
aber nur die Karkattaner verfügten über Sprache und Technologie. Wir
Karkattaner leben etwa 100 Millionen Jahre, und seit ich das Alter für
den Raumschiff-Führerschein erreicht habe, bin ich fast nur noch auf
Reisen. Eines Tages landete ich auf einem weiter entfernten Planeten,
dem besagten Tokoronron. Es war eine sehr schöne Welt, alle Bewoh-
ner waren freundlich und sie legten großen Wert auf ‚Hyupopororahyun'. Dort freundete ich mich mit Karl an, der mir viele Beispiele dafür
zeigte. Auf meinem Heimatplaneten gibt es keine Namen, also gab
Karl mir auch meinen Namen.

Eines Tages wurde ein Riesenmeteorit entdeckt, der schon bald
mit dem Planeten Tokoronron kollidieren und ihn vernichten würde.
Ich beschwor Karl und seine Freunde, in meinem Raumschiff mit
mir zu fliehen. Sie aber baten mich, stattdessen ‚Hyupopororahyun'-
Objekte an einem anderen Ort in Sicherheit zu bringen. Ich tat ihnen
den Gefallen und lud so viel ‚Hyupopororahyun' an Bord wie möglich.
Dann verließ ich mit dieser Ladung den Planeten Tokoronron allein.

Seitdem bin ich ununterbrochen unterwegs, weil ich meine Fracht
auf einen Planeten bringen möchte, auf dem es das Konzept ‚Hyupopororahyun' gibt. Fast 100 Millionen Jahre reise ich schon – beinahe
mein ganzes Leben lang –, aber bisher war die Suche erfolglos."

MATSUKATA hatte Ks Erzählung aufmerksam verfolgt. Seine Augen
blinkten blau und weiß, während er Ks Worte langsam verarbeitete.

„‚Hyupopororahyun' ist anscheinend ein eigenwilliges Konzept, das
nur auf Tokoronron existiert", fuhr K fort, „aber dennoch will ich mein
Versprechen, den richtigen Planeten zu finden, keinesfalls aufgeben.

'Eventually, I decided that "Hyupopororahyun" must be a uniquely Tokoronronian concept,' continued K. 'But I couldn't bring myself to go back on my promise to find the right planet. Difficult as it is to explain a concept I don't understand myself, I've visited planet after planet telling them what Karl and the others were so insistent on telling me. According to Karl, when you see "Hyupopororahyun", a flower blooms inside you.'

'A FLOWER.' MATSUKATA seemed to consider this. Then it said, 'PLEASE GIVE ME MORE INFORMATION ABOUT "HYUPOPORORAHYUN".'

K told him everything he had learned from the Tokoron-ronians. '. . . And that's all I know,' he concluded.

MATSUKATA was silent.

After an hour of waiting, K said, 'Nothing? I suppose it must be a uniquely Tokoronronian concept after all. But I'm not much longer for this universe. Do you think I might leave my examples of "Hyupopororahyun" here? Perhaps one day an alien from a planet with that concept might come along and find them.'

'"A...R...T ,"[2] muttered MATSUKATA. '"HYUPOPORO-RAHYUN" IS QUITE SIMILAR TO THE HUMAN CONCEPT "A...R...T".'

K rose out of his chair in astonishment. 'Really?'

'THEY ARE NOT EXACTLY THE SAME,' MATSUKATA explained cautiously. 'BUT THEY ARE VERY SIMILAR. THIS PLANET WAS ONCE HOME TO CREATURES CALLED HUMANS. THEY WENT EXTINCT APPROXIMATELY TEN THOUSAND YEARS AGO. WHEN ONLY APPROXIMATELY ONE HUNDRED HUMANS WERE LEFT, THEY DECIDED TO STORE EXAMPLES OF THEIR "A...R...T". I WAS MADE FOR THIS PURPOSE. I CONTAIN MANY EXAMPLES OF "A...R...T".'

MATSUKATA's robotic face opened down the middle, the parts swinging to either side to reveal a large cavity inside. Inside the cavity was a staircase leading down. K descended the stairway into the robot's body.

Es ist für mich sehr schwierig, einen Begriff zu erklären, den ich selber nicht verstehe, also wiederhole ich immer wieder, was Karl und die anderen unermüdlich versucht haben, mir über ‚Hyupopororahyun‘ beizubringen. Laut Karl erblüht eine Blume in dir, sobald du es siehst.“

„BLUME“, wiederholte MATSUKATA und fuhr fort:

„‚HYUPOPORORAHYUN‘. BITTE GIB MIR MEHR INFORMATIONEN DARÜBER.“

K erzählte ihm alles, was er auf dem Planeten Tokoronron erfahren hatte … Schließlich schloss er mit den Worten: „Mehr weiß ich auch nicht.“

MATSUKATA schwieg.

Nachdem er etwa eine Stunde gewartet hatte, sprach K ihn vorsichtig an: „Aussichtslos, was? Das ist wohl ein Konzept, das nur auf dem Planeten Tokoronron existiert. Ich werde vermutlich nicht mehr lange in diesem Universum bleiben. Wäre es möglich, die ‚Hyupopororahyun‘-Objekte hierzulassen? Vielleicht werden sie dann eines Tages von Aliens eines Planeten mit diesem Konzept gefunden.“

„KUN-ST²“, knarrte MATSUKATA.

„‚HYUPOPORORAHYUN‘ IST DEM MENSCHLICHEN KONZEPT KUN-ST SEHR ÄHNLICH.“

K erhob sich staunend aus seinem Stuhl. „Wirklich?“

„NICHT HUNDERTPROZENTIG, ABER SEHR ÄHNLICH“, ergänzte MATSUKATA vorsichtig.

„AUF DIESEM PLANETEN GAB ES EINST SOGENANNTE MENSCHEN. SIE SIND VOR ETWA ZEHNTAUSEND JAHREN AUS-GESTORBEN. ALS NOCH HUNDERT VON IHNEN ÜBRIG WAREN, HABEN DIESE MENSCHEN ENTSCHIEDEN, EINE GROSSE MENGE KUN-ST AUFZUBEWAHREN. DAFÜR HABEN SIE MICH ERSCHAFFEN. IN MEINEM INNEREN BEFINDET SICH VIEL KUN-ST.“

MATSUKATAs Kopf öffnete sich wie eine Flügeltür und dahinter wurden eine große Höhle und eine in die Tiefe führende Treppe sichtbar. K kletterte ins Innere des Roboters hinab. Dort stieß er auf zahlreiche sorgfältig angeordnete Gegenstände. Einige von ihnen ähnelten den Dingen, die ihm von den Bewohnern des Planeten Tokoronron anvertraut worden waren, aber es gab auch ganz andere.

There he found many carefully arranged objects. Some looked like the examples of 'Hyupopororahyun' that he had received from the Tokoronronians. Others were very different.

When he came back out of the cavity in MATSUKATA's face, K said, 'Thank you. I feel hopeful about "Hyupopororahyun" and "A...R...T" being very similar concepts.'

K asked MATSUKATA to tell him more about 'A...R...T', as well as the activities of the beings called 'humans' who had loved it. He was particularly interested in their practice of holding 'Exhibitions'.

'Why don't we try that, too?' he said. 'Perhaps aliens will cross the stars to see "Hyupopororahyun" or "A...R...T".'

'THAT WOULD MAKE ME VERY HAPPY. I AM TIRED OF WAITING.'

Just then, the sky began to lighten. Pale vermillion and blue blended at the horizon, and K saw luminous colours shine.

'What is that?'

'DAY.'

'"Day". Of, of course—the light from that big star I saw must reach this planet. I've visited a few planets like this. I've seen the sky lighten before, but these colours are quite mysterious.'

K gazed at the sky for a while. As he did, MATSUKATA printed out data on 'A...R...T' and 'Exhibitions'.

Next, K and MATSUKATA discussed what to put on the invitation for their 'Exhibition'. By the time they were finished, the sky was black as space again.

CARE FOR A NEW CONCEPT?
'Hyupopororahyun'; 'A...R...T'.
I found these words on two planets on a hundred-million-year journey. Perhaps the concept exists on your planet, too, but unnamed.

Here are its characteristics:
—It often takes physical form. Sometimes it may take other forms, like sound or language.

Als K wieder aus der Höhle herausgeklettert war und vor dem Gesicht des Roboters stand, sagte er zu MATSUKATA:

„Vielen Dank. Ich kann mir gut vorstellen, dass ‚Hyupopororahyun‘ und KUN-ST ähnliche Konzepte zugrunde liegen.“

K fragte MATSUKATA nach weiteren Einzelheiten über KUN-ST und auch über das Verhalten der sogenannten Menschen, die kunstliebend waren. Besonders der Hinweis, dass sie dafür AUSSTELLUNGEN veranstalteten, weckte Ks Interesse.

„Wollen wir das nicht auch versuchen? Vielleicht kommen dann Wesen von anderen Sternen hierher, um sich ‚Hyupopororahyun‘ beziehungsweise KUN-ST anzuschauen.“

„DAS WÄRE TOLL. ICH BIN MÜDE VOM WARTEN.“

In diesem Moment hellte sich der Himmel auf - blasses Zinnoberrot und ein Himmelblau erschienen am Horizont und K sah leuchtende Farben.

„Was ist das denn?“

„DER TAG.“

„Der Tag - verstehe. Das Licht des großen Sterns dort hinten reicht bis hierher. Planeten, auf denen es hell wurde, habe ich schon erlebt. Diese bunten Farben aber wundern mich sehr.“

K betrachtete eine Weile den Himmel. Währenddessen druckte MATSUKATA Daten zu KUN-ST und AUSSTELLUNG aus.

Sie berieten miteinander, wie sie die Einladungskarte für die AUS-STELLUNG gestalten sollten. Als sie damit fertig waren, hatte der Himmel wieder die pechschwarze Farbe des Weltraums angenommen.

Wie wäre es mit einem neuen Konzept?
HYUPOPORORAHYUN & KUN-ST
Ich bin 100 Millionen Jahre gereist und diesen Begriffen nur auf zwei Planeten begegnet. Vielleicht existieren sie auch auf Ihrem Planeten - aber ohne einen Namen.

Hier die Merkmale:
— Es handelt sich meistens um Gegenstände. Mitunter gibt es aber auch andere Formate wie Klänge oder Worte.
— Viele Gegenstände sind bunt bemalt. Es gibt aber auch unbemalte.

—These physical forms are often colourfully
painted. Sometimes they are not.
—They can be big or small. Flat examples are particularly common, and are often hung on walls.
Three-dimensional examples are sometimes placed
on stands.
—If you see it, apparently, a flower blooms inside
you.

If this sounds familiar, please come to our exhibition.
The exhibition will continue until Planet Earth is
no more.

'I'll have to leave in fifty years or so. The humans might all
be gone, but there are still lots of insects around. My remains
could damage their ecosystem.'

'I UNDERSTAND.'

The invitation had a map showing Earth's location. K's
spaceship was equipped with a fleet of miniature craft
designed to seek help in emergencies. He and MATSUKATA
loaded these craft with invitations and sent the whole fleet
out into the stars.

K was new to holding 'Exhibitions', but according to the
data MATSUKATA had printed out, it was important to
preserve the exhibits safely. So, he made a big glass tank
with a lid and door and put the exhibits inside that.

When preparations for the 'Exhibition' were complete,
K and MATSUKATA settled down to wait for patrons.
MATSUKATA's body was empty now, so K lived inside it.
It was a bit like a basement, and the lack of windows
made it quite gloomy. He came out when the sky lightened.

K had plenty of plants to eat and water to drink, so
he spent most of his time beside MATSUKATA's head.
MATSUKATA told him stories about how the humans had
lived, and K told MATSUKATA about his home planet
and the many other worlds he had seen on his travels.

— Es werden große und kleine Gegenstände gezeigt. Vor
allem gibt es viele flache Gegenstände, die an die Wand
gehängt werden können, aber auch plastische, die auf Sockel
gestellt werden.
— Beim Betrachten dieser Gegenstände erblühen Blumen
in Ihrem Inneren.

Besuchen Sie unbedingt diese AUSSTELLUNG, wenn
Sie sich angesprochen fühlen.
Die AUSSTELLUNG währt so lange, bis der Planet ERDE
erloschen ist.

„Ich muss in etwa fünfzig Jahren den Ort hier verlassen. Es gibt
zwar keine Menschen mehr auf dem Planeten, aber noch zahlreiche
Insekten. Und wenn mein Leichnam hier verwest, könnte er ihr Ökosystem durcheinander bringen."
„VERSTEHE."
Jeder Einladung fügte K eine geografische Karte der Erde bei.
In seinem Raumschiff gab es mehrere kleine Rettungssatelliten, um
im Notfall Hilfe zu rufen. Nachdem er und MATSUKATA sie mit den
Einladungen bestückt hatten, schickten sie sie so weit wie möglich
ins Weltall.
K wusste nicht so recht, wie er die AUSSTELLUNG gestalten
sollte, aber nach den Daten, die MATSUKATA ausgedruckt hatte, war
es wichtig, die Objekte beschützt aufzubewahren. Deshalb baute er
einen riesigen Glasbehälter, den er überdachte und mit Türen versah.
Darin arrangierte er die Objekte.
Nachdem sie mit den Vorbereitungen für die AUSSTELLUNG
fertig waren, ließen K und MATSUKATA sich nieder, um auf Gäste
zu warten.
K wohnte in dem nun leeren Körper von MATSUKATA. Darin
war es dämmrig wie in einem Souterrain. Sobald der Himmel
sich aufhellte, ging K nach draußen. Dort gab es viele essbare Pflanzen, auch Wasser zum Trinken, sodass K die meiste Zeit neben
MATSUKATAs Kopf verbrachte. Der Roboter berichtete ihm von
den Lebensumständen der Menschen, während K ihm von seinem
Heimatplaneten und den anderen Sternen erzählte, die er auf seiner
Fahrt durchs All erkundet hatte.

At the end of the day, when the sky grew dark and the wind grew cold, K would say, 'Well, excuse me,' step inside MATSUKATA's body, and go to sleep. If it was raining or snowing in the morning, MATSUKATA would warn K before he came outside.

'I WOULD LIKE TO TRAVEL ONE DAY, TOO,' MATSUKATA grumbled.

'Travel's a wonderful thing. Oh! I should have written this on the invitation, but Karl said that "Hyupopororahyun" was also a journey.'

'IT IS?'

K nodded. 'He said there were striking similarities.'

*

Forty years passed. K could sense the end of his life approaching. He resolved to leave Earth while he was still able to move freely. As he was tuning up his spaceship, he saw a distant silver sphere in the sky. At first he thought it might be the 'Moon' he sometimes saw during the day, but it approached with surprising speed and landed nearby. A being like a silver stick came out of it.

'Hello,' K said.

'Are you the one who sent this out?' asked the silver stick creature, holding up the invitation.

'That's right. Are you here to see the "Exhibition"?'

'I am here to kill you.'

The silver stick creature pulled out a gun and pointed it at K.

K remained calm.

'I see. And why is that?' he asked.

'Because of the danger.'

'Are "Exhibitions" dangerous? Do you have these concepts on your planet?'

'We do not. However, one day, I was overcome by a kind of convulsion. For a long time, I did not understand what it was. All I knew was that I had been possessed by something monstrous. When this invitation reached me,

Wenn der Tag zur Neige ging und es dunkel wurde, zog ein
kühler Wind auf. Dann verabschiedete sich K und kletterte wieder
ins Innere von MATSUKATA, um zu schlafen. An Tagen, an denen
es regnete oder schneite, gab ihm der Roboter Bescheid, bevor
er nach draußen kam.

„IRGENDWANN ... MÖCHTE ICH ... AUCH ... REISEN", murmelte
MATSUKATA.

„Reisen ist eine wunderbare Sache - das hätte ich auf die
Einladungskarte schreiben sollen. Karl sagte mir nämlich, dass
‚Hyupopororahyun' auch eine Art Reise sei."

„WIRKLICH?"

K nickte.

„Es gibt eine Menge Ähnlichkeiten. Das hat er mir erzählt."

*

Inzwischen waren vierzig Jahre vergangen und K spürte, dass sein
Ende nahe war. Er dachte daran, dass er den Planeten Erde recht-
zeitig verlassen musste, solange seine körperliche Verfassung es noch
zuließ. Während er sein Raumschiff wartete, erschien eine silberne
Kugel in der Ferne. Zunächst hielt er sie für den „Mond", der manchmal auch tagsüber sichtbar war, aber das Objekt näherte sich mit
rasanter Geschwindigkeit und landete in seiner Nähe.

Aus der Kapsel trat ein silbernes, stabförmiges Wesen.

„Hallo", sagte K.

„Sind Sie derjenige, der dies hier abgeschickt hat?", antwortete
das Silberstabwesen auf Ks Begrüßung und hielt die Einladung hoch.

„Ja, der bin ich. Sind Sie gekommen, um die AUSSTELLUNG
zu besichtigen?"

„Ich bin hier, um Sie zu töten."

Der Silberstab-Alien zog eine Waffe und richtete sie auf K.

K blieb ruhig.

„Aha. Dürfte ich den Grund erfahren?"

„Weil sie gefährlich ist."

„Was soll denn an einer AUSSTELLUNG gefährlich sein? Haben
Sie denn auch ein solches Konzept auf Ihrem Planeten?"

„Nein, bei uns gibt es so etwas nicht. Aber eines Tages bekam
ich eine Art Anfall. Ich begriff erst gar nicht, wie mir geschah.

I was horrified. I thought I was the only one in the universe suffering from this terrifying condition. I thought that when I died it would vanish with me. But I see now that I was wrong. I must put an end to this monstrosity at once.'

'I see. I didn't know about the danger. But won't you at least look at the exhibition while you're here? You're our first visitor.'

The silver stick creature peered at each exhibit in turn, keeping the muzzle of its gun trained on K. Every so often, K saw the creature tremble. What was happening beneath that silver skin? Was a flower blooming? Was the stick creature on a journey? K did not know.

After the stick creature had carefully inspected all the exhibits, it spoke again in a low voice. 'Dangerous, just as I thought. Such monstrous things, and so many of them! I feel like I might be sick. It's disgusting. Unbelievable.'

'Do you think? Well, before you kill me, would you mind telling me something? What is it like for you? The aliens who entrusted these items to me spoke of things like flowers that bloomed inside you, or journeys that didn't require a single step of physical movement.'

'There is nothing so beautiful here. When you awaken to it, it captures your heart. Your heart changes shape to forms it never knew before, chemical reactions occur, and you become a different person altogether. When the convulsions took me, I was sure the nightmare would soon depart. But once my heart was captured, I remained in that state my whole life. I have borne this concept alone, suffering all the while.'

'That must have been hard for you.'

'Don't think ill of me for killing you. If this concept were to escape into the universe, all life would go extinct. Spirits would be captured, controlled, remade. This curse has hounded me all my life. It must be kept from taking any more victims.'

The silver stick creature was trembling. He must have lived his life tormented by the most awful thoughts, K thought. But he also seemed somehow ecstatic.

Mir war lediglich klar, dass ich von etwas Schrecklichem besessen war. Als ich diese Einladung bekam, war ich entsetzt. Ich glaubte immer, ich sei der Einzige im ganzen Universum, den diese schreckliche Besessenheit plagte. Ich war davon überzeugt, dass sie mit meinem Tod verschwinden würde. Aber nun wurde ich eines Besseren belehrt. Diese furchtbare Angelegenheit muss sofort ein Ende haben."

„Aha. Verstehe. Die Gefahr war mir nicht bewusst. Wollen Sie sich nicht wenigstens erst einmal die AUSSTELLUNG anschauen? ... Sie wären doch immerhin der erste Besucher."

Der Alien hielt weiterhin die Mündung seiner Waffe auf K gerichtet, während er um die Objekte herumlief und sie betrachtete.

K bemerkte, dass der Außerirdische gelegentlich erschauderte. Was geschah unter der silbernen Haut? Erblühte eine Blume? Hatte es mit einer inneren Reise zu tun? K wusste es nicht.

Als das fremde Wesen mit der eingehenden Betrachtung der AUSSTELLUNG fertig war, sagte es mit gedämpfter Stimme:

„Es ist in der Tat gefährlich. Wie kann man nur derart schreckliche Dinge in einer solchen Menge ansammeln! Mir ist ganz schlecht davon. Wirklich abscheulich! Kaum zu glauben!"

„Finden Sie? Könnten Sie mir vielleicht noch eins erklären, bevor Sie mich töten? Was ist in Ihnen vorgegangen? Die Wesen, die mir diese Gegenstände anvertraut haben, sprachen von Dingen wie Blumen, die in einem aufblühen, oder von Reisen, die keinen einzigen Schritt der körperlichen Bewegung erfordern."

„So schön sind die Sachen doch gar nicht. Wenn man sie wahrnimmt, gewinnt das Innenleben die Oberhand. Die Seele wird auf eine unerhörte Weise transformiert, chemisch verwandelt und man wird ein völlig anderer. Als ich diesen ‚Anfall' hatte, glaubte ich, dass der Albtraum gleich wieder vorüber sein würde. Aber sobald dieses Zeug den Verstand beherrscht, wird der Zustand lebenslang andauern. Ich musste mich mutterseelenallein mit dieser Sache herumschlagen."

„Das war sicher schlimm für Sie."

„Denken Sie nicht schlecht von mir, wenn ich Sie umbringe. Aber wenn sich solch ein Konzept im Universum verbreitete, würden alle Lebewesen zugrunde gehen. Ihr Verstand würde eingenommen, kontrolliert und umgemodelt werden. Ich selbst war mein Leben lang dazu verdammt, mich vor Sehnsucht nach diesen Objekten zu verzehren. Es darf nicht noch mehr Opfer wie mich geben."

'All right,' K said. 'My life has almost run its course anyway. Let my journey, and "Hyupopororahyun", and "A...R...T", all meet their end at your hands.'

The silver stick creature shot K with its gun. K offered no resistance.

As K ruptured and collapsed, covered in blood, the silver stick creature exploded. Its remains were scattered outside the exhibition.

'K!' called MATSUKATA. It could not run to him, being buried from the neck down.

The bleeding K had collapsed into the glass tank. With some effort, he turned to face MATSUKATA, and smiled what was meant as a reassuring smile.

'I'm glad you told me those stories,' he said. 'About humans stealing "A...R...T" from each other, and then stealing it back, with things sometimes escalating into serious conflict. It looks like our safeguards worked as intended.'

'K, PLEASE KILL ME. I WANT TO GO ON A JOURNEY.'

'A journey. Of course. You've been here a long time, after all. But look how much "Hyupopororahyun" and "A...R...T" you had inside you. I thought that *was* your journey.'

'IF THAT IS SO, I WILL END MY JOURNEY, TOO.'

There was no reply from K. MATSUKATA shot itself in the head with the gun the silver stick creature had dropped. The robot's head went flying and rolled toward K. Its eyes stopped glowing and all the sounds it made ceased. The Exhibition was left in silence.

*

K and MATSUKATA were dead, but the Exhibition endured. The silver stick creature's remains, outside the Exhibition venue, were eaten by insects, but K's body was protected by the large glass tank. Its moisture evaporated little by little until K was completely mummified. There was none of the damage to the ecosystem that K had feared.

Fifty thousand years later, a large crowd of green aliens arrived.

Der silberstabförmige Alien zitterte am ganzen Körper. Er hatte anscheinend eine traumatische Erfahrung gemacht, dachte K, aber es schien auch beinahe so, als befände sich der Außerirdische in Ekstase.

„In Ordnung. Mein Leben ist sowieso gleich vorbei. Sie können also getrost sowohl meine Reise als auch ‚Hyupopororahyun' und KUN-ST nach Ihrem Gutdünken beenden."

Der Silberstab feuerte seine Waffe ab. K leistete keinen Widerstand.

Als K blutüberströmt zusammenbrach, explodierte im gleichen Moment der silberstabförmige Alien. Er zerbarst in Einzelteile, die außerhalb der AUSSTELLUNG durch die Gegend flogen.

„K!", rief MATSUKATA.

Er konnte ihm nicht zu Hilfe eilen, da er ja halsabwärts im Boden eingegraben war.

K war blutend in der Glashalle zusammengebrochen. Mit letzter Kraft gelang es ihm, sich MATSUKATA zuzuwenden und ihm beruhigend zuzulächeln.

„Ich bin froh, dass du mir die Geschichten erzählt hast, wie KUN-ST die MENSCHEN zu Raubzügen verleiten und zu Konflikten und Streitigkeiten führen kann. Offenbar haben die von uns geschaffenen Sicherheitsvorkehrungen gut funktioniert."

„K, BITTE TÖTE MICH. ICH MÖCHTE REISEN."

„Reisen? Ja klar, du warst ja auch die ganze Zeit hier an einem Fleck. Aber du hast doch so viele Objekte von ‚Hyupopororahyun' und KUN-ST in deinem Körper beherbergt. Da dachte ich, das wäre deine Art zu reisen."

„WENN DEM SO IST, DANN BEENDE AUCH ICH MEINE REISE."

Von K kam keine Antwort mehr. MATSUKATA schaffte es, die Waffe des Aliens, die bei der Explosion in seine Nähe geschleudert worden war, auszulösen. Sein Kopf riss ab und rollte zu Ks Leiche. Die blinkenden Augen und seine Stimme erloschen. Die AUSSTELLUNG war in Schweigen gehüllt.

*

'How mysterious! An Exhibition that's been running forever on an otherwise empty planet!'

'Mommy! This one is my favourite!'

A little girl pointed at K and MATSUKATA's remains. The mummified K looked as if he were sleeping, cradling MATSUKATA's head in his arms.

'It is lovely, isn't it? It gives you such a bright feeling. I could almost skip!'

'It makes me feel a bit uncomfortable.'

'I think it's provocative and erotic. It stirs the imagination.'

'I wonder what kind of artist made it. It certainly is an artistic sculpture. Look at those gently curving lines.'

The green aliens spread the word, and Earth soon became famous as the home of an eternal Exhibition.

Aliens from planets of all sorts came to visit. Most of them paused before K and MATSUKATA, when they reached the end of the Exhibition. K and MATSUKATA bloomed countless times within these visitors, and for countless visitors, the time spent gazing at K and MATSUKATA became an unforgettable journey.

When the sky brightened, the Exhibition was even livelier.

Eventually, even insects vanished from Earth. Most living things, in fact, had gone extinct. But it seemed that the planet Earth would continue to exist for some time yet.

K and MATSUKATA's Exhibition showed no sign of closing.

1 The robot MATSUKATA's speech is written in the original text in katakana, a Japanese syllabic script used for loan words or foreign terms. In the English translation, capital letters are used in the corresponding places. TN.

2 In the Japanese original, the robot shortens the word for art to 'Geiju' instead of 'Geijutsu'. This disruption of the reading flow is solved typographically in English with ellipsis points: 'A...R...T.' TN.

Auch nach Ks und MATSUKATAs Tod blieb die AUSSTELLUNG erhalten. Die sterblichen Überreste des silberstabförmigen Aliens lagen außerhalb des Ausstellungsgeländes am Boden und wurden dort von Insekten gefressen. Ks Leichnam blieb geschützt in dem großen Glasbehälter, wo seine Körpersäfte allmählich verdunsteten, bis er verdorrte wie eine Mumie. Dadurch wurde das Ökosystem entgegen seiner Befürchtung nicht zerstört.

Fünfzigtausend Jahre später traf eine Schar grüner Außerirdischer ein.

„Merkwürdig! Obwohl es hier auf diesem Planeten kein einziges Lebewesen gibt, scheint die AUSSTELLUNG schon ewig zu existieren."

„Mama, ich mag die hier am liebsten."

Das kleine Mädchen zeigte auf die beiden sterblichen Überreste von K und MATSUKATA. Die Mumie K sah aus, als würde sie schlafen, mit MATSUKATAs Kopf in ihrem Arm.

„Hier, das sieht fantastisch aus. Das macht mich so heiter, dass ich am liebsten hüpfen möchte."

„Auf mich wirkt es ein wenig bedrückend."

„Ich finde es reizvoll und erotisch, es regt die Fantasie an."

„Welcher Künstler hat das wohl erschaffen? Ein außerordentlich ästhetisches Objekt. Schau dir nur diese sanften Kurven an."

Die grünen Außerirdischen verbreiteten schnell die Kunde von dem Planeten Erde mit der ewig währenden AUSSTELLUNG, der dadurch allseits bekannt wurde.

Aliens von unterschiedlichsten Planeten besuchten die AUSSTELLUNG. An deren Ende angelangt, blieben viele vor K und MATSUKATA stehen. Die beiden erblühten in ihnen immer wieder. Dieser andächtige Moment beim Anblick von K und MATSUKATA wurde für viele zu einer unvergesslichen Reise.

Tagsüber, wenn es hell war, wurde die AUSSTELLUNG immer voller.

Irgendwann verschwanden sogar die Insekten von der Erde und die Lebewesen waren so gut wie ausgestorben. Aber es sah so aus, als würde der Planet Erde noch einige Zeit weiterbestehen. Ks und MATSUKATAs Ausstellung schien noch lange kein Ende zu haben.

1 Die wörtliche Rede des Roboters MATSUKATA ist im Originaltext in Katakana geschrieben, einer speziellen japanischen Silbenschrift, die besonders für Lehnwörter bzw. ausländische Begriffe verwendet wird. In der deutschen Übersetzung werden an den entsprechenden Stellen Großbuchstaben eingesetzt. A. d. Ü.

2 Im japanischen Original verkürzt der Roboter das Wort für Kunst auf „Geiju" statt „Geijutsu". Diese Störung des Leseflusses wird zur besseren Verständlichkeit im Deutschen durch den Einsatz eines Bindestriches wiedergegeben: „KUN-ST". A. d. Ü.

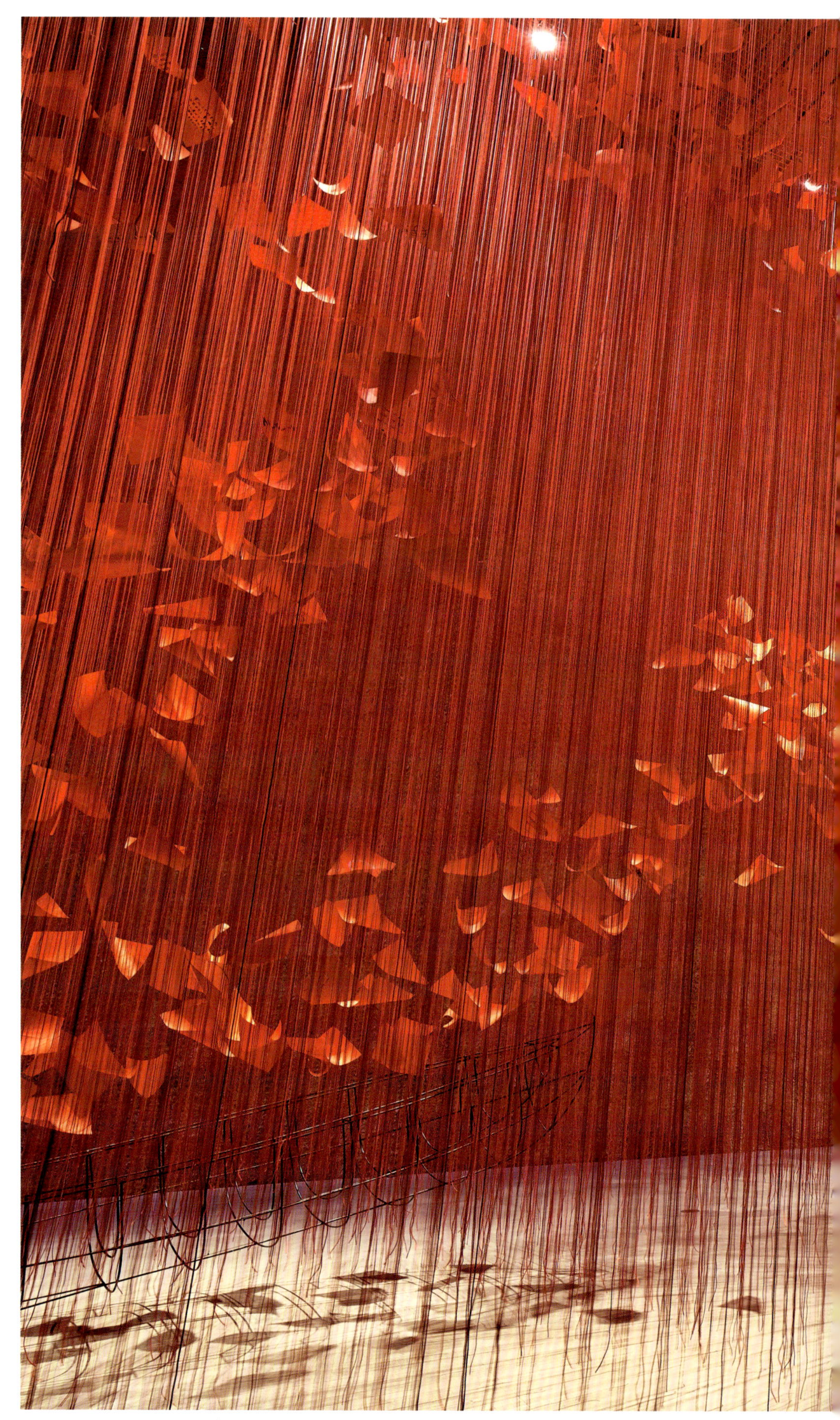

Chiharu Shiota
I hope …, 2021
Courtesy of König Galerie, Berlin

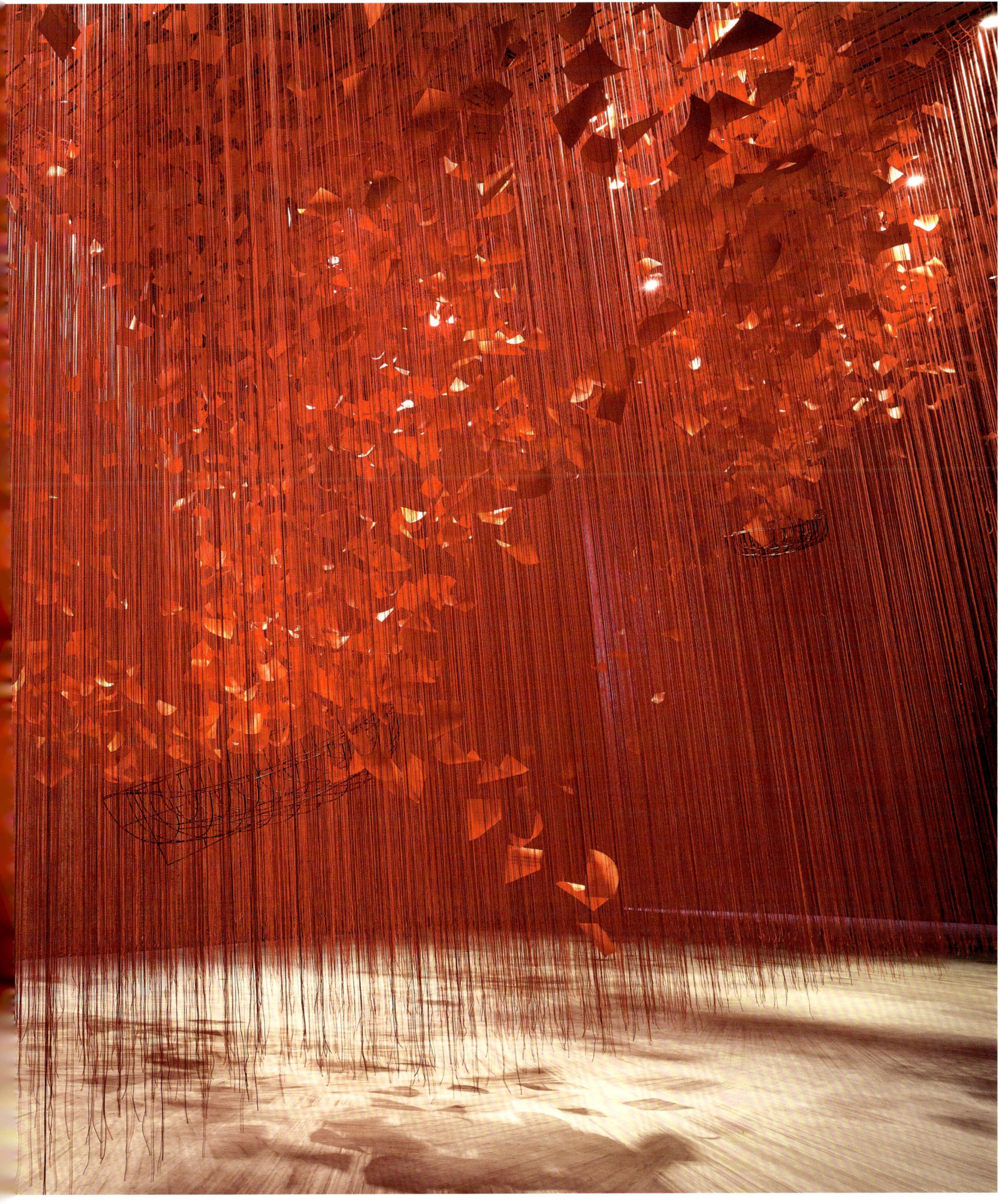

ENTREPRENEURIAL COLLECTORS AND THE TASTE FOR IMPRESSIONISM AND POST-IMPRESSIONISM

Frances Fowle

In 1976, Albert Boime explored the relationship between entrepreneurs and art collecting in his ground-breaking essay 'Entrepreneurial Patronage in Nineteenth-Century France.'[1] Boime's 'amateurs', like the artists they patronized, not only took an aesthetic pleasure in modern art, but also understood the potential for investment and were prepared to take risks. Invariably they were guided by an equally entrepreneurial, but also knowledgeable, agent or dealer, an individual who understood the product and the market. Karl Ernst Osthaus' fortune came from banking, while Kōjirō Matsukata made his wealth from shipping. Both were businesslike and even risk-taking in their approach to collecting art. They represented a new generation of enlightened collectors who contributed to the global spread and appreciation of modern French art in the first few decades of the twentieth century. To create a context for their collecting, this essay focuses on a selection of entrepreneurial collectors in Europe and the USA who, like them, developed an early taste for Impressionism and Post-Impressionism. In particular, it explores the impact of industrial prosperity on collecting practices, as well as the role of agents, advisors, critics and dealers in influencing taste.

Frances Fowle

Im Jahr 1976 untersuchte Albert Boime in seinem bahnbrechenden Essay „Entrepreneurial Patronage in Nineteenth-Century France"[1] das Verhältnis zwischen Unternehmertum und Kunstsammeln. Boimes *amateurs,* das heißt Kunstliebhaber, zeigten, ebenso wie die Künstler:innen, die sie förderten, nicht nur ästhetisches Interesse an moderner Kunst, sondern sahen auch das Potenzial für Investitionen und waren bereit, Risiken einzugehen. Sie wurden ausnahmslos von gleichermaßen unternehmerischen wie sachkundigen Agent:innen oder Händler:innen beraten, die sowohl die Handelsware als auch den Markt kannten. Karl Ernst Osthaus' Vermögen stammte aus Geschäften im Banksektor, während Kōjirō Matsukata seinen Reichtum mit der Schifffahrt erwirtschaftet hatte. Beide gingen an das Sammeln von Kunst wie an ihre Geschäfte und sogar risikofreudig heran. Sie standen für eine neue Generation aufgeklärter Sammler:innen, die in den ersten Jahrzehnten des 20. Jahrhunderts zur weltweiten Verbreitung und Anerkennung moderner französischer Kunst beitrugen. Um einen Kontext für ihre Sammlungstätigkeit aufzuzeigen, greift dieser Essay eine Auswahl Sammler-Unternehmer:innen in Europa und den USA heraus, die – wie die oben genannten – schon früh eine Vorliebe für Impressionismus und Post-Impressionismus erkennen ließen. In besonderem Maße befasst er sich mit dem Einfluss industriellen Reichtums auf Sammlungspraktiken, aber auch damit, wie Agent:innen, Berater:innen, Kritiker:innen und Händler:innen den Geschmack beeinflussten.

SAMMLER-UNTERNEHMER:INNEN UND IHRE VORLIEBE FÜR IMPRESSIONISMUS UND POST-IMPRESSIONISMUS

Pioneer Collectors ca. 1870–1916

The earliest entrepreneurial collectors were prepared to invest in avant-garde French art well before the market for such art had taken off.[2] Some were innovators in business, as well as collecting; the engineer-artist Henri Rouart, for example, was a pioneer in the field of refrigeration, as well as exhibiting alongside and supporting the Impressionists; the Rouennais François Depeaux was a patron of both Claude Monet and Alfred Sisley and also ran a highly successful coal business; an early supporter of Paul Cézanne, Auguste Pellerin made his fortune through the manufacturing of margarine. Like many of the entrepreneurial collectors discussed below, he applied business methods to collecting. In 1910, for example, he speculated on thirty-five works by Edouard Manet by selling them on at a profit to a consortium of art dealers.[3]

While most early collectors were more altruistic than Pellerin, it was only those prepared to play the 'long game' who capitalized on Impressionism and Post-Impressionism. The art dealer Paul Durand-Ruel faced bankruptcy in the 1870s through speculating in Impressionism and was only saved by the opening up of the American market in the 1880s (pp. 282, 309).[4] Ambroise Vollard built up a monopoly of Cézanne's work well before receiving any dividends (pp. 292, 293), and sensibly diversified into printing and publishing.[5] Before the First World War, relatively few collectors outside France risked investing in avant-garde French painting, and even fewer dealers promoted their work. An exception was Paul Cassirer in Berlin who promoted Impressionism and Post-Impressionism, especially the work of Cézanne and Vincent van Gogh, in the early 1900s (p. 315). However, it was mainly through the intercession of an agent or advisor, rather than a dealer, that these pioneer collectors developed an interest in modern French Art. In Osthaus's case this was Henry van de Velde (p. 211), while Matsukata was advised by Frank Brangwyn (p. 197). Modernism was also promoted by art historians such as Julius Meier-Graefe and the British critics Roger Fry and Clive Bell, among others.

The first British art dealer to stock and sell Impressionism on a regular basis was Alex Reid, who sold works by Monet, Edgar Degas, Camille Pissarro and Sisley to Glasgow's wealthy merchants and industrialists, such as the ship owner Sir William Burrell, in the 1890s and beyond.[6] However, in the period leading up to the First World War, few British collectors established noteworthy collections of modern French art. An exception was the Leeds educationalist Sir Michael Sadler, who not only bought works by Paul Gauguin, Cézanne and Van Gogh, but also lectured on Post-Impressionism. His buying was largely financed by his wife Mary, whose father, Charles Harvey, owned a large linen factory in Yorkshire. By 1911, inspired by the thirty-seven works by Gauguin on show at Fry's 1910 exhibition *Manet and the Post-Impressionists*, Sadler had acquired such masterpieces as Gauguin's *Manao Tupapau* (*Spirit of the Dead Watching*; 1892), *Le Christ au jardin des oliviers* (*Christ on the Mount of Olives*; 1889) and *Vision du sermon* (*Vision of the Sermon: Jacob Wrestling with the Angel*; 1888; fig. 1) and soon added works by Cézanne, Van Gogh and Wassily Kandinsky.[7] He was almost evangelical about this group of artists and not only lent key works to public exhibitions, but also invited young British artists to visit his collection. Nevertheless, as the market for Post-Impressionism developed in the 1920s, he sold his Post-Impressionist pictures in order to make way

Wegbereitende Sammler:innen
um 1870–1916

Die frühesten Sammler-Unternehmer:innen waren bereit, in französische Kunst der Avantgarde zu investieren, schon lange bevor sich der Markt für diese Kunst etabliert hatte.[2] Einige waren sowohl im unternehmerischen Bereich als auch beim Sammeln Vorreiter:innen, so wie der Ingenieur und Künstler Henri Rouart, der nicht nur ein Pionier im Bereich der Kältetechnik war, sondern auch gemeinsam mit den Impressionist:innen ausstellte und diese unterstützte; oder François Depeaux aus Rouen, ein Förderer von Claude Monet und Alfred Sisley, der ein äußerst erfolgreiches Kohleunternehmen führte; aber auch Auguste Pellerin, ein früher Unterstützer von Paul Cézanne, der sein Vermögen mit der Produktion von Margarine machte. Wie viele der weiter unten besprochenen Sammler-Unternehmer:innen wandte auch er beim Sammeln Geschäftsmethoden an. So spekulierte er 1910 mit 35 Arbeiten von Edouard Manet und verkaufte sie mit Gewinn an ein Konsortium von Kunsthändler:innen.[3]

Obwohl die meisten frühen Sammler:innen altruistischer als Pellerin waren, gelang es nur jenen, die auf lange Sicht investierten, mit Impressionismus und Post-Impressionismus auch zu verdienen. Der Kunsthändler Paul Durand-Ruel geriet in den 1870er-Jahren durch Spekulationen mit impressionistischer Kunst in den Bankrott und erst die Öffnung des amerikanischen Kunstmarktes in den 1880er-Jahren rettete ihn (S. 282, 309).[4]

Ambroise Vollard hatte sich das Monopol auf die Arbeiten von Cézanne gesichert, ehe er Dividenden daraus bezog (S. 292, 293), und war daneben klugerweise auch als Drucker und Verleger tätig.[5] Vor dem Ersten Weltkrieg riskierten nur relativ wenige Sammler:innen außerhalb Frankreichs eine Investition in französische Avantgardemalerei und noch weniger Händler:innen propagierten die Werke der entsprechenden Künstler:innen. Eine Ausnahme bildete Paul Cassirer in Berlin, der Anfang der 1900er-Jahre die Kunst des Impressionismus und des Post-Impressionismus – vor allem die Arbeiten von Cézanne und Vincent van Gogh – förderte (S. 315). Es war jedoch in erster Linie auf die Fürsprache von Agent:innen oder Berater:innen zurückzuführen, und nicht auf Händler:innen, dass die wegbereitenden Sammler:innen ein Interesse an moderner französischer Kunst entwickelten. Im Fall von Osthaus war dies Henry van de Velde (S. 211), während Matsukata von Frank Brangwyn (S. 197) beraten wurde. Die moderne Kunst wurde zudem von Kunsthistorikern wie Julius Meier-Graefe oder den britischen Kritikern Roger Fry und Clive Bell gefördert.

Der erste britische Kunsthändler, der impressionistische Kunst regelmäßig führte und verkaufte, war Alex Reid, der ab den 1890er-Jahren Arbeiten von Monet, Edgar Degas, Camille Pissarro und Sisley an die wohlhabenden Kaufleute und Industriellen von Glasgow veräußerte, etwa an den Schiffseigner Sir William Burrell.[6] In der Zeit vor dem Ersten Weltkrieg trugen jedoch nur wenige britische Sammler:innen bedeutende Sammlungen moderner französischer Kunst zusammen. Eine Ausnahme bildete der Pädagoge Sir Michael

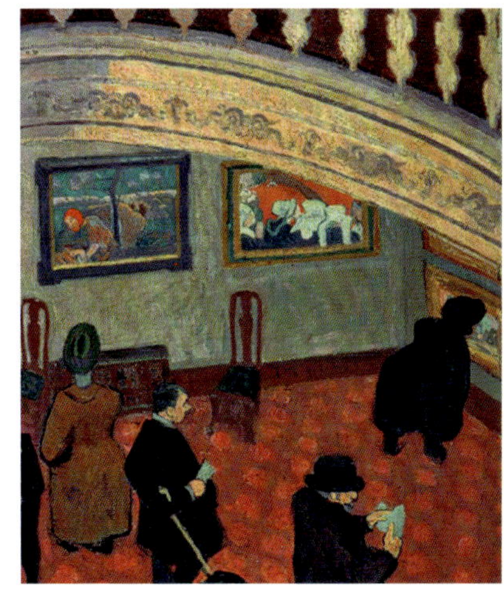

Abb. | Fig. 1
Spencer Gore, *Gauguins and Connoisseurs at the Stafford Gallery*, 1911, Detail, Privatsammlung (rechts außen Gauguins *Vision du sermon* aus der Sammlung von Michael Sadler) | detail, private collection (far right Gauguin's *Vision du sermon* from Michael Sadler's collection)

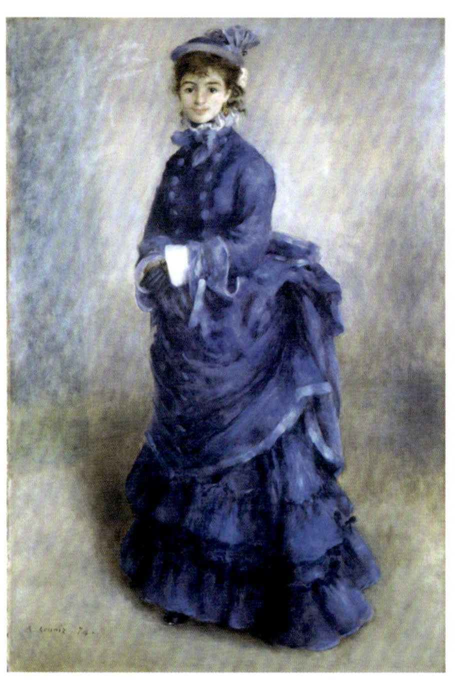

Abb. | Fig. 2
Auguste Renoir, *La parisienne*, 1874,
National Museum of Wales, Cardiff

for more contemporary British art. The Irish dealer
and collector Sir Hugh Lane made more impact,
therefore, when, following his tragic death aboard
RMS Lusitania in 1915, he controversially left his
small collection of Impressionist paintings to
London's National Gallery, rather than Dublin. Equally influential were the Welsh sisters Gwendoline
and Margaret Davies, who inherited their fortune
through their grandfather's investment in the coal
industry, railways and docks.[8] Advised by the agent
Hugh Blaker, it was Gwendoline who built up the
sisters' outstanding collection of late works by
Monet, acquired in Paris before the First World
War, and individual masterpieces such as Pierre-
Auguste Renoir's *La parisienne* (*The Parisian Girl*;
fig. 2), Cézanne's *Nature morte avec pot de thé*
(*Still Life with Teapot*; ca. 1902–06) and van Gogh's
Paysage d'Auvers sous la pluie (*Rain at Auvers*;
1890).[9] Like Sadler, they lent their pictures to public
exhibitions, inspiring future collectors such as the
textile magnate Samuel Courtauld.

Women also played a key role in the early reception of Impressionism in the USA. Like the Davies
sisters, Louisine Havemeyer and Bertha Honoré
Palmer financed their collecting through industry
and commerce. Advised by Mary Cassatt (fig. 3),
Havemeyer bought modern French art in tandem
with her husband, Henry O. Havemeyer, who
became President of the American Sugar Refining
Company in 1891. Thanks to Louisine Havemeyer's
enthusiasm for the Impressionists they built up
an important collection which hung in the Tiffany-
designed interiors of their three-storey mansion

Sadler aus Leeds, der nicht nur Arbeiten von Paul Gauguin, Cézanne und van Gogh erwarb, sondern auch Vorträge zum Post-Impressionismus hielt. Seine Ankäufe wurden größtenteils durch seine Frau Mary finanziert, deren Vater Charles Harvey eine große Leinenfabrik in Yorkshire besaß. Bis 1911 hatte Sadler – auch inspiriert durch die 37 Arbeiten Gauguins, die 1910 in Frys Ausstellung *Manet and the Post-Impressionists* zu sehen gewesen waren – Meisterwerke wie Gauguins *Manao Tupapau (Der Geist der Toten wacht,* 1892), *Le Christ au jardin des oliviers (Christus am Ölberg,* 1889) und *Vision du sermon (Die Vision der Predigt: Jakobs Kampf mit dem Engel,* 1888; Abb. 1) erworben und schon bald kamen Werke von Cézanne, van Gogh und Wassily Kandinsky hinzu.[7] Was diese Gruppe von Künstlern betraf, war er beinahe missionarisch: Er verlieh seine Schätze nicht nur an öffentliche Ausstellungen, sondern lud auch junge britische Künstler:innen ein, seine Sammlung zu besichtigen. Als der Markt für die Post-Impressionisten in den 1920er-Jahren jedoch einen Aufschwung erlebte, verkaufte er seine post-impressionistischen Arbeiten, um Platz für aktuellere britische Kunst zu machen. Noch größer war die Wirkung des irischen Händlers und Sammlers Sir Hugh Lane, der nach seinem tragischen Tod auf der *RMS Lusitania* im Jahr 1915 seine kleine Sammlung impressionistischer Gemälde der National Gallery in London hinterließ, anstatt sie in Dublin zu belassen. Ebenso einflussreich waren die walisischen Schwestern Gwendoline und Margaret Davies, die ihr Vermögen von ihrem Großvater erbten, der es wiederum durch Investitionen in Kohleindustrie, Eisen-

bahn und Hafenanlagen erwirtschaftet hatte.[8] Beraten von dem Agenten Hugh Blaker baute Gwendoline die herausragende Sammlung der Schwestern auf, bestehend aus Spätwerken Monets, die sie vor dem Ersten Weltkrieg in Paris erworben hatte, sowie aus Einzelarbeiten wie Pierre-Auguste Renoirs *La parisienne (Die Pariserin;* Abb. 2), Cézannes *Nature morte avec pot de thé (Stillleben mit Teekanne,* ca. 1902–1906) und van Goghs *Paysage d'Auvers sous la pluie (Landschaft bei Auvers im Regen,* 1890).[9] Wie Sadler verliehen auch Gwendoline und Margaret ihre Bilder für öffentliche Ausstellungen und inspirierten damit zukünftige Sammler:innen wie den Textilmagnaten Samuel Courtauld.

Frauen spielten auch eine Schlüsselrolle bei der frühen Rezeption des Impressionismus in den USA. Wie die Davies-Schwestern finanzierten auch Louisine Havemeyer und Bertha Honoré Palmer ihre Sammeltätigkeit mithilfe von Industrie und Handel. Beraten von Mary Cassatt (Abb. 3) kaufte Havemeyer moderne französische Kunst zusammen mit ihrem Ehemann Henry O. Havemeyer, der 1891 Präsident der American Sugar Refining Company wurde. Dank Louisine Havemeyers Begeisterung für die Impressionisten trugen die beiden eine bedeutende Sammlung zusammen, die in den von Tiffany ausgestatteten Innenräumen ihres dreistöckigen Hauses an der New Yorker Fifth Avenue hing. Ihre Sammlung wurde nur von jener Bertha Palmers in den Schatten gestellt, zweifellos die wichtigste frühe Sammlerin impressionistischer Kunst außerhalb Frankreichs, die neunzig Arbeiten von Monet erwarb, darunter eine große

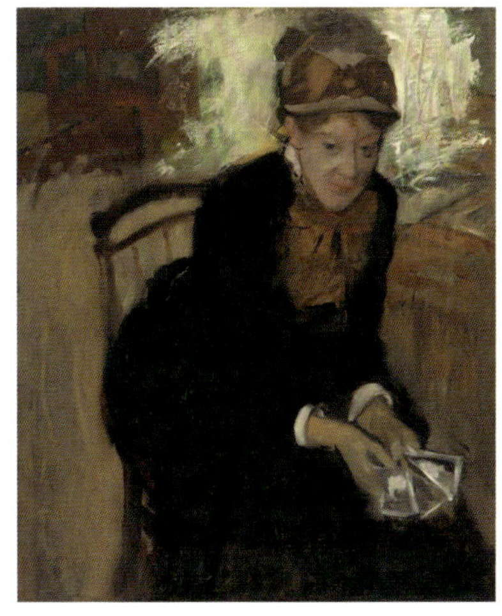

Abb. | Fig. 3
Edgar Degas, *Mary Cassatt,* ca. 1880–1884, National Portrait Gallery, Washington. Ehemals Sammlung Matsukata | formerly Matsukata Collection

Abb. | Fig. 4
Claude Monet, *Les meules*, 1890/91,
Art Institute of Chicago

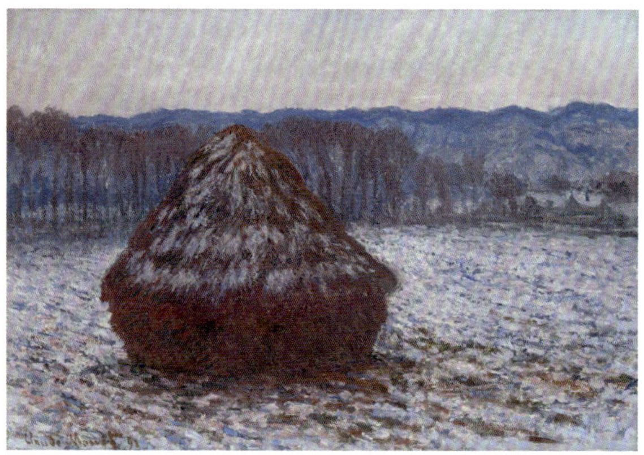

on Fifth Avenue, New York. Their collection was eclipsed only by that of Bertha Palmer, who was without question the most important early collector of Impressionism outside France, acquiring as many as ninety works by Monet, among them a large number of the 'series' paintings (fig. 4). Her extravagant tastes and lifestyle were supported by her husband Potter Palmer, a self-made man, who made his fortune from the retail industry and developing real estate in Chicago. Their mansion on Lake Shore Drive was known as 'The Castle', and in 1893, Bertha added a ninety-foot ballroom and picture gallery to accommodate the expanding art collection. She relied on the curator Sara Tyson Hallowell, as well as Cassatt, to assist her in building up her magnificent collection, which she bought mainly from Durand-Ruel in the early 1890s.[10] Palmer selected each work independently and kept a careful note of each transaction, but all purchases were made on her husband's account.[11] Like Pellerin, she was not averse to speculation, and often bought and resold works quickly at a profit, thus pushing up the value of her collection.[12]

Another major group of collectors of modern French art emerged in Russia in the early twentieth century. The textile entrepreneur Sergei Shchukin financed his collecting entirely from income generated through the family business, I.V. Shchukin and Sons, which he took over in 1890. Celebrated for his early recognition of Matisse and Picasso, Shchukin built up an important collection of Impressionist and Post-Impressionist art, acquired mainly through Durand-Ruel and Vollard. He initially focused on Monet but, from 1903, began to shift his interests to Post-Impressionism, acquiring his first Cézanne that year and his first Gauguin in 1904. He also owned several works by van Gogh, among them the portrait of *Dr Félix Rey* (fig. 5).

All trips to Paris were interrupted by the first Russian Revolution of 1905, and Shchukin faced financial ruin. However, during the period of economic depression that ensued, he risked everything by buying up all available stocks of textile goods at deflated prices. With the recovery of the economy in 1906 he was able to realize a huge profit, with the result that Shchukin and Sons became one of the largest textile manufacturing and wholesale companies in Russia.[13] One can draw parallels between his business practice and his approach to buying art, since he preferred supporting artists who were still undiscovered. As a result, he made some spectacular purchases, including Cézanne's *Le fumeur de pipe* (*The Smoker*; fig. 6) in 1908, and creating his famous Gauguin iconostasis in the dining hall of his Moscow mansion.

Shchukin's main Russian rival in the market for Impressionism and Post-Impressionism was Ivan Morozov, another textile baron.[14] Despite their enormous wealth, both men were careful to finance their collecting from income, rather than capital, limiting their spending to spring and autumn when dividends were calculated.[15] By 1906, Morozov had acquired works by Monet, Sisley, Pissarro, Degas and Renoir, which decorated his magnificent Moscow mansion at 16 Vozdvi-

Zahl seiner seriellen Gemälde (Abb. 4). Ihr extravaganter Geschmack und ihre Lebensführung wurden von ihrem Ehemann Potter Palmer, einem Selfmademan, unterstützt, der sein Vermögen im Einzelhandel und am Immobilienmarkt in Chicago erwirtschaftet hatte. Ihr herrschaftlicher Wohnsitz am Lake Shore Drive war als *The Castle* bekannt, und 1893 erweiterte Bertha Palmer diesen um einen 27 Meter langen Festsaal und eine Bildergalerie, um die wachsende Gemäldesammlung unterzubringen. Bei der Zusammenstellung ihrer prachtvollen Sammlung, die sie Anfang der 1890er-Jahre hauptsächlich von Durand-Ruel erworben hatte, verließ sie sich auf die Kuratorin Sara Tyson Hallowell, aber auch auf Cassatt.[10] Palmer wählte jede Arbeit eigenständig aus und vermerkte sorgfältig alle Transaktionen; sämtliche Erwerbungen erfolgten jedoch auf das Konto ihres Mannes.[11] Wie Pellerin war auch sie Spekulationen gegenüber nicht abgeneigt und kaufte und verkaufte Arbeiten oft rasch mit Gewinn, wodurch sie den Wert ihrer Sammlung in die Höhe trieb.[12]

Eine weitere bedeutende Gruppe von Sammler:innen moderner französischer Kunst bildete sich Anfang des 20. Jahrhunderts in Russland heraus. Der Textilunternehmer Sergei Schtschukin finanzierte seine Sammlungstätigkeit ausschließlich mit Einnahmen aus dem Familiengeschäft I. V. Schtschukin und Söhne, das er 1890 übernommen hatte. Schtschukin, der vor allem für seine frühe Würdigung von Henri Matisse und Pablo Picasso bekannt ist, stellte eine bedeutende Sammlung impressionistischer und post-impressionistischer Kunst zusammen, die er in erster Linie über

Durand-Ruel und Vollard erwarb. Ursprünglich lag sein Fokus auf Monet, doch ab 1903 verlagerte sich sein Interesse auf den Post-Impressionismus; in diesem Jahr erwarb er seinen ersten Cézanne und 1904 seinen ersten Gauguin. Zudem besaß er einige Arbeiten von van Gogh, darunter das Bildnis des *Félix Rey* (Abb. 5).

Seine Reisen nach Paris wurden 1905 durch die erste Russische Revolution unterbrochen, und Schtschukin stand vor dem finanziellen Ruin. Im Zuge der darauf folgenden Wirtschaftsdepression riskierte er jedoch alles, indem er sämtliche verfügbaren Lagerbestände von Textilwaren zu deflationierten Preisen erwarb. Mit der Erholung der Wirtschaft im Jahr 1906 konnte er so riesige Gewinne erwirtschaften, mit dem Ergebnis, dass Schtschukin und Söhne zu einem der größten Textilhersteller und -großhandelsunternehmen in Russland wurde.[13] Es finden sich durchaus Parallelen zwischen seinen Geschäftspraktiken und seiner Herangehensweise an den Erwerb von Kunst, unterstützte er doch mit Vorliebe noch unentdeckte Künstler:innen. In der Folge tätigte er einige spektakuläre Käufe, darunter Cézannes *Le fumeur de pipe (Mann mit der Pfeife,* Abb. 6) im Jahr 1908, und schuf seine berühmte Gauguin-Ikonostase bzw. -Bilderwand im Speisesaal seines Moskauer Stadtpalais. Schtschukins russischer Hauptrivale auf dem Markt für Impressionismus und Post-Impressionismus war Iwan Morosow, ein weiterer Textilbaron.[14] Trotz ihres immensen Reichtums waren beide Männer darauf bedacht, ihre Sammlungsleidenschaft über ihr Einkommen, nicht über Kapital zu finanzieren, was ihre Ausgaben

81

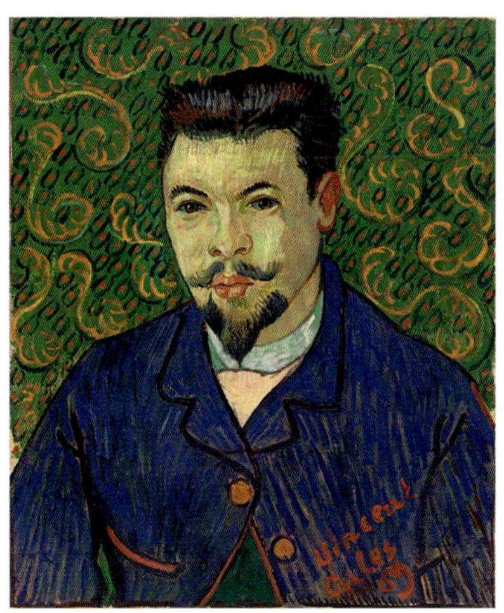

Abb. | Fig. 5
Vincent van Gogh, *Dr Félix Rey,* 1889,
The Pushkin State Museum of Fine Arts,
Moskau | Moscow

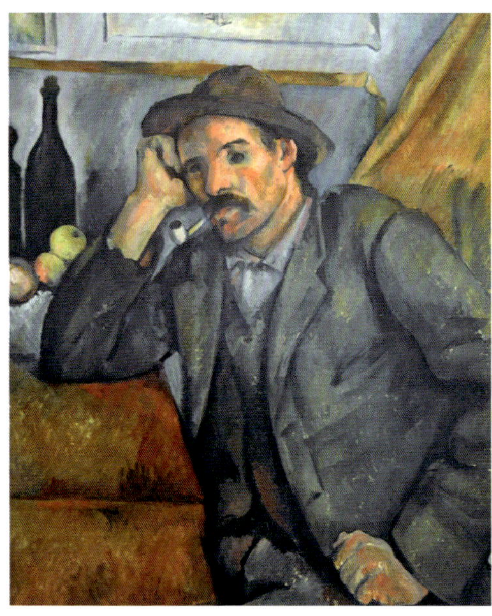

Abb. | Fig. 6
Paul Cézanne, *Le fumeur de pipe,* ca. 1891,
State Hermitage Museum, St. Petersburg

zhenka Street. However, the following year, under
Vollard's influence, he began to focus on Post-
Impressionism, acquiring a total of eleven works
by Gauguin and eighteen by his favourite artist,
Cézanne.

Entrepreneurial Collectors in the 1920s

Just before the First World War, aware of the
growing interest in Impressionism and Post-
Impressionism among collectors outside Europe,
the Danish dealer Tyge Møller advised his clients
to invest in modern French art before prices began to soar. Among those who took his advice was
Wilhelm Hansen, whose work for an insurance
company took him frequently to Paris. From 1916
onwards, Hansen built up his collection, developing a particular interest in Gauguin (fig. 7), whose
wife Mette was Danish. His tastes were encouraged by an elderly Théodore Duret, one of the
earliest champions of Impressionism, but he was
also motivated by commercial gain, and engaged
in speculation through the creation of a consortium
with the collectors Herman Heilbuth and the art
dealers Winkel & Magnussen.[16] Financial support
from the Danish Landsmansbank, whose board of
directors included Heilbuth, enabled them to buy
modern French paintings in bulk, select the best
examples for their personal collections and sell the
remainder at a profit. Their purchases included
the collection of the French dentist George Viau,
an early supporter of the Impressionists. As a result,
important works such as Gauguin's *Petite crique
devant le port de Pont-Aven* (*Landscape at Pont-
Aven*; 1888) and *Deux vases de fleurs* (*Two Vases
with Flowers*; 1890/91), as well as Berthe Morisot's
Jeune fille sur l'herbe (*Young girl on the Grass*;
1885) were acquired by Hansen and eventually

83

auf Frühling und Herbst beschränkte, wenn die Dividenden berechnet wurden.[15] Bis 1906 hatte Morosow Werke von Monet, Sisley, Pissarro, Degas und Renoir erworben, die sein prachtvolles Moskauer Palais in der Vozdvizhenka-Straße 16 schmückten. Im darauffolgenden Jahr begann er sich unter dem Einfluss von Vollard jedoch den Post-Impressionisten zuzuwenden und erwarb insgesamt 11 Arbeiten von Gauguin und 18 von Cézanne, seinem Lieblingskünstler.

Sammler-Unternehmer:innen in den 1920er-Jahren

Unmittelbar vor dem Ersten Weltkrieg und im Bewusstsein des wachsenden Interesses an Impressionismus und Post-Impressionismus unter den Sammler:innen außerhalb Europas riet der dänische Händler Tyge Møller seinen Kund:innen, in französische Kunst der Moderne zu investieren, ehe die Preise dafür in schwindelerregende Höhen steigen würden. Unter jenen, die seinem Rat folgten, war auch Wilhelm Hansen, dessen Arbeit für ein Versicherungsunternehmen ihn regelmäßig nach Paris führte. Ab 1916 trug Hansen seine Sammlung zusammen und entwickelte dabei ein besonderes Interesse für Gauguin (Abb. 7), dessen Frau Mette Dänin war. In dieser Vorliebe wurde er von dem betagten Kunstkritiker und Schriftsteller Théodore Duret bestärkt, einem der frühesten Förderer des Impressionismus; aber Hansen war auch von Gewinnstreben getrieben und gründete zusammen mit dem Sammler Herman Heilbuth und den Kunsthändlern Winkel & Magnussen ein

Konsortium.[16] Die finanzielle Unterstützung von der dänischen Landmansbank, deren Vorstandsmitglied Heilbuth war, versetzte sie in die Lage, moderne französische Malerei in großen Mengen zu kaufen, die besten Exemplare für ihre persönlichen Sammlungen auszuwählen und den Rest mit Profit zu verkaufen. Zu ihren Erwerbungen gehörte auch die Sammlung des französischen Zahnarztes George Viau, eines frühen Förderers der Impressionisten. In der Folge erwarb Hansen bedeutende Werke wie Gauguins *Petite crique devant le port de Pont-Aven (Landschaft bei Pont-Aven,* 1888) und *Deux vases de fleurs (Zwei Vasen mit Blumen,* 1890/91), aber auch Berthe Morisots *Jeune fille sur l'herbe (Junges Mädchen im Grünen,* 1885), die schließlich in die Sammlung in Ordrupgaard gelangten. 1922 ging die Landmansbank Bankrott und Hansen war leider gezwungen, eine beträchtliche Anzahl impressionistischer Gemälde zu verkaufen, von denen einige von Matsukata erworben wurden. Wie Hansen war auch Matsukata Teil dieser neuen Welle Sammler-Unternehmer:innen und erwarb seine ersten Werke im Jahr 1916.[17] Er stand für eine aufstrebende Generation von *nouveaux riches* und kaufte mit hoher Wahrscheinlichkeit aus Statusgründen, war sich jedoch auch des Investitionspotenzials moderner französischer Kunst bewusst. Als Präsident der Kawasaki-Werft erwirtschaftete er während des Ersten Weltkriegs ein beträchtliches Vermögen durch den Verkauf von Schiffen nach Europa. Diesbezüglich bietet sich ein Vergleich mit Alex Reids Kunde Sir William Burrell an, Eigentümer der Reederei Burrell & Son in Glasgow. Burrell kam zu enormem Reichtum, als er

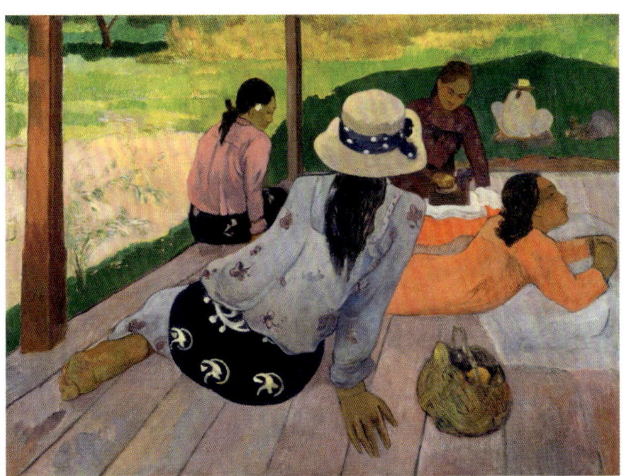

Abb. | Fig. 7
Paul Gauguin, *La sieste,* ca. 1891–1894, The Metropolitan Museum of Art, New York. Ehemals Sammlungen Hansen und Matsukata | formerly Hansen and Matsukata Collections

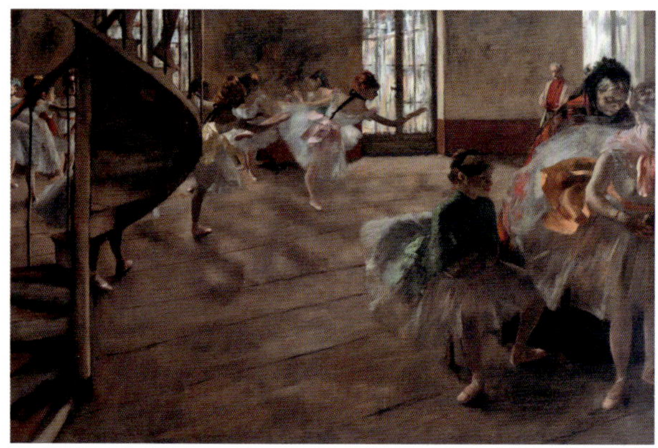

ended up in the collection at Ordrupgaard. In 1922, the Landsmansbank was bankrupted, and Hansen was unfortunately forced to sell a large number of Impressionist pictures, some of which were acquired by Matsukata. Like Hansen, Matsukata was part of this new wave of entrepreneurial collectors, acquiring his first works in 1916.[17] Representing a rising generation of nouveau riche, he almost certainly bought for reasons of status, but was also aware of the investment potential of modern French art. As president of Kawasaki Dockyard, he built up a considerable fortune through selling cargo boats to Europe during the First World War. A comparison can be drawn with Alex Reid's client Sir William Burrell, proprietor of the shipping firm Burrell & Son in Glasgow. Burrell became enormously wealthy through buying his entire fleet of ships during an economic downturn and selling during a boom period. Between 1890 and 1930, the company achieved this not once, but twice, realizing huge dividends during the First World War when steam ships were in high demand.[18] Burrell later applied his business acumen to collecting. Always one with an eye for a bargain, he developed the bulk of his collection of modern French art in the late 1920s and 1930s, when the market was depressed. His collection, which deserves to be better known, included fourteen sculptures by Auguste Rodin, twenty-four oils and pastels by Degas and nine pictures by Manet, as well as works by Sisley, Renoir, Pissarro and Cézanne. Among the major works that passed through his hands were Manet's *Portrait de Victorine Meurent*

(*Portrait of Victorine Meurent*; 1862), Degas's *La répétition* (*The Rehearsal*; fig. 8), described by Burrell as Degas's 'greatest work', his 1879 portrait of the French critic Edmond Duranty, and Cézanne's *Château de Médan* (*The Chateau of Medan*; 1879/80).[19]

Where Burrell succeeded in the shipping industry, others failed, among them the Scottish collector Elizabeth Workman, who financed her taste for Post-Impressionism through her husband's income from the Northumberland shipping company and the Belfast firm Workman, Clark & Co. Unfortunately, Workman's timing was less fortunate than either Burrell or Matsukata; the economic crisis of the late 1920s resulted in his financial ruin and Elizabeth was forced to sell the entire art collection, which included such masterpieces as Degas's *Portrait de Diego Martelli* (*Portrait of Diego Martelli*; 1879), Monet's *Boulevard des Capucines* (1873–74), Van Gogh's *Vase aux lauriers roses* (*Oleanders*; fig. 9) and Gauguin's *Portrait charge de Gauguin* (*Self-Portrait with Halo and Snake*; 1889).[20]

A similar fate nearly befell the magnificent collection of Van Gogh pictures amassed by Helene Kröller-Müller. Her father was CEO of the German shipping company Wm H. Müller & Co, who supplied and transported iron and steel products. Helene's husband Anton Kröller was appointed director in 1889, by which date their main office was in Rotterdam. The company was extremely profitable in the first two decades of the twentieth century and Kröller-Müller invested the couple's accumulated wealth in modern French

85

seine gesamte Flotte während einer Wirtschaftsflaute erwarb und dann während einer Hochkonjunkturphase wieder verkaufte. Zwischen 1890 und 1930 gelang dem Unternehmen dieser Coup sogar zwei Mal, wodurch es im Laufe des Ersten Weltkriegs, als Dampfschiffe äußerst gefragt waren, unglaubliche Dividenden erzielen konnte.[18] Später setzte Burrell seinen Geschäftssinn für das Sammeln von Kunst ein. Stets auf der Suche nach Schnäppchen, trug er den Hauptteil seiner Sammlung moderner französischer Kunst gegen Ende der 1920er- und in den 1930er-Jahren zusammen, als der Markt am Boden lag. Seine Sammlung, die einen größeren Bekanntheitsgrad verdient hätte, umfasste 14 Skulpturen von Auguste Rodin, 24 Ölgemälde und Aquarelle von Degas und 9 Bilder von Manet sowie Arbeiten von Sisley, Renoir, Pissarro und Cézanne. Andere bedeutende Werke, die durch seine Hände gingen, waren zum Beispiel Manets *Portrait de Victorine Meurent (Bildnis Victorine Meurent,* 1862), Degas' *La répétition (Die Probe;* Abb. 8), das Burrell als Degas' „beste Arbeit" bezeichnete, dessen Porträt des französischen Kritikers Edmond Duranty von 1879 und Cézannes *Le Château de Médan (Das Schloss von Médan,* 1879/80).[19]

Wo Burrell in der Schifffahrtsindustrie Erfolge feierte, scheiterten andere, darunter die schottische Sammlerin Elizabeth Workman, die ihre Vorliebe für den Post-Impressionismus mit dem Einkommen ihres Mannes aus der Northumberland-Reederei und dem Unternehmen Workman, Clark & Co. in Belfast finanzierte. Leider war Workmans Timing weniger glücklich als das von Burrell oder

Matsukata und die Wirtschaftskrise der späten 1920er-Jahre hatte den Ruin der Firma zur Folge. Elizabeth Workman war daraufhin gezwungen, die gesamte Kunstsammlung zu veräußern, darunter Meisterwerke wie Degas' *Portrait de Diego Martelli (Bildnis Diego Martelli,* 1879), Monets *Boulevard des Capucines* (1873/74), van Goghs *Vase aux lauriers roses (Oleander;* Abb. 9) und Gauguins *Portrait charge de Gauguin (Selbstporträt mit Heiligenschein und Schlange,* 1889).[20]

Ein ähnliches Schicksal drohte auch der prachtvollen Sammlung von Gemälden van Goghs, die Helene Kröller-Müller zusammengetragen hatte. Ihr Vater war Generaldirektor der deutschen Reederei Wm H. Müller & Co., die Eisen- und Stahlprodukte lieferte und transportierte. Helenes Ehemann Anton Kröller wurde 1889 zum Geschäftsführer ernannt, als die Zentrale sich in Rotterdam befand. Das Unternehmen erwies sich in den ersten beiden Jahrzehnten des 20. Jahrhunderts als äußerst profitabel und Kröller-Müller investierte das Vermögen des Paares in moderne französische Kunst. Auf Ratschlag des Kunsthistorikers H. P. Bremmer legte sie den Fokus auf Arbeiten von van Gogh (Abb. 10) und, wenn auch in geringerem Umfang, auf die Neo-Impressionisten, deren Werke sie hauptsächlich bis 1921 erwarb. Aufgrund von Anton Kröllers umfangreichen Krediten bei der Rotterdamsche Bank geriet die Firma im Laufe des folgenden Jahrzehnts jedoch in finanzielle Schwierigkeiten.[21] Unternehmen und Bank entgingen nur knapp dem Kollaps und Kröller war 1931 zum Rücktritt gezwungen. Die Sammlung konnte jedoch gerettet werden, da sie bereits 1928 in eine

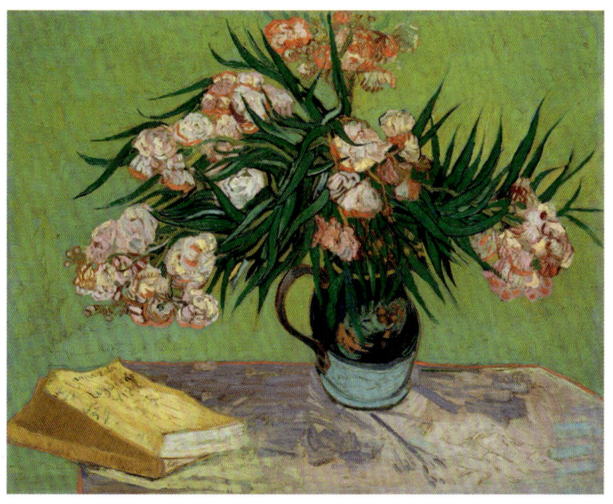

Abb. | Fig. 9
Vincent van Gogh, *Vase aux lauriers roses,*
1888, The Metropolitan Museum of Art,
New York

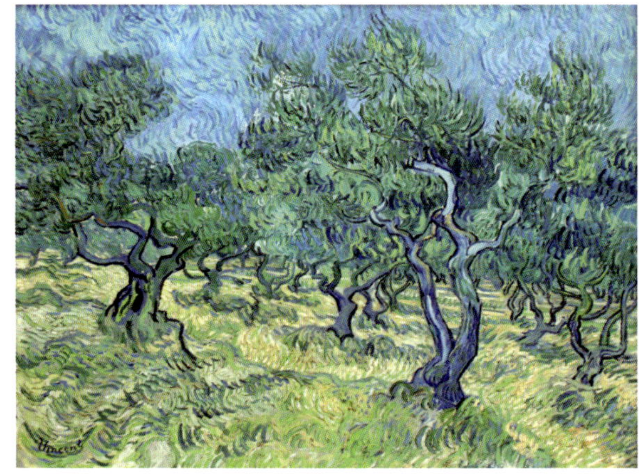

art. On the advice of the art historian H. P. Bremmer, she specialized in works by Van Gogh (fig. 10) and, to a lesser extent, the Neo-Impressionists, which were mostly acquired by 1921. However, for the next ten years the company ran into financial difficulties, thanks to Anton Kröller's extensive borrowing from the Rotterdamsche Bank.[21] The company and the bank narrowly avoided collapse, and Kröller was forced to resign in 1931. However, the collection was saved, having been placed in a foundation in 1928, and the Dutch state agreed to finance the construction of what became the Kröller-Müller Museum at Otterlo.

Other industrialist collectors managed to sidestep the economic crisis of the late 1920s. These included Samuel Courtauld, who in 1921 became chairman of Courtaulds, originally a modest manufacturer of silk and crêpe, but by then the world's leading manufacturer of man-made fibres, including rayon. It was largely through income from the company that he financed his important collection of Impressionist and Post-Impressionist art, mostly formed between 1923 and 1928. Encouraged by his wife Elizabeth and advised by Fry and by the dealer Percy Moore Turner, Courtauld developed a particular taste for Cézanne, acquiring such masterpieces as *La Montagne Saint-Victoire au grand pin* (*Mont Sainte-Victoire with Large Pine*; fig. 11), *Les Joueurs de cartes* (*The Card Players*; ca. 1892–5), *Nature morte avec amour en plâtre* (*Still Life with Plaster Cast*; ca. 1894) and *Le Lac d'Annecy* (1896).[22] Philanthropic in outlook, Courtauld believed in the importance of art for the benefit of the public, and in 1923 established a fund at the National Gallery in London solely for the purchase of modern French art.

Another textile magnate largely unaffected by the crash was Stephen Clark, who, like Osthaus, inherited his wealth initially from an entrepreneurial grandfather, Edward Clark.[23] Clark senior was co-founder of the Singer Company who manufactured domestic sewing machines in the USA and Scotland. His grandson was of a similarly business-like mindset and invested heavily in New York City land, well before it was developed as real estate. As director of the Singer Company during the First World War he endorsed the company's diversification into providing munitions, including artillery shells, aeroplane parts, grenades and even horseshoes for the UK government.[24] Taking advantage of the economic downturn of the 1930s, he made some of his most spectacular purchases at this time, acquiring major Post-Impressionist masterpieces such as Cézanne's *Les Joueurs de cartes* (*The Card Players*; 1890–92), Van Gogh's *Le café de nuit* (*The Night Café*; 1888) and Seurat's *Parade de cirque* (*Circus Sideshow*; fig. 12), all through the dealer Knoedler.[25]

Among the most fascinating industrialist collectors of this period was Albert C. Barnes, who generated his wealth through patenting an antiseptic called Argyrol, used in the treatment of ophthalmic infections in infants. Barnes's company was bought over in 1929, just before the crash, by which date he had already established the Barnes

Stiftung überführt worden war, und der niederländische Staat stimmte zu, den Bau des künftigen Kröller-Müller Museums in Otterlo zu finanzieren.

Anderen industriellen Sammler:innen gelang es, die Wirtschaftskrise der späten 1920er-Jahre unbeschadet zu überstehen. Darunter war Samuel Courtauld, der 1921 Vorstandsvorsitzender von Courtaulds wurde, ursprünglich ein mittelständischer Hersteller von Seide und Krepp, später jedoch führender Produzent von synthetischen Fasern wie etwa Viskose. Seine bedeutende Sammlung impressionistischer und post-impressionistischer Kunst, die vor allem zwischen 1923 und 1928 entstand, wurde größtenteils aus Einnahmen aus dem Unternehmen finanziert. Ermutigt von seiner Frau Elizabeth und beraten von Fry und dem Händler Percy Moore Turner entwickelte Courtauld eine besondere Vorliebe für Cézanne und erwarb Meisterwerke wie *La Montagne Saint-Victoire au grand pin (Mont Sainte-Victoire mit großer Pinie;* Abb. 11), *Les Joueurs de cartes (Die Kartenspieler,* ca. 1892–1895), *Nature morte avec amour en plâtre (Stilleben mit Gipsfigur [Cupido],* ca. 1894) und *Le Lac d'Annecy* (1896).[22] Der Philanthrop Courtauld glaubte an die Bedeutung von Kunst zum Wohle der Öffentlichkeit und gründete 1923 eine Stiftung in der Londoner National Gallery, die sich einzig und allein dem Ankauf moderner französischer Kunst widmete.

Ein weiterer Textilmagnat, der den Zusammenbruch der Wirtschaft größtenteils unbeschadet überstand, war Stephen Clark, der – wie Osthaus – sein Vermögen ursprünglich von seinem unternehmerisch tätigen Großvater Edward Clark geerbt

hatte.[23] Clark Senior war Mitbegründer der Singer Company, die in den USA und Schottland Haushaltsnähmaschinen herstellte. Sein Enkel verfügte über ein ähnlich unternehmerisches Denken und tätigte großzügige Landinvestitionen in New York City, noch ehe diese Grundstücke erschlossen waren. Als Direktor der Singer Company während des Ersten Weltkriegs unterstützte er die Erweiterung der Produktion zur Herstellung von Munition, darunter Artilleriegeschosse, von Flugzeugteilen, Granaten und sogar Hufeisen für die britische Regierung.[24] Er profitierte vom wirtschaftlichen Abschwung der 1930er-Jahre und tätigte in dieser Zeit einige seiner spektakulärsten Erwerbungen post-impressionistischer Hauptwerke, wie Cézannes *Les Joueurs de cartes (Die Kartenspieler,* 1890–1892), van Goghs *Le café de nuit (Das Nachtcafé,* 1888) und Seurats *Parade de cirque (Zirkusparade;* Abb. 12), die alle über den Händler Knoedler erfolgten.[25]

Zu den faszinierendsten industriellen Sammler:innen dieser Epoche gehörte Albert C. Barnes. Er verdankte sein Vermögen der Patentierung eines Desinfektionsmittels namens Argyrol, das bei der Behandlung von Augenentzündungen bei Kleinkindern zum Einsatz kam. Barnes verkaufte sein Unternehmen 1929, kurz vor dem Börsen-Crash, als er bereits die Barnes Foundation in Meryon (Pennsylvania) gegründet hatte. Aus der Arbeiterklasse stammend und mit einem ausgeprägten Geschäftssinn ausgestattet, hielt auch Barnes stets nach guten Gelegenheiten Ausschau. Außerdem war er von der Philosophie John Deweys beeinflusst und legte großen Wert darauf,

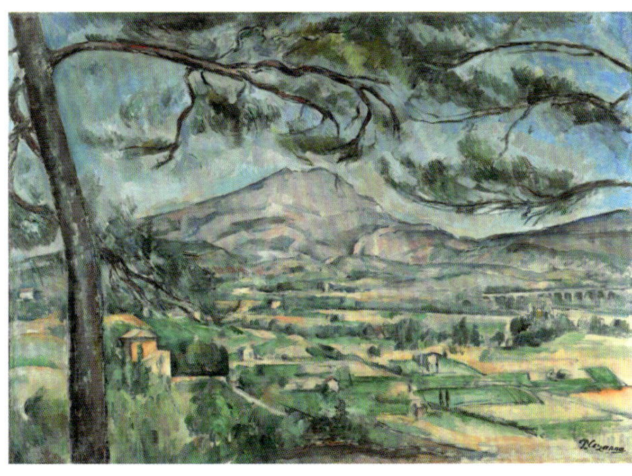

Abb. | Fig. 11
Paul Cézanne, *La Montagne Saint-Victoire au grand pin,* ca. 1887, Courtauld Gallery, London

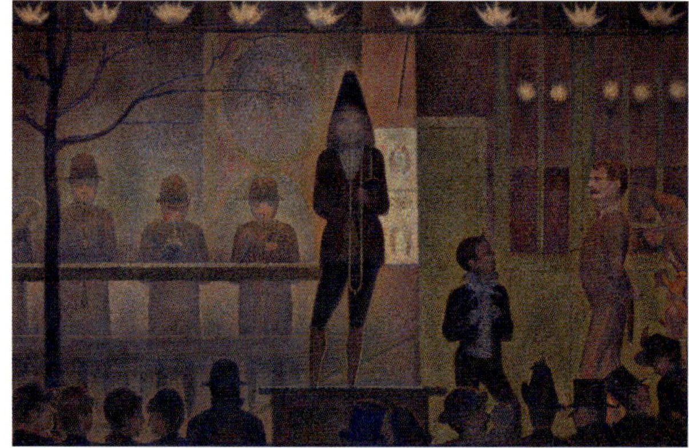

Abb. | Fig. 12
Georges Seurat, *Parade de cirque,* 1888,
The Metropolitan Museum of Art, New York

Foundation at Meryon. Coming from a working-class background and with a keen business sense, Barnes was always looking out for a bargain while, influenced by the philosophy of John Dewey, he was also concerned that his collection should serve an educational purpose. Like Courtauld, he was inspired by aesthetic theory, reading Meier-Graefe in the original German, as well as guided by agents and dealers such as William Glackens, Alfred Maurer and Paul Guillaume. As a result, he developed a particular taste for the work of Cézanne and the late work of Renoir, which he incorporated into aesthetic wall tableaux, known as 'ensembles' (fig. 13).[26] His taste for installations was shared by the Washington-based art critic Duncan Phillips, whose collection of Impressionist and Post-Impressionist art, amassed in collaboration with his wife Marjorie, was funded through his grandfather James Laughlin's pioneering role in the Pittsburgh steel industry. Influenced by Fry and Bell, both Barnes and Phillips developed their own aesthetic theories, articulated in publications such as the former's *The Art in Painting* (1925) and the latter's *A Collection in the Making* (1926).[27] In this way, they used their collections to distance and elevate them from the world of commerce, the source of their wealth.

In the main, then, the major collections of Impressionist and Post-Impressionist art formed in the late nineteenth and early twentieth centuries were financed by industrial wealth and created by women and men who, like Osthaus and Matsukata, were as progressive in their tastes as they were businesslike in their approach to collecting. Without exception they were philanthropic in their outlook and believed in the primacy of French Art, thanks to its endorsement by art historians such as Fry and Meier-Graefe, and by key events like the London Post-Impressionist Exhibitions of 1910 and 1912, or the New York *Armory Show* of 1913. Among those pioneer collectors who contributed to the latter was Lillie P. Bliss, the daughter of a prominent textile merchant, whose 1929 bequest formed the basis of the Museum of Modern Art in New York. Even before Bliss, the artist Frederick Clay Bartlett – whose father was a 'rags to riches' hardware merchant – donated such masterpieces as van Gogh's *La chambre à coucher* (*The Bedroom*, 1888), to the Art Institute of Chicago. That the taste for these artists was almost global at this time is evidenced by the rich collections of Impressionist and Post-Impressionist art that were established by industrialist collectors in the interwar period, among them Ordrupgaard (1918), Shchukin's First Museum of New Western Painting (1919), the Phillips Collection (1921), the Barnes Foundation (1922), the Courtauld Institute for Art (1931) and the Kröller-Müller Museum (1938). Thus, in creating his own Museum Folkwang as early as 1902, Osthaus was a true pioneer, ushering in a period of enlightened collecting, while Matsukata represents its culmination, through the founding of the National Museum of Western Art in Tokyo, in 1959.

dass seine Sammlung auch pädagogische Zwecke erfüllen sollte. Wie Courtauld war er von der ästhetischen Theorie inspiriert, las Meier-Graefe im deutschen Original und ließ sich von Agenten und Händlern wie William Glackens, Alfred Maurer und Paul Guillaume beraten. In der Folge entwickelte er eine besondere Vorliebe für die Arbeiten von Cézanne und das Spätwerk von Renoir, die er in als „Ensembles" bekannten ästhetischen Wandtableaus inszenierte (Abb. 13).[26] Seine Vorliebe für stilübergreifende Installationen wurde von dem in Washington ansässigen Kritiker Duncan Phillips geteilt, dessen gemeinsam mit seiner Frau Marjorie zusammengetragene Sammlung impressionistischer und post-impressionistischer Kunst durch die Pionierrolle seines Großvaters James Laughlin in der Pittsburgher Stahlindustrie finanziert wurde. Beeinflusst von Fry und Bell entwickelten sowohl Barnes als auch Phillips ihre eigenen ästhetischen Theorien, die in Publikationen wie *The Art in Painting* (1925) von Barnes und *A Collection in the Making* (1926) von Phillips zum Ausdruck kamen.[27] So setzten sie ihre Sammlungen ein, um sich von der Welt des Kommerzes, der Quelle ihres Reichtums, zu distanzieren und abzuheben.

Hauptsächlich wurden die bedeutenden Sammlungen impressionistischer und post-impressionistischer Kunst Ende des 19. und Anfang des 20. Jahrhunderts also durch industriellen Wohlstand und von Frauen und Männern geschaffen, die – wie Osthaus und Matsukata – in ihrem Geschmack ebenso fortschrittlich waren, wie sie in ihrer Herangehensweise an das Sammeln geschäftsmäßig agierten. Ohne Ausnahme waren sie philanthropisch eingestellt und glaubten, dank der Unterstützung von Kunsthistorikern wie Fry und Meier-Graefe, an die Vorherrschaft französischer Kunst, waren aber auch beeinflusst von Schlüsselereignissen wie den Londoner Ausstellungen der Post-Impressionisten in den Jahren 1910 und 1912 oder der New Yorker *Armory Show* von 1913. Zu den wegbereitenden Sammler:innen, die zu Letzterer beitrugen, gehörte auch Lillie P. Bliss, die Tochter eines bekannten Textilhändlers, deren Vermächtnis von 1929 die Grundlage für das Museum of Modern Art in New York bildete. Noch vor Bliss stiftete der Künstler Frederick Clay Bartlett – dessen Vater es als einfacher Eisenwarenhändler zu Reichtum gebracht hatte – Meisterwerke wie van Goghs *La chambre à coucher (Vincents Schlafzimmer in Arles,* 1888) an das Art Institute of Chicago. Dass die Vorliebe für jene Künstler zu dieser Zeit beinahe weltumspannend war, belegen die reichen Sammlungen impressionistischer und post-impressionistischer Kunst, die industrielle Sammler:innen in der Zwischenkriegszeit zusammentrugen, darunter das Ordrupgaard Museum (1918), Schtschukins Erstes Museum für neue westliche Malerei (1919), die Phillips Collection (1921), die Barnes Foundation (1922), das Courtauld Institute for Art (1931) und das Kröller-Müller Museum (1938). Was also die Gründung seines Museum Folkwang schon im Jahr 1902 anging, kann Osthaus als wahrer Pionier, als Wegbereiter einer Epoche aufgeklärter Sammlungstätigkeit gelten, während Matsukatas Gründung des National Museum of Western Art in Tokio im Jahr 1959 gewissermaßen den krönenden Abschluss dieser Entwicklung bildet.

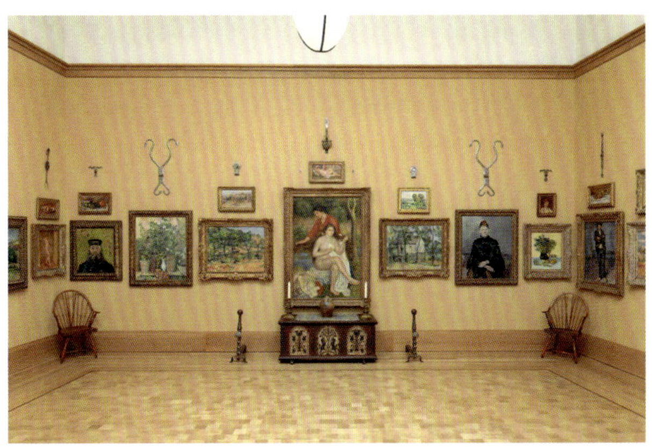

Abb. | Fig. 13
Barnes Foundation, Philadelphia, Hauptraum,
Nordwand mit Werken von Renoir und
Cézanne | Main Room, North Wall with works
by Renoir and Cézanne

1 Albert Boime, 'Entrepreneurial Patronage in Nineteenth-Century France', in Edward C. Carter II, Robert Foster and Joseph N. Moody (eds.), *Enterprise and Entrepreneurs in Nineteenth- and Twentieth-Century France* (Baltimore and London, 1976), 138–60.

2 On early French collectors of Impressionism, see, Anne Distel, *Impressionism: the First Collectors* (New York, 1990).

3 Catherine Krahmer and Ingrid Grüninger (eds.), Julius Meier-Graefe: *Kunst ist nicht für Kunstgeschichte da: Briefe und Dokumente* (Darmstadt, 2002), 275.

4 Sylvie Patry (ed.), *Inventing Impressionism: Paul Durand-Ruel and the Modern Art Market* (London and New Haven, 2015).

5 Rebecca A. Rabinow (ed.), *Cézanne to Picasso: Ambroise Vollard, Patron of the Avant-Garde* (New Haven and London, 2007).

6 Frances Fowle, *Van Gogh's Twin: The Scottish Dealer Alexander Reid (1854–1928)* (Edinburgh, 2010).

7 Albright Knox Art Gallery, Buffalo; Norton Simon Museum, Pasadena; National Galleries of Scotland respectively. *Gauguin's Vision*, exh. cat. National Galleries of Scotland (Edinburgh, 2005), 102–7.

8 Equally influential were the Welsh sisters Gwendoline (1882–1951) and Margaret Davies (1884–1963), Mark Evans, 'The Davies sisters of Llandinam and Impressionism for Wales, 1908–1923', *Journal of the History of Collections*, 16, 2, (November 2004), 219–53.

9 All held by Amgueddfa Cymru National Museum Wales.

10 Erica E. Hirshler, '"Helping Fine Things Across the Atlantic": Mary Cassatt and Art Collecting in the United States', in *Mary Cassatt: Modern Woman*, exh. cat. Art Institute of Chicago (Chicago, 1998), 177–211; see also, Carolyn Kinder Carr, *Sara Tyson Hallowell: Pioneer Curator and Art Adviser in the Golden Age* (Washington DC, 2019).

11 Richard R. Brettell, 'Monet's Haystacks Reconsidered', *Art Institute of Chicago Museum Studies*, 11 (1984), 4–21 (pp. 19, 21, note. 19).

12 Ibid., 19.

13 Albert Kostenevich, 'Russian Clients of Ambroise Vollard', in Rebecca A. Rabinow (ed.), *Cézanne to Picasso: Ambroise Vollard, Patron of the Avant-Garde* (New Haven and London, 2007), 243–56, 245.

14 Cf. Georg-Wilhelm Költzsch (ed.), *Monet bis Picasso. Morosow und Schtschukin – die russischen Sammler*, exh. cat. Museum Folkwang, Essen (Cologne, 1993).

15 Ibid., 254.

16 Anne-Birgitte Fonsmark, 'An introduction to Wilhelm Hansen's Collection of French Art at Ordrupgaard', *Gauguin and the Impressionists: The Ordrupgaard Collection*, exh. cat. Royal Academy of Arts (London, 2020) 13–24, here 16–18.

17 Cf. Léa Saint-Raymond's and Maxime Georges Métraux's essay in this catalogue, pp. 142–157.

18 Isobel MacDonald, *Sir William Burrell (1861–1958): the Man and the Collector*, unpublished PhD thesis, University of Glasgow, 2018, 47–8.

19 Apart from Manet's *Portrait de Victorine Meurent* (Museum of Fine Arts, Boston), all are in the Burrell Collection, Glasgow. On Burrell's collection of Impressionism see, Vivien Hamilton, 'William Burrell and Impressionism' in *Impressionism and Scotland*, exh. cat. National Galleries of Scotland (Edinburgh, 2008), 109–18.

20 National Galleries of Scotland; Nelson Atkins Museum, Kansas; Metropolitan Museum of Art, New York and National Gallery of Art, Washington D.C. respectively. See, Frances Fowle, 'A Woman of No Importance? Elizabeth Workman's Collection of Impressionist and Post-Impressionist Art in Context', in *19: Interdisciplinary Studies in the Long Nineteenth Century*, 31, (2021). https://19.bbk.ac.uk/article/id/3001/ [last accessed June 2021].

21 See further, Ariëtte Dekker, *Leven op kredit: Anton Kröller 1862–1941* (Amsterdam, 2015).

22 All at the Courtauld Institute Gallery, London. See further, *The Courtauld Cézannes*, exh. cat., The Courtauld Gallery (London, 2008).

23 *The Clark Brothers Collect Impressionist and Early Modern Paintings* (New Haven and London, 2006), 13.

24 Robert Bruce Davies, *Peacefully Working to Conquer the World: Singer Sewing Machines in Foreign Markets 1854–1920* (New York, 1976), 170.

25 Metropolitan Museum of Art; Yale University Art Gallery; Metropolitan Museum of Art.

26 Colin B. Bailey, 'The Origins of the Barnes Collection, 1912–15', *The Burlington Magazine*, vol. 150, no. 1265, 2008, 534–43.

27 Phillips' personal copy of Roger Fry's *Vision and Design* (1921) was heavily annotated. On Phillips see, Erika D. Passantino, *The Eye of Duncan Phillips: A Collection in the Making* (New Haven and London, 1999).

1 Albert Boime, „Entrepreneurial Patronage in Nineteenth-Century France", in: *Enterprise and Entrepreneurs in Nineteenth- and Twentieth-Century France,* hrsg. von Edward C. Carter II., Robert Foster und Joseph N. Moody, Baltimore und London 1976, S. 138–160.

2 Zu den frühen französischen Sammler:innen des Impressionismus siehe Anne Distel, *Impressionsim. The First Collectors,* New York 1990.

3 Julius Meier-Graefe, *Kunst ist nicht für Kunstgeschichte da. Briefe und Dokumente,* hrsg. von Catherine Krahmer und Ingrid Grüninger, Darmstadt 2002, S. 275.

4 *Inventing Impressionism. Paul Durand-Ruel and the Modern Art Market,* hrsg. von Sylvie Patry, London und New Haven 2015.

5 *Cezanne to Picasso. Ambroise Vollard, Patron of the Avant-Garde,* hrsg. von Rebecca A. Rabinow, New Haven und London 2007.

6 Frances Fowle, *Van Gogh's Twin. The Scottish Dealer Alexander Reid (1854–1928),* Edinburgh 2010.

7 Heute in der Albright Knox Art Gallery, Buffalo, im Norton Simon Museum, Pasadena bzw. in den National Galleries of Scotland. *Gauguin's Vision,* Ausst.-Kat. National Galleries of Scotland, Edinburgh, Edinburgh 2005, S. 102–107.

8 Mark Evans, „The Davies sisters of Llandinam and Impressionism for Wales, 1908–1923", in: *Journal of the History of Collections,* 16, 2, November 2004, S. 219–253.

9 Alle im Besitz des Amgueddfa Cymru National Museum Wales.

10 Erica E. Hirshler, „,Helping Fine Things Across the Atlantic'. Mary Cassatt and Art Collecting in the United States", in: *Mary Cassatt. Modern Woman,* Ausst.-Kat. Art Institute of Chicago, Chicago 1998, S. 177–211; siehe auch Carolyn Kinder Carr, *Sara Tyson Hallowell. Pioneer Curator and Art Adviser in the Golden Age,* Washington (DC) 2019.

11 Richard R. Brettell, „Monet's Haystacks Reconsidered", in: *Art Institute of Chicago Museum Studies,* 11, 1984, S. 4–21, hier S. 19, 21, Anm. 19.

12 Ebd., S. 19.

13 Albert Kostenevich, „Russian Clients of Ambroise Vollard", in: *Cezanne to Picasso. Ambroise Vollard, Patron of the Avant-Garde,* hrsg. von Rebecca A. Rabinow, New Haven und London 2007, S. 243–256, hier S. 245.

14 Vgl. *Monet bis Picasso. Morosow und Schtschukin – die russischen Sammler,* hrsg. von Georg-Wilhelm Költzsch, Ausst.-Kat. Museum Folkwang, Essen, Köln 1993.

15 Ebd., S. 254.

16 Anne-Birgitte Fonsmark, „An introduction to Wilhelm Hansen's Collection of French Art at Ordrupgaard", in: *Gauguin and the Impressionists. The Ordrupgaard Collection,* Ausst.-Kat. Royal Academy of Arts, London, London 2020, S. 13–24, hier S. 16 ff.

17 Vgl. den Beitrag von Léa Saint-Raymond und Maxime Georges Métraux in diesem Band, S. 142–157.

18 Isobel MacDonald, *Sir William Burrell (1861–1958). The Man and the Collector,* unveröff. Diss., University of Glasgow, 2018, S. 47 f.

19 Mit Ausnahme von Manets *Bildnis Victorine Meurent* (Museum of Fine Arts, Boston) befinden sich alle Bilder in der Burrell Collection, Glasgow. Zu Burrells Impressionismus-Sammlung siehe Vivien Hamilton, „William Burrell and Impressionism", in: *Impressionism and Scotland,* Ausst.-Kat. National Galleries of Scotland, Edinburgh, Edinburgh 2008, S. 109–118.

20 Heute in den National Galleries of Scotland, Edinburgh, im Nelson Atkins Museum, Kansas, im Metropolitan Museum of Art, New York und in der National Gallery of Art, Washington (DC). Siehe Frances Fowle, „A Woman of No Importance? Elizabeth Workman's Collection of Impressionist and Post-Impressionist Art in Context", in: *19: Interdisciplinary Studies in the Long Nineteenth Century,* 31, 2021, https://19.bbk.ac.uk/article/id/3001/ [zuletzt aufgerufen im Juni 2021].

21 Siehe auch Ariëtte Dekker, *Leven op kredit. Anton Kröller 1862–1941,* Amsterdam 2015.

22 Alle in der Courtauld Institute Gallery, London. Siehe auch *The Courtauld Cézannes,* Ausst.-Kat. The Courtauld Gallery, London, London 2008.

23 *The Clark Brothers Collect Impressionist and Early Modern Paintings,* Ausst.-Kat. Sterling and Francine Clark Art Institute, Williamstown; Metropolitan Museum of Art, New York, New Haven und London 2006, S. 13.

24 Robert Bruce Davies, *Peacefully Working to Conquer the World. Singer Sewing Machines in Foreign Markets 1854–1920,* New York 1976, S. 170.

25 Heute im Metropolitan Museum of Art, New York, in der Yale University Art Gallery und ebenfalls im Metropolitan Museum of Art.

26 Colin B. Bailey, „The Origins of the Barnes Collection, 1912–15", in: *The Burlington Magazine,* 150, 1265, 2008, S. 534–543.

27 Phillips' persönliche Ausgabe von Roger Frys *Vision and Design* (1921) war mit zahlreichen Anmerkungen versehen. Zu Phillips siehe Erika D. Passantino, *The Eye of Duncan Phillips. A Collection in the Making,* New Haven und London 1999.

FROM A HALL OF FAME OF GERMAN ART TO A GALLERY OF FRENCH MODERNISM –

THE MUSEUM FOLKWANG AS A COLLECTION OF FRENCH (POST–)IMPRESSIONISM

Rainer Stamm

When Karl Ernst Osthaus opened the Museum Folkwang in the Westphalian industrial city of Hagen in June 1902, he hoped – with pride and certainly desiring recognition – to be able to receive as a guest at the opening celebrations Hugo von Tschudi, the director of the National Gallery in Berlin (fig. 1). Along with the director of the Berlin Picture Gallery, Wilhelm von Bode, who specialized in old masters, and Alfred Lichtwark, the director of the Hamburger Kunsthalle, Tschudi was one of the most prominent museum directors in the German Reich at the time. Above all, he was one of Germany's most visible champions of French modernism. Just a few months after assuming his office, Tschudi had begun to transform the Nationalgalerie 'from a national hall of fame of art into an international art museum,'[1] and acquired its first works by French Impressionists. With his acquisitions in the years 1896 and 1897, Edouard Manet's *Dans la serre* (*In the Conservatory*; fig. 2), Claude Monet's *Maisons d'Argenteuil* (*Houses in Argenteuil*, 1873) and *Vétheuil sur Seine* (*View of Vétheuil*, 1880), a pastel by Edgar Degas and *Le moulin sur la Couleuvre à Pontoise* (*The Mill on the Couleuvre*, 1881) by Paul Cézanne became the first works of French modernism in a German public collection. The defenders of German nationalist art opposed these new acquisitions. After all, the Nationalgalerie's was dedicated 'to German art' (*DER DEUTSCHEN KUNST*), as one can still read on its tympanum today. To the champions of modernism, however, these acquisitions were a sign of a new dawn.

Tschudi was therefore one of Osthaus's most important role models; no wonder then that he hoped the museum director from Berlin would be his guest of honour. Although Tschudi disappointed the twenty-eight-year-old museum founder, he

Als Karl Ernst Osthaus im Juni 1902 in der westfälischen Industriestadt Hagen das Folkwang-Museum
eröffnete, hoffte er – stolz und durchaus geltungs-
bewusst – den Direktor der Berliner Nationalgalerie
Hugo von Tschudi als Gast der Eröffnungsfeierlich-
keiten empfangen zu können (Abb. 1). Tschudi
gehörte – gemeinsam mit dem auf die Kunst Alter
Meister spezialisierten Leiter der Berliner Gemäldegalerie Wilhelm von Bode und dem Direktor der
Hamburger Kunsthalle Alfred Lichtwark – zu den
prominentesten Museumsdirektoren im damaligen
Deutschen Reich. Vor allem jedoch war er zu dem
exponiertesten Vorkämpfer für die Anerkennung
der französischen Moderne in Deutschland geworden. Bereits wenige Monate nach seinem Amtsan-
tritt hatte Tschudi begonnen, die Nationalgalerie
„von einem nationalen Ruhmestempel der Kunst zu
einem internationalen Kunstmuseum"[1] zu verwan-
deln, und die ersten Werke der französischen
Impressionisten erworben: Mit seinen Ankäufen
der Jahre 1896 und 1897 gelangten Edouard Manets
Dans la serre (Im Wintergarten; Abb. 2), Claude
Monets *Maisons d'Argenteuil (Häuser in Argenteuil*,
1873), dessen *Vétheuil sur Seine (Ansicht von
Vétheuil*, 1880), ein Pastell von Edgar Degas und *Le
moulin sur la Couleuvre à Pontoise (Die Mühle an
der Couleuvre*, 1881) von Paul Cézanne als erste
Werke der französischen Moderne in öffentlichen
Besitz. Den Verfechter:innen einer deutschnationa-
len Kunst widerstrebten diese Neuerwerbungen.
Immerhin war die Nationalgalerie, wie bis heute
in ihrem Giebelfeld zu lesen ist, „DER DEUTSCHEN
KUNST" gewidmet. Den Vorkämpfer:innen der

93   Rainer Stamm

VON EINER RUHMESHALLE DEUTSCHER KUNST ZU EINER GALERIE DER FRANZÖSISCHEN MODERNE

DAS MUSEUM FOLKWANG ALS SAMMLUNG DES FRANZÖSISCHEN (POST–)IMPRESSIONISMUS

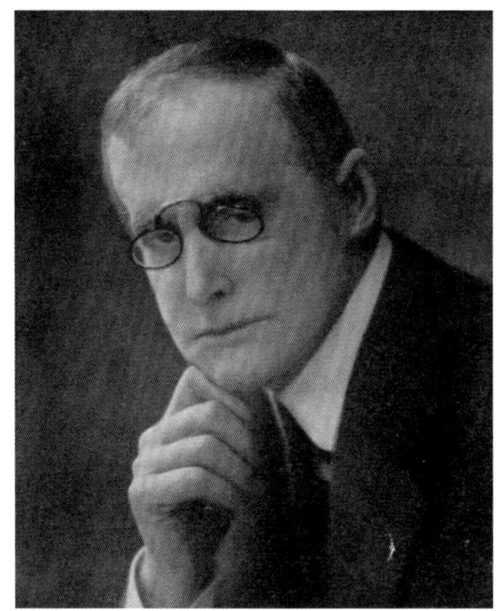

was well aware of the transformation in taste that this son of a Hagen banker had undergone: in 1897, Osthaus was still acquiring works by the Düsseldorf School of painters and above all by his cousin Theodor Rocholl, who painted battle scenes, which had also been in the collections of the Nationalgalerie, the temple of fame for the German empire. Yet by the turn of the century and the opening of his museum in July 1902, he had acquired a major work by Pierre-Auguste Renoir (p. 209) and works by the Post- and Neo-Impressionists Vincent van Gogh (p. 315), Paul Signac (p. 288), Henri Edmond Cross (p. 289), Maximilien Luce (p. 205) and Théo van Rysselberghe (p. 303) had found their way into the collection. Even at the time of its opening, the Museum Folkwang had taken the lead among modern museums in Germany: 'Its picture collection is currently the only one, perhaps not only in Germany, in which one can find the main proponents of Neo-Impressionism with important creations',[2] announced the *Westfälisches Tageblatt* proudly on the occasion of the opening.

Whereas, until finally he moved to Munich as director of the Alte and Neue Pinakothek in 1909, Tschudi had to have every acquisition of a modern French work approved by the Kaiser himself,[3] Osthaus was indebted only to his own taste and the evolution of his preferences. Tschudi therefore paid him respect, and not without envy: 'Esteemed and dear Mr Osthaus', he wrote:

Sincere thanks for your kind invitation to the opening of your 'Museum' Folkwang, which, unfortunately, my wife and I cannot attend. [...] You know that I follow with greatest interest your so unusual creation and wish you joyous success and a providential venture. All other museum directors, who are constricted and watched over by commissions and the like, will view you with envy as the completely sovereign director of the Folkwang. That which for the rest of us must largely remain a good intention can be made vital reality by you. So, once again: 'Glückauf' ('Good luck')![4]

How did the young offspring of a Westphalian entrepreneurial family come to command such respect from the director of the Nationalgalerie in Berlin? From the age of eighteen, Osthaus had been committed to the goal of serving the true, the beautiful and the good. On the death of his grandparents in 1896, their immense fortune of three million Marks became available to him and he decided to use two-thirds of this inheritance to benefit the common good by founding a public museum.[5] At first, however, its direction remained unclear: Osthaus considered a natural history museum, for which he acquired specimens of snails, beetles, scorpions, fossils and butterflies to illustrate the archetypal forms of beauty. Later his focus shifted to fine art; after his journey to North Africa and the countries of the Ottoman Empire he pictured for a time founding a museum for Islamic art and crafts.

Moderne jedoch erschienen die Ankäufe als ein Zeichen des Aufbruchs.

Für Osthaus zählte Tschudi daher zu den wichtigsten Vorbildern; kein Wunder also, dass er sich den Berliner Museumsdirektor als Ehrengast erhoffte. Auch wenn Tschudi die Hoffnung des 26-jährigen Museumsgründers enttäuschte, wusste er um die Wandlung, die der Hagener Bankierssohn durchlaufen hatte: Hatte Osthaus 1897 noch Werke der Düsseldorfer Malerschule und vor allem seines Vetters, des Schlachtenmalers Theodor Rocholl, erworben, wie sie auch in den Sammlungen der Nationalgalerie als Ruhmestempel des Kaiserreichs vorhanden gewesen waren, so hatten zwischen 1900 und der Eröffnung seines Museums im Juli 1902 ein Hauptwerk Pierre-Auguste Renoirs (S. 209) sowie Werke der Post- und Neo-Impressionisten Vincent van Gogh (S. 315), Paul Signac (S. 288), Henri Edmond Cross (S. 289), Maximilien Luce (S. 205) und Théo van Rysselberghe (S. 303) ihren Weg in die Sammlung gefunden. Schon bei seiner Eröffnung hatte sich das Museum Folkwang damit an die Spitze der modernen Museen in Deutschland gesetzt: „Die Gemäldesammlung ist zur Zeit die einzige, vielleicht nicht nur in Deutschland, in der man die Hauptvertreter des Neo-Impressionismus mit wichtigen Schöpfungen finden kann",[2] verkündete das *Westfälische Tageblatt* anlässlich der Eröffnung stolz.

Während Tschudi seit der Öffnung der Neuen Abteilung der Nationalgalerie im Kronprinzenpalais jeden Ankauf moderner französischer Werke durch den Kaiser genehmigen lassen musste, bis er schließlich 1909 als Direktor der Alten und Neuen

Pinakothek nach München wechselte,[3] war Osthaus allein seinem Geschmack und der Entwicklung seiner Vorlieben verpflichtet. Tschudi zollte ihm daher nicht ohne Neid Respekt: „Geehrter und lieber Herr Osthaus", schrieb er ihm, „besten Dank für Ihre freundliche Einladung zur Einweihung Ihres ‚Museums' Folkwang, der meine Frau und ich leider nicht Folge leisten können. [...] Sie wissen dass ich mit grösstem Interesse an Ihrer so eigenartigen Schöpfung theilnehme und ihr fröhliches Gedeihen und segensreiche Wirkung wünsche. Mit Neid werden alle anderen von Commissionen und dergleichen beengte und behütete Museumsdirectoren auf Sie als den völlig souverainen Folkwangdirector blicken. Was bei uns anderen zum grossen Theil gute Intention bleiben muss, kann sich bei Ihnen in lebendige That umsetzen. Also nochmals ‚Glückauf!'"[4]

Wie war es also gekommen, dass der junge Sprössling einer westfälischen Unternehmerfamilie dem Direktor der Berliner Nationalgalerie diesen Respekt abnötigte? Schon als 18-Jähriger hatte Osthaus das Ziel vor Augen, sein Engagement in den Dienst des Wahren, Schönen und Guten zu stellen. Als ihm 1896 – mit dem Tod der Großeltern – deren immenses Vermögen von drei Millionen Mark zur Verfügung stand, beschloss er, zwei Drittel des Ererbten für das Allgemeinwohl einzusetzen und ein öffentliches Museum zu gründen.[5] Unklar blieb jedoch vorerst dessen Ausrichtung: Zunächst dachte Osthaus an ein naturkundliches Museum, für das er präparierte Schnecken, Käfer, Skorpione, Fossilien und Schmetterlinge erwarb, die die Urformen der

95

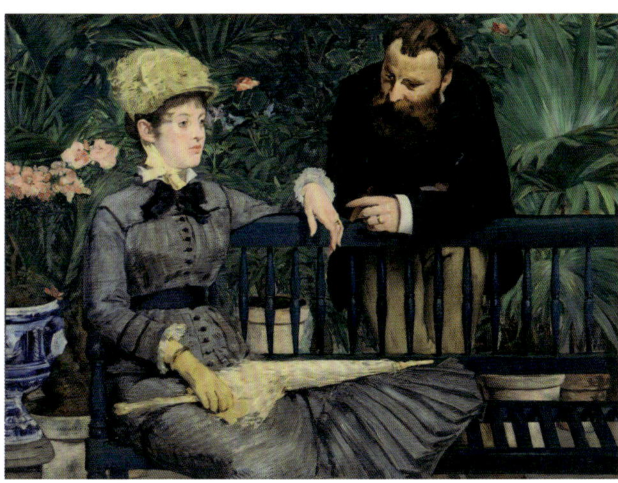

Abb. | Fig. 2
Edouard Manet, *Dans la serre*, 1878/79,
Alte Nationalgalerie, Berlin

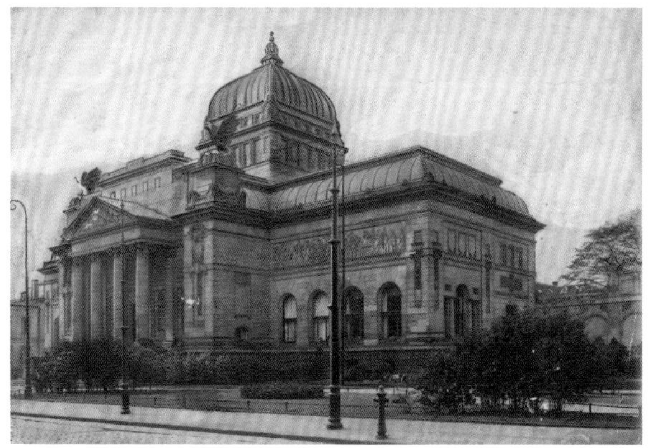

Abb. | Fig. 3
Barmer Ruhmeshalle, ca. 1910

96

In the spring of 1897, with help from his cousin, he acquired paintings by the Düsseldorf School.[6] Rocholl encouraged him to make them the nucleus of his own museum, without taking his lead from Tschudi's acquisition policies:

You have made an excellent start for a worthy collection. Continue that, do not go astray with the French and the Old Masters. I would like to make the same appeal to you that I would like to make to the real privy councillors here, who are squandering the nation's wealth on Old Masters and the foreign: reflect, look around you. Wherever you look if you have healthy, normal eyes you will see talents in all variations in Germany.[7]

As a role model, Rocholl pointed to the Ruhmeshalle (hall of fame) under construction in the neighbouring city of Barmen, now part of Wuppertal, which was in the process of becoming a 'deliberate combination of art museum and Hohenzollern temple' (fig. 3).[8]

The works acquired by the Düsseldorf painters Heinrich Hermanns, Martin Kurreck, Hugo Mühlig, Ludwig Munthe and Rocholl had almost no influence on subsequent planning for the museum and were not even included in Museum Folkwang's first catalogue of its collection in 1912. Moreover, Osthaus tried to offload the majority of these paintings from 1917 onwards. While the painful sale of several paintings by Anselm Feuerbach, Albert Weisgerber, Paul Gauguin, Van Gogh, Cross and Ferdinand Hodler had been necessary to reduce

liquidity problems that had arisen, Karl Ernst and Gertrud Osthaus also used a series of auctions to cause 'some things to disappear'[9] that no longer seemed suited to their museum. They tried to ensure as far as possible that neither their name nor the connection to the Folkwang collection was mentioned in the process (fig. 4).

Henry van de Velde:
The Cicerone on the Path to Modernity

To prepare for the founding of his own museum, Osthaus accepted an offer from Justus Brinckmann to sit in on the workings of the Museum für Kunst und Gewerbe in Hamburg for two weeks in the summer of 1899. The shell of the future Museum Folkwang was already under construction at that time. As the architect for his residential and museum building, Osthaus had hired the Berlin planning department surveyor, Carl Gérard, who had previously built his father's villa Elfriedenhöhe.[10]

Before his experience in the Hamburg museum, the choice of architect and the decision in favour of a museum building in the Neo-Renaissance style must have seemed obvious to Osthaus. During his time there, however, the young museum founder realized that a museum built in historicising Renaissance forms could never document a contemporary aesthetic and hence could hardly be the ideal place for a museum of the sort the progressive Brinckmann imagined as a 'living organism'.[11]

It was during this time that the work of the Flemish designer Henry van de Velde first came

Schönheit vergegenwärtigten. Später geriet die bildende Kunst in seinen Fokus; nach seiner Reise nach Nordafrika und in die Länder des Osmanischen Reiches schwebte ihm zeitweilig die Gründung eines Museums für islamische Kunst und Kunstgewerbe vor.

Im Frühjahr 1897 erwarb er durch Vermittlung seines Vetters, des Malers Theodor Rocholl, Gemälde der Düsseldorfer Malerschule.[6] Dieser ermutigte ihn auch, daraus den Nukleus eines eigenen Museums werden zu lassen, jedoch ohne sich an den Ankaufstätigkeiten Tschudis zu orientieren: „Sie haben für eine würdige Sammlung einen vorzüglichen Anfang gemacht. Fahren Sie doch fort, irren Sie nicht bei Franzosen und alten Meistern herum. Ich möchte Ihnen dasselbe zurufen, was ich den wirklichen Geheimräten hier zurufen möchte, welche das Nationalvermögen verplempern für alte Meister und Fremde: Besinnt Euch, seht um Euch. Wohin Ihr seht, wenn Ihr vorders gesunde normale Augen habt, seht Ihr Talente in allen Variationen in Deutschland.“[7] Als Vorbild verwies Rocholl auf die in der benachbarten Stadt Barmen, heute ein Teil Wuppertals, im Bau befindliche „Ruhmeshalle", die im Begriff war, eine „bewusste Verbindung von Kunstmuseum und Hohenzollern‚tempel'" zu werden (Abb. 3).[8]

Die erworbenen Werke der Düsseldorfer Malerfreunde Heinrich Hermanns, Martin Kurreck, Hugo Mühlig, Ludwig Munthe und Rocholl blieben jedoch für die weitere Entwicklung der Museumsplanungen nahezu wirkungslos und tauchen im ersten Bestandskatalog des Museum Folkwang von 1912 nicht einmal auf. Mehr noch: Ab 1917 versuchte

Osthaus, den Großteil dieser Bilder auf Auktionen abzustoßen. Während die schmerzlichen Verkäufe einiger Gemälde von Anselm Feuerbach, Albert Weisgerber, Paul Gauguin, van Gogh, Cross und Ferdinand Hodler notwendig geworden waren, um aufgetretene Liquiditätsengpässe zu lindern, nutzten Karl Ernst und Gertrud Osthaus eine Reihe von Auktionen dazu, bei dieser Gelegenheit auch „manches verschwinden" zu lassen,[9] was ihnen nicht länger in ihr Museum zu passen schien. Dabei waren sie tunlichst darauf bedacht, dass weder ihr Name noch der Zusammenhang mit der Folkwang-Sammlung dabei Erwähnung fand (Abb. 4).

Henry van de Velde – der Cicerone auf dem Weg in die Moderne

Um sich auf die Gründung eines eigenen Museums vorzubereiten, nahm Osthaus im Sommer 1899 das Angebot von Justus Brinckmann an, für 14 Tage am Hamburger Museum für Kunst und Gewerbe zu hospitieren. Zu dieser Zeit war die Hülle des künftigen Museum Folkwang bereits im Entstehen. Als Architekt seines Wohn- und Museumsgebäudes hatte Osthaus den Berliner Baurat Carl Gérard engagiert, der schon die väterliche Villa Elfriedenhöhe errichtet hatte.[10]

Vor seiner Hamburger Museumserfahrung muss Osthaus die Auswahl des Architekten ebenso wie die Entscheidung für ein Museumsgebäude im Stil der Neo-Renaissance selbstverständlich erschienen sein. Spätestens während seiner Zeit in Hamburg wird dem jungen Museumsgründer jedoch bewusst geworden sein, dass ein Museums-

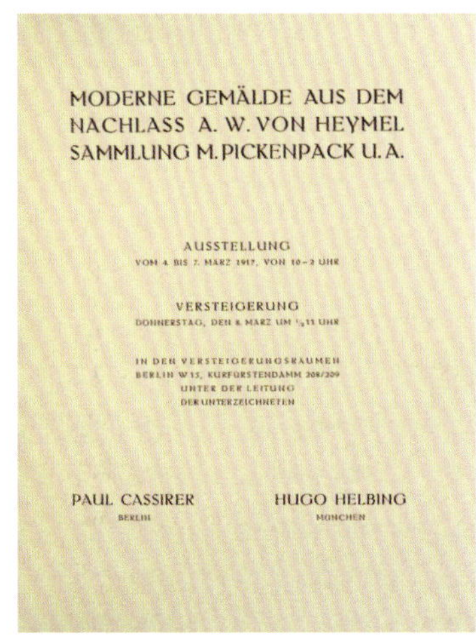

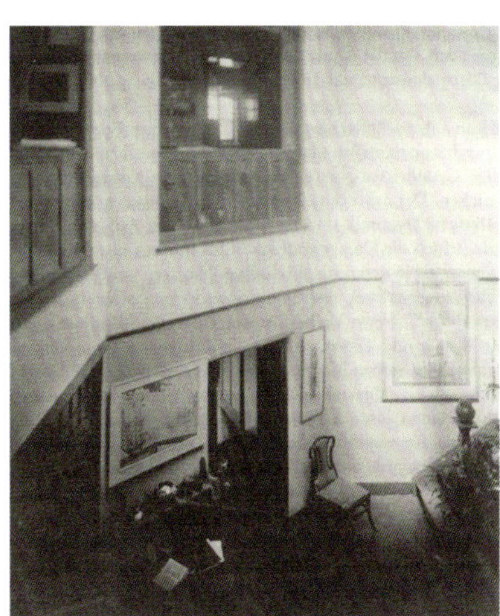

Abb. | Fig. 4
Auktionskatalog | auction catalogue
Cassirer und | and Helbing, Berlin 1917

Abb. | Fig. 5
Henry van de Velde, Haus Bloemenwerf,
Halle | Bloemenwerf House, Hall,
Uccle, 1895

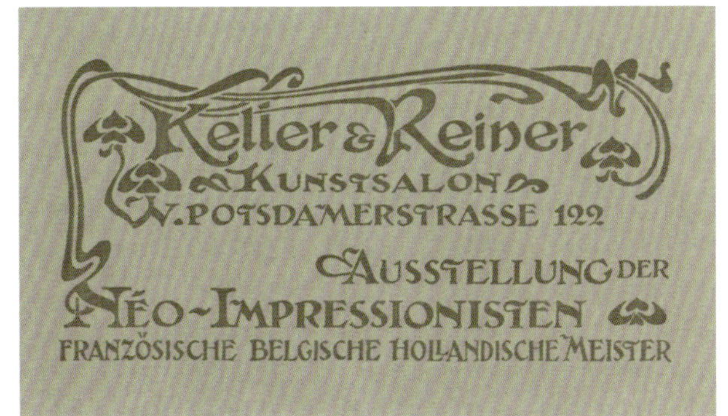

to Osthaus's attention. In the summer of 1899, the *Internationale Kunst-Ausstellung* (International Art Exhibition) of the *Verein bildender Künstler* (Association of Fine Artists) in Munich, showed his furniture designs, which had previously been exhibited at Siegfried Bing's gallery Maison de l'Art Nouveau in Paris. Inspired by the British Arts and Crafts movement, they were nevertheless un-precedented in their autonomous formal language. Osthaus was overwhelmed by this interior deco-ration in the 'New Style'. He wrote to his fiancée, Gertrud Colsman, with dismay: 'It is truly a shame that we cannot wait another half-year with the trousseau, because by then I would have learned a lot once again. I still know, I see now, far too little about the modern impulses.'[12]

The discovery of the 'New Style' radically called into question the decisions that had already been made. Within a few months, Osthaus finally turned away from historicism and towards modernism. The trigger for this was Julius Meier-Graefe's lengthy essay on Van de Velde in the journal *Dekor-ative Kunst*: 'Reading and action were one',[13] Osthaus recalled. In April 1900, he contacted Van de Velde and visited him en route to the *Exposition Universelle* in Paris in Van de Velde's self-designed residence in the Brussels suburb of Uccle (fig. 5). In the telegram announcing his visit, Osthaus had already told Van de Velde about his particular situation:

> I am working on founding a museum whose goal is to win over our art-forsaken industrial region on the Ruhr to modern art. As the free owner of

my institution, I am in the fortunate position not to have to take any prejudices into account and therefore cherish the wish to create an appeal-ing institution based entirely on modern views that is – as far as my means permit – exemplary.[14]

Henry van de Velde became not only the architect responsible for the museum's interior design but also the crucial cicerone for Osthaus on his path to modernism – above all French modernism. In the course of designing the museum's interior, Osthaus moved the natural history collection begun in 1898 to the basement of the building, where it was protected from light, and 'nothing more was to be seen of the Düsseldorf landscape painters', as he proudly recalled:

> Since our encounter, a complete transforma-tion in Osthaus's taste had occurred, especially after I brought him together with the art dealers Ambroise Vollard in Paris and Paul Cassirer in Berlin. His conversion had occurred spontane-ously [...]. In less than a year he had acquired works by [...] Renoir, Seurat, Signac, Cross, Van Gogh, Gauguin and sculptures by Minne, Rodin and Constantin Meunier.[15]

If one compares the names mentioned to those of Van de Velde's circle of friends in Paris, Brussels and Antwerp in the 1890s, the degree of his influ-ence on Osthaus and the direction of his pur-chases becomes clear. Several acquisitions can be identified specifically. Early in 1901, the Berlin gal-lery Keller & Reiner, whose interior Van de Velde

bau in historisierenden Renaissance-Formen kein Dokument einer zeitgenössischen Ästhetik und schwerlich der ideale Ort für ein Museum werden würde, wie es sich der progressive Brinckmann als „lebendigen Organismus"[11] vorstellte.

In dieser Zeit wurde Osthaus auch erstmals auf das Werk des flämischen Gestalters Henry van de Velde aufmerksam. Im Sommer 1899 waren auf der *Internationalen Kunst-Ausstellung* des Vereins bildender Künstler in München seine von der englischen Arts-and-Crafts-Bewegung inspirierten und in ihrer eigenständigen Formensprache dennoch vorbildlosen Möbelentwürfe zu sehen, die zuvor in Siegfried Bings Pariser Galerie Maison de l'Art Nouveau gezeigt worden waren. Osthaus war von dieser Zimmereinrichtung im „Neuen Stil" überwältigt. Seiner Verlobten Gertrud Colsman schrieb er konsterniert: „Es ist wirklich schade, daß wir mit der Aussteuer nicht noch ein halbes Jahr warten können, dann hätte ich wieder viel gelernt. Die modernen Regungen kenne ich, wie ich nun sehe, noch viel zu wenig."[12]

Die Entdeckung des „Neuen Stils" stellte die bereits getroffenen Entscheidungen radikal infrage. Innerhalb weniger Monate wandte sich Osthaus schließlich endgültig vom Historismus ab und der Moderne zu. Der Auslöser dafür war Julius Meier-Graefes umfangreicher Aufsatz über van de Velde in der Zeitschrift *Dekorative Kunst*: „Lesen und Handeln war eins",[13] erinnerte sich Osthaus: Im April 1900 meldete er sich bei van de Velde an und besuchte – auf dem Weg zur Pariser Weltausstellung – dessen selbst entworfenes Wohnhaus im Brüsseler Vorort Uccle (Abb. 5). In dem Telegramm,

mit dem er seinen Besuch ankündigte, berichtete er van de Velde bereits von seiner besonderen Situation: „Ich bin mit der Gründung eines Museums beschäftigt, das den Zweck haben soll, unsern kunstverlassenen Industriebezirk an der Ruhr für das moderne Kunstschaffen zu gewinnen. Als freier Besitzer meiner Anstalt bin ich in der glücklichen Lage, mit keinen Vorurteilen rechnen zu müssen und hege daher den Wunsch, eine reizvolle, durchaus auf modernen Anschauungen beruhende und – soweit es mir meine Mittel gestatten – mustergültige Anlage zu schaffen."[14]

Henry van de Velde wurde nicht nur zum Architekten des Innenausbaus des Museums, sondern für Osthaus zum entscheidenden Cicerone auf dem Weg in die – vor allem französische – Moderne. Die 1898 angelegte naturkundliche Sammlung verlegte er im Rahmen der Ausgestaltung des Museums in das lichtgeschützte Untergeschoss des Gebäudes und auch von „den Düsseldorfer Landschaftsmalern war nichts mehr zu sehen", erinnerte sich van de Velde stolz: „Seit unserer Begegnung hatte sich eine vollständige Wandlung in Osthaus' Geschmack vollzogen, besonders nachdem ich ihn mit den Kunsthändlern Ambroise Vollard in Paris und Paul Cassirer in Berlin zusammengebracht hatte. Seine Bekehrung war spontan eingetreten [...]. In weniger als einem Jahr hatte er Werke von [...] Renoir, Seurat, Signac, Cross, van Gogh, Gauguin und Skulpturen von Minne, Rodin und Constantin Meunier erworben."[15]

Vergleicht man die genannten Namen mit denen des Freundeskreises van de Veldes in Paris, Brüssel und Antwerpen der 1890er-Jahre, so wird dessen

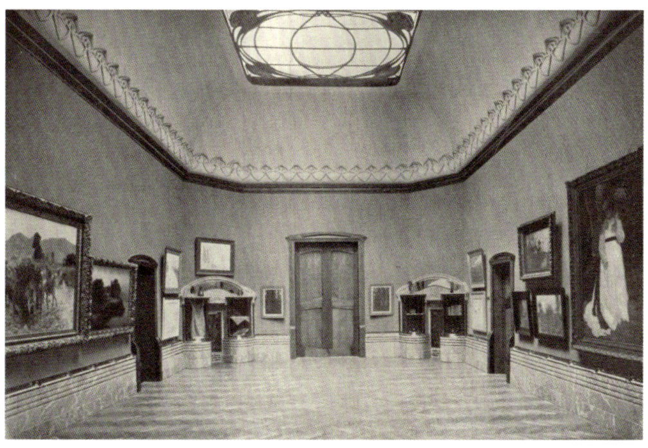

Abb. | Fig. 7
Museum Folkwang, Hagen,
Großer Bildersaal | Great picture hall, 1902

100

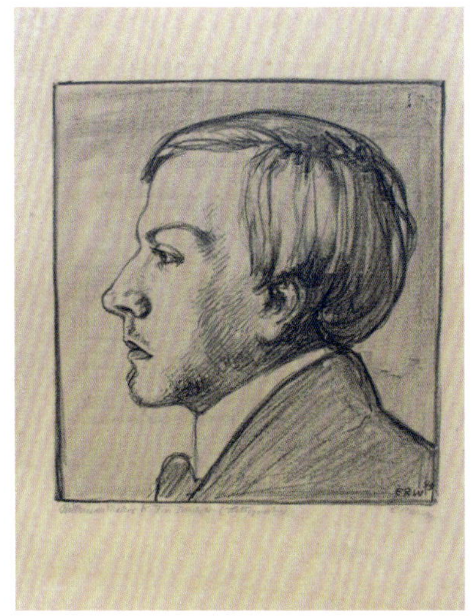

Abb. | Fig. 8
Emil Rudolf Weiß, *Bildnis F. K. von Freyhold*,
1899, Museum Folkwang, Essen

designed in 1899, showed another exhibition of
Belgian and French Neo-Impressionists with works
by Cross, Luce, Rysselberghe and Signac (fig. 6) –
artists who had exhibited with Henry van de Velde
as part of the *Association pour l'Art* in Antwerp
as early as 1892.[16] Here, Osthaus acquired his first
painting by Signac, and possibly all four works
by the Neo-Impressionists, which were among the
most modern in the collection when the museum
opened, as reviews of the exhibition and a note
in Signac's diary in 1901 suggest: 'We barely sold
a painting each (me "La Seine à St Cloud" for
650 F to a museum founded by a private collector
in Hagen)' (p. 288).[17] Along with *La moisson* (*The
Wheatfield behind Saint Paul's Hospital with a
Reaper*, 1889; p. 315), the painting by Van Gogh acquired at Paul Cassirer in the spring of 1902, the
paintings by Cross, Luce, Rysselberghe and Signac
formed an ensemble at the opening of the museum that made its picture gallery the first in the
world, 'perhaps not only in Germany, in which one
can find the main proponents of Neo-Impressionism with important creations'.[18]

The acquisition of the large-format painting
Lise – La femme à l'ombrelle (*Lise with a Parasol*,
1867; p. 209) by Renoir had been suggested by
Van de Velde, as evidenced by a letter from
Osthaus to his wife: 'Today with Van de Velde in
the Secession', he reported to her from Berlin in
May 1901: 'A Renoir fantastic, 18,000 marks, a lady
with parasol in the forest, museum piece, worth
three times that', and on the following day: 'But
now: I'm 18,000 marks lighter. What do you say to

that? The Renoir is so madly beautiful that I
couldn't resist'.[19]

Overcoming Impressionism

When the Museum Folkwang opened in the summer of 1902, it was still a document of the history
of its founder's searching and collecting. The picture gallery on the building's upper storey was not
yet the statement of modernity that the Museum
Folkwang was to later appear, but a reflection
of the taste of its owner and its diverse influences
(fig. 7). Although the paintings by Renoir and the
Neo-Impressionists mark the museum's opening
up to French modernism, they were hung in the
same room as a battle scene by Rocholl and the
Neo-Romantic landscape painting *Küste bei Recco*
(*Coast near Recco*, ca. 1890) by the soon-to-be-
forgotten painter Theodor Her.

Until he reached the point from 1906 onwards,
where he could visit Cézanne and Henri Matisse
in their own studios, Osthaus was dependent on
advisors, who showed him the path to modernity.
The most important mentor of this interim period
was Emil Rudolf Weiss, who was less influential
as a painter than as a promoter of post-Impressionist Parisian modernism. Weiss, who had lived in
Paris for a time, encouraged Osthaus to continue
decisively on the path to a modern art collection
that he had already begun, and advised him to
acquire colour lithographs by Maurice Denis and
Edouard Vuillard at Ambroise Vollard's gallery on
his next visit to Paris. He recommended as a local

101

immenser Einfluss auf Osthaus und seine Ankäufe deutlich. Etliche Erwerbungen lassen sich konkret nachvollziehen: Als die Berliner Galerie Keller & Reiner, deren Interieur van de Velde 1899 gestaltet hatte, Anfang 1901 erneut eine Ausstellung belgischer und französischer Neo-Impressionisten mit Werken von Cross, Luce, Rysselberghe und Signac zeigte (Abb. 6) – Künstlern also, die schon 1892 im Rahmen der Antwerpener Association pour l'Art gemeinsam mit Henry van de Velde ausgestellt hatten[16] –, erwarb Osthaus sein erstes Gemälde Signacs und, wie sich aus Rezensionen der Ausstellung und dem folgenden Zitat vermuten lässt, eventuell sogar alle vier Werke der Neo-Impressionisten, die bei der Eröffnung seines Museums zu den modernsten der Sammlung zählten: „Mit Mühen verkaufen wir jeder ein Bild (von mir ‚La Seine à St Cloud' für 650 F an ein von einem Privatsammler gegründetes Museum in Hagen)", notierte Signac 1901 in sein Tagebuch (S. 288).[17] Gemeinsam mit dem noch im Frühjahr 1902 bei Paul Cassirer erworbenen Gemälde *La moisson (Die Ernte, Kornfeld mit Schnitter,* 1889; S. 315) von van Gogh bildeten die Gemälde von Cross, Luce, Rysselberghe und Signac bei der Eröffnung des Museums ein Ensemble, das die Gemäldegalerie zu der ersten weltweit machte, „in der man die Hauptvertreter des Neo-Impressionismus mit wichtigen Schöpfungen"[18] vertreten fand.

Auch den Erwerb des großformatigen Gemäldes *Lise – La femme à l'ombrelle (Lise mit dem Sonnenschirm,* 1867; S. 209) von Renoir hatte van de Velde angeregt, wie ein Brief von Osthaus an seine Frau belegt: „Heute mit van de Velde in der Secession", berichtete er ihr im Mai 1901 aus Berlin: „ein Renoir fabelhaft, 18.000 Mark, Dame mit Sonnenschirm im Wald, Museumsstück, 3-fach soviel wert", und am folgenden Tag: „Nun aber: Ich bin 18.000 Mark leichter. Was sagst Du dazu? Der Renoir ist so rasend schön, daß ich nicht widerstehen konnte."[19]

Die Überwindung des Impressionismus

Als das Museum Folkwang im Sommer 1902 eröffnet wurde, war es noch ein Dokument der Such- und Sammelgeschichte seines Gründers. Die Gemäldegalerie im Obergeschoss des Gebäudes war noch nicht das Statement der Modernität, als das das Folkwang-Museum später erscheinen sollte, sondern ein Spiegel des von vielfältigen Einflüssen geprägten Geschmacks ihres Eigentümers (Abb. 7). Zwar dokumentierten die Gemälde Renoirs und der Neo-Impressionist:innen die Öffnung des Museums für die französische Moderne, aber noch hingen diese Werke im selben Saal wie ein Schlachtengemälde Rocholls oder das neo-romantische Landschaftsbild *Küste bei Recco* (ca. 1890) des alsbald vergessenen Malers Theodor Her.

Bis Osthaus ab 1906 selber so weit war, Paul Cézanne und Henri Matisse in ihren Ateliers zu besuchen, war er auf Berater:innen angewiesen, die ihm den Weg in die Moderne aufzeigten. Der wichtigste Mentor dieser Zwischenzeit war Emil Rudolf Weiß, der als Maler weniger wirkungsreich war denn als Vermittler der nach-impressionistischen Pariser Moderne. Weiß hatte zeitweise in

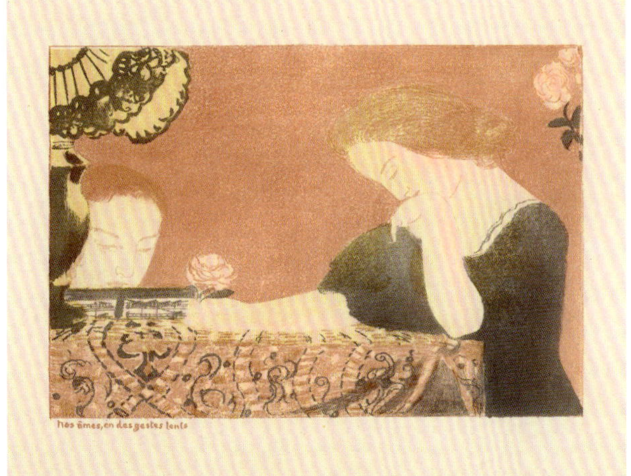

Abb. | Fig. 9
Maurice Denis, *Nos âmes, en des gestes lents,* Blatt 9 aus dem Mappenwerk *Amour* | Sheet 9 from the portfolio *Amour,* 1898, Museum Folkwang, Essen

Abb. | Fig. 10
Paul Gauguin, *Te tiai na oe ite rata*
(Tu attends une lettre?), 1899,
Privatsammlung | Private collection

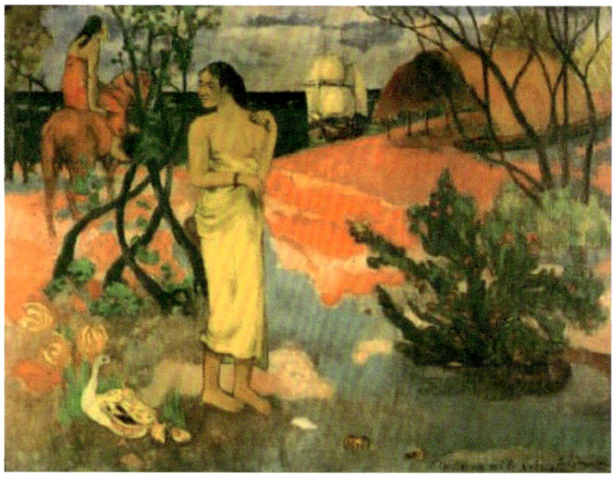

consultant his friend since their academy days, Konrad Ferdinand Edmund von Freyhold, who was living on the rue Boulard in Montparnasse (fig. 8).

The next trip to Paris in April 1903, turned out to be a crucial shopping tour that thrust the museum's collection into the modern era: Osthaus visited Rodin in his studios on rue de l'Université and in Meudon and acquired the bronzes *L'âge d'airain* (*The Bronze Age*, ca. 1880; p. 290) and *Ève* (*Eve*, 1881; p. 227) as well as the marble sculpture *Le Minotaure (Faune et nymphe)* (*The Minotaur [Faun and Nymph]*, 1885–86). With Freyhold, he also visited the studio of Edvard Munch, from whom he purchased the paintings *Vinter ved Nordstrand* (*Winter in Nordstrand,* ca. 1900–1903), and the Galerie Vollard, where he purchased not only the *Amour* album of lithographs by Maurice Denis (fig. 9), as Weiss had recommended, but also Van Gogh's *Portrait d'Armand Roulin* (*Portrait of Armand Roulin,* 1888; p. 321) and his first two Gauguin paintings (pp. 331, 339).[20]

When Osthaus had returned to Hagen, and news had arrived in Paris of Gauguin's death in French Polynesia in May, Freyhold urgently advised him to purchase additional works by the painter:

In early November Vollard wants to organize an estate exhibition [...]. Today I saw several paintings, including quite fabulous ones; the rest, and 4 or 5 paintings 'he has not shown anyone at all yet', I will see on Monday morning. – The prices have risen very much, of course, and with the exhibition will probably rise even more. Nevertheless, the prices are still low compared

to Monet, Pissarro, etc. Because his *highest* price is only 4–5000 fr. or so. A magnificent landscape was 2000 fr.; one much more beautiful that those we saw back then.[21]

'I really advise you, if you can do it, so secure several more paintings. That is truly art',[22] enthused Freyhold on the first day of the memorial exhibition at the Galerie Vollard. Osthaus then asked him to make a selection, and Vollard sent five paintings to Hagen, including *Te tiai na oe ite rata (Tu attends une lettre?)* (*Are you expecting a letter?*; fig. 10), which later hung in Gertrud Osthaus's salon in the villa Hohenhof, and *Contes barbares* (1902; p. 339), which is still today one of the major works of the Folkwang collection.[23]

Just a year and a half after its opening, the Museum Folkwang was able to present seven paintings by Gauguin that enable one to comprehend the overcoming of Impressionism; in 1907, they were joined by two paintings by Cézanne (pp. 292, 293) and *Nature morte aux asphodèles* (*Still Life with Asphodels,* 1907; fig. 11) by Matisse.

The Museum Folkwang had thus further transformed: from a collector's museum in the provinces with few high points of contemporary art, it had become an avant-garde collection and the most modern museum open to the public of its time. Tschudi's not unenvious hopes had been fulfilled. With Museum Folkwang, Osthaus took advantage of the beautiful privilege of the private gallery' to 'be different from the museum with its partially historical obligations, to work more freely, more one-sidedly.'[24]

103

Paris gelebt, ermutigte Osthaus, den eingeschlagenen Weg zu einer Sammlung moderner Kunst entschieden weiterzuverfolgen, und riet ihm, bei seinem nächsten Besuch in Paris in der Galerie von Ambroise Vollard Farblithografien von Maurice Denis und Edouard Vuillard zu erwerben. Als Berater vor Ort empfahl er ihm seinen Studienfreund Konrad Ferdinand Edmund von Freyhold, der in der Rue Boulard am Montparnasse lebte (Abb. 8).

Tatsächlich wurde die folgende Parisreise, die Osthaus im April 1903 unternahm, zu der entscheidenden Einkaufstour, die der Sammlung des Museums den Schub in die Moderne versetzte: Osthaus besuchte Auguste Rodin in seinen Ateliers in der Rue de l'Université und in Meudon und erwarb die Bronzen *L'âge d'airain (Das eherne Zeitalter,* ca. 1880; S. 290) und *Ève (Eva,* 1881; S. 227) sowie die Marmorskulptur *Le Minotaure (Faune et nymphe) (Der Minotaurus (Faun und Nymphe),* 1885/86). Gemeinsam mit Freyhold besuchte er auch das Atelier Edvard Munchs, von dem er das Gemälde *Vinter ved Nordstrand (Winter in Nordstrand,* ca. 1900/03) kaufte, und die Galerie Vollard, wo er – wie von Weiß vorgeschlagen – das Album *Amour* mit Lithografien von Maurice Denis erwarb (Abb. 9), aber auch van Goghs *Portrait d'Armand Roulin (Porträt Armand Roulin,* 1888; S. 321) sowie die ersten beiden Gemälde Gauguins (S. 331, 339).[20]

Als Osthaus wieder nach Hagen zurückgekehrt war und in Paris bekannt wurde, dass Gauguin im Mai in Französisch-Polynesien verstorben war, riet Freyhold ihm eindringlich, weitere Werke des Malers zu kaufen: „Anfang November will Vollard

eine Nachlass Ausstellung veranstalten [...]. Einige Bilder habe ich heute gesehen darunter ganz fabelhafte; den Rest, und 4 oder 5 Bilder ‚die er noch garniemand gezeigt hat', werde ich Montag früh sehen. – Die Preise sind natürlich sehr gestiegen und werden mit der Ausstellung voraussichtlich noch mehr steigen. Immerhin sind die Preise im Vergleich zu Monet, Pissarro etc. gering. Denn sein *höchster* Preis sind nun so 4–5000 fr. Eine herrliche Landschaft war 2000 fr; eine viel schönere, als die die wir damals sahen."[21]

„Ich rate Ihnen wirklich, wenn Sie es machen können sich noch einige der Bilder zu sichern. Das ist wirklich Kunst",[22] schwärmte Freyhold am ersten Tag der Gedächtnisausstellung in der Galerie Vollard. Osthaus bat ihn daraufhin, eine Auswahl zu treffen, und Vollard sandte fünf Gemälde nach Hagen, darunter *Te tiai na oe ite rata (Tu attends une lettre?) (Das Mädchen mit den Enten;* Abb. 10), das später im Salon von Gertrud Osthaus in der Villa Hohenhof hing und *Contes barbares* (1902; S. 339), das bis heute zu den Hauptwerken der Folkwang-Sammlung zählt.[23]

Bereits anderthalb Jahre nach seiner Eröffnung konnte das Folkwang-Museum sieben Gemälde Gauguins präsentieren, die die Überwindung des Impressionismus nachvollziehbar werden ließen, 1907 kamen zwei Gemälde Cézannes (S. 292, 293) und *Nature morte aux asphodèles (Stillleben mit Affodillen,* 1907; Abb. 11) von Henri Matisse hinzu.

Das Museum Folkwang hatte sich damit weiter verwandelt: Aus einem Sammlermuseum in der Provinz mit zunächst wenigen Höhepunkten zeitgenössischer Kunst war eine Avantgarde-

Abb. | Fig. 11
Henri Matisse, *Nature morte aux asphodèles,* 1907,
Museum Folkwang, Essen

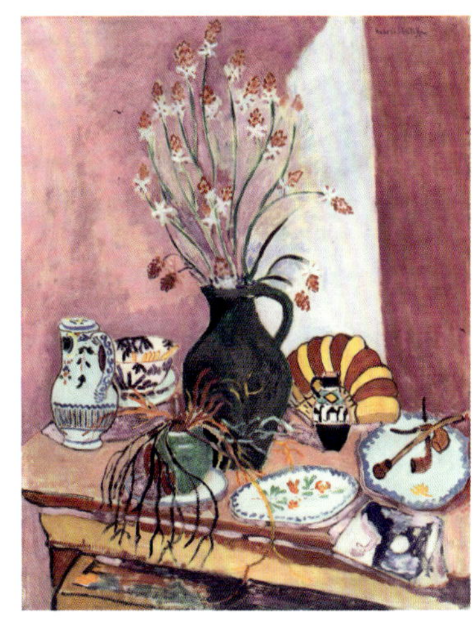

1 Peter-Klaus Schuster, 'Hugo von Tschudi und der Kampf um die Moderne', in Johann Georg Prinz von Hohenzollern and Peter-Klaus Schuster (eds.), *Manet bis van Gogh: Hugo von Tschudi und der Kampf um die Moderne* (Munich, 1996), 21–40, here 27.

2 *'Die Gemäldesammlung ist zur Zeit die einzige, vielleicht nicht nur in Deutschland, in der man die Hauptvertreter des Neo-Impressionismus mit wichtigen Schöpfungen finden kann.'* 'Folkwang', in *Westfälisches Tageblatt*, no. 167 (19 July 1902).

3 See, von Hohenzollern and Schuster, *Manet bis van Gogh*.

4 Letter from Hugo von Tschudi to Karl Ernst Osthaus, 28 June 1902, Bayerische Staatsbibliothek, Munich.

5 See, Walter Erben, 'Karl Ernst Osthaus: Lebensweg und Gedankengut', in *Karl Ernst Osthaus: Leben und Werk*, Recklinghausen 1971), 15–115, here 35.

6 See, Herta Hesse-Frielinghaus, 'Folkwang 1. Teil', in ibid., 119–241, here 120.

7 Letter from Theodor Rocholl to Karl Ernst Osthaus, 18 April 1897, Karl Ernst Osthaus-Archiv, Osthaus-Museum Hagen, V5/3.

8 Ulrike Becks-Malorny, *Der Kunstverein in Barmen 1866–1946. Bürgerliches Mäzenatentum zwischen Kaiserreich und Nationalsozialismus* (Wuppertal, 1992), 29.

9 See, Letter from Karl Ernst Osthaus to Gertrud Osthaus, 19 July 1916, quoted in Birgit Schulte, "'Kunstfragen sind nicht Friedensfragen': Das Hagener Folkwang-Museum und der Erste Weltkrieg", in Ralf Blank, Tayfun Belgin and Birgit Schulte (eds.), *Weltenbrand: Hagen 1914* (Essen, 2014), 101–26, here 115.

10 'Built of red brick, decorated with battlements and towers, it is resplendent above the soot-blackened city; the entry gate to the front garden is flanked by two sculptures of lions. Inside, a stylistic mishmash reigns: walls and ceilings with stucco borders, window and door frames hung with plush curtains, imitation Rococo furniture.' Erben, 'Karl Ernst Osthaus', here 22.

11 Alfred Lichtwark, 'Justus Brinckmann: Einleitung zur Festschrift von 1902', quoted in Lichtwark, *Eine Auswahl seiner Schriften*, ed. Wolf Mannhardt, 2 vols. (Berlin, 1917), 2:196–257, here 250.

12 Herta Hesse-Frielinghaus, 'Karl Ernst Osthaus und Henry van de Velde – eine Freundschaft (1987)', in Birgit Schulte (ed.), *Henry van de Velde in Hagen* (Hagen, 1992), 47–61, here 47.

13 Karl Ernst Osthaus, *Henry van de Velde. Leben und Schaffen des Künstlers* (Hagen, 1920), 21.

14 Letter from Karl Ernst Osthaus to Henry van de Velde, 26 April 1900, in *Karl Ernst Osthaus: Leben und Werk*, Recklinghausen 1971, facsimile following p. 38.

15 Henry van de Velde, *Geschichte meines Lebens*, ed. Hans Curjel, 2nd ed. (Munich and Zurich, 1986), 217–18.

16 See, Marcel Daloze, 'Gemeinsame Argumente und individuelles Schicksal: Henry van de Velde und die "Association pour l'Art" (1892–1893)', Klaus-Jürgen Sembach and Birgit Schulte (eds.), *Henry van de Velde: Ein europäischer Künstler in seiner Zeit* (Cologne, 1992), 81–91.

17 *'Nous vendons à peine chacun une toile (moi, La Seine à Saint-Cloud 650 F pour musée créé par une particulier de Hagen)'*. Paul Signac, diary entry, 1 February 1901, quoted in Marina Ferretti-Bocquillon, 'Paul Signac au temps d'harmonie, 1892–1913', in *Signac et la libération de la couleur de Matisse à Mondrian*, exh. cat. Musée de Grenoble (Grenoble, 1997), 51–73, here 66.

18 *'[…] in der man die Hauptvertreter des Neo-Impressionismus mit wichtigen Schöpfungen.'* 'Folkwang', in *Westfälisches Tageblatt*.

19 Letter from Karl Ernst Osthaus to Gertrud Osthaus, 23(?) May 1901 and 24 May 1901; quoted in Hesse-Frielinghaus, 'Karl Ernst Osthaus und Henry van de Velde', here 52.

20 The acquisitions that Karl Ernst Osthaus made, probably together with his wife, Gertrud, at Vollard in the spring of 1903 are evident from Karl Ernst Osthaus's correspondence with Emil Rudolf Weiss and Konrad Ferdinand von Freyhold in the archive of the Museum Folkwang in Essen as well as from a receipt from the Galerie Vollard that confirms the purchase of two paintings by Gauguin, a painting by Van Gogh, and an 'album' by Maurice Denis; see, Karl Ernst Osthaus-Archiv, Osthaus-Museum Hagen, F1/104.

21 Letter from Konrad Ferdinand von Freyhold to Karl Ernst Osthaus, 17 October 1903, Archiv Museum Folkwang Essen, MF X/3.

22 Letter Konrad Ferdinand von Freyhold to Karl Ernst Osthaus, 4 November 1903, Archiv Museum Folkwang Essen, MF X/3.

23 On the acquisition of Gauguin's works, see, Emil Rudolf Weiss, 'Paul Gauguin: Fragmentarische Bemerkungen anlässlich der Ausstellung von sieben Gemälden Gauguins im Folkwang', in *Hagener Zeitung*, 19 December 1903.

24 Emil Waldmann, 'Der Sammler', in *Die Neue Rundschau*, no. 12, 1915, 1620–43, here 1627.

Sammlung geworden, die als öffentlich zugängliches Museum das modernste seiner Zeit war. Tschudis nicht neidlose Hoffnungen hatten sich erfüllt: Mit dem Museum Folkwang nutzte Osthaus „das schöne Vorrecht der Privatgalerie", „anders zu sein als das Museum mit seinen teils historischen Pflichten, freier zu sein, einseitiger zu arbeiten."[24]

1 Peter-Klaus Schuster, „Hugo von Tschudi und der Kampf um die Moderne", in: *Manet bis van Gogh. Hugo von Tschudi und der Kampf um die Moderne,* hrsg. von Johann Georg Prinz von Hohenzollern und Peter-Klaus Schuster, München 1996, S. 21–40, hier S. 27.

2 „Folkwang", in: *Westfälisches Tageblatt,* 167, 19.7.1902.

3 Vgl. *Manet bis van Gogh. Hugo von Tschudi und der Kampf um die Moderne,* hrsg. von Johann Georg Prinz von Hohenzollern und Peter-Klaus Schuster, München 1996.

4 Hugo von Tschudi an Karl Ernst Osthaus, Brief vom 28.6.1902, Bayerische Staatsbibliothek München.

5 Vgl. Walter Erben, „Karl Ernst Osthaus. Lebensweg und Gedankengut", in: Herta Hesse-Frielinghaus u. a., *Karl Ernst Osthaus. Leben und Werk,* Recklinghausen 1971, S. 15–115, hier S. 35.

6 Vgl. Herta Hesse-Frielinghaus, „Folkwang 1. Teil", in: ebd., S. 119–241, hier S. 120.

7 Theodor Rocholl an Karl Ernst Osthaus, Brief vom 18.4.1897, Karl Ernst Osthaus-Archiv, Osthaus-Museum Hagen, V5/3.

8 Ulrike Becks-Malorny, *Der Kunstverein in Barmen 1866–1946. Bürgerliches Mäzenatentum zwischen Kaiserreich und Nationalsozialismus,* Wuppertal 1992, S. 29.

9 Vgl. Karl Ernst Osthaus an Gertrud Osthaus, Brief vom 19.7.1916, zit. nach Birgit Schulte, „‚Kunstfragen sind nicht Friedensfragen'. Das Hagener Folkwang-Museum und der Erste Weltkrieg", in: *Weltenbrand. Hagen 1914,* hrsg. von Ralf Blank, Tayfun Belgin und Birgit Schulte, Essen 2014, S. 101–126, hier S. 115.

10 „Aus rotem Backstein gebaut, mit Zinnen und Türmen verziert, prangt sie oberhalb der rußgeschwärzten Stadt; das Eingangstor zum Vorgarten ist von zwei Löwenskulpturen flankiert. Im Innern herrscht ein Stil-Mischmasch: Wände und Decken sind mit Stuckbordüren versehen, Fenster- und Türrahmen mit Plüschvorhängen behangen, die Möbel nachgemachtes Rokoko". Walter Erben, „Karl Ernst Osthaus. Lebensweg und Gedankengut", hier S. 22.

11 Alfred Lichtwark, „Justus Brinckmann. Einleitung zur Festschrift von 1902", zit. nach: ders., *Eine Auswahl seiner Schriften, Bd. 2,* hrsg. von Wolf Mannhardt, Berlin 1917, S. 196–257, hier S. 250.

12 Herta Hesse-Frielinghaus, „Karl Ernst Osthaus und Henry van de Velde – eine Freundschaft (1987)", in: *Henry van de Velde in Hagen,* hrsg. von Birgit Schulte, Hagen 1992, S. 47–61, hier S. 47.

13 Karl Ernst Osthaus, *Van de Velde. Leben und Schaffen des Künstlers,* Hagen 1920, S. 21.

14 Karl Ernst Osthaus an Henry van de Velde, Brief vom 26.4.1900, in: Herta Hesse-Frielinghaus u. a., *Karl Ernst Osthaus. Leben und Werk,* Recklinghausen 1971, Faksimile nach S. 38.

15 Henry van de Velde, *Geschichte meines Lebens,* hrsg. von Hans Curjel, 2. Aufl., München und Zürich 1986, S. 217 f.

16 Vgl. Marcel Daloze, „Gemeinsame Argumente und individuelles Schicksal. Henry van de Velde und die ‚Association pour l'Art' (1892–1893)", in: *Henry van de Velde. Ein europäischer Künstler in seiner Zeit,* hrsg. von Klaus-Jürgen Sembach und Birgit Schulte, Köln 1992, S. 81–91.

17 Paul Signac, Tagebucheintrag vom 1.2.1901, zit. nach: Marina Ferretti-Bocquillon, „Paul Signac in der Zeit der Harmonie, 1892–1913", in: *Farben des Lichts. Paul Signac und der Beginn der Moderne von Matisse bis Mondrian,* hrsg. von Erich Franz, Ausst.-Kat. Westfälisches Landesmuseum für Kunst und Kulturgeschichte, Münster u. a., Ostfildern 1996, S. 51–76, hier S. 66.

18 „Folkwang", in: *Westfälisches Tageblatt.*

19 Karl Ernst Osthaus an Gertrud Osthaus, Briefe vom 23.(?) und 24.5.1901; zit. nach: Herta Hesse-Frielinghaus, „Karl Ernst Osthaus und Henry van de Velde", hier S. 52.

20 Die Erwerbungen, die Karl Ernst Osthaus, vermutlich gemeinsam mit seiner Frau Gertrud, im Frühjahr 1903 bei Vollard getätigt hat, gehen aus dem Briefwechsel von Karl Ernst Osthaus mit Emil Rudolf Weiß und Konrad Ferdinand von Freyhold im Archiv Museum Folkwang Essen hervor sowie aus der Quittung der Galerie Vollard, die den Erwerb von zwei Bildern Gauguins, einem Gemälde van Goghs und einem „Album" von Maurice Denis bestätigt, vgl. Karl Ernst Osthaus-Archiv, Osthaus-Museum Hagen, F1/104.

21 Konrad Ferdinand von Freyhold an Karl Ernst Osthaus, Brief vom 17.10.1903, Archiv Museum Folkwang Essen, MF X/3.

22 Konrad Ferdinand von Freyhold an Karl Ernst Osthaus, Brief vom 4.11.1903, Archiv Museum Folkwang Essen, MF X/3.

23 Vgl. zu den Erwerbungen von Werken Gauguins Emil Rudolf Weiß, „Paul Gauguin. Fragmentarische Bemerkungen anläßlich der Ausstellung von sieben Gemälden Gauguins im Folkwang", in: *Hagener Zeitung,* 19.12.1903.

24 Emil Waldmann, „Der Sammler", in: *Die Neue Rundschau,* 12, 1915, S. 1620–1643, hier S. 1627.

THE RUHR REGION AND JAPAN –
A SKETCH

Shingo Shimada

Rūru-kōgyō-chitai – how auspicious that Japanese name for the Ruhr region sounded to the ears of a thirteen-year-old pupil in geography class. The teacher spoke of the cities of the region as places of longing. The name was a promise, a promise of modernity and industry. At the time I knew nothing of the relations between the Ruhr and Japan, but I already understood that this region was linked to positive emotions and perspectives on the future.

At the time, Japanese society was still in the phase of economic boom and people were trying to catch up to the West's lead in modernization and industrialization. The Ruhr's name possessed a kind of symbolic power with which it was believed the goal of modernization could be achieved.

That was not new: even earlier the Ruhr had symbolized modernization for Japan. The historical relations between the Ruhr and Japan were to a great extent characterized by industry and technology and were closely connected to the armed conflicts of the twentieth century.

What role did art play in this context? Museums such as the Museum Folkwang in Essen and the National Museum of Western Art in Tokyo are inconceivable without the background of industry and business. To put it simply, the different spheres of industry and art, which influenced each other, only developed with modernization. This is how a global art market emerged from the end of the nineteenth century. Several successful industrialists such as Kōjirō Matsukata and entrepreneurial heirs to fortunes such as Karl Ernst Osthaus began collecting works of art, which only in a few cases were transferred to museums as large collections.[1] Japan was surely also a straggler in this regard. The term for art, *bijutsu*, only came into use as a result of the encounter with the West and was therefore initially reserved for artworks from the West. Only

Shingo Shimada

Rūru-kōgyō-chitai – wie verheißungsvoll klang 1970 diese japanische Bezeichnung für das Ruhrgebiet in den Ohren eines 13-jährigen Schülers im Geografieunterricht. Der Lehrer sprach von den Städten der Region wie von einem Sehnsuchtsort. Der Name war ein Versprechen, ein Versprechen für Moderne und Industrie. Ich wusste damals nichts von den Beziehungen zwischen dem Ruhrgebiet und Japan, verstand aber, dass mit dieser Region positive Emotionen und Zukunftsperspektiven verbunden waren.

Zu diesem Zeitpunkt befand sich die japanische Gesellschaft noch in der Phase des wirtschaftlichen Aufschwungs und man bemühte sich, den westlichen Vorsprung in der Modernisierung und Industrialisierung aufzuholen. Der Name Ruhrgebiet besaß eine symbolische Zugkraft, mit der man das Ziel der Modernisierung zu erreichen glaubte. Das war nicht neu – schon früher symbolisierte das Ruhrgebiet in Japan die Modernisierung. Die historischen Beziehungen zwischen dem Ruhrgebiet und Japan waren weitestgehend von Industrie und Technologie geprägt und hingen eng mit den kriegerischen Auseinandersetzungen des 20. Jahrhunderts zusammen.

Welche Rolle spielt aber die Kunst in diesem Zusammenhang? Museen wie das Museum Folkwang in Essen oder das National Museum of Western Art in Tokio sind ohne den Hintergrund von Industrie und Wirtschaft nicht denkbar. Sehr vereinfacht betrachtet entwickelten sich erst mit der Modernisierung die unterschiedlichen Sphären Industrie und Kunst, die sich gegenseitig beeinflussten. So entstand seit Ende des 19. Jahrhunderts auch ein globaler Kunstmarkt. Mehrere erfolgreiche Industrielle wie Kōjirō Matsukata oder Unternehmererben wie Karl Ernst Osthaus begannen mit dem Sammeln von Kunstwerken, die nur in wenigen Fällen als größere Konvolute in Museen trans-

DAS RUHRGEBIET UND JAPAN – EINE SKIZZE

108

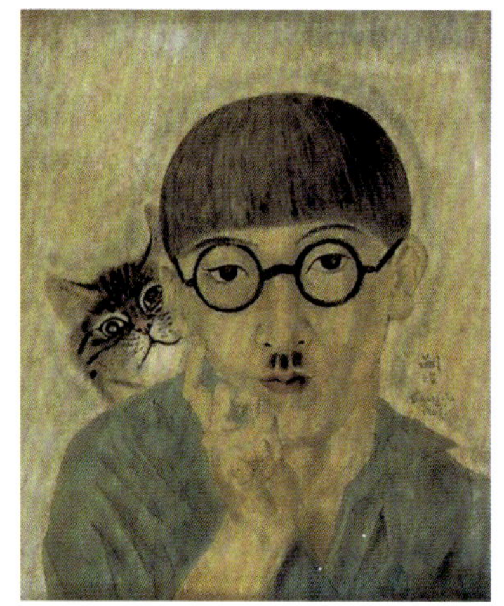

after the American art historian, Ernest Fenollosa, explicitly advocated Japanese art while teaching in Japan, and his student Tenshin Okakura had established a college for Japanese art in 1887, at which, among others, Tsuguharu Foujita studied (fig. 1), did the idea gain acceptance that Japan, too, already had its own art.[2] Only then did the concept of 'Japanese fine art' (*nihonga*) (fig. 2), as distinct from Western fine art (*yōga*), emerge.[3] The idea of making works of art accessible to the public in museums was also new to Japan. There was, therefore, a long way to go before a national museum for modern Western art could be opened in 1959, for which the Matsukata Collection provided the occasion.[4] In this evolution, the two protagonists of the present exhibition, Karl Ernst Osthaus and Kōjirō Matsukata, embody the intersection of industry and art. In what follows, I would like to outline this close connection between industry, politics, military and art from the perspective of interactions between the Ruhr and Japan.

German Steel in Japan

As early as 1864, two envoys of the Shogun, Takeaki Enomoto and Noriyoshi Akamatsu, came to see Alfred Krupp in Essen.[5] They ordered eighteen cannons from Krupp.[6] This predated the emergence of the modern Japanese state, and the two envoys were direct subordinates of the Shogun. They also stopped on his behalf in the Netherlands to supervise and attend to the building of a warship, a frigate, that had been ordered for the

shogunate. Before the frigate was completed in 1866, the two envoys were observers in the German-Danish war of 1864. Deeply impressed by the effectiveness of the Krupp cannons, they decided to order the cannons for the frigate directly from the Krupp factory. The completed ship was christened the *Kaiyōmaru*, based on the Dutch name *Voorlichter* (Educator) and transferred to Japan in 1867.[7] During the wars between the party of the shogunate and that of the new Meiji state, Enomoto fled to Hokkaidō in 1868 in the frigate he had ordered and entrenched himself in the fortress of Hakodate. The ship was caught in a storm and sank.[8] Today one can see the reconstructed frigate as well as the Krupp cannons, which were recovered from the seabed, in the Kaiyōmaru Museum in Esashi. Although he had fought in the civil war against the new Meiji state, Enomoto later went on to have a considerable career as a navy officer and politician.

The next important event was the 1873 visit from the Iwakura Mission, named after its leader the politician Tomomi Iwakura, which toured North America and Europe on behalf of the Meiji state to gather fundamental knowledge from the West necessary to modernize the country (fig. 3).[9] En route from Amsterdam to Berlin, the envoys inspected the Krupp factory in Essen, which impressed them deeply. They saw here the close cooperation between industry, military and politics and recognized that as one of the reasons for Germany's successes at the time.[10] This experience led to the Meiji state increasingly taking its

feriert wurden.[1] Japan war sicherlich auch in diesem Punkt ein Nachzügler. Der Begriff der Kunst, *bijutsu*, wurde überhaupt erst durch die Begegnung mit dem Westen bekannt und war zunächst den Kunstwerken des Westens vorbehalten. Erst nachdem sich der amerikanische Kunsthistoriker Ernest Fenollosa während seiner Lehrtätigkeit in Japan explizit für die japanische Kunst eingesetzt und sein Schüler, Tenshin Okakura, 1887 eine Hochschule für japanische Kunst eingerichtet hatte, an der unter anderen Tsuguharu Foujita lernte (Abb. 1), setzte sich die Vorstellung durch, dass auch in Japan schon eine eigene Kunst existierte.[2] Erst daraus entstand das Konzept der „japanischen Bildkunst (*nihonga*)" (Abb. 2) in Abgrenzung zur westlichen Bildkunst (*yōga*).[3] Auch die Idee, Kunstwerke in Museen öffentlich zugänglich zu machen, war neu für Japan. Es war daher ein langer Weg, bis im Jahr 1959 ein Nationalmuseum für moderne westliche Kunst eröffnet werden konnte, zu dem die Sammlung Matsukatas den Anlass gegeben hatte.[4] In dieser Entwicklung verkörpern die beiden Protagonisten dieser Ausstellung, Karl Ernst Osthaus und Kōjirō Matsukata, die Schnittstelle zwischen Industrie und Kunst. Diesen engen Zusammenhang zwischen Industrie, Politik, Militär und Kunst möchte ich im Folgenden aus der Perspektive der Wechselbeziehungen zwischen dem Ruhrgebiet und Japan skizzenhaft aufzeigen.

Deutscher Stahl in Japan

Bereits 1864 kamen zwei Gesandte des Shoguns zu Alfred Krupp nach Essen.[5] Es waren Takeaki Enomoto und Noriyoshi Akamatsu, die 18 Kanonen bei Krupp bestellten.[6] Dies geschah noch vor der Entstehung des modernen japanischen Staates und die beiden Gesandten waren direkte Untergebene des Shoguns. In dessen Auftrag hielten sie sich auch in den Niederlanden auf, um den Bau eines vom Shogunat bestellten Kriegsschiffes, einer Fregatte, zu überwachen und zu begleiten. Vor der Fertigstellung der Fregatte im Jahr 1866 waren die beiden Gesandten 1864 Beobachter im Deutsch-Dänischen Krieg. Tief beeindruckt von der Wirkung der Krupp-Kanonen beschlossen sie, die Kanonen für die Fregatte direkt im Krupp-Werk zu bestellen. Das fertige Schiff wurde auf den Namen „Kaiyōmaru" entsprechend der holländischen Bezeichnung „Voorlichter" getauft und 1867 nach Japan überführt.[7] Während der kriegerischen Auseinandersetzungen zwischen der Partei des Shogunats und jener des neuen Staates flüchtete Enomoto 1868 mit der von ihm bestellten Fregatte nach Hokkaidō und verschanzte sich in der Festung von Hakodate. Das Schiff wurde von einem Sturm erfasst und versank.[8] Heute kann man die rekonstruierte Fregatte und auch die Krupp-Kanonen, die vom Meeresboden geborgen wurden, im Kaiyōmaru-Museum (Kaiyōmaru kinenkan) in Esashi besichtigen. Enomoto machte, obwohl er einen Bürgerkrieg gegen den neuen Meiji-Staat geführt hatte, später in eben diesem

Abb. | Fig. 2
Shimomura Kanzan, Szene aus dem
Nō-Theaterstück *Yoroboshi* |
Scene from the Noh Play *Yoroboshi*, 1915,
Tokyo National Museum

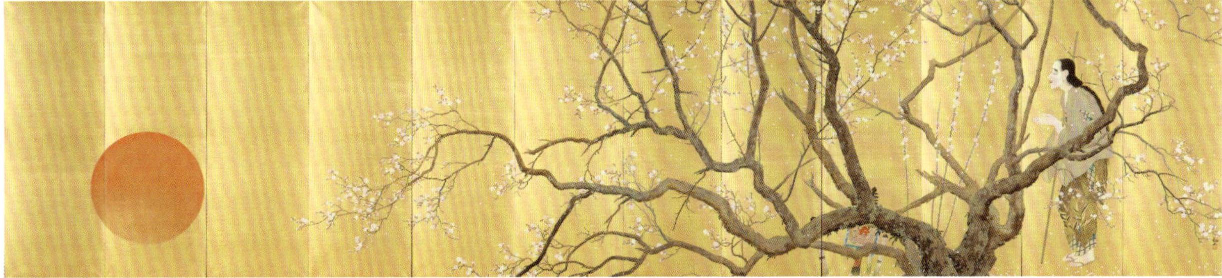

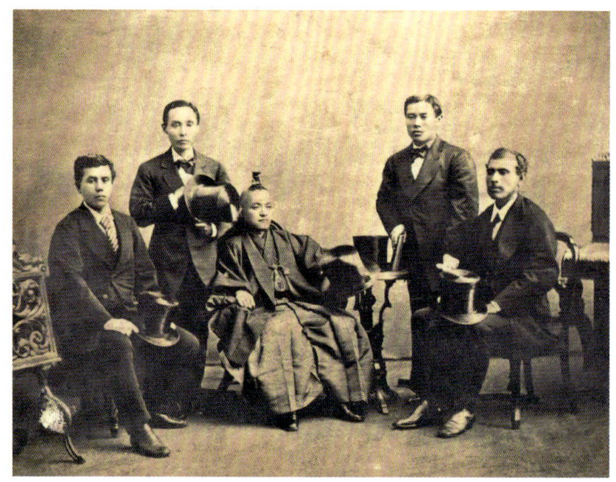

lead from Germany in its further development and also to it reforming its army on the German model, for which purpose Major Klemens Wilhelm Jakob Meckel was engaged from 1885 to 1888 as advisor to the Japanese general staff and instructor at the military college.[11]

After the Iwakura Mission, it was taken for granted that the still young Meiji state could survive in an international political situation shaped by imperialism only by further and rapid industrial development. Building heavy industry was therefore regarded as one of the most important goals of the state. It made sense to look to the Ruhr region on this point as well. For the planned steelworks, they first turned to the Krupp factory, but to no avail.[12] The mining and metallurgical company Gutehoffnungshütte (GHH) in Oberhausen – one of the largest complexes of the mining industry in the Ruhr– was hired in 1897 to build the steelworks in the Yawata District of the city of Kitakyūshū on Kyūshū Island, which had rich coal deposits. GHH sent fifteen engineers and foremen to work with the machines and materials, most of which were also from their factory.[13] Carl Haase was particularly important. He had been working in a steelworks in Bochum since 1896 and was recruited for the Yawata project in Japan in 1897. There he trained numerous co-workers, remaining until 1902. Whereas collaboration with other German engineers in this early period was not without friction, Haase apparently settled into the Japanese working world and became a popular local trainer, for which he was awarded a prestigious order by the

Emperor Meiji.[14] After initial technical difficulties, the Yawata Steelworks become one of the market leaders in Japan and contributed to the country's further industrialization. Japan's military success in the Russo-Japanese War of 1904–05 would have been inconceivable without the contribution of the steelworks.[15]

Art and U-Boats

The beginnings of Japan's industrialization described above and the associated connections to the Ruhr are the background against which Kōjirō Matsukata's activities should be viewed here.[16] The period during which Matsukata was internationally active can be seen as a phase between the two world wars in which international traffic between nation states increased. Matsukata, as the successful businessman at the head of the Kawasaki Dockyard Company (Kawasaki Zōsensho, later Kawasaki Jūkō: famous in Japan for its motorcycles), travelled both to the United States and to Europe as part of its commercial development and from 1916 and 1926 frequently spent extended periods on both continents. There he discovered his love of art and began to put together a collection. As a result of the great economic success his company enjoyed during the First World War, among other times, he had sufficient means to do so. As president of the Kawasaki Dockyard, he was able to make great profits selling prefabricated ships, so-called stock boats, in part because German U-boats were sinking numerous Allied ships.

III

Staat eine beachtliche Karriere als Marineoffizier und Politiker.

Das nächste wichtige Ereignis in Bezug auf das Ruhrgebiet war der Besuch einer japanischen Gesandtschaft im Jahr 1873. Diese drei Jahre dauernde Iwakura-Mission – benannt nach ihrem Leiter, einem der wichtigsten Politiker dieser Zeit, Tomomi Iwakura – bereiste im Auftrag des Meiji-Staates Nordamerika und Europa, um im Westen grundlegende Kenntnisse für die Modernisierung des Landes zu sammeln (Abb. 3).[9] Auf dem Weg von Amsterdam nach Berlin besichtigten die Gesandten das Krupp-Werk in Essen, von dem sie tief beeindruckt waren. Sie sahen hier die enge Kooperation zwischen Industrie, Militär und Politik und erkannten darin einen der Gründe für die damaligen Erfolge Deutschlands.[10] Diese Erfahrung führte dazu, dass sich der Meiji-Staat in seiner weiteren Entwicklung immer stärker an Deutschland orientierte und auch das Heer nach deutschem Vorbild reformierte, wofür Major Klemens Wilhelm Jakob Meckel für die Zeit von 1885 bis 1888 als Berater des japanischen Generalstabs und Lehrer an der Heereshochschule engagiert wurde.[11]

Seit der Iwakura-Mission stand fest, dass der noch junge Meiji-Staat in der vom Imperialismus geprägten weltpolitischen Lage nur durch industrielle Weiterentwicklung überleben konnte. Daher galt der Aufbau der Schwerindustrie als eines der wichtigsten Ziele des Staates. Es lag nahe, sich auch in diesem Punkt am Ruhrgebiet zu orientieren. Für das geplante Stahlwerk wandte man sich zunächst an das Krupp-Werk, allerdings erfolglos.[12] Dafür konnte die Gutehoffnungshütte in Ober-

hausen – einer der größten montanindustriellen Komplexe des Ruhrgebiets (Abb. 4) – im Jahr 1897 für den Bau der Stahlwerke im Stadtteil Yawata der Stadt Kitakyūshū auf der Insel Kyūshū gewonnen werden, wo ein reiches Steinkohlevorkommen vorhanden war. Die Gutehoffnungshütte entsandte 15 Ingenieure und Vorarbeiter, welche die ebenfalls größtenteils vom eigenen Werk stammenden Maschinen und Materialien bedienten.[13] Hierbei kam Carl Haase besondere Bedeutung zu. Er war seit 1896 zunächst in einem Stahlwerk in Bochum beschäftigt gewesen und wurde 1897 für das Yawata-Projekt in Japan rekrutiert. Er bildete dort zahlreiche Mitarbeiter aus und blieb bis 1902. Während die Zusammenarbeit mit anderen deutschen Ingenieuren in diesem frühen Projekt wohl nicht reibungslos vonstattenging, lebte Haase sich offensichtlich in die japanische Arbeitswelt ein und wurde zu einem beliebten Ausbilder vor Ort, wofür er vom Kaiser Meiji mit einem Orden ausgezeichnet wurde.[14] Nach anfänglichen technischen Schwierigkeiten entwickelte sich das Yawata-Stahlwerk zu einem der Marktführer Japans und trug zur weiteren Industrialisierung des Landes bei. Der militärische Erfolg Japans im Russisch-Japanischen Krieg der Jahre 1904/05 wäre ohne den Beitrag des Stahlwerkes kaum denkbar gewesen.[15]

Kunst und U-Boote

Der oben beschriebene Anfang der Industrialisierung Japans und die damit verbundenen Beziehungen zum Ruhrgebiet sind der Hintergrund, vor dem die Tätigkeit von Kōjirō Matsukata hier

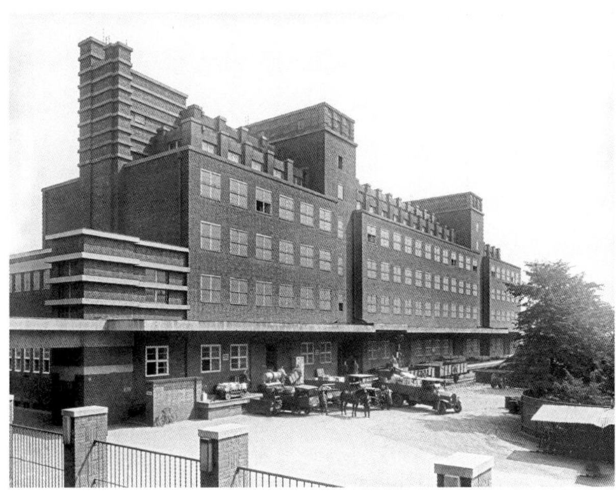

Abb. | Fig. 4
Ehemaliges Hauptlagerhaus der Gutehoffnungshütte, heute Zentraldepot des LVR-Industriemuseums | Former main warehouse of the Gutehoffnungshütte, today the central depot of the LVR Industrial Museum, Oberhausen, ca. 1929

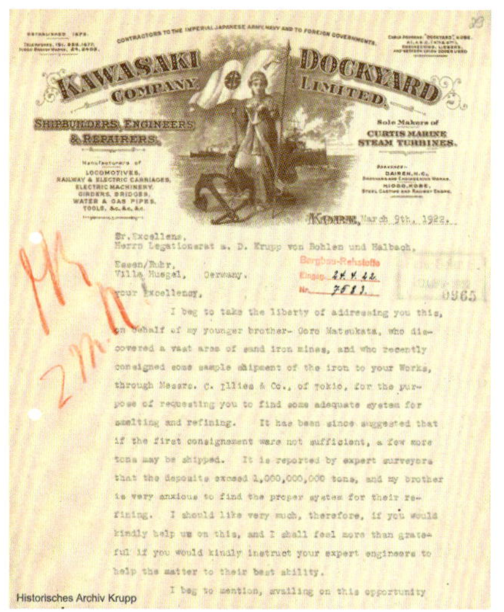

Abb. | Fig. 5
Brief von Kōjirō Matsukata an Gustav Krupp
von Bohlen und Halbach, 9. März 1922 |
Letter from Kōjirō Matsukata to Gustav Krupp
von Bohlen und Halbach, 9 March 1922

With the aid of various advisors, including the art historian Yukio Yashiro, who later became a famous scholar and director of the Institute for Art Research in Tokyo, Matsukata acquired numerous paintings, which also brought him to the attention of the international gallery scene. This may have been behind a secret assignment that Matsukata is said to have been given to help the Japanese navy gain access to the construction plans of German U-boats. Their superiority became clearly evident in the First World War, and so the secret services of many nations were trying to get the plans. For this quite dangerous mission, writers such as Nobuo Tajima suggest Matsukata was well suited because he had good connections to the upper class of various European countries, which he had established in part through his activities as a major collector of art.[17] The current director of the National Museum of Western Art, however, doubts whether Kōjirō Matsukata was ever actually active for the secret service.[18] Matsukata did, however, visit Essen several times, as documented in the Krupp Historical Archive. There is evidence of visits to the Krupp factory and personal meetings with Gustav Krupp von Bohlen und Halbach in 1902, 1911 and 1926 (fig. 5).[19] He also contacted Dr Hans Techel of the former Friedrich Krupp Germaniawerft ship-building company, who, because Germany was prohibited from building U-boats under the Versailles Treaty, was running an engineering office for shipbuilding in The Hague. Dr Techel was invited to Japan in 1924 and supervised the construction of two U-boats,[20] and from 1926 onwards Kawasaki built several U-boats under contract to the Japanese navy that would later be deployed in the Second World War. In this respect, the connection to the armed forces of his country was not independent of the business interests of Matsukata's company. Here we see how the at times bloody network of military, technology, business and politics can be behind the aesthetics of an art collection.[21]

Japanese-German Relations in Mining

After the Second World War, relations between the Ruhr and Japan initially appear to have broken off. Japan was occupied by the American military, and it was unclear what would happen with Japanese industry in general. American culture increasingly dominated the Japanese society that emerged after defeat in the Second World War. In mining, too, it was the United States that offered cooperation. The Japanese, however, quickly realized that requirements for mining coal were completely different in the United States than those of Japan. There, coal did not have to be mined underground, as was the case in Japan, so that American technology was not suited to the country. It was known that coal mining in the Ruhr region was dominated by conditions similar to those of Japan, so it seemed to make more sense to adopt the technology used there. Thus, in 1954 the GHH received another commission, this time to construct a coal pit in the city of Tagawa, one of the centres of coal mining in northern Kyūshū.

betrachtet werden soll.[16] Die Zeit, in der Matsukata international tätig wurde, kann als eine Phase zwischen dem Ersten und dem Zweiten Weltkrieg gesehen werden, in der der internationale Verkehr zwischen den Nationalstaaten zunahm. Matsukata als erfolgreicher Unternehmer der Kawasaki-Werft (Kawasaki Zōsensho, später Kawasaki Jūkō: hierzulande allgemein bekannt für ihre Motorräder) ging im Rahmen dieser Entwicklung sowohl in die USA als auch nach Europa und verweilte zwischen 1916 und 1926 öfter und länger auf beiden Kontinenten. Hier entdeckte er seine Liebe zur Kunst und begann eine Sammlung anzulegen. Aufgrund der großen wirtschaftlichen Erfolge, die sein Unternehmen unter anderem während des Ersten Weltkriegs erzielte, besaß er dafür genügend finanzielle Mittel. Als Präsident der Kawasaki-Werft konnte er mit dem Verkauf vorgefertigter Schiffe, sogenannter *stock boats*, große Gewinne erzielen, unter anderem da deutsche U-Boote zahlreiche Schiffe der Entente versenkten.

Mithilfe verschiedener Berater:innen, etwa des später bekannt gewordenen Kunsthistorikers Yukio Yashiro, erwarb Matsukata zahlreiche Gemälde, wodurch er auch in der internationalen Galerieszene bekannt wurde. Das mag der Hintergrund für einen geheimen Auftrag gewesen sein, den Matsukata erhalten haben soll, um der japanischen Marine Zugang zu den Konstruktionsplänen der deutschen U-Boote zu verschaffen. Deren besondere Leistungsfähigkeit wurde im Ersten Weltkrieg deutlich sichtbar und in der Folge bemühten sich Geheimdienste verschiedener Natio-

nen um die Konstruktionspläne. Für den durchaus gefährlichen Auftrag erscheint Matsukata Autoren wie Nobuo Tajima als geeignete Person, da er über gute Beziehungen zur Oberschicht verschiedener europäischer Länder verfügte, die er zum Teil durch seine Aktivitäten als großzügiger Kunstsammler aufgebaut hatte.[17] Ob Kōjirō Matsukata aber tatsächlich für den Geheimdienst tätig war, wird vom derzeitigen Direktor des National Museum of Western Art angezweifelt.[18] Aber zumindest besuchte Matsukata, wie im Historischen Archiv Krupp dokumentiert ist, mehrmals Essen. Für die Jahre 1902, 1911 und 1926 sind Werksbesichtigungen bei der Firma Krupp und persönliche Treffen mit Gustav Krupp von Bohlen und Halbach belegt (Abb. 5).[19] Vor diesem Hintergrund nahm er auch Kontakt zu Dr. Hans Techel von der ehemaligen Fried. Krupp Germaniawerft auf, der nach dem Ersten Weltkrieg aufgrund des Verbotes der U-Boot-Rüstung in Deutschland nach dem Versailler Vertrag das Ingenieurbüro für Schiffbau in Den Haag leitete. Dr. Techel wurde 1924 nach Japan eingeladen und betreute den Bau zweier U-Boote,[20] und Kawasaki baute im Auftrag der japanischen Marine ab 1926 mehrere U-Boote, die später im Zweiten Weltkrieg zum Einsatz kamen. Insofern war die Verbindung zu den Streitkräften seines Landes nicht unabhängig vom wirtschaftlichen Interesse von Matsukatas Unternehmen. Wir sehen hier, welches zum Teil blutige Netzwerk zwischen Militär, Technik, Wirtschaft und Politik hinter der Ästhetik einer Kunstsammlung stehen kann.[21]

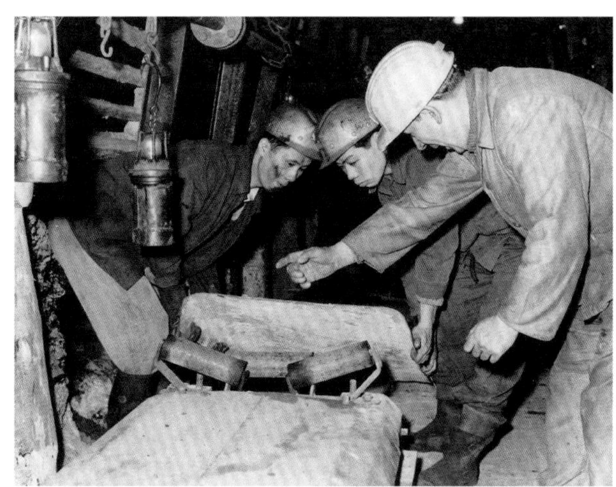

Abb. | Fig. 6
Japanische Bergleute mit Ausbilder |
Japanese miners with instructor,
Duisburg-Hamborn 1961

In 1956, the GHH fulfilled two contracts for mines in Japan.[22]

In parallel with this, there was close scholarly exchange between Germany and Japan in the field of mining studies. *Das Lehrbuch der Bergbaukunde* (The Mining Textbook) (1949) by Fritz Heise, Friedrich Herbst and Carl Hellmut Fritzsche was highly regarded in Japan and was translated into Japanese in 1955. As part of this exchange, Fritzsche, who was teaching at the Technische Hochschule Aachen, was invited to Japan and spent nearly six months there. The trade journal *Glückauf* (Good Luck) was also published in Japanese from 1952 onwards; and in 1961, the Japan Coal Association published the *Fachwörterbuch für Bergbau, Deutsch – Japanisch – Englisch* (Technical Terms for Mining: German – Japanese – English). The appendix of the book is particularly informative about Japan's relationship to the Ruhr, listing specific technical terms and information that refer to the region.[23] This intensive relationship was further reinforced when, around the same time, Japanese miners were sent to the Ruhr (fig. 6). This programme, based on an agreement between the German and Japanese governments in 1955, enabled 436 Japanese miners to come to Germany between 1957 and 1965 and work in the Ruhr region; thirty-two of them remained in Germany.[24] It is scarcely possible to imagine from today's perspective the foreignness of the environment that confronted the miners. There were none of the Japanese restaurants or Asian grocery shops that are taken for granted in Düsseldorf today. One of the miners from that time, Takehiko Kōguchi, offers an especially memorable account of the lack of Japanese food. He describes very vividly how he and two Japanese colleagues surreptitiously fished a carp from the pond in Gelsenkirchen's municipal park in order to eat it (raw) as sashimi.[25] Other reports testify to diverse intercultural exchanges between the German population and the Japanese miners.[26] The programme was, however, not concluded according to plan. From around 1961, many miners lost their jobs due to structural changes in the Japanese economy. Despite this, they showed no interest in the work abroad programme, probably because they were offered attractive alternative jobs in Japan thanks to the economic boom.[27]

The Matsukata Collection in the
Context of Industry and Politics

It may have become clear that the Matsukata Collection cannot be evaluated adequately without addressing the complex contemporary historical context of industry and politics. That impression only becomes stronger if one considers the circumstances in which its valuable collection survived the Second World War, when it was moved to a village near Paris in 1940 by Kōzaburō Hioki, who had accompanied Matsukata to Europe as his personal secretary, until it was confiscated by the French state in 1944.[28]

The historical events of the twentieth century crystallize in the Matsukata Collection, because Matsukata not only collected works of art with the capital he had acquired in the First World War but was also directly working in the armaments industry, so that he was more or less involved in the preparations for the Second World War. His art collection was in turn endangered by the events of that war and, according to Maha Harada, saved by a Japanese migrant in a French provincial village.[29] The paintings shown in this exhibition should not, therefore, be viewed independently of this history.

Japanisch-deutsche Beziehungen im Bergbau

Nach dem Zweiten Weltkrieg schien die Beziehung zwischen dem Ruhrgebiet und Japan zunächst abzubrechen. Japan war vom US-amerikanischen Militär besetzt und es war unklar, wie es mit der japanischen Industrie überhaupt weitergehen sollte. Die amerikanische Kultur dominierte zunehmend die nach der Niederlage des Zweiten Weltkriegs neu entstandene japanische Gesellschaft. Auch im Bereich der Bergbauindustrie waren es zunächst die USA, die Kooperationen anboten. Doch man erkannte auf japanischer Seite schnell, dass die Förderbedingungen für Steinkohle in den USA vollkommen andere waren als in Japan. Die Steinkohle musste dort nicht wie in Japan in der Tiefe gefördert werden, sodass die US-amerikanische Technologie für das Land ungeeignet war. Man wusste, dass beim Steinkohlebau im Ruhrgebiet ähnliche Bedingungen wie in Japan herrschten, sodass die Übernahme der dort eingesetzten Technologie sinnvoller erschien. So erhielt 1954 wieder die Gutehoffnungshütte den Auftrag, in der Stadt Tagawa als einem der Zentren des Steinkohlebaus in Nordkyūshū eine Schachtanlage für Steinkohle zu bauen. Auch im Jahr 1957 führte die Gutehoffnungshütte zwei Aufträge für Schachtanlagen in Japan aus.[22]

Parallel dazu bestand auf dem Gebiet der Bergbaukunde ein enger wissenschaftlicher Austausch zwischen Deutschland und Japan. *Das Lehrbuch der Bergbaukunde* (1949) von Fritz Heise, Friedrich Herbst und Carl Hellmut Fritzsche war auch in Japan hoch angesehen und wurde 1955 ins Japanische übersetzt. Im Rahmen dieses Austausches wurde der an der Technischen Hochschule Aachen tätige Fritzsche nach Japan eingeladen und hielt sich fast sechs Monate dort auf. Auch die Fachzeitschrift *Glückauf* wurde ab dem Jahr 1952 auf

Japanisch publiziert; und 1961 veröffentlichte die Japan Coal Association das *Fachwörterbuch für Bergbau. Deutsch-Japanisch-Englisch*. Der Anhang des Buches ist besonders aufschlussreich für die Beziehung Japans zum Ruhrgebiet. Dort werden spezifische, auf das Ruhrgebiet bezogene Fachausdrücke und Informationen aufgelistet.[23] Die intensive Beziehung wurde etwa zur gleichen Zeit durch die Entsendung japanischer Bergarbeiter an die Ruhr noch weiter verstärkt (Abb. 6). Dieses Programm, das zwischen der deutschen und der japanischen Regierung im Jahr 1955 beschlossen worden war, ermöglichte 436 japanischen Bergarbeitern, von denen 32 in Deutschland blieben, zwischen 1957 und 1965 nach Deutschland zu kommen und im Ruhrgebiet zu arbeiten.[24] Es ist aus heutiger Sicht kaum vorstellbar, mit welch einer fremden Umgebung diese Bergarbeiter damals konfrontiert waren. Es gab weder japanische Restaurants noch Lebensmittelläden, die heute in Düsseldorf so selbstverständlich sind. Besonders eindrücklich schildert einer der damaligen Bergarbeiter, Takehiko Kōguchi, den Mangel an japanischen Lebensmitteln. Er beschreibt sehr plastisch, wie er mit zwei japanischen Kollegen heimlich im Stadtpark Gelsenkirchens einen Karpfen aus dem Teich fischte, um ihn als *sashimi* (roh) zu essen.[25] Andere Berichte zeugen von vielfältigen interkulturellen Austauschbeziehungen zwischen der deutschen Bevölkerung und den japanischen Bergarbeitern.[26] Doch wurde das Programm nicht wie vorgesehen zu Ende geführt. Etwa ab 1961 verloren viele Bergarbeiter aufgrund des Strukturwandels der japanischen Wirtschaft ihre Arbeit. Dennoch interessierten sie sich nicht für das Entsendungsprogramm, weil ihnen wohl angesichts des Wirtschaftsaufschwungs attraktive alternative Arbeitsplätze innerhalb Japans angeboten wurden.[27]

1   On this, see the essay by Frances Fowle in the present volume, 74–91.

2   See, Victoria Weston, *Japanese Painting and National Identity: Okakura Tenshin and His Circle* (Ann Arbor, MI, 2003).

3   On these two terms, see, Keitarō Kondo, *Nihonga tanjō* (Tokyo, 2003).

4   See, the essays by Robert Maximilian Woitschützke and Yoshiyuki Yamana, 158–171, and Marie Yasunaga, 172–193, in the present volume.

5   The Shogun was the supreme prince of the shogunate, the Japanese military regime, until 1868.

6   See, Kazumichi Motozuna, 'Bakufu gunkan kaiyōmaru no yōmoku ni tsuite', *Techno Marine: Nihon zōsen gakkai shi*, no. 867 (2002), 341–44. This visit to Krupp occurred in the final years of the shogunate before the Meiji Restoration (1868) laid the groundwork for the emergence of the modern Japanese state.

7   See, Fujio Ishihashi, *Bakumatsu Kaiyōmaru* (Tokyo, 2013).

8   On Enomoto's life see, Ryūichirō Usui, *Enomoto Takeaki kara sekaishiga mieru* (Tokyo, 2005).

9   See, Ulrich Wattenberg, 'Die Iwakura-Mission in Preussen', in Gerhard Krebs (ed.), *Japan und Preussen*, Monographien aus dem Deutschen Institut für Japanstudien 32 (Munich, 2002), 103–24.

10 Kunitake Kume, *Tokumei zenken taishi: Bei ō kairan jikki*, vol. 3 (Tokyo, 1979), 292ff. For an account in English of the Iwakura mission see, Kunitake Kume, *Japan Rising: The Iwakura Embassy to the USA and Europe, 1871–73* (Cambridge, UK, 2002).

11 See, Gerhard Krebs, 'Japan und die Preussische Armee', in idem (ed.), *Japan und Preussen*, 125–44.

12 Michael Rauck, 'Preussisch-japanische Beziehungen auf wirtschaftlich-industriellem Gebiet', in ibid., 287–304.

13 See, Norikazu Shimizu, 'The Establishment of the State-Owned Yawata Steel Works: (1) The Integrated Steel Works That Promoted Japan's Industrialisation: When the Country Entered the Modern Industrial World as a Latecomer', *Kyushu kokusai daigaku keiei keizai ronshu* 16 February 2010, 109–45.

14 See, Hiroto Saigusa and Ken-ichi Iijima, *Nihon kindai seitetsu gijutsu hattatsushi: Yawata seitetsusho no kakuritsu katei* (Tokyo, 1957).

15 See, ibid.

16 On Matsukata's life, see the essay by Detmar Westhoff in the present volume, 350–361.

17 See, Nobuo Tajima, 'The Berlin-Tokyo Axis Reconsidered: From the Anti-Comintern Pact to the Plot to Assassinate Stalin', in Christian W,. Spang and Rolf Harald Wippich (eds.) *Japan-German Realtions, 1895–1945: War, Diplomacy and Public Opinion* (London and New York, 2006), 161–79.

18 On this, see p. 18 in the present volume.

19 Historisches Archiv Krupp, Essen, FAH 4 C 336, C 194 and WA 48-104. Information kindly provided by Historisches Archiv Krupp to Nadine Engel on 7 September 2020.

20 See, ibid.; according to Eberhard Rössler, Techel was already in Japan in 1920: Eberhard Rössler, 'Die deutschen UBoot-Konstruktionsbüros', in *Deutsches Schiffahrtsarchiv* 20 (1997), 297–340; on the engineering office for shipbuilding, see, Sebastian J. De Groot, *Ein Wolf im Schafspelz: Verdeckte deutsch-niederländische Rüstungsproduktion und die Firma IvS, 1922–1945* (Leiden and Paderborn, 2021).

21 On Matsukata's art collection, see, Akira Nakano, *Maboroshi no godai bijutsukan to meiji nojitsugyousha tachi* (Tokyo, 2018).

22 See, Sven Holst, 'Deutsch-japanische Kontakte: Die GHH, Japan und die Schachtanlage Ikari', in *OAG Notizen* (May 2016), 11–35, esp. 11–15.

23 Japan Coal Association, *Fachwörterbuch für Bergbau. Deutsch-Japanisch-Englisch* (Tokyo, 1961).

24 On this see, Hiromasa Mori, 'Japanische Bergleute in Deutschland', in Atsushi Kataoka et al. (eds.), *'Glückauf' auf Japanisch: Bergleute aus Japan im Ruhrgebiet* (Essen, 2012), 19–44.

25 See, Kōguchi, 'Erinnerungen an Westdeutschland', in ibid., 193–217.

26 See, Kataoka, *'Glückauf' auf Japanisch*.

27 See, Mori, 'Japanische Bergleute in Deutschland'.

28 See, Nakano, *Maboroshi no godai bijutsukan to meiji nojitsugyousha tachi*.

29 On Hioki see, Maha Harada, *Utsukushikinoroka monotachi no taburō* (Tokyo, 2019).

116

Die Sammlung Matsukata im Kontext
von Industrie und Politik

Es mag deutlich geworden sein, dass die Sammlung Matsukata ohne den komplexen zeithistorischen Kontext von Industrie und Politik kaum gebührend zu würdigen ist. Der Eindruck verstärkt sich, berücksichtigt man die Umstände, unter denen die wertvolle Sammlung die Zeit des Zweiten Weltkriegs überstand, von ihrer Auslagerung in ein Dorf nahe Paris im Jahr 1940 durch Kōzaburō Hioki, der Matsukata als persönlicher Sekretär nach Europa begleitet hatte, bis zu ihrer Beschlagnahmung durch den französischen Staat 1944.[28]

In der Sammlung Matsukatas kristallisieren sich die historischen Ereignisse des 20. Jahrhunderts. Denn Matsukata sammelte die Kunstwerke nicht nur mit dem im Ersten Weltkrieg gewonnenen Kapital, sondern er war direkt in der Rüstungsindustrie aktiv, womit er mehr oder weniger in die Vorbereitung des Zweiten Weltkriegs involviert war. Seine Kunstsammlung war wiederum durch das Kriegsgeschehen des Zweiten Weltkriegs gefährdet und wurde, nach der Interpretation von Maha Harada, durch einen Migranten aus Japan in einem französischen Provinzdorf gerettet.[29] Die Gemälde dieser Ausstellung sind daher nicht losgelöst von dieser historischen Verdichtung zu sehen.

1 Vgl. dazu den Beitrag von Frances Fowle in diesem Band, S. 74–91.

2 Vgl. Victoria Weston, *Japanese Painting and National Identity. Okakura Tenshin and His Circle*, Ann Arbor 2003.

3 Vgl. zu den beiden Bezeichnungen: Keitarō Kondo, *Nihonga tanjō*, Tokio 2003.

4 Vgl. die Beiträge von Robert Maximilian Woitschützke und Yoshiyuki Yamana, S. 158–171, und Marie Yasunaga, S. 172–193, in diesem Band.

5 Der Shogun war der oberste Fürst des japanischen Militärregimes Shogunat bis 1868.

6 Vgl. Kazumichi Motozuna, „Bakufu gunkan kaiyōmaru no yōmoku ni tsuite", in: *Techno Marine, Nihon zōsen gakkai shi*, 867, 2002, S. 341–344.

7 Vgl. Fujio Ishihashi, *Bakumatsu Kaiyōmaru*, Tokio 2013.

8 Vgl. zum Leben von Enomoto: Ryūichirō Usui, *Enomoto Takeaki kara sekaishiga mieru*, Tokio 2005.

9 Vgl. Ulrich Wattenberg, „Die Iwakura-Mission in Preußen", in: *Japan und Preußen*, hrsg. von Gerhard Krebs (*Monographien aus dem Deutschen Institut für Japanstudien*, 32), München 2002, S. 103–124.

10 Kunitake Kume, *Tokumei zenken taishi. Bei ō kairan jikki*, Bd. 3, Tokio 1979, S. 292 ff.

11 Vgl. Gerhard Krebs, „Japan und die Preußische Armee", in: *Japan und Preußen*, hrsg. von dems. (*Monographien aus dem Deutschen Institut für Japanstudien*, 32),

München 2002, S. 125–144.

12 Michael Rauck, „Preußisch-japanische Beziehungen auf wirtschaftlich-industriellem Gebiet", in: ebd., S. 287–304.

13 Vgl. Norikazu Shimizu, „The Establishment of the State-Owned Yawata Steel Works. (1) The Integrated Steel Works That Promoted Japan's Industrialisation. When the Country Entered the Modern Industrial World as a Latecomer", in: *Kyushu kokusai daigaku keiei keizai ronshu*, 16, 2, 2010, S. 109–145.

14 Vgl. Hiroto Saigusa und Ken-ichi Iijima, *Nihon kindai seitetsu gijutsu hattatsushi – Yawata seitetsusho no kakuritsu katei*, Tokio 1957.

15 Vgl. ebd.

16 Zum Leben Matsukatas vgl. den Beitrag von Detmar Westhoff in diesem Band, S. 350–361.

17 Vgl. Nobuo Tajima, „The Berlin-Tokyo Axis reconsidered. From the Anti-Comintern Pact to the Plot to Assassinate Stalin", in: *Japan-German Relation, 1895–1945. War, Diplomacy and Public Opinion*, hrsg. von Christian W. Spang und Rolf-Harald Wippich, London und New York 2006, S. 161–179.

18 Vgl. dazu S. 18.

19 Historisches Archiv Krupp. Essen, FAH 4 C 336, C 194 sowie WA 48/104. Freundliche Mitteilung des Historischen Archivs Krupp an Nadine Engel vom 7.9.2020.

20 Vgl. ebd.; nach Rössler war Techel bereits 1920 in Japan: Eberhard Rössler, „Die deutschen UBoot-Konstruktionsbüros", in: *Deutsches Schiffahrtsarchiv*, 20, 1997,

S. 297–340; vgl. zum Ingenieurbüro für Schiffbau: Sebastian J. De Groot, *Ein Wolf im Schafspelz. Verdeckte deutsch-niederländische Rüstungsproduktion und die Firma IvS 1922–1945*, Leiden und Paderborn 2021.

21 Vgl. zur Kunstsammlung Matsukatas: Akira Nakano, *Maboroshi no godai bijutsukan to meiji nojitsugyousha tachi*, Tokio 2018.

22 Vgl. Sven Holst, „Deutsch-japanische Kontakte – die GHH, Japan und die Schachtanlage Ikari", in: *OAG Notizen*, Mai 2016, S. 11–35, hier S. 11–15.

23 Japan Coal Association, *Fachwörterbuch für Bergbau. Deutsch-Japanisch-Englisch*, Tokio 1961.

24 Vgl. dazu: Hiromasa Mori, „Japanische Bergleute in Deutschland", in: *„Glückauf" auf Japanisch. Bergleute aus Japan im Ruhrgebiet*, hrsg. von Atsushi Kataoka u. a., Essen 2012, S. 19–44.

25 Vgl. Takehiko Kōguchi, „Erinnerungen an Westdeutschland", in: ebd., S. 193–217.

26 Vgl. *„Glückauf" auf Japanisch. Bergleute aus Japan im Ruhrgebiet*, hrsg. von Atsushi Kataoka u. a., Essen 2012.

27 Vgl. Hiromasa Mori, „Japanische Bergleute in Deutschland".

28 Vgl. Akira Nakano, *Maboroshi no godai bijutsukan to meiji nojitsugyousha tachi*.

29 Vgl. zu Hioki: Maha Harada, *Utsukushikinoroka monotachi no taburō*, Tokio 2019.

THE MATSUKATA COLLECTION, OR
A MUSEUM WITH 'NO BOUNDARY LINES'

Megumi Jingaoka

'No boundary lines'

'Western Art for Japan. Treasure House in Tokyo'
(*The Times,* 6 Oct. 1921); 'Matsukata Museum
Largest in World' (*American Art News*, 21 Jan. 1922);
'Gallery of Western Art, Tokio, Japan' (*The Building
News,* 9 June 1922) – From 1921 to 1922, the news-
papers and magazines of the West published a
steady stream of articles about 'Japanese shipbuild-
er' Kōjirō Matsukata's art collection and his plan
to build a museum named the 'Sheer Pleasure Arts
Pavilion' (the official English name of the Japanese
Kyōraku Bijutsukan). As reported by these articles,
plans called for the museum to be built on high
ground overlooking Tokyo Bay. As Marie Yasunaga
details in her essay in this volume, it would have
included a main wing with a comprehensive fine
art collection, a courtyard garden complete with
fountain, a separate wing for the applied arts,
an annex containing an art library and even a guest
house.

Kōjirō Matsukata became the first president
of the Kawasaki Dockyard Company in 1896 and
set about expanding the business while actively
adopting the latest technology from the West.
Recognizing that demand for oceangoing vessels
would soar during the First World War, he steered
the company toward mass production of stock
boats. In March 1916, he went to Europe and the
United States on business, seeking to arrange steel
imports and boat sales. It was during his time in
London before returning to Japan in November
1918 that he began his collection. On another visit
to Europe from 1921 to 1922, he expanded his
collection through further acquisitions, mostly in
Paris. However, after the Great Kantō Earthquake
of 1923 and Japan's financial panic of 1927, the
dockyard's business collapsed. Matsukata took

„Western Art For Japan. Treasure House in Tokyo"
(*Times*, 6. Oktober 1921), „Matsukata Museum
Largest in World" (*American Art News*, Januar 1922),
„Gallery of Western Art, Tokyo, Japan" (*The Building News*, 9. Juni 1922) … In den Jahren 1921/22
erschien in europäischen und amerikanischen
Zeitungen und Magazinen eine Reihe von Artikeln,
in denen die Kunstsammlung des japanischen
Schiffsbau-Unternehmers Kōjirō Matsukata sowie
seine Idee für ein Museum namens „Kyōraku
Bijutsukan" beschrieben wurden, das im Englischen
den Titel „Sheer Pleasure Arts Pavilion" trug und
sich im Deutschen frei mit „Museum für den gemeinsamen Genuss" übersetzen lässt. Diesen
Artikeln zufolge war die Museumsanlage auf einem
Hügel mit Blick auf die Bucht von Tokio als groß
angelegter Komplex geplant: Wie Marie Yasunaga
in ihrem Aufsatz in diesem Band ausführt, sollte sie
aus einem Hauptgebäude für die umfangreiche
Kunstsammlung, einem Innenhof mit Springbrun-
nen sowie einem Nebengebäude für die Abteilung
angewandter Kunst bestehen und außerdem eine
Kunstbibliothek und ein Gästehaus umfassen.

1896 wurde Kōjirō Matsukata der erste Firmenpräsident der Kawasaki-Werft und baute das Unternehmen aus, indem er engagiert neueste westliche Technologien einführte. Während des Ersten
Weltkriegs begann Matsukata mit der Massenproduktion sogenannter *stock boats*, nachdem
er frühzeitig den wachsenden Bedarf an Fracht-
schiffen erkannt hatte. Im März 1916 reiste er nach
Europa und in die USA, um Stahl zu importieren
und Schiffe zu verkaufen. Bis zu seiner Rückkehr in
seine Heimat im November 1918 hielt er sich in
London auf, wo er mit dem Erwerb von Kunstwerken begann. Bei seinem nächsten Europa-Besuch in
den Jahren 1921/22 erweiterte er seine Sammlung

119 Megumi Jingaoka

DIE SAMMLUNG MATSUKATA ODER
DAS MUSEUM OHNE GRENZEN

responsibility by resigning and the art he had collected was sold off to repay the company's debts.

Why did Matsukata, a man who had never showed any particular interest in art, suddenly start collecting it in the latter half of his life? The initial impetus is unknown, but we do know his reasons for continuing to buy artworks in the years that followed: 'What motivates me to buy up paintings is the conclusion, arrived at while wandering London to kill time, that art and industry are closely connected'.[1] For some reason, the newspaper chose the phrase 'TO KILL TIME' to print in large characters as a subhead, but the important point is Matsukata's motive: the fact that 'art and industry are closely connected'. By the time of this interview, Matsukata was already planning to build a museum for Western art and donate it to his country. He expected the art he collected in the West to become a new source of ideas for Japanese art and industry, and he explained this repeatedly when interviewed by reporters in Japan and around the world in the years to come. What he aimed to facilitate was not mere mechanical imitation but an understanding of Western psychology, as revealed in works of art, and the application of those principles to production and daily life. The application of art to industry was a challenge that had been addressed by the various Western nations in the modern period, and in Japan, too, a movement seeking protection and patronage for the arts through the establishment of public museums had been especially prominent since the beginning of the twentieth century, and Matsukata conceived of his museum within that context.

Kōjirō Matsukata was born in 1866 to a low-ranking samurai family in the Satsuma Domain (present-day Kagoshima Prefecture). Satsuma was one of the leaders in the movement that resulted in the Meiji Restoration which ended the Tokugawa Shōgunate, and Kōjirō's father, Masayoshi Matsukata, became a high-ranking official in the new government. In 1878, he was sent to France as vice president of administration for the Paris International Exposition. He later served in posts such as Minister of Finance and Prime Minister and was made a marquess in 1907. His children returned from being educated in the West to take up positions at the centre of Japanese business and politics. Kōjirō was no exception, having spent six years studying in the United States and then touring Europe before returning to Japan, and he continued to visit Europe and the United States even after becoming president of the Kawasaki Dockyard Company. With Japan hurriedly establishing a modern state in order to stand with the nations of the world, Kōjirō may have viewed contributing to these efforts as a social responsibility he was expected to fulfil as a matter of course, as much as, if not more than, other Japanese people of the time. The accession of the Taishō Emperor in 1912 ushered in the Taishō Era, which witnessed the spread of democratic ideals and the development of mass society. The Factory Law of 1911 was Japan's first labour protection law, but even ahead of its promulgation, Matsukata – who was well versed in the trends of the West – introduced systems at the dockyard evincing consideration for the education and welfare of employees.[2] He may have seen museums as 'proof of a mature society'.[3] Some argue that he also had international relations in mind, envisaging the museum as a place to entertain foreign guests among art from their native lands.[4]

In a 1922 interview with a London-based magazine, Matsukata said, 'I care nothing about your

durch Ankäufe überwiegend in Paris. Die Finanzkrise im Jahr 1927, die auf das Große Kantō-Erdbeben von 1923 folgte, führte allerdings zum Konkurs der Werft und zu Matsukatas Rücktritt als Firmenpräsident. Um seine Schulden zu tilgen, war er gezwungen, Teile seiner Sammlung zu veräußern.

Warum begann Matsukata, der nie ein besonderes Interesse an Kunst gezeigt hatte, in seiner zweiten Lebenshälfte plötzlich mit dem Sammeln von Kunst? Seine ursprüngliche Motivation bleibt unklar, aber seine Gründe für die Fortsetzung dieser Aktivitäten sind bekannt: In einem Interview mit der japanischen Zeitung *Tokyo Asahi Shimbun* vom 27. November 1918 erzählte Matsukata nach seiner Abreise aus London, dass er Streifzüge durch die Stadt unternommen habe, „um die Zeit totzuschlagen". Dabei sei ihm der enge Zusammenhang von angewandter Kunst und schönen Künsten bewusst geworden und er habe begonnen, Kunstwerke zu erwerben. Aus irgendeinem Grund wurde die Formulierung „um die Zeit totzuschlagen" in dem Artikel als zweite Überschrift fett gedruckt; wesentlich aber ist, dass Matsukata hier als wichtigstes Motiv für das Sammeln die enge Beziehung von bildender und angewandter Kunst bzw. Industrie nennt. Zu diesem Zeitpunkt hatte er bereits mit dem Gedanken gespielt, ein Museum für westliche Kunst zu gründen und es dem Staat zu vermachen. Seine Erwartung, dass die zusammengetragenen westlichen Artefakte der japanischen Kunst und Industrie neue Impulse geben würden, äußerte er auch später immer wieder gegenüber in- und ausländischen Berichterstatter:innen. Er bezweckte damit nicht, rein mechanische Reproduktion anzuregen, sondern wollte ein Verständnis für die in den Kunstwerken zum Ausdruck kommende westliche Psyche erreichen, sodass entsprechende Prinzipien dann in der

Produktion und im täglichen Leben auch in Japan Anwendung fänden. Die Zusammenführung von Kunst und Industrie war eine Aufgabe, die verschiedene westliche Nationen sich in dieser Zeit stellten, und auch in Japan gab es seit 1900 ausgeprägte Bestrebungen, öffentliche Museen zum Erhalt und zur Förderung der Künste einzurichten. Matsukatas Museumskonzept entwickelte sich in diesem Kontext.

Kōjirō Matsukata wurde 1866 als Nachkomme eines rangniedrigen Samurai-Geschlechts aus der Provinz Satsuma geboren, der heutigen Provinz Kagoshima. Die Lehnsherren von Satsuma, die Shimazu-Familie, führten maßgeblich die Bewegung an, aus der die Meiji-Restauration resultierte (sie beendete wiederum das Tokugawa-Shogunat), und Kōjirōs Vater Masayoshi Matsukata wurde ein hochrangiger Beamter in der neuen Regierung. 1878 wurde er als stellvertretender Verwaltungsdirektor zur Pariser Weltausstellung nach Frankreich entsandt. Später bekleidete er die hochrangigen Ämter des Finanzministers sowie des Premierminsters und erhielt 1907 einen Adelstitel. Seine Kinder absolvierten Auslandsstudien im Westen, bevor sie Schlüsselstellungen in wirtschaftlichen Kreisen besetzten. Kōjirō war hier keine Ausnahme. Er studierte sechs Jahre lang in den USA und bereiste Europa vor seiner Rückkehr nach Japan, wo er die Führung der Kawasaki-Werft übernahm. Auch danach hielt sich Kōjirō Matsukata mehrfach in Europa und den USA auf. Für sein Vaterland, das sich zu einem modernen Staat wandelte, um mit den übrigen Weltnationen Schritt zu halten, empfand er eine vielleicht sogar noch stärkere soziale Verpflichtung als die meisten seiner Zeitgenoss:innen während der Meiji-Periode. Die anschließende Taishō-Ära, die 1912 mit der Thronbesteigung des gleichnamigen Kaisers einsetzte, war eine Zeit, die von der Verbreitung demokratischer Ideen,

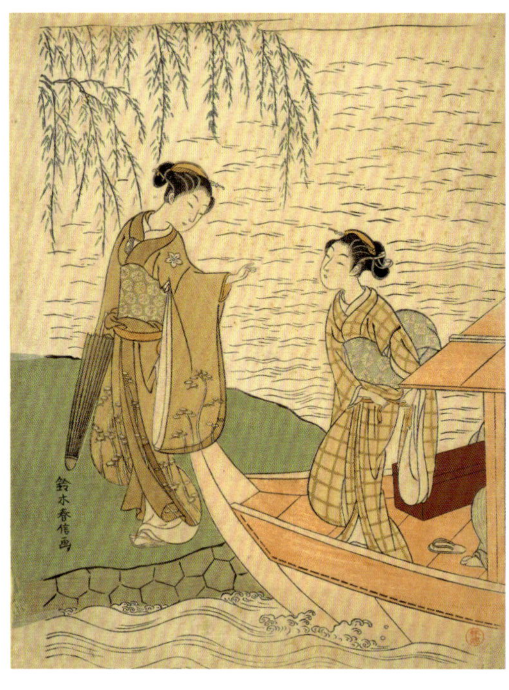

Abb. | Fig. 1
Harunobu Suzuki, *Beauties Alighting from a Boat*, ca. 1766, Tokyo National Museum. Ehemals Sammlung Matsukata | formerly Matsukata Collection

controversies over different schools of art; I buy examples of them all, for all are expressive of your psychology.'[5] Whether his use of 'schools' here referred only to countries and regions, or also included categories marked by controversies in art history such as Academism or modern art, we do not know. However, Matsukata would ultimately collect more than 3000 pieces of Western art, and his collection included not only examples of modern French art, such as Impressionist paintings and sculptures by Auguste Rodin, but also of works from a wide range of countries and regions, including England, Italy, Germany, the Netherlands, Scandinavia and the United States. Media represented include prints, drawings and even applied arts, and while most of the works were created in the nineteenth and early twentieth century, the collection also included some old masters.[6] The number of individual artists represented easily exceeded 600. There were more than 700 works by the English artist Frank Brangwyn, who advised Matsukata in his collecting activities, and his print works in particular pushed the numbers up. Even so, however, the sheer scale involved is startling for a collection assembled during a short period by a single person. Matsukata also bought back around 8000 *ukiyo-e* (woodblock prints) from the collection of Parisian jeweller Henri Vever 'for Japan' (figs. 1, 2; pp. 256–261). He was highly appreciative of how influential *ukiyo-e* had been on Western art, and if he was considering exhibiting these works in his museum as well, his intention may have been to encourage greater understanding and appreciation among the Japanese people of their own country's art.

The fall of the French franc after the First World War, combined with the strong Japanese yen, were particularly useful to Matsukata as he collected

der zunehmenden Industrialisierung und dem damit einhergehenden Wandel Japans zu einer modernen Industrienation geprägt war. Matsukata, der mit westlichen Entwicklungen vertraut war, führte in seiner Werft ein System ein, mit dem die Ausbildung und das Wohlergehen der Arbeiter:innen geregelt wurden – ein bahnbrechender Vorreiter des Fabrikgesetzes von 1911, dem ersten Arbeitsgesetz in Japan.[1] Museen mögen für ihn „der Beweis für eine reife Gesellschaft"[2] gewesen sein. Noriko Minato argumentiert darüber hinaus, dass er auch die internationalen Beziehungen fördern wollte, indem er sein Museum als Ort plante, an dem auswärtige Gäste inmitten der Kunst ihrer Länder unterhalten wurden.[3]

In einem Interview mit einer Londoner Zeitschrift im Jahr 1922 betonte er: „Ich habe kein Interesse an kontroversen Streitgesprächen über verschiedene Schulen, sondern ich erwerbe exemplarische Exponate aller Stilrichtungen. Es sind schließlich alles Manifestationen Ihrer [d.h. der europäischen] Psyche."[4] Dabei ist nicht klar, ob sich der Begriff „Schulen" lokal auf ein Land oder ein Gebiet bezog oder auf kunsthistorisch umstrittene Themen wie etwa den Konflikt zwischen Akademismus und Moderne. Letztendlich umfasste Matsukatas Sammlung über 3000 Werke westlicher Kunst, und zwar nicht nur moderne französische, wie impressionistische Gemälde und Skulpturen von Auguste Rodin, sondern auch Exponate aus vielen anderen Ländern und Regionen wie Großbritannien, Italien, Deutschland, den Niederlanden, Skandinavien und den USA. Die breite Palette reicht von der Malerei über die Grafik bis zur angewandten Kunst, und obwohl die meisten Objekte aus dem 19. und frühen 20. Jahrhundert stammen, sind auch Werke alter Meister darunter.[5] Die Zahl der vertretenen Künstler:innen liegt weit über 600.

Der englische Maler Frank Brangwyn beriet Matsukata beim Aufbau des Bestandes, der schnell eine bemerkenswerte Größe für eine Privatsammlung erreichte. Brangwyn selbst war mit über 700 Werken vertreten, darunter eine Vielzahl von Druckgrafiken. Matsukata kaufte auch etwa 8000 *ukiyo-e* aus der Sammlung des Pariser Juweliers Henri Vever 1918 „für Japan" zurück (Abb. 1, 2; S. 256–261). Er hatte große Achtung vor dem Einfluss des japanischen Holzschnitts auf die westliche Kunst. Mit der Präsentation dieser Werke in seinem Museum wollte er vermutlich seine Landsleute dazu anregen, die künstlerische Tradition Japans zu verstehen und wertzuschätzen.

Insbesondere beim Aufbau seiner Sammlung französischer Kunst profitierte Matsukata vom Kursverfall des Franc nach dem Ersten Weltkrieg und der gleichzeitigen Stärke des Yen. Er sprach fließend Englisch und war ausreichend gebildet, um sich über alles, von der antiken Skulptur bis zur modernen Kunst, verständigen zu können.[6] Obwohl aus einem seiner Briefe hervorgeht, dass er sich „nach den neuesten Tendenzen in der französischen Kunst" sehnte,[7] gab er sich öffentlich nicht als Kunstliebhaber, sondern ging bei der Auswahl seiner Werke rational vor und überließ die Entscheidungen überwiegend dem fachlichen Urteil von Expert:innen.

Matsukatas Sammlung und seine Museumspläne wurden in der damaligen europäischen Presse einerseits mit Unbehagen „als Ausdruck militärischer und kommerzieller Ambitionen" von Seiten Japans aufgefasst, andererseits aber erkannte man an, dass „nie zuvor eine Sammlung in dieser Größenordnung zusammengestellt wurde, deren Auswahlkriterien so wenig von Vorurteilen und Tendenzen geprägt" seien.[8] Wir können uns nur vorstellen, wie Matsukatas Museum, das letztlich nicht gebaut wurde, in vollendeter Form ausge-

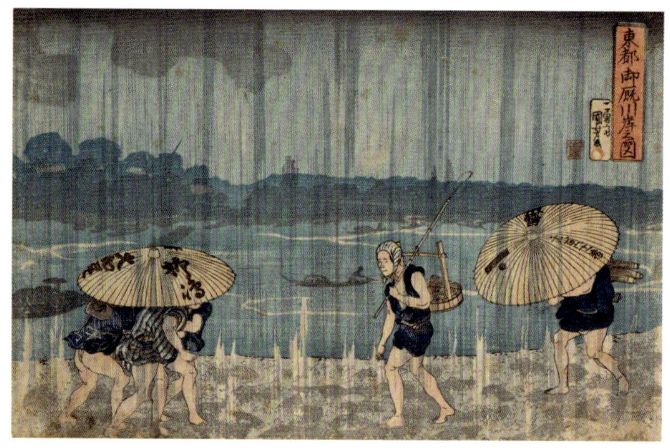

Abb. | Fig. 2
Kuniyoshi Utagawa, *View of the Umaya
River Bank*, aus der Serie | from the series
The Eastern Capital, 1830er-Jahre | 1830s,
Tokyo National Museum. Ehemals Sammlung
Matsukata | formerly Matsukata Collection

French art in particular. He had the education
and cultivation to discuss everything from ancient
sculpture to modern art in fluent English,[7] and
while he did leave behind one letter expressing
wistful longing for 'the latest artistic movements of
France',[8] he publicly denied being an art lover as
such, and took a rational approach to selecting his
works, leaving most of the decisions to specialists.

Some in the Western media at the time viewed
Matsukata's collection and his plans for a museum
as an alarming indicator of Japan's military and
commercial ambitions. Some offered a more
positive evaluation, with praise such as, 'No other
collection in the world has been planned on so
comprehensive a scale, nor with so little prejudice
or predilection'.[9] Since the museum was never
actually built, we can only imagine the final form
it might have taken, but Matsukata made his inten-
tions clear in response to media inquiries: 'It will
know no boundary lines, but will comprise works
of art expressive of the civilizations of the Western
peoples beginning three thousand years before
Christ and coming down to the present day'.[10]
As the word *kyōraku* in the Japanese name given
to the museum means 'enjoy together,' we may
perhaps assume it was to be a place with 'no
boundary lines' not just between viewers but also
between artworks – a space that gathered together works from every geographical region, historical age and artistic genre.

Brangwyn and the
Sheer Pleasure Arts Pavilion

Memoranda kept by Tomoji Okada at the London
branch of Yamanaka & Co., which handled the
shipping of Matsukata's works to Japan, allow
some insight into which London art dealers Matsukata had contact with during his 1916–18 stay in
Europe, listing names such as the Leggatt Brothers,
W. Lawson Peacock, and the Fine Art Society
(p. 217). The purchase records for some works
can also be found in the archives of some art
dealers. Matsukata was also fond of visiting artists
in their studios to buy from them directly, and
his name appears in biographies and memoirs of
contemporary artists like Walter Sickert, Augustus
John, Alfred Munnings and William Wyllie.

However, Matsukata's most important relationship in this context was with Frank Brangwyn.[11]
Born in Belgium in 1867, Brangwyn was the son of
an English architect. In his mid-teens, he entered
the William Morris workshop. In 1895, the frieze
he painted on the exterior wall of Siegfried Bing's
shop in Paris, *La Maison de l'Art nouveau,* led to
a series of commissions for murals and decorative
panels elsewhere, and his work received increasing acclaim (fig. 3). Brangwyn was largely forgotten
in the context of modernism, only recently enjoy-
ing a reappraisal, but when Matsukata met him –
in 1916, when he painted *Portrait of Mr. Kojiro
Matsukata* (p. 197) – he was viewed as one of the
leading lights of the British art world. The fact that
many of his works depicted the sea, ships, and

sehen haben könnte, aber der Presse gegenüber betonte er, dass „es keine Grenzen kennen und Kunstwerke beherbergen würde, die als Ausdruck der Zivilisation westlicher Völker von der Antike 3000 v. Chr. bis in die heutige Moderne gelten mögen."[9] Bedeutet „kyōraku" gemeinsam genießen, so sollte Matsukatas gleichnamiges Museum ein Ort sein, an dem Kunstwerke aus allen Regionen, Epochen und Gattungen zusammengetragen würden, wo nicht nur für die Betrachter:innen jegliche Grenze aufgehoben sein sollte, sondern auch für die Werke selbst.

Brangwyn und der
Sheer Pleasure Arts Pavilion

Dank einer Notiz von Tomoji Okada von der Londoner Filiale des Yamanaka-Unternehmens, das für die Verschiffung der von Matsukata angekauften Werke nach Japan zuständig war, sind uns die Namen der Londoner Kunsthändler:innen bekannt, mit denen der Sammler während seines Europa-Aufenthalts von 1916 bis 1918 zu tun hatte, darunter Leggatt, Lawson-Peacock und die Fine Art Society (S. 217). Die Kaufbelege eines Teils der Werke sind in den Archiven dieser Kunsthandlungen einsehbar. Matsukata suchte Künstler:innen für seine Ankäufe auch gern persönlich in ihren Ateliers auf, sodass sein Name in den Biografien und Memoiren einiger zeitgenössischer Maler:innen wie Walter Sickert, Augustus John, Alfred Munnings und William Wyllie Erwähnung findet.

Am wichtigsten war jedoch seine Bekanntschaft mit Frank Brangwyn.[10] Brangwyn wurde 1867 in Belgien als Sohn eines englischen Architekten geboren. Nach der Rückkehr der Familie nach England ging er als Jugendlicher bei William Morris als Glaser in die Lehre. 1895 beauftragte ihn der Pariser Kunsthändler Siegfried Bing, das Äußere

seiner Galerie La Maison de l'Art nouveau zu gestalten, was zu einer Reihe weiterer Aufträge führte (Abb. 3). Mit großflächigen Wandmalereien und Wanddekorationen an vielen Orten machte er sich schon bald einen Namen. Im Kontext der Moderne ist Brangwyn in Vergessenheit geraten und erst in jüngster Zeit wiederentdeckt worden. Als er jedoch Matsukatas Bekanntschaft machte und ihn porträtierte (ca. 1916; S. 197), galt er als einer der führenden Köpfe der damaligen britischen Kunstszene. Einer der Gründe für Matsukatas Faszination für seine Bilder mag gewesen sein, dass Brangwyn häufig Sujets wie Meer, Schiffe und Hafenarbeiter für seine Werke wählte. Darüber hinaus unterhielt der Künstler enge Beziehungen nach Japan. Zu seinen Schüler:innen gehörte Chuji Kurihara und Brangwyn war ein alter Freund von Shōsaku Matsukata, Kōjirōs älterem Bruder, der als Diplomat tätig und ein bekannter Kunstliebhaber war. Es heißt, dass Kōjirō den englischen Künstler auf Anraten seines Bruders aufgesucht hatte.[11] Fortan verließ sich Kōjirō auf Brangwyn beim Erwerb von Bildern auch anderer Künstler:innen, ließ sich durch ihn vertreten und beauftragte ihn sogar mit dem Entwurf seines geplanten Museums.

Vermutlich entstand die Idee für das Museum ziemlich bald nach ihrer ersten Begegnung.[12] Brangwyns Assistent Frank Alford schrieb am 12. Januar 1921 über Matsukatas Museumspläne in sein Tagebuch: „Im Sommer 1918 begann ich, die halb fertigen Skizzen zu bearbeiten, die dann im September nach Japan geschickt wurden. Mehr als ein Jahr später, im November 1919, wurden sie mit Matsukatas Zustimmung wieder an uns zurückgegeben."[13] Im August 1918, als Matsukata nach einem zweijährigen Auslandsaufenthalt seine Heimreise antrat, waren die Entwürfe also „halb fertig". Nachdem Brangwyns Lehrlinge sie bearbeitet hatten, wurden sie im September nach Japan

dock workers may also have endeared him to Matsukata. Brangwyn had deep connections to Japan, as well. The artist Chūji Kurihara was one of his pupils, and he was an old friend of Shōsaku Matsukata, Kōjirō's diplomat older brother and a well-known art lover. In fact, Kōjirō is said to have first visited Brangwyn's house at Shōsaku's recommendation.[12] Matsukata put his trust in Brangwyn, enlisting him to act as his agent in selling paintings and buying work by other artists, and ultimately even asking him to design the planned museum in Japan.

Conceptual work on the museum is believed to have begun not long after the two first met.[13] Brangwyn's assistant Frank Alford's diary entry for 12 January 1921, includes the following comments about the matter: 'when I commenced the semi-finished drawings in Summer 1918 they were posted to Japan in September and over one year afterwards were returned from Japan in November 1919 bearing Mr Matsukata's approval.'[14] Thus, the sketches were 'semi-finished' by August 1918, as Matsukata was preparing to end his two-year sojourn and return to Japan, and then sent in September after Brangwyn's students worked on them further. Matsukata left London at the end of August and arrived in Japan in November after passing through the United States.

Exactly why it took a full year for the plans to be returned is unclear, but we do know that the art that Matsukata purchased began arriving from London in June 1919. Gatherings were held at the Tokyo residence of Masayoshi Matsukata, Kōjirō's father, to view these works on numerous occasions, with key figures in finance and politics, artists, and various other luminaries in attendance.[15] For his part, Kōjirō must have found his hands utterly full upon returning to his company after such a long absence. When the First World War ended in October 1918, the Kawasaki Dockyard Company was left with a surplus of unsold stock. To put these vessels to use, Kōjirō established the *Kawasaki Kisen Kaisha,* Ltd. (Kawasaki Steamship Company) in April 1919 and helped establish the *Kokusai Kisen Kaisha* (International Steamship Company) in July of the same year, aiming to compete with the Western powers' cargo trade. Meanwhile, amid a rash of labour disputes at various locations around Japan, negotiations between the dockyard and its workers resulted in the September 1919 announcement of new conditions for labour that included Japan's first eight-hour day, earning it a lasting place in Japanese labour history.

Perhaps finally able to take some time away from work, on 28 November 1919, Matsukata gathered a small group at his father's residence in Tokyo for a conference on the plans for the Sheer Pleasure Arts Pavilion.[16] As well as members of the Matsukata family and Shōsaku's old friend, the painter Seiki Kuroda, the attendees included British studio potter Bernard Leach, who was using a residence provided by Kuroda as a studio; portrait painter Kazunori Ishibashi, recently returned from London for the first time in fifteen years, and Kaneo Nanjō of Mitsui & Co.[17], a well-known art collector also recently returned from London; and Shintarō Ōe, an architect at the construction department at Meiji Jingu shrine. The choice to invite Kuroda makes sense not only given his relationship to the Matsukata family and status within the art world, but also because he was chairman of the *Kokumin Bijutsu Kyōkai* (National Society of Art), for which the importance of establishing public art museums was a fundamental tenet.[18] Leach's participation was presumably related to his having learned etching from Brangwyn at the London School of

geschickt. Matsukata verließ London im August und kehrte über die USA im November nach Japan zurück.

Es ist nicht geklärt, weshalb es über ein Jahr dauerte, bis die Zeichnungen wieder nach London gelangten, bekannt ist jedoch, dass seit Juni 1919 in Japan die Kunst eintraf, die Matsukata in London zu kaufen begonnen hatte. Auf dem Tokioter Anwesen von Matsukatas Vater Masayoshi fanden mehrfach Veranstaltungen statt, um diese Werke zu präsentieren; eingeladen waren Schlüsselfiguren aus Politik und Finanzwelt, Künstler:innen und andere angesehene Persönlichkeiten.[14] Es ist zu vermuten, dass Kōjirō Matsukata nach seiner langen Abwesenheit in der Firmenzentrale geschäftlich viel zu tun hatte. Als Reaktion auf das Ende des Ersten Weltkriegs im Oktober 1918 wurde im April 1919 die Kawasaki Kisen Kaisha Ltd. (Kawasaki Dampfschifffahrtsgesellschaft) gegründet, um den unverkauften Bestand an Schiffen der Werft zu nutzen. Im Juli des gleichen Jahres beteiligte sich Matsukata an der Gründung der Kokusai Kisen Kaisha Ltd. (Internationale Dampfschifffahrtsgesellschaft), um mit dem Frachtverkehr der Westmächte zu konkurrieren. Außerdem erhielt er besondere Anerkennung in der japanischen Arbeiterbewegung in einer Zeit heftiger Streiks, als er im September 1919 bei einer Verhandlung auf einer Werft neue Arbeitsbedingungen ankündigte und erstmals in Japan den Acht-Stunden-Tag einführte.

Am 28. November 1919 versammelte Matsukata während einer Geschäftspause in der Tokioter Residenz des Vaters eine kleine Gruppe von Leuten, um seine Pläne für den Sheer Pleasure Arts Pavilion zu erörtern.[15] Neben Mitgliedern der Familie Matsukata und Shōsakus altem Freund, dem Maler Seiki Kuroda, waren auch der britische Keramiker Bernard Leach anwesend, der eine von Kuroda zur Verfügung gestellte Wohnung als Atelier nutzte; außerdem der Porträtmaler Kazunori Ishibashi und der Kunstsammler Kaneo Nanjō von Mitsui & Co.[16] – beide soeben aus London zurückgekehrt – sowie der Architekt Shintarō Ōe von der Bauleitung des Meiji-Jingū-Schreins. Kuroda war nicht nur wegen seiner Verbindungen zur Familie Matsukata und seiner Position in der Kunstwelt eingeladen, sondern auch wegen seiner Führungsrolle als Präsident der Kokumin Bijutsu Kyōkai (Nationale Gesellschaft für Kunst), die sich die Gründung öffentlicher Kunsteinrichtungen auf die Fahnen geschrieben hatte.[17] Leachs Teilnahme mochte darauf zurückzuführen sein, dass er aus England stammte und bei Brangwyn an der London School of Art die Radiertechnik gelernt hatte.[18] Ishibashi assistierte Matsukata beim Ankauf von Kunstwerken und hatte im Juni 1918 eine Ausstellung zu Wohltätigkeitszwecken in Tokio veranstaltet, die neben anderen Werken 104 Radierungen von Brangwyn umfasste. Nanjō hatte beim Transport der Kunstwerke für diese Ausstellung geholfen.[19] Beide kannten also Brangwyn und die Situation in Europa. Ōe, bekannt für seine Mitwirkung bei der Restaurierung des Nikkō-Tōshōgu-Schreins, war auch der Architekt der Schatzkammer des Meiji-Jingū-Schreins (vollendet 1920), eines der ersten vollständig aus Stahlbeton konstruierten Bauten im japanischen Stil, die erdbebensicher und feuerfest waren.

Die Skizzen und Entwürfe für Matsukatas Museum wurden nach eingehender Prüfung durch dieses Expertengremium nach London zurückgeschickt. Ob die Planfassungen sich erhalten haben, ist nicht bekannt, aber es haben sich mehrere Entwürfe gefunden, die im Zusammenhang mit dem Sheer Pleasure Arts Pavilion stehen; zwei von ihnen befinden sich nun in der Sammlung des National Museum of Western Art (S. 20, 243). Kürzlich ist darüber hinaus eine großformatige Zeich-

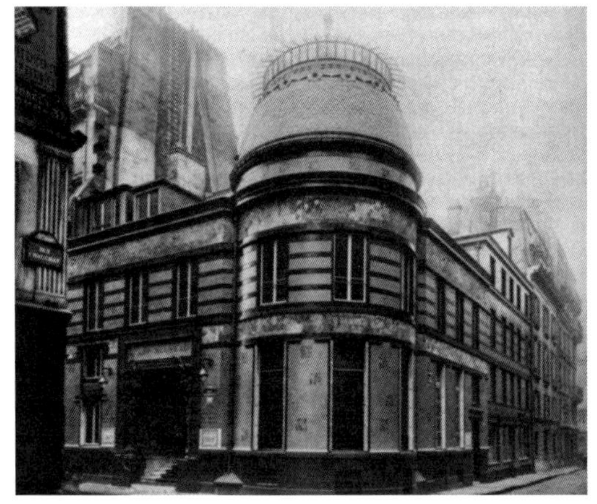

Abb. | Fig. 3
Frank Brangwyn, Fries auf der Außenwand
von | frieze on the exterior wall of La Maison
de l'Art nouveau, Paris, 1895

128

Arts, as well as his identity as a British artist.[19] Ishibashi had not only assisted Matsukata with his collecting, in June 1918 he had also organized a charity exhibition of 104 of Brangwyn's etchings, among other artworks. Meanwhile, Nanjō had assisted with shipping the works for this exhibition.[20] Both men were acquainted with Brangwyn and knowledgeable about current circumstances in Europe. As for Ōe, known for overseeing repairs to Nikkō Tōshōgū shrine, he was the architect of the Meiji Jingū treasure hall. Under construction at the time, the treasure hall is considered one of the earliest examples of Japanese-style architecture executed in ferro-concrete throughout for resistance to earthquake and fire.

After scrutiny by this panel of specialists in Japan, the plans were sent back to London. Whether this version of the plans is still extant somewhere is unknown, but multiple sketches relating to the Sheer Pleasure Arts Pavilion have been found, and two of these are now in the collection of the National Museum of Western Art (pp. 20, 243). We have also recently learned that Tomita Kumasaku, head of Yamanaka & Co.'s London branch, was in possession of a large drawing. Alford's mention of 'November 1919' likely refers to the 28 November date of the conference at which the plans were officially approved.

The Turn to French Art

Alford's diary entry for 12 January 1921, goes on to note that, although the plans were returned from Matsukata, '[s]ince that date comparatively little has been done to the work except details as designs for the fountain, walls, and doorways. The trouble Matsukata faced with is the storing the large number of pictures he has bought since the gallery idea emanated.' Indeed, from 1919 to 1920, more than 1000 works were sent from London to Japan. Works not sent to Japan due to lack of storage space or issues with customs law were stored in the London Pantechnicon, as were the works bought after that. These works were lost in the Pantechnicon fire in 1939, and a detailed accounting of them was made only in recent years.[21] This portion of the collection included over 900 individual pieces. Like the works that were sent to Japan, they were chiefly British art. As has been suspected, most were oils by painters with whom Matsukata enjoyed cordial relations, and important works by Brangwyn accounted for half of these, including Brangwyn's paintings, friezes, and the bedroom ensemble for the villa of the Edmund J. Davis couple (fig. 4). During his stay in London, starting in late 1917, Matsukata had contacted Léonce Bénédite, hoping to purchase sculptures by Rodin. Bénédite was director of the Musée du Luxembourg in Paris, and at that time hard at work on preparing to open the Musée Rodin. The two signed their first contract in Paris in August 1918, and this proved a turning point, clearing the way

nung im Nachlass von Tomita Kumasaku, dem Londoner Filialleiter des Kunsthandels Yamanaka & Co., bekannt geworden. Alfords Erwähnung des „November 1919" bezieht sich vermutlich auf die Besprechungsrunde vom 28. November des gleichen Jahres, bei der die Pläne mit Matsukatas Vermerk „Genehmigt" versehen wurden.

Die Hinwendung zur französischen Kunst

In Alfords Tagebucheintrag vom 12. Januar 1921 heißt es weiter: „Seitdem die Pläne von Matsukata an uns zurückgeschickt wurden, hat sich daran – abgesehen vom Brunnen, den Wänden und den Zugängen – nicht viel verändert. Das Problem für Matsukata ist die Lagerung der immensen Anzahl von Objekten, die er seit der Planung der Gemäldegalerie erworben hat."

Tatsächlich wurden in den Jahren 1919/20 mehr als 1000 Werke aus London nach Japan verschifft. Hinzu kamen die Arbeiten, die im Londoner Pantechnicon zwischengelagert wurden, weil ihr Versand aufgrund von Platzmangel und Zollbestimmungen aufgeschoben werden musste, wie auch später gekaufte Objekte. 1939 wurden diese Werke bei einem Brand im Pantechnicon zerstört, erst kürzlich entdeckte man die Inventarliste: [20] Der Bestand umfasste über 900 Einzelwerke; ebenso wie bei den in Japan eingetroffenen Werken handelte es sich vorwiegend um britische Kunst. Wie bereits zuvor vermutet waren es vor allem Ölgemälde von Künstler:innen, die Matsukata nahestanden, die Hälfte davon bedeutende Arbeiten

von Brangwyn, etwa das Schlafzimmer-Ensemble für die Villa des Ehepaares Edmund J. Davis (Abb. 4).

Schon während seines Aufenthalts in London gegen Ende des Jahres 1917 hatte Matsukata für den Erwerb von Rodin-Skulpturen Kontakt zu Léonce Bénédite, dem damaligen Direktor des Musée du Luxembourg in Paris, aufgenommen, als dieser gerade die Eröffnung des Rodin-Museums vorbereitete. Im August 1918 unterzeichneten die beiden einen ersten Vertrag, was sich als Wendepunkt erwies und Matsukata den Weg für das Sammeln französischer Kunst, insbesondere in Paris, ebnete. Matsukata erteilte Bénédite nicht nur einen Großauftrag zum Erwerb von Bronzegüssen von Rodins Hauptwerken – darunter auch die *porte de l'enfer (Das Höllentor;* Abb. 5) –, sondern betraute ihn auch mit dem Ankauf von Werken anderer französischer Künstler:innen. Das Musée Rodin wurde zum Aufbewahrungsort der meist in Paris erworbenen Werke.[21] Bénédite besaß ein ausgezeichnetes Gespür für die internationale Kunst seiner Zeit, was sich auch in seinen zahlreichen Schriften und der Sammlungsstrategie des Musée du Luxembourg widerspiegelte.[22] In Anbetracht von Matsukatas Plänen für sein Museum ist es gut vorstellbar, dass die beiden Männer eine gemeinsame Basis fanden. Aus Bénédites Schriftverkehr, aufbewahrt im Archiv des Pariser Institut national d'histoire de l'art, geht hervor, dass er nicht nur mit dem Erwerb von Kunstwerken für Matsukata betraut war, sondern auch bereits einen Sammlungskatalog für dessen zukünftiges Museum vorbereitete.

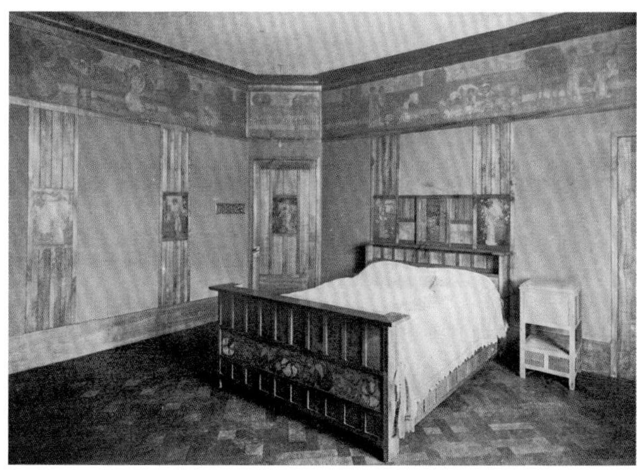

Abb. | Fig. 4
Frank Brangwyn, Schlafzimmer für |
bedroom for Mr. and Ms. Edmund Davis,
London, 1899–1900, derzeitiger Standort
unbekannt (wahrscheinlich zerstört) | current
location unknown (probably destroyed)

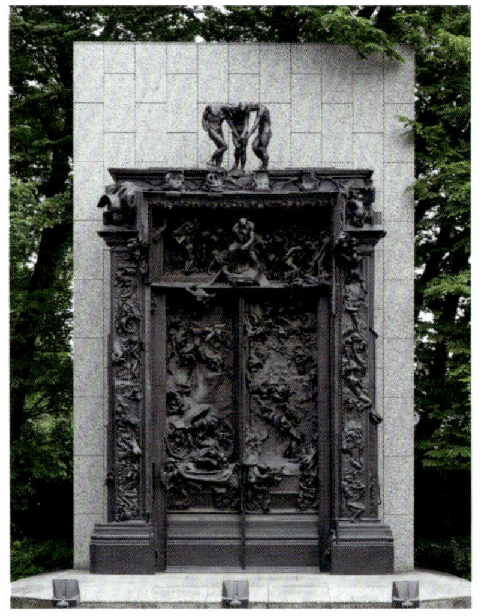

Abb. | Fig. 5
Auguste Rodin, *La porte de l'enfer,*
1880–1890/1917 (Guss | cast: 1930–1933),
The National Museum of Western Art, Tokyo.
Sammlung Matsukata | Matsukata Collection

for Matsukata to begin collecting French art, particularly in Paris. Not only did Matsukata place significant orders with Bénédite for bronzes of Rodin's major works, including *La porte de l'enfer* (*The Gates of Hell*; fig 5), he also engaged his services as an intermediary for purchasing the works of other French artists. These works, purchased mostly in Paris, would then be stored at the Musée Rodin.[22] Bénédite strove to see the art of his time from an international perspective, as is evident from his many writings and the acquisition policies of the Musée du Luxembourg.[23] Given Matsukata's plans for his museum, it is not difficult to imagine the two men finding common ground. The materials on Bénédite stored at the Institut national d'histoire de l'art in Paris reveal that he was preparing a catalogue for the proposed museum as well as purchasing works on Matsukata's behalf.

In April 1921, Matsukata departed Japan once more to tour the West in his role as a company president. He returned early the following year, having purchased a great number of important works of modern art during his sojourn. He enlisted various Japanese people to accompany him in September and October, and the diaries of Eisaku Wada, a painter staying in Paris at the time, describe Matsukata visiting important Parisian galleries such as the Galerie Durand-Ruel, M. Knoedler & Co., and the Galerie Paul Rosenberg.[24] Along with these detailed records of the galleries he toured, the artworks he viewed, and his companions on these outings, purchase records can also be found in the archives of individual galleries and the letters

and accounting documents stored by Bénédite. Matsukata also visited Belgium, Germany, and Scandinavia in August, purchasing modern French art and other works by artists such as Edvard Munch from sources including Ernst Cassirer, the Galerie van Diemen, and the Thannhauser Galleries. In Berlin he obtained tapestries said to have been sold off by 'former German royalty' (fig. 6).[25] According to the *History of Kawasaki Heavy Industries, Ltd.,* for this visit to Europe, Matsukata was also on a secret mission for the Japanese navy to bring back information about construction techniques for German submarines, and in fact did obtain plans for submarines.[26] This story has led some to suggest that Matsukata's ostentatious buying spree in the continent's galleries was partly to camouflage for this secret mission, and there are many tales, unverifiable but rich in adventurous fantasy, of him slipping submarine plans in between paintings to smuggle them out of Berlin.

Matsukata's acquisition of works by Monet were of great interest to contemporary observers. It is clear that he was intent on obtaining these paintings: as early as 1920, before even arriving in Europe, he began negotiating with the artist through intermediaries like Bénédite and Sanji Kuroki, the husband of Matsukata's niece, who was living in Paris at the time. He also enlisted the help of painters resident in Paris, such as Torajirō Kojima and Toyosaku Saitō, to assist in his careful preparations.[27] After arriving in Europe in 1921, Matsukata visited Monet's studio on at least two occasions, and presumably decided which pieces to buy

131

Im April 1921 brach Matsukata erneut zu einer Geschäftsreise nach Europa auf, in deren Verlauf er zahlreiche bedeutende moderne Kunstwerke erwarb, bevor er Anfang des folgenden Jahres wieder in seine Heimat zurückkehrte. Der Maler Eisaku Wada, der sich zeitgleich in Paris aufhielt, berichtet in seinem Tagebuch ausführlich über Matsukatas Besuche von Händler:innen wie Durand-Ruel, Knoedler und Paul Rosenberg in Begleitung mehrerer japanischer Vermittler: innen im September und Oktober 1921.[23] Die Aufzeichnungen enthalten detaillierte Angaben zu den Galerien, den besichtigten Werken und den Namen der Begleiter:innen. Belege für die Käufe befinden sich in den Archiven der einzelnen Kunsthandlungen sowie in den Briefen und Geschäftsunterlagen, die Bénédite aufbewahrte.

Schon im August war Matsukata nach Belgien, Deutschland und Skandinavien gereist, wo er etwa in den Galerien von Cassirer, van Diemen und Thannhauser moderne französische Gemälde sowie unter anderem Werke von Edvard Munch erwarb. In Berlin soll er Wandteppiche der „ehemaligen deutschen Königsfamilie" erstanden haben (Abb. 6).[24] Laut der Firmengeschichte von Kawasaki Heavy Industries Ltd. soll Matsukata von der japanischen Marine den geheimen Auftrag erhalten haben, während seiner Reise Informationen zur deutschen U-Boot-Technologie nach Japan zu schleusen. Tatsächlich gelangten derartige Baupläne in seinen Besitz.[25] Dies hat Spekulationen beflügelt, dass Matsukatas auffällige Kunsterwerbungen zur Tarnung seiner geheimen Mission gedient haben sollen, und eine ganze Reihe von nicht bestätigten, abenteuerlichen Anekdoten hervorgebracht; so habe er etwa Blaupausen in den Kunstwerken versteckt aus Berlin geschmuggelt.

Zu jener Zeit erregte auch Matsukatas Kauf von Gemälden Claude Monets große Aufmerksamkeit; diese wollte er offensichtlich unbedingt erwerben: Bereits 1920, schon vor seiner Europareise, hatte er begonnen, über Bénédite und Sanji Kuroki, den Ehemann seiner in Paris lebenden Nichte, mit Monet zu verhandeln. Für die sorgfältige Vorbereitung dieser Ankäufe sicherte er sich auch die Unterstützung der in Paris ansässigen Maler Torajirō Kojima und Toyosaku Saitō.[26] 1921 suchte Matsukata mindestens zweimal Monets Atelier auf und entschied sich vermutlich erst zum Kauf, nachdem er die Werke selbst in Augenschein genommen hatte. Rund fünfzehn Arbeiten erwarb er direkt vom Künstler, darunter zwei Seerosen-Gemälde (Abb. 7, 8).[27] Matsukatas Sammlung enthielt am Ende etwa dreißig Werke Monets, darunter auch sieben Bilder aus der bedeutenden Sammlung des dänischen Industriellen Wilhelm Hansen, die zwischen 1922 und 1923 auf Vermittlung von Bénédite erworben wurden.

Als Mitte der 1930er-Jahre Teile der Sammlung Matsukata abgestoßen wurden, ließ er insgesamt 34 moderne französische Gemälde nach Japan verschiffen, die er bei jener Gelegenheit gekauft hatte. Die meisten davon wurden vermutlich direkt an führende Sammler:innen weiterveräußert.[28] Dass sie heute zu den wichtigsten Werken in Museen des In- und Auslands zählen, unterstreicht paradoxerweise ihre Bedeutung.

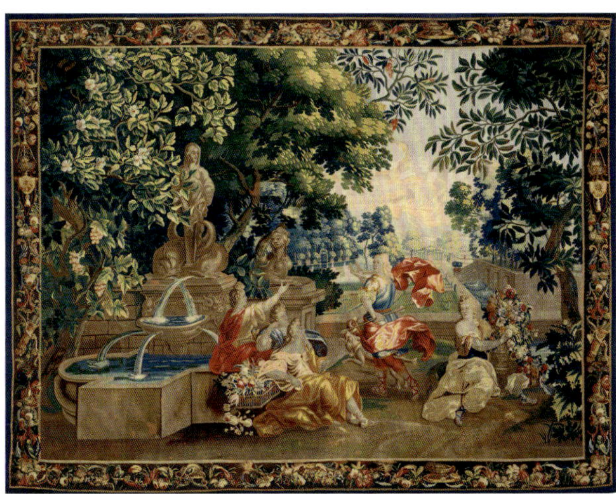

Abb. | Fig. 6
Belgien | Belgium, Oudenaarde, unbekannte Werkstatt, frühes 18. Jh. | unidentified workshop, early 18th century, The National Museum of Western Art, Tokyo. Ehemals Sammlung Matsukata | Ex-Matsukata Collection, Schenkung der | Donated by The Industrial Bank of Japan, Ltd.

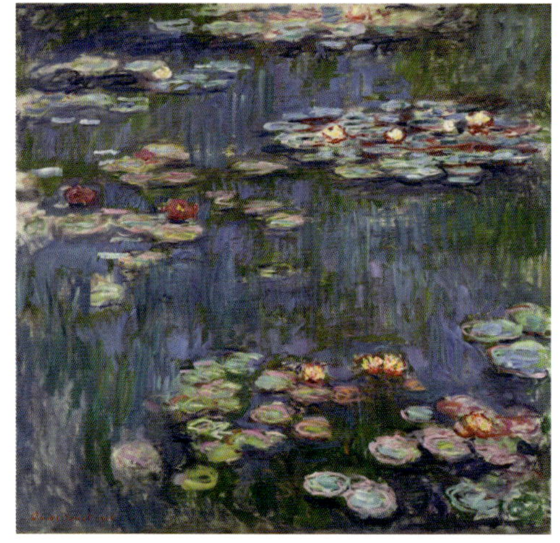

Abb. | Fig. 7
Claude Monet, *Les nymphéas,* 1916,
The National Museum of Western Art, Tokyo.
Sammlung Matsukata | Matsukata Collection

after inspecting the works for himself. He bought around fifteen works directly from the artist, including two paintings in the *Nymphéas* or *Water Lilies* series (figs. 7, 8).[28] Combined with other works purchased from galleries, Matsukata was ultimately able to collect almost thirty paintings by Monet. Among these, next in importance to the pieces bought directly from Monet were the seven pieces he obtained from the collection of Danish industrialist Wilhelm Hansen after negotiations through Bénédite that lasted from 1922 to 1923. The modern French artworks purchased on this occasion – thirty-four pieces in total – were sent to Japan in the mid-1930s as the Matsukata Collection was being dispersed, most probably for direct sale to prominent collectors.[29] The fact that they are currently counted among the best-known works at museums in Japan and around the world paradoxically speaks to their significance.

Post-Impressionism and Japan

One of Matsukata's companions on his gallery tours of Paris and London was art historian Yukio Yashiro. Yashiro had little time for Brangwyn's work, calling it 'overdone'; as for Bénédite, he judged him as 'a man behind the times', questioning his credentials as a leader in a revolutionary age where 'new movements of modern art come one after another like great waves' crashing on the shore.[30] Yashiro describes the works by artists like Henri Martin, Paul-Albert Besnard, and Edmond Aman-Jean that Bénédite bought for Matsukata in Paris as 'largely along the outdated lines of the Musée du Luxembourg,' and was so dismayed at the paucity of works by Vincent van Gogh or Edgar Degas – and lack of any by Paul Cézanne – that he concluded that he would have to personally help Matsukata in his collecting efforts. He follows this recollection with the tale of how, with considerable effort, he persuaded Matsukata to buy Van Gogh's *La chambre de Van Gogh à Arles* (*Vincent's Bedroom in Arles;* fig 9) from the Galerie Paul Rosenberg.

From a modern-day perspective, Yashiro's appraisal seems unfair; we should rather say that Bénédite did not favour 'modern painting' with special treatment. However, most Japanese artists of Yashiro's generation were fervent admirers of artists like Cézanne, Van Gogh and Paul Gauguin, and heavily influenced by art magazines like *Shirakaba* (White Birch), which echoed the modernist view of art history that had begun to take form in Great Britain and Germany. Through the 1910s and 1920s, an increasing number of Japanese artists travelled to Europe – and particularly to Paris – and direct familiarity with the contemporary avant-garde became more widespread. Indeed, it appears that Yashiro was not the only one who was eager to turn Matsukata's gaze in new directions. Jūtarō Kuroda and Gen'ichirō Adachi contacted Matsukata in around May of 1918, while waiting in London to embark on their ship home after finishing their studies in Europe. Kuroda wrote to Japan about Matsukata as follows: 'When we laid out almost all our thoughts for him, he was delighted.

Post-Impressionismus und Japan

Der Kunsthistoriker Yukio Yashiro, der Matsukata auf seinen Galerierundgängen in Paris und London begleitete, macht in seinen Erinnerungen kein Hehl daraus, dass er Brangwyns Gemälde nicht besonders schätzte, weil sie ihm „allzu übertrieben" erschienen. Auch Bénédite handelte seiner Auffassung nach in einer Zeit des Wandels mit ihren „vielen aufwallenden neuen Bewegungen in der modernen Kunst" zu „rückständig".[29] Enttäuscht reagierte Yashiro auf die für Matsukata in Paris erworbenen Werke von Henri Martin, Paul-Albert Besnard und Edmond Aman-Jean, die sich seiner Meinung nach alle an „dem altmodischen Geschmack des Musée du Luxembourg" orientierten. Dagegen gab es nur wenige Arbeiten Vincent van Goghs und Edgar Degas' und kein einziges Werk von Paul Cézanne, weshalb Yashiro beschloss, Matsukata beim Sammeln fortan zu beraten. Weiterhin berichtet er, dass es ihm erst durch eindringliche Bemühungen gelang, Matsukata zum Kauf von van Goghs *La Chambre de Van Gogh à Arles (Vincents Schlafzimmer in Arles*; Abb. 9) in der Galerie Rosenberg zu bewegen.

Aus heutiger Sicht ist dies eine einseitige Einschätzung: Tatsächlich konzentrierte Bénédite sich nur nicht speziell auf die Malerei der Moderne. Viele japanische Künstler:innen aus Yashiros Generation wurden hingegen von Kunstzeitschriften wie *Shirakaba* (Weiße Birke) beeinflusst, die auf die in England und Deutschland sich abzeichnenden avantgardistischen Kunsttendenzen reagierten, und waren begeisterte Bewunderer von Cézanne,

van Gogh und Paul Gauguin. In den 1910er- und 1920er-Jahren reisten daher immer mehr von ihnen nach Europa, vor allem aber nach Paris, und lernten die Avantgarde-Kunst ihrer Zeit aus erster Hand kennen. Offenbar war Yashiro nicht der Einzige, der Matsukatas Aufmerksamkeit eifrig in die neue Richtung lenken wollte. Um Mai 1918 zum Beispiel trafen Jūtarō Kuroda und Gen'ichirō Adachi Matsukata in London, während sie darauf warteten, an Bord des Schiffes zu gehen, mit dem sie ihre Rückreise nach dem Auslandsstudium antraten. Kuroda schrieb über seine Eindrücke nach Japan: „Wir haben fast über alles geredet, was uns bewegte, und er [Matsukata, A.d.Ü.] wirkte äußerst erfreut. Wir haben dann gemeinsam zu Mittag gegessen und ein paar Ausstellungen und Kunsthändler besucht. Einer der Händler hatte ein Aquarell von [Johan] Jongkind, und Adachi und ich empfahlen es ihm zum Kauf. Ich finde es bedauerlich, dass heutzutage in Japan europäische Künstler nur dem Namen nach oder mittels Fotografien, jedoch ohne das originale Anschauungsmaterial vor Augen zu haben, imitiert werden. Deshalb hoffe ich inständig, dass so viele Originale westlicher Kunst wie nur möglich nach Japan gelangen."[30]

Abgesehen von Jongkind erwähnte Kuroda keine weiteren Künstler:innen, die er Matsukata empfahl, aber seinen damaligen Schriften zufolge kann man vermuten, dass er begeistert von Gauguin, van Gogh, Cézanne und vielleicht Maurice Denis sprach. Interessanterweise findet Gauguins Porträt *Le peintre Slewinski (Portrait des Malers Slewinski*; Abb. 10), das Matsukata später erwarb, in Kurodas Reisebericht *Dōkei no chi (Land*

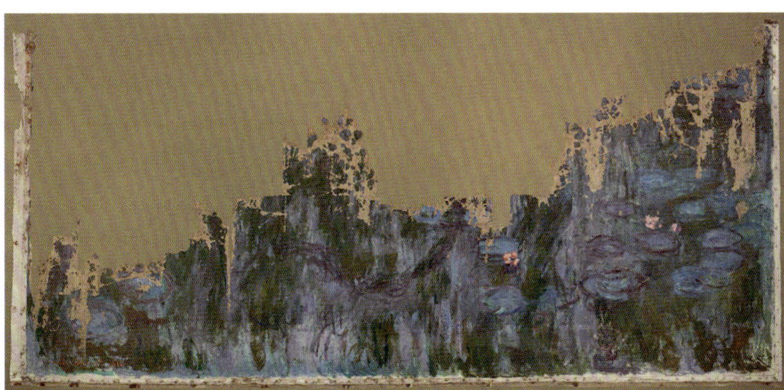

Abb. | Fig. 8
Claude Monet, *Les nymphéas, reflets du saule,* 1916, The National Museum of Western Art, Tokyo. Ehemalige Sammlung Matsukata; Schenkung der Erben von | Ex-Matsukata Collection; Donated by the heirs of Mr Kōjirō Matsukata

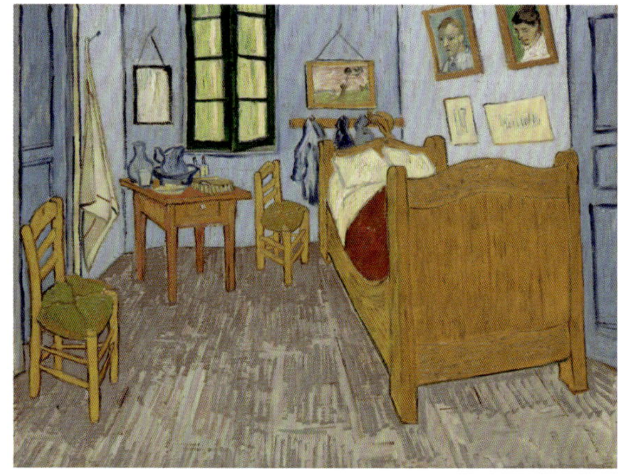

Then we had lunch together and visited two or three exhibitions and galleries. One gallery had a watercolour by [Johan] Jongkind, so Adachi and I recommended that he buy it. It is unfortunate when people only look at photographs and learn names, as they do in Japan today, rather than viewing the real thing, so it is my earnest desire that as many real works of Western art as possible – works worth introducing – make the journey to Japan.'[31]

Kuroda does not record what other artists he recommended to Matsukata, but based on his writings at the time, he presumably made a passionate case for painters like Gauguin, Van Gogh, Cézanne, and perhaps Maurice Denis. Intriguingly, in Kuroda's book about his experiences in Europe from 1916 to 1918, *Dōkei no chi* (*Lands of longing,* 1920), a work by Gauguin appears that Matsukata would later acquire: *Le Peintre Slewinski* (*Portrait of the Painter Slewinski;* fig. 10). Kuroda and Adachi had spent from July to September of 1917 in Brittany, following in the footsteps of Gauguin, whom they revered. With guidance from local residents, they were able to visit Władysław Ślewiński at his home in the fishing village of Doëlan and see this portrait along with other works by Gauguin.[32]

In 1921, Matsukata purchased eight works by Gauguin, including this one, from the John Levy Galleries in Paris. The Matsukata Collection would ultimately include twenty paintings by Gauguin, and Yashiro's reminiscences about the influence of the painter Bakusen Tsuchida are often quoted in this context. According to Yashiro, Matsukata met Tsuchida in Paris, and the painter praised Gauguin to the skies. When Matsukata later expressed interest in seeing works by Gauguin in a gallery, word spread rapidly, and from the galleries not only of Paris but also of London and Berlin, new Gauguins arrived.'[33] It is true that Tsuchida set out on a tour of Europe in 1921 with the artists of *Kokuga Sōsaku Kyōkai* (the National Painting Creation Society), which aimed to create new forms of painting by fusing Western and Eastern art, reaching Paris in mid-November. However, according to Tsuchida, he had not yet met Matsukata even in 1922.[34] Furthermore, in November 1921, Matsukata was actually in London. Incidentally, the guide engaged by Tsuchida and the other artists for their visit to Europe was none other than Kuroda, who had returned to the continent by then.

As for Gen'ichirō Adachi, tales of his efforts to recommend French paintings to Matsukata became family lore. 'In Paris, Matsukata asked Adachi his opinion of the works he had purchased (the artworks that formed the basis of the 'First' Matsukata Collection). The pieces he was arranging to buy at the time were chiefly by English painters, nothing but hunting scenes and pictures of bulldogs, smoking pipes and the like, so Adachi recommended that he start over entirely. Instead, Adachi emphasized the importance of works by painters working in France, from the Impressionists to the Fauves, with a central core of paintings by Pissarro, Monticelli, and Picasso, and a selection of pieces by Courbet, Daumier, and Renoir. "That's quite arrogant of you," said Matsukata, but he was

der Sehnsucht; erschienen 1920) Erwähnung, in dem er seinen Aufenthalt in Europa in den Jahren 1916–1918 beschreibt. Von Juli bis September 1917 hatten sich Kuroda und Adachi auf den Spuren des von ihnen verehrten Gauguin gemeinsam in der Bretagne aufgehalten. Vermittelt durch etliche Beziehungen besuchten sie Władysław Ślewiński in seinem Haus im Fischerdorf Doëlan und sahen dort das genannte Bildnis neben weiteren Werken Gauguins.[31]

1921 kaufte Matsukata von der Galerie John Levy in Paris acht Werke des Künstlers, darunter das Porträt Ślewińskis. Die Sammlung Matsukata sollte schließlich zwanzig Gemälde von Gauguin umfassen, und der Einfluss des Malers Bakusen Tsuchida ist in diesem Zusammenhang aus Yashiros Memoiren oft zitiert worden. Laut Yashiro traf Matsukata Tsuchida in Paris und dieser lobte Gauguin in den höchsten Tönen. Als Matsukata später Interesse daran bekundete, dessen Werke in Galerien zu besichtigen, verbreitete sich diese Nachricht so schnell, dass nicht nur aus Paris, sondern „bald darauf auch aus London und Berlin neue Gauguins eintrafen"[32].

Erwiesen ist, dass Tsuchida Mitte November 1921 mit Maler:innen der Kokuga Sōsaku Kyōkai (Gesellschaft zur Erschaffung einer nationalen Malerei), denen ein neuartiger Malstil auf der Grundlage einer Verschmelzung von westlicher und östlicher Kunst vorschwebte, auf einer gemeinsamen Rundreise durch Europa in Paris eintraf. Tsuchida betonte hingegen, er sei Matsukata 1922 noch nicht begegnet.[33] Tatsächlich hielt sich Matsukata im November 1921 in London auf. Der Führer, den Tsuchida und die anderen Künstler:innen für ihren Besuch in Europa engagierten, war

übrigens kein anderer als Kuroda, der inzwischen auf den Kontinent zurückgekehrt war.

Was Gen'ichirō Adachi anbelangt, so erzählte er seiner Familie über seine Bemühungen, Matsukata französische Gemälde zu empfehlen: „In Paris wurde ich von Kōjirō Matsukata um meine Meinung zum Kauf von Gemälden gebeten (die Werke, die den Grundstock von Matsukatas „erster" Sammlung bildeten). Zu jener Zeit hatte Matsukata hauptsächlich Bilder von englischen Künstlern zum Ankauf vormerken lassen – nichts als Jagdhunde und Bulldoggen mit Pfeifen im Maul –, weshalb ich ihm einen inhaltlich kompletten Wechsel nahelegte. Meine Wahl bestand aus Werken französischer Impressionisten, darunter Pissarro, Monticelli, Picasso, Courbet, Daumier und Renoir, bis hin zu den Fauves. Zu mir sagte er zwar, dass ich ‚ziemlich arrogant auftrat', aber er traf einen schnellen Entschluss und ersetzte fast alle vorgemerkten Werke [...]".[34]

Adachi meint sich zu erinnern, dass die Begegnung „in Paris" stattfand, aber hinsichtlich des Zeitpunkts ihres Aufenthalts und der Ausrichtung von Matsukatas Sammlung ist es wahrscheinlicher, dass dies 1918 in London geschah, also im selben Jahr, als Kuroda sich dort aufhielt. Es gibt eine Reihe von Werken von Adolphe Monticelli und Gustave Courbet, die Matsukata möglicherweise während seines Aufenthalts in London kaufte, sowie Werke von Camille Pissarro und Léon Augustin Lhermitte, die er während der Rückkehr nach Japan im Jahr 1918 in den USA erwarb,[35] aber das jeweilige genaue Kaufdatum ist unbekannt. Jedenfalls begann Matsukata erst zu dem Zeitpunkt richtig französische Kunst zu sammeln, als er im August 1918 Bronzen von Rodin bestellte.

quick to make his decisions, and he did end up replacing almost his entire collection [...].'[35]

Although Adachi recalled speaking to Matsukata 'in Paris,' given the timing of their visits to Europe and the types of paintings being collected, it seems more likely that this conversation took place, like Kuroda's, in London in 1918. Matsukata is believed to have bought several works by artists like Adolphe Monticelli and Gustave Courbet while in London, and there is a Camille Pissarro and a Léon Augustin Lhermitte he is thought to have purchased in the United States on his way back to Japan in 1918,[36] but the exact dates of these acquisitions are unclear. In any case, the order Matsukata placed in August 1918 for bronzes by Rodin marks the beginning of his serious attempts to collect French art.

'Kyōraku Bijutsukan'

The name *Kyōraku Bijutsukan* has a rather old-fashioned ring to it for a museum of Western art founded by a man educated in the West, but how it was chosen is unknown. Matsukata's youngest brother Saburō recalled that Kōjirō, born before the Meiji Restoration, grew up in 'an age and household strongly coloured by Confucianism';[37] on the other hand, according to Shizuka Saka-zaki, who accompanied Matsukata on gallery tours in Paris, the name was originally to be *Namu Kyōraku Bijutsukan*, which is more suggestive of Buddhism.[38]

The official English name, presumably selected through discussion with Brangwyn, was not a direct translation of the Japanese. Instead, it was called the 'Sheer Pleasure Arts Pavilion,' a name with a hint of Zen elegance to it. Discussing this name in 1924, Herbert Furst said: 'At first I imagined that "Sheer Pleasure Art" was a flowery Japanese manner of expressing the *fine arts* in contradistinction from the *applied* arts, which are not *sheer* pleasure; but the meaning is far deeper.' According to him, Brangwyn's aim was to make a museum where works of art, architecture, and environmental elements bring together true pleasure to visitors. Under the outdoor light, shadows of trees or architectures themselves are decorations, and 'flowers in the garden, and a murmuring fountain, and the panoramic view of Tokyo and its harbour, and the Sacred Fuji in the distance will be seen framed as so many ever-changing pictures through the arches [...] The contrast of the beauty of nature and the beauties of art in reciprocal action, that is what I aimed at [...].'[39]

Turning once more the Japanese name, some have pointed out its correspondence with the name of the *'Kyōraku-tei'*, a tearoom that Matsu-daira Sadanobu, head of Shirakawa Domain, had built on the shores of Lake Nanko at the beginning of the nineteenth century. Nagako Kamiyasu argues that *'Kyōraku-tei'* is based on the idea that those who found themselves at the same gathering there should 'enjoy it together' in circle – one of the underlying principles of the conception of public parks in modern Japan – and posits a possible connection to Matsukata's *'Kyōraku Bijutsukan'*.[40] Actually, the Matsukata family had several connections to the area near Shirakawa Domain. It was adjacent to Nasu, where the Matsukata family had a summer house and where Kōjirō's father, Masayoshi, had founded the first Western-style farm in Japan, which is called *Senbonmatsu Bokujō* (Thousand Pines Pastures). Not far to the north was the Inawashiro Hydroelectric Power Company, established in 1914, where

137

„Kyōraku Bijutsukan"

Die Bezeichnung „Kyōraku Bijutsukan" für das
von Matsukata erträumte Bauwerk mag antiquiert
anmuten in Anbetracht der Tatsache, dass es europäischer moderner Kunst gewidmet sein sollte
und sein Gründer auf eine westliche Ausbildung
zurückgreifen konnte. Die genauen Umstände für
die Namensgebung sind allerdings nicht bekannt.
Sein jüngster Bruder Saburō Matsukata berichtet,
dass Kōjirō, der zum Ende des Tokugawa-Shogunats geboren wurde, in einer „Ära und Familie mit
starkem konfuzianischem Einschlag" aufwuchs,[36]
während Shizuka Sakazaki, der Matsukata einst
auf einem Galerierundgang in Paris begleitet hatte,
sich daran erinnert, dass der ursprüngliche Name
„Namu Kyōraku Bijutsukan" lauten sollte, was einen
eher buddhistischen Anklang hat.[37]

„Sheer Pleasure Arts Pavilion", die englische
Bezeichnung des geplanten Museums, wurde
dagegen höchstwahrscheinlich von Matsukata und
Brangwyn ersonnen, um eine wörtliche Übersetzung zu vermeiden, und hatte einen Hauch von
Zen-Eleganz. 1924 schrieb der Kunsthistoriker
Herbert Furst: „Zuerst dachte ich, dass ‚Kunst des
reinen Vergnügens' eine blumige japanische
Ausdrucksweise für die schönen Künste im Gegensatz zu den angewandten Künsten ist, die kein
reines Vergnügen sind; aber die Bedeutung geht
viel tiefer." Brangwyns Ziel sei es gewesen, ein
Museum zu schaffen, in dem Kunstwerke, Architektur und Umweltelemente den Besucher:innen
wahre Freude bereiten. Es gehe dabei nicht nur um
den Inhalt der Präsentation, sondern ihr läge eine

„tiefere Bedeutung" zugrunde, indem der „Kontrast zwischen der Schönheit der Natur und der
Schönheit der Kunst zusammenwirkt – das ist
es, was mir vorschwebte."[38] Dies erklärt die Idee,
die hinter dem Bau stand: Elemente aus der
natürlichen Umgebung wie der Brunnen im Hof,
die Blumen, die im Wind rauschenden Blätter der
Bäume, das Spiel von Licht und Schatten und der
„Heilige Fuji" im Hintergrund seien nach dem
japanischen Prinzip der „geliehenen Szenerien"
(*shakkei*) die beste Kulisse für die mannigfaltige
Präsentation von Kunstwerken.

Was den japanischen Namen anbelangt, so
haben einige darauf hingewiesen, dass er dem
Namen des Kyōraku-tei ähnelt, einer Teestube,
die Matsudaira Sadanobu, Daimyō des japanischen
Fürstentums Shirakawa, zu Beginn des 19. Jahrhunderts an den Ufern des Nanko-Sees errichten
ließ. Nagako Kamiyasu erklärt, dem Bau liege der
Gedanke zugrunde, dass diejenigen, die sich
dort versammelten, „gemeinsam genießen" sollten (eines der grundlegenden Prinzipien der Konzeption öffentlicher Parks im modernen Japan),
und stellt eine mögliche Verbindung zu Matsukatas
Kyōraku Bijutsukan her.[39]

Tatsächlich hat die Familie Matsukata mehrere
Verbindungen zu dem Gebiet nahe Shirakawa.
Die Gegend grenzt an Nasu, wo Masayoshi Matsukata die erste westlich geprägte Ranch Japans,
die Senbonmatsu-Farm, eröffnete und wo sich
auch das Sommerhaus der Matsukatas befand.
Etwas weiter nördlich stand das Wasserkraftwerk
der Inawashiro Hydroelectric Power Company
(gegründet 1914), zu dessen Direktor Kōjirōs Bruder

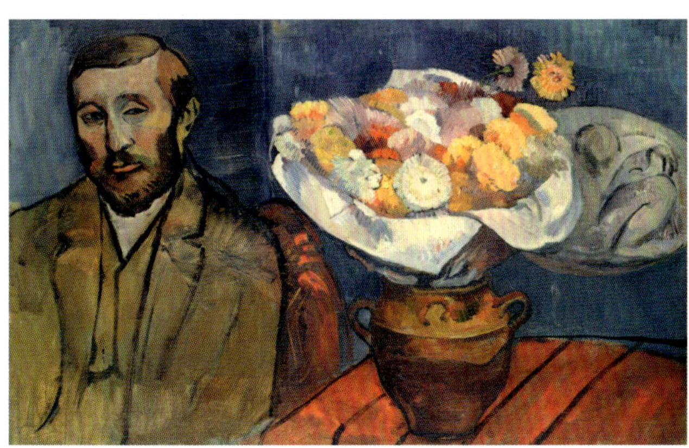

Abb. | Fig. 10
Paul Gauguin, *Le peintre Slewinski*, 1891,
The National Museum of Western Art, Tokyo.
Sammlung Matsukata | Matsukata Collection

Kōjirō's brother Shōsaku accepted a post as director after retiring from the diplomatic corps. Shirakawa was also the site of the largest battle in the Boshin War of 1868–69, the civil war between the former Tokugawa Shogunate forces and the new Meiji government forces, and in 1915 a shared grave was erected there for fallen Satsuma Domain samurai; Masayoshi, a former samurai of Satsuma himself, supplied the calligraphy for the inscription on it. The Meiji Era had begun under a new government after much bloodshed; in 1911, it ended with the death of the Meiji Emperor. Is it too fanciful to suppose that the name *'Kyōraku Bijutsukan'* expressed a kind of sentiment for a vanished age and hope for a new one on Matsukata's part?

At the end of the 1920s, the Matsukata Collection, assembled in just ten years, was forcibly dispersed, as if following the example of the short-lived Taishō Era. However, that agonizingly protracted sale, lasting from 1928 to 1941, supplied the Japanese market with a great deal of Western art and played a major role in exhibitions. Similarly, while the works left behind in France were tossed on the waves of war for a time, they ultimately led to the establishment of the National Museum of Western Art in 1959. The significance of the Matsukata Collection in the history of the reception of Western art in Japan is beyond question.

1 *Tokyo Asahi Shimbun,* 27 Nov. 1918.

2 Kawasaki Heavy Industries, Ltd (ed.), *Kawasaki jūkōgyō kabushiki kaisha shi* (1959), 746–748.

3 Mina Oya, 'Venetsia, Hento, Pari: Kyōraku Bijutsukan sekkei ni mukatte', in Mina Oya (ed.), *Furanku Burangwin ten* exh. cat., NMWA (Tokyo, 2010), 72.

4 Noriko Minato, 'Matsukata Kōjirō no Kyōraku Bijutsukan', *Bijutsukan no yume,* exh. cat., Hyōgo Prefectural Museum of Art (Kobe, 2002), 27–28.

5 W. Slater, 'Why Japan Collects Western Art', *International Studio,* 9 April 1922, 151.

6 Masako Kawaguchi and Megumi Jingaoka (eds.), *Matsukata Korekushon seiyō bijutsu zensakuhin,* 2 vols., (Tokyo: NMWA, 2018–2019).

7 Slater, 'Why Japan Collects', 151.

8 Letter from Matsukata to Léonce Bénédite, 3 November 1923, Paris, Institut national d'histoire de l'art, MS375 (6.5.1), fol. 202.

9 Mrs Gordon-Stables, 'Tokio's Occidental Museum', *International Studio,* September 1922, 461–462.

10 Slater, 'Why Japan Collects', 151.

11 The earliest work to consider in detail the relationship between the two was Noriko Minato, 'Matsukata Kōjirō to sono bijutsukan kōsō ni tsuite (jō, ge)', *MUSEUM: Tokyo Kokuritsu Hakubutsukan Bijutsushi* [MUSEUM: The art magazine of the Tokyo National Museum], 1984, No. 395: 31–40; No. 396: 27–39. See also the essays and documents in Oya (ed.), *Furanku Buranguin.*

12 A. Alford and L. Horner, *Brangwyn in His Studio: The Diary of His Assistant Frank Alford* (Guildford: Roger Alford, 2004), 37–38.

13 Minato, *'Matsukata Kōjirō'* (1984), 27; Oya (ed.), *Furanku Buranguin,* 72.

14 Alford and Horner, *Brangwyn in His Studio,* 108.

15 Noriko Minato, 'Korekutaa Matsukata Kōjirō to sono shūhin', *Matsukata Korekushon* exh. cat., Kobe City Museum, (Kobe, 2016), 26. According Kyūji Satō', who repaired the picture frames and paintings that arrived in Japan, there were also young painters who accompanied him pretending to be his workshop craftsman. See, Kyūji Satō, 'Matsukata Collection ga hajimete shōrai sareta toki no omoide', Sansai, 1959, no. 116, 56–58.

16 https://www.tobunken.go.jp/ materials/kuroda_diary. (Last accessed September 2021).

17 The *Kuroda nikki* [Kuroda diary] says 'Nanjō of Shōkin', but 'Shōkin' (Yokohama Shōkin Bank) would appear to be an error in Kuroda's recollection.

18 Regarding the Kokumin Bijutsu Kyōkai detailed research has recently been published. There is room for more detailed study of the relationship between Matsukata's museum concept and modern Japan's art system. See, Eiko Imabashi, *Kindai Nihon no bijutsu shisō: Bijutsu hihyōka Iwamura Tōru to sono jidai,* Vols. 1–2 (Hakusuisha, 2021).

19 Sadahiro Suzuki, *Higashi to nishi no kekkon* (Minerva Shobo, 2006), 11–13, 8183.

Shōsaku ernannt wurde, nachdem er aus dem diplomatischen Dienst ausgetreten war. Das Gebiet war auch Schauplatz heftigster Kämpfe im Boshin-Krieg (1868/69), einem Bürgerkrieg zwischen den ehemaligen Truppen des Tokugawa-Shogunats und jenen der neuen Meiji-Regierung. 1915 wurde dort das Gemeinschaftsgrab der Shimazu aus der Region Satsuma errichtet, dessen Inschrift von Matsukatas Vater Masayoshi, einem Abkömmling des Samuraigeschlechts, beauftragt wurde. Dem großen Blutvergießen folgte unter der neuen Regierung die friedliche Meiji-Ära, die schließlich 1911 mit dem Tod des gleichnamigen Kaisers endete. Der Name „Kyōraku Bijutsukan" mag auch darauf hindeuten, dass Kōjirō Matsukata noch von tiefen Gefühlen gegenüber der vergangenen Epoche bewegt war und sich zugleich eine neue wünschte.

Ende der 1920er-Jahre wurde die Sammlung Matsukata, die über einen Zeitraum von nur etwa zehn Jahren aufgebaut worden war, gewaltsam aufgelöst, als folgte sie dem Beispiel der kurzlebigen Taishō-Periode (1912–1926). Die zwischen 1928 und 1941 stattfindenden Auktionen versorgten den japanischen Kunstmarkt mit einer Flut an westlichen Werken und spielten eine wichtige Rolle bei Ausstellungen. Die in Frankreich verbliebenen Werke gerieten in die Wirren des Zweiten Weltkriegs, führten im Jahr 1959 aber schließlich zur Gründung des National Museum of Western Art. Die Bedeutung der Sammlung Matsukata für die Geschichte der Rezeption westlicher Kunst in Japan steht außer Frage.

1 *Kawasaki jūkōgyō kabushiki kaisha shi,* hrsg. von Kawasaki Heavy Industries, Ltd., o. O. 1959, S. 746–748.

2 Mina Oya, „Venetsia, Hento, Pari. Kyōraku Bijutsukan sekkei ni mukatte", in: *Furanku Burangwin,* Ausst.-Kat. The National Museum of Western Art, Tokio, Tokio 2010, S. 72.

3 Noriko Minato, „Matsukata Kōjirō no Kyōraku Bijutsukan", in: *Bijutsukan no yume,* Ausst.-Kat. Hyōgo Prefectural Museum of Art, Kobe, Kobe 2002, S. 27 f.

4 Willard Slater, „Why Japan Collects Western Art", in: *International Studio,* 75, April 1922, S. 151.

5 Masako Kawaguchi und Megumi Jingaoka (Hrsg.), *Matsukata Korekushon seiyō bijutsu zensakuhin,* 2 Bde., Tokio 2018/19.

6 Willard Slater, „Why Japan Collects Western Art", S. 151.

7 Matsukata an Bénédite, Brief vom 3.11.1923, Institut national d'histoire de l'art, MS375 (6.5.1), fol. 2020.

8 Mrs. Gordon-Stables, „Tokio's Occidental Museum", in: *International Studio,* 75, September 1922, S. 461 f.

9 Willard Slater, „Why Japan Collects Western Art", S. 151.

10 Die früheste Erörterung über die Beziehung zwischen den beiden findet sich in Noriko Minato, „Matsukata Kōjirō to sono bijutsukan kōsō ni tsuite (jō, ge)", in: MUSEUM. Tokyo Kokuritsu Hakubutsukan Bijutsushi, 1984, Nr. 395: S. 31–40, Nr. 396: S. 27–39. Siehe auch verschiedene Beiträge im Ausst.-Kat. *Furanku Burangwin.*

11 A. Alford und L. Horner, *Brangwyn in His Studio. The Diary of His Assistant Frank Alford,* Guildford 2004, S. 37 f.

12 Noriko Minato, „Matsukata Kōjirō no Kyōraku Bijutsukan", S. 27; Mina Oya, „Venetsia, Hento, Pari", S. 72.

13 A. Alford und L. Horner, *Brangwyn in His Studio,* S. 108.

14 Noriko Minato, „Korekutaa Matsukata Kōjirō to sono shūhin", in: *Matsukata Korekushon,* Ausst.-Kat. Kobe City Museum, Kobe 2016, S. 26. Laut Kyūji Satō, der die nach Japan gelangten Bilderrahmen und Gemälde restaurierte, gab es auch junge Maler:innen, die ihn begleiteten und sich als seine Werkstattmitarbeiter:innen ausgaben. Vgl. Kyūji Satō, „Matsukata Collection ga hajimete shōrai sareta toki no omoide", in: *Sansai,* 116, 1959, S. 56–58.

15 Siehe: https://www.tobunken.go.jp/ materials/kuroda_diary [zuletzt aufgerufen am 6.10.2021].

16 Im „Kuroda-Tagebuch" wird „Nanjō von Shōkin" (statt von „Mitsui") erwähnt, aber da es sich bei „Shōkin" um die Yokohama Shōkin Bank handelt, hat Kuroda sich offenbar falsch erinnert.

17 Vor Kurzem wurde eine detaillierte Studie über die Kokumin Bijutsu Kyōkai veröffentlicht. Matsukatas Vision eines Kunstmuseums sollte auch in Bezug auf moderne japanische Kunstinstitutionen näher untersucht werden. Vgl. Eiko Imahashi, *Kindai Nihon no bijutsu shisō. Bijutsu hihyōka Iwamura Tōru to sono jidai,* 2 Bde., Hakusuisha 2021.

18 Sadahiro Suzuki, *Higashi to nishi no kekkon,* Kyoto 2006, S. 11–13, 81–73.

19 Michiko Hayashi, „Kokuritsu Seiyō Bijutsukan kitaku Furanku Burangwin hanga 104 ten no rireki ni tsuite", in: *Kokuritsu Seiyō Bijutsukan kenkyū kiyō,* 3, 1999, S. 45–60.

20 Masako Kawaguchi, „Rondon ni nokosareta Matsukata Korekushon. Pantekunikan soko hokan sakuhin o meguru shiryō chōsa hōkoku", in: *Kokuritsu Seiyō Bijutsukan kenkyū kiyō,* 21, 2017, S. 5–17.

21 Die Sammlung Matsukata und ihre Lagerung in Frankreich wird andernorts beschrieben: siehe Megumi Jingaoka, „Matsukata Korekushon. Hyakunen no rute", in: *Matsukata Korekushon ten,* Ausst.-Kat. The National Museum of Western Art, Tokio, Tokio 2019, S. 11–26, 291–307.

22 Caroline Mathieu, „Reonsu Beneditto to Matsukata Kōjirō", in: *Matsukata Korekushon,* Ausst.-Kat. Kobe City Museum, Kobe 2016, S. 196.

20 Michiko Hayashi, 'Kokuritsu Seiyō Bijutsukan kitaku Furanku Burang-win hanga 104 ten no raireki ni tsuite', in *Kokuritsu Seiyō Bijutsukan kenkyū kiyō* No. 3 (1999), 45–60.

21 Masako Kawaguchi, 'Rondon ni nokosareta Matsukata Korekushon: Pantekunikan soko hokan sakuhin o meguru shiryō chōsa hōkoku', in *Kokuritsu Seiyō Bijutsukan kenkyū kiyō* No. 21 (2017), 5–17.

22 I have written elsewhere about the collection and storage of the Matsukata Collection in France. See, Megumi Jingaoka, 'Matsukata Korekushon: Hyakunen no ruten', in *Matsukata Korekushon ten* exh. cat., NMWA (2019), 11–26, 291–307 (in English).

23 Caroline Mathieu, *Reonsu Beneditto to Matsukata Kōjirō*, in *Matsukata Korekushon* exh. cat. (2016), 196.

24 Emiko Tezuka, 'Wada Eisaku nikki (1921/8/16–1922/2/7)' (August 16, 1921–February 7, 1922), *Kindai gasetsu*, No. 16 (2007), 1–43.

25 Sakurō Hashimoto, 'Matsukata Korekushon yuraiki', *Kawasaki*, No. 9, (Kawasaki Heavy Industries, Ltd., 1970), 45. (M2971–2987).

26 *Kawasaki jūkōgyō*, 228.

27 Jingaoka, 'Matsukata Korekushon', 16–17.

28 Claude Monet's *Les nymphéas, reflets du saule* (1916) was rediscovered in France in 2016. Regarding its post-war fate, see the following: Geneviève Lacambre, "Sensō to bijutsuhin no yukue", in *Matsukata Korekushon* exh. cat., 49–55. (M776, 788).

29 Jingaoka, 'Matsukata Korekushon', 21–22.

30 Yukio Yashiro, *Geijutsu no patoron* (Shinchōsha, 1958), 38–42.

31 Postcard sent to Japan (address and date unclear) included at the end of *Botsugo 35 nen: Kuroda Jūtarō ten* exh. cat., (Shiga Prefectural Museum of Modern Art, 2005). The author thanks Akiko Mabuchi for drawing her attention to this information.

32 Jūtaro Kuroda, *Dōkei no chi: Geijutsu kankyo*, (Nihon Bijutsu Gakuin, 1920), 115–16.

33 Yashiro, *Geijutsu no patoron*, 34.

34 'Tsuchida Bakusen taiō shokan – tsuma Chiyo ate fūsho', in Seijō University, vol. 6 (1985), 96.

35 Akira Adachi, *Gaka Adachi Gen'ichirō no kiroku* (Miyoshi Kikaku, 2002), 53–54.

36 Minato, 'Korekutaa Matsukata Kōjirō', (2016), 26.

37 Saburō Matsukata, "Matsukata Kōjirō to sono korekushon", in *Bijutsu techō*, No. 159 (1959), 5.

38 "Matsukata Korekushon: Sono 40 nen no wadai", in *Asahi Shimbun*, 23 May 1959. "Namu" is the Buddhist word transliterated into Chinese of the Sanskrit exclamation "Namo," which means respect, reverence and veneration.

39 H. Furst, *The Decorative Art of Frank Brangwyn* (London/NY, 1924), 164–65.

40 Nagako Kamiyasu, "Matsukata Kōjirō no 'Kyōraku Bijutsukan' kōsō to 'kyōraku' no shisō", in *Hakuō Daigaku ronshū*, Vol. 32, No. 2, 2018, 77–102.

23 Emiko Tezuka, „Wada Eisaku nikki [16.8.1921–7.2.1922]", in: *Kindai Gasetsu,* 16, 2007, S. 1–43.

24 Sakurō Hashimoto, „Matsukata Korekushon yuraiki", in: *Kawasaki,* 9, 1970, S. 45.

25 *Kawasaki jūkōgyō kabushiki kaisha shi,* S. 228.

26 Megumi Jingaoka, „Matsukata Korekushon", S. 16 f.

27 Zur Nachkriegsgeschichte des Werks *Les nymphéas, reflets du saule* (1916) von Claude Monet, das 2016 in Frankreich wiederentdeckt wurde, siehe Geneviève Lacambre, „Sensō to bijutsuhin no yukue", in: *Matsukata Korekushon,* Ausst.-Kat., S. 49–55.

28 Megumi Jingaoka, „Matsukata Korekushon", S. 21 f.

29 Siehe Yukio Yashiro, „Geijutsu no patoron", in: *Shinchosha,* 1958, S. 38–42.

30 Postkarte nach Japan (Adresse und Datum unbekannt), abgedruckt in: *Botsugo 35 nen. Kuroda Jūtarō ten,* Ausst.-Kat. Shiga Prefectural Museum of Modern Art, Shiga 2005. Ich danke Akiko Mabuchi für ihren Hinweis.

31 Jūtarō Kuroda, *Dōkei no chi. Geijutsu kankyo,* Tokio 1920, S. 115 f.

32 Yukio Yashiro, „Geijutsu no patoron", S. 34.

33 „Tsuchida Bakusen taiō shokan – tsuma Chiyo ate fūsho", in: *Bigaku Bijutsushi Ronshū,* 6, 1985, S. 96.

34 Akira Adachi, *Gaka Adachi Gen'ichirō no kiroku,* Matsudo 2002, S. 53 f.

35 Noriko Minato, „Korekutaa Matsukata Kōjirō to sono shūhin", S. 26.

36 Saburō Matsukata, „Korekutaa Matsukata Kōjirō", in: *Bijutsu Techō,* 159, 1959, S. 5.

37 „Matsukata Korekushon: Sono 40 nen no wada", in: *Asahi Shimbun,* 23.5.1959. „Namu" ist das ins Chinesische transliterierte buddhistische Wort des Sanskrit-Ausrufs „Namo", was Respekt, Ehrfurcht und Verehrung bedeutet.

38 Herbert Furst, *The Decorative Art of Frank Brangwyn,* London/New York 1924, S. 164 f.

39 Nagako Kamiyasu, „Matsukata Kōjirō no ‚Kyōraku Bijutsukan' kōsō to ‚kyōraku' no shisō", in: *Hakuō Daigaku ronshū,* 32, 2, 2018, S. 77–102.

141

'A GREAT PRIDE FOR FRANCE' –

FRENCH MUSEUMS AND
THE MATSUKATA COLLECTION

Léa Saint-Raymond
and Maxime Georges Métraux

The history of the Matsukata Collection is closely linked to that of French museums, whether at the time of its constitution, its conservation at the Rodin Museum, or its eventful trajectory between its sequestration in 1944 and its partial 'donation' to Japan's National Museum of Western Art in 1959. This essay looks at the mutual interests between Kōjirō Matsukata and French curators, who, like Léonce Bénédite, considered that the collection of the rich Japanese industrialist was and would be 'a great pride for France':[1] How can this paradoxical interest of French museums be explained, with respect to a Japanese collection?

France, 'so well represented
thanks to you'[2]

Kōjirō Matsukata founded his collection on a very precise idea: to establish a museum in Japan. Indeed, he wanted to propagate 'the taste and admiration for the masterpieces of your great artists'[3] – by which he meant the great French artists – in order to inspire, in return, Japanese artists and craftsmen.[4] Wishing to acquire bronzes by the sculptor Auguste Rodin, who had just died, Matsukata was introduced in December 1917 to Léonce Bénédite, the curator for contemporary art at the Musée du Luxembourg, who was then preparing for the opening of the Rodin Museum, of which he would also become the curator and director (fig. 1). From 1918 until his death in 1925, Léonce Bénédite agreed not only to help this rich collector to acquire Rodin's bronzes but also to build up a collection of French art, since, as he wrote to him, 'it will be a great pride for France to be so well represented thanks to you in the land of the rising sun.'[5]

143 Léa Saint-Raymond
und Maxime Georges Métraux

Die Geschichte der Sammlung Matsukata ist eng mit jener der französischen Museen verbunden, sei es zur Zeit ihrer Begründung, ihrer Unterbringung im Musée Rodin oder ihrer ereignisreichen Reise zwischen der Beschlagnahmung im Jahr 1944 und ihrer teilweisen „Schenkung" an das japanische National Museum of Western Art im Jahr 1959. Dieser Essay befasst sich mit den Interessen von Kōjirō Matsukata auf der einen und den französischen Kurator:innen, die – wie Léonce Bénédite – der Ansicht waren, dass die Sammlung des reichen japanischen Industriellen „ein großer Stolz für Frankreich"[1] sei und sein würde, auf der anderen Seite. Wie lässt sich dieses paradoxe Interesse französischer Museen an einer japanischen Sammlung erklären?

Frankreich, „dank Ihnen
so hervorragend vertreten"[2]

Kōjirō Matsukata begann seine Sammlung mit einer sehr genauen Vorstellung: ein Museum in Japan zu gründen. Tatsächlich wollte er „den Geschmack und die Bewunderung für die Meisterstücke Ihrer großartigen Künstler"[3] fördern – womit er die großen französischen Künstler:innen meinte –, um im Gegenzug japanische Künstler:innen und Kunsthandwerker:innen zu inspirieren.[4] Nachdem er den Wunsch geäußert hatte, Bronzen des kurz zuvor verstorbenen Bildhauers Auguste Rodin zu erwerben, wurde Matsukata im Dezember 1917 Léonce Bénédite vorgestellt, dem Kurator für Gegenwartskunst im Musée du Luxembourg. Dieser bereitete gerade die Eröffnung des Musée Rodin vor, deren

„EIN GROSSER STOLZ FÜR FRANKREICH" –

FRANZÖSISCHE MUSEEN UND DIE SAMMLUNG MATSUKATA

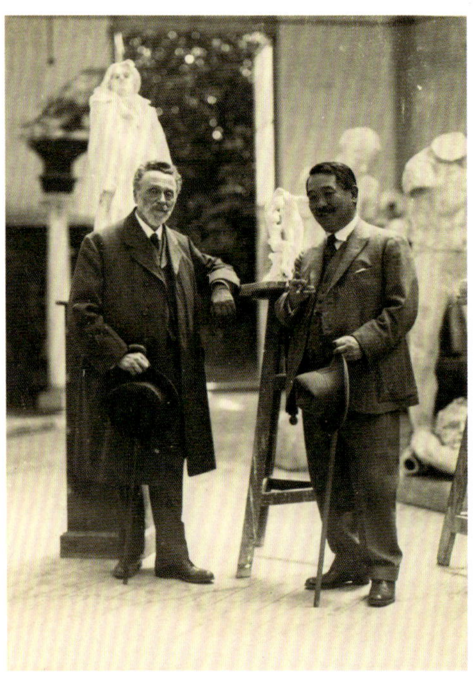

Abb. | Fig. 1
Kōjirō Matsukata und | and Léonce Bénédite
in Meudon, vermutlich | probably 1921

Matsukata commissioned two bronze casts of Rodin's *La porte de l'enfer* (*Gates of Hell*), one for the Rodin Museum as a generous donation, the other for the museum he wished to open in Japan (fig. 2; p. 228).[6] To complete his museum to the glory of French art, he trusted the expertise of Bénédite, providing him with the extraordinary sum of 1.2 million francs at the Suzuki & Co bank to pay for the artworks that the curator was to choose for him.[7] Bénédite put a lot of energy, in addition to his work as curator of both the Rodin Museum and Musée du Luxembourg, into helping the Japanese collector. He succeeded in obtaining essential pieces from major art dealers, such as Paul Durand-Ruel for works by Claude Monet (p. 275), Pierre-Auguste Renoir (p. 219) and Pierre Puvis de Chavannes (fig. 3),[8] or Paul Rosenberg for paintings by Henri de Toulouse-Lautrec (fig. 4) or Camille Pissarro (p. 306). Bénédite also recommended the acquisition of works by living French artists who were successful at the official Salon, such as Charles Cottet, Etienne Dinet, Ernest Quost and Paul Dardé, and he also succeeded in getting Monet to agree to sell works from his studio, although admittedly at a high price (pp. 278, 279, 281).

Bénédite's biggest coup was the Hansen collection. In November 1922, the curator wrote to Matsukata about 'the most extraordinary affair':

> The director of a large insurance company in Denmark, Mr [Wilhelm] Hansen has for many years recruited a truly unique collection of first-rate pieces of the modern French school. It is an incomparable museum of which the Louvre and the Luxembourg Museum could be jealous. This museum was intended, in Mr Hansen's mind, to be offered to the Danish nation. Unfortunate speculations force him to dispose of part of his collection to pay part of his debts.[9]

145

Kurator und Direktor er ebenfalls werden sollte (Abb. 1). Von 1918 bis zu seinem Tod 1925 erklärte sich Léonce Bénédite nicht nur bereit, den wohlhabenden Sammler beim Erwerb von Rodins Bronzen, sondern auch beim Aufbau einer Sammlung französischer Kunst zu unterstützen, da es, so schrieb er, „ein großer Stolz für Frankreich sein wird, dank Ihnen so hervorragend im Land der aufgehenden Sonne vertreten zu sein"[5]. Matsukata beauftragte zwei Bronzegüsse von Rodins *La porte de l'enfer (Das Höllentor)*, von denen der eine als großzügige Schenkung an das Musée Rodin gedacht war, der andere für das Museum, das er in Japan eröffnen wollte (Abb. 2; S. 228).[6] Zur Vervollständigung seiner Sammlung zum Ruhme französischer Kunst vertraute er auf die Expertise von Bénédite und stattete ihn mit der außerordentlichen Summe von 1,2 Millionen französischer Francs bei der Bank Suzuki & Co aus, um damit die Kunstwerke zu bezahlen, die der Kurator für ihn auswählen würde.[7] Zusätzlich zu seiner Arbeit als Kurator des Musée Rodin wie auch des Musée du Luxembourg investierte Bénédite eine Menge Energie in die Aktivitäten für den japanischen Sammler. Es gelang ihm, wesentliche Arbeiten von bedeutenden Kunsthändlern zu erwerben, darunter Werke von Claude Monet (S. 275), Pierre-Auguste Renoir (S. 219) und Pierre Puvis de Chavannes (Abb. 3)[8] bei Paul Durand-Ruel oder Gemälde von Henri de Toulouse-Lautrec (Abb. 4) und Camille Pissarro (S. 306) bei Paul Rosenberg. Bénédite empfahl auch den Ankauf von Arbeiten lebender französischer Künstler:innen, die im offiziellen Salon Erfolge feierten,

wie Charles Cottet, Étienne Dinet, Ernest Quost und Paul Dardé; er überzeugte sogar Monet davon, Arbeiten direkt aus seinem Atelier zu verkaufen, wenn auch zugegebenermaßen zu einem hohen Preis (S. 278, 279, 281).

Bénédites größter Coup war jedoch die Sammlung Hansen. Im November 1922 berichtete der Kurator Matsukata über „die absolut außergewöhnliche Angelegenheit":

„Der Direktor eines großen Versicherungsunternehmens in Dänemark, Herr [Wilhelm] Hansen, hat viele Jahre lang eine wahrhaft einzigartige Sammlung erstklassiger Werke der modernen französischen Schule zusammengetragen. Es handelt sich um ein beispielloses Museum, auf das der Louvre und das Musée du Luxembourg neidisch sein könnten. Dieses Museum sollte Herrn Hansens Vorstellung zufolge der dänischen Nation angeboten werden. Unglückliche Spekulationen zwingen ihn dazu, sich von Teilen seiner Sammlung zu trennen, um einen Teil seiner Schulden zu begleichen."[9]

Dank eines günstigen Wechselkurses müsste Matsukata „nur" 1,8 Millionen Francs bezahlen, um ein gutes Geschäft zu machen und „auf einen Schlag ein wunderbares Museum"[10] zu besitzen. Der japanische Sammler willigte ein und setzte, ohne die Werke überhaupt gesehen zu haben, sein Vertrauen wieder einmal in Bénédite. Im März 1923 ging die Transaktion über die Bühne. Bénédite wählte 34 erstklassige Stücke für eine Gesamtsumme von 1.678.000 Francs aus, die Matsukata noch

Abb. | Fig. 2
Auguste Rodin, *La porte de l'enfer,*
1880–1890/1917, Musée Rodin, Paris

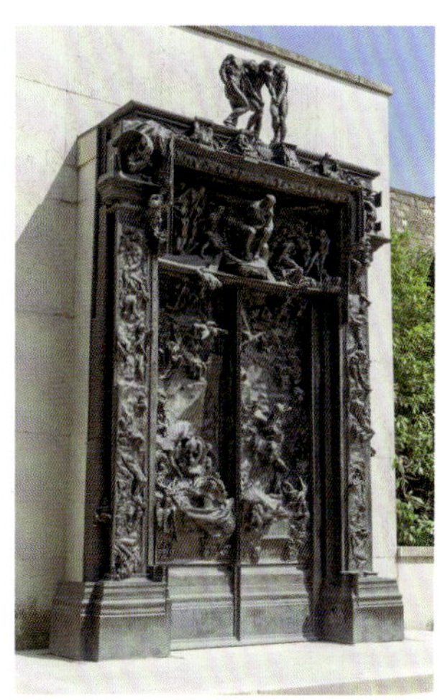

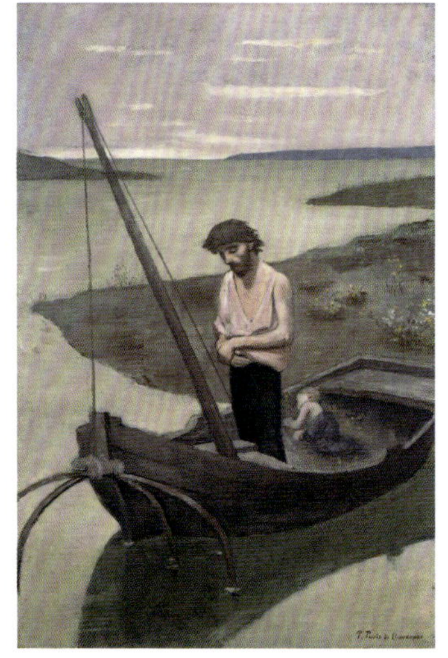

Abb. | Fig. 3
Pierre Puvis de Chavannes, *Le pauvre pêcheur*,
ca. 1887–1892, The National Museum of
Western Art, Tokyo, Sammlung Matsukata |
Matsukata Collection

Thanks to a favourable exchange rate, Matsukata would have to pay 'only' 1.8 million francs to make a good deal and own 'in one fell swoop a wonderful museum'.[10] The Japanese collector accepted and, without even seeing the works, once again placed his trust in Bénédite. In March 1923, the transaction was concluded. Bénédite chose thirty-four first-rate pieces for a total of 1,678,000 francs that Matsukata hastened to pay in March 1923.[11] 'You have the best of the Hansen collection,'[12] Bénédite wrote, listing seven paintings by Monet (fig. 6), five by Pissarro, seven by Alfred Sisley, two by Renoir, two by Edouard Manet (p. 220), two by Edgar Degas, three by Paul Gauguin, two by Henri Fantin-Latour, two by Jean-Baptiste Camille Corot (p. 268), one by Honoré Daumier and one by Paul Cézanne. As curator of the Musée du Luxembourg, Bénédite could have been in competition with Matsukata to buy these works for the museum he directed. However, there seemed to be no conflict of interest: the Paris museum only acquired a small Degas head from the Hansen collection.[13]

An Artistic Showcase at
Lower Risk and Lower Costs

The relationship between Léonce Bénédite and Kōjirō Matsukata could have been asymmetrical – the curator serving the interests of the collector in the short term, and, in the medium term, the museum in Japan promoting French art. Never-theless, the French museums quickly found where they could benefit, taking advantage of a profitable artistic showcase.

Indeed, at the same time that Matsukata made the important acquisition of the Hansen collection, a new museum in San Francisco, the California Palace of the Legion of Honor, was preparing to open its doors. Bénédite was in the front row: a member of the organizing committee of the inaugural exhibition dedicated to 'French Art', he wrote the preface to the catalogue and lent eighty-two artworks by young French artists, from the Musée du Luxembourg.[14] But the curator played a master stroke and made French art shine at a lower cost. On 4 December 1924, he informed Kōjirō Matsukata – who still had not seen the works in his collection – that he had 'taken the liberty [...] to include in the San Francisco exhibition of French art almost all the works from the Hansen collection in Copenhagen'.[15] Bénédite forgot to mention that he had also loaned other works acquired for Matsukata, which remained in the Rodin Museum's storerooms: nearly fifty works in all, many by the greatest Impressionists, but also works by Corot, Gustave Courbet, Cézanne, Gauguin, Puvis de Chavannes, Toulouse-Lautrec, Maurice Denis and Pierre Bonnard (fig. 5).

Thanks to the Japanese collector, France was proud to exhibit in San Francisco 'the most beautiful and most important core of the French retrospective exhibition,'[16] which was extended for six months in 1925. While reassuring Matsukata that these works were 'duly insured,' Léonce Bénédite

im selben Monat beglich.[11] „Sie besitzen das Beste aus der Sammlung Hansen"[12], schrieb Bénédite und listete sieben Gemälde von Monet (Abb. 6), fünf von Pissarro, sieben von Alfred Sisley, zwei von Renoir, zwei von Edouard Manet (S. 220), zwei von Edgar Degas, drei von Paul Gauguin, zwei von Henry Fantin-Latour, zwei von Jean-Baptiste Camille Corot (S. 268), eines von Honoré Daumier und eines von Paul Cézanne auf. Als Kurator des Musée du Luxembourg hätte Bénédite eine Konkurrenz für Matsukata darstellen können, um diese Arbeiten für das von ihm geführte Museum zu erwerben. Es schien jedoch keinerlei Interessenskonflikt zu bestehen: Das Pariser Museum erwarb aus der Sammlung Hansen lediglich einen kleinen Kopf von Degas.[13]

Ein künstlerisches Vorzeigeprojekt mit geringem Risiko und geringen Kosten

Die Beziehung zwischen Léonce Bénédite und Kōjirō Matsukata hätte durchaus asymmetrisch sein können – der Kurator diente kurzfristig den Interessen des Sammlers und das Museum in Japan bewarb mittelfristig französische Kunst. Dennoch fanden die französischen Museen rasch heraus, wie sie profitieren konnten, und zogen ihren Nutzen aus einem vorteilhaften künstlerischen Vorzeigeprojekt.

Tatsächlich bereitete genau zu der Zeit, als Matsukata den bedeutenden Ankauf der Sammlung Hansen tätigte, ein neues Museum in San Francisco – der California Palace of the Legion of Honor – seine Eröffnung vor. Bénédite stand dabei in der ersten Reihe, denn als Mitglied des Organisationskomitees der Eröffnungsausstellung, die der „French Art" gewidmet war, verfasste er nicht nur das Vorwort zum Katalog, sondern lieh auch 82 Arbeiten junger französischer Künstler:innen aus dem Musée du Luxembourg.[14] Dem Kurator gelang außerdem ein geradezu meisterlicher Schachzug, mit dem er die französische Kunst zu niedrigen Kosten glänzen lassen konnte. Am 4. Dezember 1924 informierte er Kōjirō Matsukata – der die Werke in seiner Sammlung immer noch nicht gesehen hatte – darüber, dass er sich „die Freiheit genommen habe [...] in der Ausstellung französischer Kunst in San Francisco nahezu alle Arbeiten aus der Sammlung Hansen in Kopenhagen zu präsentieren"[15]. Bénédite vergaß dabei zu erwähnen, dass er für die Ausstellung auch andere für Matsukata erworbene Arbeiten ausgeliehen hatte, die im Depot des Musée Rodin untergebracht waren: alles in allem fast fünfzig Arbeiten, viele davon Werke bedeutender Impressionist:innen, aber auch Arbeiten von Corot, Gustave Courbet, Cézanne, Gauguin, Puvis de Chavannes, Toulouse-Lautrec, Maurice Denis und Pierre Bonnard (Abb. 5).

Dank des japanischen Sammlers konnte Frankreich in San Francisco voll Stolz „den schönsten und bedeutendsten Kern der französischen Retrospektive"[16] präsentieren, die 1925 um weitere sechs Monate verlängert wurde. Bénédite versicherte Matsukata, dass die Werke „ordnungsgemäß versichert" seien, und rechtfertigte die Leihgabe durch einen Steuertrick zugunsten des japanischen Sammlers:

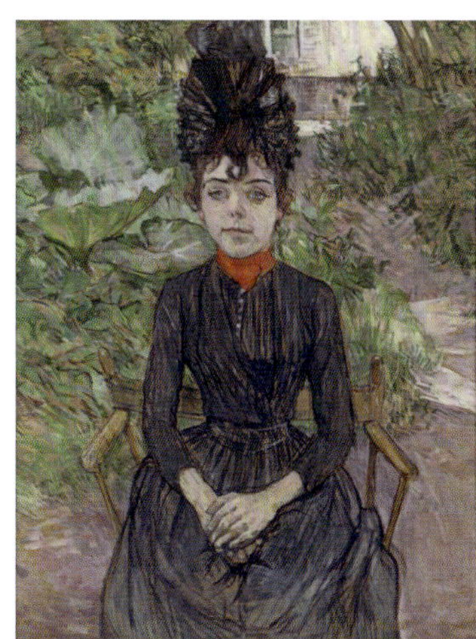

Abb. | Fig. 4
Henri de Toulouse-Lautrec,
Justine Dieulh, 1891, Musée d'Orsay, Paris.
Ehemals Sammlung Matsukata |
formerly Matsukata Collection

GAUGUIN (Eugene Henri Paul)

Born in Paris, June 7, 1848. Died at Dominica, Marquesas, May 6, 1903.

His early youth was spent in Peru, his mother's country. After many vicissitudes he devoted himself to painting, at which he was little more than an amateur. Exhibited at the Salon in 1876, he almost at once came under the influence of Pissarro, then of Cézanne, and came in contact with Van Gogh, whom he accompanied to Provence in 1888, in order to find his personal formula decorative, synthetic and symbolic, which he divided into two styles: his Brittany manner (having stayed at Pont-Aven and at Pouldu in 1886 and 1888) and his oceanic manner. He voyaged to the Antilles (1887-1888), lived in Tahiti (1891-1893), and again in 1895-1901; then at Dominica, 1901-1903.

The first exposition of his works was at Boussod and Valadon (1888), then at the Durand-Ruel Galleries (1893); a posthumous exposition was held at the Autumn Salon in 1906.

23. Still Life. *Private collection.*
24. Coast of Brittany (Bathers). *Private collection.*
25. Farm in Brittany (Mill). *Private collection.*
26. South Sea Island (Woman of Tahiti). *Private collection.*
27. Mother and Daughter. *Private collection.*
28. Vai Ru Mati. *Private collection.*

GUILLAUMIN (Armand)

28a. Le Moulin de la Folie a Crozant.

INGRES (Dominique)

Born at Montauban in 1780. Died in Paris in 1867. Pupil of Jean-Marie Joseph Ingres, his father, miniature painter and sculptor; then of David. First grand prize in Rome in 1802. Member of the Institute in 1825, senator in 1867.

Unconsciously dropped the heroic style of David. Was a great admirer of Raphael. Always attracted by design, has in certain cases voluntarily neglected color, although at times he has proved himself to be a marvelous colorist. Historical and portrait painter, and painter of feminine grace.

29. The Martyrdom of Sain-Symphorien.

LA TOUCHE

Born at Saint Cloud, October 29, 1854. Died in Paris, July 13, 1913. Painter and engraver, worked with Manet at the beginning of Impressionism, and studied with Bracquemond. Exhibited realistic subjects for the first time in 1875, was afterwards attracted by the style of the French eighteenth century, and painted in that

manner some great compositions like the Fête de Nuit du Palais de l'Elysée, and the panels of the Ministry of Justice; executed for Mr. Dougall Hawkes of New York; celebrated water-colorist, founder of the Society of Water-colorists. He was an officer of the Legion of Honor.

30. Le Bassin de Latone à Versailles.
31. The Indiscreet One.
32. In the Roses.

MANET (Edouard)

Born in Paris, January 23, 1832, died there April 30, 1883. After many changes of fortune at the beginning of his career, he entered the studio of Thomas Couture, traveled in Holland, Germany, Italy, and then in Spain. Up to about 1866, he painted contemporary realistic subjects under the influence of Franz Hals and Spanish masters. About this time he introduced new methods and became associated with the new Impressionist group which had been formed and of which he was the outstanding personality at that time.

Refused admittance to the Salon of 1859, and many times afterwards. He, however, received a medal in 1881, and was decorated with the Legion of Honor in 1882.

The Louvre and the Luxembourg Museum possess paintings of this master. Many of his works are to be found in the public and private collections of the United States.

33. Bock Server. *Private collection.*
34. Stormy Sea. *Private collection.*
34a. The Painter. *Private collection.*

MILLET (J. F.)

Born in 1814, died in 1875, Millet was one of the strongest men, if strength be uncompromising and vigorous adherence to personal ideals, when these are furthest emancipated from and opposed to popularly accepted routine and formulary. The keynote of his art lies in his own expressions, "To characterize the type" and "Nothing counts but what is fundamental." He did this in such largeness of style, such monumental conception, that, although his art has undoubtedly a literary side, this sentimental appeal is always subordinate to his pictorial potency. His superb feeling for color alone would make him a painter rather than a story-teller, even though every one of his peasant subjects not only represents but proclaims loudly all that is noblest and most pathetic in that peasant life with its deeper meanings and larger truths, its dignity of labor, its poetry of common things.

34b. The Man with the Hoe.
Lent by William H. Crocker, Esq.

149

„Indem wir sie für eine gewisse Zeit gehen ließen, ergab sich die Möglichkeit, die 10 Prozent Rechte zu vermeiden, die bei ihrem Eintritt nach Frankreich zu begleichen gewesen wären, wo Werke auf der Durchreise nur ein Jahr verbleiben können: Für die Summe von 1.600.000 Francs hätten Sie also 160.000 Francs bezahlen müssen! Dieses vielumjubelte Ensemble [...] kann entweder für ein weiteres Jahr nach Frankreich zurückkehren oder direkt von San Francisco zu Ihnen gesandt werden."[17]

Nachdem die Kunstwerke sich bereits in San Francisco befänden, sei da nicht der Transport nach Kobe oder Tokio bereits „zur Hälfte erledigt"?[18] Schließlich sandte Kōjirō Matsukata ein Telegramm an Bénédite: „Bitte Übersendung Kopenhagen Bilder Yamanaka London".[19]

Frankreich profitierte also von der Sammlung Matsukata, und zwar zum Nachteil des japanischen Industriellen: Im Ausstellungskatalog wurden die Arbeiten als Teil einer „Privatsammlung" beschrieben, ohne jede Erwähnung des Namens Kōjirō Matsukata. Es war nicht das letzte Mal, dass eine solche absichtliche Unterlassung stattfand. Ein großer Teil der Sammlung Matsukata wurde 1944 vom französischen Staat konfisziert und kam erneut als internationales Vorzeigeprojekt für Frankreich zum Einsatz, diesmal in einem völlig anderen Kontext.

Eine „unerwartete Bereicherung"[20] für französische Museen

Der Großteil der Sammlung Matsukata sollte eigentlich nicht in Frankreich bleiben. Unglücklicherweise fiel jedoch der Tod von Léonce Bénédite im Jahr 1925 nicht nur mit Matsukatas finanziellen Schwierigkeiten zusammen, sondern auch mit einer Erhöhung der japanischen Zolltarife, was den Sammler davon abhielt, all seine Arbeiten nach Japan zurückzuführen. Somit verblieben etwa fünfzig Skulpturen von Rodin und über dreihundert Gemälde, Aquarelle und Zeichnungen im Musée Rodin, was den neuen Direktor, Georges Grappe, zur Verzweiflung brachte. Grappe war äußerst besorgt über die sich verändernden geopolitischen Umstände und schrieb im Mai 1936 an Kosaburo Hioki, Matsukatas Vertreter in Paris:

„Angesichts der allgemeinen Vorschriften für staatliche Gebäude bezüglich der Vorsichtsmaßnahmen, die in Kriegszeiten zu treffen sind, ist klar, dass das Musée Rodin keinesfalls vorhersagen kann, was mit Herrn Matsukatas Sammlung in einem solchen Fall geschehen könnte. Es liegt deshalb an Ihnen, sich bereits jetzt über Maßnahmen für die Gemälde und Skulpturen, die Herrn Matsukata gehören, Gedanken zu machen. [...] Das Musée Rodin sieht sich im Fall eines Krieges von jeglicher Verantwortung enthoben, was die Sammlung des japanischen Mäzens anbelangt."[21]

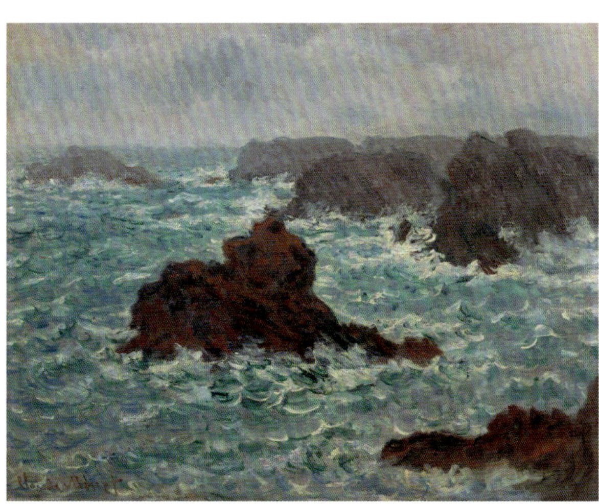

Abb. | Fig. 6
Claude Monet, *Belle-Île, effet de pluie,* 1886, Artizon Museum, Ishibashi Foundation, Tokyo. Ehemals Sammlung Matsukata | formerly Matsukata Collection

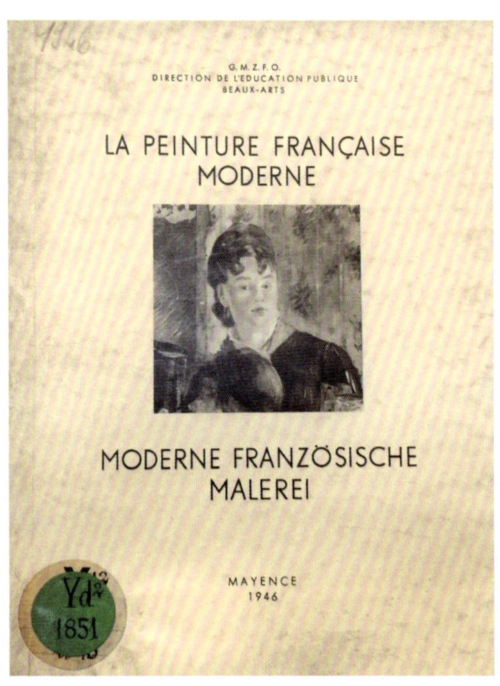

Abb. | Fig. 7
Ausst.-Kat. | exh. cat. Baden-Baden, Mainz, 1946,
Cover

justified this loan by a tax trick, which would
benefit the Japanese collector:

> It was a way, by having them leave tempo-
> rarily, to avoid the 10 per cent rights that would
> have been paid upon their entry into France,
> where works in transit can only remain for
> one year: on the sum of 1,600,000 francs, you
> would have had to pay 160,000 francs! This
> much-admired ensemble [...] can either return
> to France for another year, or be sent directly
> from San Francisco to you.[17]

With the artworks already in San Francisco wasn't
the shipping to Kobe or Tokyo 'halfway done'?[18]
Finally, Kōjirō Matsukata sent a telegram to
Bénédite: 'Please Transfer Copenhagen Pictures
Yamanaka London.'[19]

France thus benefited from the Matsukata Collection to the detriment of the Japanese industrialist: in the exhibition catalogue, the works were
described as belonging to a 'private collector',
with no mention of Kōjirō Matsukata's name. This
was not the last time such a deliberate omission
would occur: a large part of the Matsukata Collection, confiscated by the French state in 1944, was
again used as an international showcase for France,
in a completely different context.

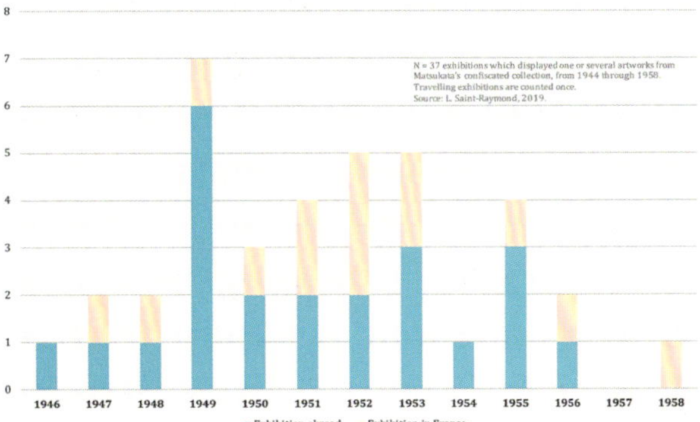

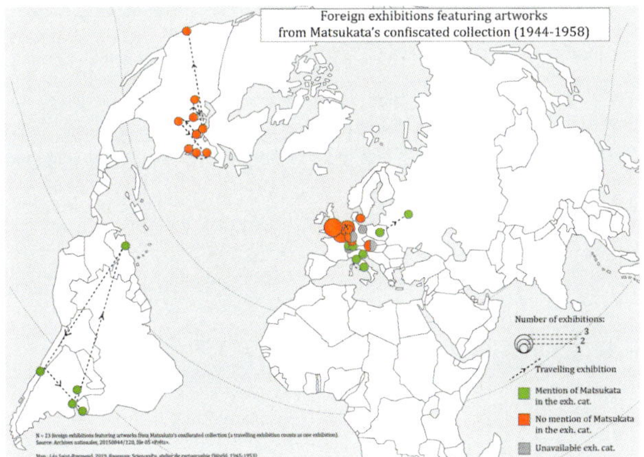

Abb. | Fig. 8
Gesamtzahl der Ausstellungen, bei denen Werke
aus der beschlagnahmten Sammlung Matsukata
gezeigt wurden | total number of exhibitions that
solicited works from Matsukata's confiscated
collection

Abb. | Fig. 9
Ausländische Ausstellungen mit Kunstwerken
aus der beschlagnahmten Sammlung Matsukata |
foreign exhibitions featuring artworks from
Matsukata's confiscated collection, 1944–1958

Bedauerlicherweise brach der Zweite Weltkrieg aus und nach der Befreiung betrachtete der französische Staat die Werke aus der Sammlung Matsukata als „feindliches Vermögen".[22] Die beschlagnahmte Sammlung kam in die Bergungsräume des Musée National d'Art Moderne – die Skulpturen verblieben im Musée Rodin – und weckte, unter der Kontrolle der *Administration des Domaines,* das Interesse französischer Kurator:innen, besonders des Kurators am Musée National d'Art Moderne, Bernard Dorival. In einem Brief an Georges Salles, den Generaldirektor der französischen Museen, erklärte er, dass „es von größtem Interesse für die Abteilungen für Gemälde, Skulpturen, Zeichnungen, moderne Kunst sowie für die Provinzmuseen wäre, wenn ihnen, wenn schon nicht alles, so doch zumindest ein Teil von Herrn Matsukatas konfiszierter Sammlung zugeteilt würde."[23]

Die Sammlung Matsukata geriet somit nach dem Krieg unter französische Kontrolle und diente als Instrument für die Sicherung von Frieden und für den kulturellen Einfluss Frankreichs. In dieser Rolle kam sie erstmals 1946 in Deutschland zum Einsatz und zwar im Rahmen einer Wanderausstellung in Baden-Baden und Mainz mit dem Titel *Moderne Französische Malerei vom Impressionismus bis zur Gegenwart* (Abb. 7). Im April 1947, einige Monate nach der Rückkehr der Arbeiten nach Paris, organisierte Salles eine weitere „Ausstellung französischer Kunst", die auch nach Straßburg, Nancy und Besançon reiste und in deren Rahmen 26 Kunstwerke aus der Sammlung Matsukata gezeigt wurden. Darunter war auch Gauguins Gemälde *Vairumati* (1897; Musée d'Orsay, Paris), das den Umschlag des Katalogs zierte. Von da an wurde die Sammlung Matsukata in den Händen der Museumskurator:innen und der *Association française d'action artistique* unter der Leitung von

An 'Unexpected Enrichment'[20]
for French Museums

For the largest part, the Matsukata Collection was not supposed to remain in France. Unfortunately, the death of Léonce Bénédite in 1925 coincided with Matsukata's financial difficulties and an increase in customs tariffs in Japan, preventing Kōjirō Matsukata from repatriating all his works to Japan. Thus, some fifty sculptures by Rodin and more than three hundred paintings, watercolours and drawings remained in the Rodin Museum, to the great despair of the new director, Georges Grappe. Grappe, worried about the changing geopolitical context, wrote in May 1936 to Kosaburo Hioki, Matsukata's representative in Paris:

> In view of the general instructions concerning state buildings on the precautions to be taken in time of war, it is clear that the Rodin Museum cannot in any way foresee what might happen to Mr Matsukata's collection in such a case. It would therefore be appropriate for you to already consider the measures to be taken for the paintings and statues belonging to Mr Matsukata. [...] The Rodin Museum intends, in the event of war, to be relieved of all responsibility for the collections of the Japanese patron.[21]

Unfortunately, the Second World War broke out and, at the Liberation, the French state considered the works of the Matsukata Collection to be 'enemy property'.[22] The sequestered collection was placed in the reserves of the Musée National d'art Moderne – the sculptures remained at the Rodin Museum – and, under the control of the *Administration des Domaines*, it raised French curators' interest. In particular, the curator of the Musée National d'Art Moderne, Bernard Dorival,

who wrote to Georges Salles, the general director of the Museums of France, explaining that 'it would be of the utmost interest to the departments of painting, sculpture, drawings, modern art and provincial museums to be allocated, if not all, at least part of Mr Matsukata's confiscated collection.'[23]

The Matsukata Collection thus came under French control after the war and served as an instrument for the construction of peace and for French cultural influence. It was first used in Germany in 1946, for a travelling exhibition in Baden-Baden and Mainz, entitled *La Peinture française moderne de l'impressionisme à nos jours / Moderne Französische Malerei vom Impressionismus bis zur Gegenwart* (fig. 7). In April 1947, a few months after the return of the works to Paris, Salles organized another 'exhibition of French art,' also traveling to Strasbourg, Nancy and Besançon, and showed twenty-six artworks from the Matsukata Collection, including Gauguin's *Vairumati* (1897; Musée d'Orsay, Paris), which was chosen to illustrate the cover of the catalogue. From then on, the Matsukata Collection became an artistic showcase for France and its cultural influence abroad, in the hands of the museum curators and of the *Association française d'action artistique* (AFAA), directed by Philippe Erlanger. Through his action, between 1947 and 1955 the main works of the Matsukata Collection travelled all around the world: to the Venice Biennale, Brussels, Stuttgart, Vienna, London, Basel, Copenhagen, Amsterdam, Zurich, Rome, Florence, Moscow, Warsaw, and also to cities in North and South America (figs. 8, 9).[24]

By sparking comparisons between national pavilions, the 1948 Venice Biennale triggered an awakening of French museums. Dorival wrote to the Ministry of Foreign Affairs of 'the unique

153

COLLECTION MATSUKATA

Tableaux souhaités par le Département des Peintures :

VAN GOGH	La chambre à Arles
TOULOUSE-LAUTREC	Portrait de femme
MANET	La serveuse de bock
RENOIR	Parisiennes habillées en Algériennes
GAUGUIN	Vaïrumati
–	Paysage au moulin
–	Nature morte
COURBET	La vague
–	Les paysans dé Flagey revenant de la foire
BONVIN	Trois natures mortes décoratives

Oeuvres souhaitées par le Cabinet des Dessins :

CEZANNE	Aquarelle – Sainte Victoire
–	Le concert champêtre
–	Nature morte aux verres
Gustave MOREAU	Dessin

Tableaux souhaités par le Musée d'Art Moderne :

PICASSO	Femme lisant
SOUTINE	Le groom
–	Volailles

Sculpture souhaitée par le Musée Rodin :

| RODIN | Les Bourgeois de Calais – bronze |

Abb. | Fig. 10
Liste von Werken aus der Sammlung
Matsukata, die für die französischen
Nationalmuseen „um jeden Preis erhalten
werden müssen", Bernard Dorival an
Georges Salles, 5./6. Juli 1950 | list of works
from the Matsukata Collection 'to be kept at
all costs' for the national museums, Bernard
Dorival to Georges Salles, 5/6 July 1950

Philippe Erlanger ein Vorzeigebeispiel für Frankreich und dessen kulturellen Einfluss im Ausland. Auf Betreiben Erlangers reisten die Hauptwerke aus der Sammlung Matsukata zwischen 1947 und 1955 um die ganze Welt: zur Biennale von Venedig, nach Brüssel, Stuttgart, Wien, London, Basel, Kopenhagen, Amsterdam, Zürich, Rom, Florenz, Moskau, Warschau und auch in nord- und südamerikanische Städte (Abb. 8, 9).[24]

Die Biennale entfachte den Vergleich zwischen den nationalen Pavillons und löste damit eine Art Erwachen der französischen Museen aus. Dorival schrieb an das Ministerium für auswärtige Angelegenheiten über „die einzigartige Bedeutung dieser Sammlung und das Interesse Frankreichs daran, diese für seine Museen zu erhalten"[25] und übersandte eine Liste der Stücke aus „dieser Sammlung, eine der schönsten in Frankreich, [die] weltweit beinahe einzigartig"[26] sei.

Ohne näher auf all die Wendungen und Verwicklungen dieser Angelegenheit einzugehen,[27] sei lediglich erwähnt, dass zwei Ereignisse die Abwicklung der Beschlagnahmung beschleunigten. Zunächst übersandte Dorival nach dem Tod von Matsukata am 24. Juni 1950 an Salles eine Liste von Werken aus der Sammlung, die für die französischen Nationalmuseen „um jeden Preis erhalten werden müssen"[28] (Abb. 10). Dann machte der Friedensvertrag von San Francisco vom 8. September 1951, der am 28. April 1952 in Kraft trat, den französischen Staat zum Eigentümer der Sammlung Matsukata. Schließlich gelangte man zu dem Entschluss, den Großteil der Sammlung an den japanischen Staat zu „übergeben", um – wie Matsukata es sich erträumt hatte – ein Museum französischer Kunst in Japan zu begründen, die Meisterwerke jedoch in französischen Nationalsammlungen zu behalten. Germain Bazin, Kurator für Gemälde im Louvre, informierte Salles über seinen Wunsch,

importance of this collection and the interest that France would have in keeping it for its museums',[25] and he sent a note listing the pieces of 'this collection, one of the most beautiful in France, [which] is almost unique in the world'.[26]

Without going into all the twists and turns of the affair,[27] two events accelerated the settlement of the confiscation. First, after the death of Matsukata on 24 June 1950, Dorival sent Salles a list of works from the collection 'to be kept at all costs'[28] for the French national museums (fig. 10). Then, on 8 September 1951, the Treaty of San Francisco made the French state the owner of the Matsukata Collection as soon as it came into force on 28 April 1952. It was finally decided to 'give' the majority of the collection to the Japanese state in order to create, as Matsukata had dreamed, a museum of French art in Japan, but to keep the masterpieces in the French national collections. Germain Bazin, curator of paintings at the Louvre, informed Salles of his wish to increase the Louvre's claims, in particular with the entry of seven paintings by Gauguin: 'I don't need to tell you how much this Matsukata sequestration constitutes for the provincial museums and the Louvre an unexpected enrichment, much more important than anything we have recovered in Germany,'[29] he wrote to his superior. Together with him, Jacqueline Bouchot-Saupique, curator of the Louvre's *Cabinet des Dessins*, Dorival and Jean Cassou expanded their wish list but they came up against Robert Schuman, Minister of Foreign Affairs, who considered that 'the claims of the national museums [were] excessive.'[30] He finally reduced their claims and reached the current division of artworks between the French museums and the NMWA in Tokyo.[31]

If in Japan the importance of the Matsukata Collection remains notable and its memory alive, the situation is quite different in France. Most of the labels of works from Matsukata's collection mention only the following provenance: 'entered in application of the peace treaty with Japan, 1959' (*entré en application du traité de paix avec le Japon, 1959*). Similarly, while his proximity to Monet is often mentioned, his fruitful relationship with Léonce Bénédite is only rarely reported. The link between Kōjirō Matsukata and the French museums remains indelible, the history of this relationship continues to be written and is rich in many possibilities.

die Ansprüche des Louvre zu erweitern, besonders durch den Eingang von sieben Gemälden
Gauguins: „Ich muss Ihnen nicht erst sagen, welch
unerwartete Bereicherung diese Matsukata-Be-
schlagnahmung für die Provinzmuseen und den
Louvre darstellt, weitaus bedeutender als alles, was
wir in Deutschland wiedererlangt haben",[29] schrieb
er an seinen Vorgesetzten. Neben ihm erweiterten
auch Jacqueline Bouchot-Saupique, die Kuratorin
des Grafischen Kabinetts am Louvre, Dorival und
Jean Cassou ihre Wunschlisten, stießen dabei
jedoch auf den Widerstand von Robert Schuman,
dem Minister für auswärtige Angelegenheiten, der
der Ansicht war, dass „die Ansprüche der nationalen Museen überzogen"[30] seien. Schlussendlich
reduzierte er deren Forderungen und erzielte
die noch heute gültige Aufteilung der Kunstwerke
zwischen den französischen Museen und dem
National Museum of Western Art in Tokio.[31]

Während die Bedeutung der Sammlung
Matsukata in Japan weiterhin beträchtlich ist und
die Erinnerung daran immer noch lebendig, so
gestaltet sich die Situation in Frankreich anders.
Die meisten Bildunterschriften der Arbeiten aus
Matsukatas Sammlung erwähnen lediglich die
folgende Provenienz: „Zugang in Anwendung des
Friedensabkommens mit Japan, 1959" („Entrée en
application du traité de paix avec le Japon, 1959").
Ebenso wird kaum über Matsukatas fruchtbare
Beziehung zu Léonce Bénédite berichtet, während
seine Nähe zu Monet oft Erwähnung findet. Die
Verbindung zwischen Kōjirō Matsukata und den
französischen Museen bleibt jedoch unauslösch-
lich; die Geschichte dieses Verhältnisses wird nicht
nur weitergeschrieben, sie ist in vielerlei Hinsicht
auch äußerst reich an Möglichkeiten.

1 Léonce Bénédite an Kōjirō
Matsukata, Brief vom 30.6.1920,
Institut national d'histoire de l'art
(INHA) [60–2]: „une grande fierté
pour la France". Wenn nicht anders
angegeben, stammen sämtliche
Übersetzungen von Alexandra
Titze-Grabec.

2 Ebd.: „Si bien représentée grâce
à vous."

3 Kōjirō Matsukatas Begrüßungsrede
für die Ehrenlegion vom 9.7.1921,
INHA [299]: „J'espère par ce moyen
propager dans mon pays, qui est
l'ami des arts, le goût et l'admiration pour les chefs de vos grands
artistes."

4 Ebd.

5 Léonce Bénédite an Kōjirō
Matsukata, Brief vom 30.6.1920:
„Ce sera une grande fierté pour la
France d'être si bien représentée
grâce à vous dans le pays du
soleil levant."

6 Siehe Akiko Mabuchi, „Rodin's
Gate of Hell. The First Four Bronzes
and Their Destinies", in: *The Matsu-
kata Collection. A One-Hundred-
Year Odyssey*, Ausst.-Kat. National
Museum of Western Art, Tokio,
Tokio 2019, S. 308–317.

7 Quittung der Bank Suzuki & Co
an Léonce Bénédite, 10.9.1918,
INHA [4].

8 Kōjirō Matsukata an Léonce
Bénédite, Brief vom 4.11.1920,
INHA [83].

9 Léonce Bénédite an Kōjirō
Matsukata, Brief vom 2.11.1922, INHA
[180–182]: „Le directeur d'une
grande compagnie d'assurances
au Danemark, M. Hansen a recruté
depuis de longues années un
ensemble vraiment unique de
pièces de premier ordre de l'école
française moderne. C'est un incomparable musée dont le Louvre et le
Luxembourg pourraient être jaloux.
Ce musée était destiné à la pensée
de M. Hansen à être offert à la
nation danoise. Des spéculations
malheureuses l'obligent à se défaire d'une partie de sa collection
pour payer une partie de ses
dettes."

10 Ebd.: „[...] en un seul coup un
merveilleux musée."

11 An Kōjirō Matsukata übersandte
Liste, 6.3.1923, INHA [200].

12 Léonce Bénédite an Kōjirō
Matsukata, Brief vom Juni 1923,
INHA [211–2]; 30.3.1923, Lénars & Co,
„geliefert an das Musée Rodin",
INHA [205].

13 Léonce Bénédite an Kōjirō
Matsukata, undatierter Brief (nach
Januar 1924), INHA [271–6].

14 *Catalog. Inaugural exposition of
French art in the California Palace of
the Legion of Honor, Lincoln Park,
San Francisco. California, 1924–1925*,
Ausst.-Kat. California Palace of the
Legion of Honor, San Francisco,
San Francisco 1924.

15 Léonce Bénédite an Kōjirō
Matsukata, Brief vom 4.12.1924, INHA
[245–7]: „J'ai pris la liberté [...] de
faire figurer à l'exposition d'Art
français de San Francisco à peu
près toutes les œuvres provenant
de la collection Hansen, de
Copenhague."

16 Léonce Bénédite an Kōjirō
Matsukata, Brief vom 10.2.1925,
INHA [256]: „[...] le plus beau et le
plus important noyau de l'exposition rétrospective française."

17 Léonce Bénédite an Kōjirō
Matsukata, Brief vom 4.12.1924, INHA
[245–7]: „C'était le moyen en les
faisant sortir momentanément de
nous éviter les droits de 10% qu'ils
auraient dû payer à leur entrée en
France, où les œuvres en transit ne
peuvent demeurer qu'un an, sur la
somme de 1 600 000 fr, vous auriez
donc eu 160 000 fr à payer! Cet
ensemble, dûment assuré d'ailleurs,
fort admiré, pourra donc soit
retourner encore pour un an en
France, soit être dirigé directement
de San Francisco chez vous."

18 Léonce Bénédite an Kōjirō
Matsukata, Brief vom 10.2.1925,
INHA [256]: „[...] la moitié du chemin
de fait."

19 Kōjirō Matsukata an Léonce
Bénédite, Telegramm von Januar
1925, INHA [255].

1 Letter from Léonce Bénédite to Kōjirō Matsukata, 30 June 1920. Institut national d'histoire de l'art (INHA) [60–2] : *Une grande fierté pour la France.* Unless stated otherwise, all translations are by the author.

2 Ibid. : *'Si bien représentée grâce à vous.'*

3 Kōjirō Matsukata's reception speech for the Legion of Honor, 9 July 1921. INHA [299]: *'J'espère par ce moyen propager dans mon pays, qui est l'ami des arts, le goût et l'admiration pour les chefs de vos grands artistes.'*

4 Ibid.

5 Letter from Léonce Bénédite to Kōjirō Matsukata, 30 June 1920. INHA [60–2]: *'Ce sera une grande fierté pour la France d'être si bien représentée grâce à vous dans le pays du soleil levant.'*

6 See, Akiko Mabuchi, 'Rodin's *Gate of Hell*: The First Four Bronzes and Their Destinies', in *The Matsukata Collection: A One-Hundred-Year Odyssey*, exh. cat The National Museum of Western Art, Tokyo (Tokyo, 2019), 308–317.

7 Receipt from the Suzuki & Co bank to Léonce Bénédite, 10 September 1918. INHA [4]

8 Letter from Kōjirō Matsukata to Léonce Bénédite, 4 November 1920. INHA [83]

9 Letter from Léonce Bénédite to Kōjirō Matsukata, 2 November 1922. INHA [180 to 182]: *'Le directeur d'une grande compagnie d'assurances au Danemark, M. Hansen a recruté depuis de longues années un ensemble vraiment unique de pièces de premier ordre de l'école française moderne. C'est un incomparable musée dont le Louvre et le Luxembourg pourraient être jaloux. Ce musée était destiné à la pensée de M. Hansen à être offert à la nation danoise. Des spéculations malheureuses l'obligent à se défaire d'une partie de sa collection pour payer une partie de ses dettes.'*

10 Ibid. *'en un seul coup un merveilleux musée'.*

11 List sent to Kōjirō Matsukata, 6 March 1923. INHA [200]

12 Letter from Léonce Bénédite to Kōjirō Matsukata, June 1923. INHA [211–2]; 30 March 1923, Lénars & Co, 'delivered to the Rodin Museum.' INHA [205]

13 Undated letter from Léonce Bénédite to Kōjirō Matsukata (after January 1924). INHA [271–6]

14 *Catalogue. Inaugural exposition of French art in the California Palace of the Legion of Honor, Lincoln Park, San Francisco. California, 1924–1925* (San Francisco, 1924).

15 Letter from Léonce Bénédite to Kōjirō Matsukata, 4 December 1924. INHA [245–7]: *'J'ai pris la liberté [...] de faire figurer à l'exposition d'Art français de San Francisco à peu près toutes les œuvres provenant de la collection Hansen, de Copenhague.'*

16 Letter from Léonce Bénédite to Kōjirō Matsukata, 10 February 1925. INHA [256]: *'le plus beau et le plus important noyau de l'exposition rétrospective française.'*

17 Letter from Léonce Bénédite to Kōjirō Matsukata, 4 December 1924. INHA [245–7]: *'C'était le moyen en les faisant sortir momentanément de nous éviter les droits de 10% qu'ils auraient dû payer à leur entrée en France, où les œuvres en transit ne peuvent demeurer qu'un an, sur la somme de 1 600 000 fr, vous auriez donc eu 160 000 fr à payer! Cet ensemble, dûment assuré d'ailleurs, fort admiré, pourra donc soit retourner encore pour un an en France, soit être dirigé directement de San Francisco chez vous.'*

18 Letter from Léonce Bénédite to Kōjirō Matsukata, 10 February 1925. INHA [256]: *'la moitié du chemin de fait'.*

19 Cable from Kōjirō Matsukata to Léonce Bénédite, January 1925. INHA [255].

20 Letter from Germaine Bazin to Georges Salles, 28 May 1952. Archives Nationales (AN), 20150044/120: *'un enrichissement inespéré'.*

21 Letter from Georges Grappe to Kosaburo Hioki, 19 May 1936. [Musée Rodin]: *'Étant donné les instructions générales concernant les bâtiments de l'État sur les précautions à prendre en temps de guerre, il est bien entendu que le Musée Rodin ne saurait en aucune façon prévoir ce que pourrait devenir la collection de M. Matsukata en pareil cas. Il y aurait donc lieu que vous vous occupiez dès maintenant d'envisager les mesures à prendre pour les tableaux et statues appartenant à M. Matsukata. [...] Le Musée Rodin entend bien, en cas de guerre, être déchargé de toute responsabilité à l'égard des collections du Mécène japonais.'*

22 On the trajectory of the works during the Second World War see, Léa Saint-Raymond and Maxime Georges Métraux, 'La Chambre à Arles de Van Gogh: Pièce maîtresse du séquestre Matsukata,' in *Noto – Revue Culturelle*, no 14 (2020): 99–103.

23 Letter from Bernard Dorival to Georges Salles, 30 September 1945. AN, 20150044/120.

24 Léa Saint-Raymond and Maxime Georges Métraux, 'From Enemy Asset to National Showcase: France's Seizure and Circulation of the Matsukata Collection (1944–1958).' in *Artl@s Bulletin 8*, no 3 (2019), article 2.

25 Letter from Bernard Dorival to Jean Chauvel, Secrétaire Général au Ministère des Affaires Etrangères, 3 November 1948. AN, 20150044/120: *'Vous verrez l'importance unique de cette collection et l'intérêt qu'aurait la France à la garder pour ses musées.'*

26 Note by Bernard Dorival, September 1948. AN, 20150044/120: *'Cette collection, une des plus belles de France, est à peu près unique au monde.'*

27 Léa Saint-Raymond and Maxime Georges Métraux, 'La Chambre à Arles de Van Gogh : Pièce maîtresse du séquestre Matsukata,' in *Noto – Revue Culturelle*, no 14 (2020): 94–121.

28 Letter from Bernard Dorival to Georges Salles, 5 or 6 July 1950. AN, 20150044/120: *'à conserver à tout prix'.*

29 Letter from Germain Bazin to Georges Salles, 28 May 1952. AN, 20150044/120: *'Je n'ai pas besoin de vous dire combien ce séquestre Matsukata constitue pour les Musées de Province et le Musée du Louvre un enrichissement inespéré, beaucoup plus important que tout ce que nous avons récupéré en Allemagne.'*

30 Note, 11 June 1952. Groupe Archives Municipales / Archivage Electronique (AMAE), 554 INVA 1294: *'les prétentions des Musées Nationaux sont excessives.'*

31 Eighteen artworks were kept by France, 370 were 'given' to Japan. Source: https://dataverse.harvard.edu/dataset.xhtml?persistentId=doi:10.7910/DVN/7OYPMN (last accessed 15 July 2021).

20 Germain Bazin an Georges Salles, Brief vom 28.5.1952, Archives nationales (AN), 20150044/120: „[…] un enrichissement inespéré."

21 Georges Grappe an Kosaburo Hioki, Brief vom 19.5.1936, Musée Rodin: „Étant donné les instructions générales concernant les bâtiments de l'État sur les précautions à prendre en temps de guerre, il est bien entendu que le Musée Rodin ne saurait en aucune façon prévoir ce que pourrait devenir la collection de M. Matsukata en pareil cas. Il y aurait donc lieu que vous vous occupiez dès maintenant d'envisager les mesures à prendre pour les tableaux et statues appartenant à M. Matsukata. […] Le Musée Rodin entend bien, en cas de guerre, être déchargé de toute responsabilité à l'égard des collections du Mécène japonais."

22 Zum Verbleib der Arbeiten während des Zweiten Weltkriegs siehe Léa Saint-Raymond und Maxime Georges Métraux, „La Chambre à Arles de Van Gogh. Pièce maîtresse du séquestre Matsukata", in: *Noto – Revue Culturelle*, 14, 2020, S. 99–103.

23 Bernard Dorival an Georges Salles, Brief vom 30.9.1945, AN, 20150044/120: „Il serait donc du plus haut intérêt pour les départements de la peinture, de la sculpture, des dessins, de l'art moderne et des Musées de province de se voir attribués, sinon la totalité, du moins une partie de la collection mise sous-séquestre de Monsieur Matsukata."

24 Léa Saint-Raymond und Maxime Georges Métraux, „From Enemy Asset to National Showcase. France's Seizure and Circulation of the Matsukata Collection (1944–1958)", in: *Artl@s Bulletin,* 8, 3, 2019, Absatz 2.

25 Bernard Dorival an Jean Chauvel (Secrétaire Général au Ministère des Affaires Etrangères), Brief vom 3.11.1948, AN, 20150044/120: „Vous verrez l'importance unique de cette collection et l'intérêt qu'aurait la France à la garder pour ses musées."

26 Notiz von Bernard Dorival, September 1948, AN, 20150044/120: „Cette collection, une des plus belles de France, est à peu près unique au monde."

27 Léa Saint-Raymond und Maxime Georges Métraux, „La Chambre à Arles de Van Gogh".

28 Bernard Dorival an Georges Salles, Brief vom 5. oder 6.7.1950, AN, 20150044/120: „[…] à conserver à tout prix."

29 Germain Bazin an Georges Salles, Brief vom 28.5.1952, AN, 20150044/120: „Je n'ai pas besoin de vous dire combien ce séquestre Matsukata constitue pour les Musées de Province et le Musée du Louvre un enrichissement inespéré, beaucoup plus important que tout ce que nous avons récupéré en Allemagne."

30 Notiz, 11.6.1952. Groupe Archives Municipales / Archivage Electronique (AMAE), 554 INVA 1294: „[…] les prétentions des Musées Nationaux sont excessives."

31 18 Kunstwerke blieben in Frankreich, 370 wurden an Japan „übergeben". Quelle: https://dataverse.harvard.edu/dataset.xhtml?persistentId=doi:10.7910/DVN/7OYPMN [zuletzt aufgerufen am 15.7.2021].

HOUSING THE MATSUKATA COLLECTION –

ON THE GENESIS OF THE NATIONAL MUSEUM OF WESTERN ART IN TOKYO, 1953–1955

Robert Maximilian Woitschützke
Yoshiyuki Yamana

Seen from today's perspective, the establishment in 1959 of Tokyo's National Museum of Western Art (NMWA), based on the sequestered Matsukata Collection, appears to be an almost exemplary case of well-managed bilateral cultural diplomacy. However, the genesis of this institution was by no means smooth. Although united by their aim to achieve the final goal of the collection's restitution and the creation of a new museum, Japanese and French authorities found themselves struggling with tedious and time-consuming discussions, differing expectations and mutual misunderstandings.[1] The whole process took almost ten years – far longer than either side had anticipated.

As is well known, it was Le Corbusier who in October 1955 was finally entrusted with the task of designing a new museum for the Matsukata Collection in Tokyo, where he was to create one of his most celebrated buildings. However, between 1953 and 1955, two years prior to Le Corbusier's commission, discussions under the guidance of the Monbusho (Japanese Ministry of Education) for architectural solutions for a new museum were already underway. During these two years, three ideas crystallized into more or less concrete plans. These will be portrayed on the following pages, thus highlighting the early phase of the museum's formation.

Aus heutiger Sicht erscheint die Gründung des
National Museum of Western Art (Nationalmuseum
für westliche Kunst; NMWA) in Tokio, das als
Schaufenster für die nach dem Zweiten Weltkrieg
durch Frankreich beschlagnahmte Sammlung
Matsukata dienen sollte, als Paradebeispiel für
gelungene bilaterale Kulturdiplomatie. Die Entstehung dieser Institution verlief jedoch keineswegs
reibungslos. Zwar waren sich die japanischen und
französischen Behörden darin einig, die Kunstsammlung nach Japan zurückzuführen, doch die
Verhandlungen wurden durch mühsame und
zeitaufwendige Diskussionen, unterschiedliche
Erwartungen und gegenseitige Missverständnisse
erschwert. Der Restitutionsprozess dauerte fast
zehn Jahre, deutlich länger als von beiden Seiten
erwartet.[1]

Es war schließlich Le Corbusier, der im Oktober
1955 mit der Aufgabe betraut wurde, in Tokio ein
neues Museum für die Sammlung Matsukata zu
gestalten. Das von ihm entworfene heutige National Museum of Western Art sollte eines seiner
bekanntesten Bauvorhaben werden, doch bereits
vor der Auftragserteilung an den französischen
Architekten wurden zwischen 1953 und 1955 unter
der Leitung des Monbusho (Japanisches Bildungsministerium) architektonische Lösungen für ein
neues Museum intern diskutiert. In diesen beiden
Jahren kristallisierten sich drei mehr oder weniger
ausgearbeitete Pläne heraus, die auf den folgenden Seiten dargestellt werden. Im Mittelpunkt dieser Ausführungen steht die bislang wenig bekannte
Frühphase der Museumsplanung.

159   Robert Maximilian Woitschützke
Yoshiyuki Yamana

DIE FRÜHEN JAHRE DER ENTSTEHUNG DES NATIONAL MUSEUM OF WESTERN ART IN TOKIO, 1953–1955

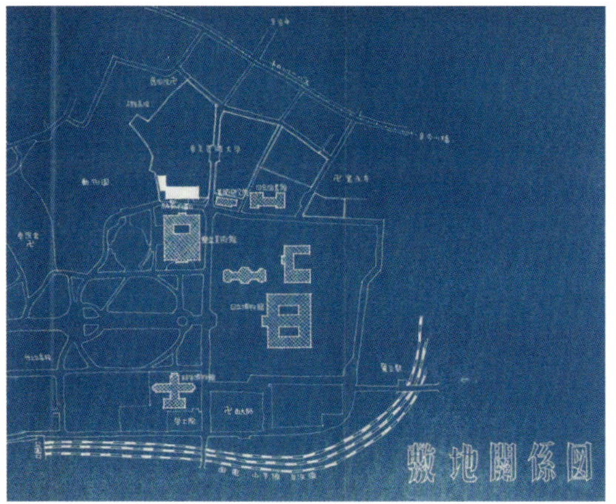

Abb. | Fig. 1
Geijutsu Daigaku, Lage des geplanten Museums
für französische Kunst im Ueno-Park, 1953.
Das Bauwerk ist links oben weiß hervorgehoben
und befindet sich auf dem Gelände der Universität |
Geijutsu Daigaku, situation of the proposed Museum
of French Art in Ueno Park, 1953. The structure is
highlighted in white on the upper left and located
on the grounds of the university

Summer 1953:
the Tokyo University of the Arts

At the end of the Second World War, the French government confiscated the collection of the Japanese Industrialist, Kōjirō Matsukata that had been stored in France, as enemy property. In the subsequent years, while both Japan and France were aware of the issue, nothing could be done until the ratification of the San Francisco Peace Treaty in 1951, when Japan regained its complete sovereignty and thus became able to fully restore its relationships with the international community.

A possible restitution of the sequestered collection was first raised in 1952 during discussions between the Japanese Prime Minister, Shigeru Yoshida, and the French Minister of Foreign Affairs, Robert Schuman. However, some years passed before the process arrived at practical steps. The restitution was agreed upon in spring 1953, and measures concerning its subsequent housing commenced soon after under the guidance of the Monbusho.

In September 1953, Charles Le Genissel, a member of the French Embassy in Tokyo, summarized the most recent developments concerning the Matsukata Collection in a letter to the French Minister of Foreign Affairs:

> At the moment, to the best of my knowledge, four ideas seem to be examined. The first one considers the use of the old Marine Museum which nowadays remains closed and occupied by private third parties. The second one [...] considers the use of a terrain on the vicinity of the National University of Arts in Ueno to erect a specially designed building. The third idea [...] proposes to temporarily offer an unutilized wing of the [National] museum to house the collection until a new building has been completed. In addition to that, the Maison Franco-Japonaise offered the use of some parts of its premises for the construction of a new museum as well.[2]

Among the ideas outlined by Charles Le Genissel, the propositions for a museum on the grounds of the Geijutsu Daigaku (Tokyo University of the Arts) must have been the earliest as they were already proposed to the Ministry of Education in July 1953, some months prior to Genissel's letter, under the title 'Museum of French Art'.[3] It seems that the idea for these plans came originally from members of the university although the apparently fostered their execution.[4] Here, for the first time, a location in Ueno Park was chosen (fig. 1).

Unlike subsequent propositions that shall be discussed below, the plans by the university had already reached a considerable degree of detail. The structure itself appears to be an almost exemplary showcase of international modernistic vocabulary (fig. 2). Seen in the context of its time, it is rather obvious that Junzo Sakakura's 1951 Museum of Modern Art in Kamakura – the first Japanese post-war exhibition building to adopt the rules of international modernism – was the design's harbinger. The influence of this structure on the plans by the University of the Arts is most clearly

Sommer 1953:
Die Pläne der Kunsthochschule Tokio

Mit Ende des Zweiten Weltkrieges erklärte die
französische Regierung die in Frankreich gelagerte
Sammlung des japanischen Industriellen Kōjirō
Matsukata zu Feindeseigentum und damit zu Staats-
besitz. Jahre diplomatischen Tauziehens vergin-
gen, ehe Japan seine volle Souveränität 1951 durch
die Unterzeichnung des Friedensvertrages von
San Francisco wiedererlangte und der Weg für
die Wiederherstellung freundschaftlicher Beziehungen mit der internationalen Gemeinschaft
geebnet war.

Erste Überlegungen bezüglich der Restitution
der Sammlung wurden 1952 in Gesprächen zwischen dem japanischen Premierminister Shigeru
Yoshida und dem französischen Außenminister
Robert Schuman angestellt. Knapp zwei Jahre
später, im Frühjahr 1953, vereinbarten beide Seiten
eine zeitnahe Rückgabe, woraufhin das Monbusho
unverzüglich mit Planungen für die Unterbringung
der Sammlung begann. Im September 1953 fasste
Charles Le Genissel, ein Mitglied der französischen Botschaft in Tokio, die aktuellen Entwicklungen bezüglich der Sammlung Matsukata in einer
Depesche an den französischen Außenminister
zusammen:

> „Im Moment werden nach meinem Wissen vier
> Entwürfe geprüft. Der erste erwägt die Verwen-
> dung des alten Marinemuseums, das zur Zeit
> zweckentfremdet und von privaten Interessen-
> ten belegt ist. Der zweite [...] schlägt die Nut-
> zung eines Geländes in der Nähe der Universität

der Künste in Ueno und die dortige Errichtung
eines neuen Gebäudes vor. Der dritte Entwurf
[...] sieht vor, vorübergehend einen ungenutzten Flügel des Nationalmuseums zu verwenden,
bis ein neues Gebäude fertiggestellt ist. Auch
die Maison Franco-Japonaise [...] äußerte sich
und bot an, einen ungenutzten Teil ihres Grund-
stückes für den Bau eines neuen Museums zu
nutzen."[2]

Von diesen Vorschlägen dürfte jener der Geijutsu
Daigaku (Kunsthochschule) als erstes in Erwägung
gezogen worden sein, denn bereits im Juli 1953 –
also Monate vor Genissels Brief – unterbreitete
die Hochschule dem Bildungsministerium entsprechende Pläne unter dem Titel „Museum für französische Kunst" (*furanzu bijutsukan*).[3] Die Pläne lassen
sich keinem Gestalter namentlich zuordnen, doch
es ist davon auszugehen, dass sie von Professor:in-
nen oder Student:innen der Hochschule ausge-
arbeitet wurden – offenbar unter der wohlwollen-
den Ägide des Monbusho.[4] Zum ersten Mal wurde
in ihnen ein prominenter Standort im Ueno-Park,
einer großflächigen Parkanlage im Herzen Tokios,
illustriert (Abb. 1).

Anders als die im weiteren Verlauf dieses Textes besprochenen Bauentwürfe erreichten die
Pläne der Geijutsu Daigaku bereits ein beträchtliches Maß an Detailfülle. Die dargestellte Struktur
erscheint dabei fast als Musterbeispiel des damals gängigen modernistischen Formvokabulars
(Abb. 2), wobei der Einfluss des erst kurz zuvor
fertiggestellten Museums für Moderne Kunst in
Kamakura, ein Werk des Corbusier-Schülers Junzō

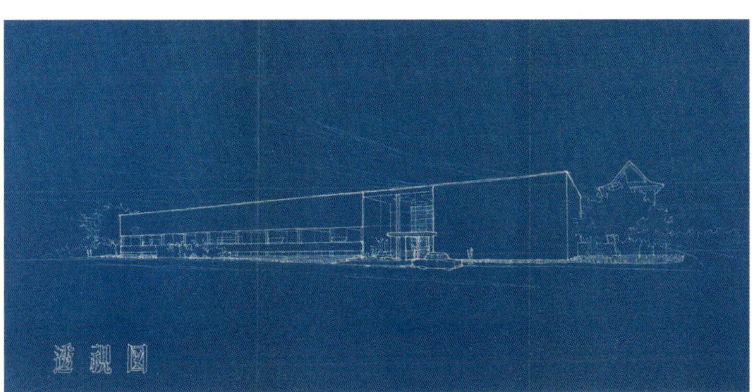

Abb. | Fig. 2
Geijutsu Daigaku, Aufriss des geplanten
Museums für französische Kunst | elevation
of the proposed museum of French Art,
1953

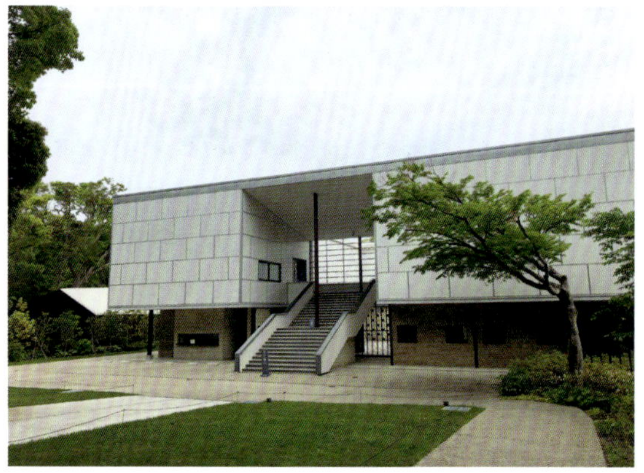

Abb. | Fig. 3
Junzō Sakakura, Museum für moderne Kunst, Kamakura (kürzlich umbenannt in Tsuru-gaoka Hachimangu Museum, Kamakura) | Museum of Modern Art, Kamakura (recently renamed Tsurugaoka Hachimangu Museum, Kamakura), 1951

seen in the open vestibule with a slim vertical pillar spanning the space from floor to ceiling, a motif Sakakura had used prominently in the facade of his museum design (fig. 3). In this regard, it is worth noting that Sakakura's design was itself already partly based on Le Corbusier's prototype of the 'Museum of Unlimited Growth', a design that would ultimately be realized by Le Corbusier himself in the NMWA.

However, despite their sophistication, these ideas do not seem to have been regarded as a serious option among Japanese officials, and no trace can be found that they were discussed with the French authorities at any time.

Spring 1954: Hyōkeikan

On 4 December 1953, just a few months after the Tokyo University of the Arts proposed the above-mentioned drawings to the Monbusho, the issue of the new museum was discussed during a Cabinet meeting. During this meeting, the Minister of Education proposed, among other things, the following unusual strategy which was subsequently officially approved: 'In case it becomes necessary to receive the collection before the completion of the new museum, a facility for temporary keeping should be considered separately.'[5] Although it was already decided at this time that a new museum building should ultimately be erected, the financing of the project was not yet clearly solved. Thus, the idea of renovating an existing building as a temporary storage was approved.[6]

The choice fell on the Hyōkeikan ('Pavilion of the Expression of Joy'; fig. 4)), a western-style, late-Meiji-era (1868–1912) building in the grounds of the National Museum in Ueno Park. Unlike the plans by the University of the Arts, the Hyōkeikan plans, despite being far less elaborate, were subject to quite lengthy discussions with the French administration and even came to be publicly announced. On 21 January 1954, the newspaper *The Asahi Shimbun* officially reported that it had been decided to display the Matsukata Collection in the Hyōkeikan.[7] During that time, the building, formerly used to display artefacts from Japanese history, was unused and in need of renovation.

It seems that no precise plans for a renovation of Hyōkeikan had been made until the director of the Louvre, Georges Salles, visited Tokyo in February 1954 to help foster negotiations between French and Japanese authorities regarding the restitution. He did not respond favourably to the Hyōkeikan solution but half-heartedly agreed that it might be used as a temporary solution under the condition that partition walls would be installed, existing showcases removed, a new lighting system implemented, and the outer façade repainted (fig. 5). [8] Several sketches that were made according to Salles's recommendations by the Ministry's inhouse architectural department have been saved in the NMWA archives (figs. 6, 7).[9]

However, Salles's diplomatic approach did not reflect the opinion of his fellow countrymen. The French Embassy in Japan rejected Hyōkeikan completely and considered it inappropriate even

Sakakura, unübersehbar ist. Am deutlichsten wird Sakakuras Vorbildwirkung im offenen Vestibül mit vertikalem Pfeiler, ein Motiv, das von ihm in der Nordfassade seines Museums verwendet wurde und das prominent Eingang in die Pläne der Geijutsu Daigaku fand (Abb. 3). Bemerkenswert ist in diesem Zusammenhang, dass Sakakuras Museum (Japans erster moderner Museumsbau der Nachkriegszeit) bereits teilweise auf Le Corbusiers Idee eines „Museums des endlosen Wachstums" basierte, einem baulichen Konzept, das letztlich von Le Corbusier im späteren NMWA realisiert werden sollte.

Trotz ihrer architektonischen Raffinessen scheinen diese Ideen jedoch innerhalb des Monbusho nicht als ernsthafte Option angesehen worden zu sein. Es finden sich keine Hinweise, dass sie zu irgendeinem Zeitpunkt mit den französischen Behörden besprochen wurden.

Frühling 1954: Hyōkeikan

163

Nur wenige Monate, nachdem die Kunsthochschule dem Monbusho die oben genannten Entwürfe vorgeschlagen hatte, wurde die Frage des neuen Museums während einer Kabinettssitzung am 4. Dezember 1953 diskutiert. Während dieses Treffens schlug der Bildungsminister unter anderem folgende ungewöhnliche Strategie vor: „Falls es notwendig wird, die Sammlung vor der Fertigstellung eines neuen Gebäudes zu übernehmen, sollte eine Einrichtung für die vorübergehende Unterbringung gesondert in Betracht gezogen werden."[5] Obwohl zu diesem Zeitpunkt bereits

beschlossen worden war, dass ein neues Museum errichtet werden solle, war dessen Finanzierung noch nicht eindeutig geklärt. So wurde der Vorschlag, ein bestehendes Gebäude für eine zwischenzeitliche Beheimatung zu renovieren, genehmigt.[6]

Die Wahl fiel auf das 1909 eröffnete Hyōkeikan (Abb. 4), ein historisches Ausstellungs- und Galeriegebäude im westlichen Baustil auf dem Gelände des Nationalmuseums im Ueno-Park in Tokio. Anders als die Entwürfe der Geijutsu Daigaku wurden die Hyōkeikan-Pläne, obwohl weit weniger elaboriert als jene der Kunsthochschule, vermutlich aufgrund ihrer Praktikabilität über längere Zeit mit der französischen Regierung diskutiert und sogar öffentlich bekannt gegeben. Bereits am 21. Januar 1954 berichtete die Zeitung *The Asahi Shimbun* offiziell, dass beschlossen worden sei, die Sammlung Matsukata im Hyōkeikan auszustellen.[7] Das Gebäude, vormals zur Ausstellung japanischer Antiken genutzt, stand zu diesem Zeitpunkt leer und war renovierungsbedürftig.

Detaillierte Pläne für die Ertüchtigung des Hyōkeikan wurden im Zuge eines Besuchs des französischen Museumsleiters Georges Salles, Direktor des Louvre, in Tokio im Januar 1954 angefertigt. Salles, der nach Japan gereist war, um die stockenden Verhandlungen zwischen Frankreich und Japan über die Rückführung der Sammlung Matsukata voranzutreiben, reagierte zwar nicht überschwänglich auf den Hyōkeikan-Kompromiss, gestand aber halbherzig, dass er als Übergangslösung dienen könne, sofern Trennwände installiert, bestehende Vitrinen entfernt,

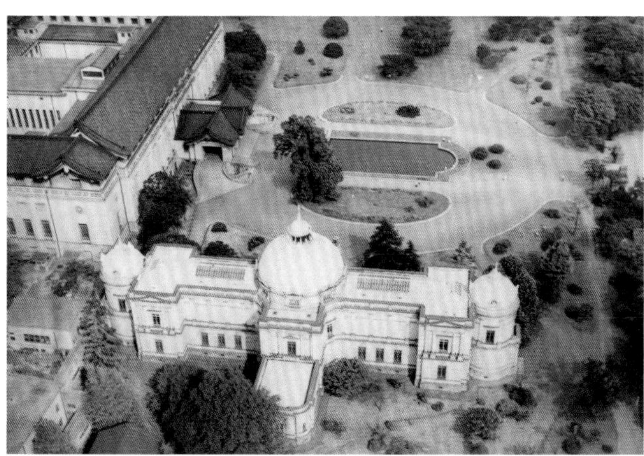

Abb. | Fig. 4
Das Hyōkeikan (Haus, das Freude ausdrückt) auf dem Gelände des Nationalmuseums Tokio | The Hyōkeikan (Pavilion of the Expression of Joy) on the grounds of the Tokyo National Museum, 1908

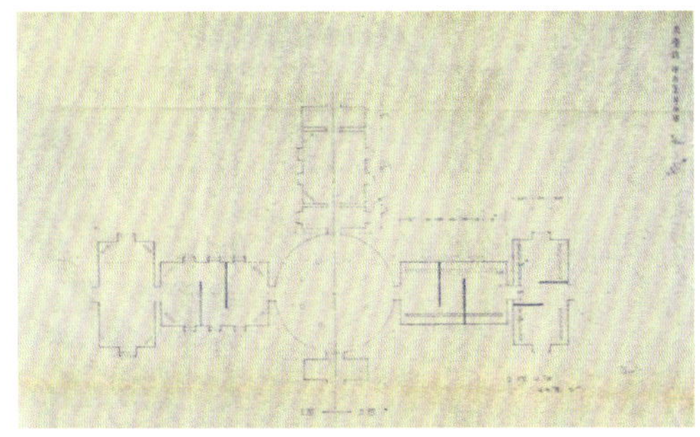

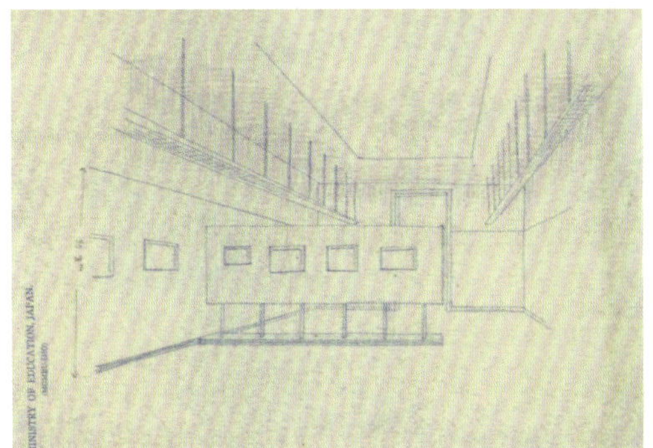

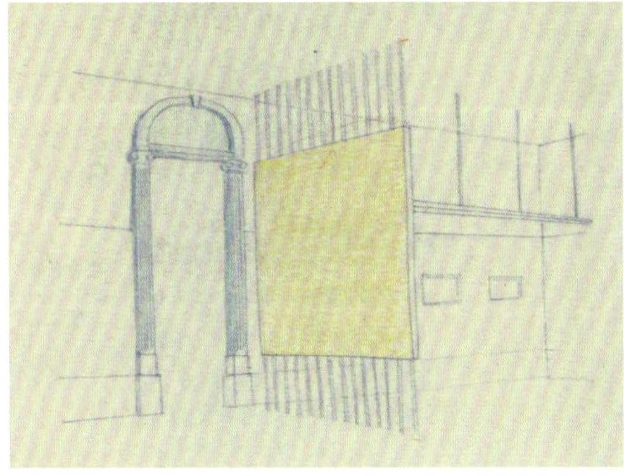

Abb. | Fig. 5
Wahrscheinlich Monbusho, Hyōkeikan, Plan
der zweiten Etage | Probably Monbusho,
Hyōkeikan, plan of the second floor, 1954

Abb. | Fig. 6
Monbusho, Hyōkeikan, Skizze des Innenraums zur
Veranschaulichung der geplanten Renovierung |
sketch of the interior to visualize proposed
renovations, 1954

Abb. | Fig. 7
Monbusho, Hyōkeikan, Skizze des Innenraums |
sketch of the interior, 1954

on a temporary basis.[10] The following quote from
a letter by a member of the French Embassy to
Salles underlines the apprehension of the French
authorities that the Hyōkeikan, once in use, would
house the collection for an indefinite period and
that a new museum building would never be
constructed at all: 'I suppose that their [the Japanese's] little intrigue aims at getting back the
collection without effort [...].'[11] In addition to these
doubts, the symbolical nature of the building – a
pre-war relic with direct connection to the Imperial
household – was problematic. The French administration was surely aware that housing the restitut-
ed Matsukata Collection in a building even distantly
linked to Japanese imperialism would contradict
the spirit of reconciliation that underlined the
restitution.

Salles, being diplomatically minded, seemed
to have avoided strong objections against the
Hyōkeikan but nevertheless insisted on a larger-
scale solution. He emphasized the necessity of a
new building and encouraged the Japanese government to increase the budget. He also suggested that if a larger budget for the construction of
a new building of appropriate dimensions could
be secured, he might help to speed up the restitution process.[12]

Possibly Spring 1954: Ryoun-In, Ueno Park

As demonstrated above, the Hyōkeikan, despite
being favoured by the Ministry of Education,
caused some irritation and rather slowed down
the restitution of the Matsukata collection instead
of speeding it up. However, the French side's
concern that this building might turn out to be the
final destination of the collection seemed to have
been unwarranted, as another internal note by the

165

ein neues Beleuchtungssystem implementiert und die Außenfassade neu gestrichen würden (Abb. 5).[8] Mehrere Skizzen, die nach Salles' Empfehlungen in der Hausarchitekturabteilung des Monbusho gefertigt wurden, finden sich heute noch im NMWA-Archiv (Abb. 6, 7).[9]

Salles' diplomatischer Ansatz spiegelte nicht die Meinung seiner Landsleute wider. Die französische Botschaft in Japan lehnte das Hyōkeikan vollständig ab und hielt es selbst als vorübergehende Lösung für unangemessen, denn die Befürchtungen, dass das Hyōkeikan die Sammlung auf unbestimmte Zeit beherbergen und ein neues Museumsgebäude niemals errichtet würde, wogen schwer.[10] Folgendes Zitat aus dem Brief eines Mitglieds der französischen Botschaft an Salles unterstreicht diese Skepsis: „Ich nehme an, dass ihre [gemeint sind die japanischen Behörden] kleine Intrige darauf abzielt, die Sammlung ohne Mühe zurückzugewinnen".[11] Neben diesen Zweifeln war aber auch die Symbolik des Hyōkeikan problematisch, da es ein Relikt aus der Vorkriegszeit mit direkter Verbindung zum kaiserlichen Hof darstellte. Der französischen Seite dürfte bewusst gewesen sein, dass die Ausstellung der restituierten Sammlung Matsukata in einem Gebäude mit Bezug zum japanischen Imperialismus den Geist der Restitution, die nicht weniger als den freundschaftlichen Neubeginn zweier vormals verfeindeter Nationen markieren sollte, ad absurdum geführt hätte.

Der überaus diplomatisch gesinnte Georges Salles schien die starken Ressentiments seiner Landsleute gegen das Hyōkeikan nicht zu teilen,

bestand aber dennoch auf eine umfassendere Lösung. Unermüdlich betonte er die Notwendigkeit eines Neubaus, ermutigte die japanische Regierung zur Erhöhung des Etats und machte ferner deutlich, dass er den Restitutionsprozess beschleunigen könne, sobald ein größeres Budget für den Bau eines neuen Gebäudes von angemessener Dimension gesichert sei.[12]

Wahrscheinlich Frühjahr 1954:
Ryoun-In, Ueno-Park

Obwohl in guter Absicht erdacht, sorgte die Hyōkeikan-Lösung für diplomatische Unruhe und verlangsamte die Verhandlungsprozesse, statt sie zu beschleunigen. Befürchtungen der französischen Seite, dass das Gebäude nach Instandsetzung zum endgültigen Hort der Sammlung Matsukata werden könnte, waren der Datenlage nach jedoch nicht begründet, wie ein weiteres internes Protokoll des Monbusho beweist.[13] Es enthält nicht nur einen detaillierten Zeitplan für die Errichtung eines Neubaus, sondern (und das ist für die folgenden Betrachtungen von Interesse) wies darüber hinaus darauf hin, dass das Monbusho die Gestaltung eines Museumsneubaus seiner hauseigenen Architekturabteilung zu übertragen gedachte.

Die Baupläne, die von namentlich nicht bekannten Beamten des Ministeriums erstellt wurden, sind insofern bemerkenswert, als sie erstmals einen Entwurf für das Gelände des ehemaligen Ryoun-In-Tempels im Ueno-Park (d. h. dem Ort, an dem sich das heutige Museumsgebäude von Le Corbusier befindet) zeigen.[14] Die auf ihnen dargestellte

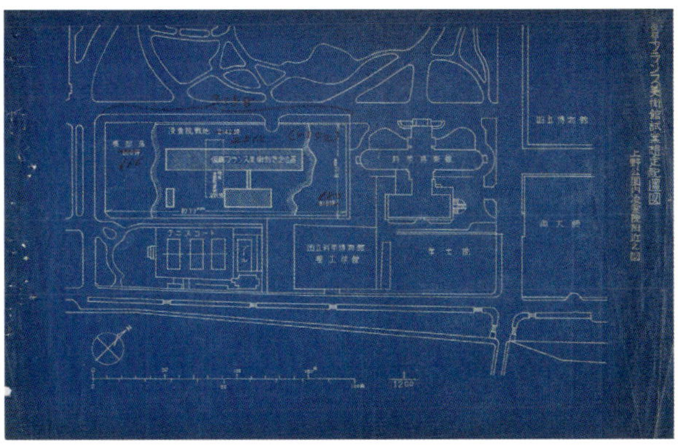

Abb. | Fig. 8
Monbusho, Plan für ein Museum für französische Kunst auf dem Gelände des ehemaligen Ryoun-In, Ueno-Park | plan for a Museum of French Art on the grounds of former Ryoun-In, Ueno Park, 1954

Abb. | Fig. 9
Monbusho, Liste der Referenzgebäude für die
Architektur des Museums für französische Kunst,
1954. Sakakuras Museum wird an der Spitze
der Liste erwähnt | List of reference buildings for
the architecture of the Museum of French Art,
1954. Sakakura's museum is mentioned on top of
the list

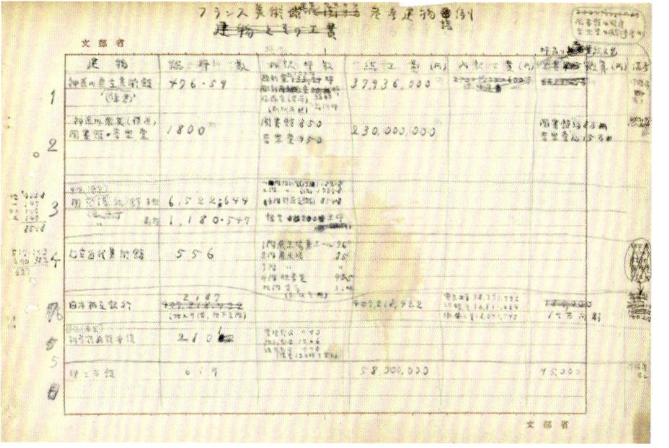

Ministry proves.[13] It not only features a detailed
timetable concerning the erection of a new building but, furthermore, indicates that the Monbusho
attempted to confer the task to its inhouse architectural department.

The plans which were subsequently carried
out by the Ministry are remarkable insofar as they
specify a design on the site of the former Ryoun-
In Temple in Ueno Park (the site of the current
museum's building by Le Corbusier) for the first
time. The structure illustrated here cannot be
called sophisticated, consisting merely of two
stretched rectangular buildings connected by a
thin corridor (fig. 8). However, the facade appears
to be strikingly similar to the NMWA main building
which Le Corbusier would later design, featuring tiles and a large laterally positioned window
(fig. 10). It would certainly be too great a reach
to suggest that Le Corbusier's ideas played a vital
role in Tokyo before he was commissioned but
still, the question arises: How can the similarity
between these early plans and Le Corbusier's final
version be explained?

The key might once again be found in Sakakura's Kamakura Museum. As mentioned above,
this building had already partly inspired the plans
by the University of the Arts. However, for the
unknown architects in the Ministry of Education,
Sakakura's design seemed to have been a true
model. A group of undated documents – possibly
conceived in spring 1954 – had been attached to
the plans and reveal the Ministry's strong interest in
buildings that might be comparable to the planned

new museum. In the first document entitled 'List
of reference buildings for the architecture of
the Museum of French Art', Sakakura's building is
mentioned on top of a list that comprises the
Kanagawa Prefectural Library and Concert Hall,
the Tokyo National Museum, the National Museum
of Modern Art in Takebashi, the Nippon Sogo
Bank and the National Science Museum with its
annex (fig. 9).[14] Another document lists the total
floor space and construction costs of the Kamakura Museum.[15]

According to these notes, one may conclude
that the plans for a new museum were created
by Ministry staff not so much to create a definitive
solution but rather as a kind of preliminary tem-
plate to help calculate the possible costs of a
new building. Obviously, the unknown draughts-
men, having been advised to take the Kamakura
Museum as a model, simply took some elements
which they found in Sakakura's composition (the
tile facade, the large window, the *pilotis*) and
thus created an architecture that unintendedly
prefigured the block-like stereometry of Le
Corbusier's final design for the same location.

1954/1955: Le Corbusier's
Commission and the Final Design

As shown, the design of the new museum had
remained a largely domestic Japanese affair
until mid-1954. However, things were about to
change. A first hint that a foreign architect was
under consideration can be traced in a note of

Struktur kann keineswegs als raffiniert oder anspruchsvoll bezeichnet werden, besteht sie doch lediglich aus zwei gestreckten rechteckigen Gebäuden, verbunden durch einen schmalen Korridor (Abb. 8). Das unscheinbare Arrangement lässt kaum erahnen, welche Überraschung sich offenbart, sobald man die Aufrisse begutachtet: Es zeigt sich dann nämlich eine Fassade, die dank ihrer Fliesenbekleidung, ihrer Pilotis und ihres seitlich angeordneten Fensterdurchbruchs jener des später von Le Corbusier entworfenen NMWA frappierend ähnlich sieht (Abb. 10). Die Annahme, dass Le Corbusiers Ideen bereits vor seiner Beauftragung eine Rolle in Tokio gespielt haben sollen, widerspricht offenkundig jeder Logik und scheint deshalb gewagt. Jedoch, die Frage bleibt: Wie kann die Ähnlichkeit zwischen diesen japanischen Plänen und Le Corbusiers finaler Version erklärt werden?

Die Erklärung dürfte erneut, wie zuvor bei der Geijutsu Daigaku, in Sakakuras Museum für Kamakura zu finden sein. Es hatte bereits die Zeichner der Kunsthochschule inspiriert, doch für die namentlich nicht bekannten Zeichner des Ministeriums muss es geradezu eine Vorbildfunktion gehabt haben. Eine Gruppe undatierter Monbusho-Dokumente – möglicherweise im Frühjahr 1954 angefertigt – war den Entwürfen beigefügt worden und beweist, dass sich Ministerialbeamte zunächst auf die Suche nach bereits in Japan bestehenden Gebäuden machten, die in Verwendung, Form und Kosten mit dem geplanten neuen Museum vergleichbar sein könnten. Im ersten Dokument mit dem Titel „Liste von Referenzgebäuden für die Architektur des Museums für französische Kunst" (*furanzu bijutsukan kenchiku no tame no sanko tatemono rei*) steht Sakakuras Museum an erster Stelle auf einer Liste, die zudem die Präfekturbibliothek und Konzerthalle von Kanagawa, das Nationalmuseum Tokio, das Nationalmuseum für Moderne Kunst in Takebashi, die Nippon Sogo Bank und das Nationalmuseum der Naturwissenschaften umfasst (Abb. 9).[15] Ein weiteres Dokument listet die Fläche und die Baukosten des Kamakura-Museums auf.[16]

Aus diesen Notizen lässt sich schlussfolgern, dass die hier besprochenen Zeichnungen für ein neues Museum nicht mit dem Anspruch einer definitiven Lösung erstellt wurden, sondern vielmehr als Schablone dienten, durch die es möglich wäre, die voraussichtlichen Kosten eines neuen Gebäudes zu berechnen. Offensichtlich nahmen die unbekannten Zeichner dabei Sakakuras Museumsbau als Vorlage, orientierten sich an charakteristischen Elementen wie der gefliesten Fassade oder den Pilotis und skizzierten so eine Architektur, die zufälligerweise die blockartige Stereometrie von Le Corbusiers endgültigem Entwurf für denselben Ort präfigurierte.

1954/55: Le Corbusiers Auftrag und der endgültige Entwurf

Wie gezeigt wurde, war das geplante neue Museum bis Mitte 1954 eine innerjapanische Angelegenheit geblieben. Die Dinge sollten sich jedoch ändern. Ein erster Hinweis, dass ausländische Baumeister berücksichtigt werden sollten, findet sich in einer Notiz des sogenannten Vorbe-

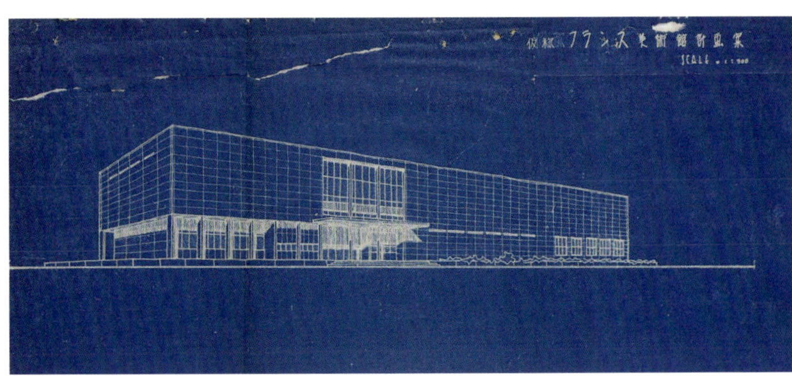

Abb. | Fig. 10
Monbusho, Aufriss für ein Museum für französische Kunst | elevation for a Museum of French Art, 1954

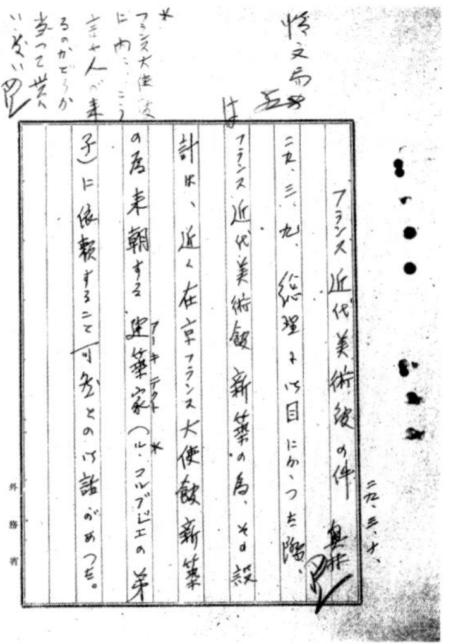

Abb. | Fig. 11
Handschriftliche Notiz des Vizeministers für
auswärtige Angelegenheiten, Katsuzō
Okumura, über ein Treffen mit Premierminis-
ter Yoshida am 9. März 1954 | Handwritten
note by the vice-minister of foreign affairs,
Katsuzō Okumura, concerning a meeting
with Prime Minister Yoshida on 9 March 1954

the so-called 'Preparatory Council', an association
that was responsible for the collection of funds
from the private sector under the guidance of
the Monbusho. One of the council's reports from
March 1954 contains the note: 'The design of the
museum shall be executed in cooperation with
a French architect if possible'[16]

Among the council's participants were members of the Matsukata family, as well as high-ranking
cultural functionaries like Sōichi Tominaga, who
would later become the NMWA's first director, or
Yukio Yashiro, a friend of Georges Salles and
former disciple of American art historian Bernard
Berenson. Obviously, the council was able to exert
considerable influence behind the scenes and it
is around this time that the Japanese Prime Minister,
Shigeru Yoshida, became more actively involved
in the museum. An internal note (fig. 11) by the
former Vice Minister of Foreign Affairs, Katsuzō
Okumura, proves the Prime Minister's interest in
the affair:

Showa 29, March 10[17]
About the Museum of Modern French Art
On 9 March 1954 I met the Prime Minister.
He asked me to consider if it was possible to
confer the design of a new Museum of Modern
French Art to an architect who is a disciple
of Le Corbusier and who will be coming to
Japan to design a new building for the French
Embassy in Tokyo.[18]

It is here in Okamura's note that Le Corbusier's
name can be detected for the first time in regard
to the Matsukata Collection. In addition to that,
the note was accompanied by a detailed hand-
written curriculum vitae of Le Corbusier in Japanese, probably executed by a member of the
Ministry of Foreign Affairs for the Prime Minister's
reference.

The Prime Minister's sudden intervention shows
that the planned museum was not only an issue
between French and Japanese authorities but also
within the Japanese government apparatus itself.
Being the head of the government, Yoshida was
obviously the only person able to overrule the
schemes already approved by the Monbusho and
it seems that he finally decided to take advantage
of his authority. A few weeks later, in April 1954, the
Ministry of Foreign Affairs was ordered to contact
Le Corbusier and commission him with the museums design.[19] It is not possible to reconstruct how
he finally came to be chosen but appears likely
that his former disciple, Kunio Maekawa, a highly
established figure with access to governmental
circles, gave the final impetus in talks with members of the Ministry of Foreign Affairs.

The decision to entrust Le Corbusier with
the design of the new museum for Matsukata's
collection unified two giants of the modern movement. Both Matsukata and Le Corbusier were
pioneers who avidly believed in the importance
of art museums for societies. Le Corbusier's
highly idealistic approach towards the institution
of the museum is reflected in the spiral form of the
building, reminiscent of his idea of a 'Museum
of Unlimited Growth'. The visitor was supposed to

169

reitungsrates, einer Vereinigung, die für die Akquirierung privater Geldmittel unter der Leitung des Monbusho verantwortlich war. Einer der Berichte des Rates vom März 1954 enthielt den Vermerk: „Der Entwurf des Museums soll nach Möglichkeit in Zusammenarbeit mit einem französischen Architekten ausgeführt werden".[17]

Unter den Teilnehmern des Rates befanden sich Mitglieder der Familie Matsukata, hochrangige Kulturfunktionäre wie der spätere Gründungsdirektor des NMWA Sōichi Tominaga sowie Yukio Yashiro, ein Freund Georges Salles' und ehemaliger Schüler des amerikanischen Kunsthistorikers Bernard Berenson. Offensichtlich konnte der Rat hinter den Kulissen erheblichen Einfluss ausüben und es dürfte kein Zufall sein, dass, wie ein interner Vermerk des ehemaligen Vize-Außenministers Katsuzō Okumura deutlich macht (Abb. 11), Premierminister Shigeru Yoshida zu diesem Zeitpunkt verstärkt persönliches Interesse an der Matsukata-Frage zu zeigen begann:

> „Showa 29, 10. März[18]
> Über das Museum für moderne französische Kunst
> Am 9. März traf ich den Premierminister. Er bat mich zu überlegen, ob es möglich sei, den Entwurf eines neuen Museums für moderne französische Kunst einem Schüler Le Corbusiers zu übertragen, der nach Japan kommen wird, um ein neues Gebäude für die französische Botschaft in Tokio zu entwerfen."[19]

In dieser für die interne Verwendung des Außenministeriums bestimmten Notiz dürfte Le Corbusiers Name zum ersten Mal in Bezug auf die Sammlung Matsukata erwähnt worden sein. Zwar ist in ihr dezidiert von einem Schüler Le Corbusiers die Rede, allerdings wurde sie von einem ausführlichen Lebenslauf Le Corbusiers auf Japanisch begleitet, vermutlich verfasst als Referenz für den Premierminister und seinen inneren Zirkel.

Die plötzliche Intervention des Premierministers zeigt, dass das geplante Museum nicht nur ein Thema zwischen französischen und japanischen Behörden war, sondern auch innerhalb des japanischen Regierungsapparats selbst. Als Regierungschef war Yoshida offensichtlich als Einziger in der Lage, die bereits genehmigten Szenarien des Monbusho zu überstimmen, und es scheint, dass er sich schließlich entschied, seine Autorität zu nutzen. Wenige Wochen später, im April 1954, ordnete das japanische Außenministerium an, Le Corbusier zu kontaktieren und ihn für den Museumsentwurf zu verpflichten.[20] Wie und warum die Wahl letztlich auf Le Corbusier fiel, lässt sich nicht rekonstruieren, aber es ist davon auszugehen, dass sein ehemaliger Schüler Kunio Maekawa, ein in Regierungskreisen vernetzter Architekt, in Gesprächen mit dem Außenministerium den finalen Anstoß gab.

Die Entscheidung, Le Corbusier mit dem Entwurf eines neuen Museums für die Sammlung Matsukata zu betrauen, vereinte seinerzeit zwei Giganten der modernen Bewegung. Sowohl der Sammler Kōjirō Matsukata als auch der Architekt Le Corbusier waren Pioniere, die von der Bedeutung von Kunstmuseen für die Gesellschaft unbeirrbar überzeugt waren. Le Corbusiers idealistischer

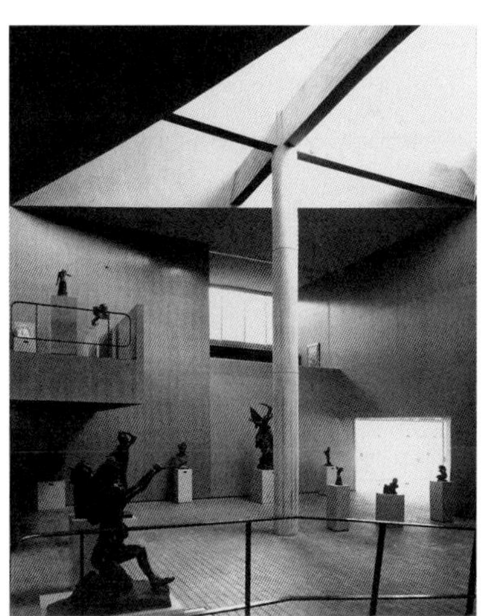

Abb. | Fig. 12
Die „Halle des 19. Jahrhunderts" im heutigen National Museum of Western Art, entworfen von Le Corbusier, wie sie kurz nach der Eröffnung des Museums 1959 aussah |
'19th Century Hall' in the current National Museum of Western Art, designed by Le Corbusier, as it appeared shortly after the museum's opening in 1959

start his tour in the central '19th Century Hall' (fig. 12) from which a 'crescendo'[20] of artworks should unfold, illustrating the development of art from the industrial era (Impressionism) to Fauvism, Cubism and so forth. The end of the spiral-shaped *parcours* marked yet another beginning: by reserving space for the 'art of the future' the museum was supposed to signal its visitors the coming of an 'era of harmony' – an era that, according to Le Corbusier, mankind was to enter once the confusions and contradictions of modernity had been overcome.[21]

The authors like to offer their gratitude to the Japan Foundation for its generous support of this article. Furthermore, they wish to offer their special thanks to the staff of the NMWA, in particular Hiroya Murakami, Megumi Jingaoka and Masako Kawaguchi.

1 The most comprehensive overview of the museum's genesis can be found in Yoko Terashima's essay 'The Construction of the National Museum of Western Art Recounted', in *Le Corbusier & The National Museum of Western Art (Commemorating the 50th Anniversary of the opening of the National Museum of Western Art)* (Tokyo, 2009), 58–65.

2 Letter from Charles Le Genissel, Chargé d'affaires de France au Japon, French Embassy in Japan to the French Minister of Foreign Affairs, 14 September 1953, NMWA Archives. (Original data from the Centre des Archives diplomatiques de Nantes) 6033f.

3 'Museum of French Art' (*furanzu bijutsukan*). Tokyo University of the Arts, Proposition for a museum of French art for the Ministry of Education, July 1953. NMWA Archives, MSO_1_0074.

4 Letter by Charles Le Genissel (op. cit.).

5 National Cabinet of Japan, Notes on a Cabinet meeting on 4 December 1953. NMWA Archives MSO_1_0173.

6 National Cabinet of Japan, Notes on a Cabinet meeting on 28 May 1954. NMWA Archives MSO_1_0283–0286.

7 Institute Franco-Japonaise du Kansai, *Note sur l'installation eventuelle de la Collection Matsukata a Kyoto*, 11 March 1954. NMWA Archives (Original data from the Archives diplomatiques de Nantes) 6348.

8 Monbusho, Summary of Georges Salles' opinions regarding the reception of the Matsukata Collection. Opinions given to Sakuo Teranaka, Director-General of Social Education Bureau at the Ministry of Education, during a meeting on 4 February 1954. NMWA Archives MSO_1_0228–0230.

9 Japanese ministries still make use of inhouse architects to realise or restore governmental or semi-governmental structures.

10 French Embassy in Japan, *Allocution de M. Odachi, Ministre de l'éducation nationale, à l'occasion de la réunion au sujet de collection Matsukata, le 10 mars 1954 à l'hôtel impérial*. NMWA Archives (original data from the Archive diplomatiques de Nantes) 6344.

11 Letter from the French Embassy in Japan to Georges Salles, 9 March 1954. NMWA Archives (original data from the Archive diplomatiques de Nantes) 6341.

12 Summary of Georges Salles' opinions (op. cit.).

13 Monbusho, timetable for the foundation of the Matsukata Museum (unofficial name), undated, possibly March 1954. NMWA Archives MSO_1_179–182.

14 Monbusho, List of reference buildings for the architecture of the Museum of French Art, undated, possibly spring 1954. NMWA Archives, FYO_1_0082.

15 Monbusho, List of technical data and building expenses concerning the architecture of the Kamakura Museum of Modern Art, undated, possibly spring 1954. NMWA Archives, FYO_1_0083.

16 Preparatory Council, Protocol of a council meeting, 31 March 1954. NMWA Archives MSO_1_0250.

17 Showa 29 is 1954 in the Western calendar.

18 Japanese Ministry of Foreign Affairs, Note by Deputy Minister of Foreign Affairs, Katsuzō Okumura, after a meeting with the Prime Minister, 10 March 1954. NMWA Archives 005.

19 Letter from Kunio Maekawa to Le Corbusier, 14 April 1954, Fondation Le Corbusier F1-12-1-001

20 Le Corbusier, note for his collaborator André Maisonnier concerning the NMWA, 9 January 1956. Fondation Le Corbusier F1-12-168-004.

21 Letter to the Japanese Minister of Education, 10 July 1956. Fondation Le Corbusier F1-12-174-003.

Ansatz gegenüber der Institution des Museums spiegelt sich in der Spiralform des NMWA wider, eine Reminiszenz an seine Idee eines „Museums des unbegrenzten Wachstums". Der Besucher sollte seinen Rundgang in der zentralen „Halle des 19. Jahrhunderts" beginnen (Abb. 12), von der ausgehend ein spiralförmiges „Crescendo" die Entwicklung moderner Kunst vom Impressionismus über den Fauvismus hin zum Kubismus veranschaulichen sollte.[21] Das Ende des Parcours markierte seinerseits einen neuen Anfang: Mit der Reservierung von Raum für die „Kunst der Zukunft" sollte das Museum seinen Besuchern die bevorstehende Ankunft einer „Ära der Harmonie" signalisieren – eine Epoche, in die die Menschheit gemäß Le Corbusier eintreten solle, sobald die Verwirrungen und Widersprüche der Moderne überwunden worden seien.[22]

Die Autoren danken der Japan Foundation für die großzügige Förderung der Recherchen sowie den Mitarbeiter:innen des National Museum of Western Art, insbesondere Hiroya Murakami, Megumi Jingaoka und Masako Kawaguchi.

1 Yoko Terashima, „The Construction of the National Museum of Western Art Recounted", in: *Le Corbusier & the National Museum of Western Art (Commemorating the 50th Anniversary of the Opening of the National Museum of Western Art)*, Tokio 2009, S. 58–65. Terashimas Aufsatz enthält die bis heute detailreichste Studie zur Genese des NMWA.

2 Französische Botschaft Tokio, Charles Le Genissel, Chargé d'affaires de France au Japon, an den französischen Außenminister, Brief vom 14.9.1953. NMWA Archiv (Original aus den Archives diplomatiques de Nantes), 6033 f. (Übers. des Autors).

3 Geijutsu Daigaku, Vorschläge für ein Museum französischer Kunst auf dem Gelände der Kunsthochschule, Juli 1953. NMWA Archiv, MSO_1_0074.

4 Charles Le Genissel an den französischen Außenminister, Brief vom 14.9.1953.

5 Nationales Kabinett von Japan, Protokoll einer Kabinettssitzung am 4.12.1953. NMWA Archiv, MSO_1_0173 (Übers. von Hiroya Murakami).

6 Nationales Kabinett von Japan, Protokoll einer Kabinettssitzung am 28.5.1954. NMWA Archiv, MSO_1_0283–0286.

7 Institut franco-japonais du Kansai, Notiz bzgl. einer möglichen Installation der Sammlung Matsukata in Kyoto, 11.3.1954. NMWA Archiv (Original aus den Archives diplomatiques de Nantes), 6348.

8 Monbusho, Notiz eines Gespräches zwischen Sakuo Teranaka, Generaldirektor des Monbusho Social Education Bureau, und Georges Salles, 4.2.1954. NMWA Archiv, MSO_1_0228–0230.

9 Bis heute beschäftigen japanische Ministerien hauseigene Architekten für den Bau beziehungsweise die Instandsetzung staatlicher oder halbstaatlicher Gebäude.

10 Französische Botschaft in Japan, Ansprache des Bildungsministers M. Odachi anlässlich einer Zusammenkunft zum Sachverhalt der Sammlung Matsukata im Hotel Imperial am 10.3.1954. NMWA Archiv (Original aus den Archives diplomatiques de Nantes), 6344.

11 Französische Botschaft in Japan an Georges Salles, Brief vom 9.3.1954. NMWA Archiv (Original aus den Archives diplomatiques de Nantes), 6341 (Übers. des Autors).

12 Zusammenfassung von Georges Salles' Meinungen bzgl. Hyōkeikan (Notiz eines Gespräches zwischen Sakuo Teranaka und Georges Salles, 4.2.1954).

13 Monbusho, Zeitplan für die Gründung eines „Matsukata-Museums" (inoffizieller Name), undatiert (wahrscheinlich März 1954). NMWA Archiv, MSO_1_179–182.

14 Die Pläne befinden sich in Register FYO_1 des Archivs des National Museum of Western Art.

15 Monbusho, Liste von Referenzgebäuden für die Architektur des Museums für französische Kunst, undatiert (wohl Frühjahr 1954). NMWA Archiv, FYO_1_0082.

16 Monbusho, Auflistung technischer Daten und Kosten des Museums für moderne Kunst, Kamakura, undatiert (wohl Frühjahr 1954). NMWA Archiv, FYO_1_0082.

17 Vorbereitungsrat, Protokoll eines Treffens des Rates, 31.3.1954. NMWA Archiv, MSO_1_0250 (Übers. von Hiroya Murakami).

18 Die japanische Bezeichnung „Showa 29" entspricht dem Jahr 1954.

19 Japanisches Außenministerium, Notiz des stellvertretenden Außenministers Katsuzō Okumura nach einem Treffen mit dem Premierminister, 10.3.1954. NMWA Archiv, 005 (Übers. von Hiroya Murakami).

20 Kunio Mayekawa an Le Corbusier, Brief vom 14.4.1954, Fondation Le Corbusier, F1-12-1-001.

21 Le Corbusier, Hinweis für seinen Mitarbeiter André Maisonnier bzgl. der Innengestaltung des NMWA, 9.1.1956. Fondation Le Corbusier, F1-12-168-004.

22 Le Corbusier an den japanischen Bildungsminister, Brief vom 10.7.1956. Fondation Le Corbusier, F1-12-174-003.

KARL ERNST OSTHAUS'S MUSEUM FOLKWANG AND KŌJIRŌ MATSUKATA'S KYŌRAKU BIJUTSUKAN –

TWO MUSEUM CONCEPTS AT THE AGE OF THE ARTS AND CRAFTS MOVEMENT

Marie Yasunaga

The two museum projects – Karl Ernst Osthaus's Museum Folkwang in Hagen and Kōjirō Matsukata's *Kyōraku Bijutsukan* or 'Sheer Pleasure Arts Pavilion' – have a remarkable resonance despite the gap between the periods of acquisition and their different historical settings. Not only did both collections consist of excellent pieces of European modern art, but their founders' collecting practices were fuelled by a shared belief in the power of art and the fervent hope that a museum of art could benefit the wider community and foster the visual literacy of the general audience. It is noteworthy that unlike many other private museums, often based on a collection acquired primarily for private enjoyment such as decorating a private residence, both Osthaus and Matsukata's acquisitions were driven by their motivation to make art accessible to the public: the concept of the museum preceded the collection. The former envisioned 'leading art back to life,'[1] and the latter aimed 'to enable my countrymen to understand the psychology of the Western peoples.'[2]

The Ambitions:
Establishing an Art Museum

Karl Ernst Osthaus, born into a successful business family, decided to devote two-thirds of his grandfather's estate, which he inherited in 1896, to construct a museum in his hometown in Westphalia.[3] He intended to redress the cultural disparity, 'the injustice that lies in the unequal distribution of art assets and blessings of art.' More than elsewhere, he believed, an industrial city like Hagen needed a museum.[4] Initially, his museum plans shifted from one idea to the other: first, a hall in honour of Westphalia,[5] then a natural history museum, and, after his trip to North Africa in 1898,

Die beiden Museumsprojekte – Karl Ernst Osthaus'
Museum Folkwang in Hagen und Kōjirō Matsukatas
Kyōraku Bijutsukan oder „Sheer Pleasure Arts
Pavilion" – weisen bemerkenswerte Ähnlichkeiten
auf, obwohl ihre Sammlungen zu unterschiedlichen
Zeiten erworben wurden und sie in einem ganz
anders gearteten historischen Kontext entstanden.
So enthalten beide nicht nur außergewöhnliche
Werke europäischer moderner Kunst, die Sammeltätigkeit ihrer Gründer beruhte zudem auf einem
ganz ähnlichen Glauben an die Macht von Kunst
sowie auf der inständigen Hoffnung, dass ein
Kunstmuseum einer größeren Gemeinschaft dienen könne und der visuellen Bildung des gewöhnlichen Publikums zuträglich wäre. Es ist bemerkenswert, dass – im Gegensatz zu vielen anderen
Privatmuseen, die oft auf Sammlungen aufbauen,
die vorrangig dem privaten Vergnügen wie etwa
der Ausstattung eines Privathauses dienten – sowohl die Ankäufe von Osthaus als auch jene von
Matsukata der Motivation entsprangen, Kunst der
Öffentlichkeit zugänglich zu machen. Das Konzept
des Museums ging der Sammlung bereits voraus.
Ersterer wollte „die Zurückführung der Kunst ins
Leben",[1] Zweiterer war bestrebt, „es meinen Landsleuten zu ermöglichen, die Psyche der Völker des
Westens zu verstehen"[2].

Das gemeinsame Ziel:
Die Gründung eines Kunstmuseums

Karl Ernst Osthaus, geboren in eine Familie erfolgreicher Geschäftsleute, entschloss sich dazu,
zwei Drittel des Besitzes seines Großvaters, den

     Marie Yasunaga

DAS MUSEUM FOLKWANG VON KARL ERNST OSTHAUS UND DAS KYŌRAKU BIJUTSUKAN VON KŌJIRŌ MATSUKATA –

ZWEI MUSEUMSKONZEPTE IM ZEITALTER DER KUNSTGEWERBEBEWEGUNG

a museum for Islamic art. Eventually, in the spring of 1900, the decisive encounter with the Belgian artist Henry van de Velde led to the birth of the Museum Folkwang, which combined modern interior design with a multifaceted collection of modern art, decorative arts, artefacts and natural history specmens.[6]

Kōjirō Matsukata, the shrewd president of the Kawasaki Dockyard Company, envisioned building a museum for Western art[7] – the *Kyōraku Bijutsukan,* which can be literally translated as 'sharing pleasure art museum,' named the 'Sheer Pleasure Arts Pavilion' in English.[8] Matsukata aimed 'to enable the lovers of art and the art students to study the best that Europe and America can show them.'[9] In the late 1910s, museum institutions in Japan underwent a transition period with a growing call for a Western art museum, and Matsukata's museum concept was in line with these nationwide campaigns. The Imperial Museums in Tokyo, Kyoto and Nara, established by the Meiji government in the 1880s as part of their modernization programme, reserved no room for Western art and its displays leaned towards nationalistic narratives.[10] Under these circumstances, the ardent advocates of Auguste Rodin and modern European artists around the *Shirakaba* (White Birch) school of writers, as well as intellectual groups such as the Association for Establishing an Art Museum (*Bijutsukan kensetsu kisei doumeikai*) and the Japanese Society of Fine Art (*Kokumin bijutsu kyōkai*) published statements and petitions calling for a modern Western art museum.[11] Matsukata enlisted British artist Frank Brangwyn to design his museum. Had it been realized as planned, the *Kyōraku Bijutsukan* would have been the first museum of this kind in Japan and one of the most prominent examples in the world.[12]

The Background:
Art, Applied Art, and Industry

In contrast to what we know about these collections with splendid masterpieces of so-called 'classical' modern art, the underlying foundational conceptions of the two museums strongly resonated with the decorative art movements at the turn of the century and were formed under its significant influence. The far-reaching international campaign that first emerged in the Arts and Crafts movement in Britain in reaction to the machine industry triggered discussions on the conceptualization of a new type of museum as an aesthetic, educational institution for the public to promote the enhanced design of the applied-arts industry, as demonstrated by the pioneering experiments at the South Kensington Museum (present-day Victoria and Albert Museum, London).[13] While being closely linked with the promotion of national industry,[14] the renewed interest in applied arts urged a rethinking of the hierarchical classification of fine and applied arts, making the museum space a new site of exploration, where artists pursued a harmonious integration of interior design and the pieces of artworks installed within.

For both Osthaus and Matsukata, fine and applied art and manufacturing were not mutually exclusive domains. They conceptualized a museum not merely as a place for the safekeeping of precious fine art but as a mediating institution for cultural enrichment and industrial development. It is suggestive, in this context, that the two projects had accidental encounters: first, at Siegfried Bing's shop *La Maison de l'Art Nouveau* in Paris – the new mecca for modern design which both Van de Velde and Brangwyn were involved in furnishing[15] – and then, although somewhat indirectly, at

er 1896 geerbt hatte, der Gründung eines Museums in seiner Heimatstadt in Westfalen zu widmen.[3] Damit wollte er die kulturelle Ungleichheit überwinden, „das Unrecht […] das in der ungleichen Verteilung des Kunstgutes und des Kunstsegens in unserm Vaterlande liegt". Er war der Ansicht, dass gerade eine Industriestadt wie Hagen dringend eines Museums bedürfe.[4] In der Anfangsphase waren die Pläne jedoch noch etlichen Änderungen unterworfen: Zunächst sollte ein Ehrenhalle für Westphalia entstehen,[5] dann ein Naturhistorisches Museum und nach seiner Reise nach Nordafrika im Jahr 1898 ein Museum für islamische Kunst. Im Frühling des Jahres 1900 gab jedoch die schicksalhafte Begegnung mit dem belgischen Künstler Henry van de Velde schließlich den Ausschlag für die Geburt des Museum Folkwang, das eine Verbindung moderner Innengestaltung mit einer komplexen Sammlung moderner Kunst, angewandter Kunst, Artefakte und naturhistorischer Präparate darstellte.[6]

Kōjirō Matsukata, der clevere Präsident der Kawasaki-Werft, plante hingegen den Bau eines Museums für westliche Kunst[7] – des Kyōraku Bijutsukan, was sich wortwörtlich als „Museum für den gemeinsamen Genuss" übersetzen ließe und im Englischen „Sheer Pleasure Arts Pavilion" benannt wurde.[8] Matsukata war bestrebt, „Kunstliebhaber:innen und Kunststudent:innen das Studium des Besten zu ermöglichen, was Europa und Amerika zu bieten haben"[9]. Gegen Ende der 1910er-Jahre waren die Museumsinstitutionen in Japan einem Wandel unterworfen und die Forderungen nach einem Museum westlicher Kunst

wurden lauter. Matsukatas Museumskonzept entsprach diesen landesweiten Kampagnen. Die Kaiserlichen Museen in Tokio, Kyoto und Nara, die in den 1880er-Jahren als Teil des Modernisierungsprogramms von der Meiji-Regierung gegründet worden waren, hatten keinen Platz für westliche Kunst vorgesehen und stützten sich in ihren Präsentationen auf nationalistische Narrative.[10] Unter diesen Bedingungen veröffentlichten die leidenschaftlichen Anhänger:innen von Auguste Rodin und modernen europäischen Künstler:innen rund um die Schriftsteller:innengruppe Shirakaba (Weiße Birke), aber auch intellektuelle Gruppen wie die Vereinigung zur Gründung eines Kunstmuseums (Bijutsukan kensetsu kisei doumeikai) und die Japanische Gesellschaft für bildende Künste (Kokumin bijutsu kyōkai) Erklärungen und Petitionen mit der Forderung nach einem Museum westlicher Kunst.[11] Matsukata beauftragte den britischen Künstler Frank Brangwyn mit dem Entwurf für das Museum. Wäre es realisiert worden wie geplant, wäre das Kyōraku Bijutsukan das erste Museum seiner Art in Japan gewesen und eines des herausragendsten Beispiele weltweit.[12]

Der Hintergrund: Kunst,
angewandte Kunst und Industrie

Im Gegensatz zu dem, was wir heute über diese beiden Sammlungen von Meisterwerken der sogenannten „klassischen" Moderne wissen, standen ihre grundlegenden Museumskonzepte in einem engen Zusammenhang mit der Kunstgewerbebewegung der Jahrhundertwende und entstanden

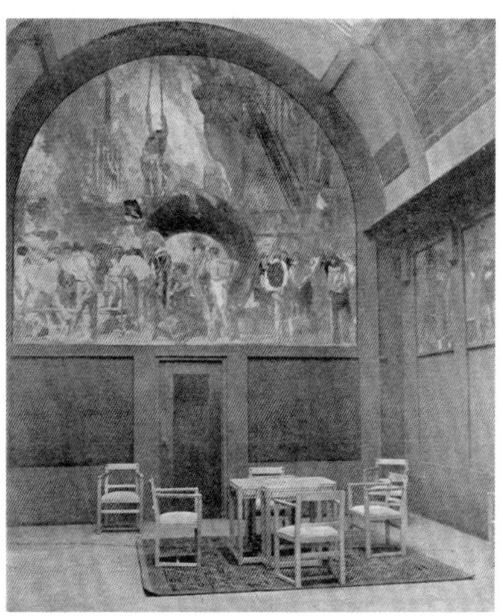

Abb. | Fig. 1
Exposition universelle et internationale de Gand, Britische Abteilung, von Frank Brangwyn entworfener Lesesaal | British section, reading room designed by Frank Brangwyn, 1913

175

the *Ghent International Exhibition (L'exposition universelle et internationale de Gand)* in 1913. Osthaus, as the director of the Deutsches Museum für Kunst in Handel und Gewerbe (German Museum of Art in Trade and Commerce)[16] that was established in close collaboration with the *Deutscher Werkbund,* as a travelling museum ('*Wandermuseum*') in 1909 with the motto of 'reintegration of art and craft,'[17] was responsible for the German sections of applied art and spatial art. He directed a large part of the interior design upholding the slogan of 'artists as a teacher of industry.'[18]

At the end of the British section, which featured the Arts and Crafts movement, was the large reading room fully designed by Brangwyn (fig. 1). Above its entrance was the artist's sizeable lunette-shaped tempera painting *Boiler Makers,* accompanied by ten rectangular paintings depicting porters in the London docks on the wall on both sides and the furniture and floor carpet designed by the artist and executed by Turpin and Co. After the exhibition closed, the ten rectangular paintings were installed in the Committee Luncheon Room of Lloyd's Register of Shipping, while *Boiler Makers* went back to the artist's atelier before coming into possession of Matsukata.[19] A design sketch of the annex building of the *Kyōraku Bijutsukan* shows the *Boiler Makers* at the centre of the wall with two stained glass panels on either side, while carpets, tapestries and several large antique vessels are scattered here and there (fig. 2). There are also glass vitrines and pieces of furniture that the artist would have designed.[20]

Decorative art was a significant component of the original Matsukata collection.[21] Contrary to the alleged character of a haphazard collector who spared no expense in randomly hunting for European Art, Matsukata had a clear policy on art

collecting.[22] His purchases shipped from London to Japan between 1919 and 1920 included not only 867 paintings and over 8000 *ukiyo-e* (woodblock prints, fig. 3) from the collection of the Paris-based jeweller Henri Vever,[23] but also 480 pieces of sculpture, furniture and interior decoration, prints and tapestries,[24] and there were many more 'awaiting the time when they can be sent to their permanent home.'[25] He attributed the 'miserable' sales of Japanese goods for export to the lack of knowledge in Japan of Western tastes, and hoped his collection could provide opportunities not only for artists 'but also applied artists and general people' to 'extensively study Western art and apply the knowledge to craftwork to mass-produce refined products for a cheaper cost.'[26] The *Kyōraku Bijutsukan* that would showcase 'examples' 'expressive of [Western] psychology' would be instrumental to 'help [his countrymen] in the application of Occidental methods in manufacturing, and in many phases of industrial life.'[27] Notably, he believed that such 'an influx of foreign art' would not corrupt the Japanese tradition but rather trigger 'a reaction' in an innovative way that would still be 'an expression of the Japanese soul.'[28]

Osthaus reviewed the Ghent show and appraised Brangwyn's execution, where 'the attempt has been made, with much luck, to deal with the modern life in a painterly way,' but he considered it as more a historical, old-fashioned example.[29] For Matsukata, on the contrary, Brangwyn's decorative works would serve as a model for the future development of Japanese art and industry. Among his collection deposited in the Pantechnicon Warehouse in London (lost in the firm's fire in 1939), were listed sixty-nine entries by the artist, including the *Brangwyn Room* – a complete set of the interior design for the main bedroom of British

unter deren ganz wesentlichem Einfluss.
Die weitreichende internationale Offensive, die
zunächst in der Arts-and-Crafts-Bewegung in
Großbritannien als Reaktion auf die Maschinen-
industrie aufkam, führte zu Debatten über die
Konzeptualisierung einer neuen Art von Museum
als einer ästhetischen, pädagogischen Institution
für die Öffentlichkeit, die eine Verbesserung des
Designs in der kunstgewerblichen Industriepro-
duktion fördern sollte, wie die bahnbrechenden
Experimente im South Kensington Museum (heute
Victoria & Albert Museum, London) zeigen.[13] Das
erneute Interesse an angewandter Kunst stand
in engem Zusammenhang mit der Förderung der
nationalen Industrie[14] und hatte ein Überdenken
der hierarchischen Klassifizierung von bildender
und angewandter Kunst zur Folge. Das Museum
wurde zu einem neuen Ort der Entdeckungen,
wo Künstler:innen eine harmonische Verbindung
von Innengestaltung und den darin befindlichen
Kunstwerken anstrebten.

Sowohl Osthaus als auch Matsukata betrach-
teten bildende Kunst, angewandte Kunst und
verarbeitendes Gewerbe nicht als klar getrennte
Bereiche. Sie planten ihre Museen nicht nur als
Orte für die Aufbewahrung kostbarer Kunstwerke
aus dem Bereich der bildenden Kunst, sondern
auch als vermittelnde Institutionen zur kulturellen
Bereicherung und industriellen Entwicklung. In
diesem Zusammenhang ist es aufschlussreich, dass
die Projekte zufällig miteinander in Berührung kamen: Zunächst in Siegfried Bings Galerie La Maison
de l'Art Nouveau in Paris – dem neuen Mekka für
modernes Design, an dessen Ausstattung sowohl

van de Velde als auch Brangwyn beteiligt waren[15] –
und dann, wenn auch eher indirekt, bei der *Exposition universelle et internationale de Gand*,
der Weltausstellung 1913 in Gent. Osthaus war als
Direktor des Deutschen Museums für Kunst in
Handel und Gewerbe,[16] das 1909 in enger Zusammenarbeit mit dem Deutschen Werkbund als
„Wandermuseum" mit dem Ziel der „Wiedervereinigung von Kunst und Gewerbe"[17] konzipiert
worden war, für die deutschen Abteilungen für
Kunstgewerbe und Raumkunst verantwortlich. Er
gestaltete einen großen Teil der Innenausstattung
unter dem Motto „Künstler als Lehrer der Gewerbe"[18]. Die britische Abteilung präsentierte die
Arts-and-Crafts-Bewegung und schloss mit dem
großen Lesesaal, der vollständig von Brangwyn
entworfen worden war (Abb. 1). Über dem Eingang befand sich in einer Lünette das beachtliche
Temperagemälde des Künstlers, *Boiler Makers
(Kesselschmiede)*, begleitet von zehn rechteckigen Gemälden zu beiden Seiten mit Trägern aus
den Londoner Hafenanlagen sowie Möbeln und
Teppich nach Entwürfen des Künstlers und ausgeführt von Turpin and Co. Nach Ende der Ausstellung wurden die zehn rechteckigen Gemälde im
Committee Luncheon Room des Lloyd's Register
of Shipping aufgehängt und *Boiler Makers* kehrte
in das Atelier des Künstlers zurück, ehe es in den
Besitz von Matsukata überging.[19] Eine Entwurfs-
skizze für den Anbau des Kyōraku Bijutsukan zeigt
Boiler Makers in der Mitte der Wand, auf jeder
Seite von einer Buntglasscheibe flankiert, während
im Raum Teppiche, Tapisserien und etliche antike
Gefäße zu sehen sind (Abb. 2). Außerdem finden

Abb. | Fig. 2
Frank Brangwyn, Entwurfszeichnung für die
Innenraumgestaltung des Kyōraku Bijutsukan
in Tokio | design drawing for the interior
room design for the Tokyo *Kyōraku Bijutsukan*,
Privatsammlung | Private collection, Mitchell
Wolfson Jr, Miami, Florida

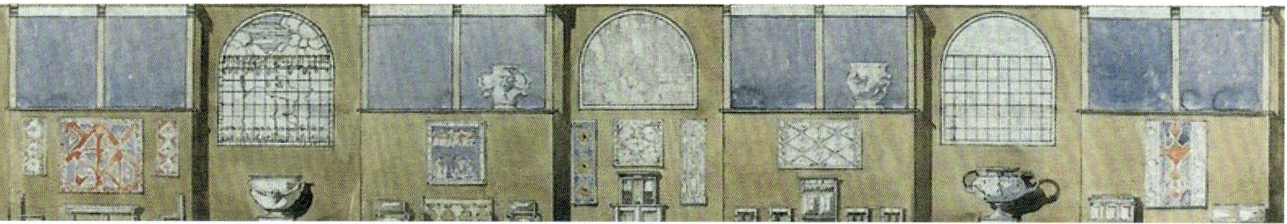

178

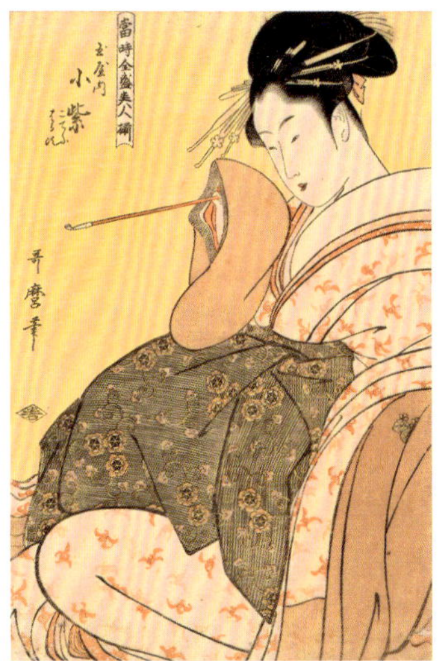

Abb. | Fig. 3
Kitagawa Utamaro, *Komurasaki of the
Tamaya Teahouse,* aus der Serie | from the
series *A Collection of Reigning Beauties,*
ca. 1794, Tokyo National Museum.
Ehemals Sammlung Matsukata | formerly
Matsukata Collection

industrialist and art collector Edmund Davis.[30]
If the museum had materialized, the room was to
have been reconstructed in the annex building.[31]

The Museum as Place for
Cultural Encounters

For proponents of the international decorative art
movements, including Brangwyn and Van de Velde,
who strived to reintegrate decorative and fine arts,
the design of exhibition space became a place
for aesthetic exploration that brought architecture,
interior decoration and fine arts together.[32] The
design for the display of art emerged as a new
issue of balancing the decorative aspect and the
functionality of exhibiting artworks to enhance
the audience's experience of viewing art.[33] Instead
of art presented as a symbol of the wealth of the
privileged classes embodied in a lavishly decorated room with walls filled with art objects from
the bottom to the top, a new way of displaying
artworks was needed. For museum directors like
Osthaus, the issue was how they could realize
a space best suited to achieving their goal of art
education, which aesthetic ideal the museum
space itself must embody.[34] At the same time, the
two museum projects were challenging experiments, creating a platform where different cultures
would encounter one another: one of the critical
features of the Museum Folkwang was the con-
glomerate nature of the thoroughly heterogeneous collection put together harmoniously on
display, and the core vision of *Kyōraku Bijutsukan*

was to introduce Western art to the Japanese
audience.

When the Museum Folkwang opened at 73
Hochstrasse on 19 July 1902, the interior executed
by Van de Velde exceeded what one might ex-
pect from its Renaissance-style exterior designed
by Carl Gérard.[35] Upon entering the three-storey
building, visitors were welcomed to the entrance
hall illuminated by Van de Velde's coloured round
skylight; from 1906, this was designated as the
'Fountain Hall' since it centred around the corre-
spondingly round-shaped white marble *La fontaine
aux agenouillés* (*Fountain with Kneeling Boys,*
1905-06; fig. 4) by George Minne.[36] The hall encap-
sulated the museum's founding concept of the
harmonious integration of interior design and
exhibits. Following the ground floor with its wide
variety of European and non-Western art and artefacts, including the Egyptian collection, Phoenician
glassworks, Islamic metalworks, Persian tapestries,
Japanese hanging scrolls (*kakemono*; pp. 253–255),
and antique furniture in Baroque and Rococo
styles, visitors were invited to the staircase with a
large window fitted with a vitrine for glassworks
(fig. 5), facing a few Japanese *kago* baskets hung
on the upper floor vestibule devoted to East Asian
art (fig. 6). Through the vestibule, they would reach
the picture gallery, the high point of the permanent exhibition with the gem of the collection in its
elaborately wrought interior (fig. 7). Surrounding
the picture gallery were an auditorium, a music
room and until 1909 the residential space, making
the building a physical realization of Osthaus's
ideal to bring everyday life and art together.[37]

sich Glasvitrinen und Möbelstücke, die wohl ebenfalls auf Entwürfe des Künstlers zurückgehen.[20]

Angewandte Kunst stellte eine bedeutende
Komponente der ursprünglichen Sammlung
Matsukata dar.[21] Im Gegensatz zum mutmaßlichen
Charakter eines planlosen Sammlers, der bei der
willkürlichen Jagd auf europäische Kunst keine
Kosten scheut, verfolgte Matsukata beim Sammeln
von Kunst eine klare Strategie.[22] Seine zwischen
1919 und 1920 von Europa nach Japan verschifften
Erwerbungen umfassten nicht nur 867 Gemälde
und mehr als 8000 *ukiyo-e* (Abb. 3) aus der
Sammlung des in Paris ansässigen Juweliers Henri
Vever,[23] sondern auch 480 Arbeiten aus den
Bereichen Bildhauerei, Mobiliar und Innenausstattung, Druckgrafik und Tapisserien.[24] Hinzu kamen
viele weitere Objekte, die „des Zeitpunkts harren,
an dem sie an ihr endgültiges Zuhause gesandt
werden können".[25] Er schrieb den „miserablen"
Verkauf japanischer Exportgüter dem mangelnden
Wissen um westlichen Geschmack in Japan zu
und hoffte, dass seine Sammlung nicht nur Künstler:
innen, „sondern auch Kunstgewerbler:innen und
gewöhnlichen Menschen" die Möglichkeit bieten
würde, „sich umfassend mit westlicher Kunst
auseinanderzusetzen und das Wissen auf das
Kunsthandwerk anzuwenden, um ausgewählte
Kunst in Massenproduktion mit niedrigeren Kosten
herzustellen".[26] Das Kyōraku Bijutsukan, das „Beispiele" zeigen würde, die als „ein Ausdruck [west-
licher] Psyche" gelten könnten, wäre entscheidend, um „[seinen Landsleuten] bei der Anwendung abendländischer Herstellungsmethoden und
in zahlreichen Phasen industriellen Lebens be-
hilflich zu sein".[27] Vor allem glaubte er daran, dass
ein solcher „Einfluss fremder Kunst" die japanische Tradition nicht korrumpieren würde, sondern
vielmehr „eine Reaktion" hervorrufen würde, die
gleichermaßen innovativ wie auch „ein Ausdruck
der japanischen Seele"[28] wäre.

In einer Rezension der Genter Schau beurteilte
Osthaus Brangwyns Fresken, „in denen mit vielem
Glück der Versuch gemacht ist, Szenen aus dem
modernen Leben malerisch zu bewältigen", er war
jedoch der Ansicht, dass dies eher auf historische,
altmodische Art und Weise geschehen sei.[29] Für
Matsukata mochten Brangwyns dekorative Arbeiten hingegen als Vorbild für die zukünftige Entwicklung japanischer Kunst und Industrie dienen.
In seiner im Pantechnicon Warehouse in London
gelagerten Sammlung (die 1939 bei einem Brand
zerstört wurde) fanden sich 69 Arbeiten des
Künstlers, darunter auch der *Brangwyn Room* – ein
komplettes Ensemble an Inneneinrichtung für das
Schlafzimmer des britischen Industriellen und
Kunstsammlers Edmund Davis.[30] Bei einer Realisierung des Museums sollte der Raum im Anbau
rekonstruiert werden.[31]

Das Museum als Ort
kultureller Begegnungen

Für Vertreter:innen der internationalen Kunstgewerbebewegung, darunter auch Brangwyn und
van de Velde, deren Ziel die Wiedervereinigung
angewandter und bildender Künste war, wurde die
Gestaltung des Ausstellungsraumes zu einem Ort
ästhetischer Erkundungen, bei denen Architektur,
Innenraumgestaltung und bildende Kunst miteinander verschmolzen.[32] Die Gestaltung der Präsentation von Kunst stellte ein ganz neues Problem
dar, bei dem es um eine Balance zwischen dekora-
tivem Aspekt und der Funktion des Ausstellens
von Kunstwerken ging – mit dem Ziel, das Kunst-
erlebnis des Publikums zu erhöhen.[33] Statt Kunst
als Symbol für den Wohlstand der privilegierten
Klassen in einem üppig dekorierten Raum zu
präsentieren, dessen Wände von oben bis unten
mit Kunstgegenständen vollgehängt waren,
brauchte es nun eine neue Art der Ausstellung.

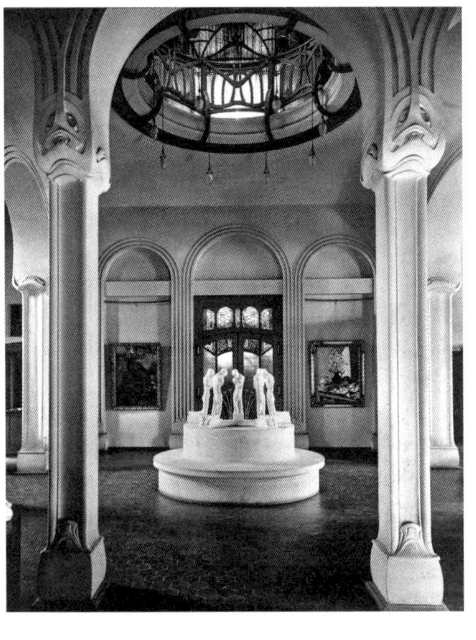

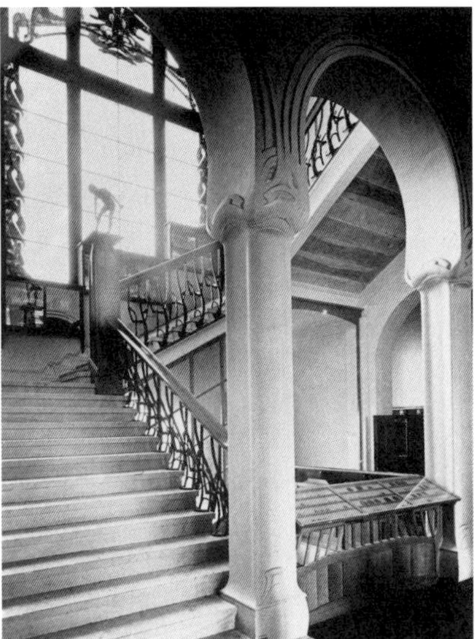

Abb. | Fig. 4
Museum Folkwang, Hagen, Foyer |
Entrance Hall, 1910

Abb. | Fig. 5
Museum Folkwang, Hagen,
Blick vom Foyer zum Treppenhaus |
View from the Entrance Hall to the
Staircase, ca. 1902–1922

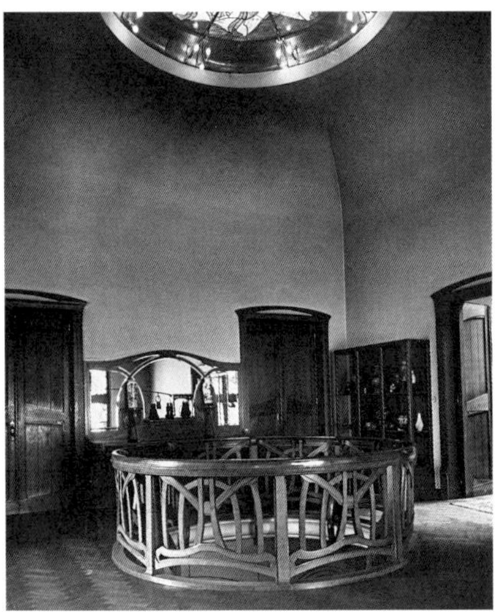

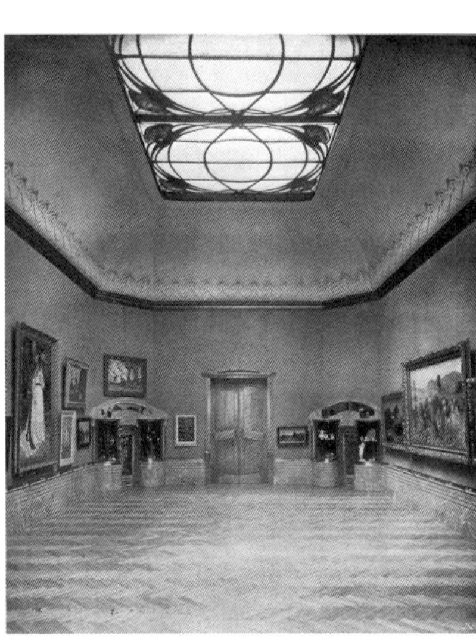

Abb. | Fig. 6
Museum Folkwang, Hagen, Empore
mit Vitrinen für ostasiatische Kunst |
Upstairs vestibule with display
cabinets for East Asian Art, 1902–1922

Abb. | Fig. 7
Museum Folkwang, Hagen,
Großer Bildersaal | Great picture hall,
ca. 1902

181

Für Museumsdirektoren wie Osthaus stellte sich die Frage, wie sie einen Raum realisieren konnten, der ihrem Ziel der Kunstvermittlung am besten entsprach, und welches ästhetische Ideal der Museumsraum selbst verkörpern sollte.[34] Gleichzeitig waren die beiden Museumsprojekte herausfordernde Experimente, die eine Plattform schufen, in deren Rahmen unterschiedliche Kulturen einander begegnen konnten: Eines der wesentlichen Elemente des Museum Folkwang war die zusammengewürfelte Natur der durch und durch heterogenen Sammlung, die für die Präsentation jedoch harmonisch kombiniert wurde. Der Hauptzweck des Kyōraku Bijutsukan lag in der Präsentation westlicher Kunst für ein japanisches Publikum. Als das Museum Folkwang am 19. Juli 1902 in der Hochstraße 73 eröffnete, übertraf das von van de Velde gestaltete Innere das, was man von dem im Stil der Renaissance gehaltenen Äußeren von Carl Gérard erwarten durfte.[35] Nach dem Eintritt in das dreigeschossige Gebäude fanden sich die Besucher:innen in der Eingangshalle wieder, die van de Velde durch ein rundes Oberlicht aus Buntglas beleuchtet hatte. Ab 1906 wurde dieser Raum als Brunnenhalle bezeichnet, da sich in seiner Mitte die runde, aus weißem Marmor bestehende *Fontaine aux agenouillés (Brunnen mit knienden Knaben,* 1905/06; Abb. 4) von George Minne befand.[36] Die Halle verkörperte das grundlegende Konzept des Museums einer harmonischen Verbindung von Innenraumgestaltung und Ausstellungsobjekten. Vom Erdgeschoss mit seiner großen Vielfalt an europäischen und nicht-abendländischen Kunstwerken und Artefakten, darunter die ägyptische Sammlung, phönizische Glasarbeiten, islamische Metallarbeiten, persische Tapisserien, japanische Rollbilder (*kakemono,* S. 253–255) und antike Möbel im Barock- und Rokoko-Stil, gelangten die Besucher:innen in das Treppenhaus mit

seinem großen Fenster, wo sich eine Vitrine für Glasarbeiten befand (Abb. 5). Im Vestibül des Obergeschosses (Abb. 6), das der ostasiatischen Kunst gewidmet war, hingen einige japanische *kago*-Körbe. Durch das Vestibül erreichte man die Bildergalerie, den Höhepunkt der Dauerausstellung mit den Schmuckstücken der Sammlung in einem kunstvoll gestalteten Interieur (Abb. 7). Um die Bildergalerie waren ein Auditorium, ein Musiksaal und bis 1909 der Wohnbereich angeordnet, was das Gebäude zu einer physischen Verkörperung von Osthaus' Ideal der Verbindung von Kunst und Alltagsleben machte.[37]

Mit Fortschreiten des Ersten Weltkriegs warfen die wirtschaftlichen Turbulenzen allmählich ihre Schatten auf die Folkwang-Aktivitäten von Osthaus. Kōjirō Matsukata, der sich auf seiner vierten Reise nach Europa befand und dessen Ankaufsprogramm in vollem Gang war, verpflichtete Brangwyn, der sich ab 1918 dem Projekt Kyōraku Bijutsukan widmete. Matsukata erhielt einige Vorzeichnungen und diskutierte den Plan im darauffolgenden Jahr in seinem Domizil in Mita, Tokio, mit einem engen Kreis aus Künstler:innen.[38] In der Zwischenzeit wurde ein weitläufiges Gelände auf der Kuppe des Sendaizaka – zur Verfügung gestellt von Kōjirōs Vater Masayoshi Matsukata – als Baugelände ausgewählt, wobei an die viertausend Quadratmeter für den Museumsbau vorgesehen waren. Eine Reihe von Skizzen und Blaupausen, die zusammen mit einigen Artikeln in englischen Zeitschriften erschienen, vermitteln einen Eindruck der architektonischen Idee (S. 243).[39] Brangwyns ursprüngliches Entwurfskonzept sah die Schaffung eines Galeriegebäudes für westliche Kunst mit maximaler „Zweckmäßigkeit" vor. Gleichzeitig war der Künstler bestrebt, durch die Umsetzung eines Prinzips der „Schlichtheit" dafür zu sorgen, dass das Gebäude „mit seiner Umgebung aus einhei-

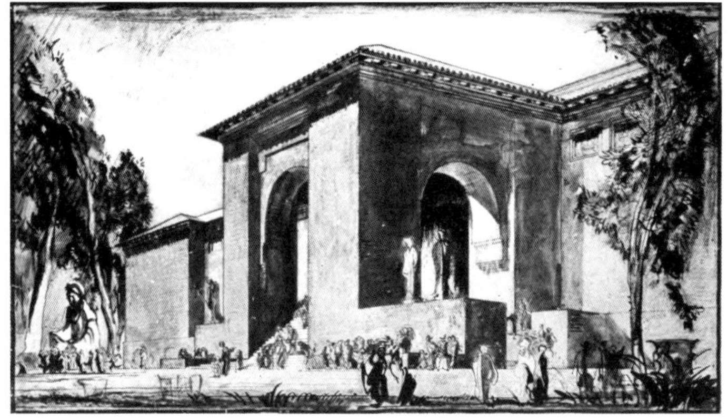

Abb. | Fig. 8
Frank Brangwyn, Entwurf des Kyōraku
Bijutsukan, Portikus am Haupteingang |
Design of the *Kyōraku Bijutsukan*,
Main Entrance Portico, 1922

As the First World War dragged on and the economic turmoil began to cast a shadow on Osthaus's Folkwang activities, Matsukata, who was on his fourth excursion to Europe and whose acquisition programme was in full swing, enlisted Brangwyn, who undertook the *Kyōraku Bijutsukan* project in 1918. Matsukata received some preparatory drawings and discussed the plan with his close artists' circle at his Tokyo residence in Mita in the following year.[38] Meanwhile, a vast site on the Sendaizaka hilltop offered by his father, Masayoshi Matsukata, was selected for the construction site with about four thousand square metres for the museum premises. A set of sketches and blueprints that accompanied some English journal articles convey the architectural idea (p. 243).[39] Brangwyn's foundational design concept was to produce a gallery building suitable for Western art with the maximum 'utility'. At the same time, it was the artist's intention, through employing the concept of 'simplicity', to make the buildings 'harmonize with its surroundings of native architecture and scenery without giving it a purely Japanese character,' so that it would not 'look like "a stranger in a strange land"'.[40]

In his unrealized designs, the main building, which is approachable from the central entrance portico, is brick in a 'warm, drab tone' covered with coarse roof tiles with 'thick pipelike ridges'. It is 'composed of four great galleries built in quadrangle form round a central court, surrounded by cloisters' and connects by way of a Japanese garden to the annex building dedicated to the decorative art department and accommodating an art library and a guest house (p. 20; fig. 8).[41] Not only the immediate surroundings but also the excellent prospect from the hill were considered 'as integral part of the decorative scheme,'[42] and a loggia was placed in front of the side entrance 'with a large pool of still water reflecting in its surface the snow-capped summit of the outstanding Fuji',[43] perhaps incorporating the principle of *shakkei* or 'borrowed scenery', an East Asian tradition of garden design that makes use of the external natural landscape as part of the garden composition (fig. 9). To make the as yet unfamiliar art approachable for the Japanese audience, providing comfort was of utmost importance. The central 'cloistered courtyard with gardens and a fountain within the inner walls' provided not only 'a beautiful *milieu* for the sculpture' but also 'a relief for the eyes of the visitor after looking at so many brilliantly coloured pictures.'[44] (fig. 11) Such visual refreshment was essential to encourage the Japanese audience to develop a 'museum habit,' and the facility should obviate the 'militating factor,' the 'rapidity with which the average visitor becomes mentally sated and physically exhausted.'[45] Destined for the presentation of Occidental art, the *Kyōraku Bijutsukan* put less emphasis on an intercultural association inside the exhibition space; nevertheless, the museum edifice itself embodied a cultural juxtaposition that was designed as 'an accompaniment to the natural surroundings in the midst of which it is placed.'[46]

mischer Architektur und Szenerie harmoniert, ohne ihm einen rein japanischen Charakter zu verleihen", damit es nicht „wie ein ‚Fremder in einem fremden Land' aussieht"[40].

In seinen nicht realisierten Entwürfen besteht das Hauptgebäude, das über die zentrale Eingangsvorhalle betreten wird, aus Ziegeln in einem „warmen Graubraun", bedeckt von rohen Dachziegeln mit „dicken, röhrenähnlichen Graten". Es „setzt sich aus vier großen Galerien in Vierecksform um einen zentralen Hof, umgeben von Säulengängen, zusammen" und ist über einen japanischen Garten mit dem Anbau verbunden, der der Abteilung für angewandte Kunst gewidmet ist und zudem eine Kunstbibliothek und ein Gästehaus umfasst (S. 20; Abb. 8).[41] Nicht nur die unmittelbare Umgebung, sondern auch der herausragende Ausblick vom Hügel galten „als wesentlicher Bestandteil des dekorativen Programms",[42] und vor dem Seiteneingang befand sich eine Loggia „mit einem großen Süßwasserbecken, in dessen Oberfläche sich der schneebedeckte Gipfel des herausragenden Fuji spiegelte"[43]. Dies kann möglicherweise als Ausdruck des Prinzips von *shakkei* oder der „geliehenen Szenerie" verstanden werden, einer ostasiatischen Tradition der Gartengestaltung, bei der man die außerhalb des Gartens liegende Naturlandschaft in die Gartenkomposition integriert (Abb. 9). Um die bislang unbekannte Kunst dem japanischen Publikum näher zu bringen, war es von größter Wichtigkeit, für eine vertraute Atmosphäre zu sorgen. Der zentrale „von einem Säulengang umgebene Hof mit Gärten und einem Brunnen innerhalb der inneren Mauern" bot nicht

nur „ein wunderschönes Umfeld für die Skulpturen", sondern auch „eine Linderung für die Augen der Betrachter nach so vielen leuchtend bunten Bildern"[44] (Abb. 11). Eine solche visuelle Labsal war ganz wesentlich, damit das japanische Publikum eine „Museums-Gewohnheit" entwickeln konnte; die Anlage sollte zudem einen „widerstreitenden Faktor" vermeiden, also die „Schnelligkeit, mit der durchschnittliche Besucher:innen geistig übersättigt und körperlich überanstrengt werden"[45]. Das für die Präsentation westlicher Kunst bestimmte Kyōraku Bijutsukan legte weniger Wert auf eine interkulturelle Verbindung im Ausstellungsraum; dennoch verkörperte das Museumsgebäude selbst ein kulturelles Nebeneinander, das als „Begleitung zur natürlichen Umgebung, in der es sich befindet"[46] entworfen wurde.

Neutralität und Farbharmonie
im Ausstellungsraum

Was die Innengestaltung des Ausstellungsraumes anging, bestand einerseits ein Konsens darüber, was die Notwendigkeit von Neutralität anging; andererseits verfolgte man eine harmonische Integration von Farbe in den Schauräumen.

In seinem Entwurf für das Kyōraku Bijutsukan behandelte Brangwyn das Museumsgebäude „als einen Hintergrund für die Kunstwerke"[47] und beließ die Galeriewände „schmucklos […] ohne Verzierungen wie Zierleisten, Pfeiler und Ornamente"[48] (Abb. 10). Die schlichten, ungeschmückten Wände waren „in einem sanften, gestreiften Grau gehalten, das bewusst gewählt wurde, damit es

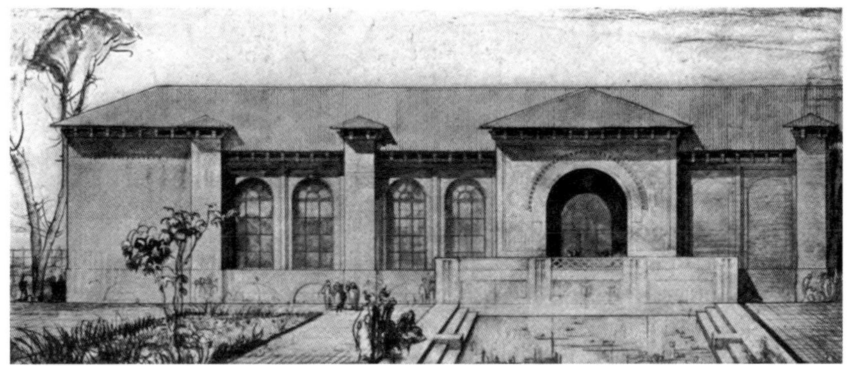

Abb. | Fig. 9
Frank Brangwyn, Entwurf des
Kyōraku Bijutsukan | Design of the
Kyōraku Bijutsukan, Loggia, 1922

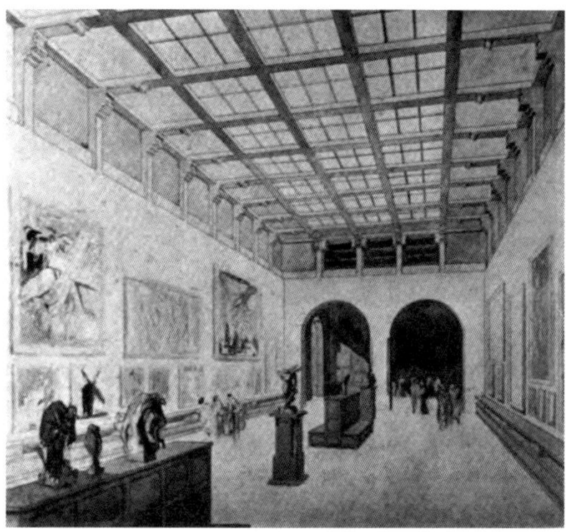

Abb. | Fig. 10
Frank Brangwyn, Entwurf des Kyōraku
Bijutsukan, Galerie mit einfach gestalteter
Teakholzdecke und grauen Wänden |
Design of the *Kyōraku Bijutsukan,* gallery
with simply designed teakwood ceiling
and grey walls, 1922

184

Neutrality and Colour Harmony in Exhibition Spaces

As regards the interior arrangement of exhibition space, on the one hand, there was a consensus on the requirement of neutrality; on the other hand, they pursued the harmonious integration of colour in the exhibitory rooms.

In his design for the *Kyōraku Bijutsukan,* Brangwyn treated the museum building 'as a background to the works of art,'[47] leaving the gallery walls 'plain' with 'no embellishments, such as mouldings, pillars and ornaments.' (fig. 10)[48] The simple, unornamented walls were 'kept a soft, striped grey, selected as being calculated not to clash in any way with the exhibits, and are very quiet, very restful, very unobtrusive,' at the base of which were wooden panels 'of extremely simple form.' The light coming through the lattice-shaped roofs of teak could be regulated according to the weather and the season.[49] While keeping the architectural elements restrained in design, spaces were reserved for mural decoration, which Matsukata wanted the artist to 'visit Tokyo to embellish.'[50]

Such an arrangement with a simple design and pictorial mural decoration had already been implemented at Brangwyn's earlier projects at Venice and Ghent (fig. 13).[51] At the Venice Biennale, he fulfilled the task of designing a space for 'a more or less considerable number of thoroughly heterogeneous works' by 'reduc[ing] his decorations to a mere, but agreeable background, positive enough to serve its purpose, but neutral enough to bestow its grace impartially.'[52] The walls were divided by a flat rail into two parts, the lower part of which 'was hung with the grey-buff coloured material only, while the upper part was further sub-divided by a frieze-rail, the frieze itself being dark-blue, powdered with a few silver stars, while below it ran a broader band of pale yellow.'[53] As such, Brangwyn paid particular attention to the colour palette and its combination inside his gallery room. In his own words: 'I have endeavoured to cause the person who enters it to feel the presence of a quiet richness, a certain sense of harmony without being able to for the moment give any reason for it.' 'The scheme of colour,' Brangwyn continues, 'is what I believe to be the very best for the purpose.'[54]

He applied the same plan at the entrance hall of the *Kyōraku Bijutsukan* with the mosaic ceiling 'patterned in arabesques of blue and gold.' (fig. 12) At the centre of the hall he installed 'the marble fountain in shell form placed on a square base, its border being of blue, its tiles of buff,' reflecting the 'glory of the ceiling' on its water surface. Adding a pictorial component, he was to design 'four stained-glass windows in illustration of forms of great modern industries such as boiler making, bridge and locomotive construction, electrical enterprise.'[55] The choice of subject matter implies another resonance of shared interest with the Museum Folkwang, where Osthaus included a painting by Maximilien Luce, *L'aciérie* (*The Ironworks in Couillet,* 1900; p. 205) on the wall at the corner of the picture gallery.

185

nicht mit den Ausstellungsstücken kontrastiert, und [sie waren] zudem sehr dezent, sehr beruhigend, sehr zurückhaltend". An ihrem Fuß befanden sich Holzpaneele „von äußerst schlichter Form". Das Licht, das durch die gitterförmigen Teak-Dächer dringen sollte, ließ sich je nach Wetter und Jahreszeit regulieren.[49] Während die Gestaltung der architektonischen Elemente äußerst zurückgenommen war, war auch Platz für Wanddekorationen vorgesehen, für „deren Verschönerung [der Künstler] Tokio besuchen" sollte, wie Matsukata sich wünschte.[50]

Eine solche Ausgestaltung mit schlichtem Entwurf und malerischer Wandgestaltung hatte der Künstler bereits bei früheren Projekten in Venedig und Gent umgesetzt (Abb. 13).[51] Im Rahmen der Biennale von Venedig gelang es ihm, einen Raum „für eine mehr oder weniger beträchtliche Anzahl von durchwegs heterogenen Arbeiten" zu entwerfen, indem er „seine Ausschmückungen auf einen bloßen, jedoch ansprechenden Hintergrund reduzierte, der überzeugend genug war, um seinem Zweck zu dienen, jedoch ausreichend neutral, damit seine Anmut unvoreingenommen zur Geltung kommt."[52] Die Wände wurden durch eine flache Leiste zweigeteilt, wodurch der untere Teil „lediglich mit dem graubräunlich gefärbten Material behängt war, während der obere Teil durch eine Friesleiste weiter unterteilt war; wobei das Fries selbst dunkelblau war, gesprenkelt mit einigen silbernen Sternen, darunter ein breiteres Band in hellem Gelb."[53] Brangwyn legte besonders großes Augenmerk auf die Farbpalette und die Farbkombinationen in seinen Galerieräumen.

Er selber sagte: „Ich habe es mir zum Ziel gesetzt, dass die Person, die den Raum betritt, die Anwesenheit einer stillen Vielfalt wahrnimmt, einen gewissen Sinn für Harmonie, ohne sofort einen Grund dafür benennen zu können." Und er fährt fort: „Die Farbgebung ist meiner Ansicht nach das Allerbeste für diesen Zweck."[54]

Den gleichen Plan wandte er auf die Eingangshalle des Kyōraku Bijutsukan an, wobei die Mosaikdecke „mit Arabesken in Blau und Gold gemustert" war (Abb. 12). Im Zentrum der Halle platzierte er einen „Marmorbrunnen in Muschelform auf einem quadratischen Sockel, die Kanten in Blau, die Fliesen in Gelbbraun", und auf der Wasseroberfläche sollte sich „die Pracht der Decke" spiegeln. Mit dem Entwurf von „vier Buntglasfenstern zur Wiedergabe von Ausprägungen großer moderner Industrien wie Kesselherstellung, Brücken- und Lokomotivenbau, elektrische Betriebe"[55] fügte er auch eine malerische Komponente hinzu. Die Themenwahl lässt auf eine weitere Gemeinsamkeit mit dem Museum Folkwang schließen, wo Osthaus das Gemälde *L'aciérie* (*Das Hüttenwerk,* 1900; S. 205) von Maximilian Luce an der schrägen Wand in einer Ecke der Bildergalerie präsentierte.

Auch im Museum Folkwang war die Raumneutralität eine ganz wesentliche Voraussetzung, die jedoch differenzierter interpretiert und umgesetzt wurde. Anstatt bildliche Elemente einzusetzen, erzielte van de Velde die Ornamentierung durch seine ausgeklügelte lineare Gestaltung der Architekturelemente wie Pfeiler, Geländer und in den Ecken der Räume eingelassene Vitrinen. Wie Gertrud Osthaus bemerkte, sollte in den

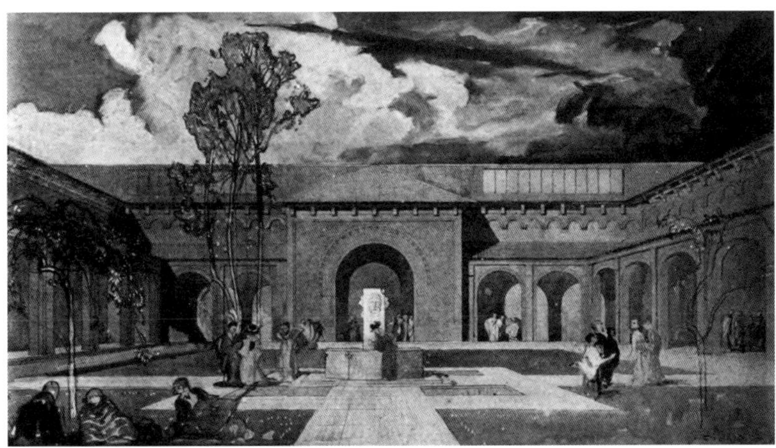

Abb. | Fig. 11
Frank Brangwyn, Entwurf des Kyōraku Bijutsukan, zentraler Innenhof mit gepflastertem Kreuzgang | Design of the *Kyōraku Bijutsukan,* the central courtyard, with stone-paved cloisters, 1922

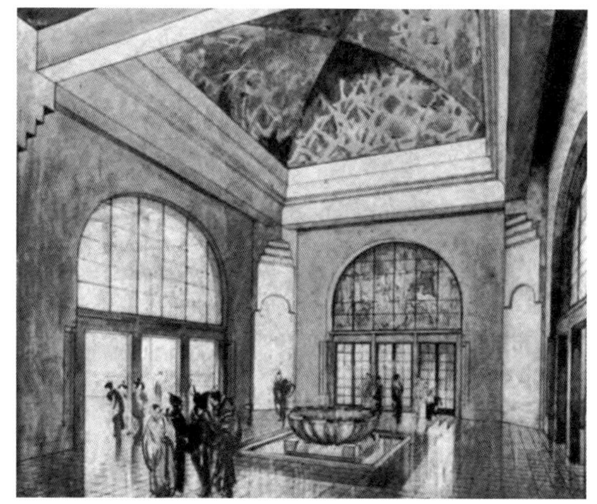

At the Museum Folkwang, space neutrality
was also an essential requisite yet executed with a
more nuanced interpretation. In place of pictorial
decorations, Van de Velde achieved the orna-
mentation through his elaborate linear design on
architectural elements such as pillars, rails and the
vitrines embedded in the corners of the room. As
Gertrud Osthaus argued exhibition spaces should
avoid any 'spurious or romantic' arrangement to
produce a 'historical mood' but instead remain
'so neutral that they do not touch the sphere of the
individual work.'[56] The neutrality meant, however,
not 'a colourless and unrelatable austerity,' but
instead would create 'an almost indiscernible but
by no means inanimate atmosphere,' in which
'every work of art can freely unfold its powers.'[57]
It was before the so-called 'white cube' developed as the standard format for a museum, and the
discussion on the wall colour was active. In 1903,
at a conference dedicated to museums as educational establishments for the people, some curators like Alfred Lichtwark and Ernst Grosse argued
for completely neutral background colour without
any ornamentations; others, such as Gustav Pauli,
argued that art museums should be decorated with
a sense of festivity.[58] Osthaus acknowledged the
pull to 'resort to yellow-brown' as it would 'save
as much nerve substance as possible,' which would
be helpful for the educational purpose, but proposed a more harmonious arrangement incorporating the 'colour triad'.

He chose 'particular colour tones' inside the
cabinets while keeping the central part of the wall
and the ceiling 'as white as possible to conserve
a fair amount of light.' Therefore 'in the vestibule,
where East Asian objects are exhibited,' 'the ceiling skylight of Tiffany glasses in violet, yellow and
green colours' was brought 'down into the cabinets, for instance, placing Japanese gold lacquer
on purple Chinese silk and other objects against a
green background.'[59] Comparing it to musical
chords, Osthaus believed in the abstract symbolic
capability of colour to produce a synergistic
effect. For him, the architectural elements were not
a mere background of the artworks, but rather all
the components should be organically harmonized
to make an entire whole.

He did not limit such interconnection to objects
from the same cultural backgrounds, but rather
overcame preset geographical or cultural boundaries, acknowledging instead what he called the
'psychological affinity'.[60] Following such an 'axis
of the display,' by the side of the entrance hall
stood the vitrine for antique handicraft,[61] and a
painting by Gauguin hung between a sacred stone
from Korea and bronze works from Laos.[62] Notably, Japanese art occupied a 'central part' of the
Folkwang collection because it was the source of
inspiration for the Western artists that, like a
'revelation' opened their eyes for the new artistic
expression,[63] as demonstrated, for example, by
Japanese paper stencils (*katagami*) hung on the
staircase (fig. 14) that anticipated the Impressionist
works in the picture gallery, across which one
could also overlook Paul Gauguin's *Contes barbares* (1902; p. 339) and Henri Matisse's *Still life with*

Ausstellungsräumen nicht mit „unechten und romantischen Mitteln" gearbeitet werden, um eine „historische Stimmung" heraufzubeschwören, sondern sie sollten „so neutral sein, daß sie die Sphäre des einzelnen Werkes nicht berühren"[56]. Bei Neutralität war jedoch nicht von einer „irrtümlich neutral genannten farb- und verhältnislosen Nüchternheit" die Rede, vielmehr sollte „eine fast unmerkliche, aber keineswegs unlebendige Atmosphäre erzeugt werden, in der nun jedes Kunstwerk frei seine Kräfte entfalten kann"[57]. Dies war noch vor der Zeit, in der der sogenannte White Cube sich zum Standardformat für Museen entwickelt hatte, und die Diskussionen zur Wandfarbe verliefen recht lebhaft. Im Rahmen einer Konferenz zum Thema Museen als Volksbildungsstätten im Jahr 1903 traten einige Kuratoren wie Alfred Lichtwark und Ernst Grosse für eine völlig neutrale Hintergrundfarbe ohne jegliche Ornamentierung ein; andere wie Gustav Pauli waren der Ansicht, dass Kunstmuseen eine feierliche Stimmung vermitteln sollten.[58] Osthaus bekräftigte, dass es in manchen Fällen „wichtig ist, möglichst viel Nervensubstanz zu sparen und zur gelbbraunen Farbe zu greifen", was dem Zweck der Belehrung zuträglich wäre, schlägt jedoch unter Einsatz eines „Farbendreiklang[s]" ein stärker harmonisch geprägtes Arrangement vor. Er wählte bestimmte „Farbenklänge" für die Schränke, während der „Hauptteil der Wand und vor allen Dingen die Decke möglichst weiß gehalten [wurden], um recht viel Licht zu sparen." Und weiter: „Wir sind im Vestibül, in dem ostasiatische Gegenstände ausgestellt sind, ausgegangen von einem

Deckenoberlicht aus Tiffany-Gläsern in violetter, gelber und grüner Farbe und haben diese Farben in die Schränke hinabgezogen, z. B. den japanischen Goldlack auf lila chinesische Seide gelegt und andere Gegenstände vor einem grünen Hintergrund gebracht."[59] Osthaus verglich dies mit musikalischen Akkorden und war der Ansicht, dass die abstrakte symbolische Kraft der Farbe einen synergistischen Effekt zur Folge hätte. Für ihn stellten die architektonischen Elemente keinen bloßen Hintergrund der Kunstwerke dar, stattdessen sollten alle Komponenten auf organische Art und Weise miteinander in Einklang gebracht werden, um so ein Ganzes zu erschaffen. Er beschränkte solche Querverbindungen jedoch nicht auf Gegenstände mit dem gleichen kulturellen Hintergrund, sondern überwand vorgegebene geografische oder kulturelle Grenzen und würdigte das, was er als „psychische Verwandtschaft"[60] bezeichnete. Gemäß einem solchen „Aufstellungsprinzip" stand an der Seite der Eingangshalle die Vitrine mit antiker Kleinkunst,[61] und ein Gemälde von Gauguin hing zwischen einem heiligen Stein aus Korea und Bronzen aus Laos.[62]

Interessanterweise bildete die japanische Kunst einen „Hauptbestandteil" der Sammlung Folkwang, da sie als Inspirationsquelle für westliche Künstler:innen galt und diesen „wie eine Offenbarung" die Augen für neue künstlerische Ausdrucksformen öffnete.[63] Dies zeigte sich zum Beispiel in den japanischen Papierschablonen (*katagami*), die im Treppenhaus hingen (Abb. 14) und die die impressionistischen Arbeiten in der Bildergalerie vorwegnahmen, von denen aus man auch Paul Gauguins

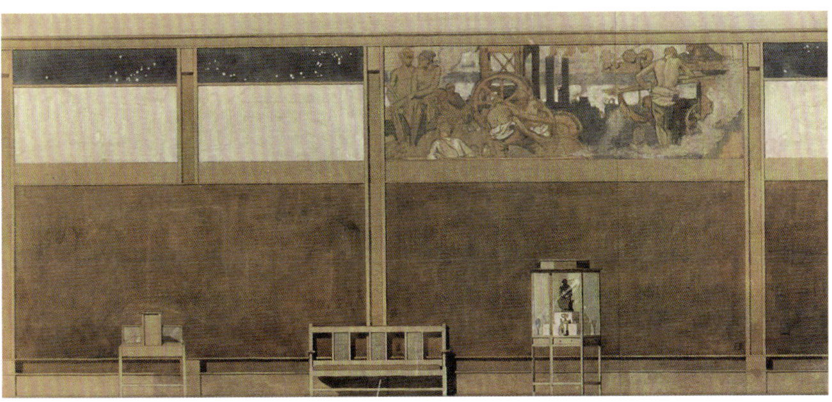

Abb. | Fig. 13
Frank Brangwyn, Schema für
Wanddekoration, Englische Abteilung,
Biennale von Venedig | Scheme
for mural decoration, English section,
Venice Biennale, 1905

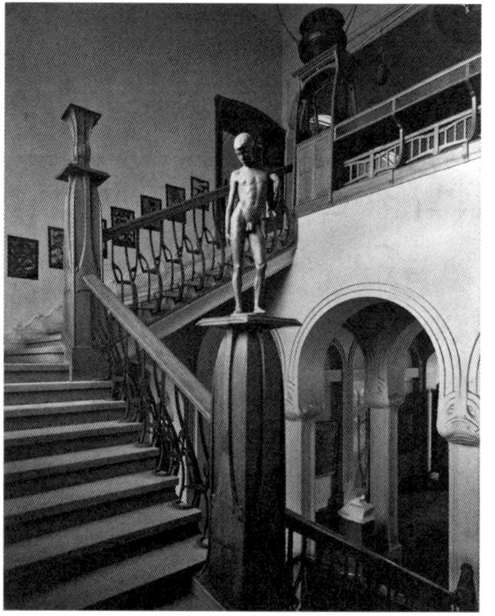

Abb. | Fig. 14
Museum Folkwang, Hagen, zentrales
Treppenhaus | the central stairwell,
ca. 1914

Asphodel (*Nature morte aux asphodèles*, 1906/07;
p. 103, fig. 11) in the entrance hall.

Though separated by decades and across
the continent, the two museum projects of Osthaus's Museum Folkwang and Matsukata's *Kyōraku Bijutsukan* demonstrated striking resonance.
Grounded in the decorative arts movement, the
two institutions shared the basic concept of the
role of a museum as an instrument for the aesthetic
education of the public leading to the promotion

of culture and industry. The two museum designs
were the embodiments of two different approach-
es to realizing a place not of self-representation
of one's own culture but rather one where people
could experience art from different backgrounds,
react to it, and reflect on it. Bringing the unfamiliar
together and encouraging such reflections, both
museum designs sought to realize a harmonious
exhibition space through deliberate application of
colour and decoration.

1   In German Osthaus described his
    mission as: '*Daß große Problem
    der Zeit war die Zurückführung
    der Kunst ins Leben…*'. Karl Ernst
    Osthaus, 'Lebenslauf', *Grundzüge
    der Stilentwicklung* (Hagener
    Verlagsnstalt, 1918), I–VI, quoted in
    Rainer Stamm, (ed.), *Karl Ernst
    Osthaus: Reden und Schriften
    Folkwang, Werkbund, Arbeitsrat,
    Kontext. Schriftenreihe für Kunst,
    Kunsterziehung und Kulturpäda-
    gogik*, 3, (Cologne, 2002), 24.

2   Willard Slater, 'Why Japan Collects
    Western Art,' *International Studio*
    (April 1922), 151.

3   On Osthaus's biography and his
    museum project, see introduction
    and the discussion in this volume
    (pp. 22–53) by Nadine Engel.
    See also Herta Hesse-Frielinghaus,
    August Hoff, Walter Erben et al.,
    Karl Ernst Osthaus. Leben und Werk
    (Recklinghausen, 1971), 35–7.

4   Karl Ernst Osthaus, 'Darstellung
    einiger bisher gemachter Versuche,
    die Schätze der Museen weiteren

    Schichten des Volkes nutzbar zu
    machen: Der Folkwang in Hagen',
    Vortrag gehalten am 21. September
    1903, *Die Museen als Folksbildungs-
    stätten: Ergebnisse der 12. Konfe-
    renz der Centralstelle für Arbeiter-
    Wohlfahrtseinrichtungen* (Berlin
    1904), 58-61, quoted from Rainer
    Stamm, (ed.), *Karl Ernst Osthaus:
    Reden und Schriften* (Cologne
    2002), 40.

5   Letter from Theodor Rocholl to
    Karl Ernst Osthaus, 11. /97 [sic]
    (1897), Kü 125, Hagen, Karl Ernst
    Osthaus Archive, cited in Hesse-
    Frielinghaus et al., *Karl Ernst
    Osthaus. Leben und Werk*, 232.

6   The entomological collection that
    Osthaus assembled from his travels
    to North Africa in the semi-base-
    ment was not yet on display at the
    museum's official opening but a
    year later. Anonymous, 'Zur Eröff-
    nung des Museum "Folkwang"',
    Hagener Zeitung, 19 July 1902;
    Hesse-Frielinghaus et al., *Karl Ernst
    Osthaus. Leben und Werk*, 133.

7   On Matsukata's biography and the
    establishment of his collection,
    see the essay by Megumi Jingaoka
    in this volume (pp. 118–141) and
    her earlier essay: Megumi Jinga-
    oka, 'The Matsukata Collection –
    A Century-Long Voyage,' trans.
    Sō Ōta and Walter Hamilton, in
    *The Matsukata Collection: A One-
    Hundred-Year Odyssey*, exh. cat.
    National Museum of Western Art
    (Tokyo, 2019), 291–307.

8   On the name of the museum and
    its origin, see, Noriko Minato,
    'Matsukata Kōjirō to sono bijutsu-
    kan kōsō ni tsuite (ge)' *Museum*,
    no. 396 (March 1984), 30–1; Noriko
    Minato, 'Matsukata Kōjirō no yume:
    Kyōraku Bijutsukan,' in *Bijutsukan
    no Yume*, exh. cat. Hyogo Prefectur-
    al Museum of Art (2002), p. 131 and
    note. 13; Nagako Kamiyasu, 'Matsu-
    kata Kōjirō no "Kyōraku Bijutsukan"
    kōsō to "kyōraku" no shisō,' *Hakuhō
    Daigaku Ronshū*, vol. 32 no. 2 (2018),
    77–102.

189

Contes barbares (1902; S. 339) und Henri Matisse' *Nature morte aux asphodèles (Stillleben mit Affodillen,* 1906/07; S. 103, Abb. 11) in der Eingangshalle sehen konnte.

Obwohl getrennt durch Jahrzehnte und Kontinente, weisen die beiden Projekte, Osthaus' Museum Folkwang und Matsukatas Kyōraku Bijutsukan, frappierende Ähnlichkeiten auf. Die beiden Institutionen, die in der Kunstgewerbebewegung verwurzelt waren, hatten ein gemeinsames Grundkonzept, nämlich die Rolle des Museums als Instrument für die ästhetische Bildung des Publikums und zur Förderung von Kultur und Industrie. Die zwei Museumsentwürfe verkörpern einen jeweils unterschiedlichen Ansatz zur Realisierung eines Ortes, dessen Zweck nicht die Selbstdarstellung der eigenen Kultur war, sondern der es den Menschen ermöglichen sollte, Kunst mit unterschiedlichem Hintergrund zu erleben, darauf zu reagieren und darüber nachzudenken. Beide Museumsentwürfe waren bestrebt, durch die bewusste Anwendung von Farbe und Ausstattung einen harmonischen Ausstellungsraum zu erzielen, der fremde Elemente zusammenführte und solche Überlegungen damit förderte.

1 „Das große Problem der Zeit war die Zurückführung der Kunst ins Leben …". Karl Ernst Osthaus, „Lebenslauf", in: *Grundzüge der Stilentwicklung,* Hagen 1918, S. I–VI, zit. nach: *Karl Ernst Osthaus. Reden und Schriften. Folkwang, Werkbund, Arbeitsrat (Kontext. Schriftenreihe für Kunst, Kunsterziehung und Kulturpädagogik,* 3), hrsg. und komm. von Rainer Stamm, Köln 2002, S. 24.

2 Willard Slater, „Why Japan Collects Western Art", in: *International Studio,* 75, April 1922, S. 151. Wenn nicht anders angegeben, stammen sämtliche Übersetzungen von Alexandra Titze-Grabec.

3 Zur Biografie von Osthaus und seinem Museumsprojekt siehe die Beiträge von Michelle Latta und Rainer Stamm sowie die Ausführungen von Nadine Engel in diesem Band (S. 22–53). Siehe auch Herta Hesse-Frielinghaus u. a., *Karl Ernst Osthaus. Leben und Werk,* Recklinghausen 1971, S. 35 ff.

4 Karl Ernst Osthaus, „Darstellung einiger bisher gemachter Versuche, die Schätze der Museen weiterer Schichten des Volkes nutzbar zu machen: Der Folkwang in Hagen", Vortrag vom 21.9.1903, in: *Die Museen als Volksbildungsstätten. Ergebnisse der 12. Konferenz der Centralstelle für Arbeiter-Wohlfahrtseinrichtungen,* Berlin 1904, S. 58–61, zit. nach: *Karl Ernst Osthaus. Reden und Schriften,* S. 40.

5 Theodor Rocholl an Karl Ernst Osthaus, Brief vom 11./97 [sic] 1897, Kü 125, Karl Ernst Osthaus Archiv, Hagen, zit. in: Herta Hesse-Frielinghaus u. a., *Karl Ernst Osthaus,* S. 133.

6 Die entomologische Sammlung im Souterrain, die Osthaus auf seinen Reisen nach Nordafrika zusammengetragen hatte, war bei der offiziellen Eröffnung des Museums noch nicht zu sehen, sondern eröffnete erst ein Jahr später. Anonym, „Zur Eröffnung des Museum ‚Folkwang'", in: *Hagener Zeitung,* 19.7.1902, zit. in: Herta Hesse-Frielinghaus u. a., *Karl Ernst Osthaus,* S. 133.

7 Zu Matsukatas Biografie und zum Aufbau seiner Sammlung siehe den Beitrag von Megumi Jingaoka in diesem Band (S. 118–141) sowie ihren früheren Essay: Megumi Jingaoka, „The Matsukata Collection – A Century-Long Voyage", in: *The Matsukata Collection. A One-Hundred-Year Odyssey,* Ausst.-Kat. National Museum of Western Art, Tokio, Tokio 2019, S. 291–307.

8 Zum Namen des Museums und dessen Ursprüngen siehe Noriko Minato, „Matsukata Kōjirō to sono bijutsukan kōsō ni tsuite (ge)", in: *MUSEUM. Tokyo Kokuritsu Hakubutsukan Bijutsushi,* 396, März 1984, S. 30 f.; Noriko Minato, „Matsukata Kōjirō no yume. Kyōraku Bijutsukan", in: *Bijutsukan no Yume,* Ausst.-Kat. Hyōgo Prefectural Museum of Art, Kobe, Kobe 2002, S. 131 und Anm. 13; Nagako Kamiyasu, „Matsukata Kōjirō no ‚Kyōraku Bijutsukan' kōsō to ‚kyōraku' no shisō", in: *Hakuhō Daigaku Ronshū,* 32, 2, 2018, S. 77–102.

9 Anonym, „Western Art for Japan", in: *Times,* 6.10.1921, S. 8. Der japanische Kunsthistoriker Yashiro Yukio, Matsukatas häufiger Kunstgalerie-Gefährte in Paris und London, liefert in seinen Memoiren einen entsprechenden Bericht: „In Japan gibt es tausende von Menschen, die Ölgemälde malen, und doch können diese Menschen niemals ein echtes Ölgemälde als Vorbild sehen. […] Ich finde das abscheulich und hoffe, dass ich auf eigene Faust echte europäische Ölgemälde sammeln und nach Japan schicken kann, damit diese Menschen sie sehen können." Yashiro Yukio, *Geijutsu no patoron,* Tokio 2019 (erstmals 1958 publiziert), S. 25. Englische Übersetzung zit. in: Mina Oya, „Venice, Ghent, and Paris. Designing the Kyoraku Bijutsukan (Sheer Pleasure Arts Pavilion)", in: *Frank Brangwyn,* Ausst.-Kat. National Museum of Western Art, Tokio, Tokio 2010, S. 229.

10 1917 reformierte Ōgai Mori, der heute in erster Linie für seine Romane bekannt ist, als Generaldirektor der Kaiserlichen Museen das museale Ausstellungskonzept, indem er die Werkstoffklassifizierung durch eine chronologische Ordnung ersetzte, und erschuf damit das Narrativ der japanischen Nationalgeschichte. Yuri Kawanishi, Yūji Takahashi u. a., *Mori Ōgai to Bijutsu,* Ausst.-Kat. Iwami Art Museum, Masuda 2006.

11 Das Tokyo-Fu Bijutsukan (Tokyo Metropolitan Art Gallery, das heutige Tokyo Metropolitan Art Museum) wurde schließlich 1926 gegründet. Zur Geschichte der Kunstmuseen in Japan siehe z. B.: *The Dream of a Museum. 120 years of the concept of the „bijutsukan" in Japan,* Ausst.-Kat. Hyōgo Prefectural Museum of Art, Kobe, Kobe, 2002.

9 Anonymous, 'Western Art for Japan,' *Times*, 6 October 1921, 8. Japanese art historian Yashiro Yukio, who was Matsukata's frequent art gallery companion in Paris and London, provides a corresponding account in his memoir: 'There are thousands of people painting oil paintings in Japan and yet those people cannot see a real oil painting as their model. [...] I find that abhorrent and, on my own, hope that I can collect real European oil paintings and send them to Japan for these people to see.' Yashiro Yukio, *Geijutsu no patoron* (Tokyo, 2019, first published in 1958), 25. English translation cited from Mina Oya, 'Venice, Ghent, and Paris: Designing the Kyoraku Bijutsukan (Sheer Pleasure Arts Pavilion),' in *Frank Brangwyn*, exh. cat. National Museum of Western Art, Tokyo (2010), 229.

10 In 1917, as the general director of the imperial museums, Ōgai Mori, best known today for his novels, reformed the museum display by replacing the material classification with chronological order producing the narrative of Japan's national history. Yuri Kawanishi, Yūji Takahashi, et al., *Mori Ōgai to Bijutsu*, eds. Masuda, et al, exh. cat., Iwami Art Museum, (2006).

11 Ultimately, the Tokyo-Fu Bijutsukan (Tokyo Metropolitan Art Gallery, present-day Tokyo Metropolitan Art Museum) was established in 1926. On the history of art museums in Japan, see, for example, *The Dream of a Museum: 120 years of the concept of the 'bijutsukan' in Japan* exh. cat, Hyogo Prefectural Museum of Art, (2002).

12 On the project of Kyōraku Bijutsukan see articles by Noriko Minato. Noriko Minato, 'Matsukata Kōjirō to sono bijutsukan kōsō ni tsuite (jō),' *Museum: Tōkyō Kokuritsu Hakubutsukan Bijutsushi*, no. 395 (February 1984), 31–40; Minato, 'Matsukata Kōjirō to sono bijutsukan kōsō ni tsuite (ge),' (1984), 27–38; Minato, 'Matsukata Kōjirō no yume' (2002), 129–32.

13 On the establishment of the South Kensington Museum and its design and decoration, see, Julius Bryant, *Designing the V&A: The Museum as a Work of Art (1857-1909)*, (Lund Humphries, 2017).

14 On the politics of the German decorative arts movement, see, John V. Maciuika, *Before the BAUHAUS: Architecture, Politics, and the German State, 1890–1920* (Cambridge University Press, 2005).

15 Van de Velde furnished four rooms, the rotunda with fresco paintings by Albert Besnard, a dining room with wall decoration by Paul Ranson, a smoking room, and a cabinet. Karl Ernst Osthaus, *Van de Velde. Leben und Schaffen des Künstlers*, (Hagen, 1920), 17–19. Brangwyn designed a frieze for the shop front and two panels for the entrance hall. Herbert Ernest Augustus Furst, *The Decorative Art of Frank Brangwyn* (London, 1924), 48–51.

16 On Deutsches Museum and the list of exhibitions, see, Sebastian Müller, 'Deutsches Museum für Kunst in Handel und Gewerbe,' in Hesse-Frielinghaus et.al, *Karl Ernst Osthaus. Leben und Werk*, 259–342; Michael Fehr, Sabine Röder, Gerhard Storck, (eds.), *Das schöne und der Alltag; Deutsches Museum für Kunst in Handel und Gewerbe*, exh. cat. Kaiser Wilhelm Museum Krefeld and Karl Ernst Osthaus Museum (Hagen, 1997).

17 '*Wiedervereinigung von Kunst und Gewerbe.*' Karl Ernst Osthaus, 'Gründung eines deutschen Museum für Kunst in Handel und Gewerbe in Hagen,' *Hagener Zeitung*, August 9, 1909, quoted in Stamm (ed.), *Karl Ernst Osthaus: Reden und Schriften*, 68.

18 In German: '*Künstler als Lehrer der Gewerbe.*' Christiane Heiser, "Der Deutsche Werkbund auf der Weltbühne oder wie Deutschland 1913 doch noch an der Weltausstellung teilnahm: das Deutsche Haus und die deutsche Abteilung für Raumkunst und Kunstgewerbe in Gent," *Archive für Kulturgeschichte*, vol. 92, 2010, 363-98, here see 381–82.

19 Noriko Minato, 'Matsukata korekushon to kōgei (The Matsukata Collection and Decorative Arts),' in *Oridasareta kaiga (Woven Pictures)*, exh. cat. The National Museum of Western Art (Tokyo, 2003) in Japanese with English summary, 24-9, here see 25.

20 Ibid., 25.

21 On the artworks in the old Matsukata collection, see, Masako Kawaguchi and Megumi Jingaoka (eds.), *The Matsukata Collection: Complete Catalogue of the European Art*, 2 vols., The National Museum of Western Art (Tokyo, 2018/ 2019); Minato, 'Matsukata korekushon to kōgei', 24–28.

22 Being a regular reader of the French art magazine *Revue de l'Art Ancien et Moderne*, he preferred to purchase works directly from artists, wisely avoiding the concerns over authenticity, and prepared diligently with his Paris advisor Léonce Bénédite ahead of negotiation with artists like Rodin and Claude Monet. See, Jingaoka, 'The Matsukata Collection – A Century-long Voyage', 293–96.

23 On the *ukiyo-e* prints (today in the Tokyo National Museum collection), see, Julia Meech, 'The Matsukata Collection of Ukiyo-e Prints: Masterpieces from the Tokyo National Museum,' in Julia Meech and Christine Guth, *The Matsukata Collection of Ukiyo-E Prints: Masterpieces from the Tokyo National Museum*, exh. cat., The Jane Voorhees Zimmerli Art Museum (Rutgers, New Jersey, 1988), 10–25.

24 Masako Kawaguchi, 'The Matsukata Collection Sales and the Practice of Personal Asset Forfeiture by Company Executives,' trans. Martha J. McClintock, in Kawaguchi and Jingaoka (eds.), *The Matsukata Collection* (Tokyo, 2019), 318–29, here see 318–19.

25 *Times* 6 October 1921, 8.26 'Taiseimeiga tenrankai. Honsha rōjyō no geijutsu no aki. Matsukata Kōjirō shi no hōfu,' *Osaka Mainichi Shimbun*, October 13, 1922, quoted in Minato, 'Matsukata korekushon to kōgei' (2003), 24.

27 Slater, 'Why Japan Collects Western Art', 151-3.

28 Ibid., 151.

29 Karl Ernst Osthaus, 'Die Genter Weltausstellung,' *Neudeutsche Bauzeitung*, vol. 9 (1913), no. 35, 601–02 and no. 39, 657–59, cited in Stamm, (ed.), *Karl Ernst Osthaus: Reden und Schriften*, 77–81, here 80.

30 Minato, 'Matsukata Kōjirō to sono bijutsukan kōsō ni tsuite (ge),' (1984); Masako Kawaguchi, 'The Matsukata Collection Artworks Stored in London,' *Journal of the National Museum of Western Art,*

190

191

12 Zum Projekt des Kyōraku Bijutsukan siehe folgende Artikel von Noriko Minato: Noriko Minato, „Matsukata Kōjirō to sono bijutsukan kōsō ni tsuite (jō)", in: *Museum: Tōkyō Kokuritsu Hakubutsukan Bijutsushi*, 395, Februar 1984, S. 31–40; Noriko Minato, „Matsukata Kōjirō to sono bijutsukan kōsō ni tsuite (ge)", S. 27–38; Noriko Minato, „Matsukata Kōjirō no yume. Kyōraku Bijutsukan", S. 129–132.

13 Zur Gründung des South Kensington Museum sowie zu dessen Entwurf und Ausstattung siehe Julius Bryant, *Designing the V&A. The Museum as a Work of Art (1857–1909)*, London 2017.

14 Zur Politik der deutschen Kunstgewerbebewegung siehe John V. Maciuika, *Before the BAUHAUS. Architecture, Politics, and the German State, 1890–1920*, Cambridge 2005.

15 Van de Velde stattete vier Räume aus, die Rotunde mit Freskobildern von Albert Besnard, ein Speisezimmer mit Wanddekorationen von Paul Ranson, einen Rauchsalon und ein kleines Zimmer. Karl Ernst Osthaus, *Van de Velde. Leben und Schaffen des Künstlers*, Hagen 1920, S. 17 ff. Brangwyn entwarf ein Fries für die Ladenfront und zwei Paneele für den Eingangsbereich. Herbert Ernest Augustus Furst, *The Decorative Art of Frank Brangwyn*, London 1924, S. 48–51.

16 Zu diesem Museum und seinen Ausstellungen siehe Sebastian Müller, „Deutsches Museum für Kunst in Handel und Gewerbe", in: Herta Hesse-Frielinghaus u. a., *Karl Ernst Osthaus*, S. 259–342; *Das Schöne und der Alltag. Deutsches Museum für Kunst in Handel und Gewerbe*, hrsg. von Michael Fehr, Sabine Röder und Gerhard Storck, Ausst.-Kat. Kaiser Wilhelm Museum, Krefeld; Karl Ernst Osthaus Museum, Hagen, Köln 1997.

17 Karl Ernst Osthaus, „Gründung eines deutschen Museum für Kunst in Handel und Gewerbe in Hagen", in: *Hagener Zeitung*, 9.8.1909, zit. nach: *Karl Ernst Osthaus. Reden und Schriften*, S. 68.

18 Christiane Heiser, „Der Deutsche Werkbund auf der Weltbühne oder wie Deutschland 1913 doch noch an der Weltausstellung teilnahm. Das Deutsche Haus und die deutsche Abteilung für Raumkunst und Kunstgewerbe in Gent", in: *Archiv für Kulturgeschichte*, 92, 2010, S. 363–398, hier S. 381 f.

19 Noriko Minato, „Matsukata korekushon to kōgei (The Matsukata Collection and Decorative Arts)", in: *Oridasareta kaiga (Woven Pictures)*, Ausst.-Kat. The National Museum of Western Art, Tokio, Tokio 2003, Japanisch mit engl. Zusammenfassung, S. 24–29, hier S. 25.

20 Ebd.

21 Zu den Kunstwerken in der alten Sammlung Matsukata siehe Masako Kawaguchi und Megumi Jingaoka (Hrsg.), *The Matsukata Collection. Complete Catalogue of the European Art*, 2 Bde., Tokio 2018/19; Noriko Minato, „Matsukata korekushon to kōgei", S. 24–28.

22 Als regelmäßiger Leser der französischen Kunstzeitschrift *Revue de l'Art Ancien et Moderne* kaufte er Werke am liebsten direkt von den Künstler:innen und vermied so Bedenken hinsichtlich der Authentizität. In Zusammenarbeit mit seinem Pariser Berater Léonce Bénédite bereitete er sich geflissentlich auf Verhandlungen mit Künstlern wie Auguste Rodin oder Claude Monet vor. Siehe Megumi Jingaoka, „The Matsukata Collection – a Century-Long Voyage", S. 293–296.

23 Zu den *ukiyo-e* (heute in der Sammlung des Tokyo National Museum) siehe Julia Meech, „The Matsukata Collection of Ukiyo-e Prints. Masterpieces from the Tokyo National Museum", in: *The Matsukata Collection of Ukiyo-e Prints. Masterpieces from the Tokyo National Museum*, hrsg. von Julia Meech, Ausst.-Kat. Zimmerli Art Museum, Rutgers University, New Brunswick (NJ) 1988, S. 10–25.

24 Masako Kawaguchi, „The Matsukata Collection Sales and the Practice of Personal Asset Forfeiture by Company Executives", in: Masako Kawaguchi und Megumi Jingaoka (Hrsg.), *The Matsukata Collection*, S. 318–329, hier S. 318 f.

25 *Times*, 6.10.1921, S. 8.

26 „Taiseimeiga tenrankai. Honsha rōjyō no geijutsu no aki. Matsukata Kōjirō shi no hōfu", in: *Osaka Mainichi Shimbun*, 13.10.1922, zit. nach: Noriko Minato, „Matsukata korekushon to kōgei", S. 24.

27 Willard Slater, „Why Japan Collects Western Art", S. 151 ff.

28 Ebd., S. 151.

29 Karl Ernst Osthaus, „Die Genter Weltausstellung", in: *Neudeutsche Bauzeitung*, 9, 1913, Nr. 35, S. 601 f., und Nr. 39, S. 657 ff., zit. nach: *Karl Ernst Osthaus. Reden und Schriften*, S. 77–81, hier S. 80.

30 Noriko Minato, „Matsukata Kōjirō to sono bijutsukan kōsō ni tsuite (ge)"; Masako Kawaguchi, „The Matsukata Collection Artworks Stored in London", in: *Journal of the National Museum of Western Art*, 21, 2017, S. 5–17; „Pantechnicon sōko hokan kaiga tō risuto", in: Masako Kawaguchi und Megumi Jingaoka (Hrsg.), *The Matsukata Collection*, S. 124 f., siehe Kat. D3, „List of the Matsukata Collection items stored in the Pantechnicon Warehouse, London. Arthur Tooth and Sons, London"; Tate Archive, London, TGA 20106/1/11/51. Die Einrichtung bestand aus Friesgemälden, Türen mit bemaltem Paneel, Randleisten, Geländern, Sockeln, Möbeln und Textilien.

31 Fujishima Takeji schrieb über Matsukatas Plan, dass „von Brangwyn entworfene Möbel, Tisch, Stühle, Wanddekoration und Schreibtisch ankommen werden und, wenn das Museum errichtet wird, ein Raum mit dem Titel ‚Brangwyn's Room' eingerichtet werden soll". Fujishima Takeji, „Matsukata shi syūsyūhin nit suite", in: *Chūō Bijutsu*, 5, 8, August 1919, S. 60. Dieser Bericht wurde als Plan fehlinterpretiert, Brangwyns eigenes Atelier zu rekonstruieren. Jüngste Untersuchungen haben diese Annahme widerlegt, siehe Masako Kawaguchi und Megumi Jingaoka (Hrsg.), *The Matsukata Collection*, S. 124 f.

32 Oftmals teilten sie die ästhetische Ausrichtung des Symbolismus und überschnitten sich mit der Gruppe der Künstler:innen der Moderne, die zur Jahrhundertwende oft auch als Sezessionisten bezeichnet wurden.

33 Das Gebäude der Wiener Secession war ein bahnbrechendes Beispiel für einen unabhängigen Ausstellungsraum, der der Präsentation von Kunstwerken und Ästhetik der Künstler:innengruppe diente. Zur Wiener Secession und ihrer Ausstellungsstrategie siehe z. B. Peter Vergo, *Art in Vienna 1898–1918. Klimt, Kokoschka, Schiele and their contemporaries*, 4. überarb. Aufl., London 2015.

vol. 21 (2017), 5–17; ---, 'Pantechnicon sōko hokan kaiga tō risuto,'
in Kawaguchi and Jingaoka (eds.),
The Matsukata Collection, 124–5,
see, cat. no. D3, 'List of the Matsukata Collection items stored in the
Pantechnicon Warehouse, London.
Arthur Tooth and Sons, London.'
TGA 20106/1/11/51, Tate Archive.
London. The set consisted of frieze
paintings, doors with the painted
panel, cornice, rails, skirting, design
furniture and textiles.

31 Fujishima Takeji wrote on Matsukata's plan that 'furniture, table,
chairs, wall decorations, and desk
designed by Brangwyn will arrive,
and, when the museum will be built,
a room called "Brangwyn's Room"
will be installed.' Fujishima Takeji,
'Matsukata shi syūsyūhin nit suite,'
Chūō Bijutsu, vol. 5 no.8 (August
1919), 60, translation mine. This
account has been misinterpreted
as a plan to reconstruct Brangwyn's
own atelier. Recent studies have
disproved this supposition, see,
Kawaguchi and Jingaoka (eds.),
The Matsukata Collection, 124–5.

32 They often shared the aesthetic
orientation of symbolism and over-
lapped with the group of modernist artists of the turn of the century
often labeled as secessionists.

33 The Secession Building in Vienna
was a pioneering example built as
an independent exhibition space
to demonstrate the group artists'
artworks and aesthetics. On the
Vienna Secession and their exhibition strategies, see, for example,
Peter Vergo, *Art in Vienna 1898–1918:
Klimt, Kokoschka, Schiele and their
contemporaries,* 4th revised ed,
(Phaidon, 2015).

34 On the design and installation of
the Museum Folkwang in Hagen,
see, among others, Hartwig Fischer,
Uwe M. Schneede et al., *'Das
Schönste Museum der Welt':
Museum Folkwang bis 1933. Essays
zur Geschichte des Museum
Folkwang*, ed. by Museum of
Folkwang (Essen and Göttingen,
2010), see especially the article by
Rainer Stamm, 'Weltkunst und
Moderne,' pp. 27–46; Katherine
Kuenzli, 'The Birth of the Modernist
Art Museum: The Folkwang as
Gesamtkunstwerk,' *Journal of the
Society of Architectural Historians,*
vol. 72, no. 4 (December 2013),
503–29.

35 Herta Hesse-Frielinghaus, 'Folkwang 1. Teil,' in Hesse-Frielinghaus
et al., *Karl Ernst Osthaus: Leben
und Werk*, 119–241, here 122–30.

36 Ibid., 174–5.

37 Ibid., 132, 134. In 1909 the Osthaus
family moved to the villa Hohenhof,
which was fully designed by
Van de Velde and decorated with
works of modern artists such as
Ferdinand Hodler, Edouard Vuillard,
and Henri Matisse. On Hohenhof,
see, among others, Birgit Schulte,
'Museutopia: Der Rückblick im
Hohenhof,' in Michael Fehr and
Thomas W. Rieger (eds.), *Muse-
utopia:Schritte in andere Welten*
(Hagen, 2003), 27–47.

38 Matsukata's circle included the
painter Kuroda Seiki (1866–1924),
the architect Ōe Shintaro (1879–
1935), the portrait painter Ishibashi
Kazunori (1876–1928) and the British
potter Bernard Leach (1887–1979).
Kuroda Seiki Nikki (diary), November 28, 1919. Kuroda Seiki Nikki
Database, Tokyo National Research
Institute for Cultural Properties.
https://www.tobunken.go.jp/
materials/kuroda_diary/119046.html
(Last accessed September 2021);
Minato, 'Matsukata Kōjirō to sono
bijutsukan kōsō ni tsuite (ge)',
28–29.

39 Anonymous, 'Our Illustrations:
Gallery of Western Art, Tokio,
Japan,' *The Building News and
Engineering Journal*, vol. 122 no. 3512
(28 April 1922), 290; Anonymous,
'Our Illustrations: Enclosed Garden
at Rear of Main Galleries: A Gallery
of Western Art, Tokio, Japan,' *The
Building News and Engineering
Journal*, vol. 122 no. 3514 (12 May
1922), 316; Anonymous, 'Our Illustra-
tions: Gallery of Western Art, Tokio,
Japan: One of the Four Galleries,'
*The Building News and Engineering
Journal*, vol. 122 no. 3515 (19 May
1922), 343; Anonymous, 'Our Illustra-
tions: Gallery of Western Art, Tokio,
Japan,' The Building News and
Engineering Journal, vol. 122 no.
3518 (9 June 1922), 395; Anonymous,
'Illustrations: A Gallery of Western
Art, Tokio, Japan,' *The Builder,*
vol. 123, no. 4148 (4 Aug 1922);
Mrs Gordon-Stables, 'Tokio's
Occidental Museum', *International
Studio*, vol. 75 no. 304 (Sep. 1922),
455–67.

40 *Times,* 6 October 1921, 8.

41 Mrs Gordon-Stables 'Tokio's
Occidental Museum', 459.

42 Ibid.

43 *Building News,* 28 April 1922, 290.

44 *Times,* 6 October 1921, 8.

45 Mrs Gordon-Stables 'Tokio's
Occidental Museum', 459.

46 Ibid., 458.

47 Ibid., 458.

48 *Times,* 6 October 1921, 8.

49 Mrs Gordon-Stables 'Tokio's
Occidental Museum', 460–61.

50 Ibid., 461.

51 Oya, 'Venice, Ghent, and Paris'
in *Frank Brangwyn*, exh. cat
(Tokyo, 2010), 72–77, 229–33.

52 Furst, *The Decorative Art of Frank
Brangwyn,* 56.

53 Furst, *The Decorative Art of Frank
Brangwyn,* 56.

54 'Frank Brangwyn's Exhibition Room
at Venice,' *International Studio*,
vol. 25 (May 1905), 284–92, here 291.

55 Mrs Gordon-Stables 'Tokio's
Occidental Museum', 460.

56 Gertrud Osthaus, 'Das Museum
Folkwang in Hagen,' *Kölnische
Zeitung*, No. 908, August 10, 1913.

57 Ibid.

58 Alexis Joachimides, *Die Museumsreformbewegung in Deutschland
und die Entstehung des modernen
Museums 1880–1940* (Dresden,
2001), 112–13.

59 Karl Ernst Osthaus, 'Zur Einrichtung
der Museen' (Contributions to the
discussions of 22 September 1903),
in *Die Museen als Volksbildungsstätten. Ergebnisse der 12. Konferenz der Centralstelle für Arbeiter-Wohlfahrtseinrichtungen* (Berlin,
1904), 140, quoted from Stamm,
ed., *Karl Ernst Osthaus: Reden und
Schriften,* 43.

60 *Psychischer Verwandtschaft.'* Frau
K. E. Osthaus [Gertrud Osthaus],
'Das Museum Folkwang in Hagen'.

61 Kurt Freyer, 'Das Folkwang-Museum
zu Hagen i.W.,' *Die Kunst für Alle*,
Bd. 27, Jg. 28, H. 19 (1 July 1913),
433–45, here p. 438.

62 Gertrud Osthaus, 'Das Museum
Folkwang in Hagen'.

63 Max Cruetz, 'Kleinkunst und
Kunstgewerbe im Folkwang',
Die Rheinlande (Düsseldorf 1905),
105–112, see 107.

34 Zu Entwurf und Anlage des Museum Folkwang in Hagen siehe u. a. *„Das schönste Museum der Welt". Museum Folkwang bis 1933. Essays zur Geschichte des Museum Folkwang (Folkwang Texte,* 1), hrsg. vom Museum Folkwang, Göttingen 2010, besonders den Beitrag von Rainer Stamm, „Weltkunst und Moderne", S. 27–46; Katherine Kuenzli, „The Birth of the Modernist Art Museum. The Folkwang as Gesamtkunstwerk", in: *Journal of the Society of Architectural Historians,* 72, 4, Dezember 2013, S. 503–529.

35 Herta Hesse-Frielinghaus, „Folkwang 1. Teil", in: dies. u. a., *Karl Ernst Osthaus,* S. 119–241, hier S. 122–130.

36 Ebd., S. 174 f.

37 Ebd., S. 132, 134. 1909 zog die Familie Osthaus in die Villa Hohenhof, die vollständig von van de Velde entworfen wurde und mit Arbeiten von Künstlern der Moderne wie Ferdinand Hodler, Edouard Vuillard und Henri Matisse ausgestattet war. Zum Hohenhof siehe u. a. Birgit Schulte, „Museutopia. Der Rückblick im Hohenhof", in: *Museutopia. Schritte in andere Welten,* hrsg. von Michael Fehr und Thomas W. Rieger, Hagen 2003, S. 27–47.

38 Zu Matsukatas Kreis gehörten der Maler Kuroda Seiki (1866–1924), der Architekt Ōe Shintaro (1879–1935), der Porträtmaler Ishibashi Kazunori (1876–1928) und der britische Keramiker Bernard Leach (1887–1979). Kuroda Seiki Nikki (Tagebuch), 28.11.1919. Kuroda Seiki Nikki

Database, Tokyo National Research Institute for Cultural Properties. https://www.tobunken.go.jp/ materials/kuroda_diary/119046.html [zuletzt aufgerufen im September 2021]; Noriko Minato, „Matsukata Kōjirō to sono bijutsukan kōsō ni tsuite (ge)", S. 28 f.

39 Anonym, „Our Illustrations. Gallery of Western Art, Tokio, Japan", in: *The Building News and Engineering Journal,* 122, 3512, 28.4.1922, S. 290; Anonym, „Our Illustrations. Enclosed Garden at Rear of Main Galleries: A Gallery of Western Art, Tokio, Japan", in: *The Building News and Engineering Journal,* 122, 3514, 12.5.1922, S. 316; Anonym, „Our Illustrations. Gallery of Western Art, Tokio, Japan: One of the Four Galleries", in: *The Building News and Engineering Journal,* 122, 3515, 19.5.1922, S. 343; Anonym, „Our Illustrations. Gallery of Western Art, Tokio, Japan", in: *The Building News and Engineering Journal,* 122, 3518, 9.6.1922, S. 395; Anonym, „Illustrations. A Gallery of Western Art, Tokio, Japan", in: *The Builder,* 123, 4148, 4.8.1922; Mrs. Gordon-Stables, „Tokio's Occidental Museum", in: *International Studio,* 75, 304, September 1922, S. 455–467.

40 *Times,* 6.10.1921, S. 8.

41 Mrs. Gordon-Stables, „Tokio's Occidental Museum", S. 459.

42 Ebd.

43 *Building News,* 28.4.1922, S. 290.

44 *Times,* 6.10.1921, S. 8.

45 Mrs. Gordon-Stables, „Tokio's Occidental Museum", S. 459.

46 Ebd., S. 458.

47 Ebd.

48 *Times,* 6.10.1921, S. 8.

49 Mrs. Gordon-Stables, „Tokio's Occidental Museum", S. 460 f.

50 Ebd., S. 461.

51 Mina Oya, „Venice, Ghent, and Paris", S. 72–77, 229–233.

52 Herbert Ernest Augustus Furst, *The Decorative Art of Frank Brangwyn,* S. 56.

53 Ebd.

54 „Frank Brangwyn's Exhibition Room at Venice", in: *International Studio,* 25, Mai 1905, S. 284–292, hier S. 291.

55 Mrs. Gordon-Stables, „Tokio's Occidental Museum", S. 460.

56 Gertrud Osthaus, „Das Museum Folkwang in Hagen", in: *Kölnische Zeitung,* 908, 10.8.1913.

57 Ebd.

58 Alexis Joachimides, *Die Museumsreformbewegung in Deutschland und die Entstehung des modernen Museums 1880–1940,* Dresden 2001, S. 112 f.

59 Karl Ernst Osthaus, „Zur Einrichtung der Museen" (Beiträge zur Diskussion vom 22.9.1903), in: *Die Museen als Volksbildungsstätten. Ergebnisse der 12. Konferenz der Centralstelle für Arbeiter-Wohlfahrtseinrichtungen,* Berlin 1904, S. 140, zit. in: *Karl Ernst Osthaus. Reden und Schriften,* S. 43.

60 Gertrud Osthaus, „Das Museum Folkwang in Hagen".

61 Kurt Freyer, „Das Folkwang-Museum zu Hagen i.W.", in: *Die Kunst für Alle,* 28, 19, 1.7.1913, S. 433–445, hier S. 438.

62 Gertrud Osthaus, „Das Museum Folkwang in Hagen".

63 Max Cruetz, „Kleinkunst und Kunstgewerbe im Folkwang", in: *Die Rheinlande,* 1905, S. 105–112, hier S. 107.

KATALOG | CATALOGUE

Kapiteleinführungen von |
chapter introductions by

Rebecca Herlemann

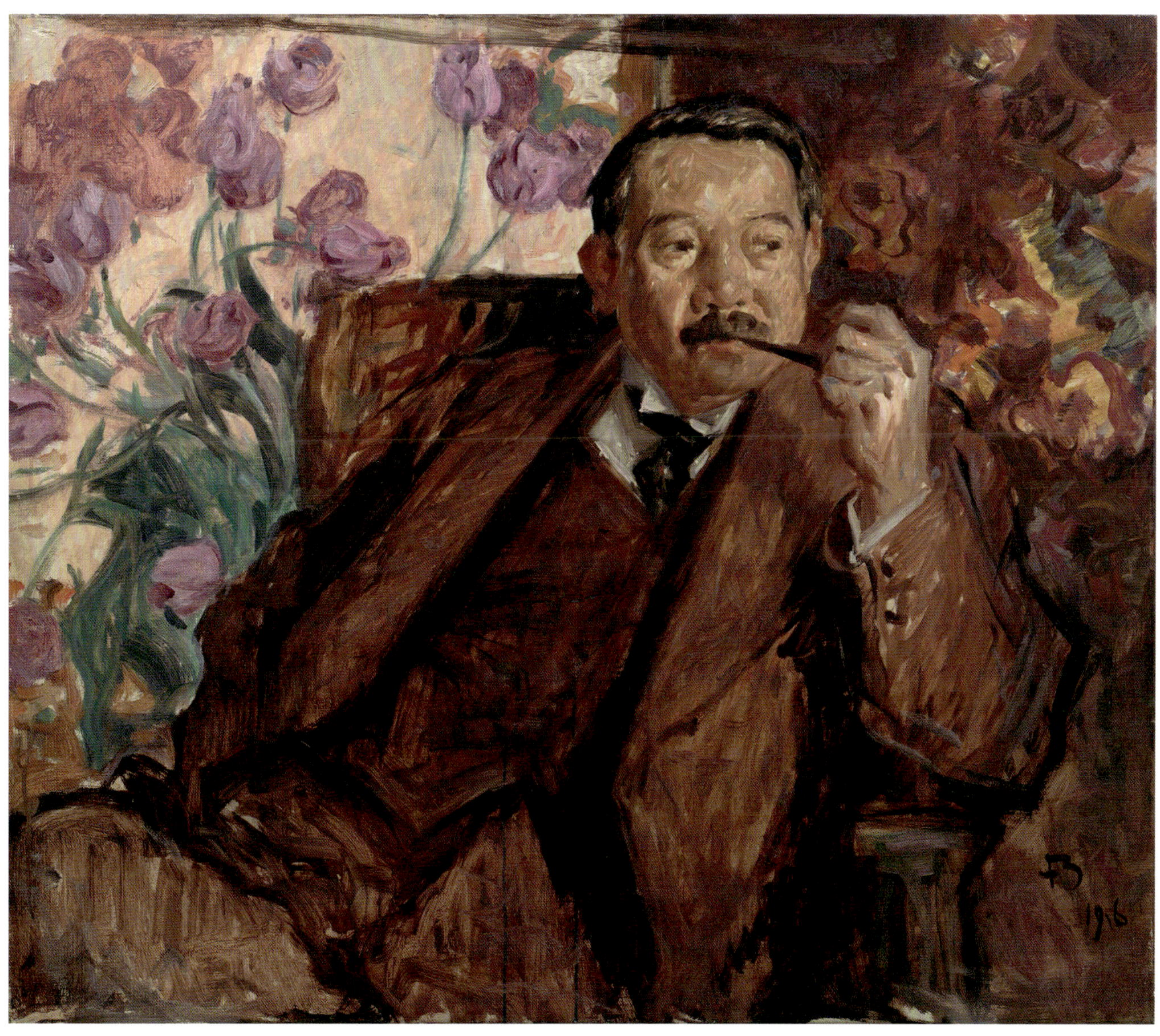

Frank Brangwyn
Portrait of Mr. Kōjirō Matsukata, 1916
The National Museum of Western Art, Tokyo

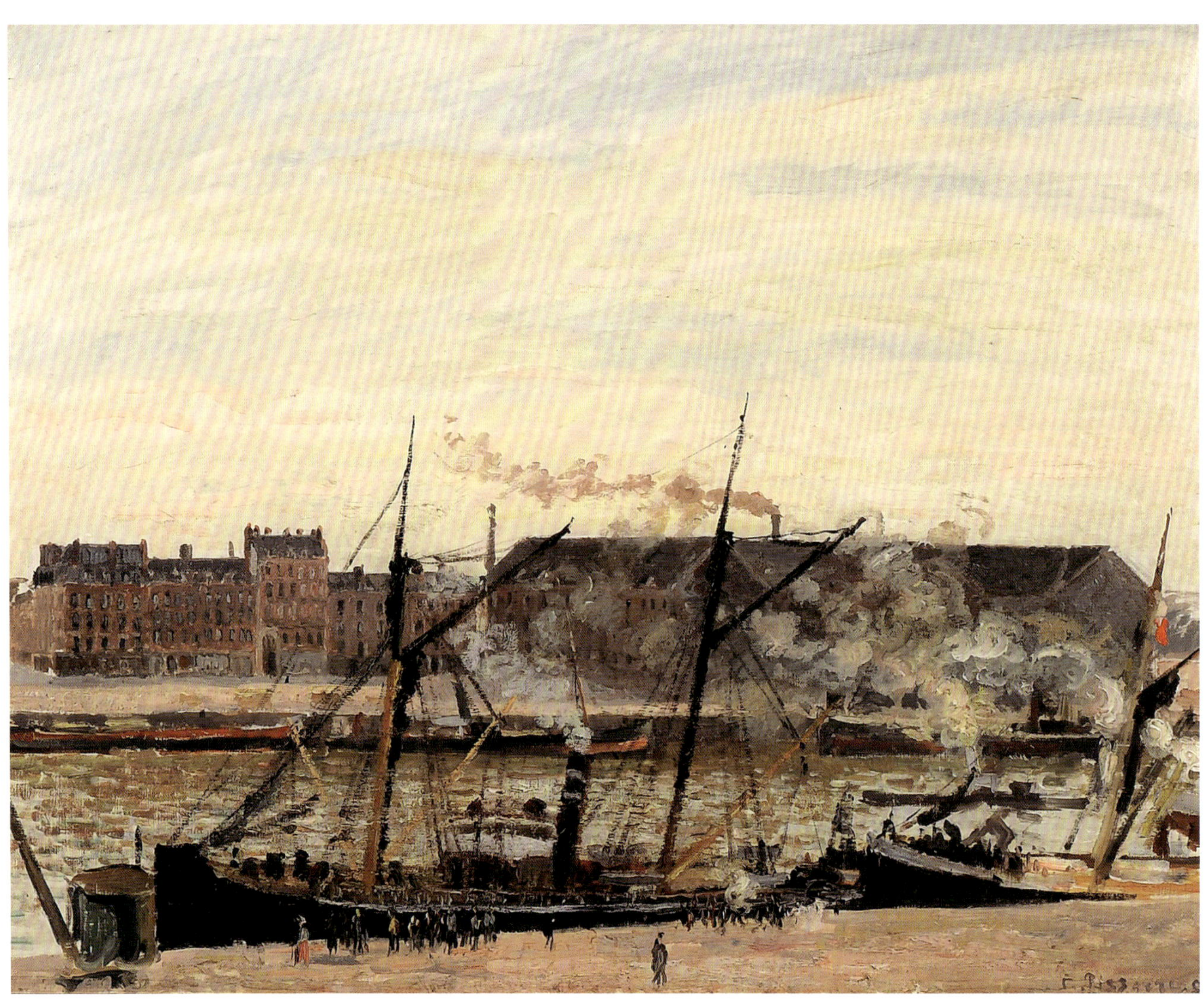

Camille Pissarro
Les docks, Saint-Sever, Rouen, fumées, 1898
Sumitomo Mitsui Banking Corporation, Tokyo

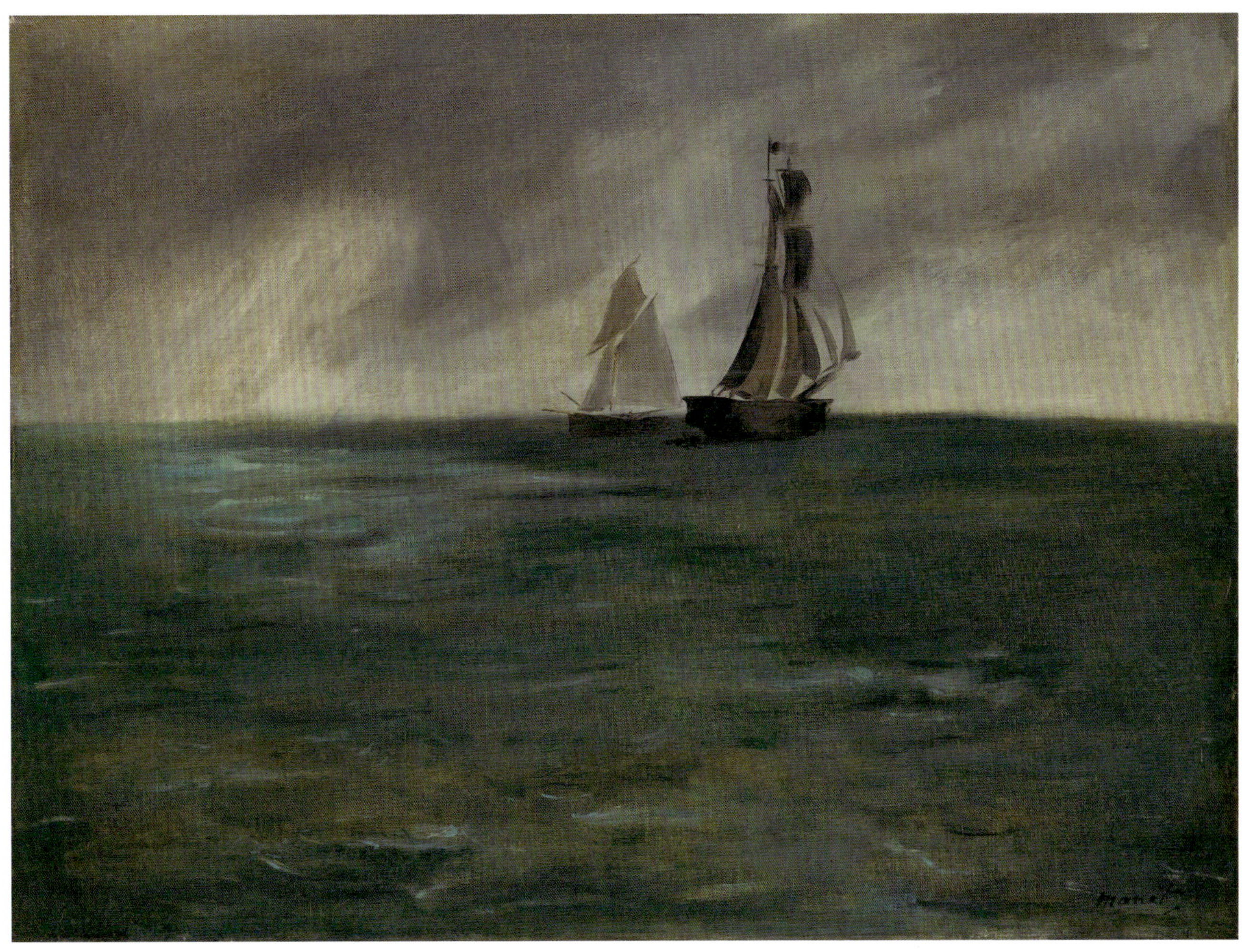

199

Edouard Manet
Marine, temps d'orage, 1873
The National Museum of Western Art, Tokyo

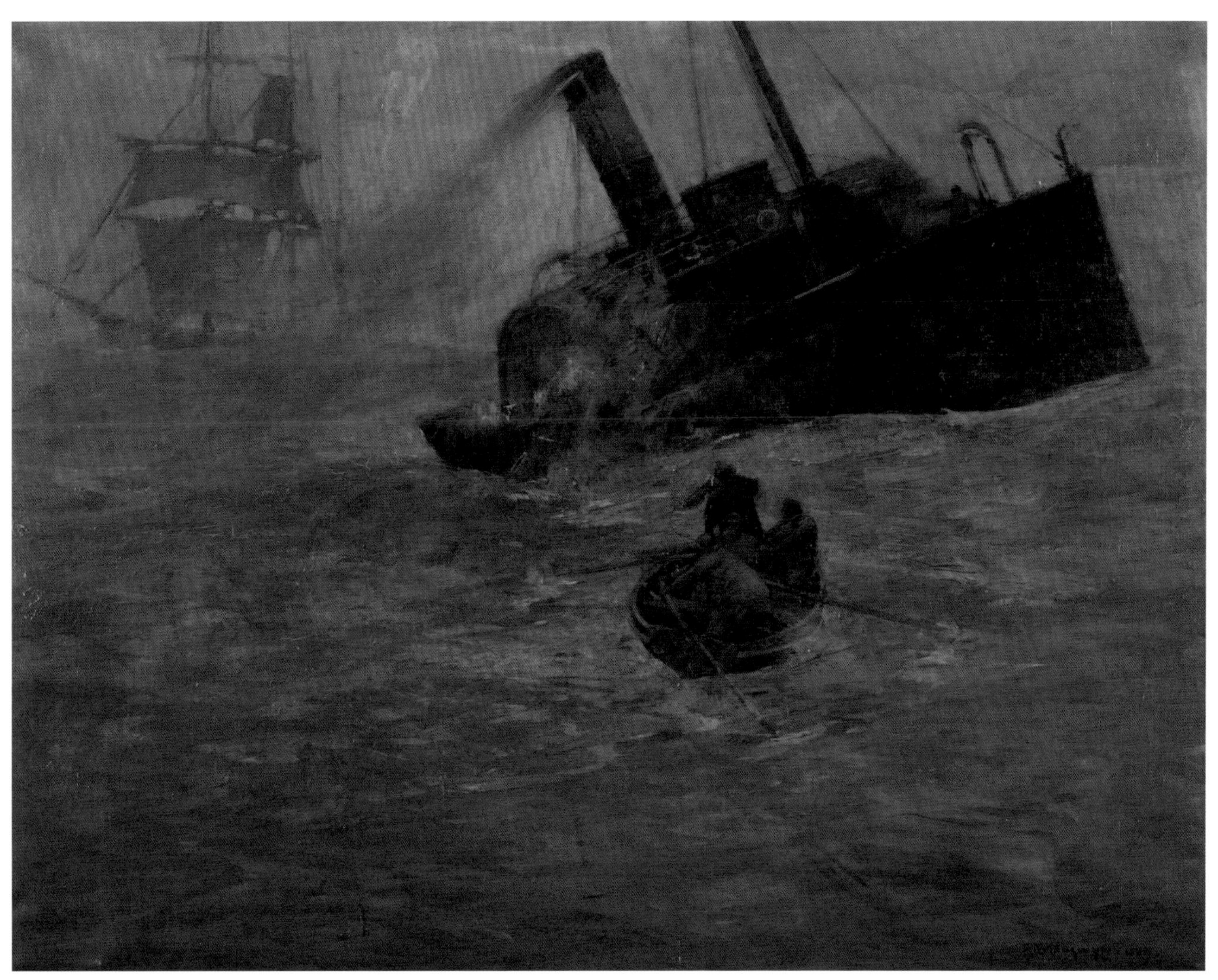

201

Frank Brangwyn
Stormy Weather at Sea, 1889
The National Museum of Western Art, Tokyo

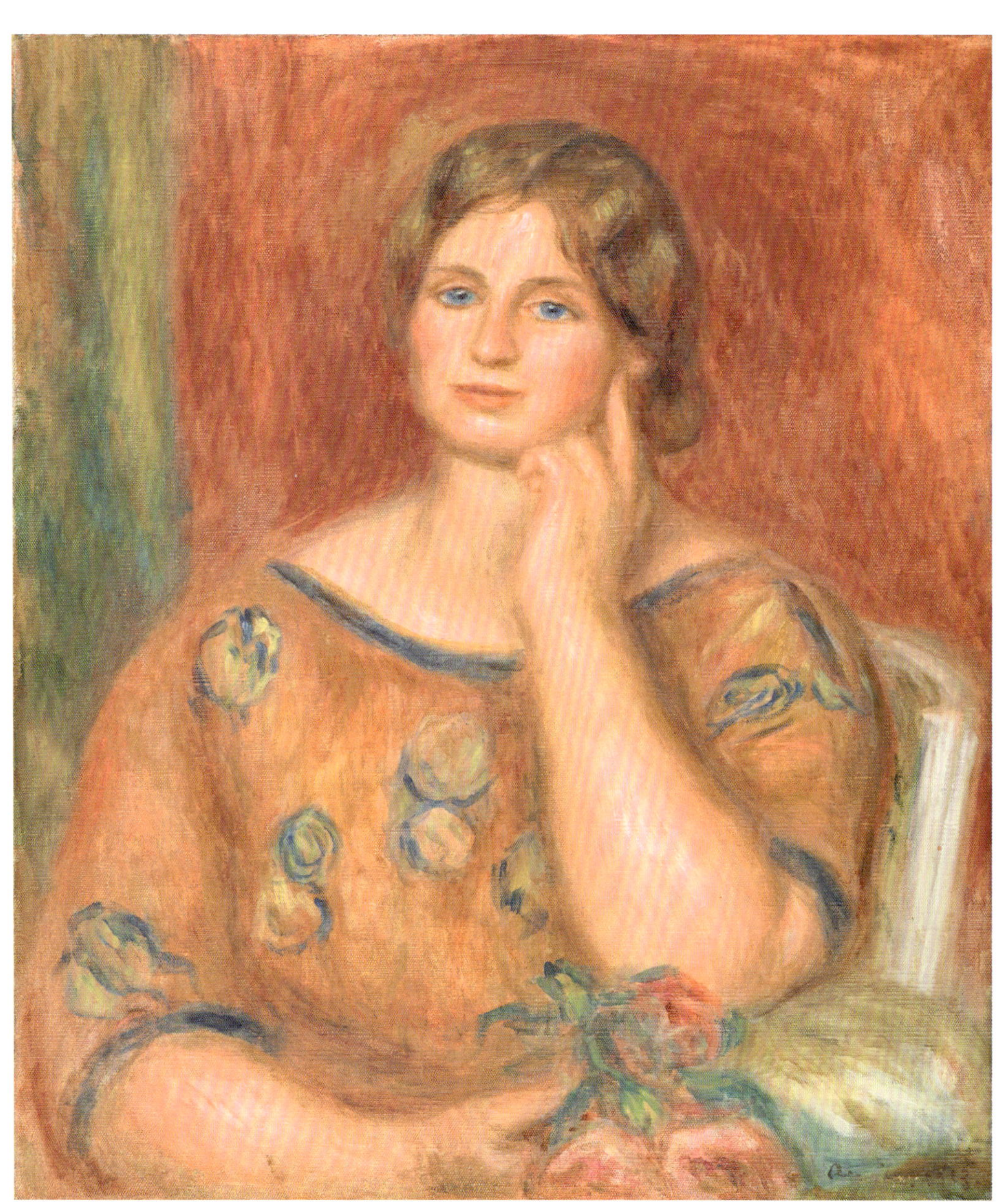

Pierre-Auguste Renoir
Bildnis Gertrud Osthaus, 1913
Museum Folkwang, Essen

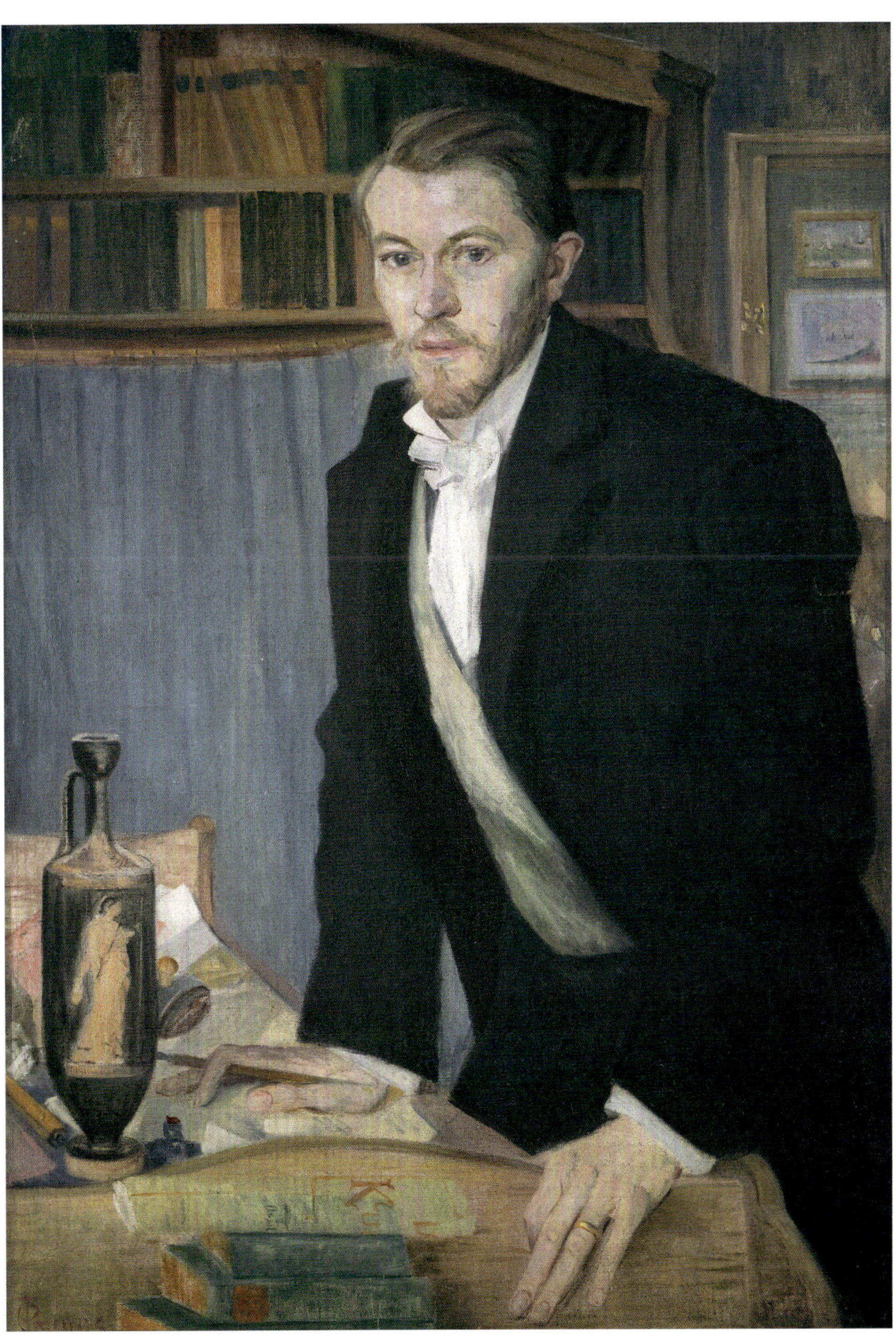

203

Ida Gerhardi
Porträt Karl Ernst Osthaus, 1903
Osthaus Museum, Hagen

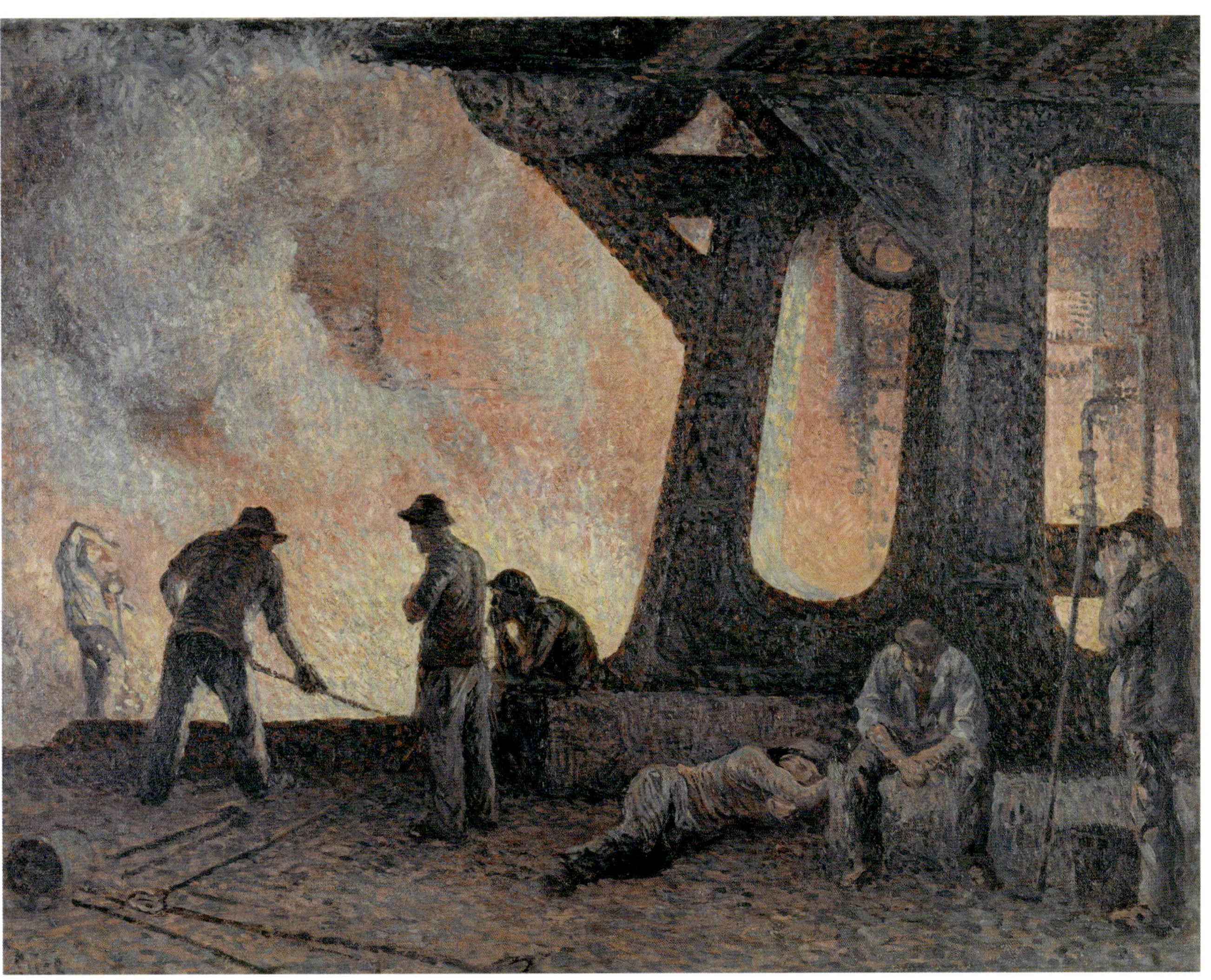

205

Maximilien Luce
L'aciérie, 1900
Museum Folkwang, Essen

OSTHAUS' AUFBRUCH MIT VAN DE VELDE

OSTHAUS' BEGINNINGS WITH VAN DE VELDE

OSTHAUS' AUFBRUCH MIT
VAN DE VELDE

A number of contemporary artists whose work Karl Ernst Osthaus esteemed and with whom he sought to establish contact acted as both influences and intermediaries for the museum founder's collection, most notably, from 1900, the Belgian architect and designer Henry van de Velde, who moved to Germany in 1901. He not only took on the decoration of the new museum building in Hagen, but also provided inspiration for numerous purchases of modern art. Through his influence the painting collection of the Museum Folkwang assumed a clear direction, and Osthaus focused increasingly on the artistic avant-garde of that time. The natural history collection to which Osthaus had initially applied himself, as well as German nineteenth-century academic art, faded into the background. Instead, Van de Velde put the collector in touch with the art dealers Ambroise Vollard in Paris and Paul Cassirer in Berlin, and drew his attention to the circle of Neo-Impressionists around Paul Signac. Van de Velde had previously exhibited along with Signac, Théo van Rysselberghe and others in 1892, and now set about making the German public familiar with their art. The purchase of Pierre-Auguste Renoir's *Lise – La femme à l'ombrelle* (*Lise with a Parasol,* 1867; p. 209) dates to a visit that Osthaus and Van de Velde paid together to the Berlin Secession in 1901, and it may also have been Van de Velde's influence that led the founder of the museum to purchase *La moisson* (*The Wheatfield behind St Paul's Hospital with a Reaper,* 1889; p. 315), the first work by Vincent van Gogh that he bought for his collection.[1] With this and other purchases, Osthaus was involved with the formation of an artistic

Vermittelnd und prägend für Karl Ernst Osthaus' Sammlung wirkte eine Reihe von zeitgenössischen Künstler:innen, deren Schaffen der Museumsgründer schätzte und deren Kontakt er suchte – ab 1900 allen voran der belgische Architekt und Gestalter Henry van de Velde, der 1901 nach Deutschland zog. Dieser übernahm nicht nur die Einrichtung des neuen Museumsbaus in Hagen, sondern gab auch den Anstoß für zahlreiche Ankäufe moderner Kunst. Durch seinen Einfluss bekam die Gemäldesammlung des Museum Folkwang eine klare Ausrichtung und Osthaus fokussierte sich mehr und mehr auf die künstlerische Avantgarde jener Zeit. Die naturwissenschaftliche Sammlung, der sich Osthaus anfangs zugewandt hatte, aber auch die deutsche Akademiekunst des 19. Jahrhunderts traten in den Hintergrund. Stattdessen brachte van de Velde den Sammler mit den Kunsthändlern Ambroise Vollard in Paris und Paul Cassirer in Berlin in Kontakt und machte ihn auf den Kreis der Neo-Impressionist:innen um Paul Signac aufmerksam. Mit Signac, Théo van Rrysselberghe und weiteren hatte van de Velde schon 1892 gemeinsam ausgestellt und bemühte sich nun darum, das deutsche Publikum mit ihrer Kunst vertraut zu machen. Der Ankauf von Pierre-Auguste Renoirs *Lise – La femme à l'ombrelle* (*Lise mit dem Sonnenschirm,* 1867; S. 209) geht auf einen gemeinsamen Besuch von Osthaus und van de Velde 1901 in der Berliner Secession zurück und van de Veldes Einfluss dürfte auch dazu geführt haben, dass der Museumsgründer im April 1902 *La moisson* (*Die Ernte, Kornfeld mit Schnitter,* 1889; S. 315) als erstes Bild von Vincent van Gogh für seine

canon in the German collecting world and
museum scene. From that time on, the Folkwang
presented itself as a museum in which the latest
trends in visual art were brought together, and
also made that claim clear in the first catalogue
of the collection in 1912 with the statement that it
had encouraged and brought to fame 'the great
initiators of modern painting' in Germany.[2] Previous purchases that no longer fit the new direction of the programme finally disappeared from
the presentation. When the Folkwang collections
were transferred from Hagen to Essen, and with
the Kunstmuseum Essen grew together into the
new Museum Folkwang Essen, an outstanding
and internationally recognized holding of French
art had been created.

1   Walter Feilchenfeldt, 'Vincent van Gogh –
seine Sammler – seine Händler', in Georg-
Wilhelm Költzsch and Ronald de Leeuw (eds.),
Vincent van Gogh und die Moderne 1890–1914,
exh. cat. Museum Folkwang, Essen, and Van Gogh
Museum, Amsterdam, (Freren, 1990), 43.

2   Karl Ernst Osthaus, 'Vorwort', in *Museum
Folkwang,* Bd. 1, *Moderne Kunst. Plastik, Malerei,
Graphik,* quoted from Kurt Freyer (ed.),
(Hagen, 1912; reprint 1983), 3–5.

Sammlung erwarb.[1] Mit diesen und weiteren
Ankäufen war Osthaus an der Herausbildung eines
künstlerischen Kanons in der deutschen Sammler-
schaft und Museumsszene beteiligt. Fortan präsentierte sich das Folkwang als ein Museum, in dem
die neuesten Strömungen der bildenden Kunst
versammelt waren, und machte diesen Anspruch
im ersten Sammlungskatalog von 1912 auch deutlich mit dem Verweis, schon früh „die großen Anreger moderner Malkunst" in Deutschland gefördert und bekannt gemacht zu haben.[2] Ankäufe, die
nicht mehr in das neu ausgerichtete Programm
passten, verschwanden schließlich aus der Präsentation. Als die Folkwang-Sammlungen von Hagen
nach Essen verbracht wurden und mit dem Kunstmuseum Essen 1922 zum neuen Museum Folkwang
Essen zusammenwuchsen, war ein herausragender,
international anerkannter Bestand an französischer
Kunst vorhanden.

1   Walter Feilchenfeldt, „Vincent van Gogh –
seine Sammler – seine Händler", in: *Vincent
van Gogh und die Moderne 1890–1914,*
hrsg. von Georg-Wilhelm Költzsch und Ronald
de Leeuw, Ausst.-Kat. Museum Folkwang,
Essen; Van Gogh Museum, Amsterdam, Freren
1990, S. 43.

2   Karl Ernst Osthaus, „Vorwort", in: *Museum
Folkwang,* Bd. 1, *Moderne Kunst. Plastik,
Malerei, Graphik,* bearb. von Kurt Freyer,
Hagen 1912 (Nachdruck 1983), S. 3–5.

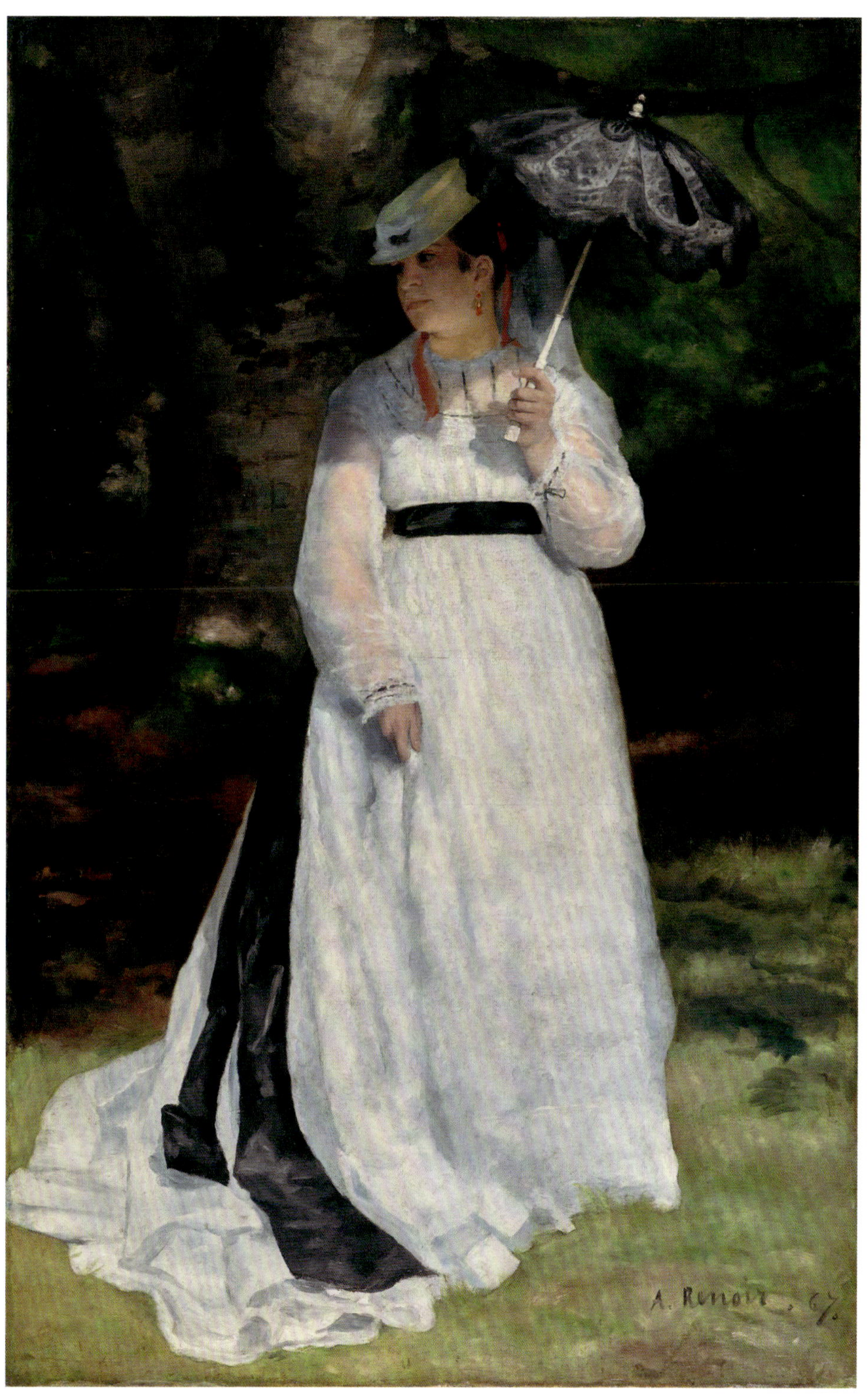

Pierre-Auguste Renoir
Lise – La femme à l'ombrelle, 1867
Museum Folkwang, Essen

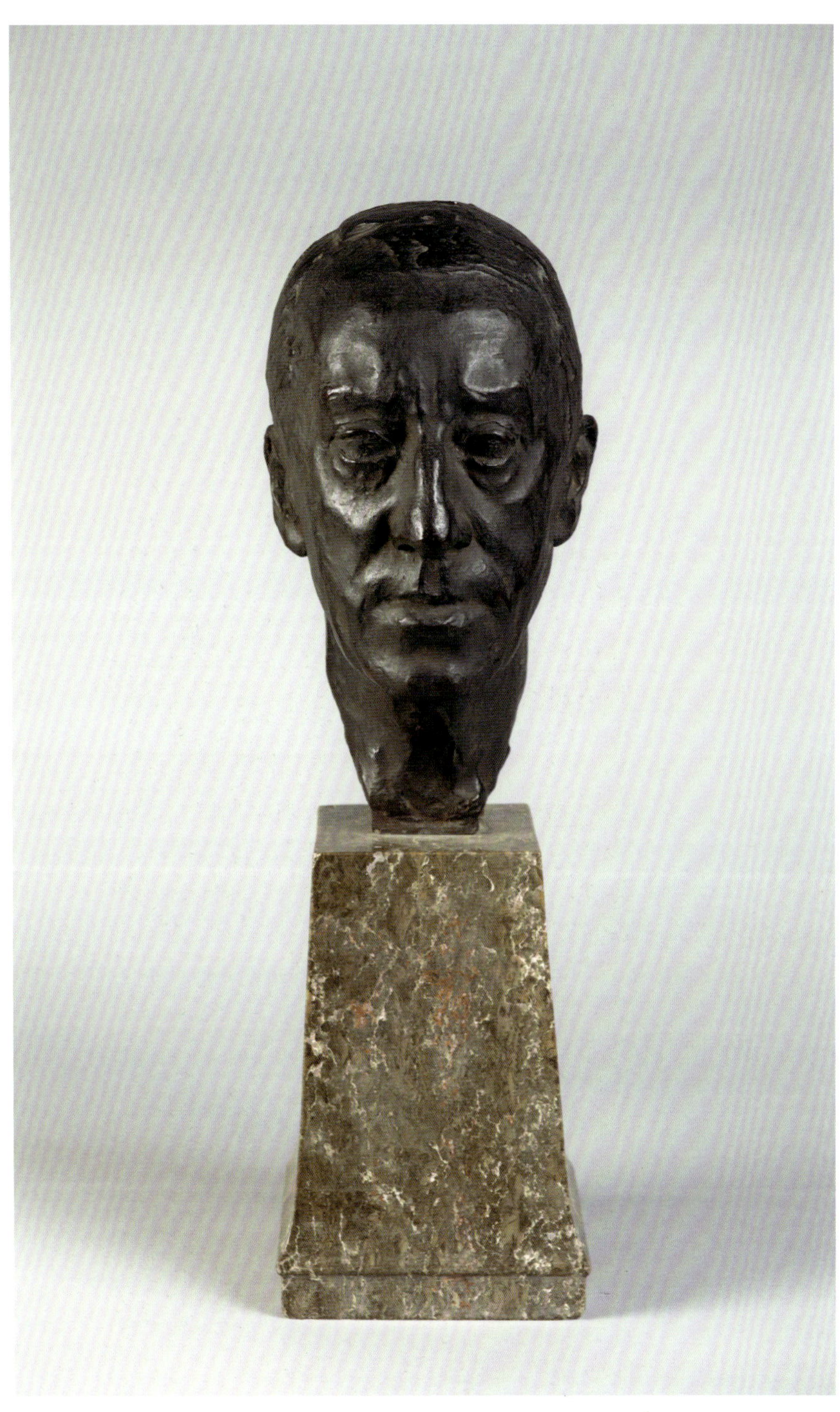

Georg Kolbe
Kopf Henry van de Velde, 1913
Museum Folkwang, Essen

211

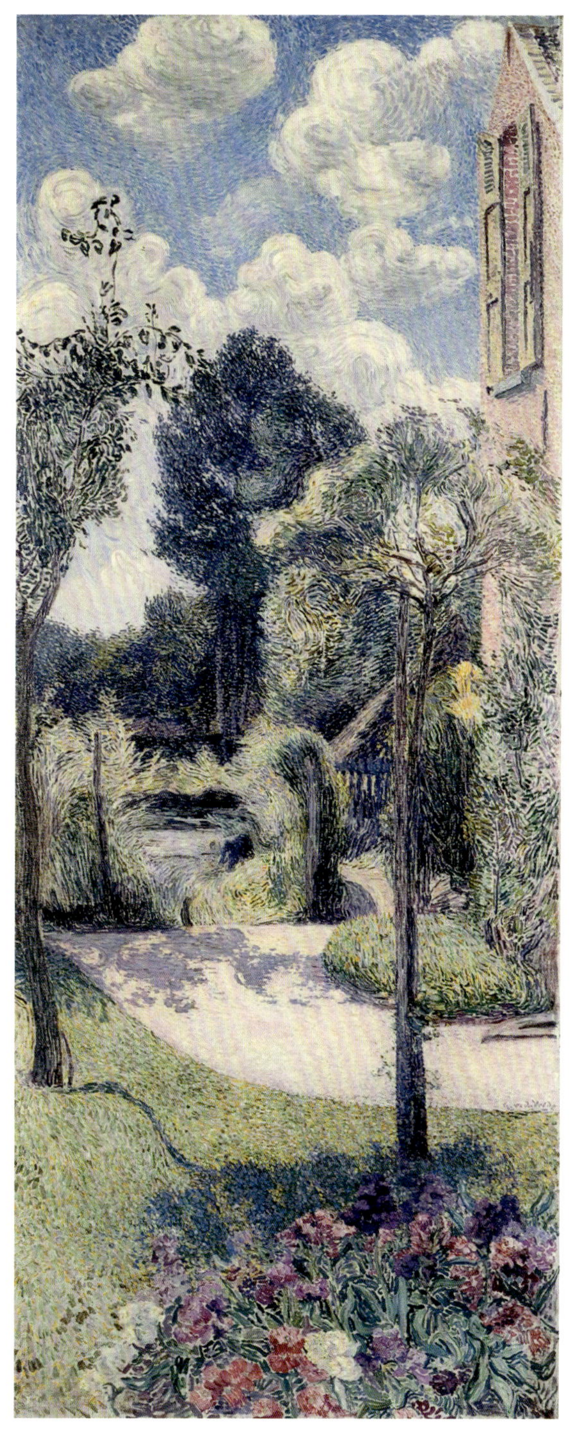

Henry van de Velde
Garten im Sommer (Wandgemälde aus dem Esszimmer
des Hauses Wagemans, Antwerpen), ca. 1892
Osthaus Museum, Hagen

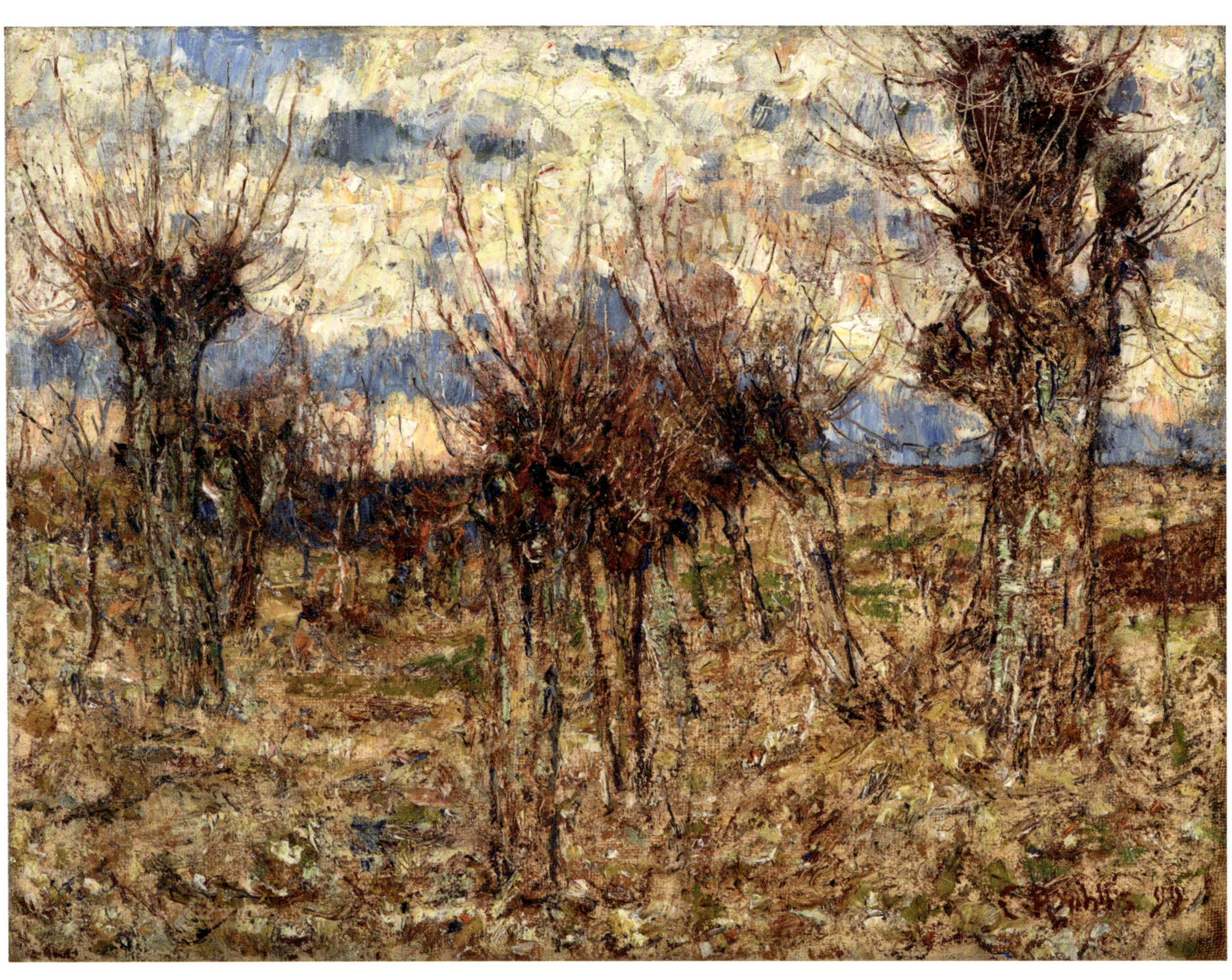

Christian Rohlfs
Weiden, 1899
Museum Folkwang, Essen

213

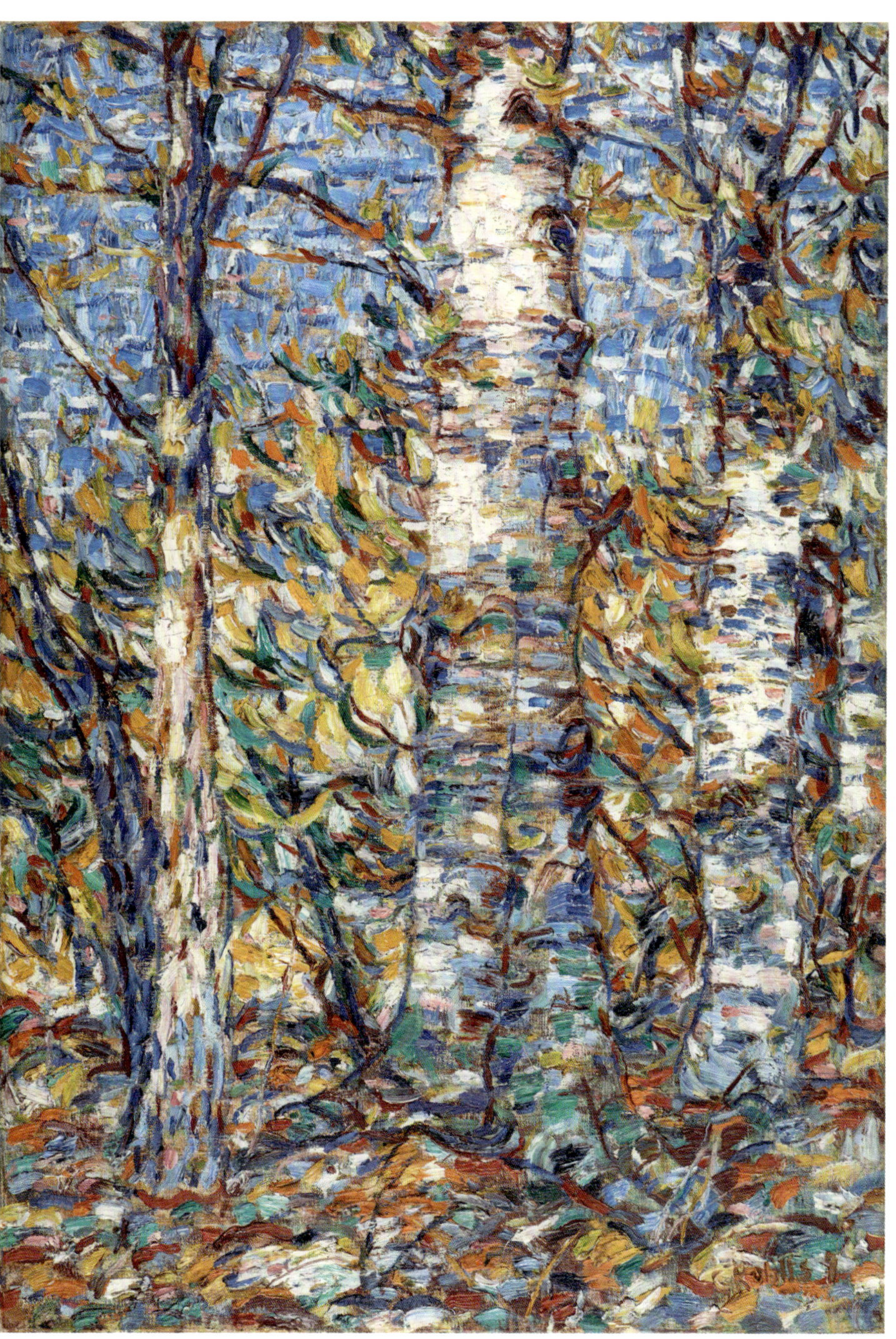

Christian Rohlfs
Birkenwald, 1907
Museum Folkwang, Essen

MATSUKATA UND SEINE BERATER BRANGWYN UND BÉNÉDITE

MATSUKATA AND HIS ADVISORS BRANGWYN AND BÉNÉDITE

When assembling his art collection, Kōjirō Matsukata relied on a large network of Japanese and Western advisors based in Europe. As his business kept him in Japan most of the time, it was important to have people on the spot to keep an eye on the market and conclude purchases, even without him.

Apart from his personal assistant Kōzaburō Hioki, he had at first the help of Frank Brangwyn, whom he had met in London in 1916, and whom he then asked to buy artworks for him as his agent. Matsukata also commissioned Brangwyn to design and plan his own museum in Tokyo. The Welshman was a celebrated architect, designer and artist at the time, and his own works soon made up half of Matsukata's collection. Together they visited galleries and local artists, and Matsukata made over 1000 purchases in London until 1918.

In 1917, Kōjirō Matsukata approached Léonce Bénédite, the director of the Musée du Luxembourg and the new director of the Musée Rodin, which was then being set up in Paris, to buy some sculptures from Auguste Rodin. Over the next few years Bénédite became his most important contact – and not only with regard to Rodin. Where Matsukata had previously bought mostly English art, applied art and Old Masters, from now on the focus of his collection was on works by French artists, most of which he bought in Paris.

With Bénédite's activities, a coherent collection of modern art emerged, which contained all current trends up to the Nabis and the Fauves. The most important sets of works which were purchased at that time included works by Edouard Manet, Claude Monet and Auguste

Kōjirō Matsukata verließ sich beim Zusammenstellen seiner Kunstsammlung auf ein großes Netzwerk aus japanischen und westlichen Berater:innen, die in Europa ansässig waren. Da ihn seine Geschäfte für die meiste Zeit in Japan hielten, war es wichtig, Personen vor Ort zu haben, die den Markt beobachteten und Ankäufe abwickeln konnten, auch ohne ihn.

Neben seinem persönlichen Assistenten Kōzaburō Hioki stand ihm dafür zunächst Frank Brangwyn zur Seite, mit dem er 1916 in London zum ersten Mal zusammentraf und den er fortan bat, für ihn als Agent Kunstwerke zu erwerben. Matsukata beauftragte Brangwyn auch mit Entwurf und Planung seines eigenen Museums in Tokio. Der Waliser war zu jener Zeit ein gefeierter Architekt, Gestalter und Künstler und seine eigenen Werke machten bald die Hälfte von Matsukatas damaliger Sammlung aus. Zusammen besuchten sie Galerien und lokale Künstler:innen und Matsukata tätigte in London bis 1918 mehr als 1000 Ankäufe.

1917 wandte Kōjirō Matsukata sich an Léonce Bénédite, den Direktor des Musée du Luxembourg und neuen Direktor des entstehenden Musée Rodin in Paris, um einige Skulpturen von Auguste Rodin zu erwerben. Bénédite wurde in den folgenden Jahren sein wichtigster Ansprechpartner – nicht nur in Bezug auf Rodin. Hatte Matsukata bisher vorwiegend englische Kunst, Kunsthandwerk und alte Meister erstanden, verlagerte sich sein Sammlungsfokus fortan auf Werke französischer Künstler:innen, die er hauptsächlich in Paris erwarb.

Rodin, which make up the core of the collection even today. Their collaboration is well attested with letters and purchase documents, which are now in the Institut national d'histoire de l'art in Paris and represent an important source for the development of the Matsukata collection. Bénédite administered a budget of his own for the purchase of new works, and also worked on a catalogue for the collection of the museum Matsukata in Tokyo, which was left uncompleted amongst other things by Bénédite's sudden death in 1925.

Mit Bénédites Tätigkeit entwickelte sich eine kohärente Sammlung moderner Kunst, die alle aktuellen Strömungen bis zu den Nabis und Fauves enthielt. Die wichtigsten Konvolute, die in jener Zeit erworben wurden, umfassten Werke von Edouard Manet, Claude Monet und Auguste Rodin, die auch heute noch das Herzstück der Sammlung ausmachen. Die Zusammenarbeit ist gut belegt durch Briefe und Ankaufsdokumente, die sich heute im Institut national d'histoire de l'art in Paris befinden und eine wichtige Quelle für die Erschließung der Sammlung Matsukata darstellen. Bénédite verwaltete ein eigenes Budget zum Ankauf neuer Werke und arbeitete darüber hinaus an einem Sammlungskatalog für das von Matsukata geplante Museum in Tokio, der aber unter anderem durch Bénédites plötzlichen Tod 1925 nicht vollendet wurde.

217

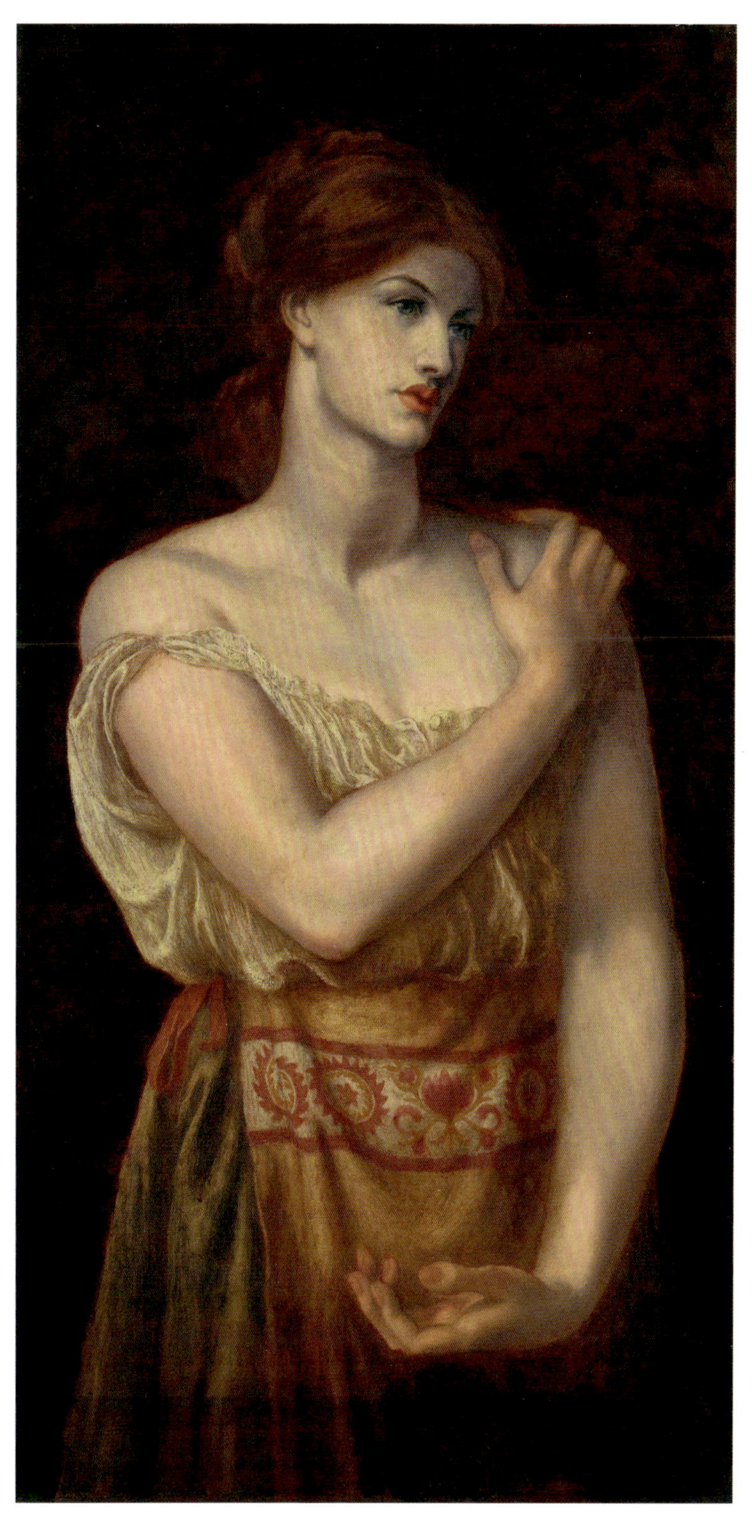

Dante Gabriel Rossetti
Risen at Dawn, 1877/78
The National Museum of Western Art, Tokyo

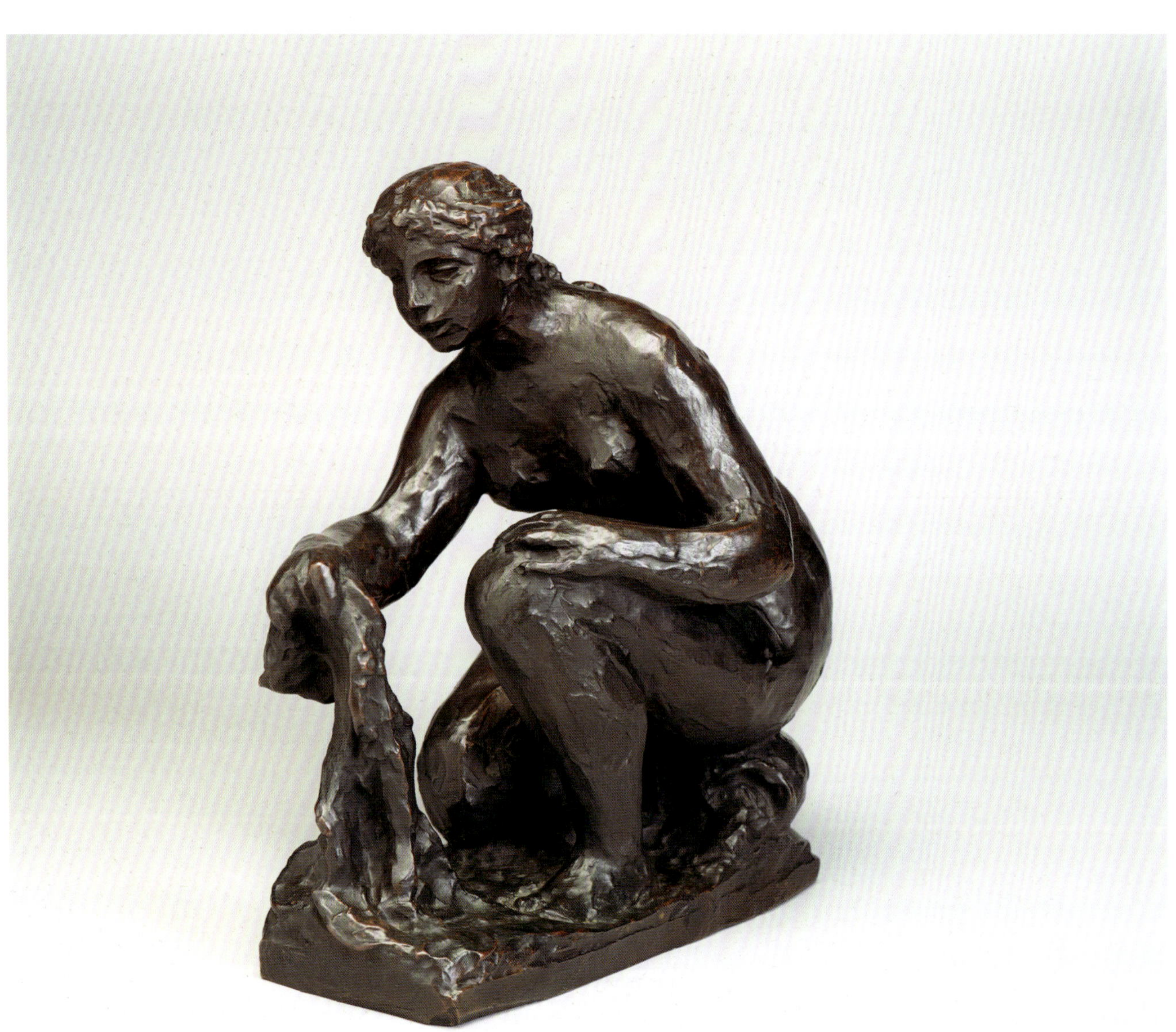

Pierre-Auguste Renoir
La laveuse, 1916
Museum Folkwang, Essen

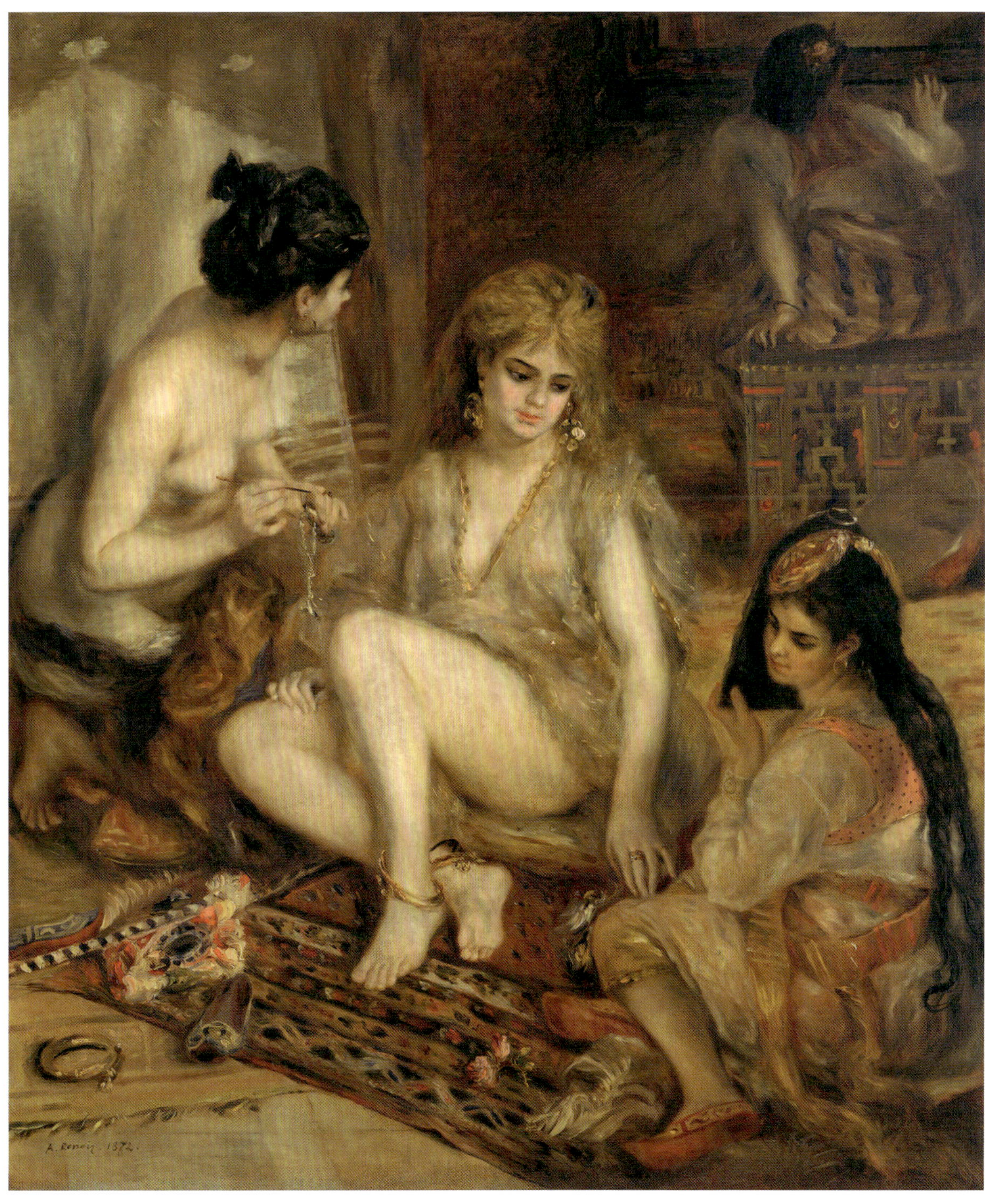

219

Pierre-Auguste Renoir
Parisiennes habillées en Algériennes, 1872
The National Museum of Western Art, Tokyo

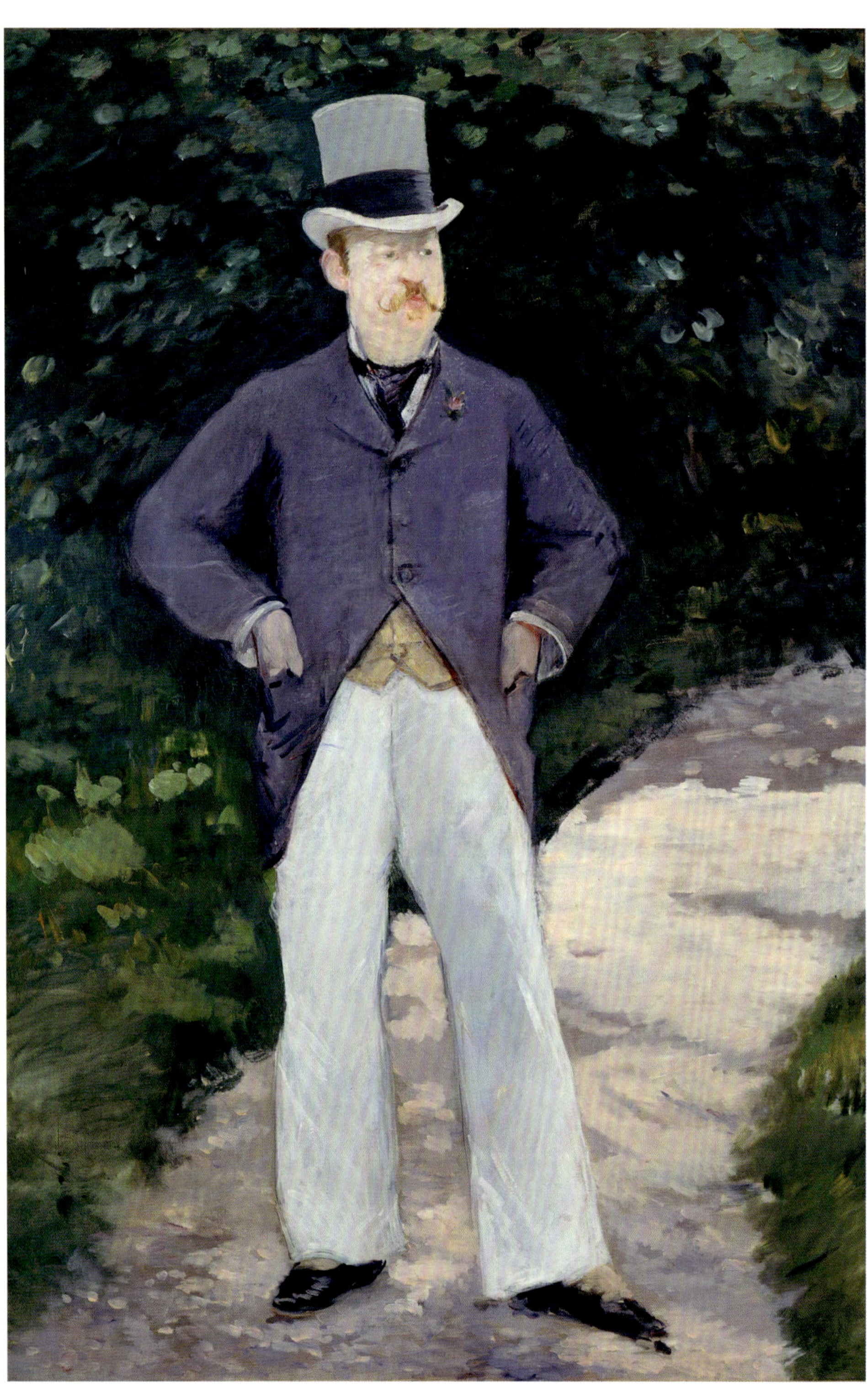

Edouard Manet
Portrait de Monsieur Brun, ca. 1879
The National Museum of Western Art, Tokyo

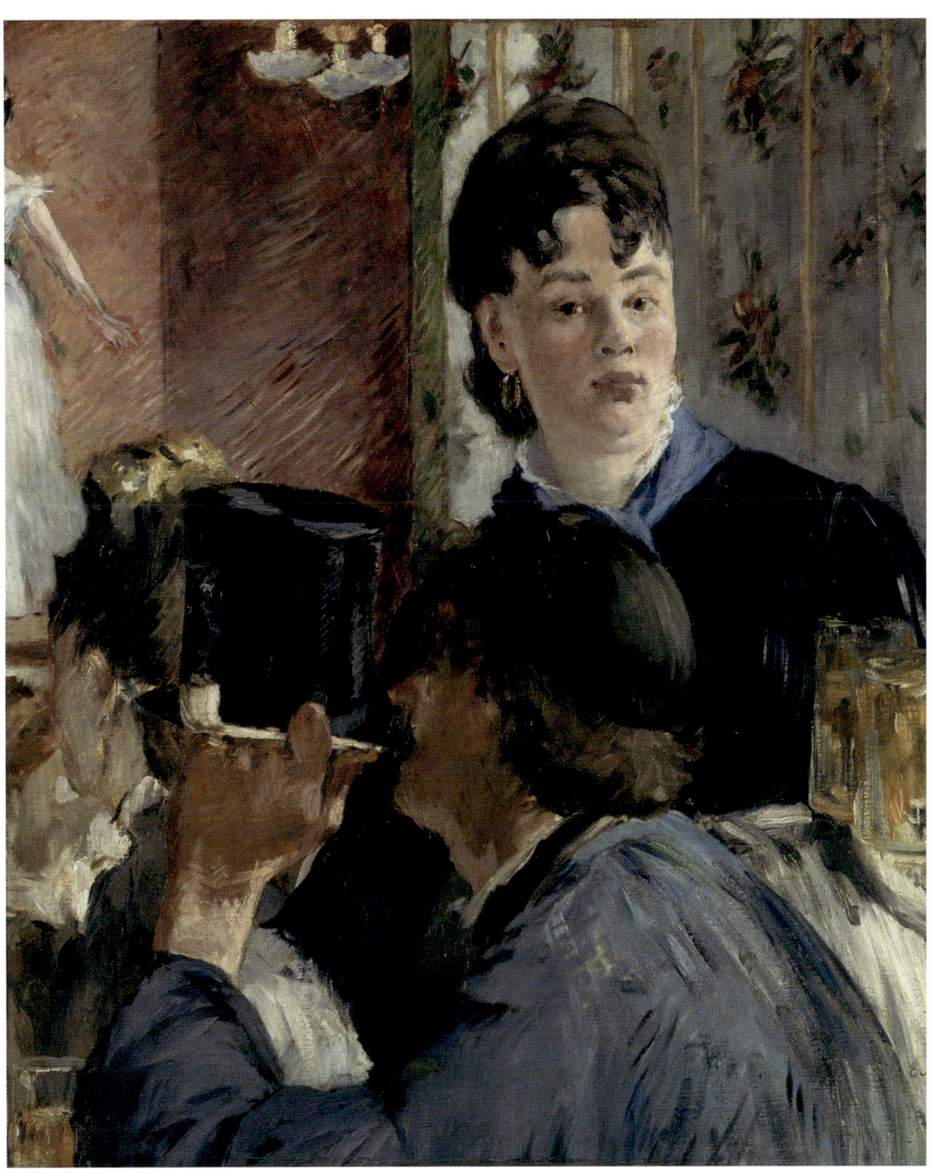

221

Edouard Manet
La serveuse de bocks, 1878/79
Musée d'Orsay, Paris

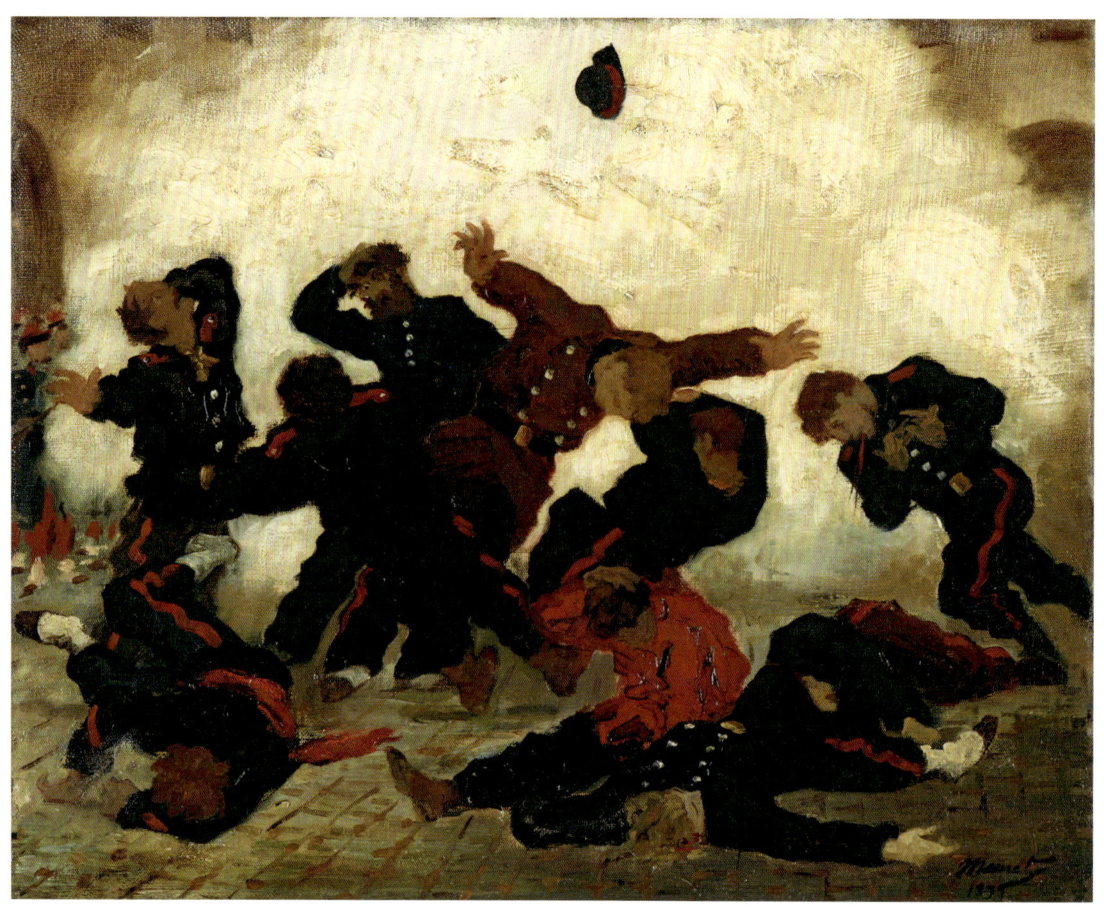

222

Edouard Manet
L'explosion, 1871
Museum Folkwang, Essen

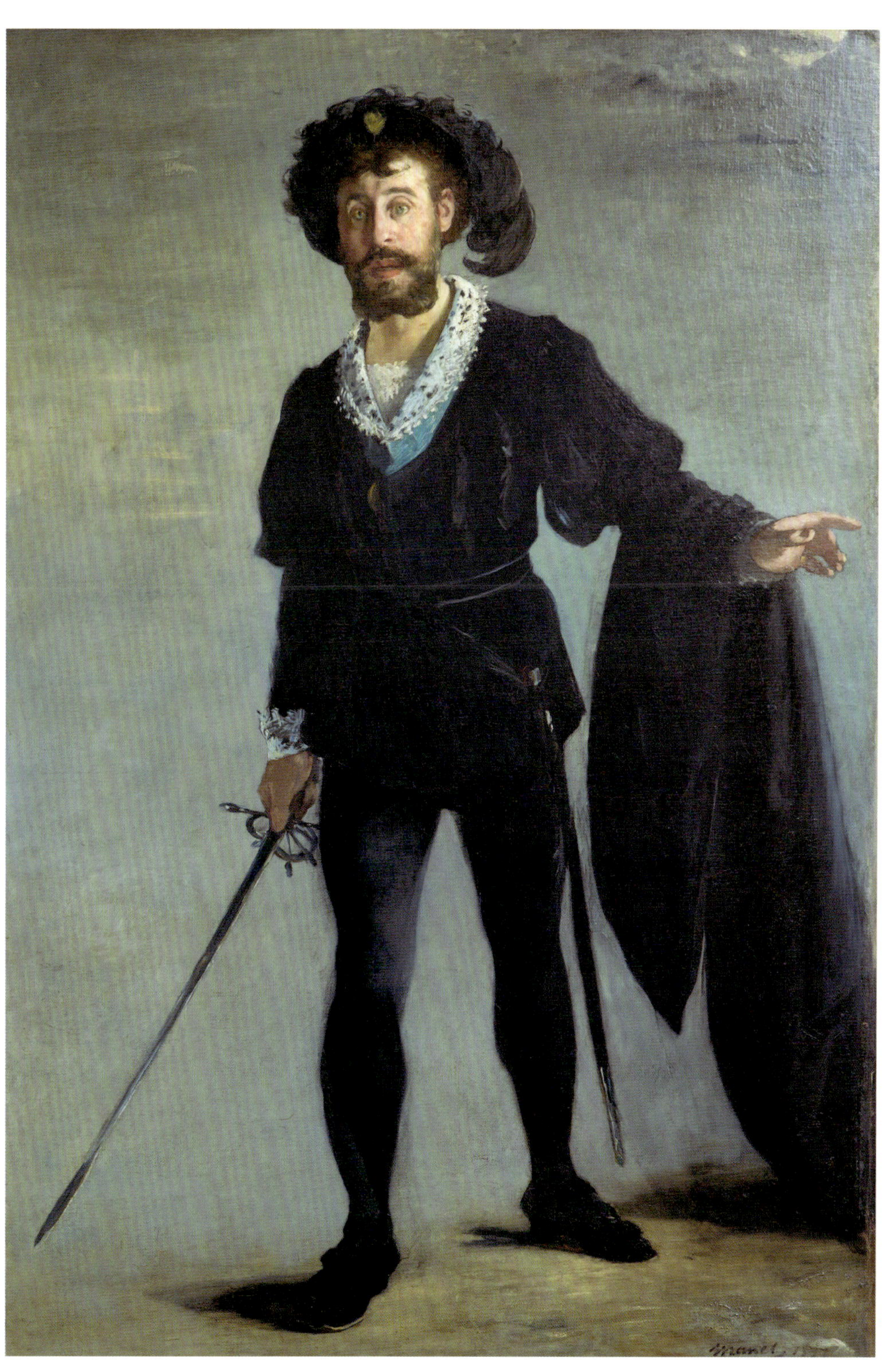

223

Edouard Manet
Portrait de Faure dans le rôle d'Hamlet, 1877
Museum Folkwang, Essen

RODIN UND DIE „PORTE DE L'ENFER"

RODIN AND THE 'PORTE DE L'ENFER'

Auguste Rodin is seen as a pioneer of modern sculpture. As early as 1901/02, via the contact of the Hagen artist Ida Gerhardi, Karl Ernst Osthaus became acquainted with the artist, and the collector regularly visited Rodin in his studios in Paris. Osthaus made the first purchases for the Museum Folkwang in 1903 with *L'âge d'airain* (*The Age of Bronze,* ca. 1880; p. 290) and *Ève* (*Eve,* 1881; p. 227). The latter is considered of particular importance in the artist's oeuvre and in the Museum Folkwang collection. Osthaus describes Rodin explaining to him that the birth of Impressionism had occurred in this work:[1] indeed, the uneven surface appears as if it was created from a swift impression.

Kōjirō Matsukata also bought a cast of *Eve.* Possibly drawing inspiration from New York's Rodin Gallery that opened at the Metropolitan Museum of Art in 1912, he tried to buy his first works during the artist's lifetime.[2] Through Léonce Bénédite, from 1918 Matsukata bought works continuously, both small and large sculptures, eventually amassing one of the biggest Rodin collections in the world. In 1920, Matsukata commissioned two bronze casts of Rodin's monumental work *La porte de l'enfer* (*The Gates of Hell,* 1880–90/1917; p. 228), one of which he gave to the Musée Rodin in Paris.[3] The other cast now stands in front of the National Museum of Western Art in Tokyo. As is the case with *Le penseur* (*The Thinker,* 1881/82; p. 229), many of Rodin's sculptures from the Matsukata collection are related to the *Gates of Hell.*

Rodin had developed the work from 1880 as a commission for a gate at the entrance of the Musée des Arts Décoratifs in Paris, borrowing

Auguste Rodin gilt als ein Wegbereiter der modernen Skulptur und Plastik. Bereits 1901/02 entwickelte sich durch die Vermittlung der Hagener Künstlerin Ida Gerhardi eine Bekanntschaft von Karl Ernst Osthaus mit dem Künstler und der Sammler besuchte Rodin regelmäßig in seinen Ateliers in Paris. Die ersten Ankäufe für das Museum Folkwang tätigte Osthaus 1903 mit *L'âge d'airain (Das eherne Zeitalter,* ca. 1880; S. 290) und *Ève (Eva,* 1881; S. 227). Letzterer kommt im Œuvre des Künstlers und in der Sammlung des Museum Folkwang besondere Bedeutung zu. So beschreibt Osthaus, wie Rodin ihm darlegte, dass sich in diesem Werk die Geburt des Impressionismus in seinem Werk vollzogen habe.[1] Die ungeglättete Oberfläche erscheint wie aus einem schnellen Eindruck heraus geschaffen.

Auch Kōjirō Matsukata erwarb einen Guss der *Eva.* Möglicherweise angeregt durch die 1912 eröffnete Rodin-Galerie im Metropolitan Museum of Art, New York, bemühte er sich noch zu Lebzeiten des Künstlers um erste Werke.[2] Über Léonce Bénédite erstand Matsukata ab 1918 dann kontinuierlich ein Konvolut aus Klein- wie auch Großplastiken und es entwickelte sich daraus schließlich eine der größten Rodin-Sammlungen weltweit. Im Jahr 1920 beauftragte Matsukata gleich zwei Bronzegüsse von Rodins Monumentalwerk *La porte de l'enfer (Das Höllentor,* 1880–1890/1917; S. 228), von denen er einen dem Musée Rodin in Paris schenkte.[3] Der andere Guss hat seinen Platz heute vor dem National Museum of Western Art in Tokio. Wie etwa im Fall von *Le penseur (Der Denker,* 1881/82; S. 229) stehen viele von Rodins

from Lorenzo Ghiberti's *Porta del Paradiso* (*Gate of Paradise,* 1425–52) on the Baptistry in Florence. He drew his inspiration for the content of the work from the *Inferno* of Dante's *Divine Comedy.* Almost two hundred individual figures appear in the gate – here Rodin also reworked earlier sculptures. New designs that were created in connection with the *Gates of Hell* were also executed separately in life-size. The first design, for example, shows the figure of Eve at the top right of the lintel. Adam was supposed to be placed opposite her to illustrate the consequences that entered the world with the Fall. In the later version Rodin rejected this idea. In the presentation of the cast in Tokyo, however, Rodin's plan for an Adam and Eve standing to the left and right of the portal is taken up again.

1 Karl Ernst Osthaus, 'Rodin', in *Feuer. Monats-schrift für Kunst und Künstlerische Kultur,* 2, 1, (1920/21), 597–604, here 598.
2 Cf. Yuko Nakama, 'The Matsukata Collection. Europe and Japan's mutual cultural interest in art', in Anna Maria Ambrosini and Giovanna Perini (eds.), *Riflessi del collezionismo, tra bilanci critici e nuovi contributi (Reflections of/on art collecting, between critical assessments and new contributions)* (Florence 2014), 359–75.
3 See Akiko Mabuchi, 'Rodin's *Gate of Hell*: The First Four Bronzes and Their Destinies' in *The Matsukata Collection: A One-Hundred-Year Odyssey,* exh. cat., The National Museum of Western Art, Tokyo (Tokyo, 2019), 308–17.

Plastiken aus der Sammlung Matsukata in Zusammenhang mit dem *Höllentor.*

Rodin hatte das Werk ab 1880 als Auftrag für ein Eingangstor zum Musée des Arts Décoratifs in Paris in Anlehnung an Lorenzo Ghibertis *Porta del Paradiso (Paradiespforte,* 1425–1452) am Florentiner Baptisterium entwickelt. Inhaltliche Inspiration lieferte ihm das *Inferno* aus Dantes *Göttlicher Komödie.* Beinahe 200 Einzelfiguren finden sich in dem Tor – Rodin verarbeitete hier auch frühere Skulpturen. Im Zusammenhang mit dem *Höllentor* entstandene neue Entwürfe führte er zudem separat lebensgroß aus. Der erste Entwurf sah etwa die Figur der *Eva* rechts oben im Türsturz vor. Ihr gegenüber gestellt werden sollte Adam, um die Konsequenzen zu verdeutlichen, die mit dem Sündenfall in die Welt kamen. In der späteren Ausführung verwarf Rodin diese Idee. In der Präsentation des Gusses in Tokio ist Rodins Planung mit den links und rechts des Portals stehenden Figuren von Adam und Eva jedoch wieder aufgegriffen worden.

1 Karl Ernst Osthaus, „Rodin", in: *Feuer. Monatsschrift für Kunst und Künstlerische Kultur,* 2, 1, 1920/21, S. 597–604, hier S. 598.
2 Vgl. Yuko Nakama, „The Matsukata Collection. Europe and Japan's mutual cultural interest in art", in: *Riflessi del collezionismo, tra bilanci critici e nuovi contributi (Reflections of/on art collecting, between critical assessments and new contributions),* hrsg. von Anna Maria Ambrosini Massari und Giovanna Perini, Florenz 2014, S. 359–375.
3 Vgl. Akiko Mabuchi, „Rodin's *Gate of Hell.* The First Four Bronzes and Their Destinies", in: *The Matsukata Collection. A One-Hundred-Year Odyssey,* Ausst.-Kat. The National Museum of Western Art, Tokio, Tokio 2019, S. 308–317.

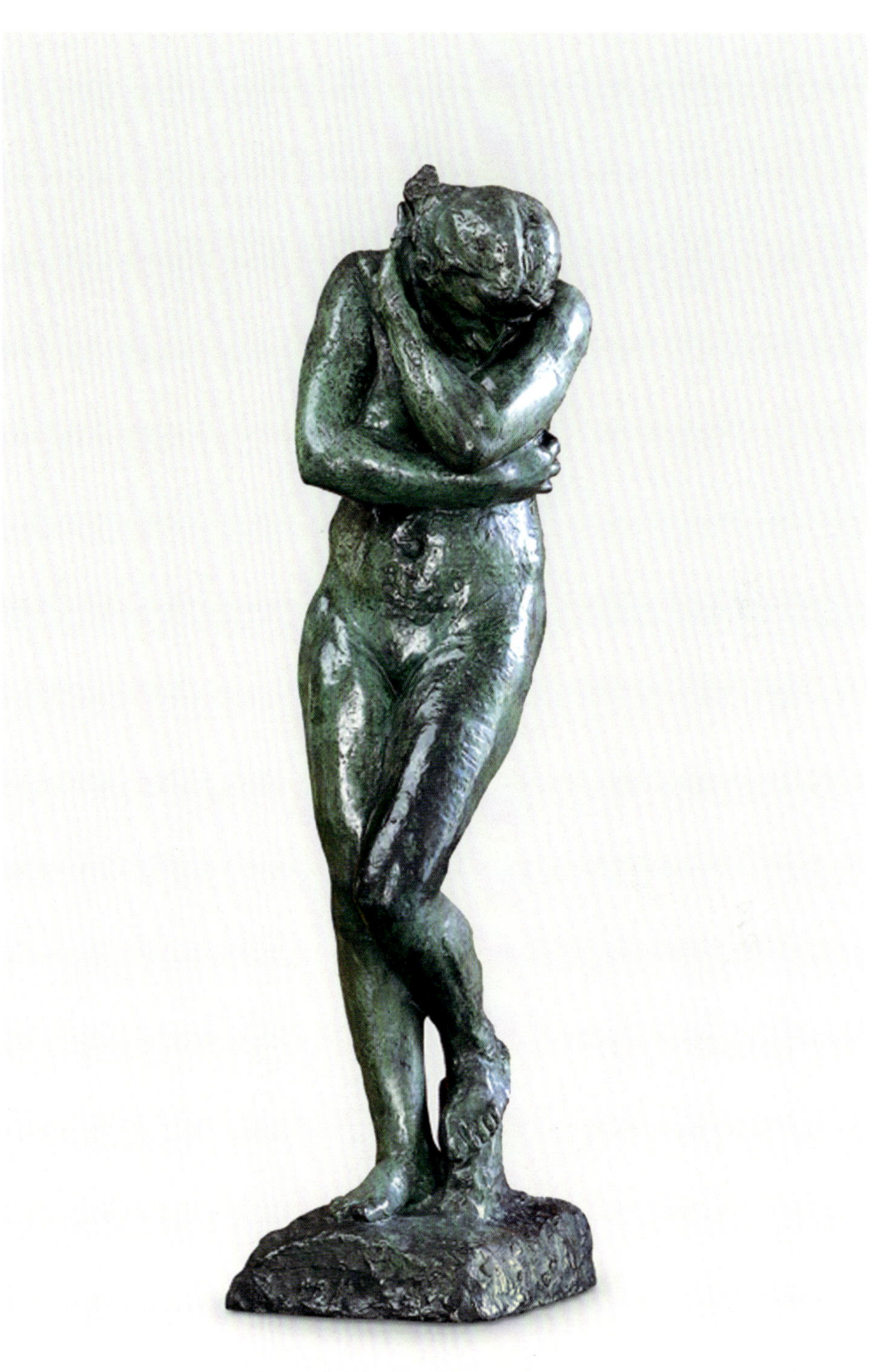

227

Auguste Rodin
Ève, 1881 (Guss: spätestens 1904 | cast: 1904 at the latest)
Museum Folkwang, Essen

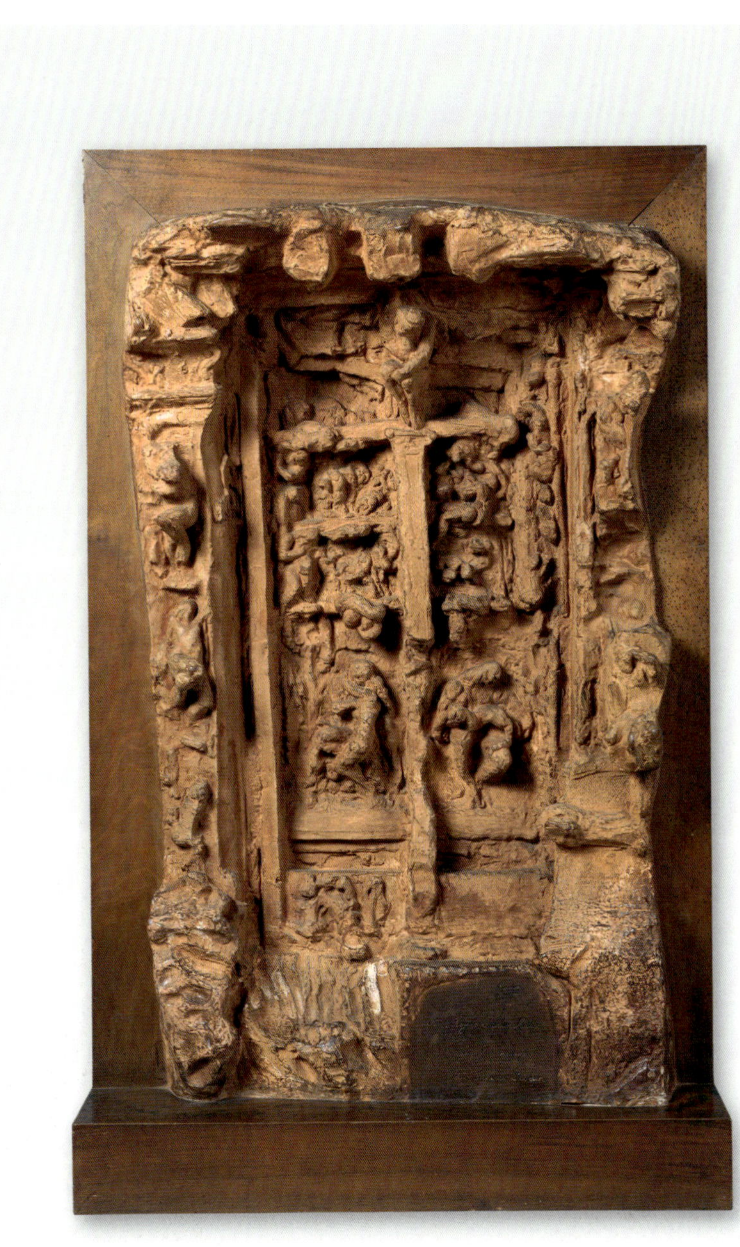

Auguste Rodin
Troisième maquette de *La porte de l'enfer*, ca. 1881/82
(Guss: vor 1926 | cast: before 1926)
The National Museum of Western Art, Tokyo

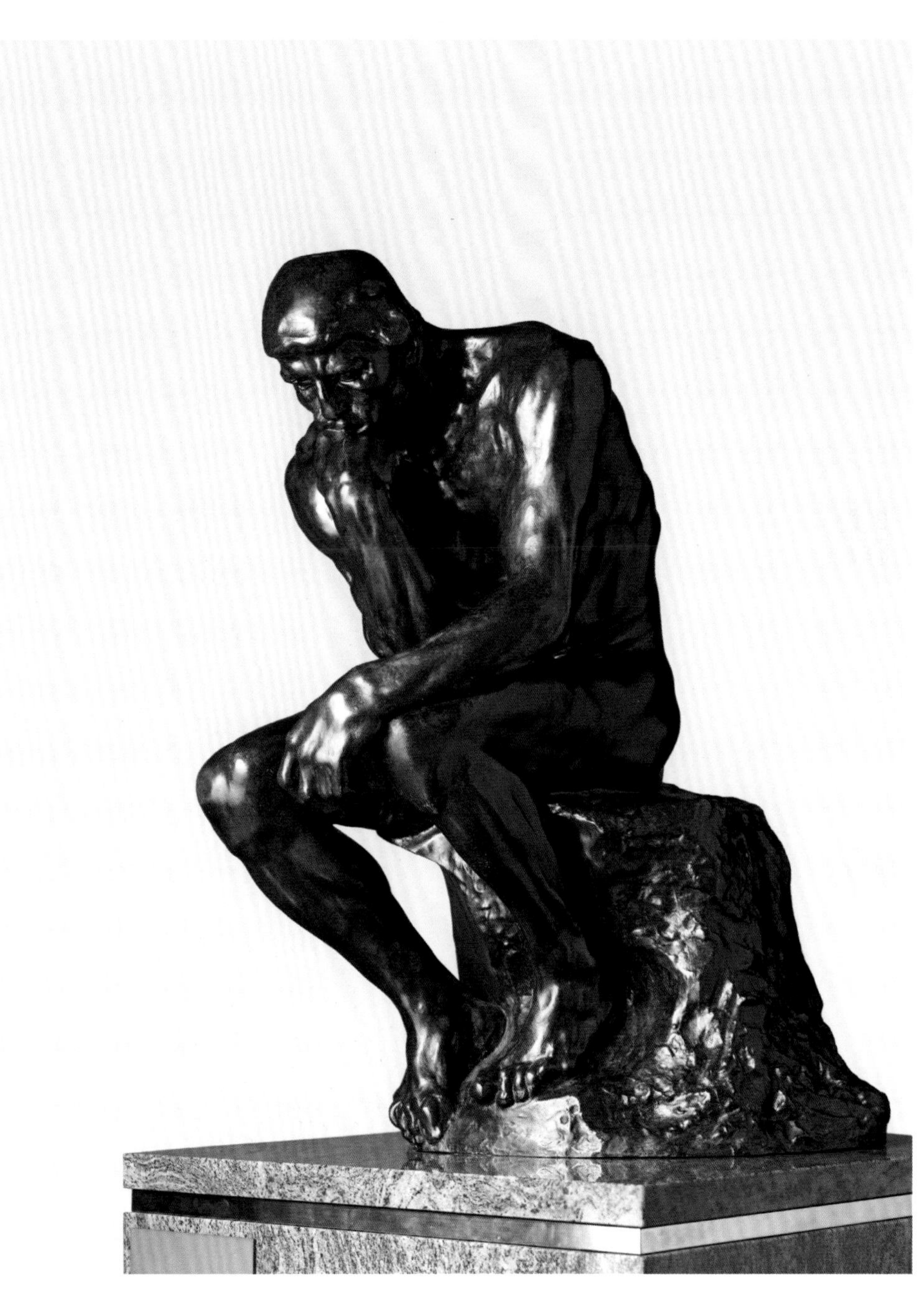

Auguste Rodin
Le penseur, 1881/82
(Guss: spätestens 1919 | cast: 1919 at the latest)
The National Museum of Western Art, Tokyo

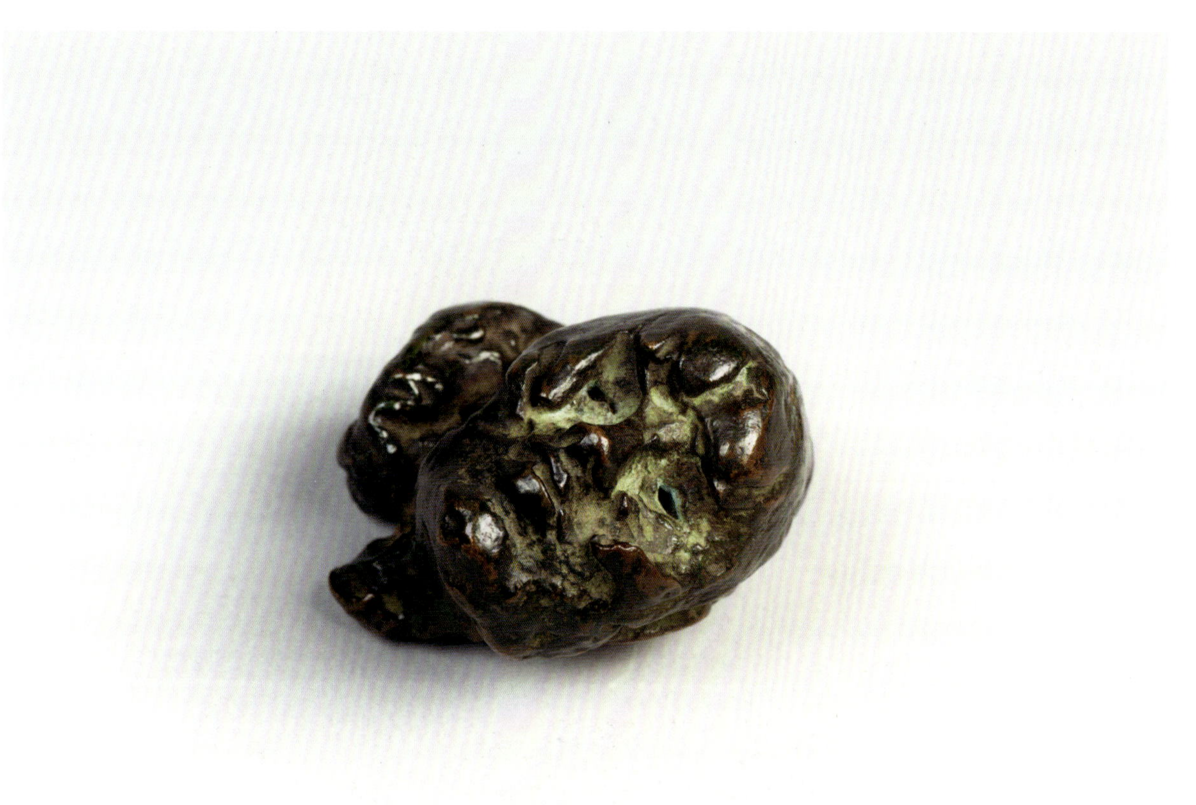

230

Auguste Rodin
Petite tête de damnée, 1885
Museum Folkwang, Essen

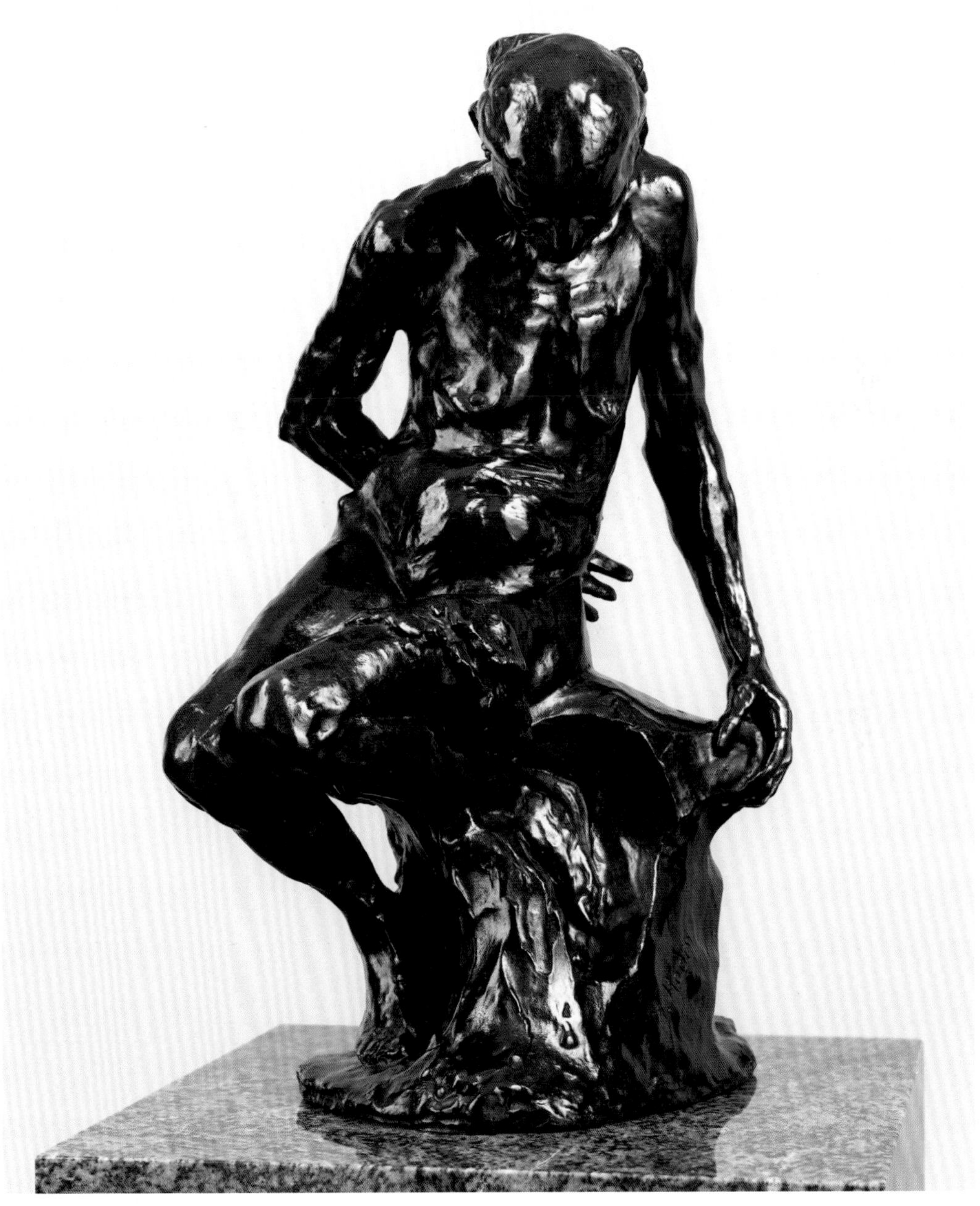

231

Auguste Rodin
Celle qui fut la belle heaulmière, 1885–1887
(Guss: spätestens 1919 | cast: 1919 at the latest)
The National Museum of Western Art, Tokyo

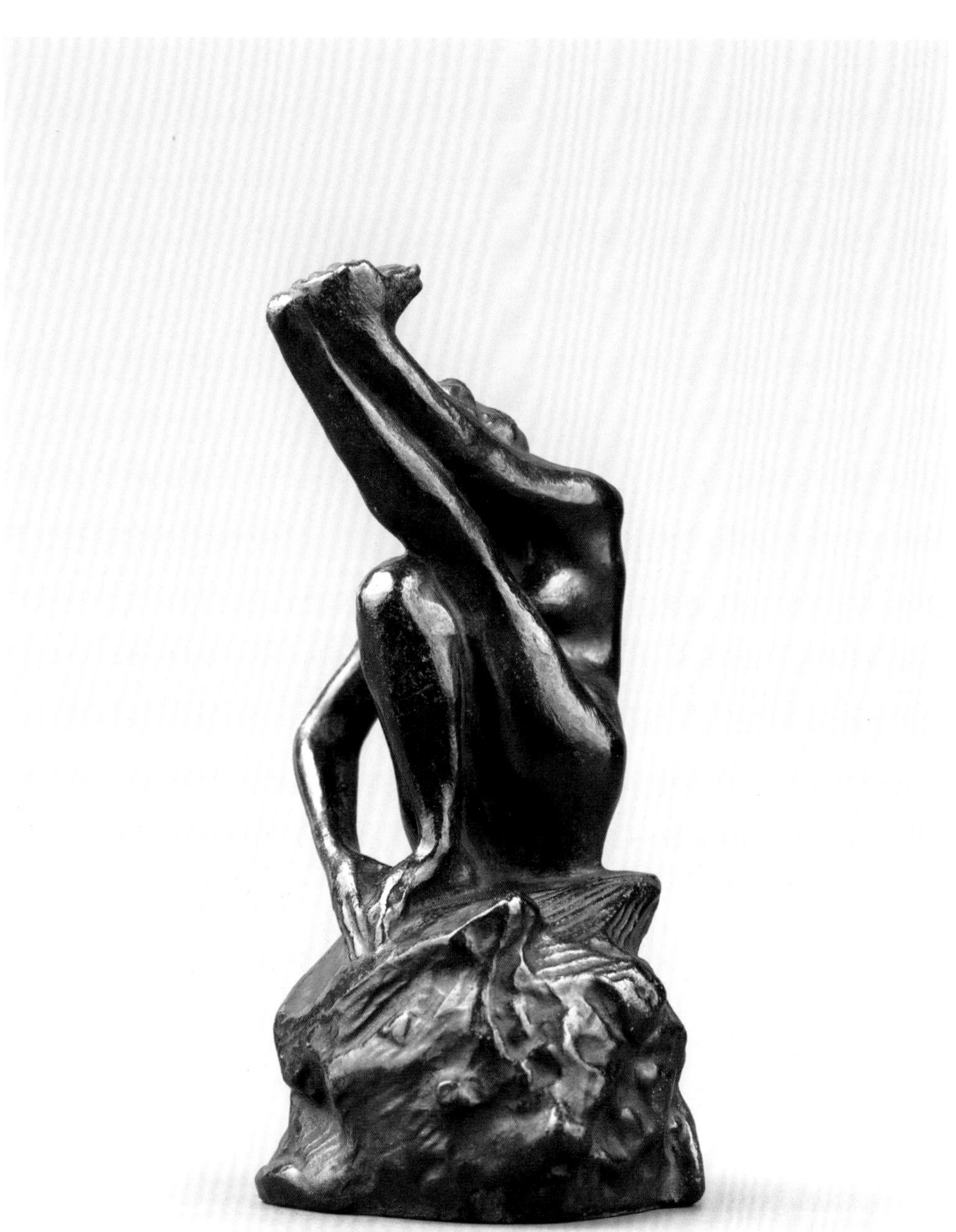

Auguste Rodin
Le désespoir, vor | before 1890
(Guss: spätestens 1937 | cast: 1937 at the latest)
The National Museum of Western Art, Tokyo

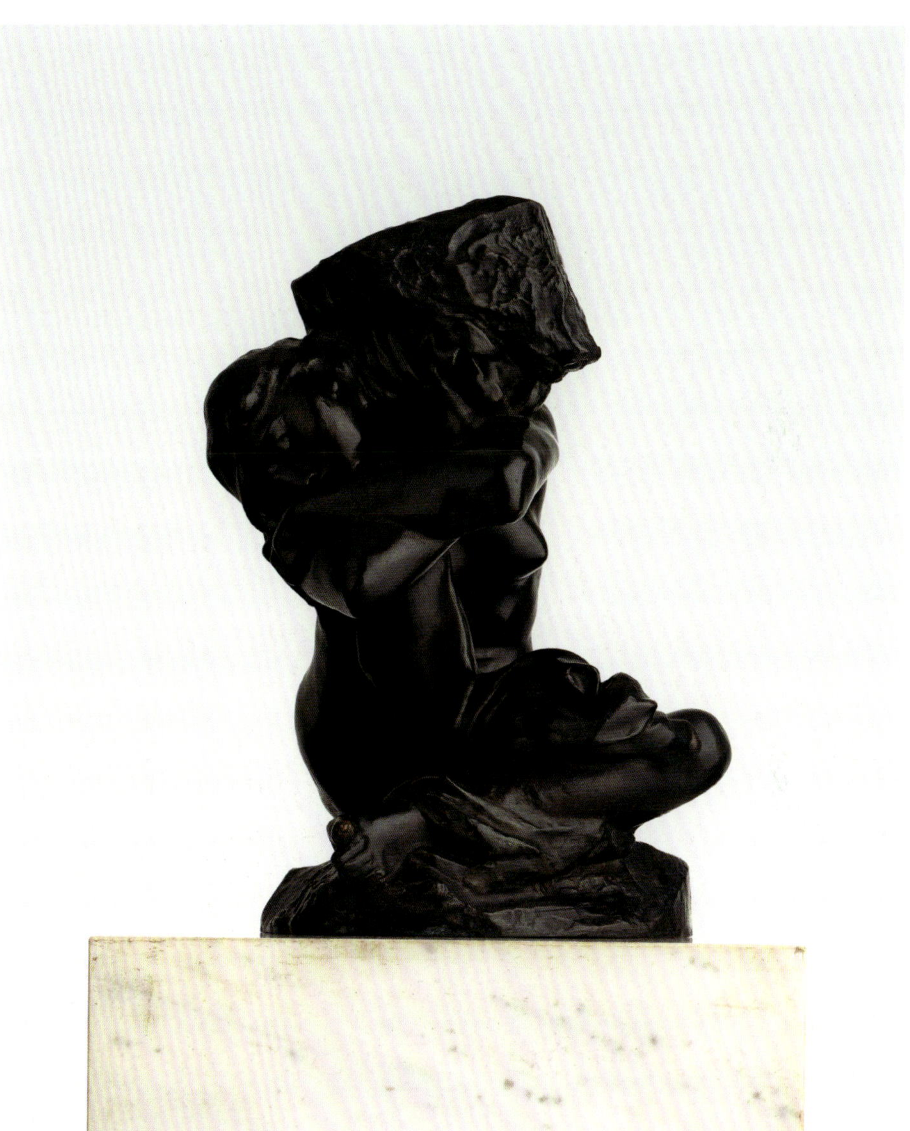

Auguste Rodin
Cariatide tombée portant sa pierre, ca. 1881/82
(Guss: spätestens 1919 | cast: 1919 at the latest)
The National Museum of Western Art, Tokyo

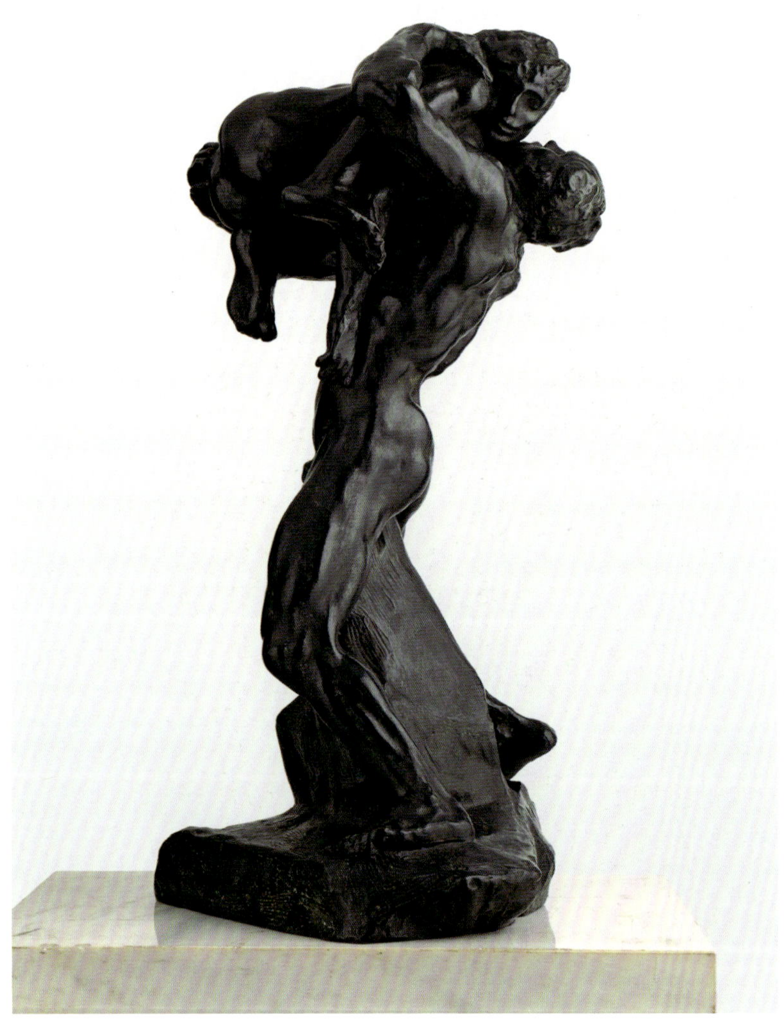

234

Auguste Rodin
Je suis belle, ca. 1885
(Guss: spätestens 1919 | cast: 1919 at the latest)
The National Museum of Western Art, Tokyo

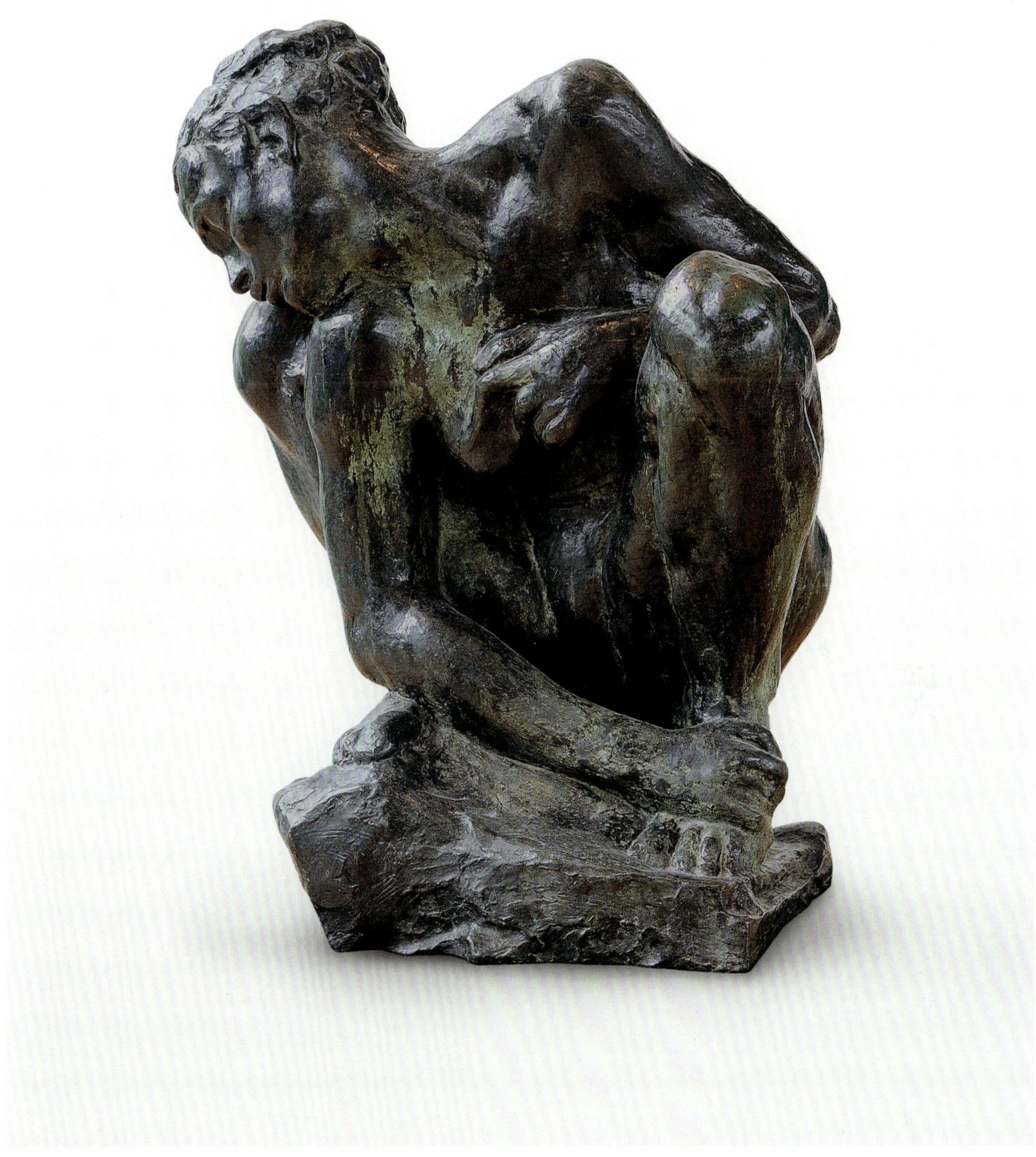

Auguste Rodin
La femme accroupie, ca. 1882
(Guss: spätestens 1913 | cast: 1913 at the latest)
Museum Folkwang, Essen

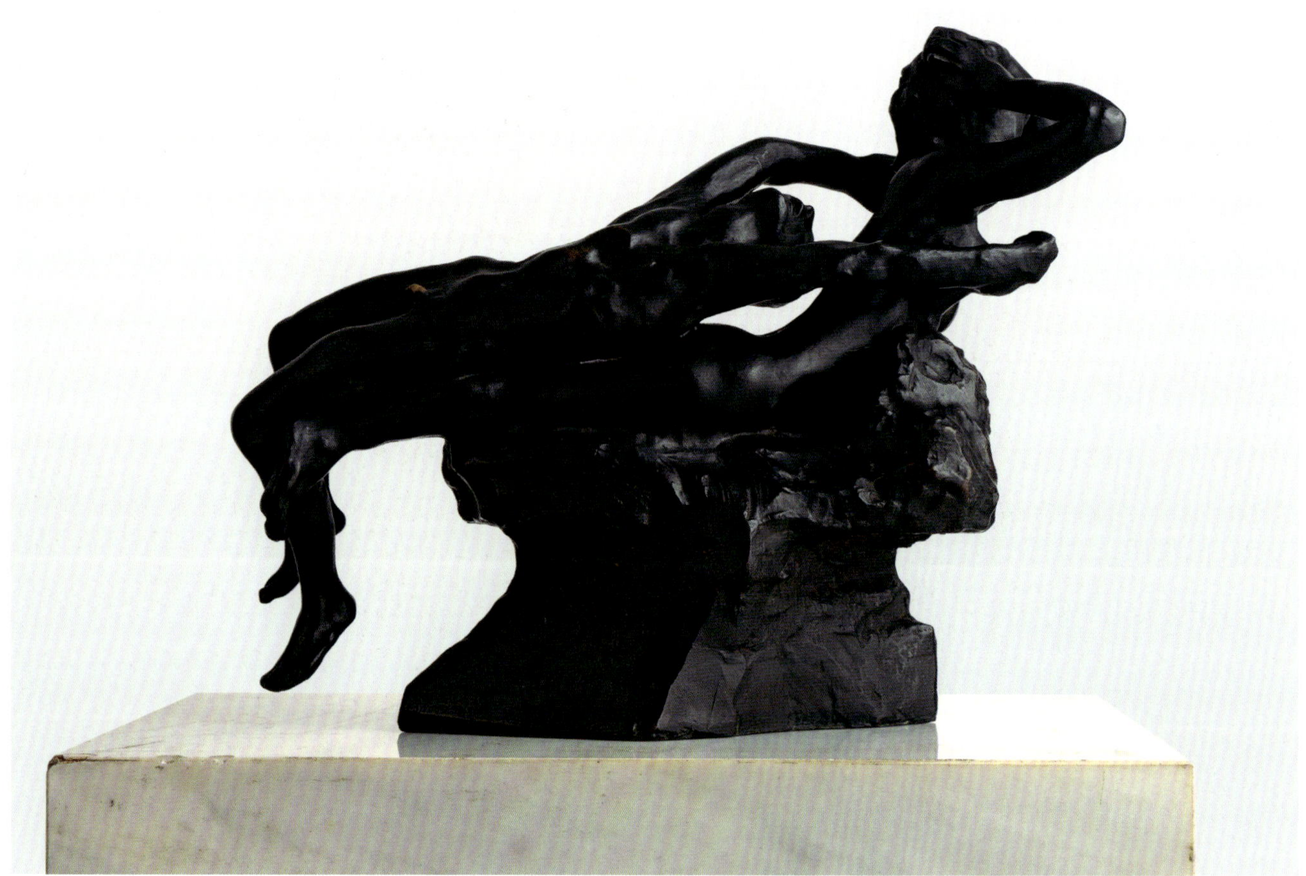

Auguste Rodin
Fugit Amor, vor | before 1887
(Guss: spätestens 1919 | cast: 1919 at the latest)
The National Museum of Western Art, Tokyo

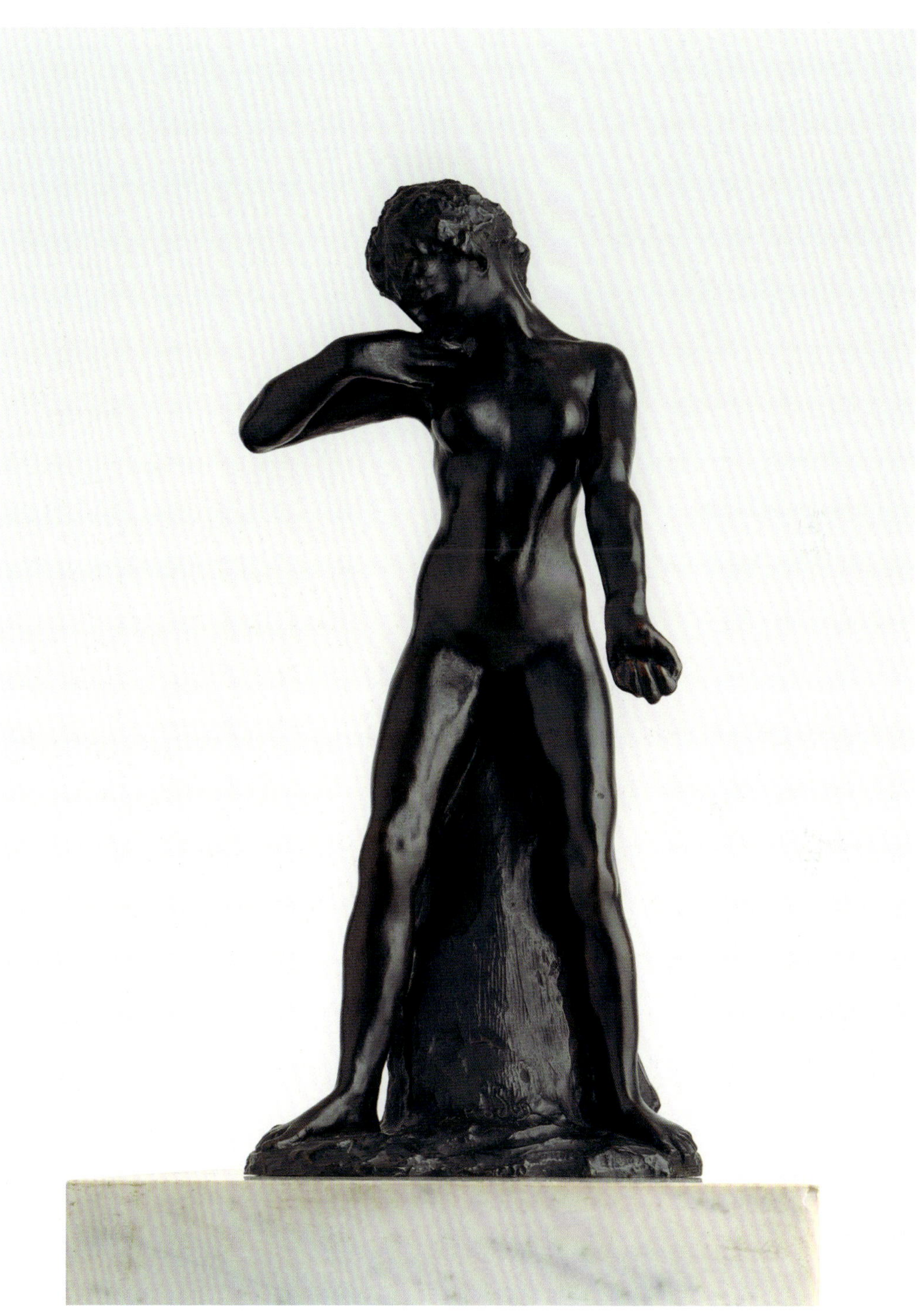

237

Auguste Rodin
Fauness debout
(Guss: spätestens 1919 | cast: 1919 at the latest)
The National Museum of Western Art, Tokyo

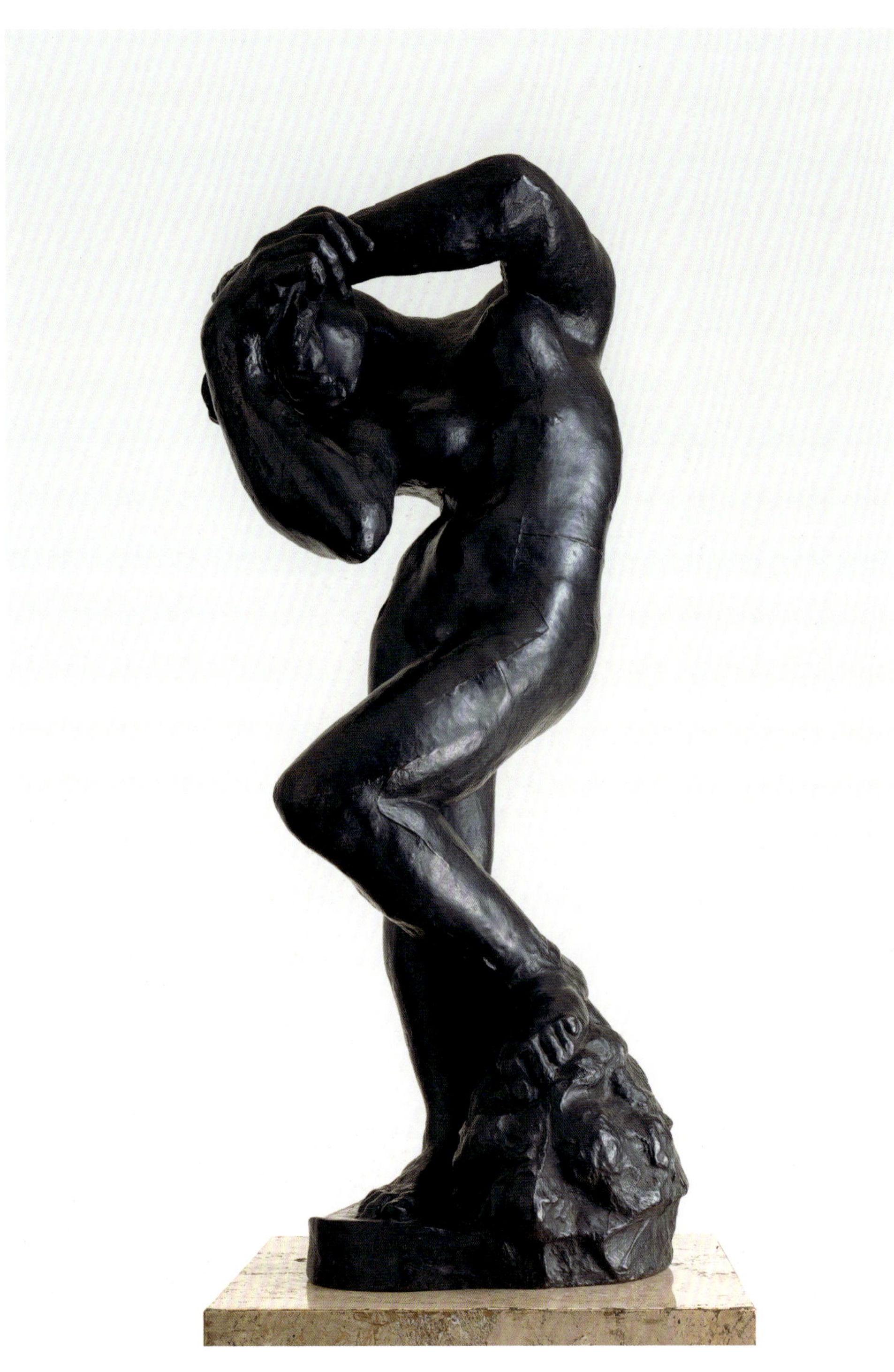

Auguste Rodin
Méditation, nach | after 1900
(Guss: spätestens 1921 | cast: 1921 at the latest)
The National Museum of Western Art, Tokyo

239

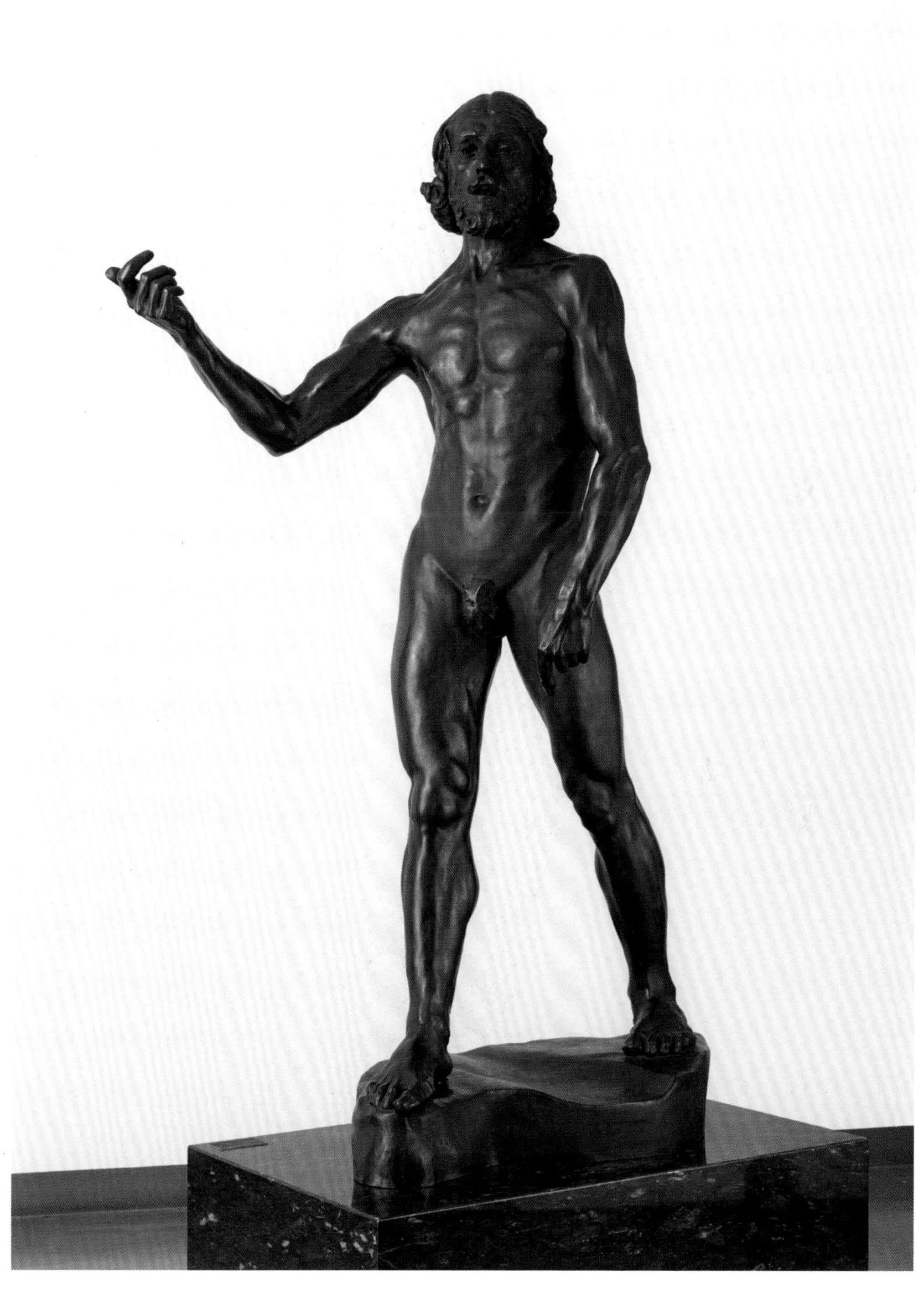

Auguste Rodin
Saint Jean Baptiste, 1880 (Guss | cast: 1944)
The National Museum of Western Art, Tokyo

RÄUME FÜR DIE KUNST

SPACES FOR ART

For the design of their planned museum buildings, Karl Ernst Osthaus and Kōjirō Matsukata relied on their respective advisors Henry van de Velde and Frank Brangwyn. When Osthaus came into contact with Van de Velde's work at the *Internationale Kunst-Ausstellung des Vereins bildender Künstler Münchens* in 1899, the construction of the Hagen Museum was fully underway as a Neo-Renaissance building under the architect Carl Gérard, but at short notice he commissioned Henry van de Velde to undertake the interior in the modern style. The architecture of the building and the exhibits were to be brought into harmony, to grant the public a unique experience and enable a 'return of art to life'.[1] This idea of a holistic design in which architecture, painting, sculpture and furniture were integrated with each other was omnipresent at the time and associated in France with the term *décoration*. Collectors such as the Wiesbaden theatre director Kurt von Mutzenbecher, for example, pursued the notion in the outline of their private reception rooms, referring back to a canon of artists: Mutzenbecher's music room was assembled from a triad formed by the architecture of Henry van de Velde, the paintings of Maurice Denis and the sculptures of Aristide Maillol. Osthaus described the whole as the 'most poetic space in Velde's entire body of work'. 'It was an atmosphere of soft, Elysian charm', he wrote in 1920 in his monograph on Van de Velde.[2]

Matsukata was also convinced by the Wiesbaden furnishing, and in 1921 he bought Maurice Denis's *L'eternel eté. La danse* (*Girls Dancing*, 1905; p. 247), a study or replica of the decoration in Mutzenbecher's music room, as part of a large

Bei der Gestaltung ihrer geplanten Museumsgebäude vertrauten Karl Ernst Osthaus und Kōjirō Matsukata auf ihre Berater Henry van de Velde bzw. Frank Brangwyn. Als Osthaus 1899 auf der *Internationalen Kunst-Ausstellung des Vereins bildender Künstler Münchens* mit dem Werk van de Veldes in Berührung kam, war zwar der Bau des Hagener Museums als Neo-Renaissanceanlage unter dem Architekten Carl Gérard bereits in vollem Gange, doch verpflichtete er kurzerhand Henry van de Velde, den Innenausbau im modernen Stil auszuführen. Die Architektur des Hauses und die ausgestellten Objekte sollten in Einklang gebracht werden, um dem Publikum eine einmalige Erfahrung und eine „Zurückführung der Kunst ins Leben"[1] zu ermöglichen. Die Idee einer Gesamtgestaltung von Räumen, in der Architektur, Malerei, Skulptur und Mobiliar aufeinander abgestimmt wurden, war zu dieser Zeit virulent und in Frankreich mit dem Begriff „décoration" verbunden. Auch Sammler:innen wie der Wiesbadener Intendant Kurt von Mutzenbecher folgten ihr bei der Einrichtung von privaten Repräsentationsräumen und griffen dabei auf einen Kanon von Künstlern zurück: Das Musikzimmer Mutzenbechers setzte sich aus dem Dreiklang der Architektur von Henry van de Velde, der Malerei von Maurice Denis und den Skulpturen von Aristide Maillol zusammen. Osthaus bezeichnete das Ensemble als den „poesievollste[n] Raum aus Veldes ganzem Schaffen". „Es war eine Stimmung aus weichem, elysischem Reiz", schrieb er 1920 in seiner Monografie zu van de Velde.[2] Auch Matsukata zeigte sich überzeugt von der Wiesbadener Ausstattung und

collection of the artist's work. This also included a series of sketches that Denis had made
for the interior of the Paris Théâtre des Champs-
Elysées, and which Matsukata bought directly
from the artist in 1921 (pp. 248/249). The first
design for the theatre building was done around
1910 by Henry van de Velde, and Osthaus described that building enthusiastically too.[3] Here,
once again, we see a closure of the circle
around the Osthaus and Matsukata collections,
which referred to the same design elements in
their museum architecture. Kōjirō Matsukata
also strove to bring together applied and visual
art in his museum building. Its galleries were to
become spaces of aesthetic exploration that
combined architecture, interior decoration and
art. In the end, however, Brangwyn's designs
were never realized (p. 243).

1   Karl Ernst Osthaus, 'Lebenslauf,' in idem.,
    Grundzüge der Stilentwicklung, Diss. Hagen
    1918, quoted in Rainer Stamm (ed.), *Reden und
    Schriften. Folkwang, Werkbund, Arbeitsrat*,
    Kontext. Schriftenreihe für Kunst, Kunsterziehung
    und Kulturpädagogik, 3, (Cologne, 2002), 23 f.
2   Karl Ernst Osthaus, *Van de Velde. Leben
    und Schaffen des Künstlers* (Hagen, 1920), 54.
3   Ibid., pp. 98–104.

erwarb 1921 Maurice Denis' *L'éternel été. La danse
(Der ewige Sommer. Der Tanz*, 1905; S. 247),
welches eine Studie oder Replik der Innenausstattung aus Mutzenbechers Musikzimmer darstellt,
als Teil eines großen Konvolutes von Werken des
Künstlers. Dazu zählte auch eine Reihe von Skizzen,
die Denis für die Dekoration des Pariser Théâtre
des Champs-Elysées gemacht hatte und die Matsukata 1921 direkt beim Künstler erstand (S. 248/249).
Der erste Entwurf zum Bau des Theaters stammte
um 1910 von Henry van de Velde und Osthaus
schilderte auch diesen Bau mit Begeisterung.[3] Hier
schließt sich abermals der Kreis zwischen den
Sammlungen Osthaus und Matsukata, die sich in
der Museumsarchitektur auf die gleichen Gestal-
tungselemente beriefen. Auch Kōjirō Matsukata
strebte bei seinem Museumsbau die Zusammenführung von angewandter und bildender Kunst
an. Die Ausstellungsräume sollten ein Ort der
ästhetischen Erkundung werden, der Architektur,
Innendekoration und Kunst zusammenbrachte.
Letztlich kamen die Entwürfe Brangwyns allerdings
nie zur Ausführung (S. 243).

1   Karl Ernst Osthaus, „Lebenslauf", in: ders.,
    Grundzüge der Stilentwicklung, Diss. Hagen
    1918, zit. nach: *Karl Ernst Osthaus. Reden und
    Schriften. Folkwang, Werkbund, Arbeitsrat
    (Kontext. Schriftenreihe für Kunst, Kunst-
    erziehung und Kulturpädagogik*, 3), hrsg. und
    komm. von Rainer Stamm, Köln 2002, S. 23 f.
2   Karl Ernst Osthaus, *Van de Velde. Leben und
    Schaffen des Künstlers*, Hagen 1920, S. 54.
3   Ebd., S. 98–104.

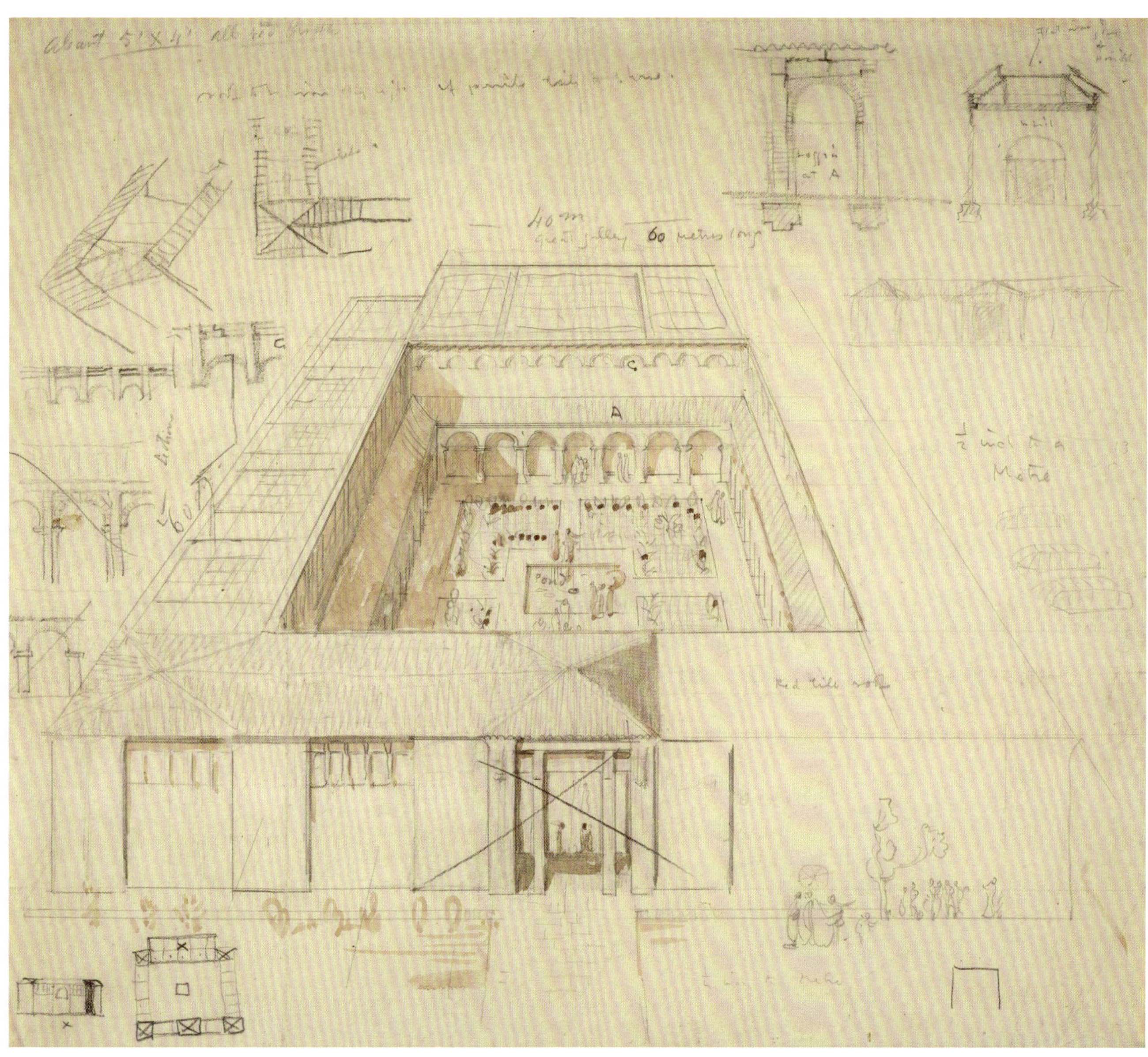

Frank Brangwyn
*Aerial Perspective of Kyōraku Bijutsukan
(Sheer Pleasure Arts Pavilion)*, 1918–1922
The National Museum of Western Art, Tokyo

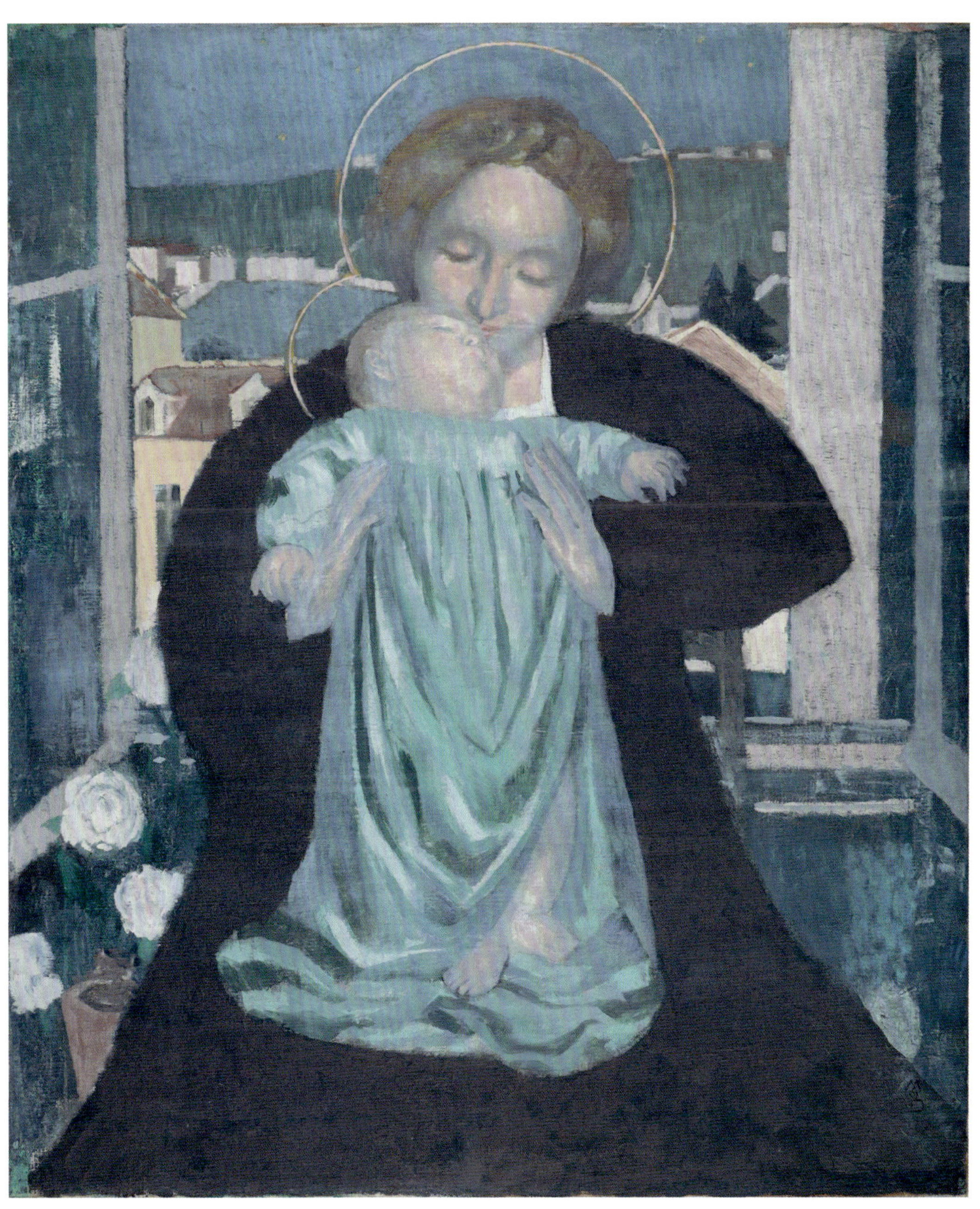

245

Maurice Denis
Vierge au baiser, 1902
Museum Folkwang, Essen

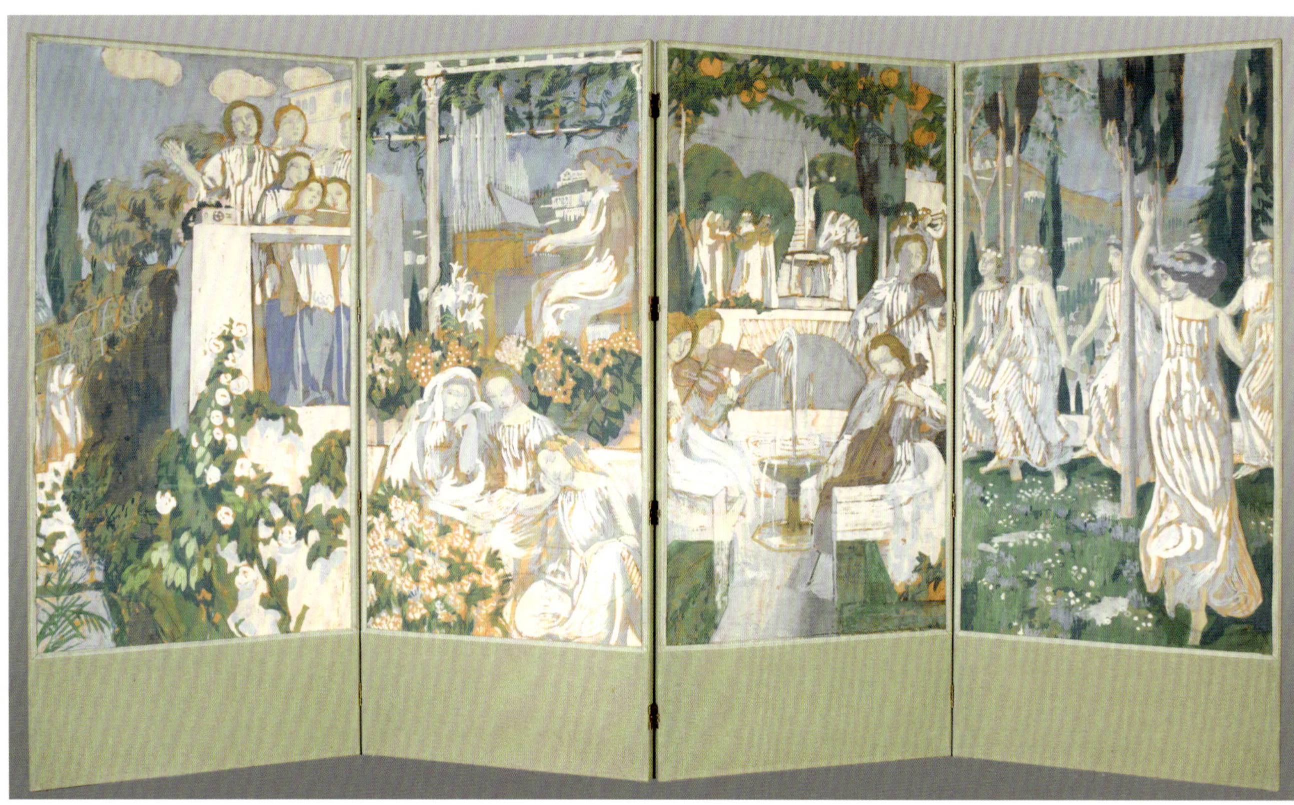

Maurice Denis
*L'éternel été. Le chant choral, l'orgue,
le quatuor, la danse*, 1905
Musée d'Orsay, Paris

247

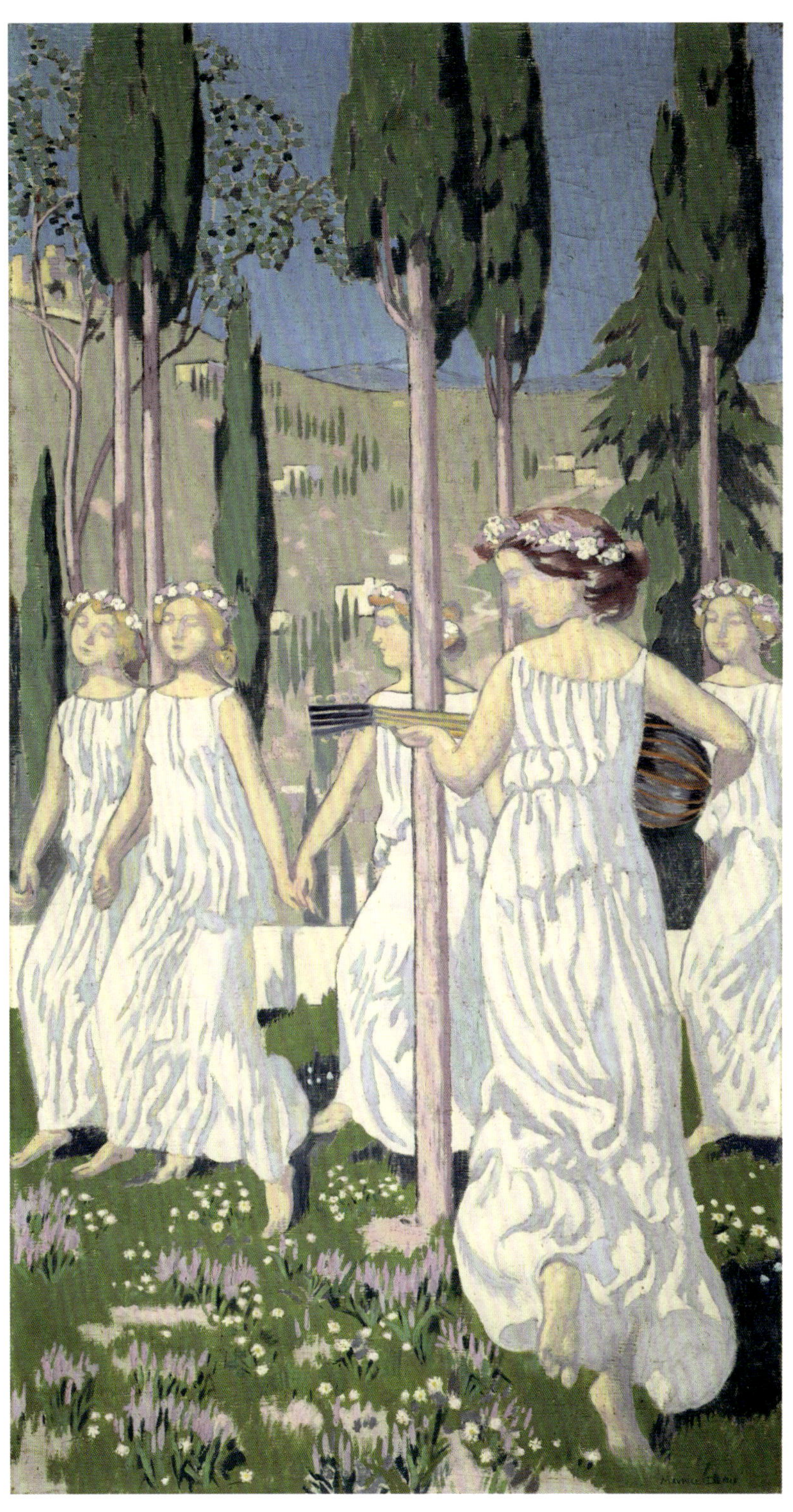

Maurice Denis
L'éternel été. La danse, 1905
The National Museum of Western Art, Tokyo

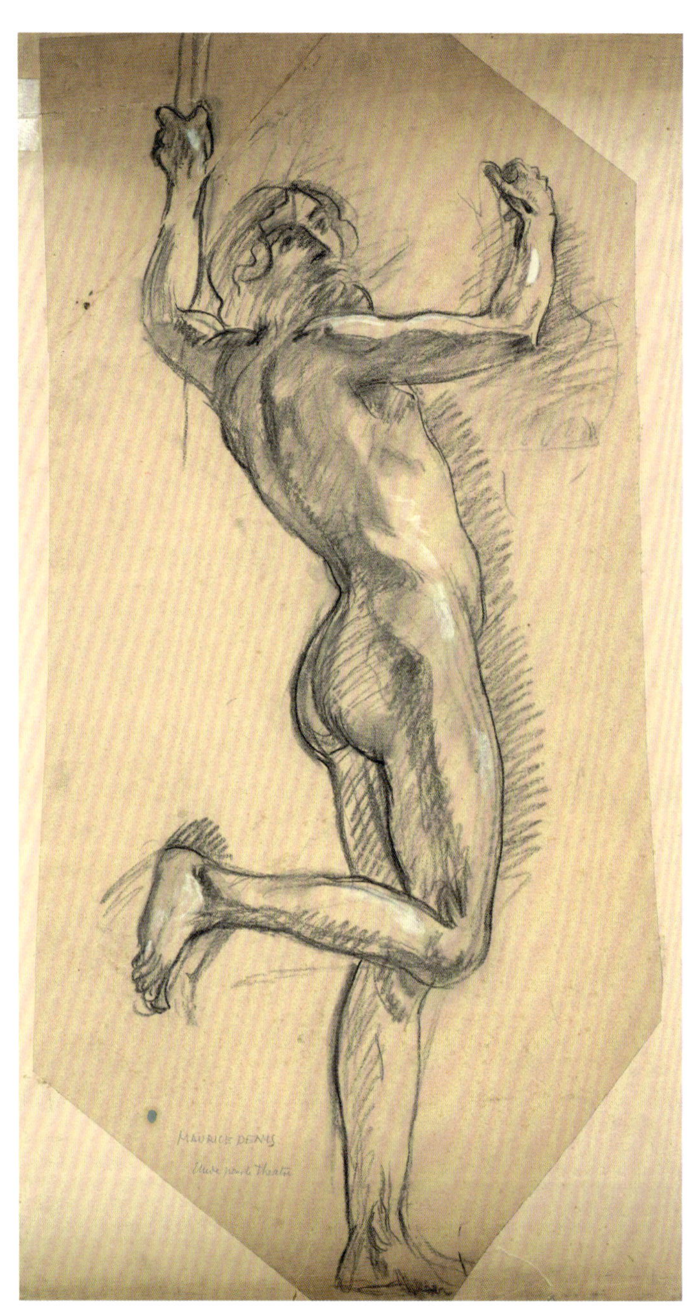

Maurice Denis
Etude pour le théâtre, zweite Hälfte
des 19. Jh. | Second half of 19th century
The National Museum of Western Art, Tokyo

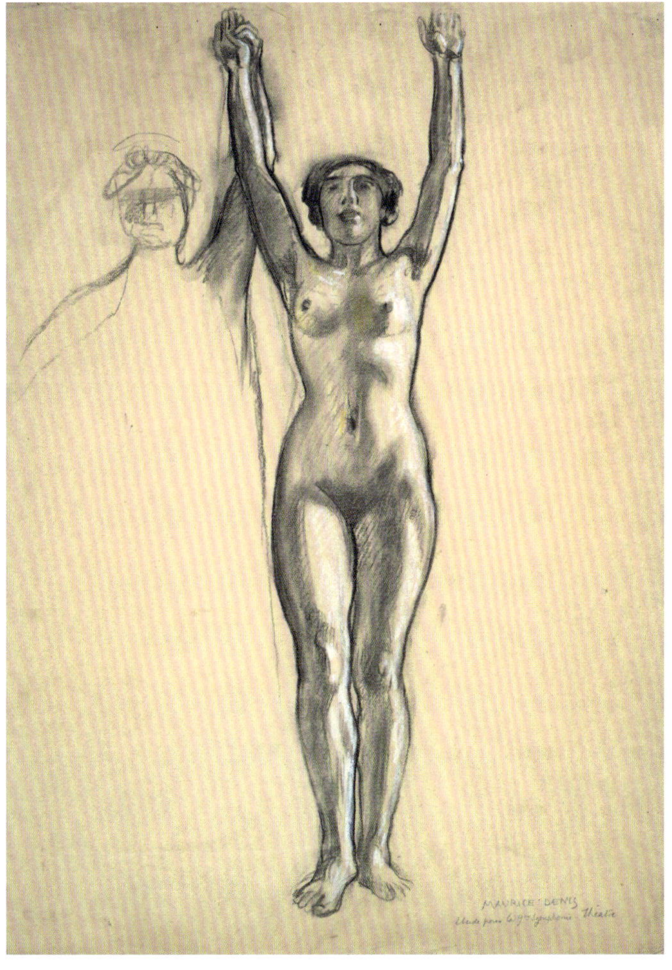

Maurice Denis
Etude pour la 9ème symphonie, théâtre, 1912
The National Museum of Western Art, Tokyo

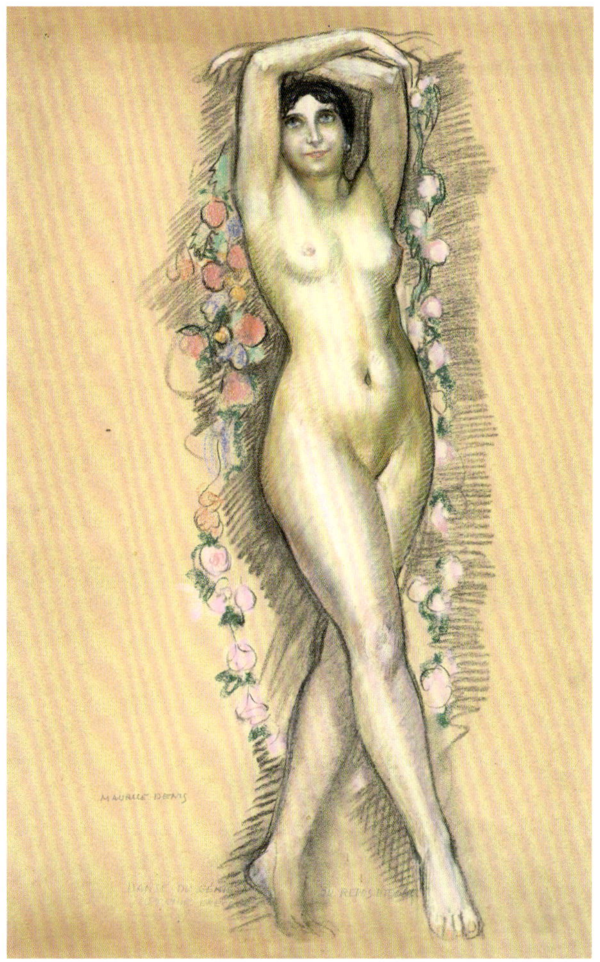

Maurice Denis
Danse du génie. Statue grecque du repos éternel,
zweite Hälfte des 19. Jh. | Second half of 19th century
The National Museum of Western Art, Tokyo

BILDER EINER
FLIESSENDEN WELT

IMAGES OF
A FLOATING WORLD

In the late nineteenth century, Japanese art was highly esteemed in Europe. This trend was given the name 'Japonisme'.[1] The artistic products of the country, which had only just opened up to trade with the West, fascinated artists and collectors and gave them new ideas and ways of seeing. From the very start of his collecting career, Karl Ernst Osthaus was among those with an interest in East Asian, and particularly Japanese, artefacts. His model in this was Justus Brinckmann, the then director of the Museum für Kunst und Gewerbe in Hamburg, for whom Osthaus worked as an intern in 1899, and who had emerged as one of the first connoisseurs of Japanese arts and crafts in Germany. Not only did Brinckmann provide Osthaus with duplicates from the Hamburg collection, but he also put him in contact with Hermann Paechter, the most important dealer of Japanese art in Germany at that time. It was from Paechter that Osthaus bought the first pieces for his collection, as early as 1899. Japan became centrally important to the Museum Folkwang, which now has around 290 Japanese objects in its holdings. One focus was on ceramics, but examples of Japanese painting and graphic arts were also part of the collection, including not only colour woodcuts, *ukiyo-e* (which translates roughly as 'images of a floating world'), but also ornate scrolls, called *kakemono*. Shortly after the opening of the Museum Folkwang Hagen, Kanō Yōsen-in Korenobu's depiction of cranes (p. 253) was prominently displayed in the entrance hall, and an East Asian cabinet was installed in the upper vestibule.

While Kōjirō Matsukata might have based his collection around European art, he did also

Ende des 19. Jahrhunderts genoss die japanische Kunst in Europa hohe Wertschätzung. Dieser Trend wird mit dem Begriff „Japonismus" beschrieben.[1] Künstler:innen und Sammler:innen gleichermaßen faszinierten die Kunsterzeugnisse des Landes, das sich dem Westen gerade erst geöffnet hatte. Sie boten ihnen neue Anregungen und Sichtweisen. Auch Karl Ernst Osthaus interessierte sich schon zu Beginn seiner Sammeltätigkeit für ostasiatische und insbesondere japanische Artefakte. Vorbild war Justus Brinckmann, der damalige Direktor des Museums für Kunst und Gewerbe in Hamburg, bei dem Osthaus 1899 hospitierte und der als einer der ersten Kenner für japanisches Kunsthandwerk in Deutschland in Erscheinung getreten war. Brinckmann vermittelte Osthaus nicht nur Dubletten aus der Hamburger Sammlung, sondern brachte ihn auch in Kontakt mit Hermann Paechter, dem seinerzeit wichtigsten Händler japanischer Kunst in Deutschland. Bei ihm erwarb Osthaus noch 1899 erste Stücke für seine Sammlung. Japan entwickelte sich zu einem Schwerpunkt im Museum Folkwang, heute befinden sich noch etwa 290 japanische Objekte im Bestand. Ein Fokus lag auf der Keramik, aber auch Beispiele japanischer Malerei und Grafik waren Teil der Sammlung, darunter neben Farbholzschnitten, den *ukiyo-e* (übersetzt etwa „Bilder einer fließenden Welt"), auch kunstvolle Hängerollen, sogenannte *kakemonos*. Schon kurz nach der Eröffnung des Museum Folkwang Hagen wurde Kanō Yōsen-in Korenobus Darstellung von Reihern (S. 253) prominent in der Eingangshalle ausgestellt und im oberen Vestibül war ein ostasiatisches Kabinett eingerichtet.

acknowledge the significance of *ukiyo-e*. In 1918, he bought over 8000 woodcuts from the famous collection of the Paris jeweller Henri Vever (and probably other sources) for his planned museum (pp. 256–261). In buying these works back from Europe Matsukata wanted to make the art of the woodcut more accessible to his compatriots and promote the artistic traditions of Japan. In 1925, Matsukata showed a selection of 200 *ukiyo-e* in a series of four exhibitions in Japan, also accompanied by an illustrated catalogue.[2] Today these holdings are in the Tokyo National Museum. Many pieces are labelled as important cultural property, which is why borrowing them is very difficult.

1 Cf. *Monet, Gauguin, van Gogh … Japanese Inspirations*, exh. cat. Museum Folkwang, Essen (Göttingen, 2014).
2 *Matsukata ukiyo-e hangashū [Catalogue of the Matsukata Collection of Woodblock Prints]*, see Julia Meech (ed.), *The Matsukata Collection of Ukiyo-e Prints. Masterpieces from the Tokyo National Museum*, exh. cat., Zimmerli Art Museum, Rutgers University (New Brunswick (NJ), 1988), 20.

Kōjirō Matsukata legte den Fokus seiner Sammlung zwar auf europäische Kunst, erkannte aber auch die Bedeutung des *ukiyo-e*. 1918 erwarb er mehr als 8000 Holzschnitte aus der berühmten Sammlung des Pariser Juweliers Henri Vever und vermutlich noch aus anderen Quellen für sein geplantes Museum (S. 256–261). Durch den Rückkauf aus Europa wollte er die Kunst des Holzschnitts seinen Landsleuten wieder zugänglich machen und sie dazu anregen, die künstlerische Tradition Japans zu verstehen und wertzuschätzen. 1925 stellte Matsukata eine Auswahl von 200 *ukiyo-e* in einer Serie von vier Ausstellungen in Japan aus, zu der auch ein bebilderter Katalog erschien.[2] Heute befindet sich der Bestand im Tokyo National Museum. Viele Stücke sind als national bedeutendes Kulturgut ausgezeichnet, weshalb eine Ausleihe nur schwer möglich ist.

1 Vgl. *Monet, Gauguin, van Gogh … Inspiration Japan*, Ausst.-Kat. Museum Folkwang, Essen, Göttingen 2014.
2 *Matsukata ukiyo-e hangashū [Catalogue of the Matsukata Collection of Woodblock Prints]*, siehe *The Matsukata Collection of Ukiyo-e Prints. Masterpieces from the Tokyo National Museum*, hrsg. von Julia Meech, Ausst.-Kat. Zimmerli Art Museum, Rutgers University, New Brunswick (NJ) 1988, S. 20.

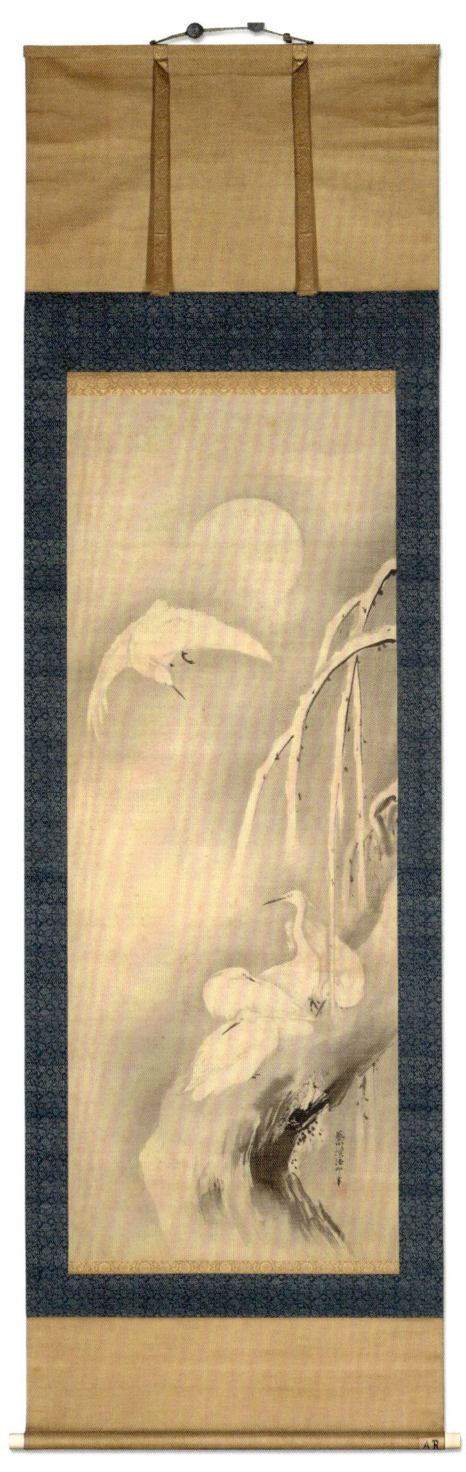

Kanō Yōsen-in Korenobu
kakemono (Hängerolle | hanging scroll), nach | after 1794
Museum Folkwang, Essen

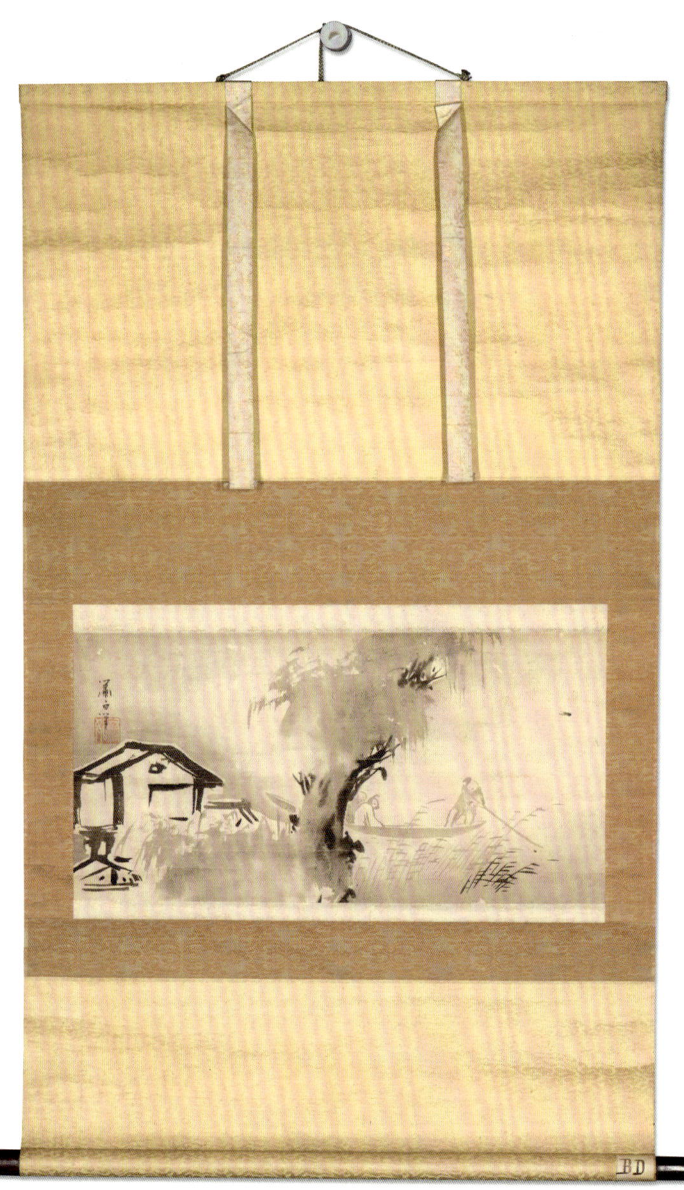

254

Soga Shōhaku
kakemono (Hängerolle | hanging scroll),
zweite Hälfte des 18. Jh. | second half of the 18th century
Museum Folkwang, Essen

255

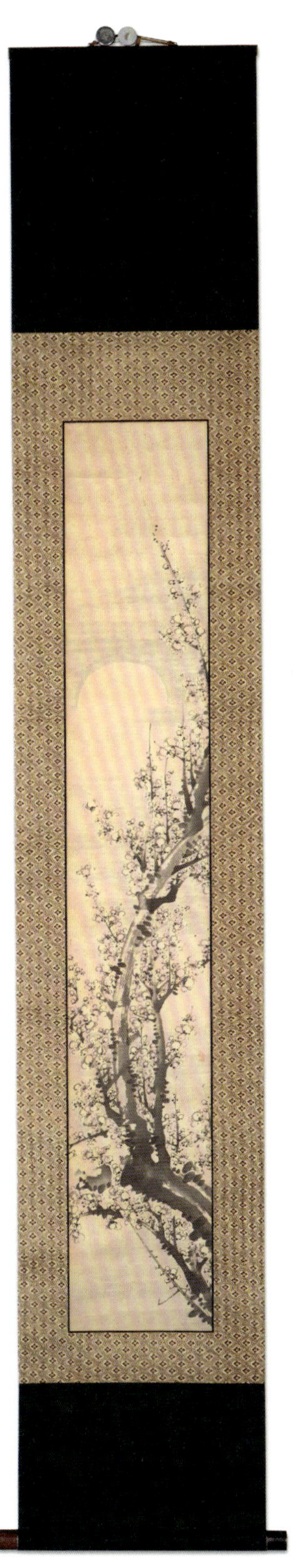

Anonymer Künstler im Stil des Hokusai Katsushika |
Anonymous artist in the style of Hokusai Katsushika
kakemono (Hängerolle | hanging scroll),
19. Jh. | 19th century
Museum Folkwang, Essen

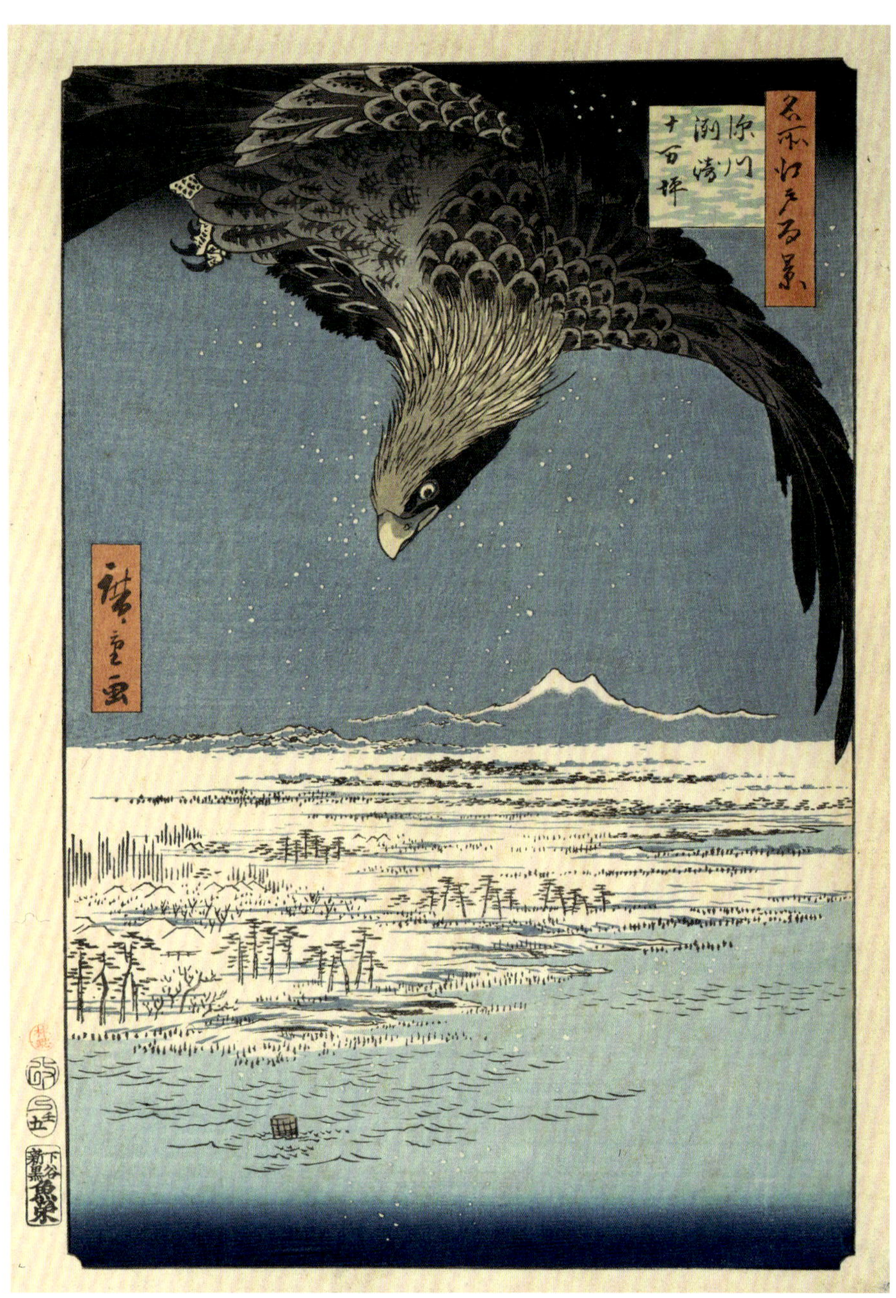

Hiroshige Utagawa
*One Hundred Thousand Tsubo Plain
at Susaki, Fukagawa,* 1857
(Aus der Serie | from the series:
One Hundred Famous Views of Edo)
Tokyo National Museum

257

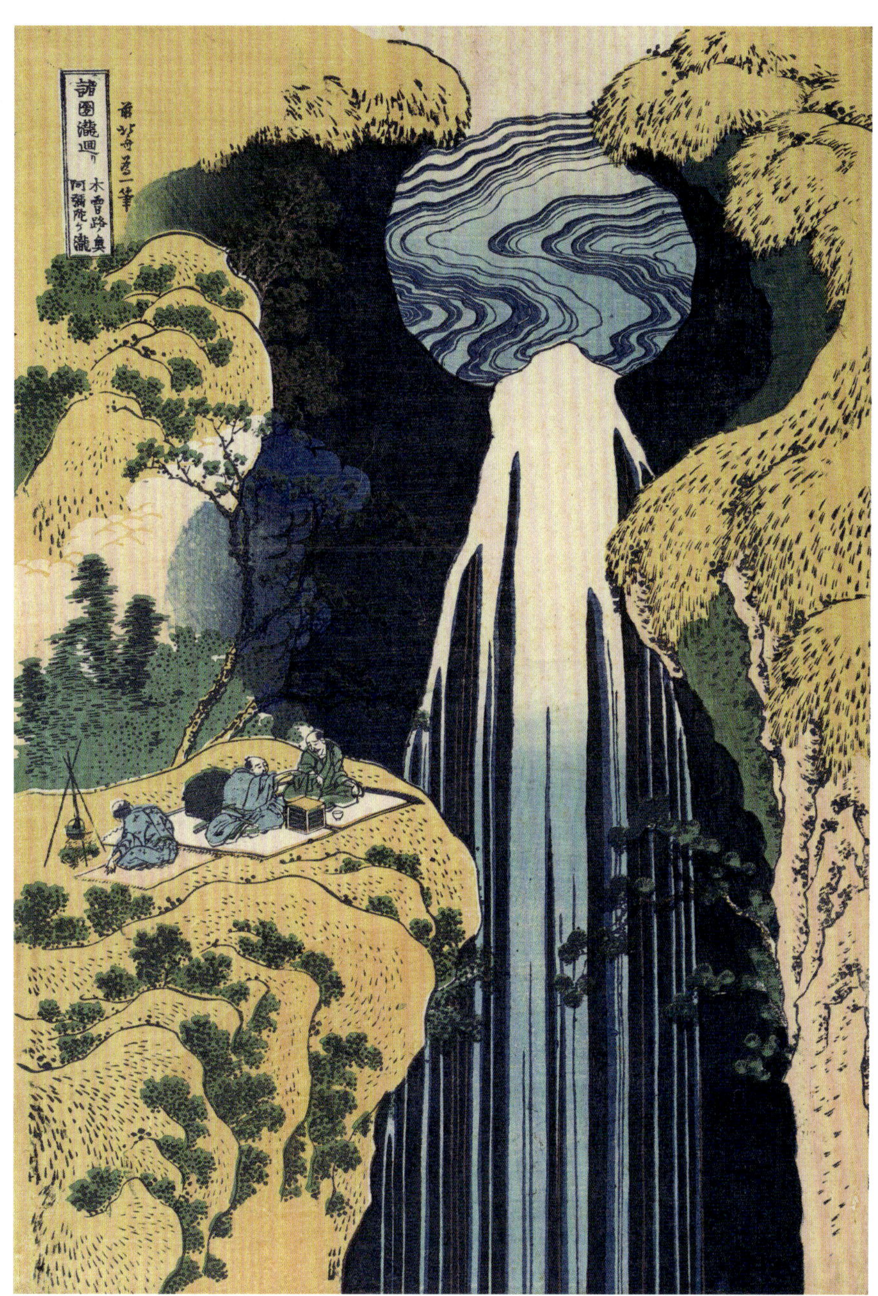

Hokusai Katsushika
The Amida Waterfall on the Kisokaido, 1833
(Aus der Serie | from the series:
A Journey to the Waterfalls of All the Provinces)
Tokyo National Museum

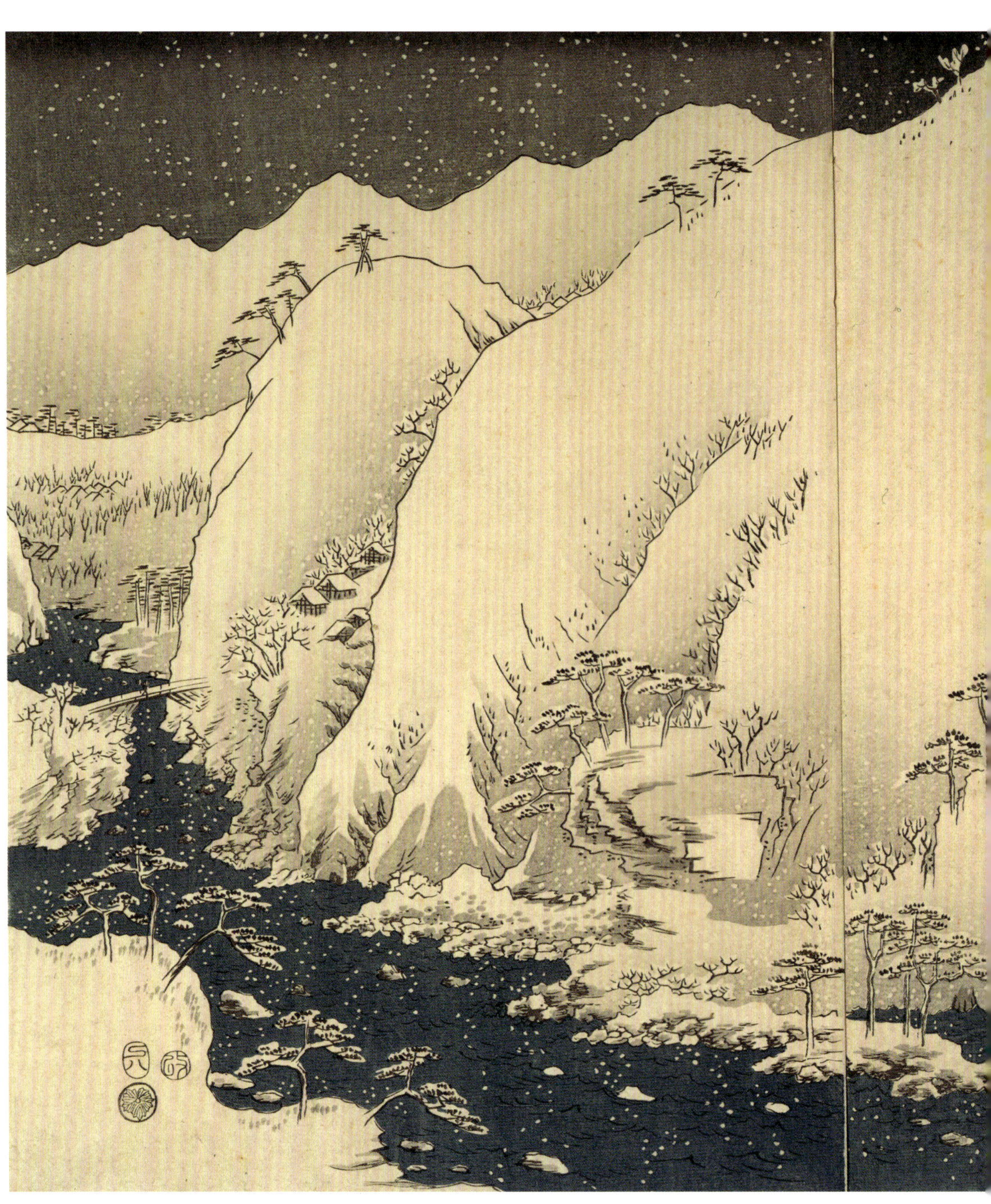

Hiroshige Utagawa
Mountains and Rivers Along the Kisokaido Highway, 1857
Tokyo National Museum

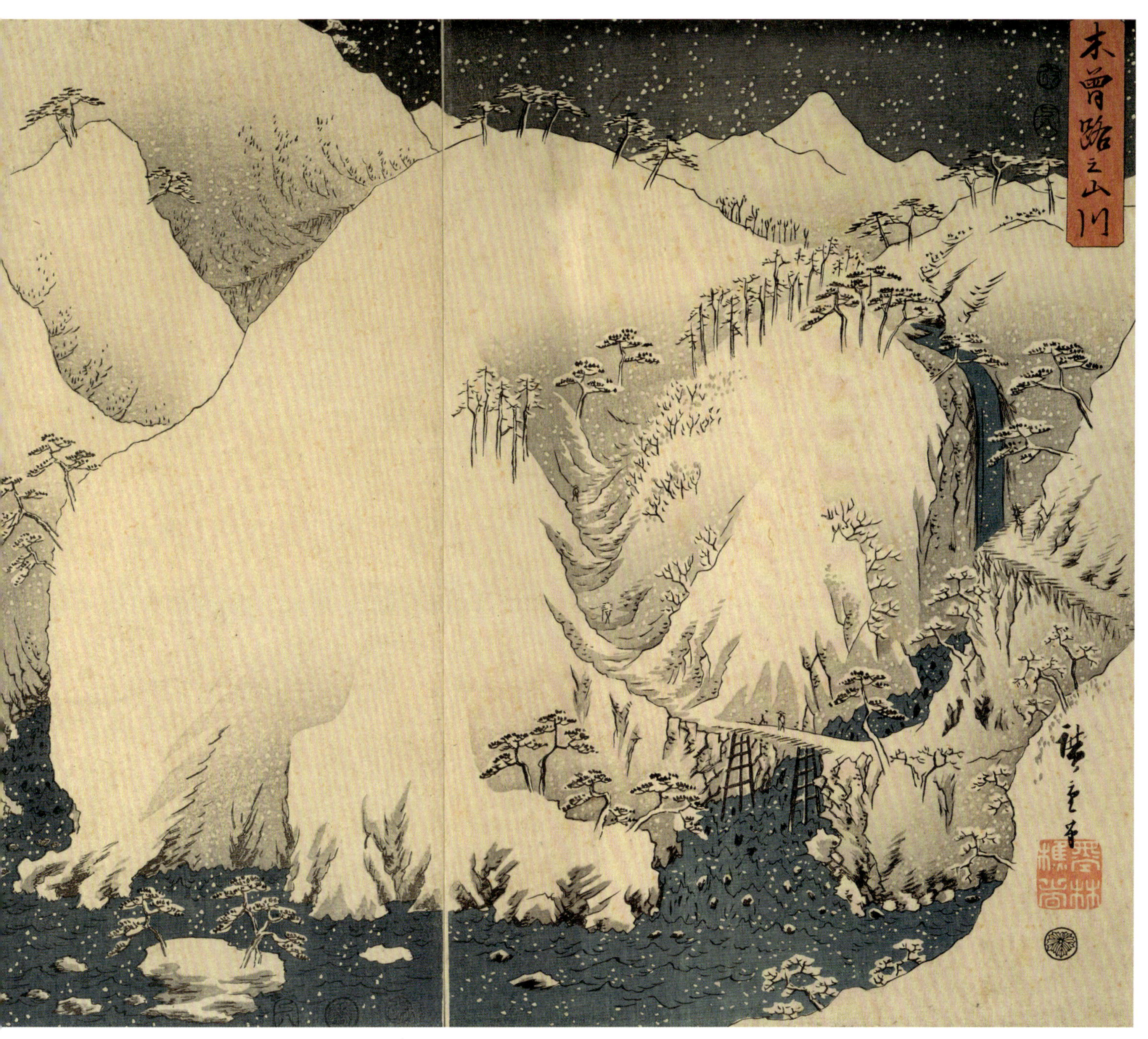

木曽路之山川
廣重筆

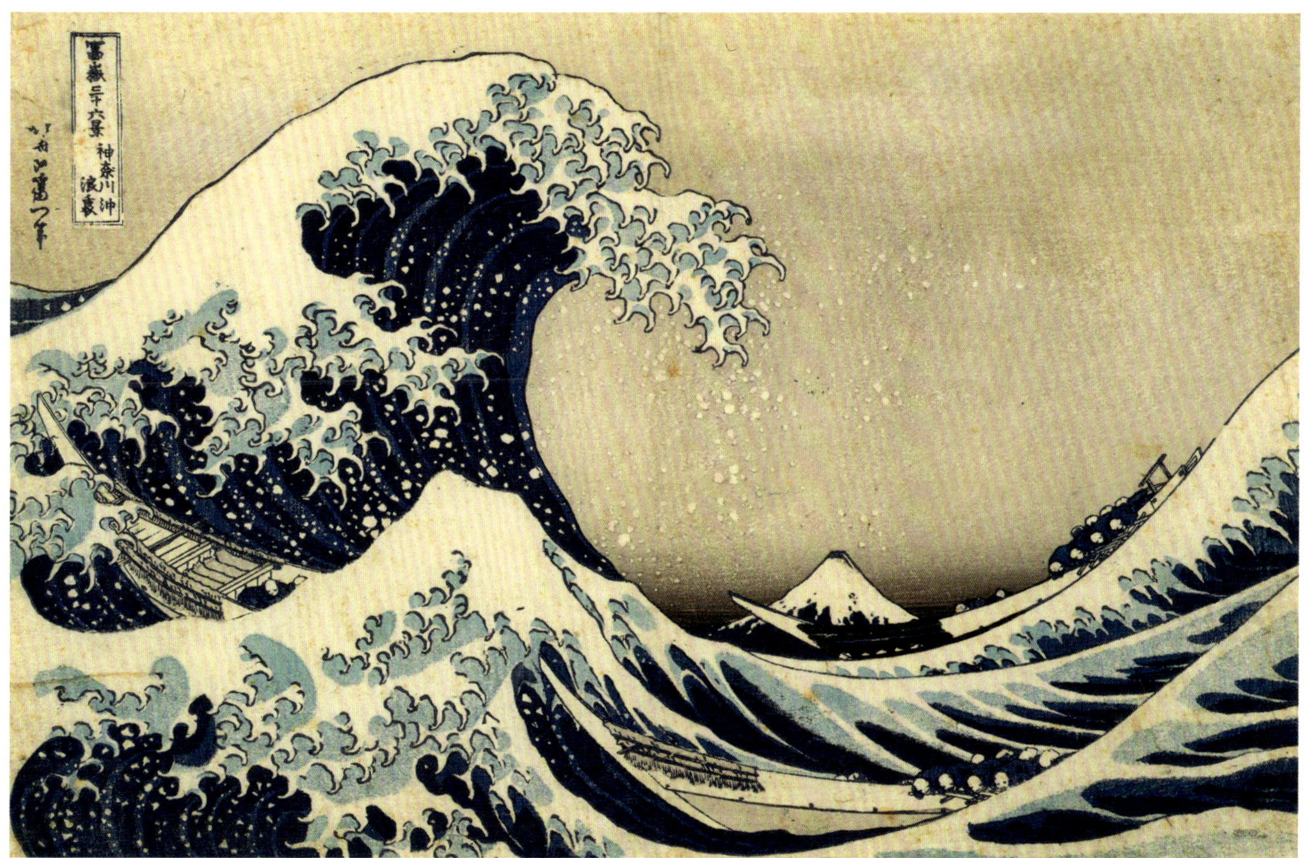

261

Hokusai Katsushika
The Great Wave off Kanagawa, 1831
(Aus der Serie | from the series:
Thirty-Six Views of Mount Fuji)
Tokyo National Museum

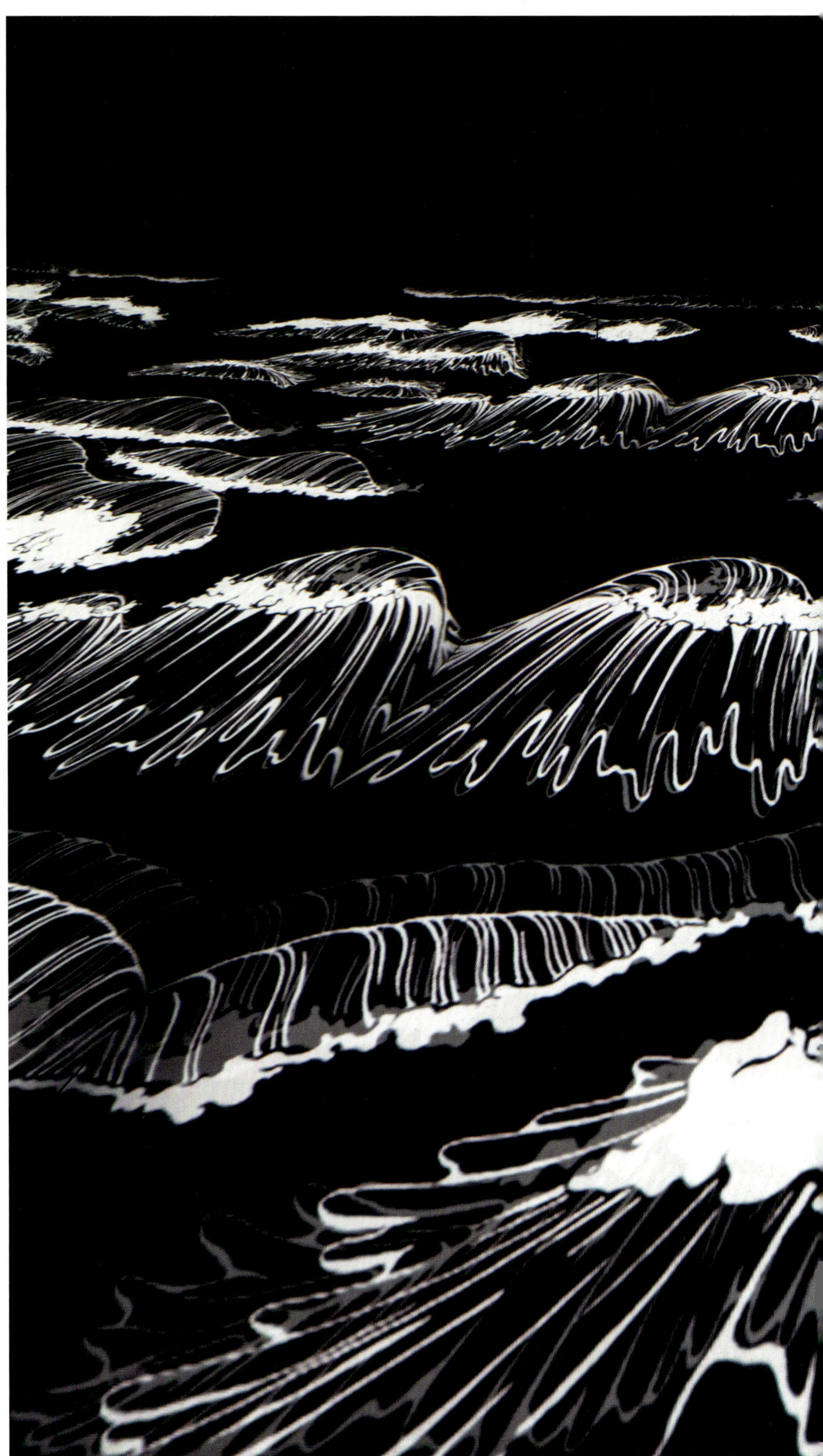

Tabaimo
midnight sea, 2006
Installationsansicht | Installation view,
Hara Museum ARC
Courtesy of James Cohan Gallery,
New York, und | and Gallery Koyanagi, Tokyo

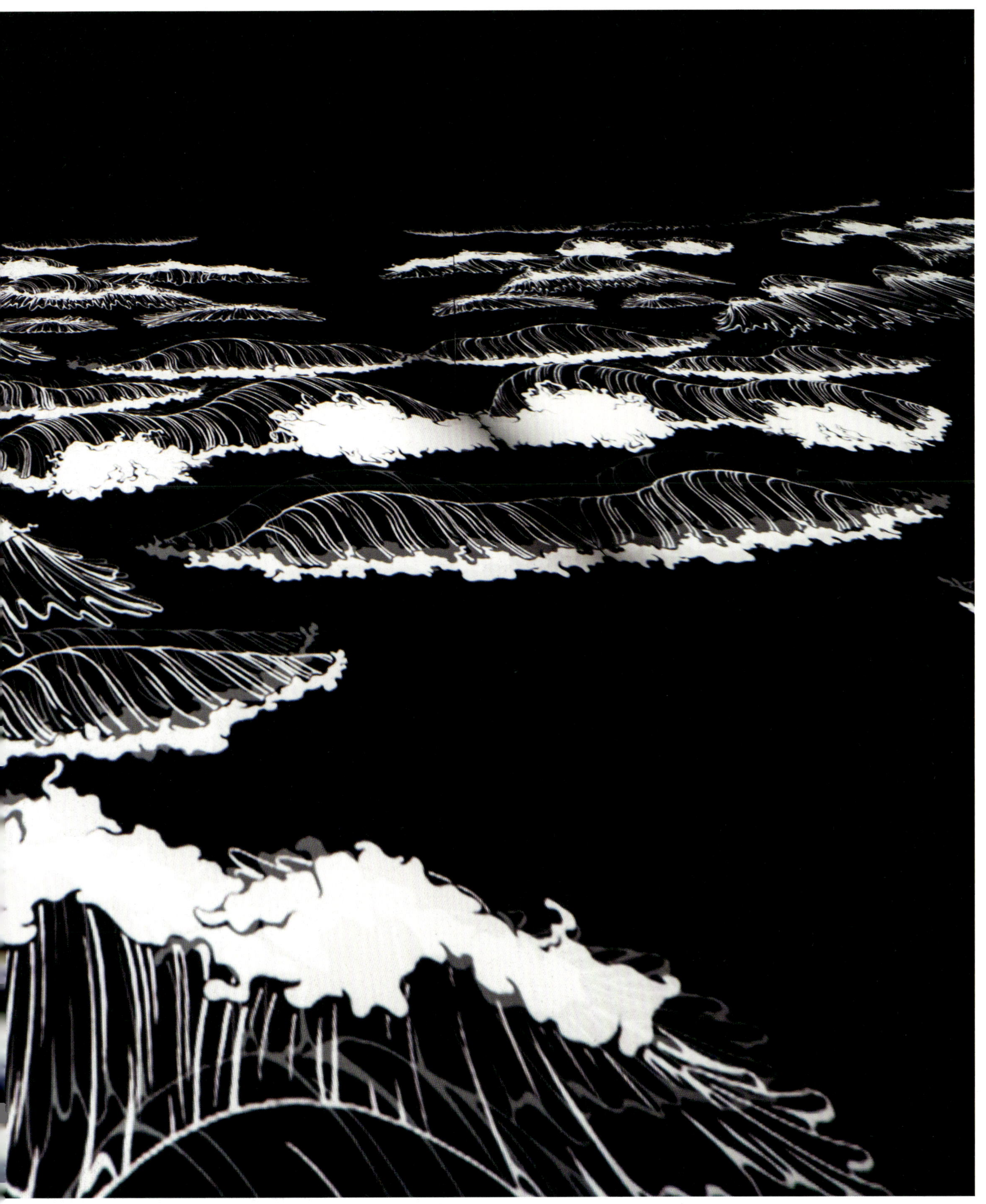

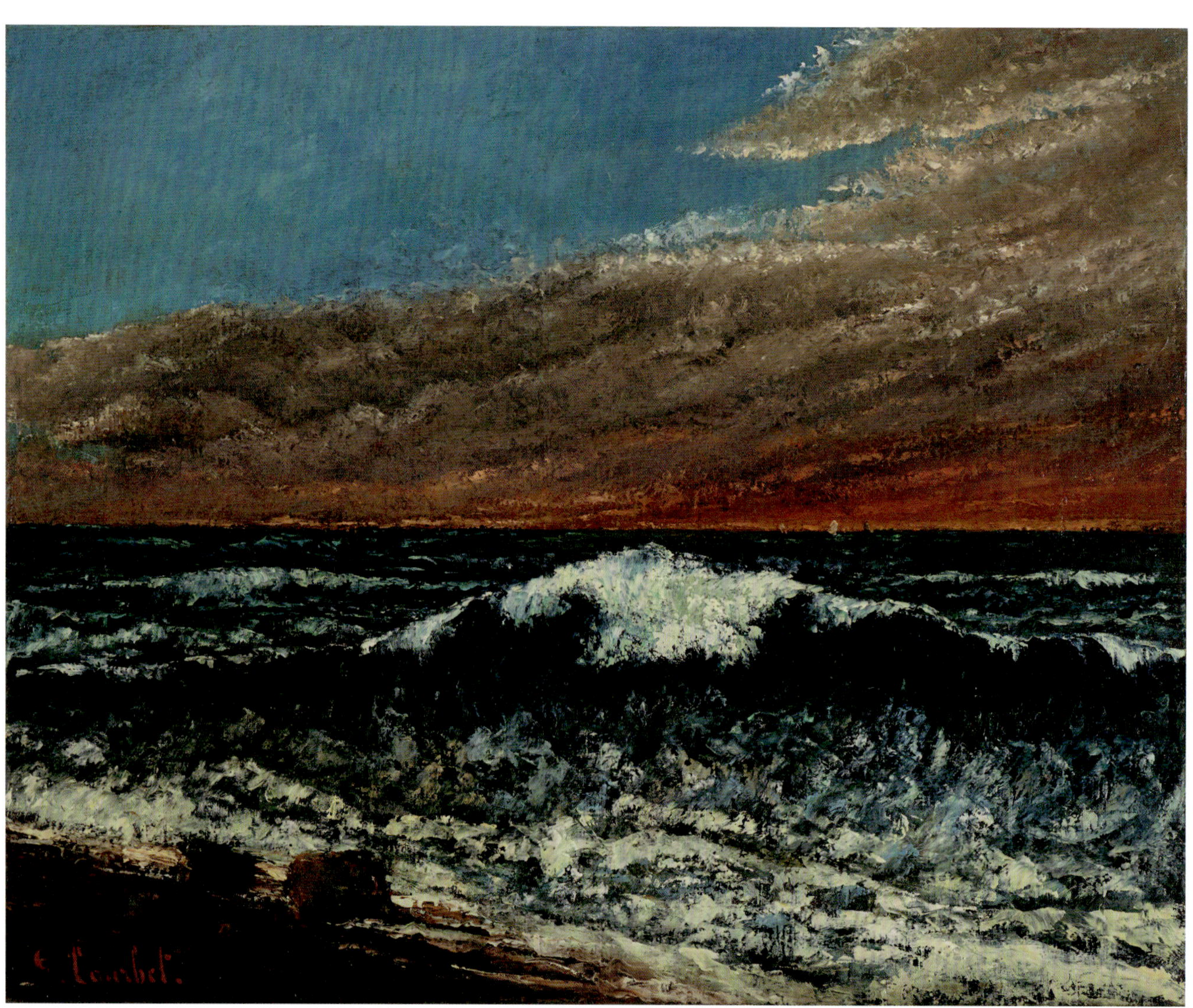

Gustave Courbet
La vague, 1870
Museum Folkwang, Essen

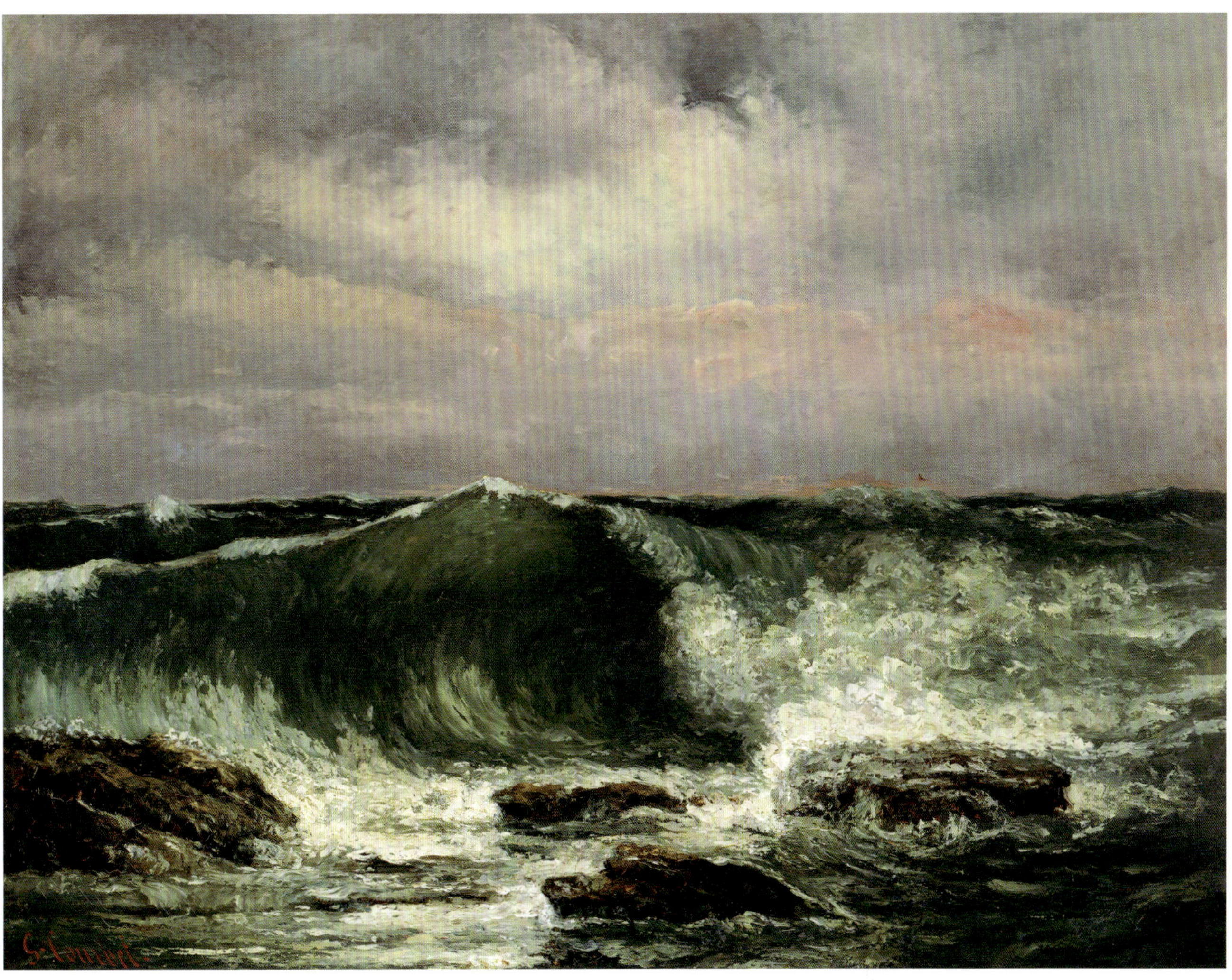

Gustave Courbet
La vague, ca. 1870
The National Museum of Western Art, Tokyo

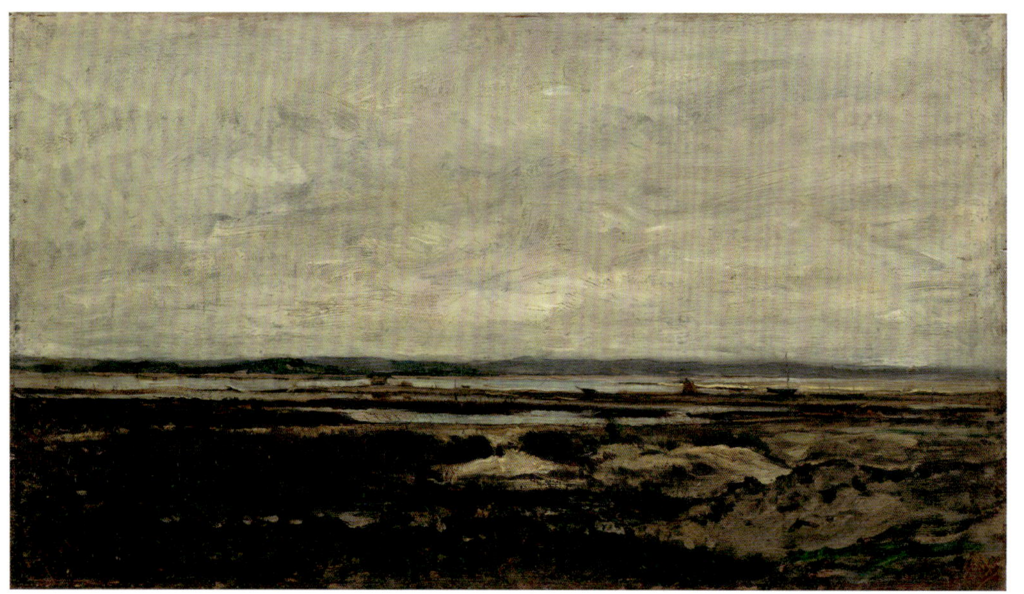

Charles-François Daubigny
Les Sables-d'Olonne
Artizon Museum, Ishibashi Foundation, Tokyo

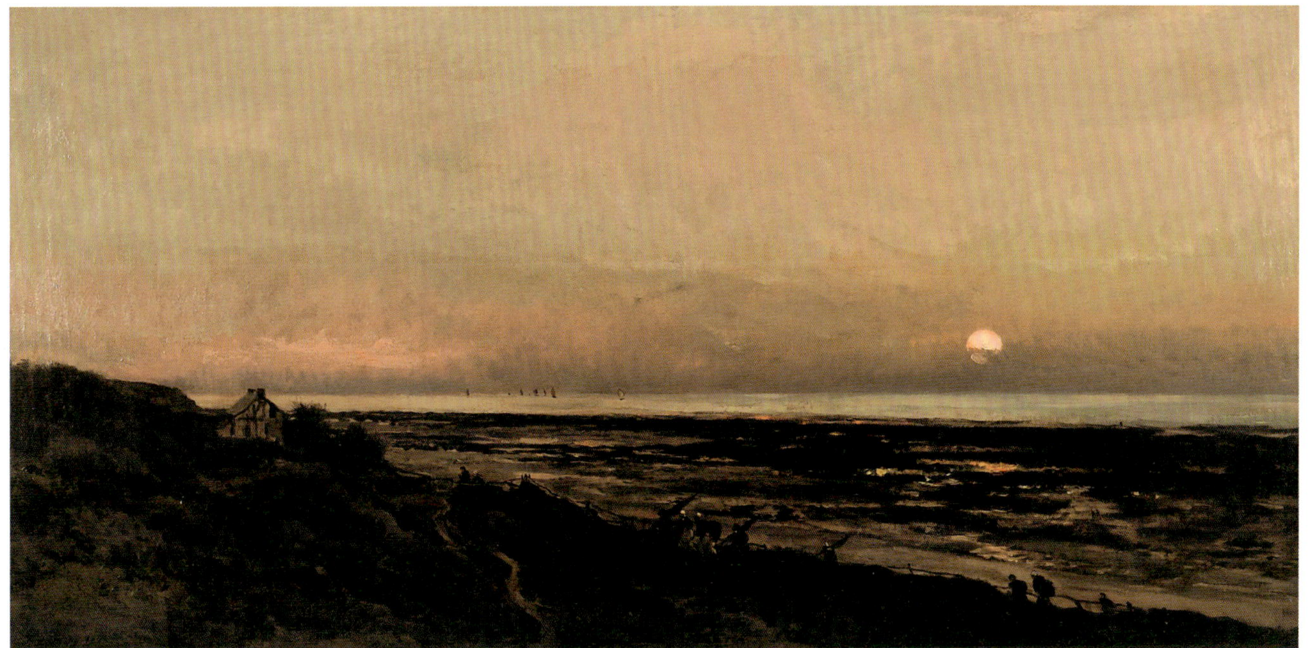

267

Charles-François Daubigny
La plage de Villerville au soleil couchant, 1870
Sumitomo Mitsui Banking Corporation, Tokyo

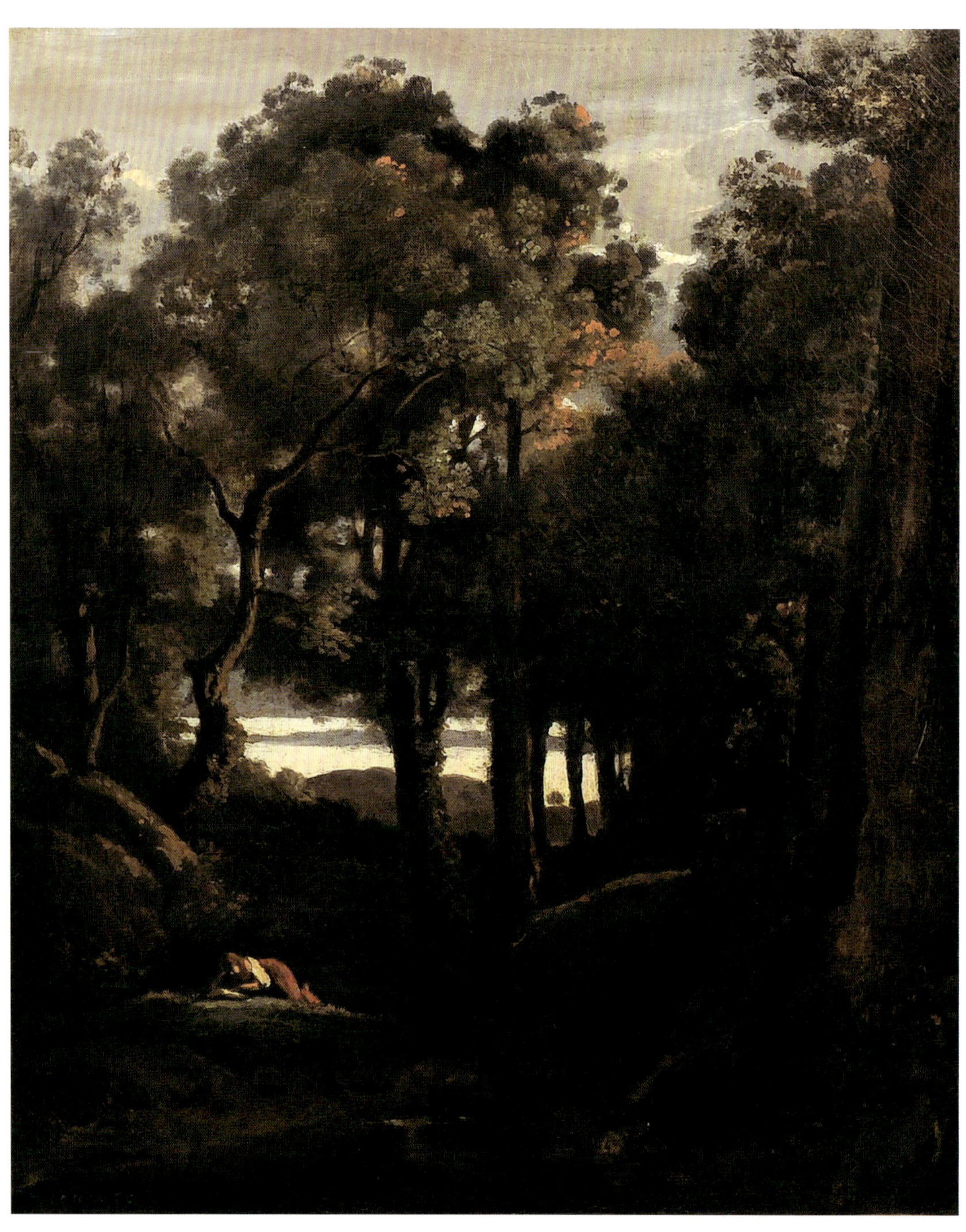

268

Jean-Baptiste Camille Corot
Madeleine
Sumitomo Mitsui Banking Corporation, Tokyo

269

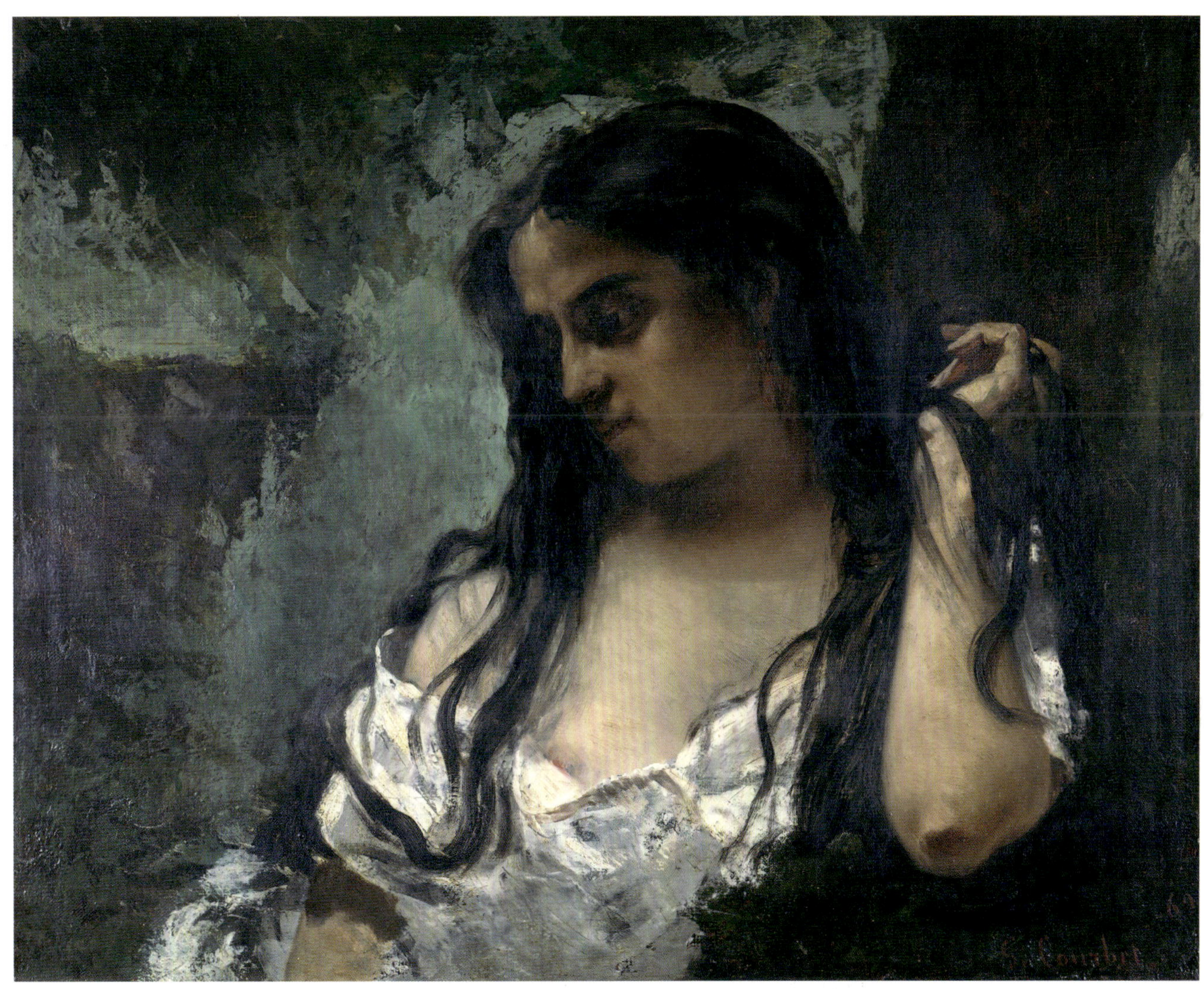

Gustave Courbet
*Rêverie tzigane**, 1869
The National Museum of Western Art, Tokyo

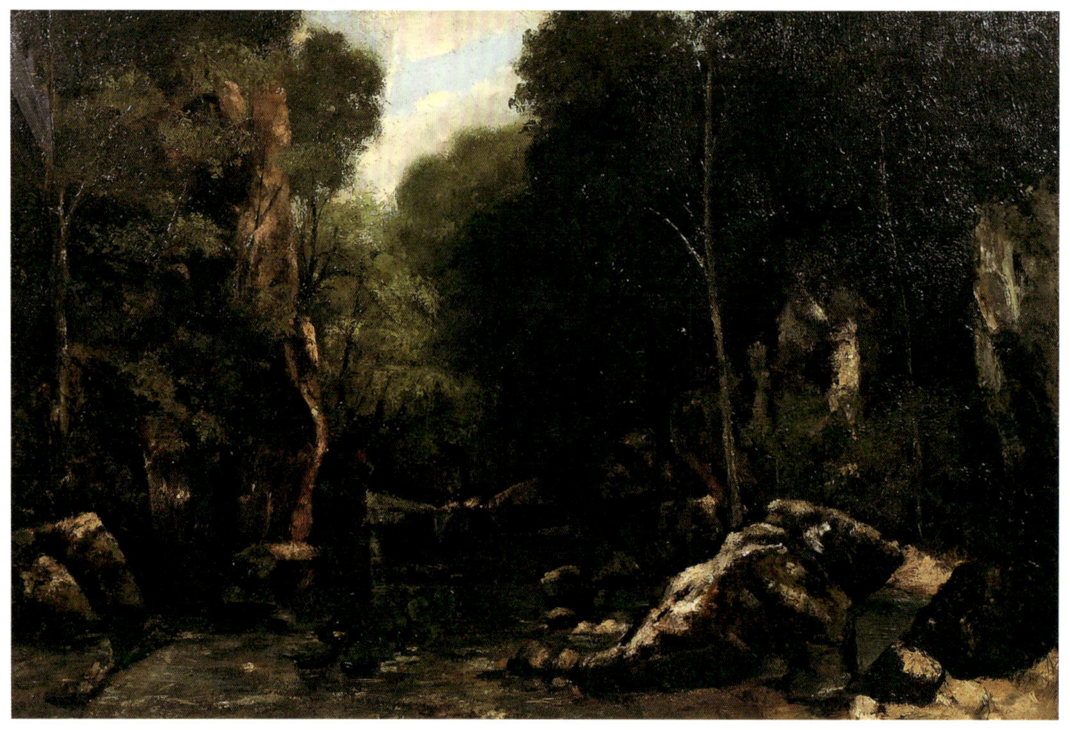

Gustave Courbet
Le puits-noir, ca. 1872
Sumitomo Mitsui Banking Corporation, Tokyo

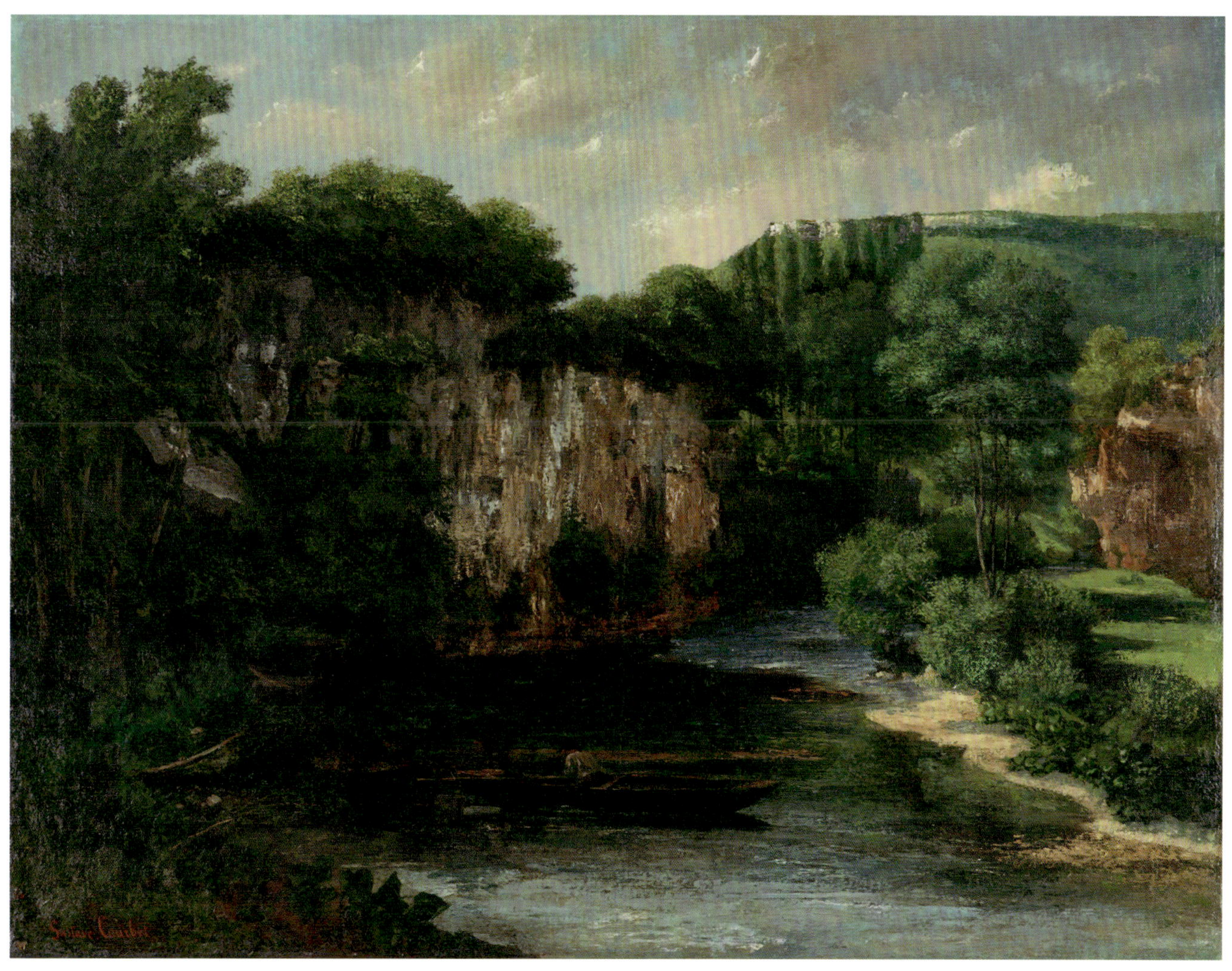

Gustave Courbet
La roche oraguay, Vallon de Maisières, Doubs, 1860
Museum Folkwang, Essen

EINE MONET-SAMMLUNG FÜR JAPAN

A MONET COLLECTION FOR JAPAN

272

Claude Monet was one of the founders of Impressionism, the movement that was named after his painting entitled *Impression, soleil levant* (1872; Musée Marmottan Monet, Paris). Among its fundamental features were *plein-air* work and the quick recording of ephemeral motifs or atmospheres with a direct painting style. This new style was inspired among other things by Japanese woodcuts (*ukiyo-e*), which were very popular in France at the time. The representation of everyday scenes and the unusual details selected here were a novelty to European painting that was picked up by the Impressionists (cf. p. 281 and p. 122, fig. 1).

In 1920, Kōjirō Matsukata first made contact with the eighty-year-old Monet, who by now seldom received buyers. The meeting was arranged by Léonce Bénédite and Matskuta's niece Takeko Kuroki, who was living with her husband in Paris at this time and knew the artist socially. The following year Matsukata visited the painter twice in his studio in Giverny and bought numerous paintings for his collection – both directly from Monet and via art dealers and collectors in Paris. Over time his collection came to include thirty-four works by the artist.[1] Matsukata prepared carefully for the purchases, and the range of his acquisitions clearly shows the esteem in which he held Monet's art. Apart from Rodin's oeuvre, Monet's work thus became the focus of Matsukata's collection. Even though Impressionism was still frowned upon by critics in the 1870s, a market quickly grew, reaching its first peak at the beginning of the twentieth century. Because of his fortune, however, unlike someone like Karl Ernst Osthaus, Matsukata was still able to invest

Claude Monet zählt zu den Begründern des Impressionismus, jener Stilrichtung, die nach seinem Gemälde mit dem Titel *Impression, soleil levant* (1872, Musée Marmottan Monet, Paris) benannt wurde. Zu ihren Grundzügen zählten die Arbeit in der Natur und das schnelle Einfangen eines flüchtigen Motivs oder einer Stimmung durch eine direkte Malweise. Inspiriert wurde diese neue Richtung unter anderem durch japanische Farbholzschnitte *(ukiyo-e)*, die zu jener Zeit in Frankreich weit verbreitet waren. Die Darstellung von Alltagsszenen und die ungewöhnlichen Bildausschnitte, die hier gewählt wurden, waren eine Neuheit für die europäische Malerei, die die Impressionist:innen aufgriffen (vgl. S. 281 und S. 122, Abb. 1).

1920 nahm Kōjirō Matsukata zum ersten Mal Kontakt mit dem achtzigjährigen Monet auf, der nur noch selten Käufer:innen empfing. Vermittelt hatten dies Léonce Bénédite sowie Matsukatas Nichte Takeko Kuroki, die zu jener Zeit mit ihrem Mann in Paris lebte und mit dem Künstler verkehrte. Im folgenden Jahr besuchte Matsukata den Maler gleich zweimal in seinem Atelier in Giverny und kaufte eine Vielzahl von Gemälden für seine Sammlung – sowohl direkt bei Monet als auch über Kunsthändler:innen und Sammler:innen in Paris. Zeitweise wuchs sein Bestand auf 34 Werke des Künstlers an.[1] Matsukata bereitete sich sorgfältig auf die Ankäufe vor und der Umfang seiner Erwerbungen zeigt deutlich die Wertschätzung, die er der Kunst Monets entgegenbrachte. Neben dem Œuvre von Rodin stand Monets Schaffen damit im Fokus der Sammlung Matsukata. Obwohl

in Monet's art. Following the devastating Kantō earthquake near Tokyo in 1923, a commemorative exhibition in support of the victims was held on January 1924 in the Galerie Georges Petit in Paris, featuring works by Claude Monet and including around thirty works from Matsukata's collection.[2] Among these were *La route de la ferme Saint-Siméon* (*The Road to the Saint-Siméon Farm*, 1861–64; p. 275) and *Mer agitée à Pourville* (*Stormy Sea at Pourville*, 1897; p. 278).

1 See Masako Kawaguchi and Megumi Jingaoka (eds.), *The Matsukata Collection. Complete Catalogue of the European Art*, Vol. 1, *Paintings* (Tokyo, 2018). Today the inventory in the NMWA Tokyo is clearly decimated.
2 Exh. cat. Galerie Georges Petit, 1924, Paris, Institut national d'histoire de l'art, 16 P192466, quoted in Marianne Mathieu, 'Tadamasa Hayashi, Kōjirō Matsukata und die westlichen Sammler und Sammlungen', in *Japans Liebe zum Impressionismus. Von Monet bis Renoir,* exh. cat. Bundeskunsthalle, Bonn (Munich, 2015), 120–128.

der Impressionismus noch in den 1870er-Jahren von der Kritik missbilligt wurde, entwickelte sich schnell ein Markt, der zu Beginn des 20. Jahrhunderts einen ersten Höhepunkt erreicht hatte. Aufgrund seines Vermögens war Matsukata anders als etwa Karl Ernst Osthaus dennoch in der Lage, in die Kunst Monets zu investieren. Nach dem großen Kantō-Erdbeben rund um Tokio 1923 fand im Januar 1924 in der Pariser Galerie Georges Petit eine Gedenkausstellung als Hilfsaktion für die Opfer des Erdbebens mit Arbeiten von Claude Monet statt – unter den Exponaten befanden sich rund dreißig Werke aus Matsukatas Sammlung.[2] Zu sehen waren damals unter anderem *La route de la ferme Saint-Siméon (Die Straße zum Hof Saint-Siméon,* 1861–1864; S. 275) und *Mer agitée à Pourville (Stürmische See bei Pourville,* 1897; S. 278).

1 Vgl. Masako Kawaguchi und Megumi Jingaoka (Hrsg.), *The Matsukata Collection. Complete Catalogue of the European Art*, Bd. 1, *Paintings*, Tokio 2018. Heute ist der Bestand im NMWA Tokio deutlich dezimiert.
2 Ausst.-Kat. Galerie Georges Petit, 1924, Paris, Institut national d'histoire de l'art, 16 P192466, nach Marianne Mathieu, „Tadamasa Hayashi, Kōjirō Matsukata und die westlichen Sammler und Sammlungen", in: *Japans Liebe zum Impressionismus. Von Monet bis Renoir,* Ausst.-Kat. Bundeskunsthalle, Bonn, München 2015, S. 120–128.

275

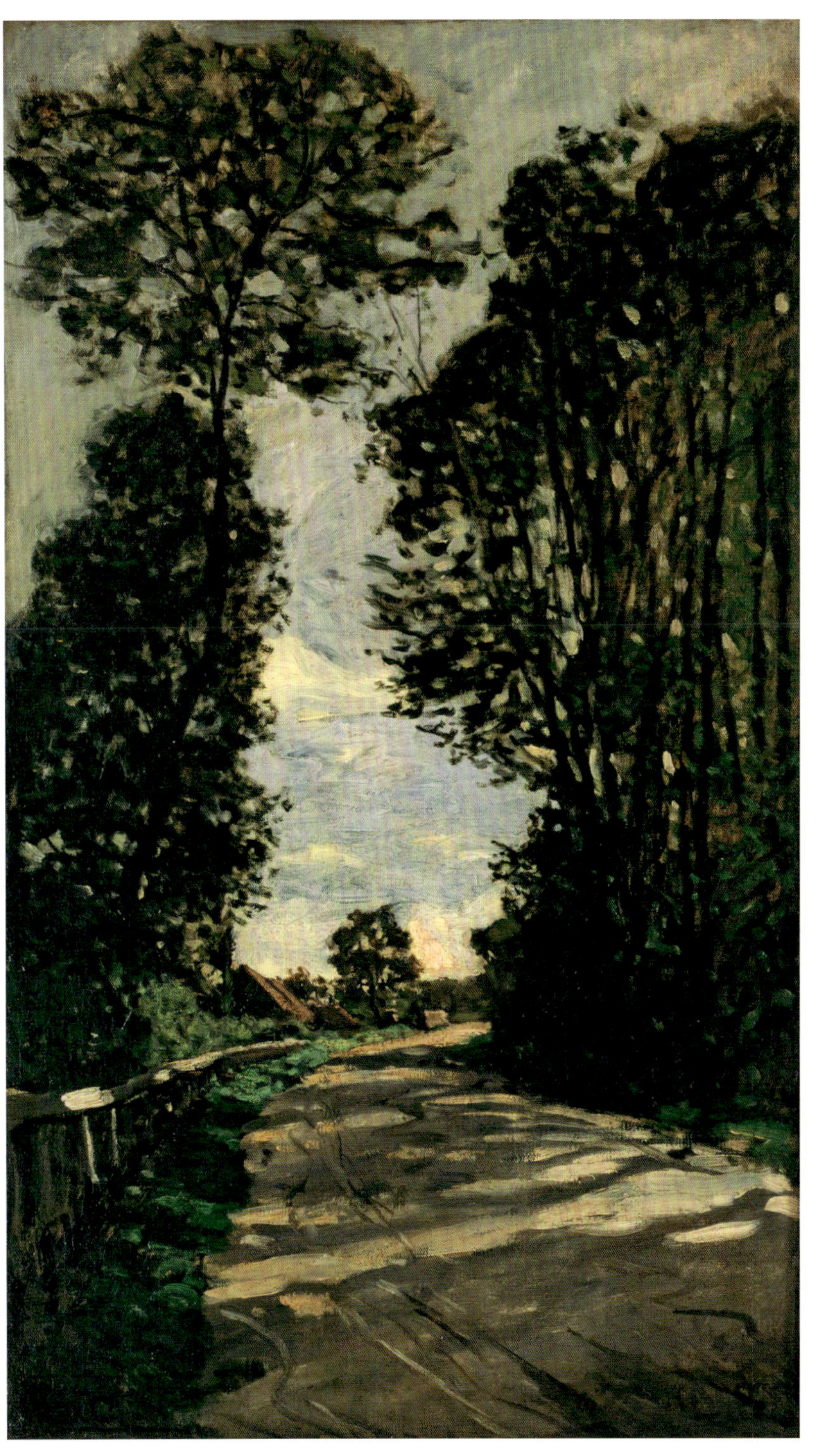

Claude Monet
La route de la ferme Saint-Siméon, 1861–1864
The National Museum of Western Art, Tokyo

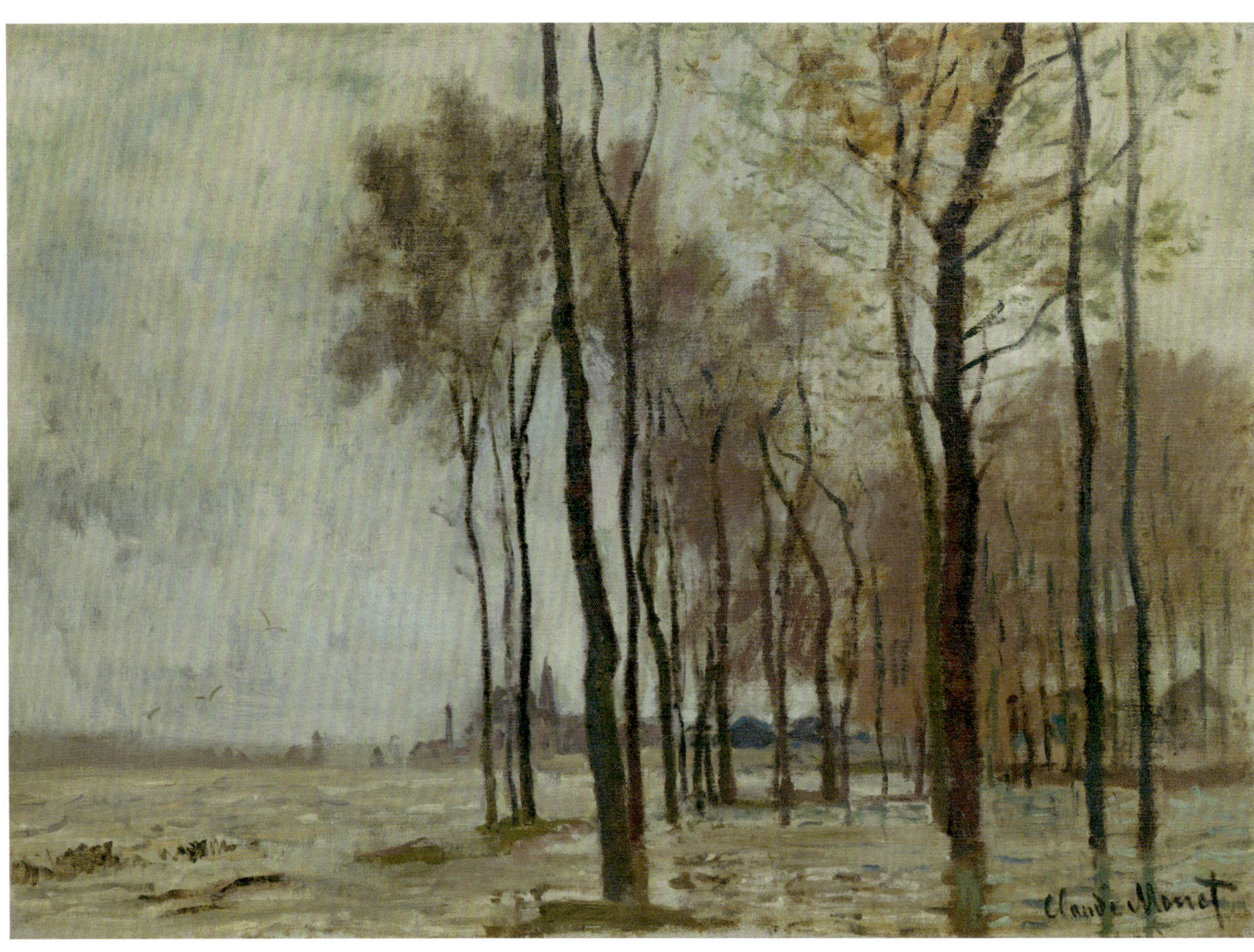

Claude Monet
L'inondation, 1872/73
Artizon Museum, Ishibashi Foundation, Tokyo

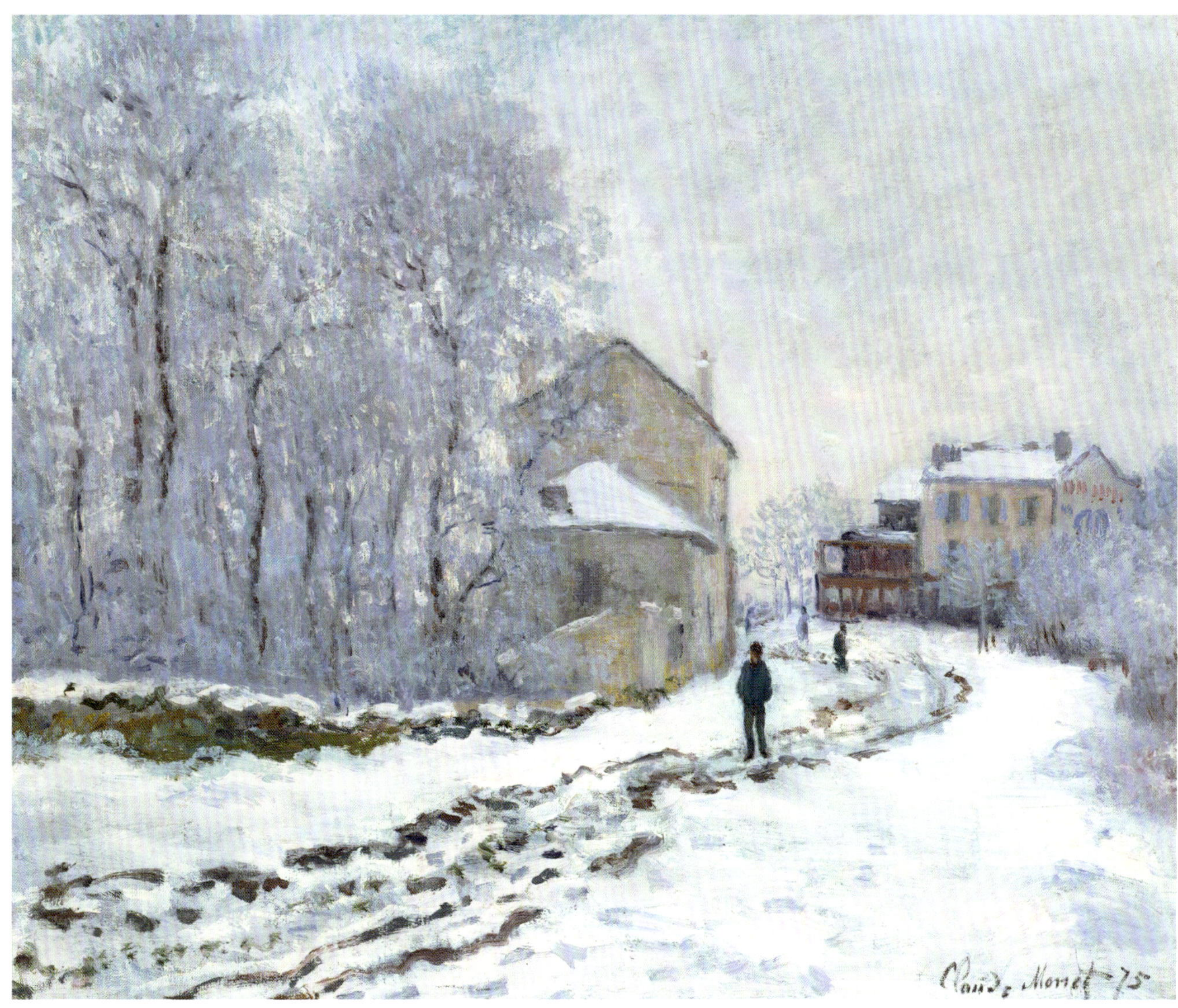

Claude Monet
Neige à Argenteuil, 1875
The National Museum of Western Art, Tokyo

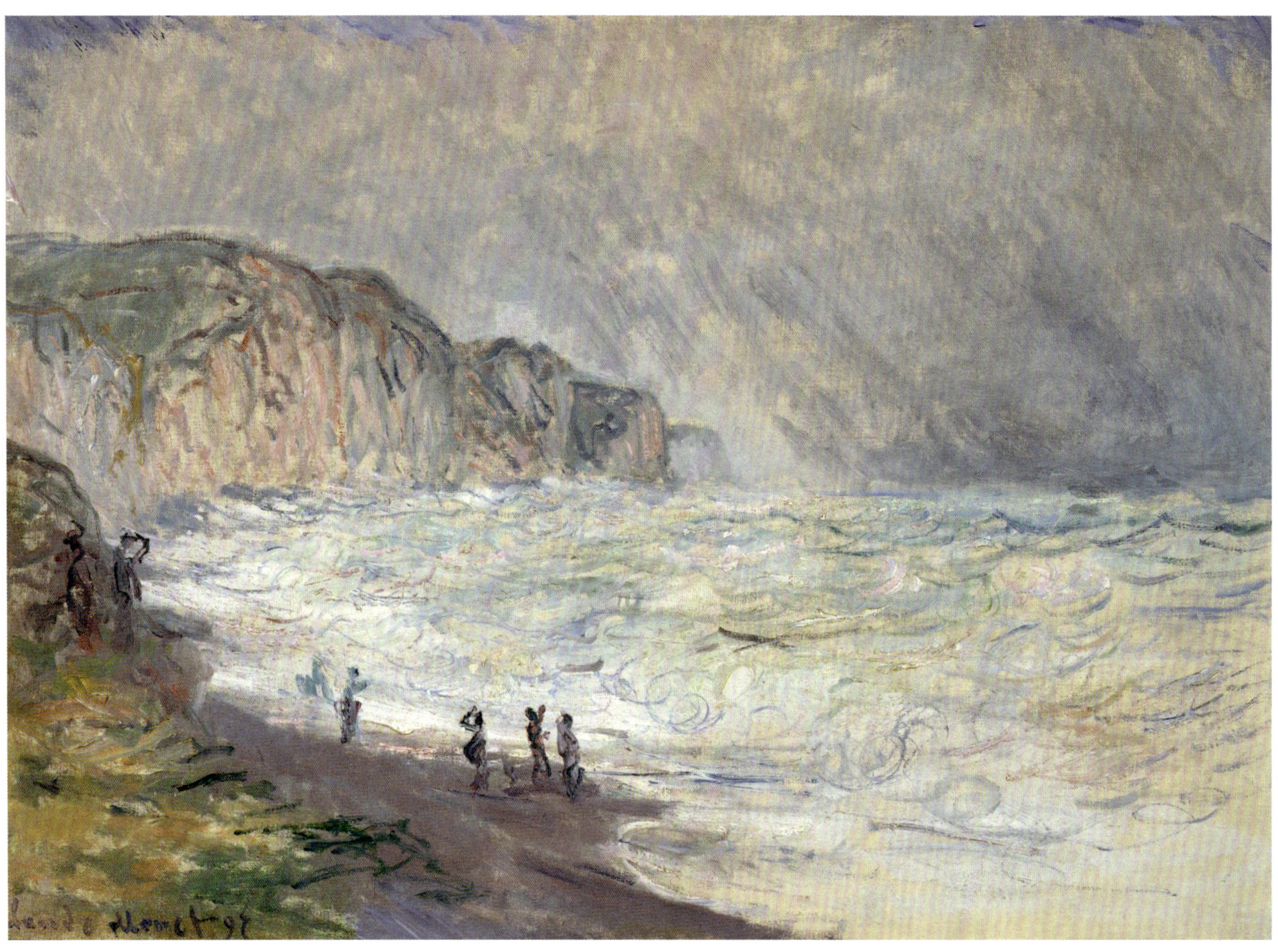

Claude Monet
Mer agitée à Pourville, 1897
The National Museum of Western Art, Tokyo

279

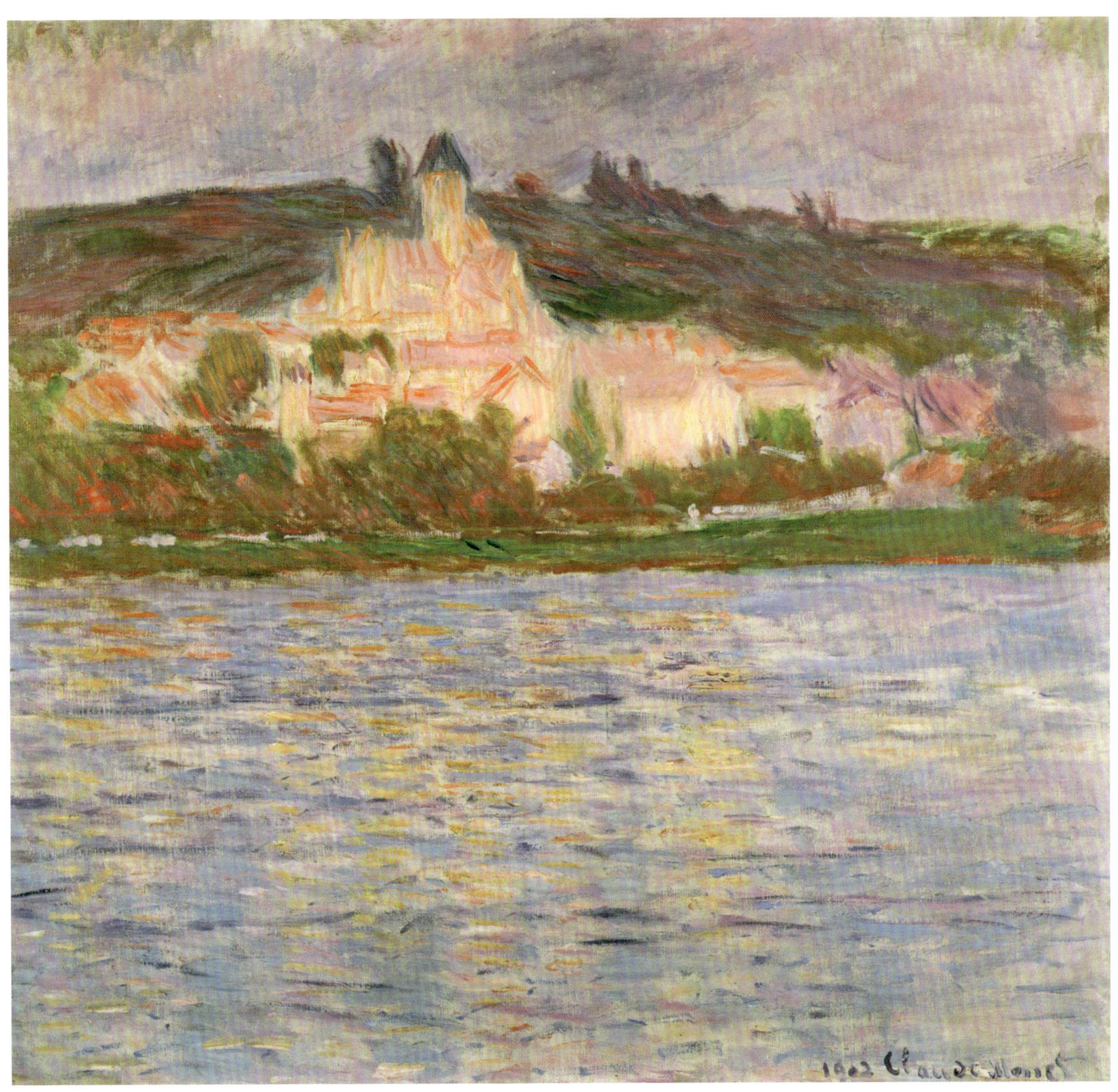

Claude Monet
Vétheuil, 1902
The National Museum of Western Art, Tokyo

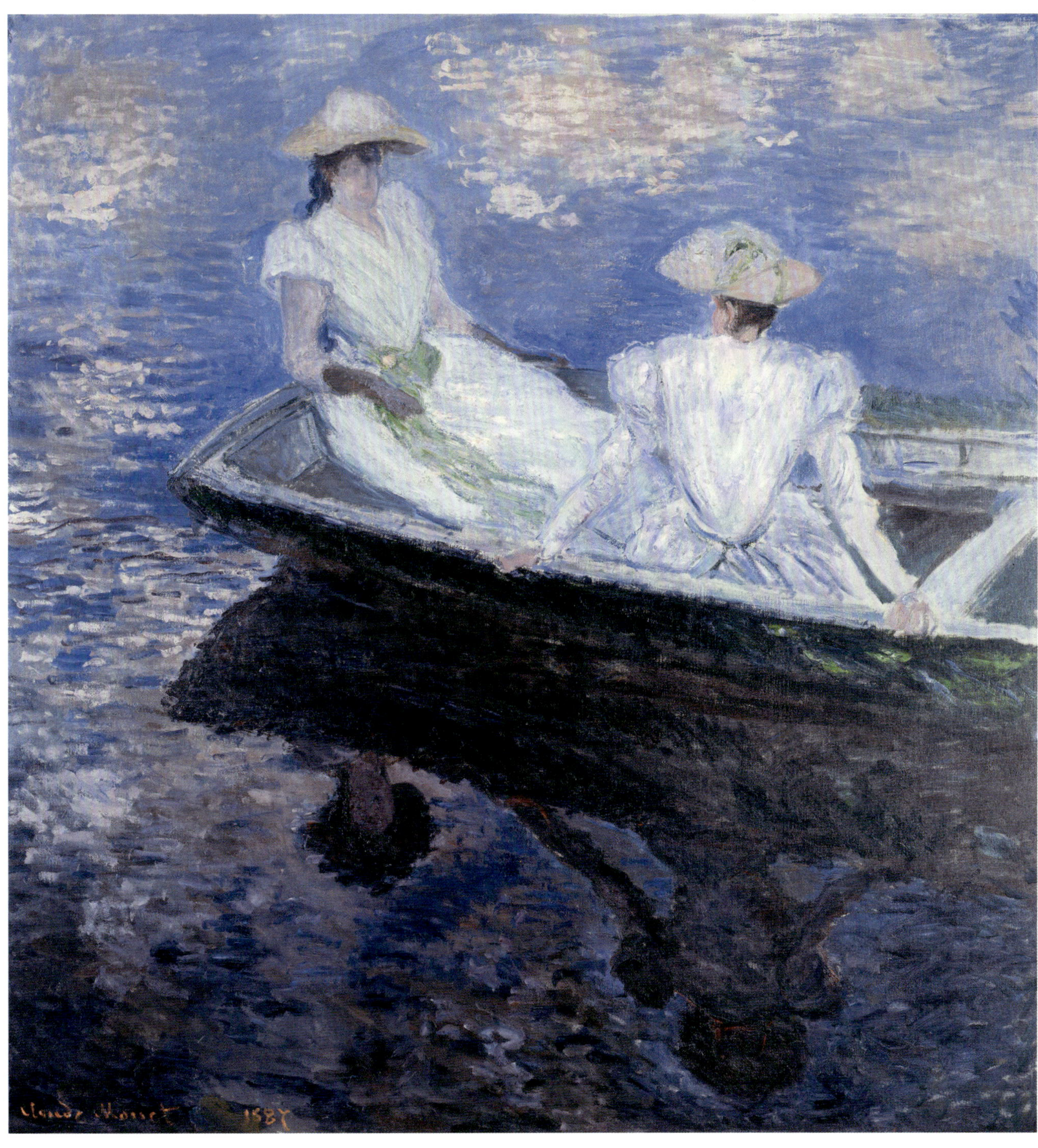

Claude Monet
Sur le bateau (Jeunes filles en barque), 1887
The National Museum of Western Art, Tokyo

282

Claude Monet
Le portail, brouillard matinal, 1894
Museum Folkwang, Essen

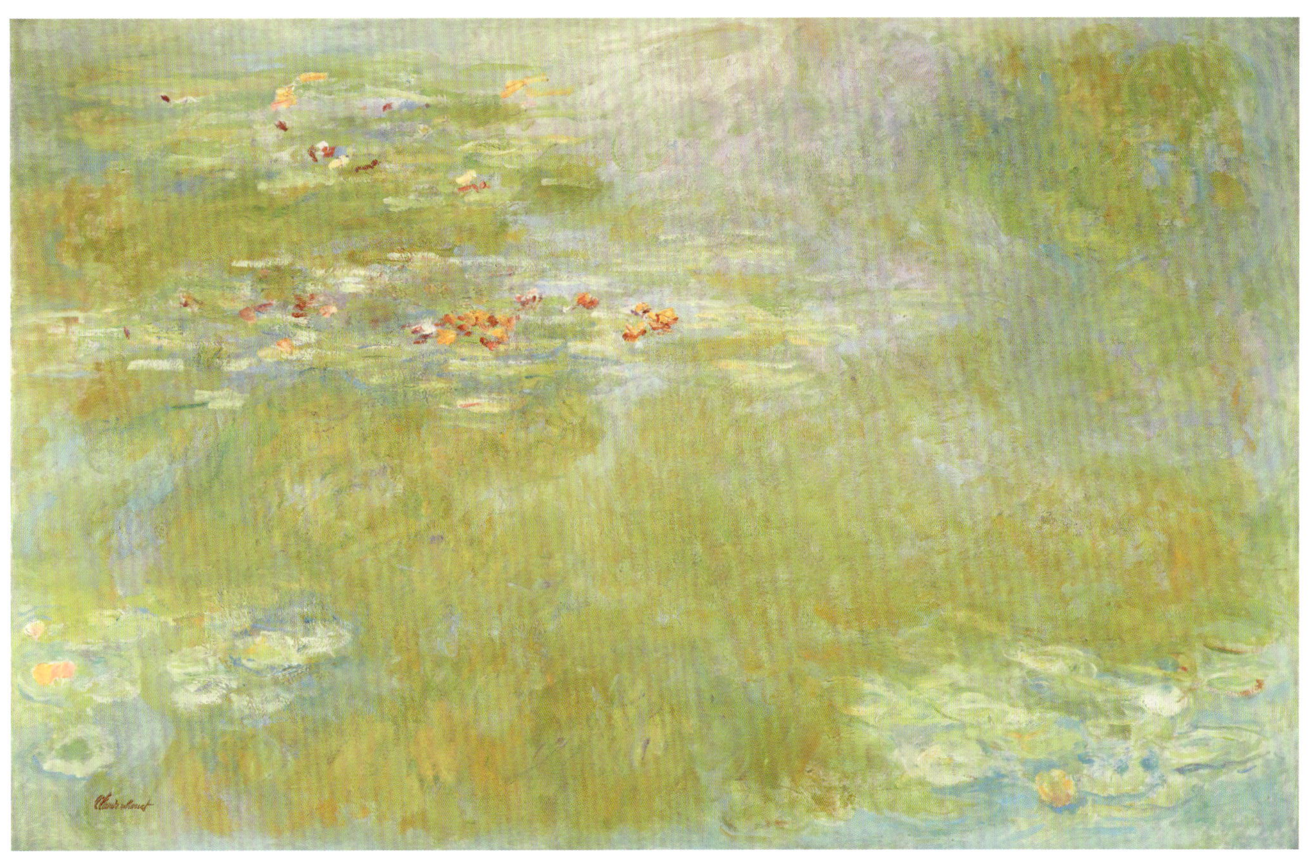

Claude Monet
Le bassin aux nymphéas, ca. 1916
Museum Folkwang, Essen

DER GROSSE BILDERSAAL
IN HAGEN

THE GREAT PICTURE HALL
IN HAGEN

The Museum Folkwang building in Hagen, which opened in 1902, housed the varied collections that its founder, Karl Ernst Osthaus assembled between about 1897 and 1920. As one can see from surviving installation views, the presentation changed several times over the years, but the underlying concept remained the same: the museum followed the history of the evolution of art, as Osthaus saw it, over three floors.

The light-protected basement level included the natural history objects that had been the initial focus of the collection to which Osthaus had intended to devote his museum.[1] They made up the formal foundation on which the art and craft collections on the ground floor were built. These ranged from ancient Egypt, classical antiquity and Islamic art through medieval art to the eighteenth century. At the centre of the sequence of rooms, the vestibule already referred in an exemplary way to what the collector saw as the highest stages of the development of art on the upper floor. An elaborately designed flight of stairs, which also served as a display area, led to the upper galleries and the East Asian cabinet. A source of inspiration for many subsequent Western artists, it formed the pathway to the Painting Hall, the core of the museum. Beneath a large skylight, situated in the interior architecture designed by Henry van de Velde, this was where the main works from the painting collection were brought together. Marble fireplaces in the corners of the room were disguised by semi-circular glass cases containing sculptures and craftwork, fitting in with the idea of a *Gesamtkunstwerk* or 'total work of art'.

Der 1902 eröffnete Bau des Museum Folkwang in Hagen nahm die weitgefächerten Sammlungen auf, die Museumsgründer Karl Ernst Osthaus von etwa 1897 bis 1920 zusammentrug. Wie sich unter anderem an den erhaltenen Installationsansichten zeigt, änderte sich die Präsentation über die Jahre mehrfach, das zugrunde liegende Konzept aber blieb gleich: Über drei Etagen zeichnete das Museum die Entwicklungsgeschichte der Kunst nach, so wie Osthaus sie verstand.

Das lichtgeschützte Kellergeschoss umfasste die naturkundlichen Objekte, die der erste Sammlungsfokus waren, dem Osthaus sein Museum hatte widmen wollen.[1] Sie bildeten das Formfundament, auf dem die Kunst- und Gewerbesammlungen im Erdgeschoss aufbauten. Diese reichten vom alten Ägypten, der klassischen Antike und der islamischen Kunst über das Mittelalter bis ins 18. Jahrhundert. Im Zentrum der Raumfolge verwies das Vestibül bereits exemplarisch auf die im Verständnis des Sammlers höchsten Entwicklungsstufen der Kunst im Obergeschoss. Ein kunstvoll gestalteter Treppenaufgang, der ebenfalls als Präsentationsfläche genutzt wurde, führte auf die Empore, wo sich das Ostasiatische Kabinett anschloss. Dieses bildete – als Inspirationsquelle für die nachfolgenden westlichen Künstler:innen – den Übergang zum Bildersaal, dem Kernstück des Museums. Unter einem großen Oberlicht in der von Henry van de Velde entworfenen Innenarchitektur wurden hier die Hauptwerke aus dem Bestand der Malerei versammelt. Marmorkamine in den Raumecken waren mit verglasten Rundschränken zur Präsentation von Skulpturen und Kleinkunst verkleidet

If at first works like Pierre-Auguste Renoir's *Lise – La femme à l'ombrelle* (*Lise with a Parasol,* 1867; p. 209) and Vincent van Gogh's *La moisson* (*The Wheatfield behind St Paul's Hospital with a Reaper,* 1889; p. 315) were hung next to battle scenes and landscape paintings by the Düsseldorf School, amongst other things, over time the display changed according to Osthaus's purchasing habits into a 'French gallery'. In 1911, Osthaus explained this key position of French modern art in his collection: 'Almost all the important problems of those years were picked up and solved in France, and German artists as diverse as Feuerbach and Leibl have gratefully acknowledged that they owe no less to Paris than they do to themselves.'[2] Osthaus, therefore, oriented the Picture Hall increasingly towards the post-Impressionist art of France, which in turn became the model for German art – particularly Expressionism that in the years after the First World War was displayed in subsequent cabinets. The transformation into a 'French gallery' was finally complete by 1920.

1 Cf. Herta Hesse-Frielinghaus, "Folkwang 1. Teil", in idem et al., *Karl Ernst Osthaus. Leben und Werk* (Recklinghausen, 1971), 133.
2 Karl Ernst Osthaus, 'Antwort auf den "Protest deutscher Künstler" (1911),' in Rainer Stamm (ed.), *Reden und Schriften: Folkwang, Werkbund, Arbeitsrat,* Kontext. Schriftenreihe für Kunst, Kunsterziehung und Kulturpädagogik, 3, (Cologne, 2002), 43.

und fügten sich in die Idee eines Gesamtkunstwerks ein.

Hingen im Bildersaal anfangs neben Werken wie Pierre- Auguste Renoirs *Lise – La femme à l'ombrelle (Lise mit dem Sonnenschirm,* 1867; S. 209) und Vincent van Goghs *La moisson (Die Ernte, Kornfeld mit Schnitter,* 1889; S. 315) unter anderem noch Schlachten- und Landschaftsbilder der Düsseldorfer Schule, wandelte sich die Präsentation mit der Zeit entsprechend Osthaus' Ankaufsverhalten zu einer „Franzosengalerie". 1911 erläuterte Osthaus diese Schlüsselstellung der französischen Moderne: „Es sind nahezu alle wichtigen Probleme dieser Jahre in Frankreich aufgegriffen und gelöst worden, und so verschiedene deutsche Künstler wie Feuerbach und Leibl haben dankbar anerkannt, daß sie Paris nicht weniger wie sich selbst verdanken."[2] So richtete Osthaus den Bildersaal mehr und mehr auf die post-impressionistische Kunst Frankreichs aus, die wiederum der deutschen Kunst – insbesondere dem Expressionismus, der spätestens in den Jahren nach dem Ersten Weltkrieg in den folgenden Kabinetten präsentiert wurde – zum Vorbild wurde. 1920 schließlich war die Umwandlung zur „Franzosengalerie" komplett.

1 Vgl. Herta Hesse-Frielinghaus, „Folkwang 1. Teil", in: dies. u. a., *Karl Ernst Osthaus. Leben und Werk,* Recklinghausen 1971, S. 133.
2 Karl Ernst Osthaus, Antwort auf den „Protest deutscher Künstler" (1911), in: *Karl Ernst Osthaus. Reden und Schriften. Folkwang, Werkbund, Arbeitsrat (Kontext. Schriftenreihe für Kunst, Kunsterziehung und Kulturpädagogik,* 3), hrsg. und komm. von Rainer Stamm, Köln 2002, S. 43.

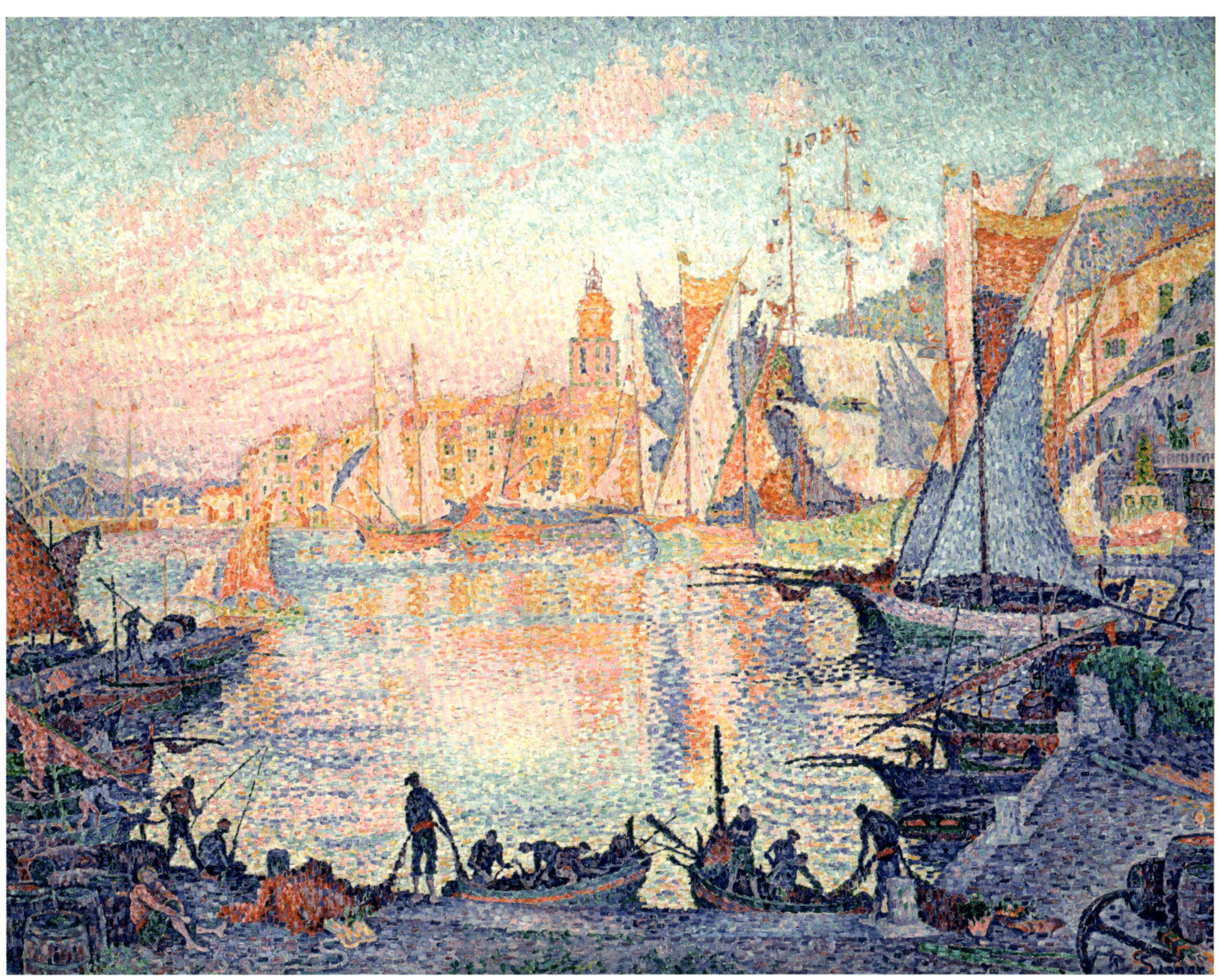

Paul Signac
Le port de Saint-Tropez, 1901/02
The National Museum of Western Art, Tokyo

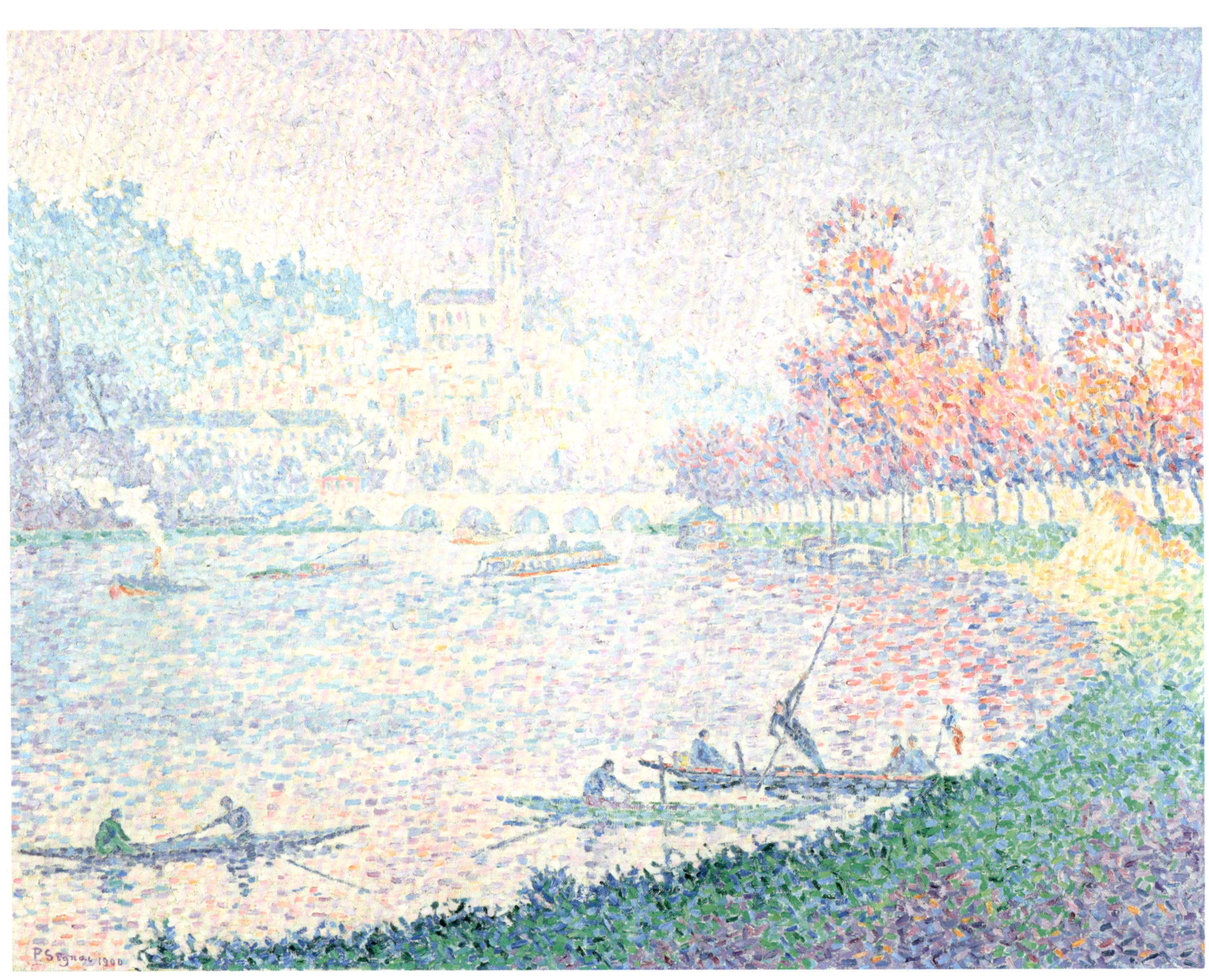

Paul Signac
Saint-Cloud, 1900
Museum Folkwang, Essen

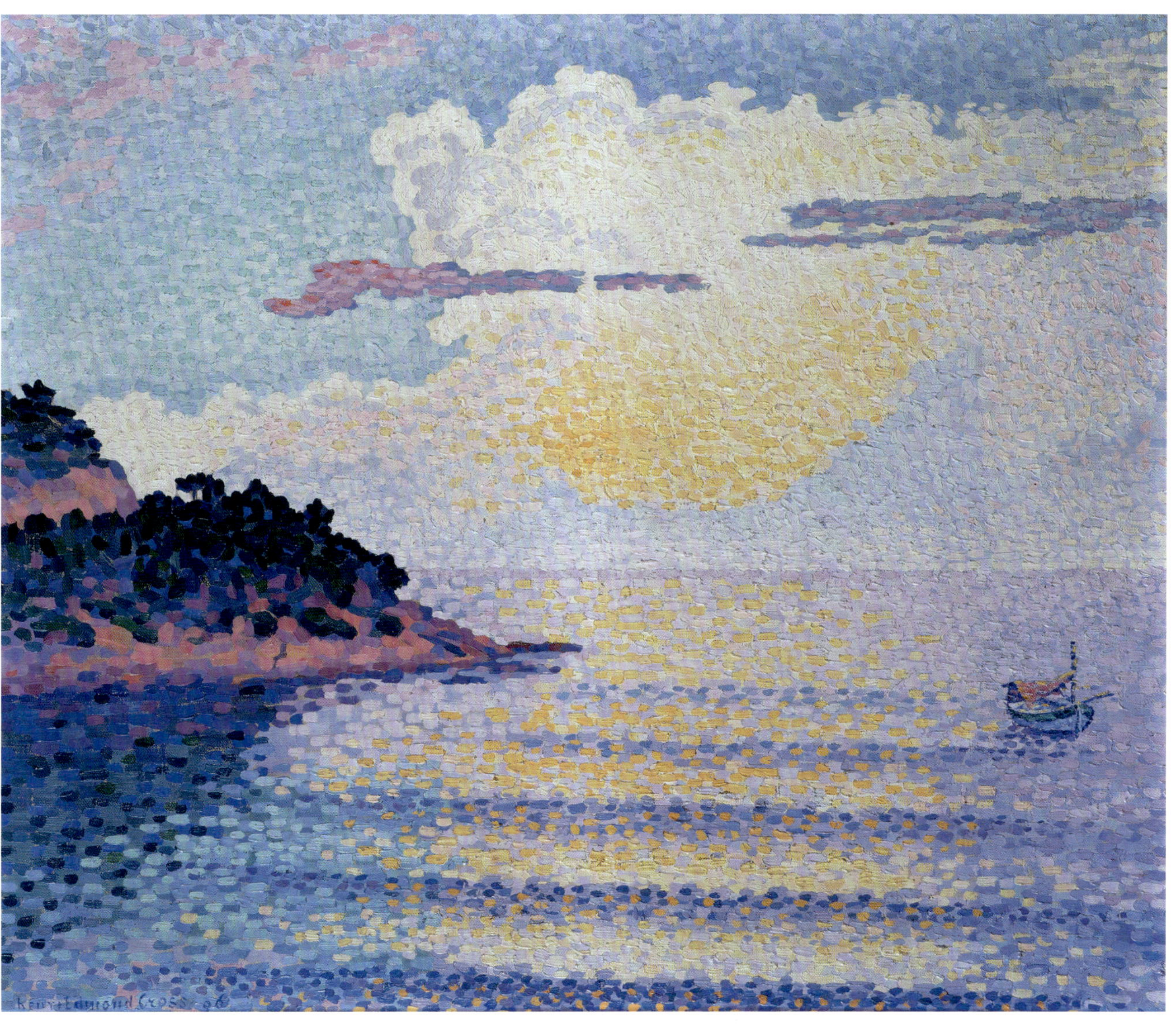

Henri Edmond Cross
Coucher de soleil sur la mer, 1896
Wallraf-Richartz-Museum & Fondation Corboud, Köln

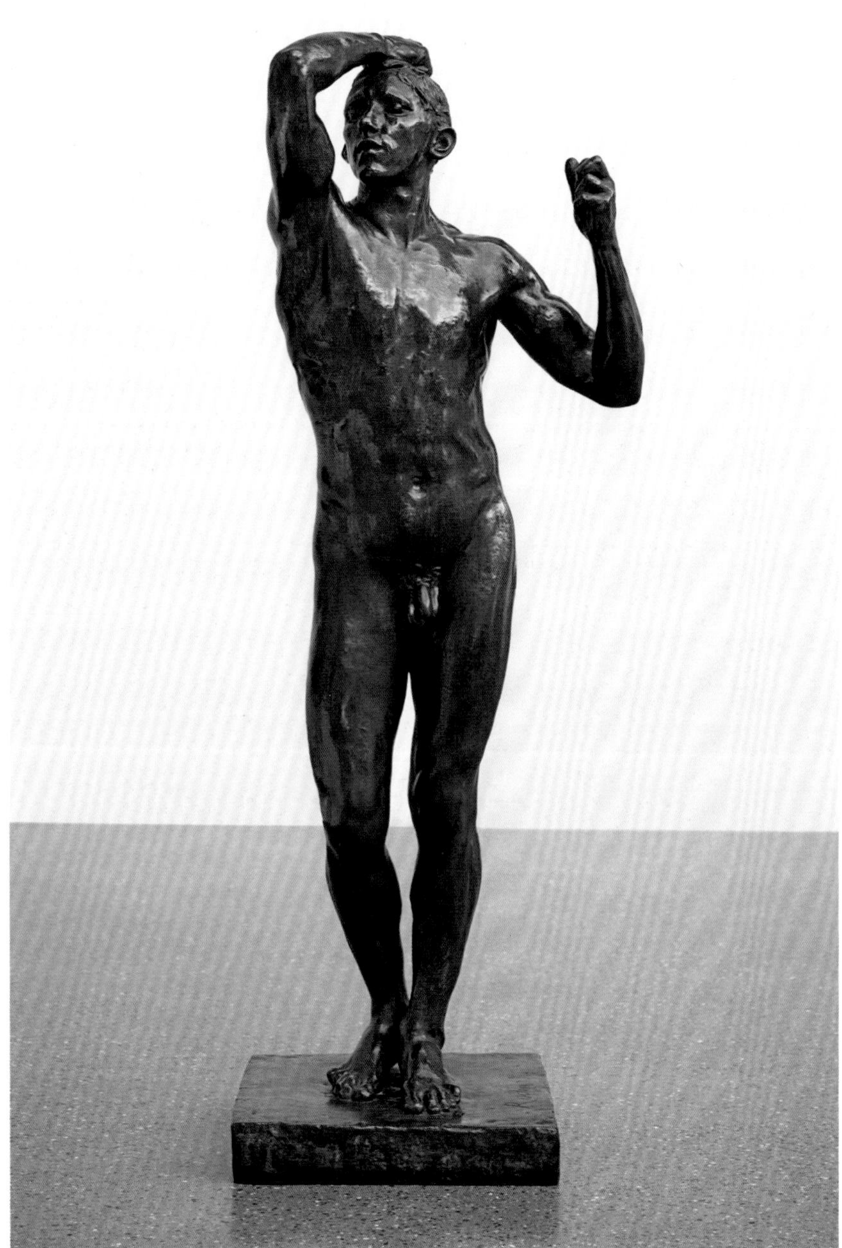

Auguste Rodin
L'âge d'airain, ca. 1880
(Guss: spätestens 1904 | cast: 1904 at the latest)
Museum Folkwang, Essen

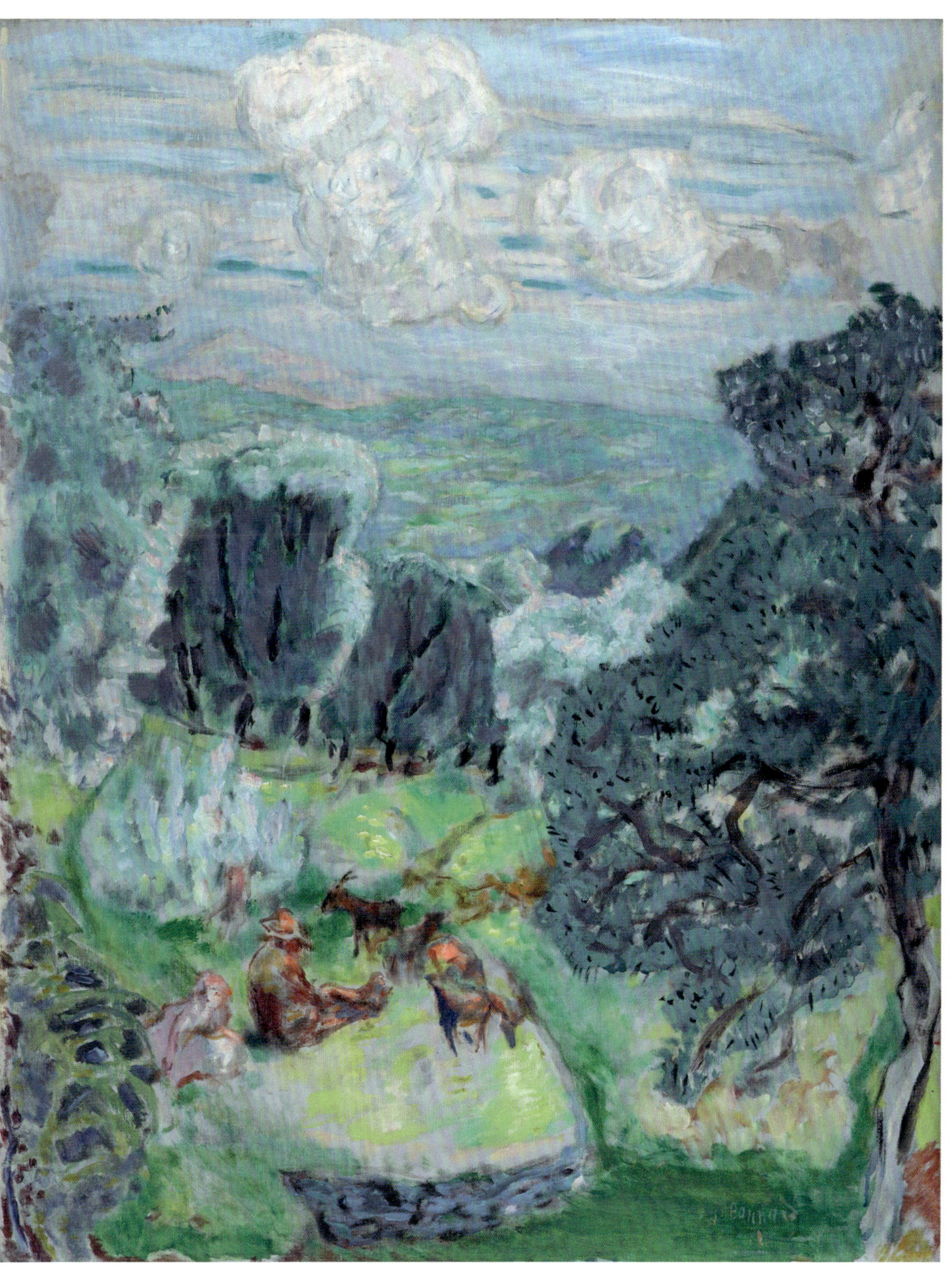

Pierre Bonnard
L'oliveraie, 1912
Museum Folkwang, Essen

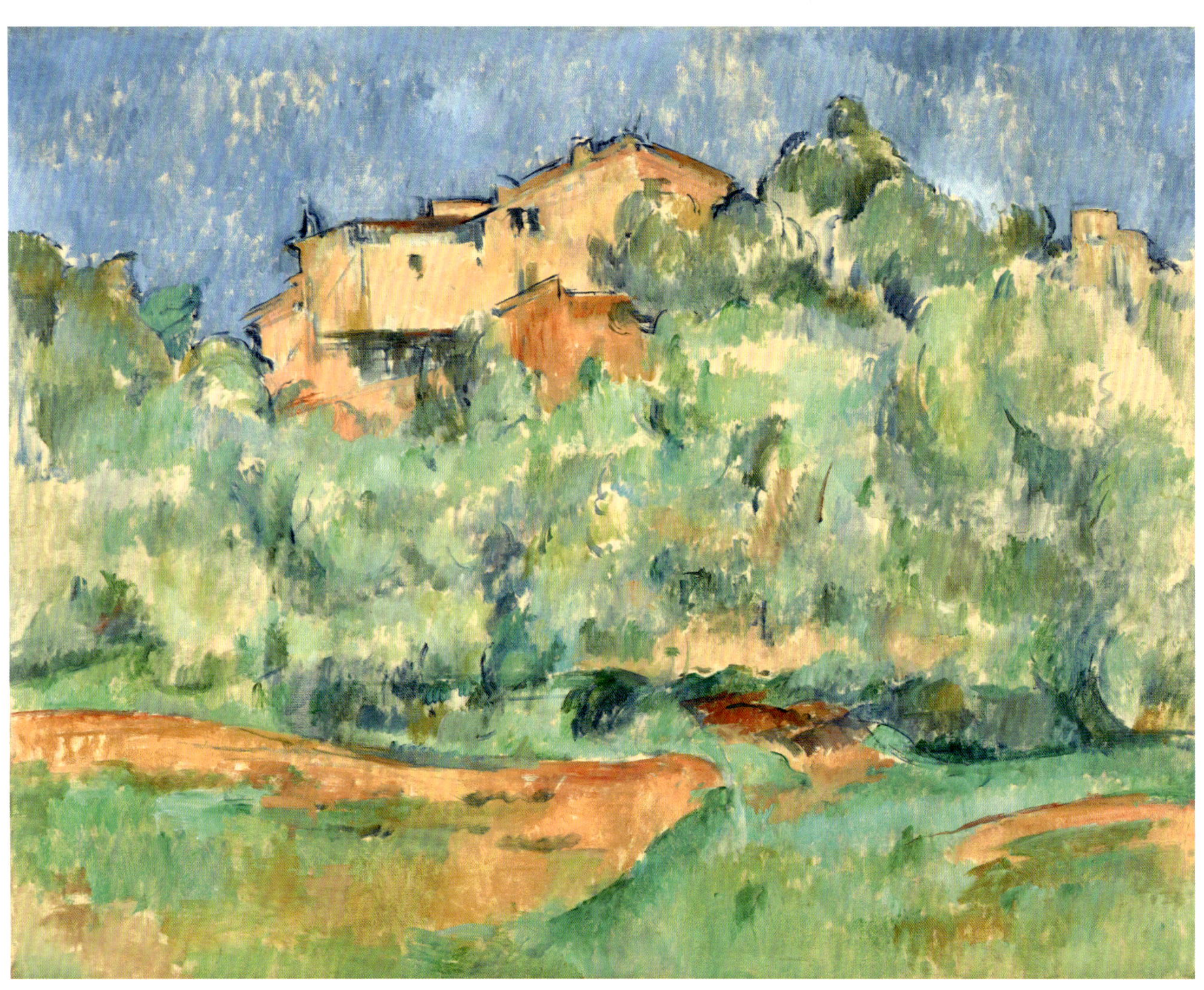

292

Paul Cézanne
Maison de Bellevue et pigeonnier, ca. 1890–1892
Museum Folkwang, Essen

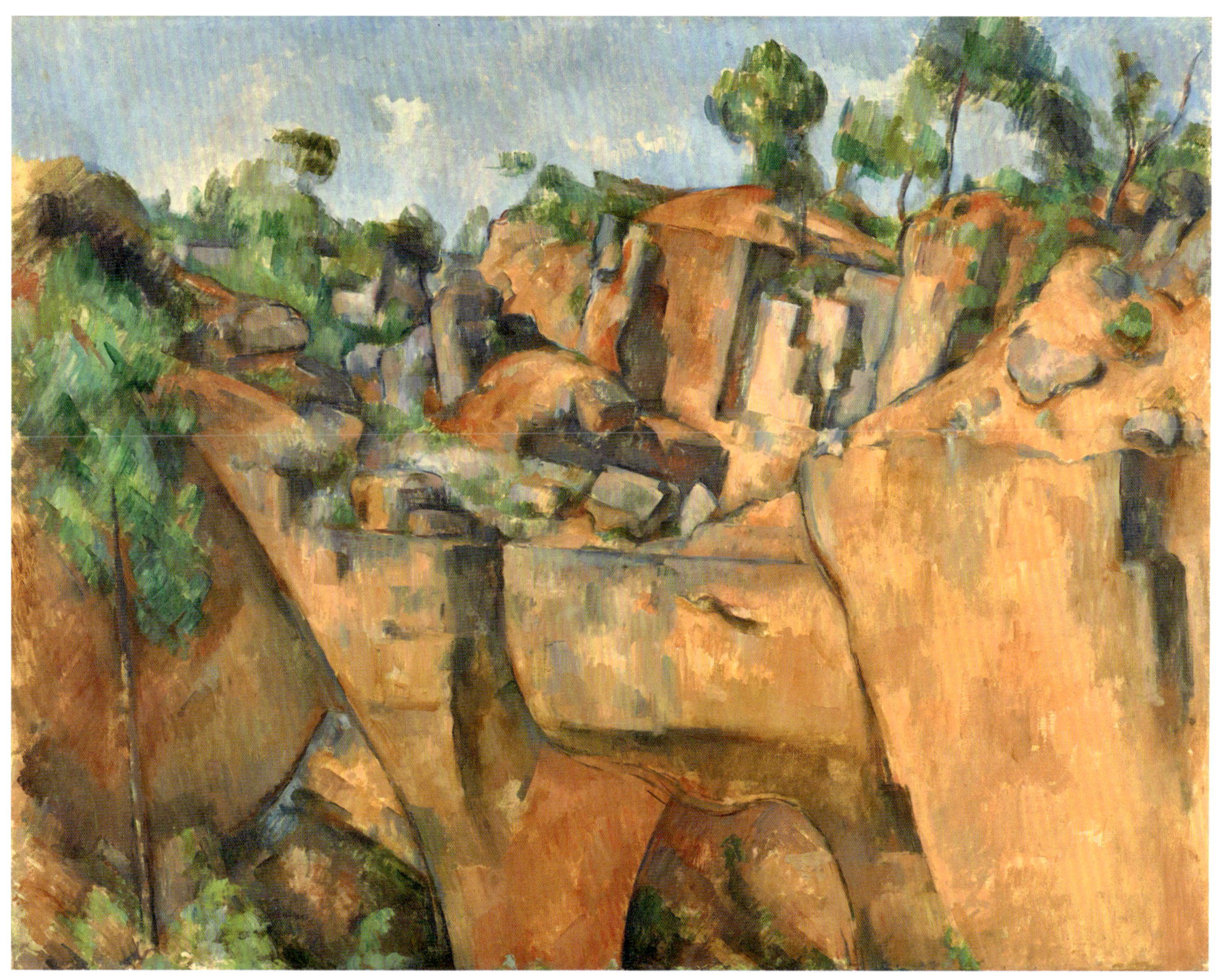

Paul Cézanne
La carrière de Bibémus, ca. 1895
Museum Folkwang, Essen

SIGNAC UND DIE ABKEHR
VOM IMPRESSIONISMUS

SIGNAC AND THE MOVE
AWAY FROM IMPRESSIONISM

At the opening of the Museum Folkwang in Hagen in 1902, Paul Signac's painting *Saint-Cloud (The Seine at Saint-Cloud,* 1900; p. 288) was already hanging in the painting gallery. Karl Ernst Osthaus had bought the painting on the advice of Henry van de Velde, making him one of the first to include so-called Neo-Impressionism in his collection before it had been recognized in large parts of the German and even the French art world. A few years previously, Richard Muther wrote in his *History of Painting in the 19th Century* of 'a certain monotony' in this artistic trend, and the permanent secretary of the Berlin Academy of the Arts, Wolfgang von Oettingen, was still warning against the purchase of Neo-Impressionist paintings in 1903. At the same time a powerful advocacy of the new art developed among a group of collectors and museum personnel in Germany, who organized exhibitions in cities such as Weimar (Harry Graf Kessler, 1903) and Krefeld (Friedrich Deneken, 1902 and 1907).

Neo-Impressionism, also known as 'Division-ism', was a painting style established by Georges Seurat in 1884. Its strict technique, based on simultaneous contrasts, was based on scientific discoveries made in the field of optics, and thus represented a move away from Impression-ism's impulsive and intuitive painting style. After Seurat's early death Signac became the group's spokesman and chief representative. Beginning in 1896, he wrote the book *From Eugène Delacroix to Neo-Impressionism*[3], which should not be seen solely as a manifesto, but rather connected Neo-Impressionist art with a painterly tradition. Signac became a model for many

Bereits bei der Eröffnung des Museum Folkwang in Hagen 1902 hing Paul Signacs Gemälde *Saint-Cloud (Die Seine bei Saint-Cloud,* 1900; S. 288) in der Gemäldegalerie.[1] Karl Ernst Osthaus hatte das Bild auf Anraten Henry van de Veldes gekauft und damit schon früh den sogenannten Neo-Impressionismus in seine Sammlung integriert, ehe dieser in weiten Teilen der deutschen und auch französischen Kunstwelt anerkannt war. Wenige Jahre zuvor noch schrieb Richard Muther in seiner *Geschichte der Malerei im 19. Jahrhundert* von „mancher Monotonie" dieser Kunstrichtung und der Ständige Sekretär der Akademie der Künste Berlin, Wolfgang von Oettingen, warnte gar noch 1903 davor, neo-impressionistische Bilder zu kaufen.[2] Gleichzeitig entwickelte sich eine starke Befürwortung der neuen Kunst durch eine Gruppe von Sammler:innen und Museumsleuten in Deutsch-land, die Ausstellungen in Städten wie Weimar (Harry Graf Kessler, 1903) und Krefeld (Friedrich Deneken, 1902 und 1907) organisierten.

Der Neo-Impressionismus oder auch Divisio-nismus war eine Malweise, die George Seurat 1884 begründet hatte. Seine strenge, auf Simultan-kontrasten beruhende Technik basierte auf wissenschaftlichen Erkenntnissen aus der Optik und war somit eine Abkehr von der impulsiven und intuitiven Malweise des Impressionismus. Nach dem frühen Tod von Seurat wurde Signac zum Wortführer und Hauptvertreter der Gruppe. Er verfasste ab 1896 das Buch *Von Eugène Delacroix zum Neo-Impressionismus*[3], das nicht nur als Manifest zu verstehen ist, sondern die neo-impressionistische Kunst an eine malerische

Tradition band. Signac wurde für viele Künstler:innen zum Vorbild, so etwa Henri Matisse, Vincent van Gogh und Paul Gauguin. Osthaus kaufte von 1901 bis 1914 kontinuierlich Gemälde und Grafiken des Künstlers an. Zum zehnten Jubiläum 1912 schenkte Signac dem Museum ein Aquarell als Ehrengabe (S. 297). Die Kunst der Neo-Impressionisten definierte zusammen mit der van Goghs und Gauguins im Museum Folkwang den Beginn der Moderne und machte Osthaus zu einem Sammler moderner Kunst.

artists, including Henri Matisse, Vincent van Gogh and Paul Gauguin. Between 1901 and 1914, Osthaus frequently bought paintings and graphic works by the artist. For its tenth anniversary in 1912, Signac gave the museum a watercolour as a gift of honour (p. 297). The art of the Neo-Impressionists, along with that of artists like Van Gogh and Gauguin, defined the beginning of modernism in the Museum Folkwang and established Osthaus as a collector of modern art.

1   Vgl. Herta Hesse-Frielinghaus, „Folkwang 1. Teil", in: dies. u. a., *Karl Ernst Osthaus. Leben und Werk*, Recklinghausen 1971, S. 134.
2   Richard Muther, *Geschichte der Malerei im 19. Jahrhundert*, Bd. 3, München 1894, S. 43; vgl. Harry Graf Kessler, *Über den Kunstwert des Neo-Impressionismus. Eine Erwiderung*, 1903, https://www.projekt-gutenberg.org/kessler/aufreden/chap003.html [zuletzt aufgerufen am 8.9.2021].
3   Erschienen zunächst 1898 in einzelnen Artikeln in der *Revue blanche*, 1899 als Buch unter dem Titel *D'Eugène Delacroix au néo-impressionisme*.

1   Cf. Herta Hesse-Frielinghaus, 'Folkwang 1. Teil', in idem et al., *Karl Ernst Osthaus. Leben und Werk* (Recklinghausen, 1971), 134.
2   Richard Muther, *Geschichte der Malerei im 19. Jahrhundert*, vol. 3 (Munich, 1894), 43; cf. Harry Graf Kessler, *Über den Kunstwert des Neo-Impressionismus. Eine Erwiderung* (1903), https://www.projekt-gutenberg.org/kessler/aufreden/chap003.html [last accessed 11.10.2021].
3   First published in 1898 in single articles in the *Revue blanche,* and as a book in 1899 under the title *D'Eugène Delacroix au néo-impressionisme*.

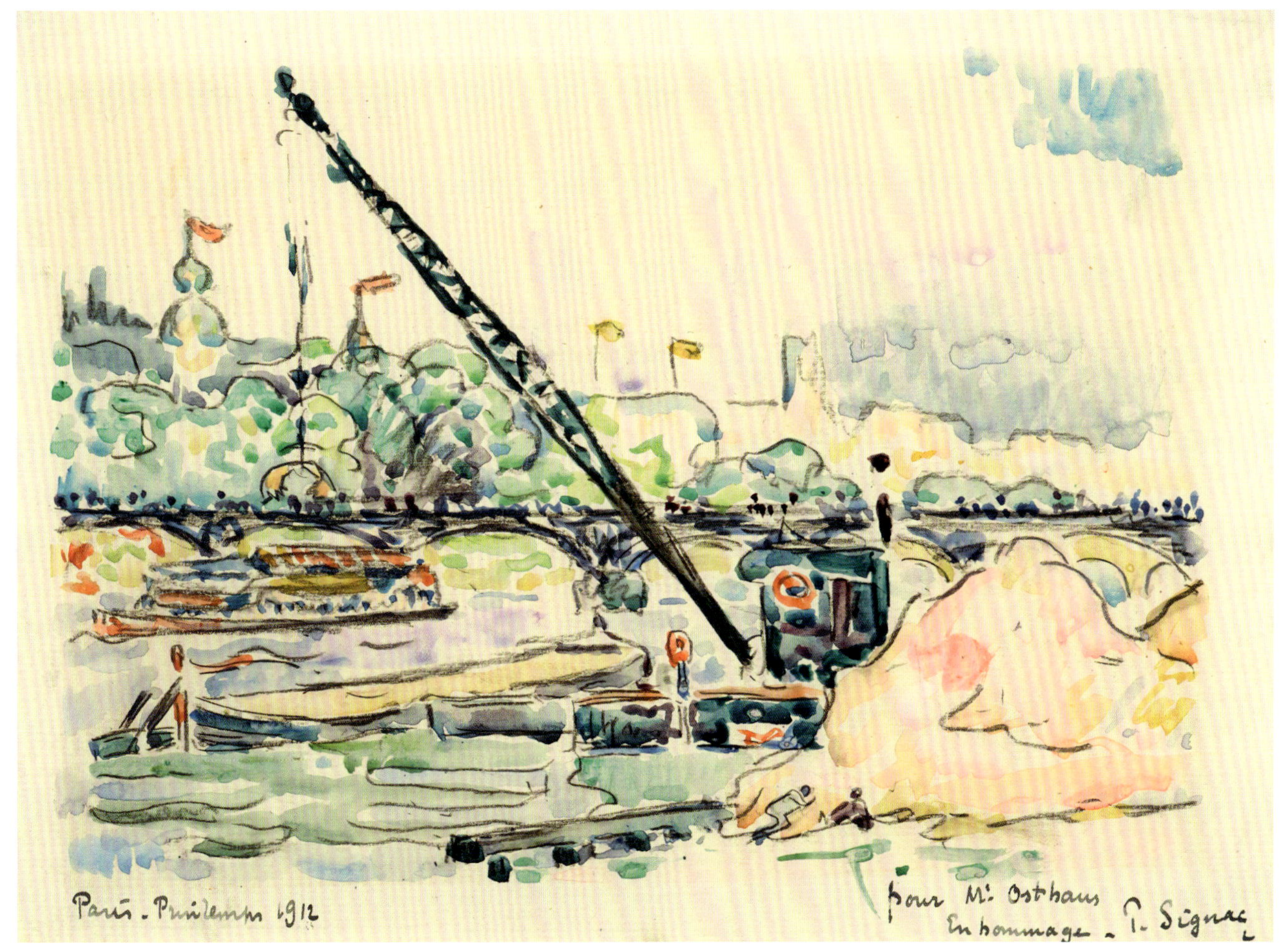

Paul Signac
Seinebrücke, 1912
Museum Folkwang, Essen

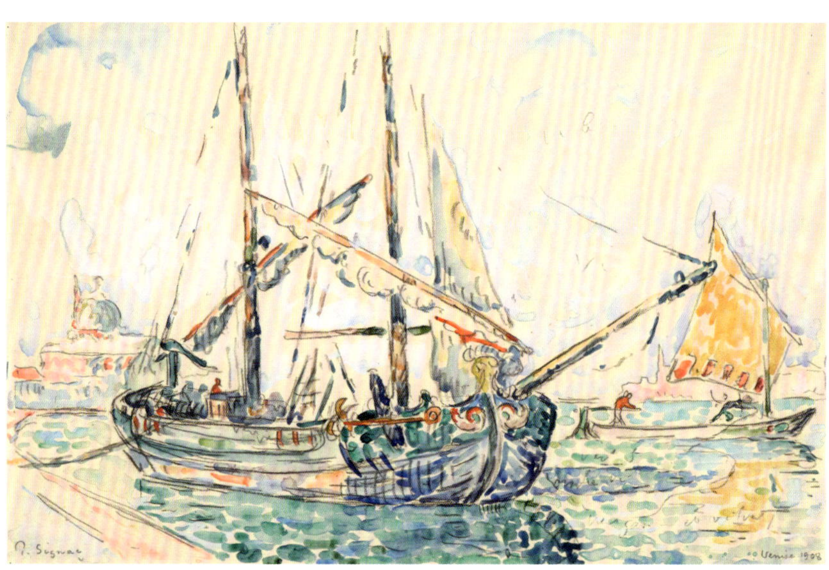

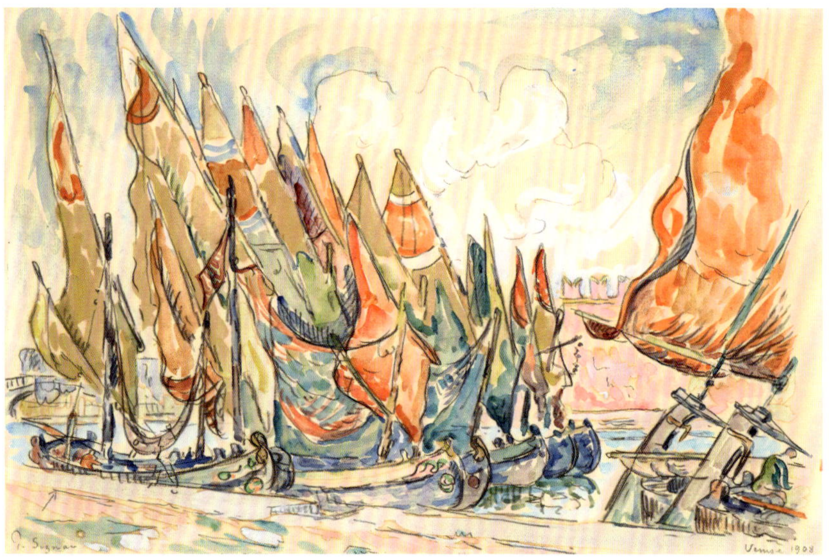

Paul Signac
Venise. Quai à la Giudecca, 1908
Museum Folkwang, Essen

Paul Signac
Segelschiffe bei Venedig, 1908
Museum Folkwang, Essen

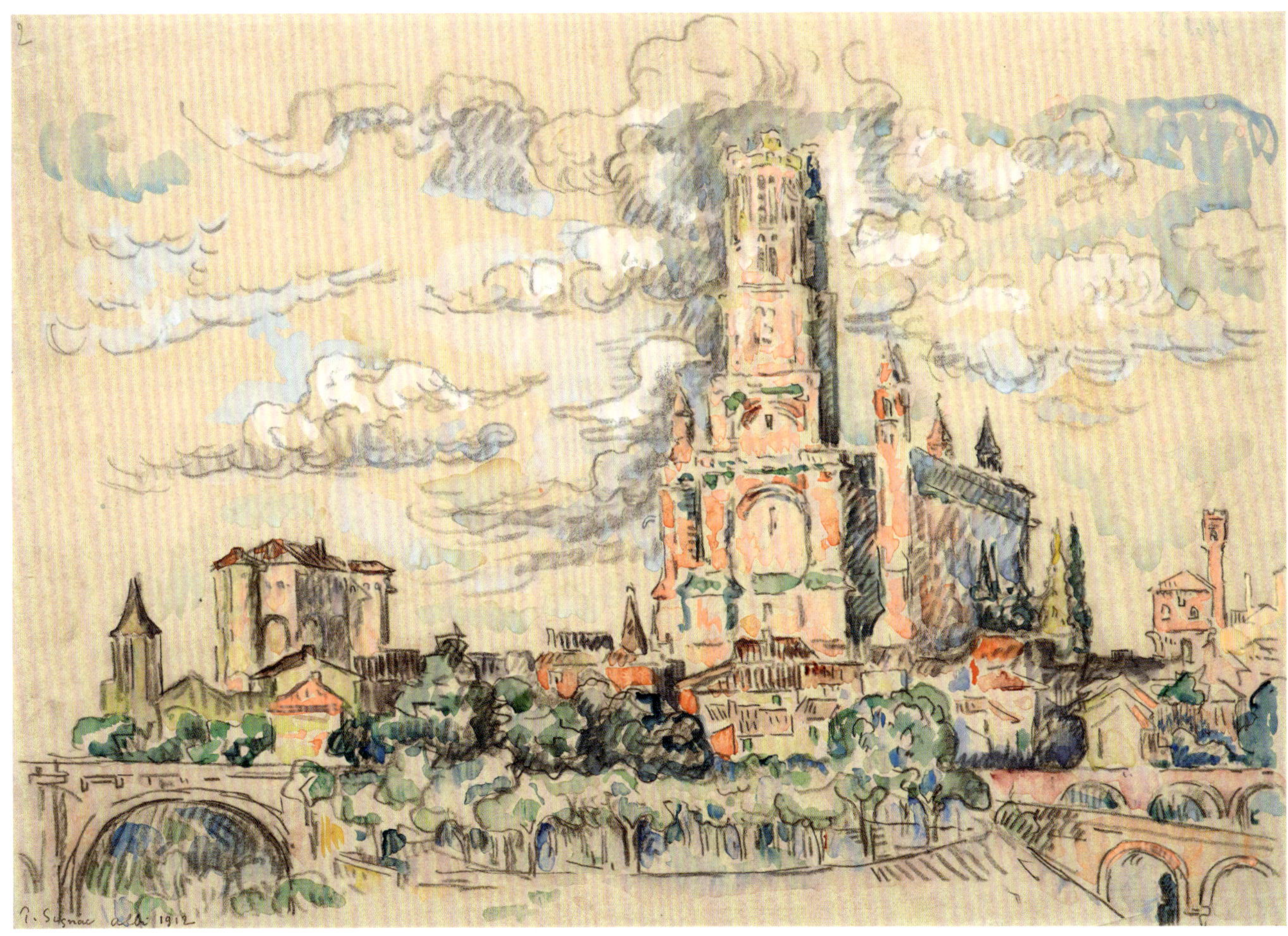

Paul Signac
Kathedrale von Albi, 1912
Museum Folkwang, Essen

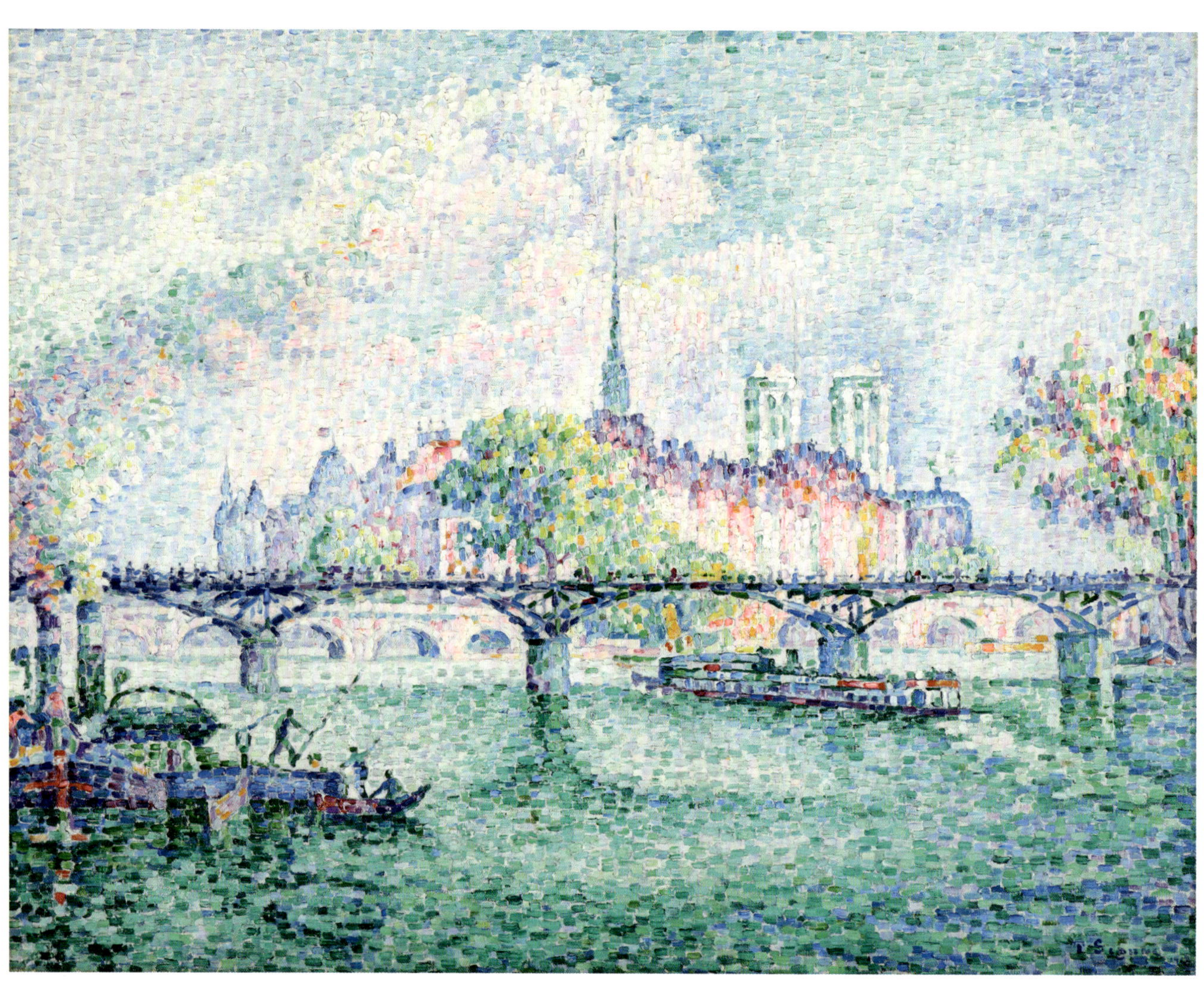

Paul Signac
Le Pont des Arts, 1912/13
Museum Folkwang, Essen

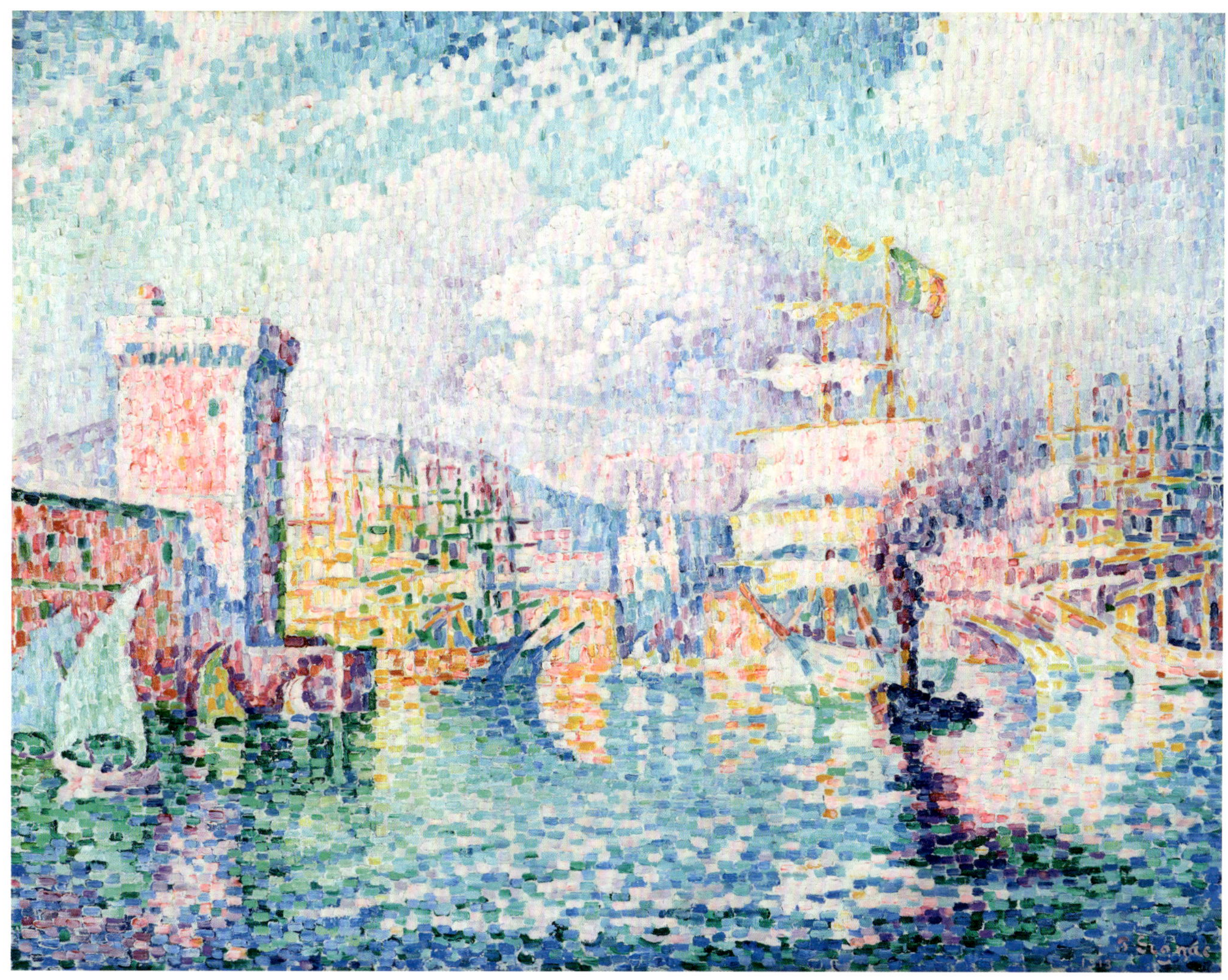

Paul Signac
La Tour Rose, Marseille, 1913
Museum Folkwang, Essen

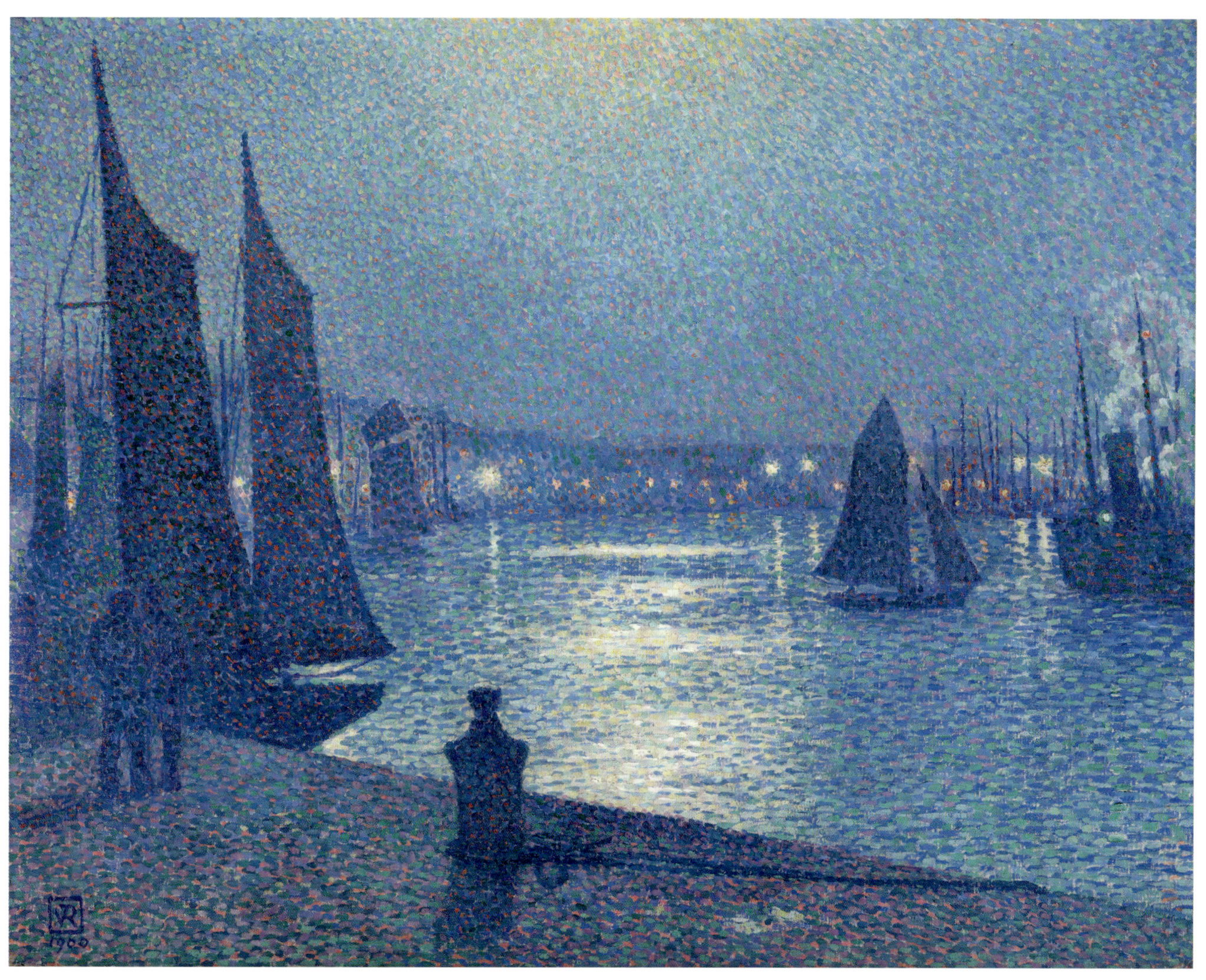

303

Théo van Rysselberghe
Claire de lune à Boulogne-sur-Mer, 1900
Museum Folkwang, Essen

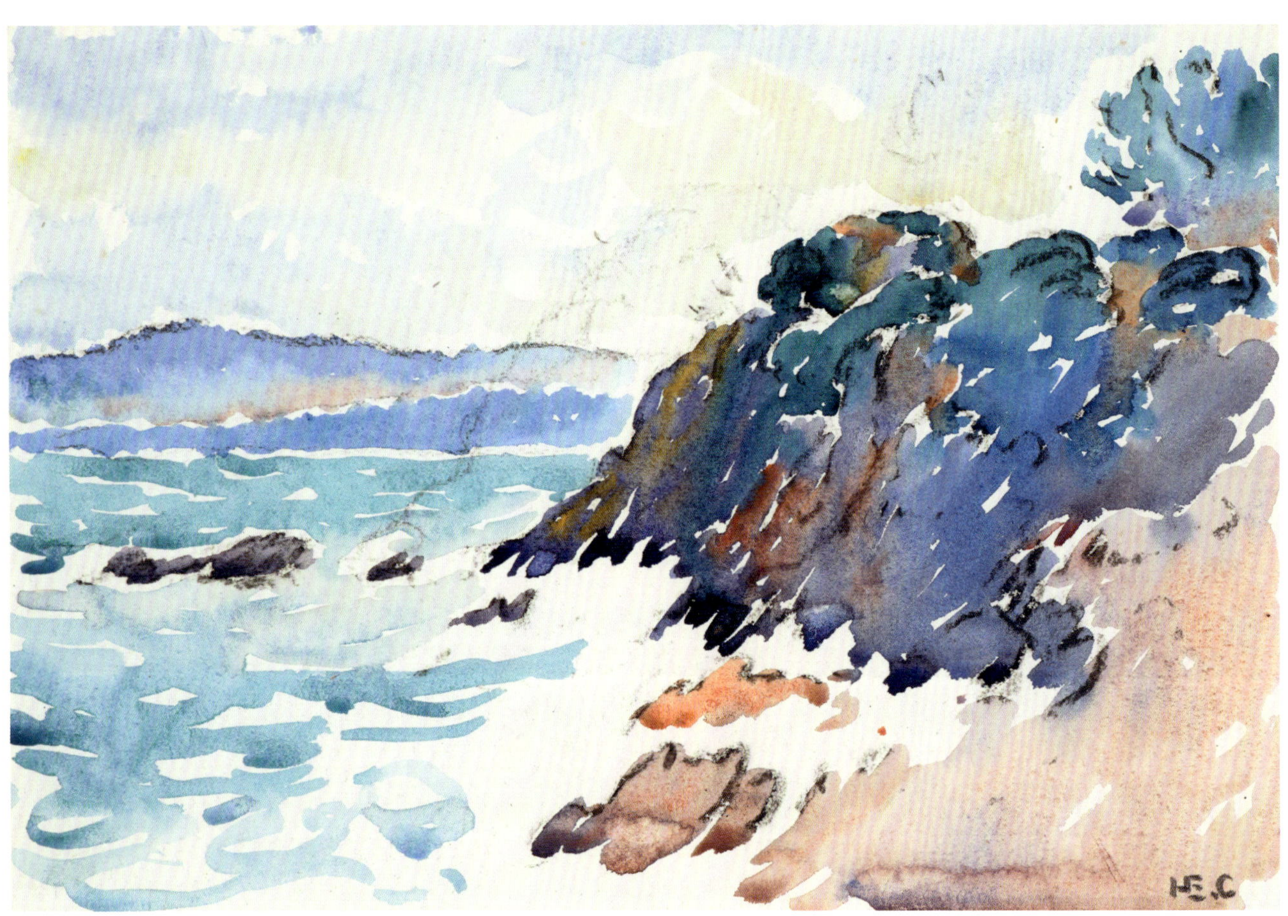

304

Henri Edmond Cross
Les vagues (Le rocher)
Museum Folkwang, Essen

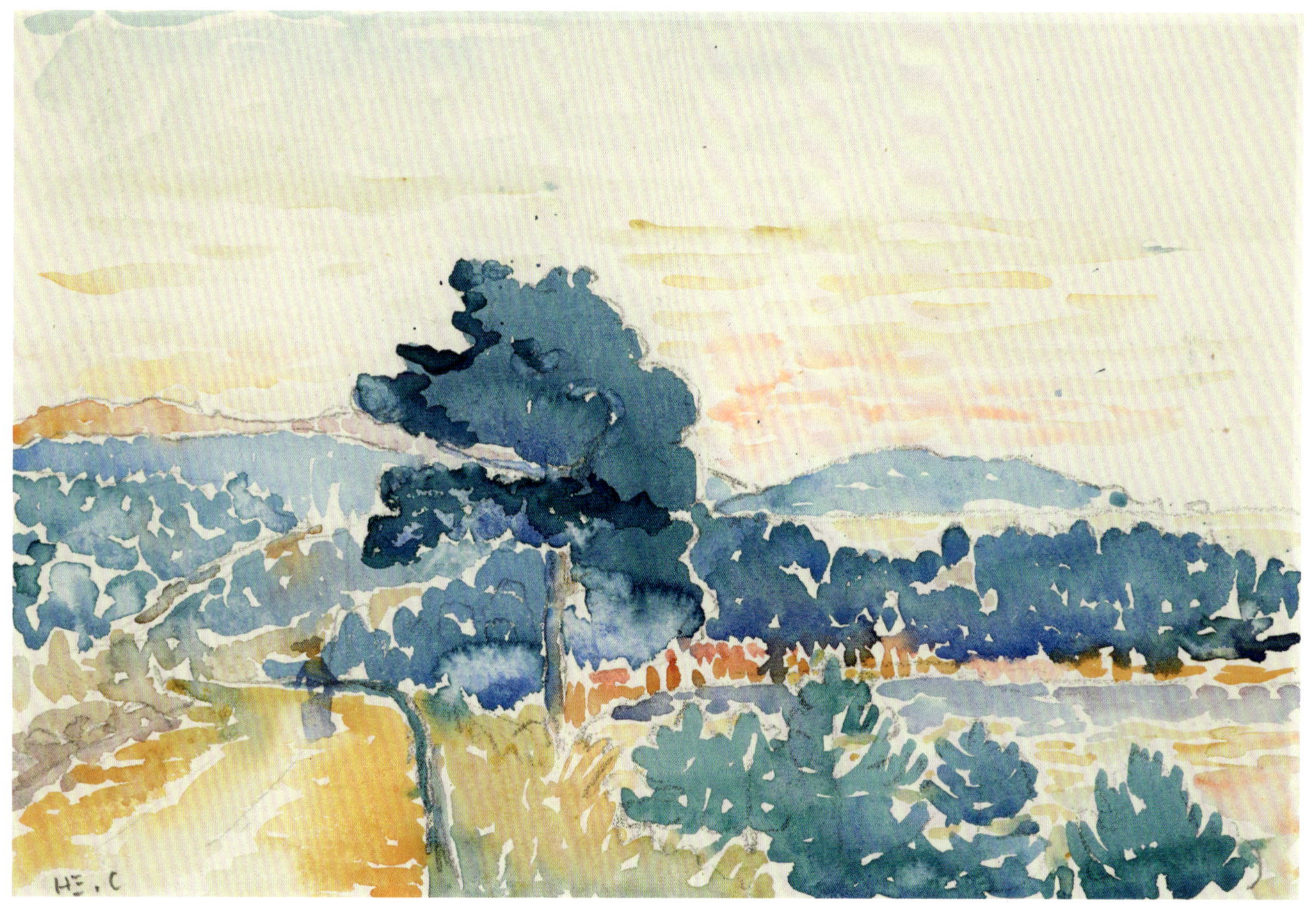

305

Henri Edmond Cross
La promeneuse
Museum Folkwang, Essen

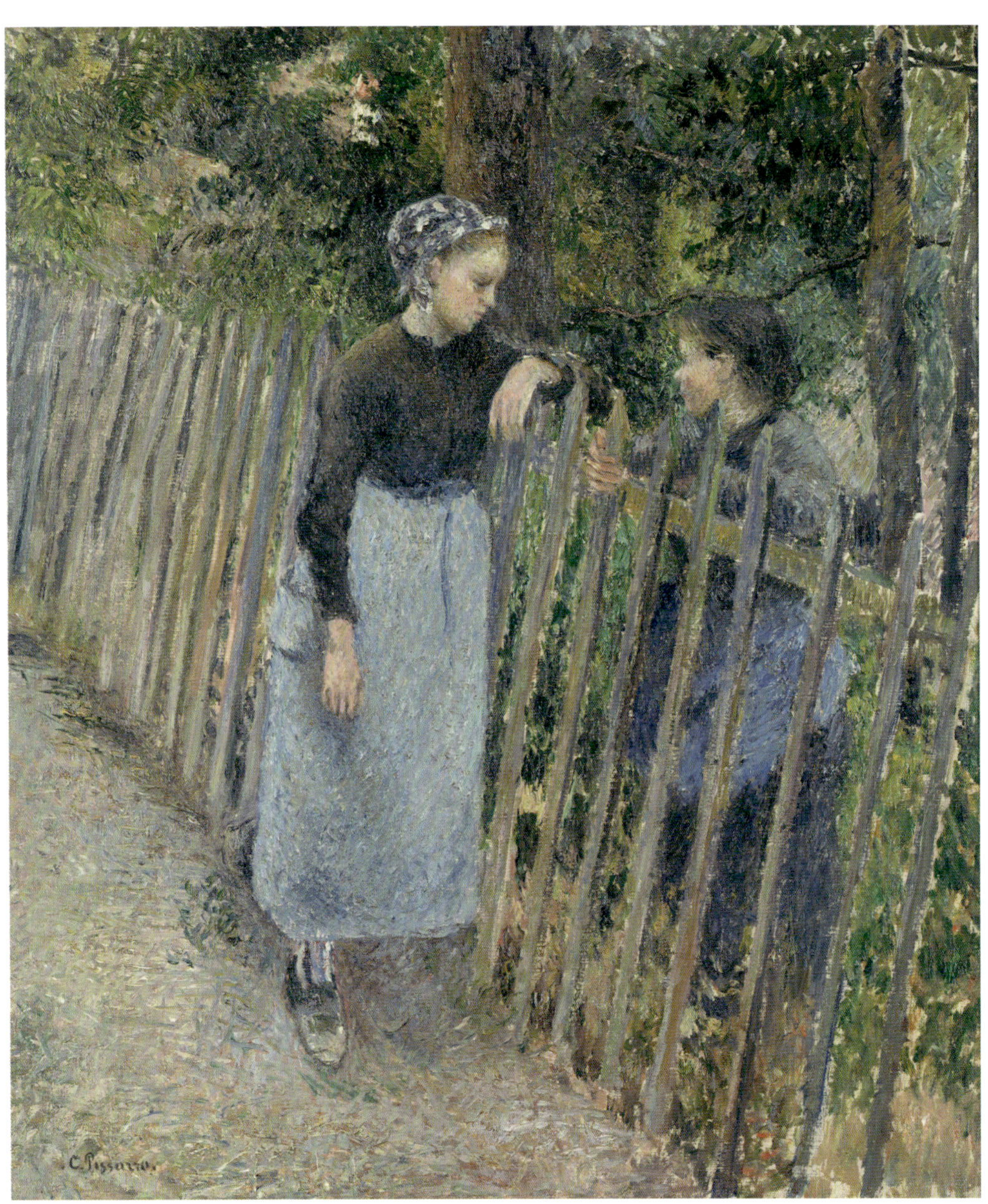

Camille Pissarro
La conversation, ca. 1881
The National Museum of Western Art, Tokyo

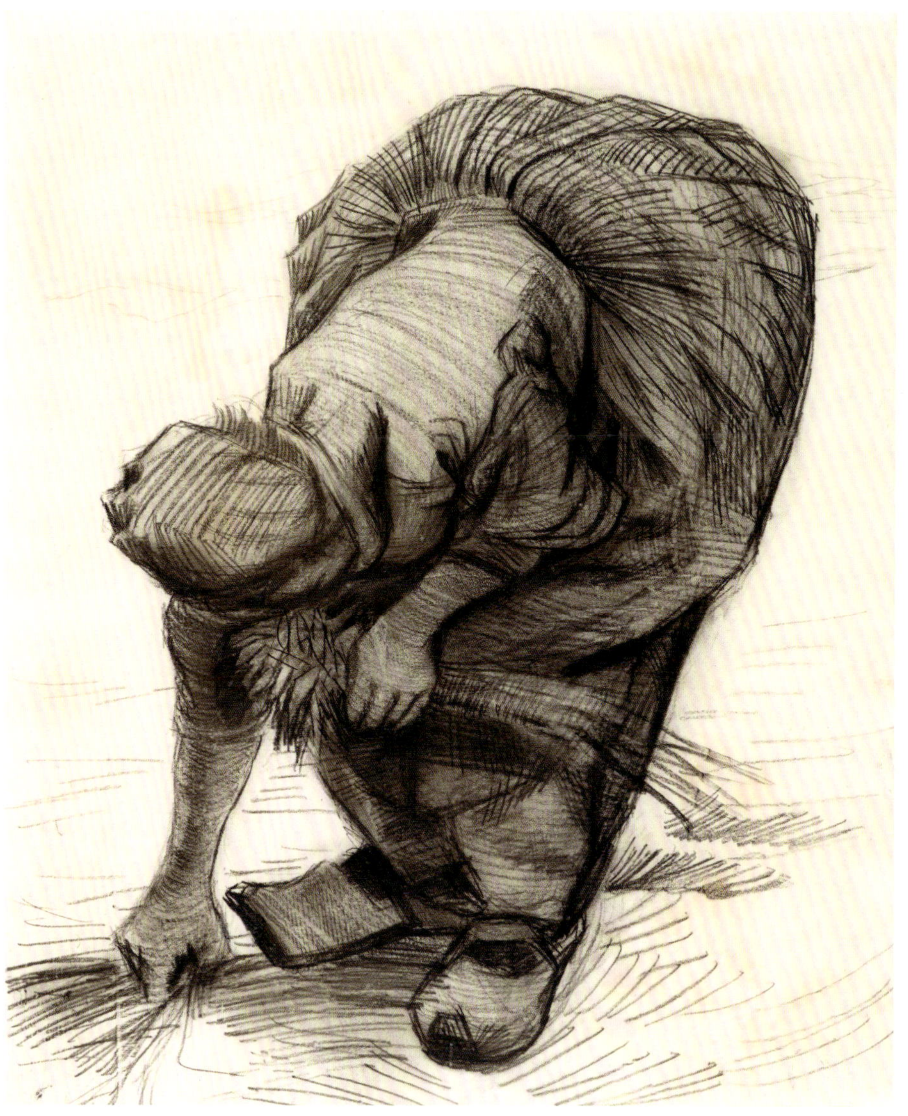

Vincent van Gogh
Paysanne arrachant de l'herbe, 1885
Museum Folkwang, Essen

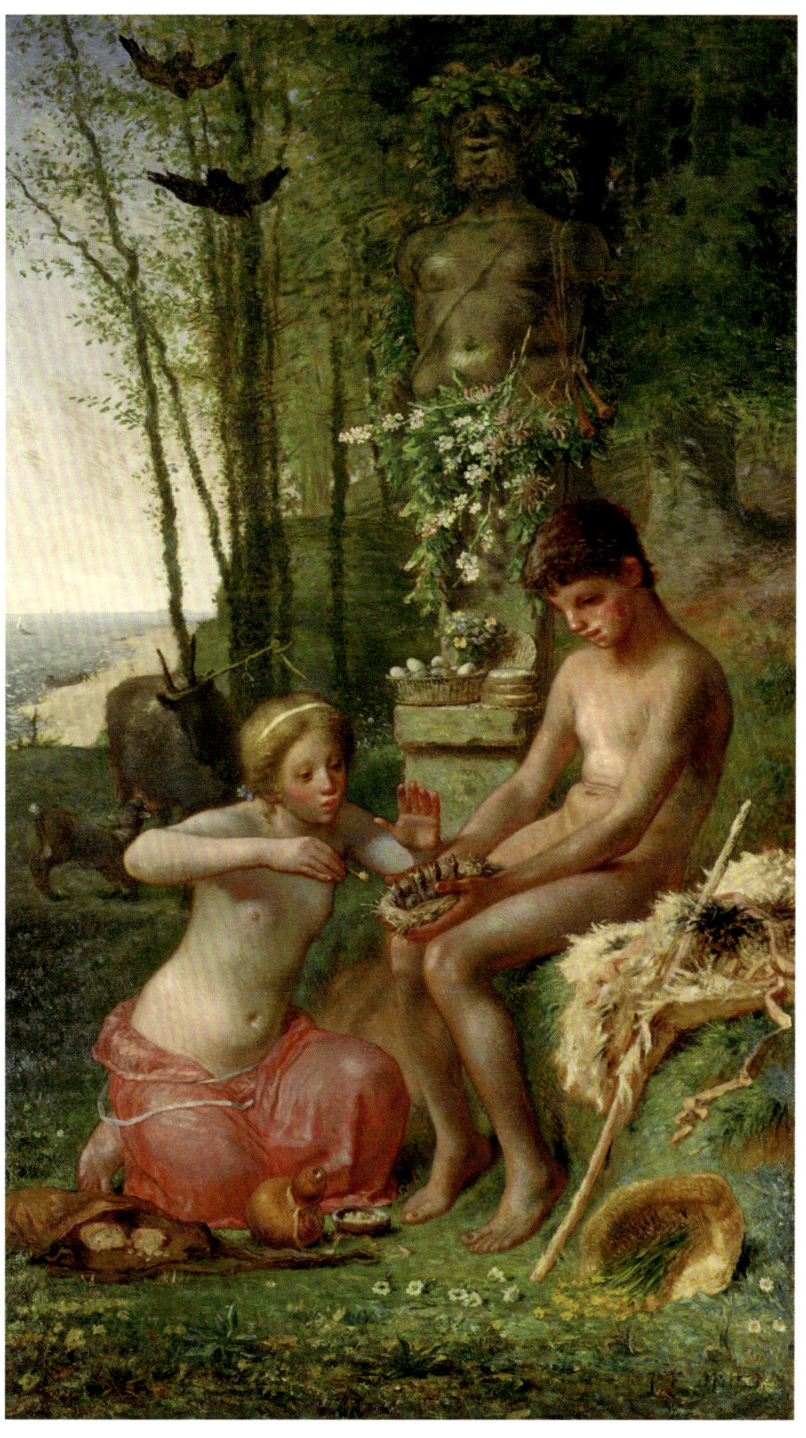

309

Jean-François Millet
Spring (Daphnis and Chloë), 1865
The National Museum of Western Art, Tokyo

Jean-François Millet
Meules de foin
The National Museum of Western Art, Tokyo

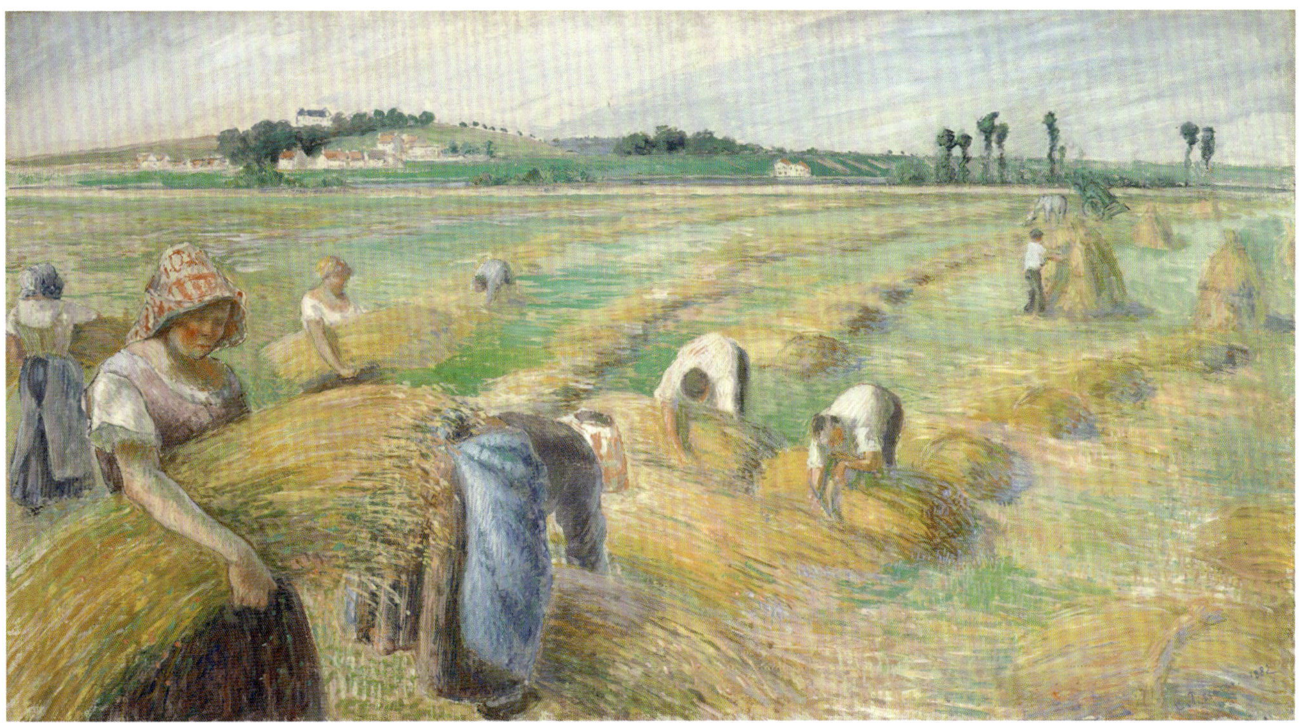

311

Camille Pissarro
La récolte, 1882
The National Museum of Western Art, Tokyo

WETTLAUF UM VAN GOGH

THE RACE FOR VAN GOGH

WETTLAUF UM VAN GOGH

The purchase of *La moisson* (*The Wheatfield behind St Paul's Hospital with a Reaper*, 1889; p. 315) was the first time that a painting by Vincent van Gogh entered a German museum collection. The Paul Cassirer Berlin art dealership had offered the work for sale on 8 February 1902, enabling Karl Ernst Osthaus to exhibit it at the opening of his museum in Hagen. This was followed soon afterwards by the acquisition of the *Portrait d'Armand Roulin* (*Portrait of Armand Roulin*, 1888; p. 321) for the Folkwang collection, laying the foundation for a portfolio that by 1905 had grown to a total of six paintings and a representative group of drawings, unparalleled at the time.

The first purchase had probably been mediated by Henry van de Velde, who had seen Van Gogh's estate in 1894 and bought a drawing. By this point the painter had been dead for four years, and his sister-in-law Johanna van Gogh-Bonger administered the estate, for which there was as yet no great appetite on the art market. This changed once Ambroise Vollard took over as Van Gogh's dealer after the death of the artist's brother Theo in 1891, and finally with Paul Cassirer's activities in Berlin. In around 1905, Osthaus entered competition with Cassirer, when he made direct contact with Johanna van Gogh-Bonger to have paintings sent for viewing for a monographic presentation at the Museum Folkwang. At this time, Cassirer was also pursuing an exhibition project with works by the artist, which was to be a travelling exhibition visiting several German cities. After the big Van Gogh retrospective in Amsterdam, a total of eleven paintings and three drawings were made

Mit dem Ankauf von *La moisson* (*Die Ernte, Kornfeld mit Schnitter*, 1889; S. 315) gelangte zum ersten Mal ein Gemälde Vincent van Goghs in eine deutsche Museumssammlung. Die Kunsthandlung Paul Cassirer aus Berlin hatte das Werk am 8. Februar 1902 angeboten, sodass Karl Ernst Osthaus es bereits zur Eröffnung seines Museums in Hagen ausstellen konnte. Kurz darauf folgte der Ankauf des *Portrait d'Armand Roulin* (*Porträt Armand Roulin*, 1888; S. 321) für die Folkwang-Sammlung, womit der Grundstein gelegt war für ein Konvolut, das bis 1905 auf insgesamt sechs Gemälde und eine repräsentative Gruppe von Zeichnungen anwuchs und damit zu jener Zeit seinesgleichen suchte.

Vermittelt hatte den ersten Erwerb vermutlich Henry van de Velde, der den Nachlass van Goghs 1894 selbst gesehen und eine Zeichnung erstanden hatte.[1] Zu diesem Zeitpunkt war der Maler bereits seit vier Jahren verstorben und seine Schwägerin Johanna van Gogh-Bonger verwaltete das Erbe, für das noch kein großes Interesse auf dem Kunstmarkt bestand. Das änderte sich erst durch das Engagement des Pariser Kunsthändlers Ambroise Vollard, welcher den 1891 verstorbenen Bruder des Künstlers Theo van Gogh als Händler ablöste, und schließlich durch Paul Cassirer in Berlin. Mit Letzterem geriet Osthaus um 1905 in direkte Konkurrenz, als er zu Johanna van Gogh-Bonger Kontakt aufnahm, um sich für eine monografische Präsentation im Museum Folkwang Bilder zur Ansicht senden zu lassen. Auch Cassirer verfolgte zu dieser Zeit ein Ausstellungsprojekt mit Werken des Künstlers, das als Wanderausstellung in mehreren deutschen

Städten zu sehen sein sollte. Nach der großen Van-Gogh-Retrospektive in Amsterdam wurden im Herbst 1905 im Museum Folkwang in Hagen insgesamt elf Gemälde und drei Zeichnungen dem Publikum zugänglich gemacht.[2] Es war die erste Ausstellung des Künstlers in einem deutschen Museum.

Im Gegensatz zu Osthaus erwarb Kōjirō Matsukata erst in den 1920er-Jahren Werke van Goghs, deren Bedeutung jedoch nicht zu unterschätzen ist. Als 1959 große Teile der während des Zweiten Weltkriegs beschlagnahmten Sammlung Matsukata an Japan restituierten wurden, verblieb etwa das Hauptwerk *La chambre de Van Gogh à Arles (Vincents Schlafzimmer in Arles, 1889)* in Frankreich. Es befindet sich heute in der Sammlung des Musée d'Orsay in Paris.

accessible to the public in the Museum Folkwang in Hagen in the autumn of 1905. It was the artist's first exhibition in a German museum.

Unlike Osthaus, it was not until the 1920s that Kōjirō Matsukata bought works by Van Gogh, although their significance should not be underestimated. When large parts of Matsukata's collection, confiscated during the Second World War, were restored to Japan, the major work *La chambre de Van Gogh à Arles (Van Gogh's Bedroom in Arles,* 1889) was one of those kept in France. It is now in the collection of the Musée d'Orsay in Paris.

1   Walter Feilchenfeldt, „Vincent van Gogh –
    seine Sammler – seine Händler", in: *Vincent van
    Gogh und die Moderne 1890–1914*, hrsg. von
    Georg-Wilhelm Költzsch und Ronald de Leeuw,
    Ausst.-Kat. Museum Folkwang, Essen; Van Gogh
    Museum, Amsterdam, Freren 1990, S. 43.
2   Vgl. Herta Hesse-Frielinghaus, „Folkwang
    1. Teil", in: dies. u. a., *Karl Ernst Osthaus. Leben
    und Werk,* Recklinghausen 1971, S. 141.

1   Walter Feilchenfeldt, 'Vincent van Gogh –
    seine Sammler – seine Händler', in Georg-Wilhelm
    Költzsch and Ronald de Leeuw (eds.), *Vincent
    van Gogh und die Moderne 1890–1914*, exh. cat.
    Museum Folkwang, Essen, and Van Gogh Museum,
    Amsterdam (Freren, 1990), 43.
2   See Herta Hesse-Frielinghaus, 'Folkwang
    1. Teil', in idem et al. *Karl Ernst Osthaus.
    Leben und Werk* (Recklinghausen, 1971), 141.

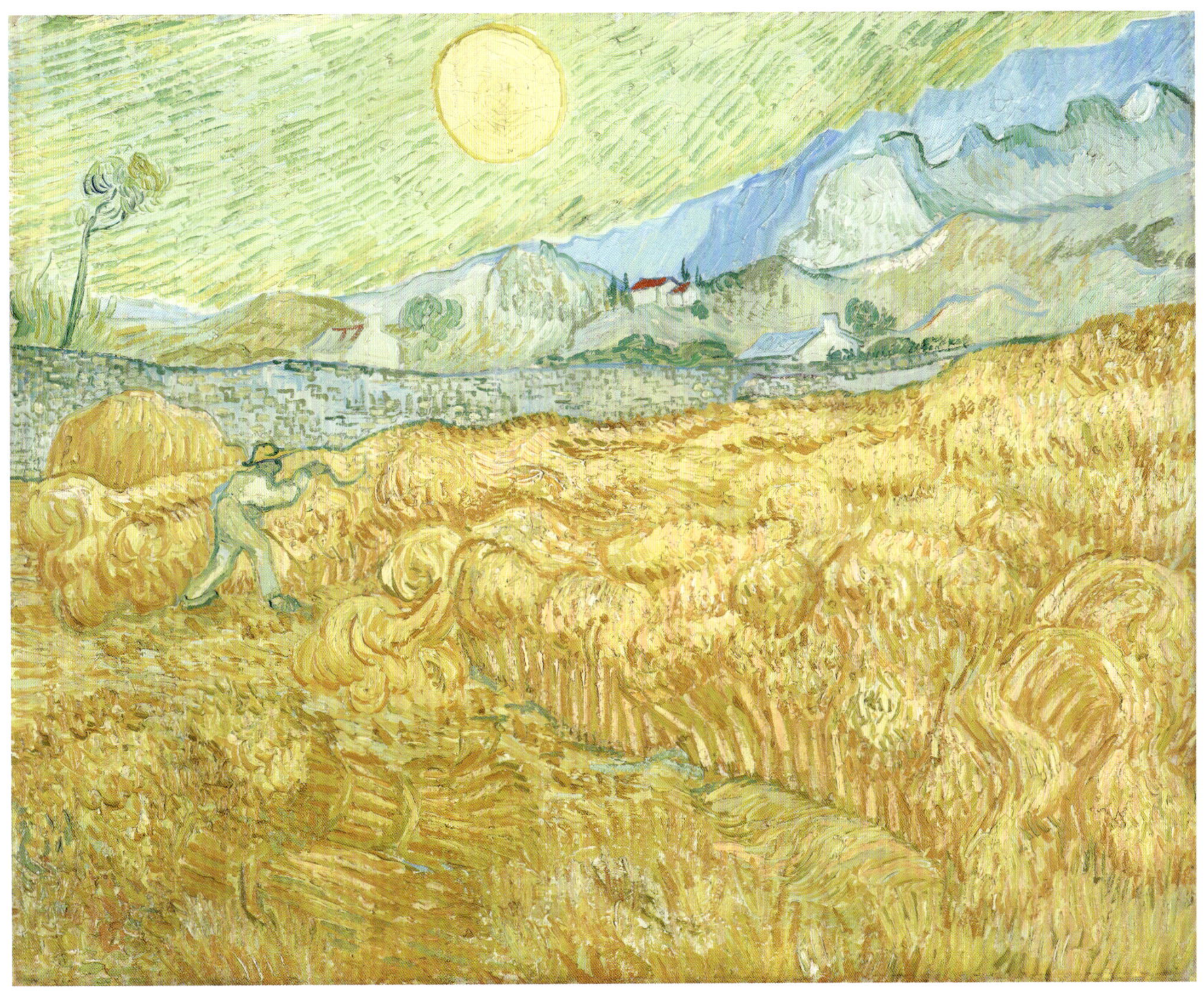

315

Vincent van Gogh
La moisson, 1889
Museum Folkwang, Essen

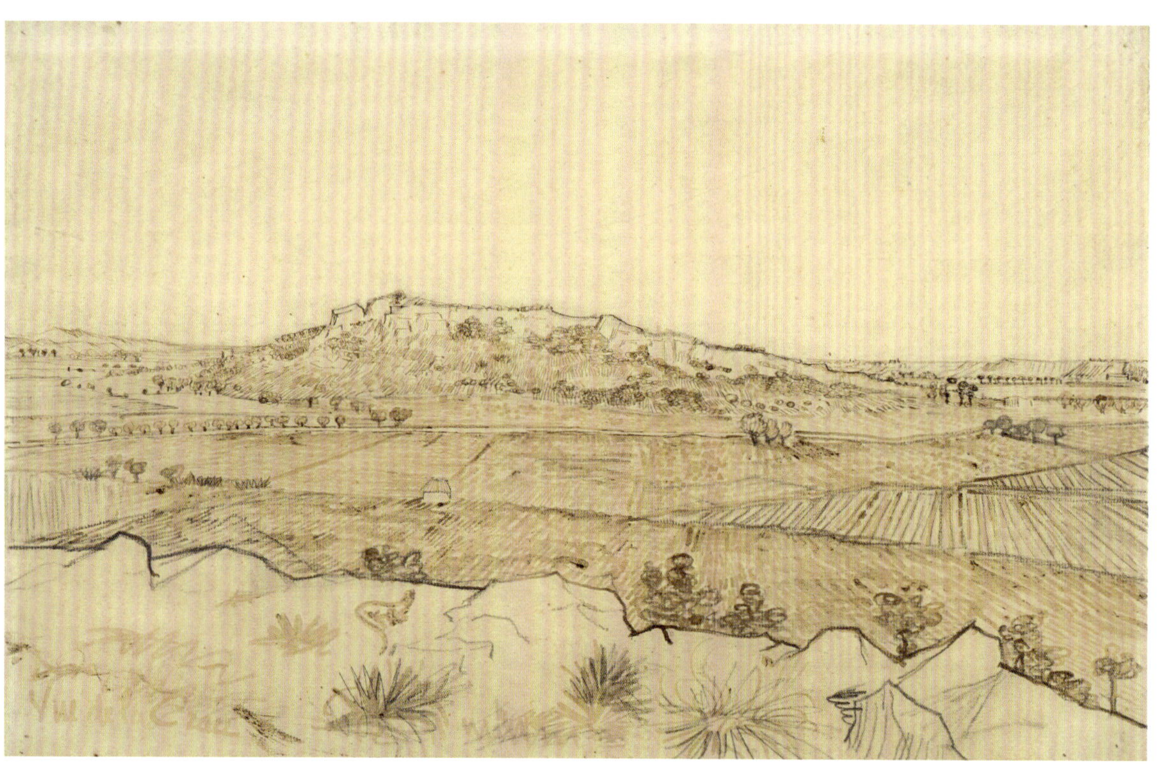

Vincent van Gogh
Vue de la Crau, 1888
Museum Folkwang, Essen

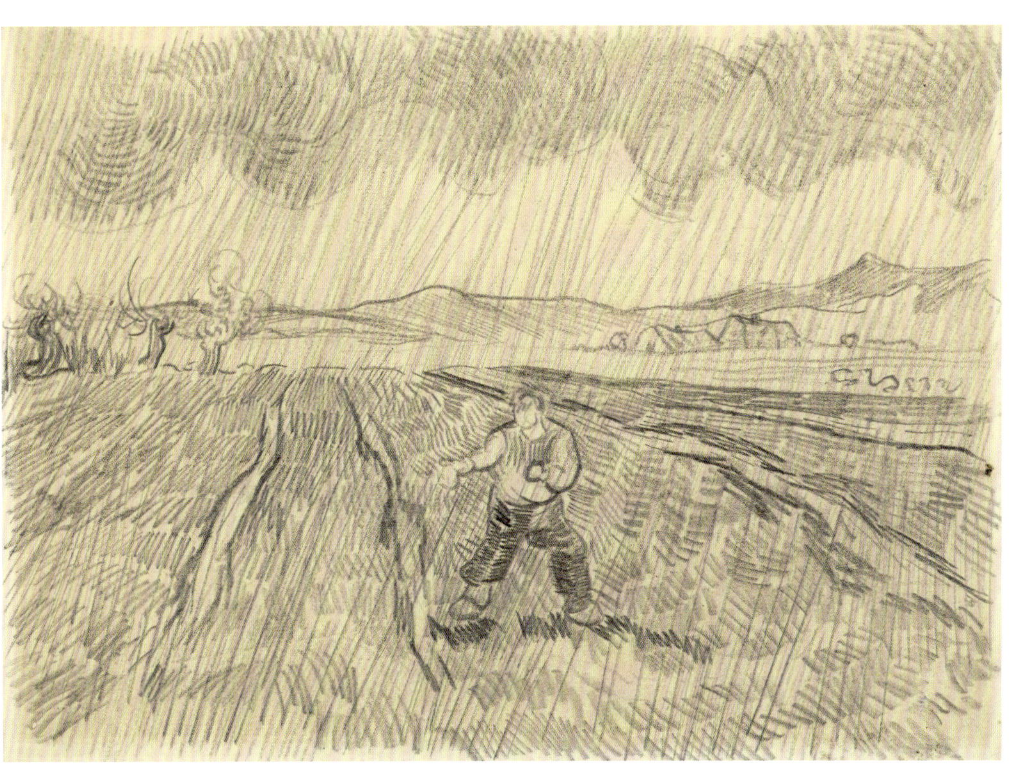

Vincent van Gogh
La pluie, 1890
Museum Folkwang, Essen

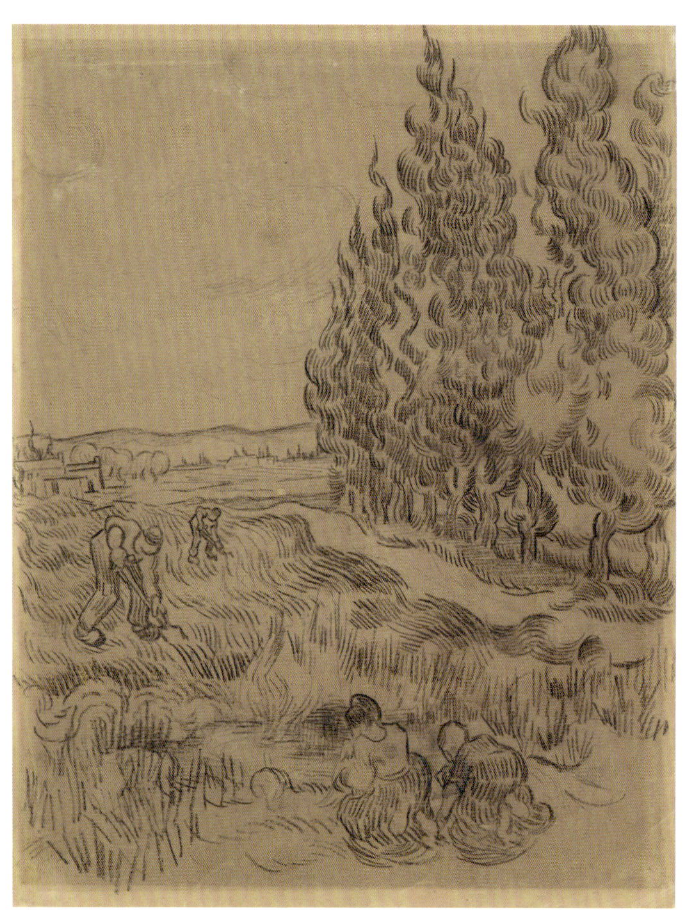

Vincent van Gogh
Paysage avec cyprès, 1889
Museum Folkwang, Essen

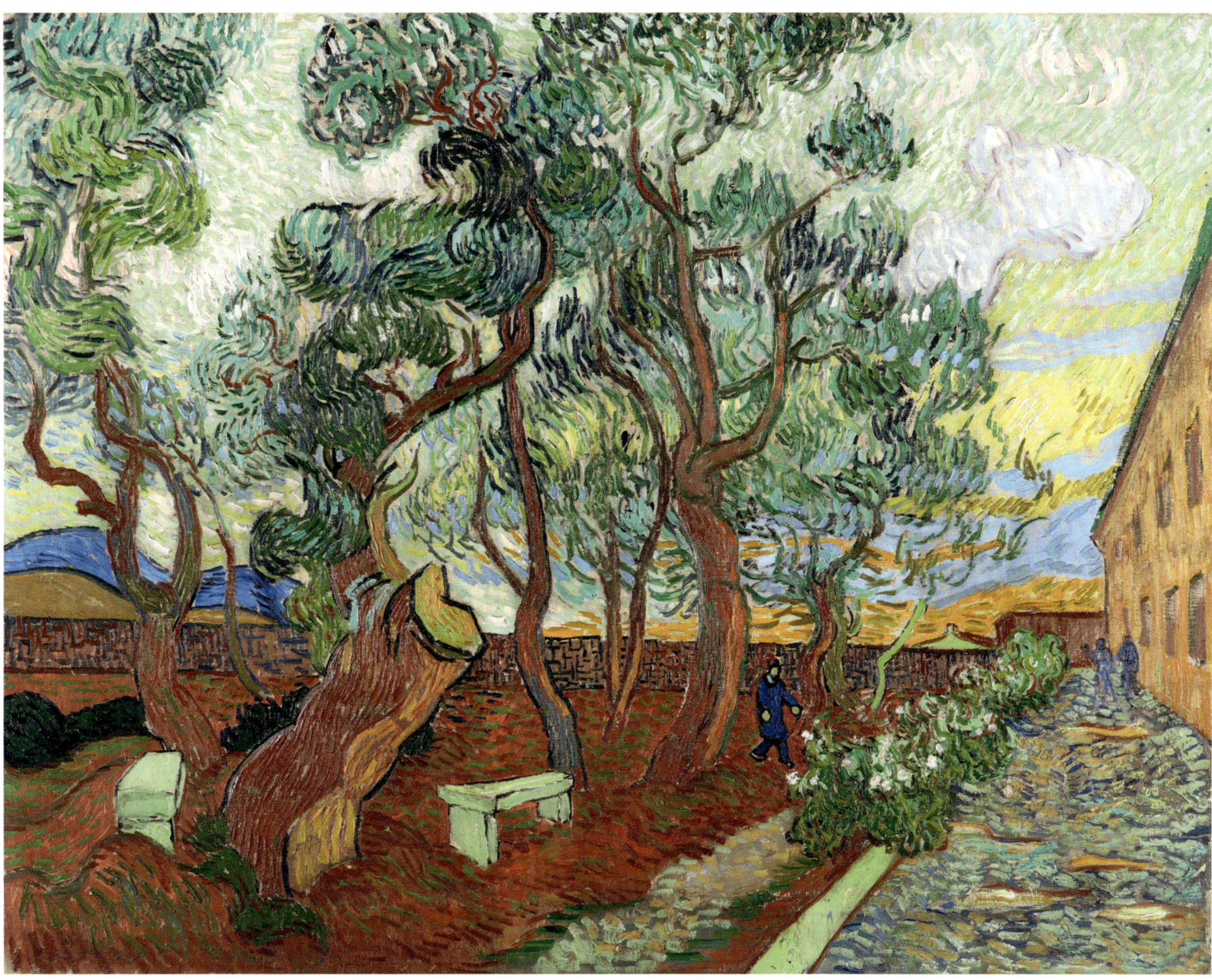

Vincent van Gogh
Le parc de l'hôpital, à Saint-Rémy, 1889
Museum Folkwang, Essen

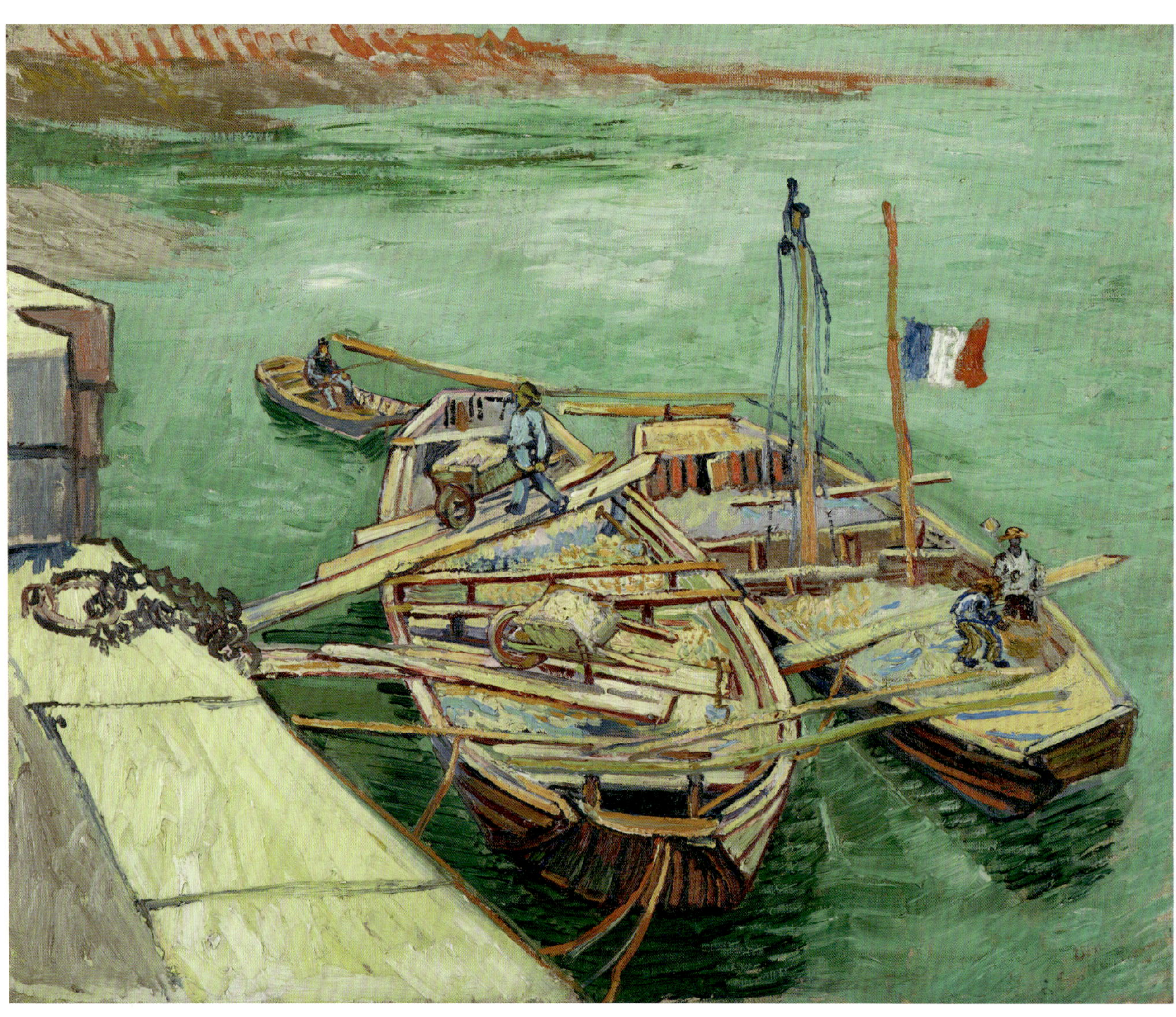

Vincent van Gogh
Les bateaux amarrés, 1888
Museum Folkwang, Essen

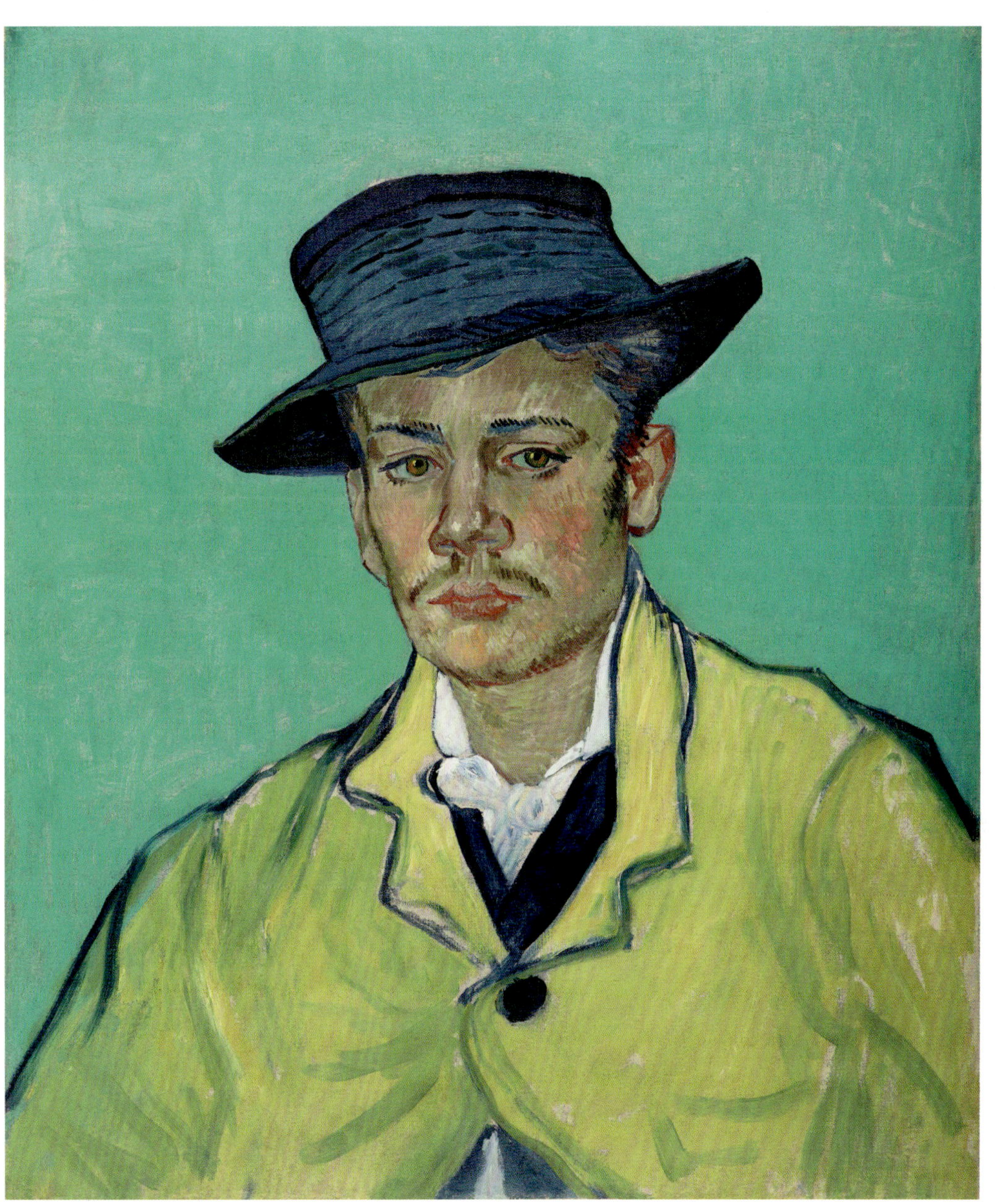

321

Vincent van Gogh
Portrait d'Armand Roulin, 1888
Museum Folkwang, Essen

AUF DEN SPUREN
VON GAUGUIN

IN THE FOOTSTEPS
OF GAUGUIN

323

Like Vincent van Gogh, Paul Gauguin had to
wait a very long time for his artistic work to attract
attention. The two painters knew one another
and briefly shared a studio in Arles in the south
of France. However, that arrangement soon came
to an end. A few years later Gauguin moved the
centre of his life to Polynesia, where he began
what is probably his best-known series of works
featuring scenes from the South Seas. For these,
Gauguin used the style of synthetism, which
he had developed in the years leading up to 1891
along with the painters of the Pont-Aven school.
The group's subjects sought to bring together
nature and emotions and capture them on
the picture support in simplified planar forms,
in clear, flat colours.

As early as 1903, a year after the opening of
his museum, Karl Ernst Osthaus bought two works
by Paul Gauguin (pp. 331, 339) from the Paris art
dealer Ambroise Vollard, whom he visited along
with the painter Konrad Ferdinand von Freyhold.
Immediately after it became known that Gauguin
had died in May 1903, on Von Freyhold's advice
Osthaus decided to buy additional works by the
artist from the posthumous exhibition organized
by Vollard in Paris. The five paintings sent to him
to view were shown in Hagen the same year
along with his earlier purchases, while four of the
new works went on to join the Osthauses' private
and museum collections (pp. 336/337). This made
Gertrud and Karl Ernst Osthaus the first German
collectors to buy Gauguin paintings, and the
Museum Folkwang the first museum in Germany
to devote an exhibition to the artist.[1]

In 1921, when Kōjirō Matsukata embarked on
his second purchasing trip across Europe and

Vergleichbar mit Vincent van Gogh erhielt auch
Paul Gauguin erst sehr spät Aufmerksamkeit für
seine künstlerische Arbeit. Die beiden Maler waren
miteinander bekannt und teilten kurzzeitig ein
Atelier im südfranzösischen Arles. Dieses Arrangement zerschlug sich jedoch schnell. Wenige Jahre
später verlegte Gauguin seinen Lebensmittel-
punkt nach Polynesien und begann dort mit seiner
wohl bekanntesten Werkreihe der Südseeszenen.
Gauguin bediente sich dazu der Malweise des
Synthetismus, den er in den Jahren bis 1891 gemeinsam mit den Maler:innen der Schule von Pont-Aven
entwickelt hatte: Die Motive der Gruppe sollten
Natur und Emotionen zusammenbringen und
vereinfacht, in klaren, flächigen Farben auf den
Bildträger aufgebracht werden.

Karl Ernst Osthaus kaufte bereits 1903, ein Jahr
nach der Eröffnung seines Museums, zwei Werke
Paul Gauguins (S. 331, 339) bei dem Pariser Kunsthändler Ambroise Vollard, den er gemeinsam mit
dem Maler Konrad Ferdinand von Freyhold besuchte. Unmittelbar nachdem bekannt wurde, dass
Gauguin im Mai 1903 verstorben war, bemühte sich
Osthaus auf Anraten von Freyholds um weitere
Werke des Künstlers aus der Nachlass-Ausstellung,
die Vollard in Paris veranstaltete. Die zur Ansicht
übersandten fünf Gemälde wurden noch im
gleichen Jahr gemeinsam mit den früheren Erwerbungen in Hagen ausgestellt, vier der neuen
Exponate gingen in der Folge in die Privat- und
Museumssammlung der Osthaus über (S. 336/337).
Damit waren Gertrud und Karl Ernst Osthaus die
ersten deutschen Sammler:innen, die Gemälde
Gauguins erwarben, und das Museum Folkwang

the USA, his large-scale museum project was already known to the art world. His desire to see works by Gauguin was soon much discussed in the trade and galleries in Paris, London and Berlin offered new works to view. Between 1921 and 1923, Matsukata bought over twenty works by the artist from such important art dealers as Heinrich Thannhauser, John Levy and Georges Bernheim. Unlike Osthaus, Matsukata concentrated more on Gauguin's early work from his time in Britanny (pp. 325, 327, 329). Today only relatively few works remain in the collection of the National Museum of Western Art in Tokyo, while the rest of the portfolio is scattered across various public and private collections. After the end of the Second World War, the Louvre in Paris alone claimed seven works for itself (p. 333).[2]

1 See Herta Hesse-Frielinghaus, 'Folkwang 1. Teil', in idem et al., *Karl Ernst Osthaus. Leben und Werk* (Recklinghausen, 1971), 142.
2 See Masako Kawaguchi and Megumi Jingaoka (eds.), *The Matsukata Collection. Complete Catalogue of the European Art*, Vol. 1, *Paintings* (Tokyo, 2018). In the end four paintings by Gauguin were assigned to the Musée du Louvre in 1959. They are now in the collection of the Musée d'Orsay, Paris.

das erste Museum Deutschlands, das dem Künstler eine Ausstellung widmete.[1]

Als Kōjirō Matsukata 1921 seine zweite Ankaufsreise durch Europa und die USA antrat, war sein großangelegtes Museumsprojekt der Kunstwelt bereits bekannt. Sein Wunsch, Werke Gauguins zu sehen, sprach sich schnell im Handel herum und Galerien in Paris, London und Berlin boten neue Werke zur Ansicht an. Matsukata erwarb zwischen 1921 und 1923 mehr als zwanzig Arbeiten des Künstlers von so wichtigen Kunsthändler:innen wie Heinrich Thannhauser, John Levy oder Georges Bernheim. Im Gegensatz zu Osthaus konzentrierte sich Matsukata dabei mehr auf das Frühwerk Gauguins aus der Zeit in der Bretagne (S. 325, 327, 329). Heute befinden sich nur noch verhältnismäßig wenige Werke in der Sammlung des National Museum of Western Art in Tokio, der Rest des Konvoluts ist über verschiedene öffentliche und private Sammlungen verstreut. Allein sieben Werke beanspruchte nach dem Ende des Zweiten Weltkriegs der Pariser Louvre für sich (S. 333).[2]

324

1 Vgl. Herta Hesse-Frielinghaus, „Folkwang 1. Teil", in: dies. u. a., *Karl Ernst Osthaus. Leben und Werk*, Recklinghausen 1971, S. 142.
2 Vgl. Masako Kawaguchi und Megumi Jingaoka (Hrsg.), *The Matsukata Collection. Complete Catalogue of the European Art*, Bd. 1, *Paintings*, Tokio 2018. Letztendlich wurden dem Musée du Louvre 1959 vier Gemälde Gauguins zugeschrieben. Sie befinden sich heute in der Sammlung des Musée d'Orsay, Paris.

325

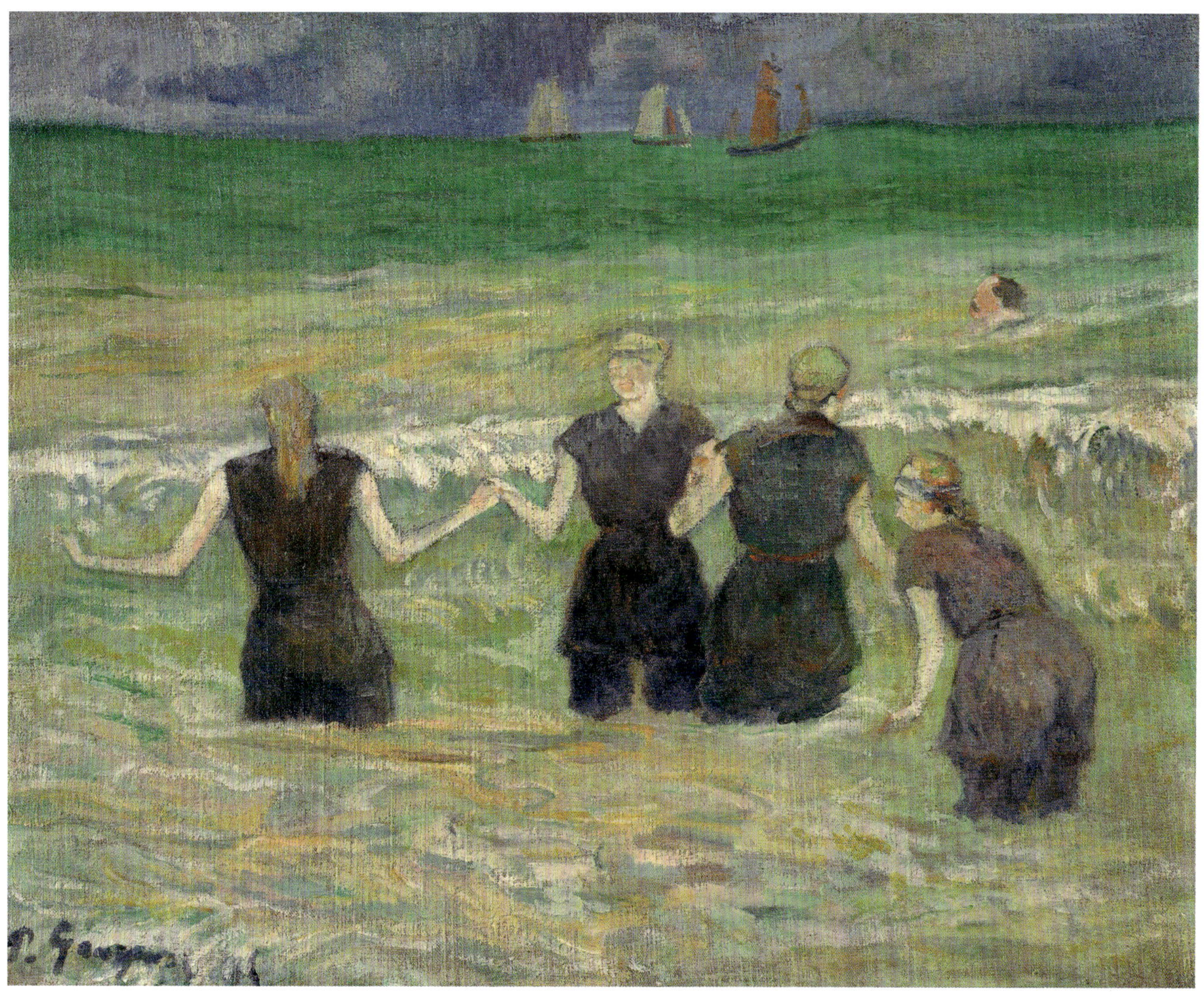

Paul Gauguin
Baigneuses à Dieppe, 1885
The National Museum of Western Art, Tokyo

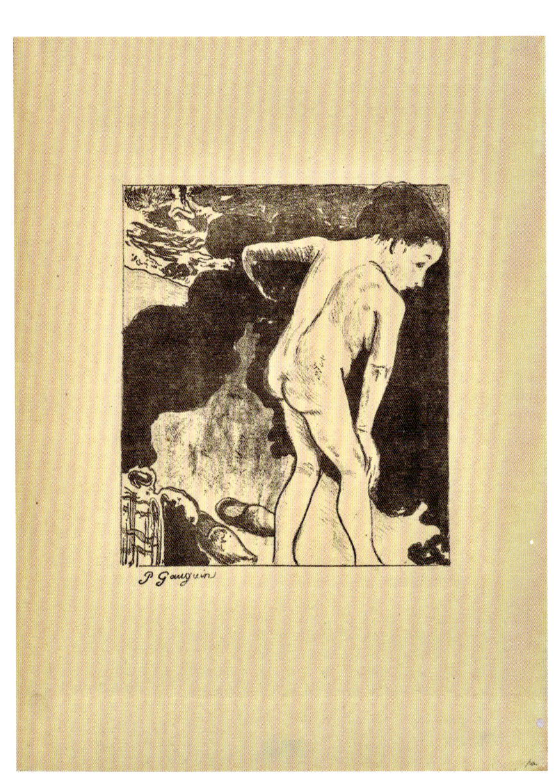

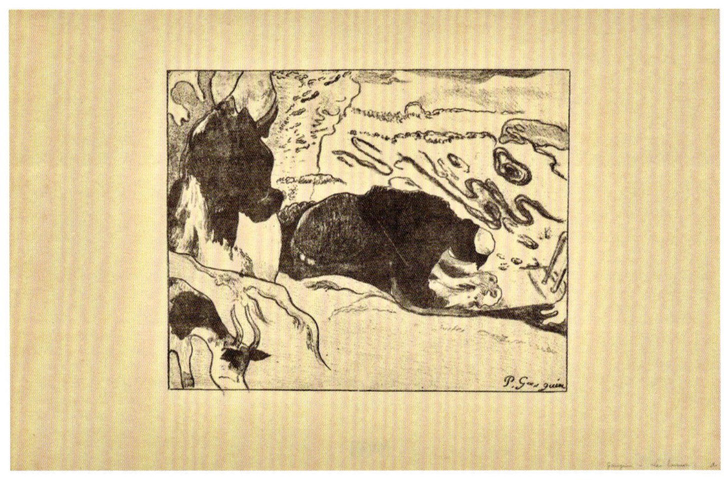

326

Paul Gauguin
Baigneuses Bretonnes, 1889
Museum Folkwang, Essen

Paul Gauguin
Les laveuses, 1889
Museum Folkwang, Essen

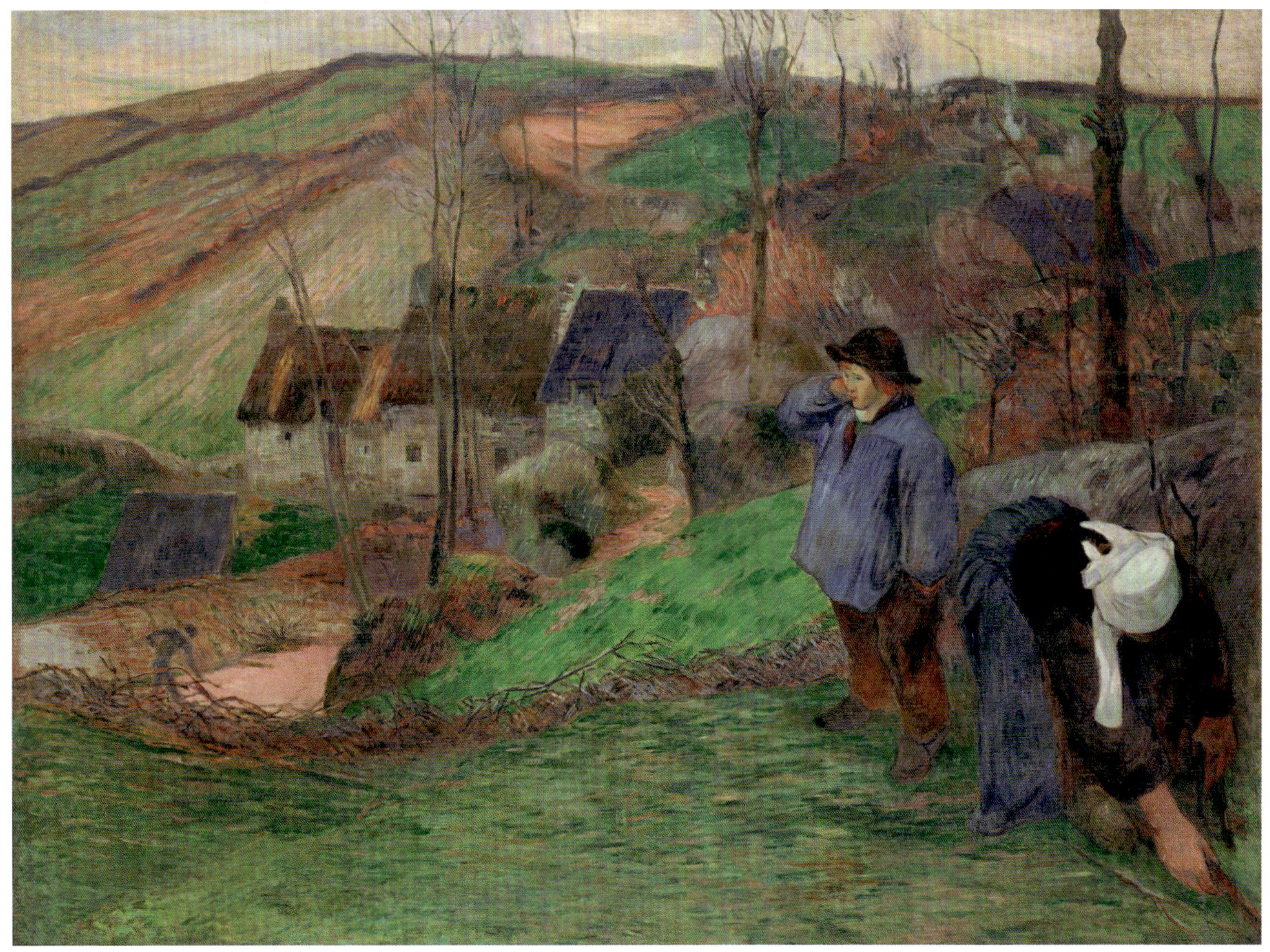

327

Paul Gauguin
Paysage de Bretagne, 1888
The National Museum of Western Art, Tokyo

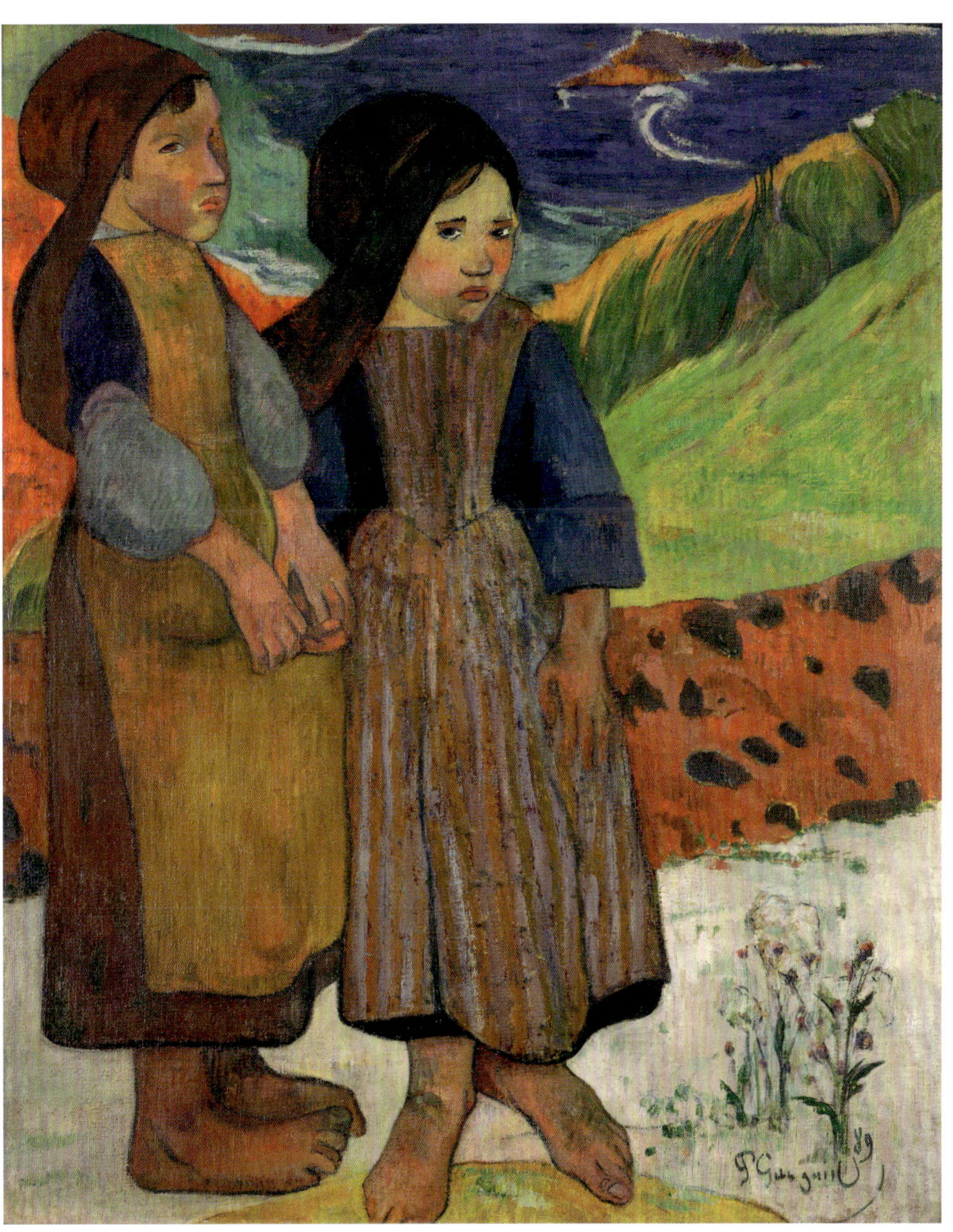

329

Paul Gauguin
Petites Bretonnes au bord de la mer, 1889
The National Museum of Western Art, Tokyo

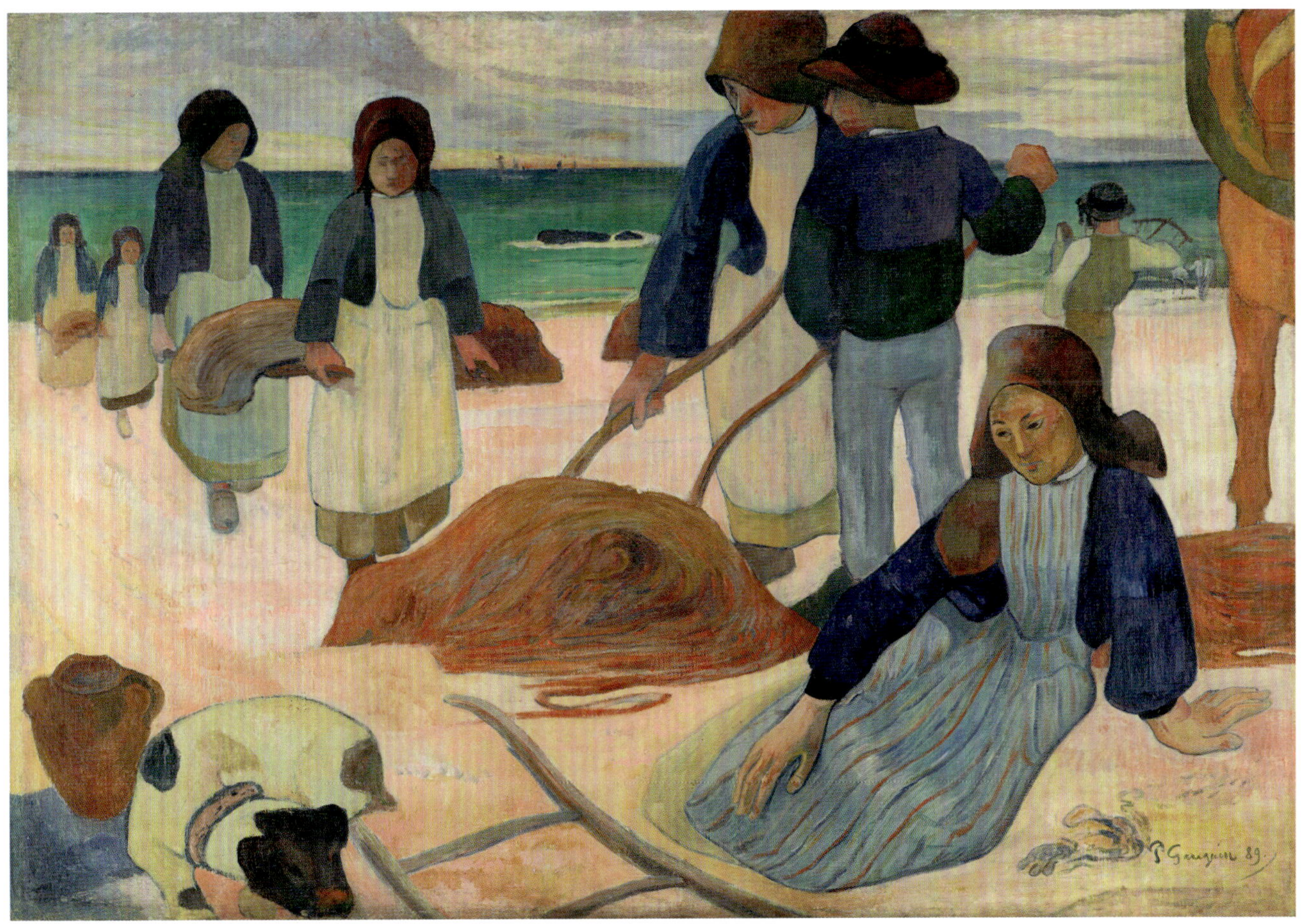

Paul Gauguin
Ramasseuses de varech (II), 1889
Museum Folkwang, Essen

331

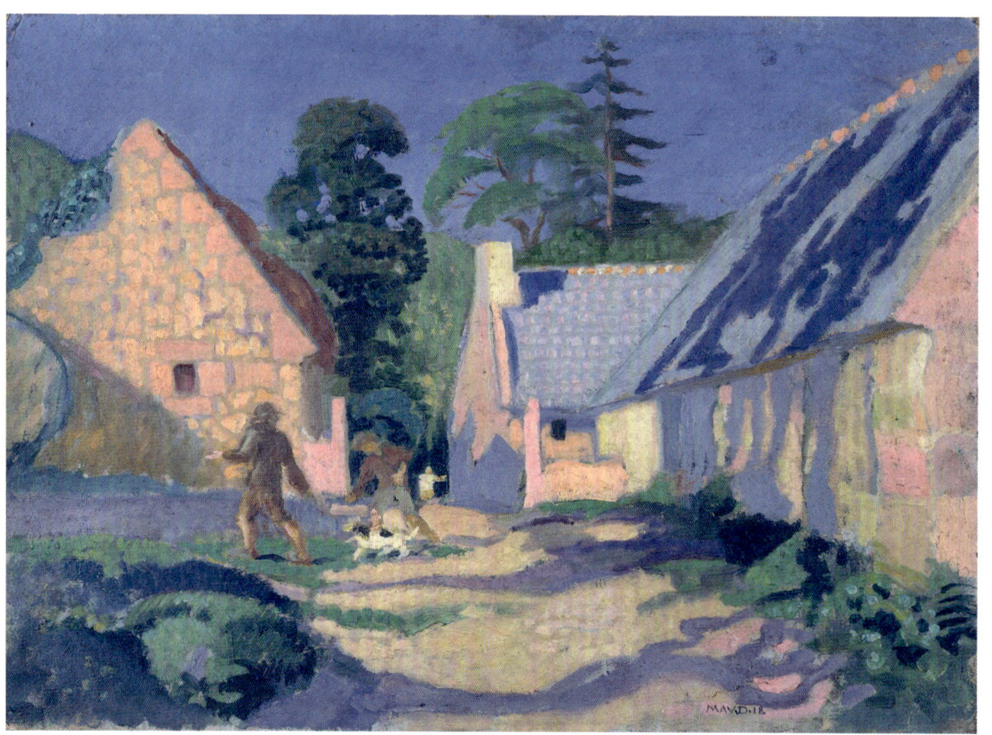

Maurice Denis
Rosmapamon, 1918
The National Museum of Western Art, Tokyo

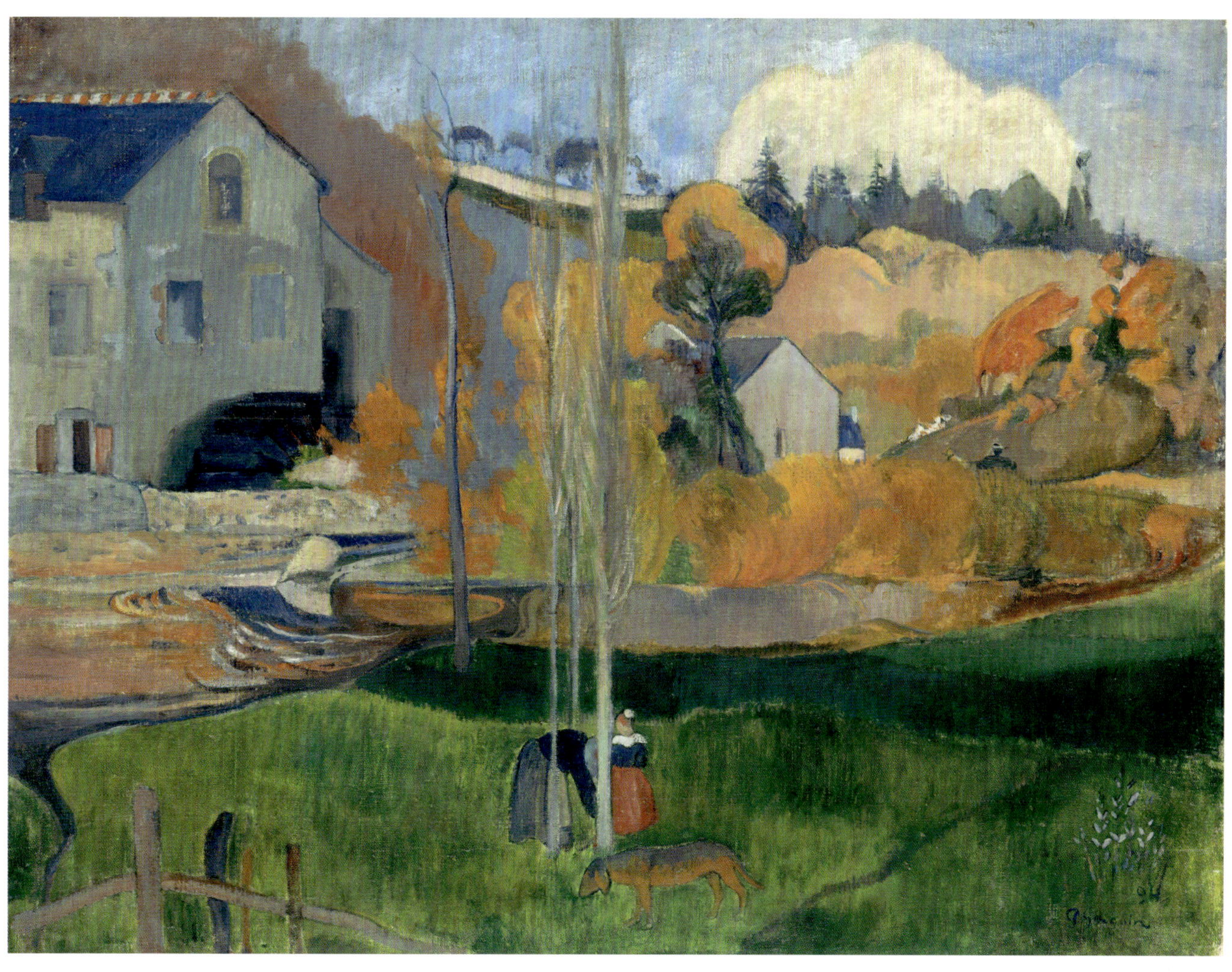

Paul Gauguin
Paysage de Bretagne. Le moulin de David, 1894
Musée d'Orsay, Paris

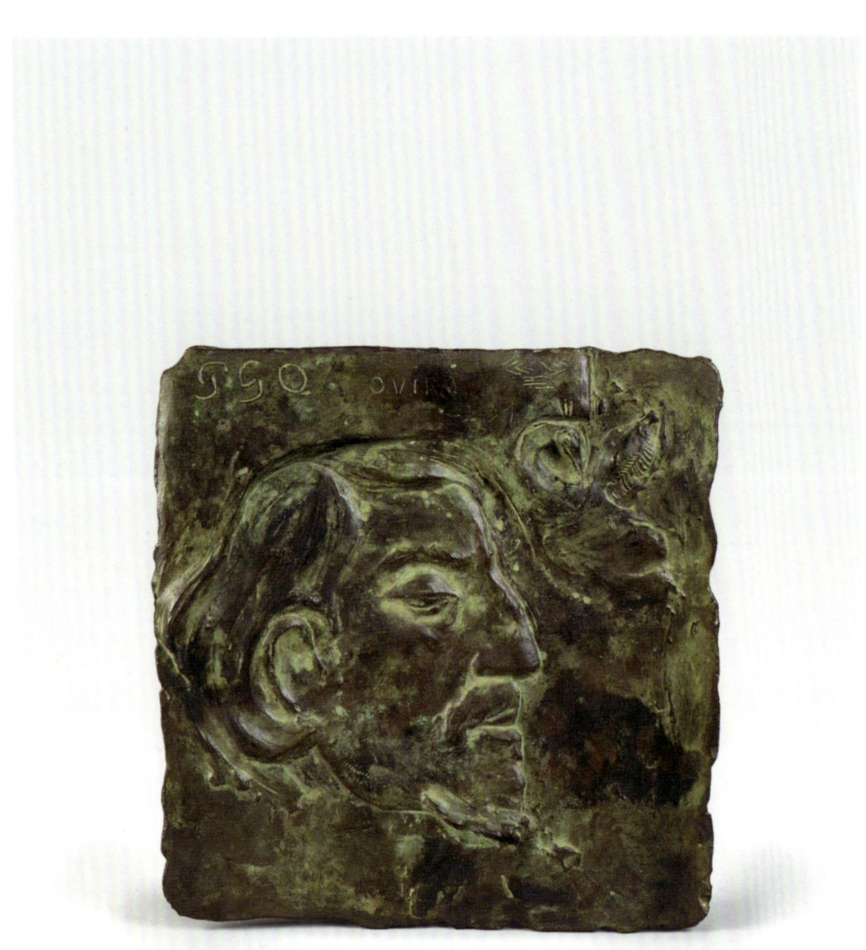

334

Paul Gauguin
Autoportrait Oviri, 1893
Museum Folkwang, Essen

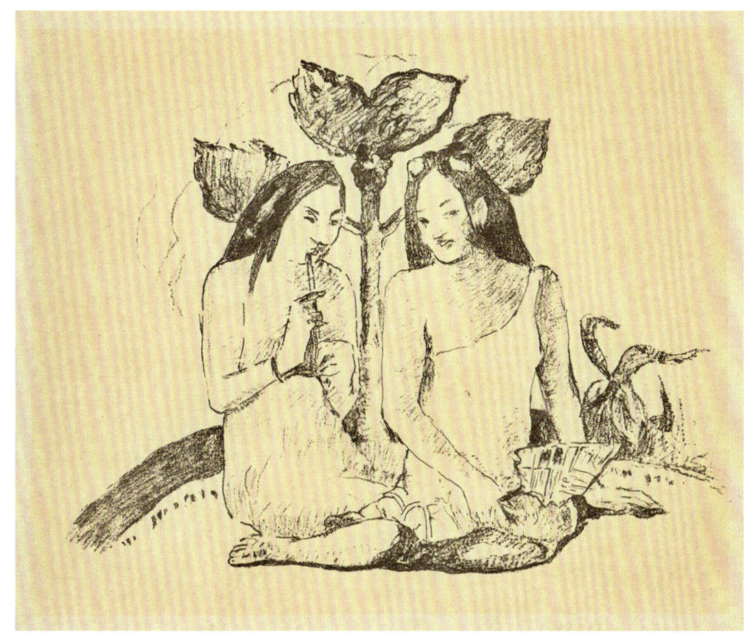

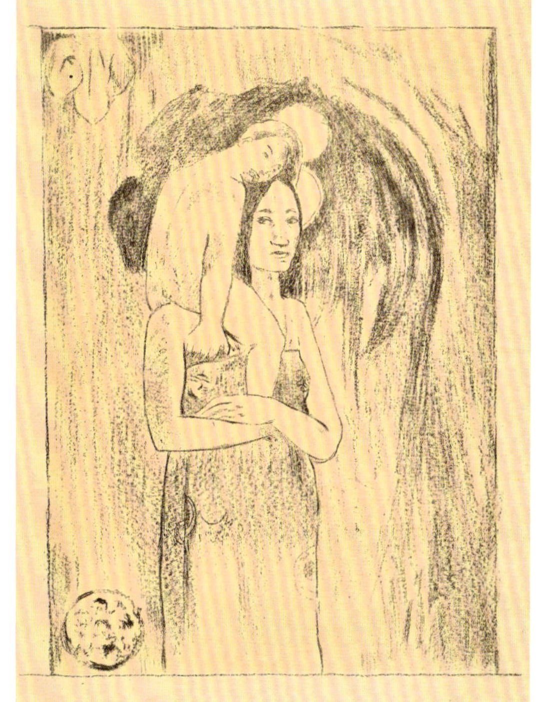

335

Paul Gauguin
Deux femmes maories accroupies, 1894/95
Museum Folkwang, Essen

Paul Gauguin
La Orana Maria, 1894/95
Museum Folkwang, Essen

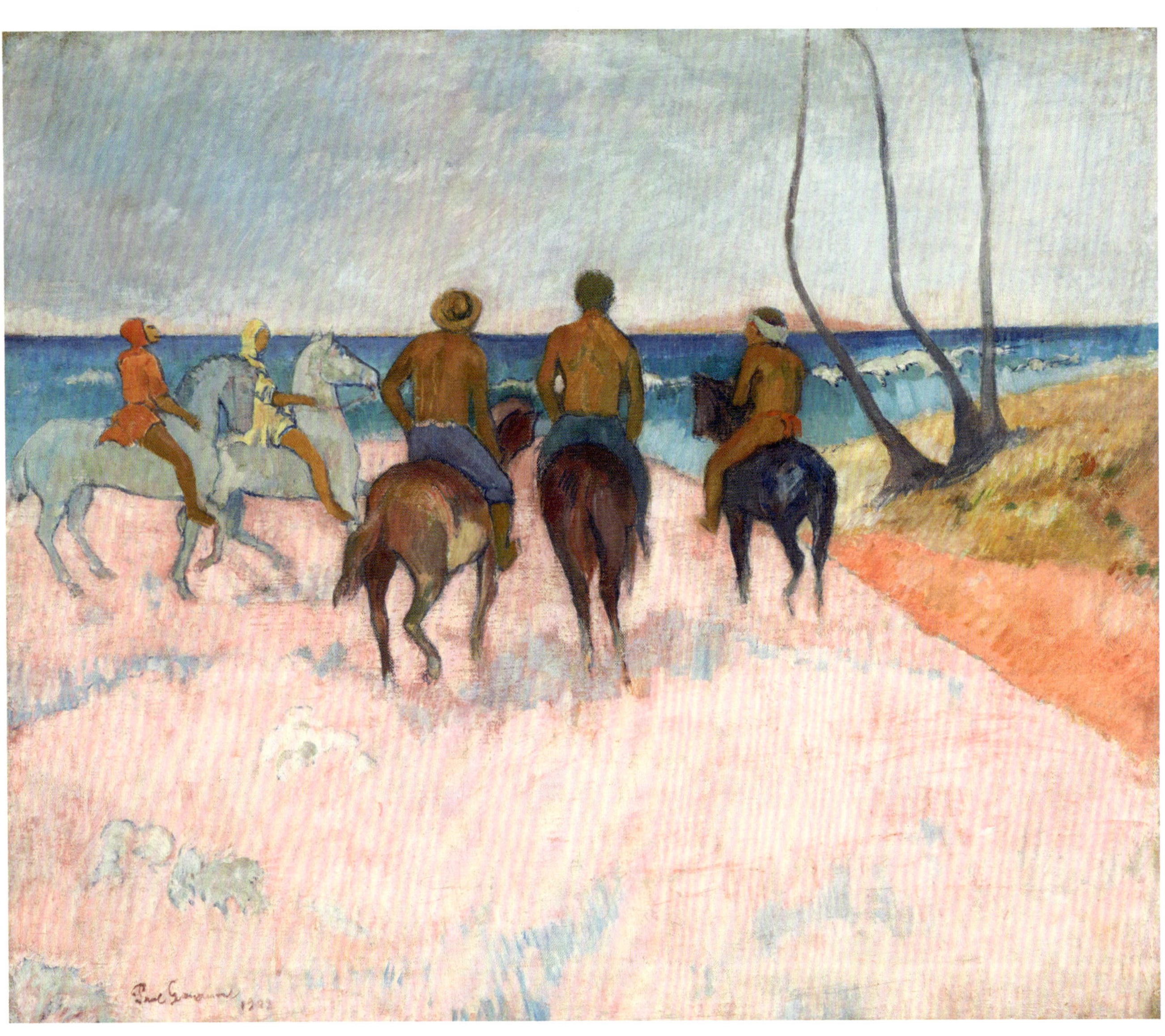

Paul Gauguin
Cavaliers sur la plage (I), 1902
Museum Folkwang, Essen

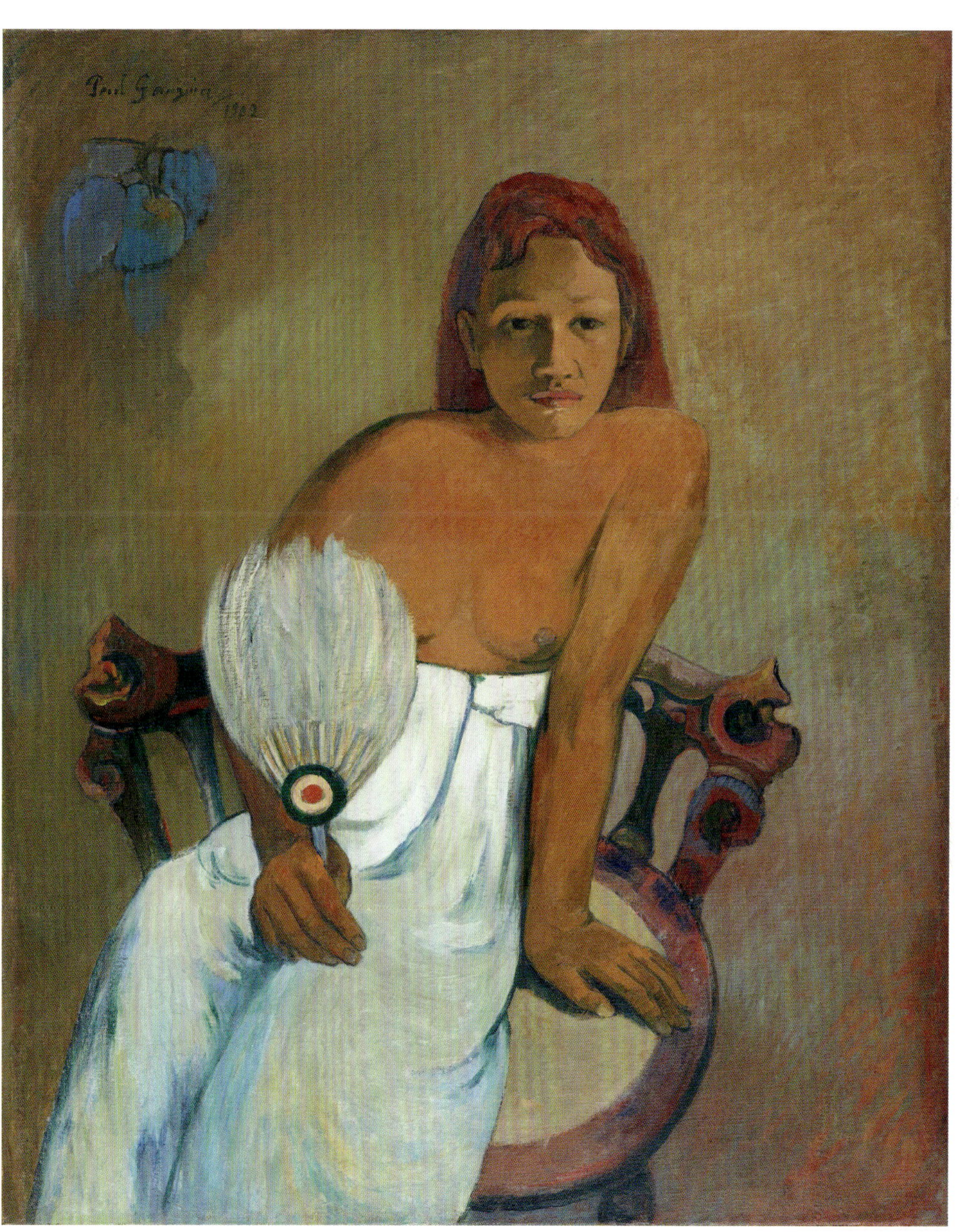

Paul Gauguin
Jeune fille à l'éventail, 1902
Museum Folkwang, Essen

339

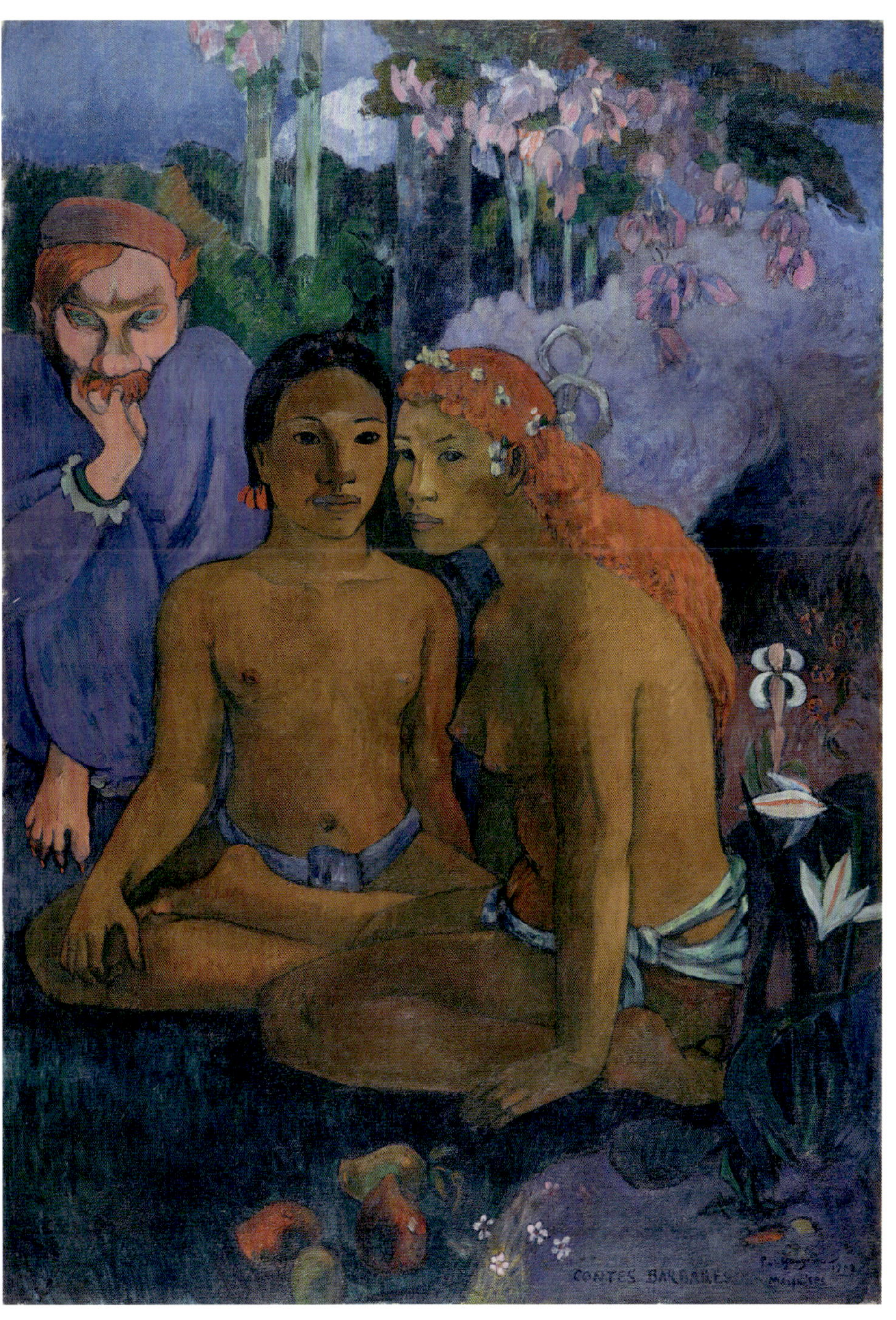

Paul Gauguin
Contes barbares, 1902
Museum Folkwang, Essen

KARL ERNST OSTHAUS:

FROM COMMERCIAL APPRENTICE TO ART COLLECTOR AND MUSEUM FOUNDER

Michelle Latta

Karl Ernst Osthaus was born on 15 April 1874, the son of Ernst Osthaus, an entrepreneur and banker, and Selma Osthaus (née Funcke), the daughter of an influential screw manufacturer (p. 203). His mother died a few days after his birth, and his father soon married Laura Funcke, the late Selma's sister.[1]

After receiving his school-leaving certificate in 1892, Osthaus initially complied with his father's wish that he complete a commercial apprenticeship at the textile company Mühlenthaler Spinnerei und Weberei A.G. in Dieringhausen. A year later, however, he switched to studying aesthetics, philosophy and literature at the Christian-Albrechts-Universität in Kiel. When he travelled to Munich in the winter of 1893, he attended lectures in art history at the university and visited important cities in the area. There were already signs of his penchant for collecting: he bought photographs and kept a notebook on important art historians. In the years that followed, he studied in Berlin, Strasbourg and Vienna. In Vienna in particular, Osthaus was politically active in the German nationalist movement as a member of the *Verein Deutscher Studenten* (Association of German Students).[2] He was even deported from Austria for that reason, and he returned to Berlin in the winter of 1896. Osthaus, however, remained associated with the *Alldeutscher Verband* (Pan-German League) and four years later held lectures for the local section in his native city of Hagen.[3] Appendicitis delayed his doctorate on Rhenish and Düsseldorf art, which he ultimately completed in 1918 with a different

Karl Ernst Osthaus kommt am 15. April 1874 als Sohn von Ernst Osthaus, Unternehmer und Bankier, und Selma Osthaus (geborene Funcke), Tochter eines einflussreichen Schraubenfabrikanten, zur Welt (S. 203). Da seine Mutter wenige Tage nach der Geburt stirbt, heiratet sein Vater bald darauf Laura Funcke, die Schwester der verstorbenen Selma.[1]

Nach seinem Abitur im Jahr 1892 entspricht Osthaus zunächst dem Wunsch seines Vaters, kaufmännischer Lehrling an der Mühlenthaler Spinnerei und Weberei A.G. in Dieringhausen zu werden. Ein Jahr später wechselt er allerdings zu einem Studium der Fächer Ästhetik, Philosophie und Literatur an der Christian-Albrechts-Universität zu Kiel. Als er im Winter 1893 nach München reist, nimmt er an kunsthistorischen Vorlesungen der Universität teil und besichtigt bedeutsame Städte in der Umgebung. Seine Sammlerneigung tritt damals bereits zutage: Er ersteht Fotografien und führt ein Notizheft über bedeutende Kunsthistoriker:innen. In den folgenden Jahren studiert er in Berlin, Straßburg und Wien. Insbesondere in Wien wirkt Osthaus politisch als Mitglied des Vereins Deutscher Studenten aktiv in der deutschnationalen Bewegung mit.[2] Er wird aufgrund dessen sogar aus Österreich ausgewiesen und kehrt im Winter 1896 nach Berlin zurück. Osthaus bleibt aber weiterhin mit dem Alldeutschen Verband assoziiert und wird noch vier Jahre später Vorträge für die Ortsgruppe in seiner Heimatstadt Hagen halten.[3] Eine Blinddarmentzündung verhindert in Berlin seine Promotion zur rheinischen und insbesondere Düsseldorfer Kunst, welche Osthaus aber letztlich im Jahr 1918 mit einem anderen Forschungsschwerpunkt

Michelle Latta

KARL ERNST OSTHAUS –

VOM KAUFMÄNNISCHEN LEHRLING ZUM KUNSTSAMMLER UND MUSEUMSGRÜNDER

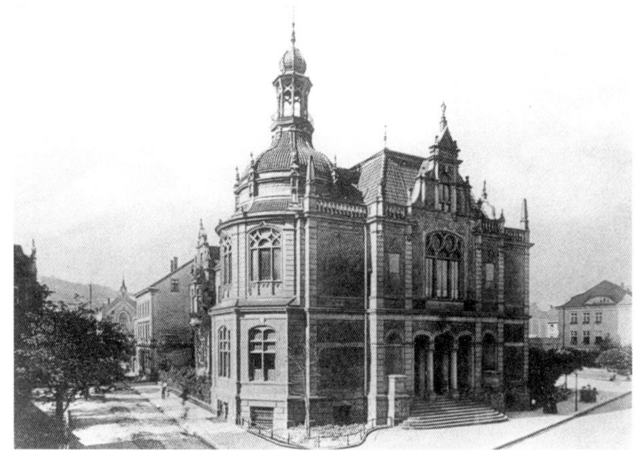

Abb. | Fig. 1
Museum Folkwang, Hagen, Außenansicht
nach Entwurf von Carl Gérard, Berlin.
Aufnahme zwischen 1902 und 1912 |
Museum Folkwang, Hagen. Exterior view
showing the design by Carl Gérard, Berlin.
Between 1902 and 1912

focus and a dissertation entitled *Grundzüge
der Stilentwicklung* (Principles of Stylistic Development) at the Julius Maximilian University of
Würzburg.

When his grandparents died in 1896, they left
him a considerable inheritance, and Osthaus used
his newly acquired financial independence to
realize his plans for a museum. With the vision of
'reintroducing art to life',[4] his museum was intended to make it possible to experience beauty in
the 'art-forsaken industrial region'[5] of western
Germany. In accordance with the original concept
of a *'Folkwang'*, the museum was supposed to
serve the people (*folk*) as a 'place of assembly'
(*vang*). In order to improve the city artistically,
the museum director also invited artists, such as
Christian Rohlfs, to move to Hagen.

Osthaus initially made natural history the focus
of his collecting: by observing beauty in nature,
museum visitors would be led to appreciate
the aesthetic in art. After acquiring two important
natural history collections, Osthaus undertook
excursions with the Hagen entomologist J. H. H.
Schmidt in the Atlas Mountains and the Sahara,[6]
which increasingly brought him to rethink: 'Here
living contact with Islamic culture led […] to an
active resumption of my art historical studies.'[7] In
the autumn of 1898, therefore, this was followed by
journeys to, among other places, Constantinople,
Greece and Egypt, where he acquired applied art
and archaeological artefacts. There, Osthaus finally became, as he himself observed, 'a collector
of works of art'.[8] During his travels, he also made

numerous contacts that would later prove useful
to the museum.

In 1899, he married Gertrud Colsman, the
daughter of a wealthy textile manufacturer, who
not only shared his interests in art but was also
increasingly cultivating contacts with artists
(p. 202).[9] Plans for the Museum Folkwang were
now taking shape. For the commission to build a
museum in the centre of his native city of Hagen,
Osthaus turned to the planning department
surveyor Carl Gérard, whose design was in the
then-common, stately Neo-Renaissance style
(fig. 1). Osthaus's fondness for the building's design
faded, however. Searching for a new architect
to finish his museum, he was so convinced by the
work of the Belgian Henry van de Velde that he
arranged to meet him – the beginning of a close
bond marked by important mutual influence. In
1900, two years after construction had begun, he
hired Van de Velde to complete the museum
building. Because the shell was already in place,
the architect redesigned the interior, not in
Gérard's Neo-Renaissance style but in a purist
design that deliberately alluded to the functional
and industrial elements of the structure: for example, he conceived a stucco cladding for the
iron-and-brick supports that employs their forms
and materiality rather than concealing them (fig. 2).

Osthaus finally opened the Museum Folkwang
in 1902.[10] Three focuses had evolved from his
collecting activities: in addition to the department
of natural history objects there was a collection
of archaeological pieces and international applied

unter dem Titel *Grundzüge der Stilentwicklung*
an der Julius-Maximilians-Universität in Würzburg
abschließen wird.

Als ihm seine im Jahr 1896 verstorbenen Großeltern ein beträchtliches Erbe hinterlassen, nutzt
Osthaus seine neugewonnene finanzielle Unabhängigkeit, um seine Pläne für ein Museum in die Tat
umzusetzen. Mit dem Leitbild einer „Zurückführung
der Kunst ins Leben"[4] soll sein Museum im „kunstverlassenen Industriebezirk"[5] des Westens die
Schönheit erfahrbar machen. Dem ursprünglichen
Begriff „Folkwang" folgend, soll das Museum dem
Volk als „Versammlungsort" dienen. Um die Stadt
künstlerisch aufzuwerten, lädt der Museumsgründer zusätzlich Künstler:innen wie Christian Rohlfs
dazu ein, nach Hagen überzusiedeln.

Osthaus legt den Schwerpunkt seiner Sammlung zunächst auf naturkundliche Objekte: Die
Museumsbesucher:innen sollen durch die Beob-
achtung der Schönheit in der Natur an das Ästhetische in der Kunst herangeführt werden. Nachdem
er zwei bedeutende naturkundliche Sammlungen
erworben hat, unternimmt Osthaus gemeinsam
mit dem Hagener Entomologen J. H. H. Schmidt
Exkursionen in den Atlas und die Sahara,[6] die ihn
zunehmend umdenken lassen: „Hier führte die
lebendige Berührung mit der islamischen Kultur [...]
zu einer lebhaften Wiederaufnahme meiner kunst-
geschichtlichen Studien"[7]. Im Herbst 1898 folgen
daher unter anderem Reisen nach Konstantinopel,
Griechenland und Ägypten, wo er Kunstgewerbe und archäologische Artefakte ersteht. Osthaus
wird dort letztlich, wie er selbst festhält, „zum
Sammler von Kunstwerken"[8]. Während seiner

Reisen knüpft er außerdem zahlreiche dem
späteren Museum dienliche Kontakte.

Im Jahr 1899 heiratet er Gertrud Colsman,
Tochter eines wohlhabenden Textil-Fabrikanten,
die nicht nur seine geistigen und künstlerischen
Interessen teilt, sondern ebenfalls zunehmend
enge künstlerische Kontakte pflegt (S. 202).[9]
Auch die Pläne für das Museum Folkwang nehmen
nun immer mehr Gestalt an. Osthaus wendet sich
mit dem Auftrag für einen Museumsbau im Zentrum seiner Heimatstadt Hagen an den Baurat Carl
Gérard, dessen Entwurf den damals üblichen
Repräsentationsstil der Neo-Renaissance vorsieht
(Abb. 1). Osthaus' Gefallen an der Gestaltung des
Baus schwindet jedoch. Auf der Suche nach einem
neuen Architekten für die Fertigstellung seines
Museums überzeugt ihn die Arbeit des Belgiers
Henry van de Velde so sehr, dass er ein Treffen mit
diesem in die Wege leitet – der Auftakt einer
engen Bindung, die von bedeutendem wechsel-
seitigem Einfluss geprägt ist. Im Jahr 1900, zwei
Jahre nach Baubeginn, beauftragt er van de Velde,
den Museumsbau fertigzustellen. Da der Roh-
bau bereits steht, gestaltet der Architekt den
Innenraum neu und orientiert sich dabei nicht wie
Gérard an der Neo-Renaissance, sondern nimmt
in seinem puristischen Entwurf bewusst Bezug auf
die funktionalen und industriellen Elemente des
Baus: So konzipiert er etwa eine Verkleidung für
die Eisen- und Backsteinstützen aus Stuck, welche
deren Formen und Materialien nutzt, anstatt diese
zu verschleiern (Abb. 2).

Im Jahr 1902 eröffnet Osthaus schließlich das
Museum Folkwang.[10] Aus seinen Sammleraktivitäten

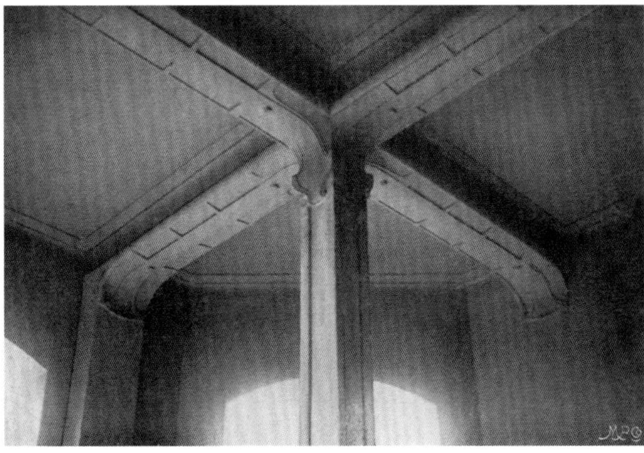

Abb. | Fig. 2
Museum Folkwang, Hagen, Stuckverkleidung
der Eisen- und Backsteinstützen |
stucco cladding for the iron and brick
supports, 1902

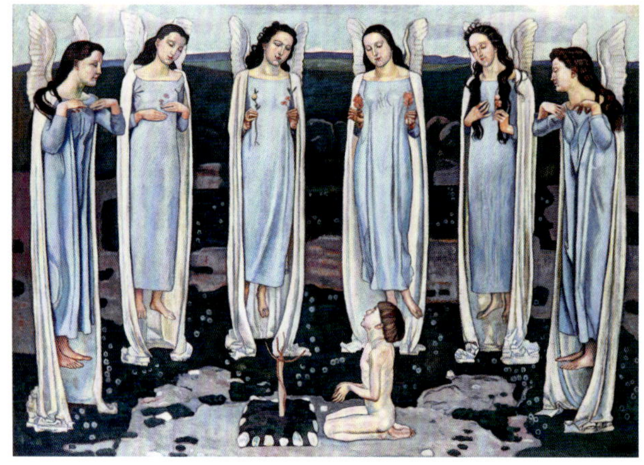

arts from the Middle Ages onwards as well
as a gallery with French and German modern art,
which after 1912 would join in a dialogue with
non-Western artefacts – a fundamental difference
from the presentation in other German art
museums.

In 1909, Osthaus also founded the Deutsches
Museum für Kunst in Handel und Gewerbe (German Museum for Art in Trade and Commerce) with
the goal of reviving the social relevance of applied
art by means of travelling exhibitions. He was
also active in, among other things, urban planning,
theatre and publishing and addressed issues of
regional art and cultural policy. In the 'Hohenhof',
the Osthaus family residence built between 1906
and 1908 to a design by Henry van de Velde, works
of art such as Ferdinand Hodler's painting *Der
Auserwählte* (*The Chosen One*, 1903; fig 3) had
places specially designed for them within spatial
ensembles.

Because both the museums and Osthaus himself were in debt during the war years, owing to
inflation and war loans, Osthaus sold selected
works from his collection privately or in auctions
in 1917, including paintings by Paul Gauguin and
Vincent van Gogh. The post-war years were also
hard on the Museum Folkwang, so that Osthaus,
who had suffered severely from pleurisy, struggled
with financial problems until his death. In order to
keep the existing holdings as cohesive as possible
after the death of its founder, his heirs contacted
suitable buyers on the German museum scene;
in addition to Hagen and Essen, Munich showed

interest.[11] A close interchange between Osthaus
and Ernst Gosebruch of the Kunstmuseum Essen
had been evolving at least since 1910. After tough
negotiations, in 1922 the collection of the Museum
Folkwang was transferred to the City of Essen
and the Folkwang-Museumsverein, which had been
created for that purpose. The holdings of the
Deutsches Museum für Kunst in Handel und Gewerbe became the property of the Kaiser-Wilhelm-
Museum in Krefeld in 1923, with whose founding
director, Friedrich Deneken, Osthaus had also
been in close contact. The buildings designed for
Osthaus, such as the former museum and the
Hohenhof, continue to be managed by the City
of Hagen. Today, the Osthaus Museum Hagen also
preserves the bulk of Osthaus's correspondence
and the archival materials of the Museum Folkwang
from the years up to the sale of the collection.

The preface to the first and only collection catalogue to be published during Osthaus's lifetime,
in 1912, speaks of the Museum Folkwang as having
initiated a new understanding of art: 'The most
important works in the collection […] were acquired at a time when their masters were still little
known or even entirely unknown in Germany.
They have contributed to improving understanding of the great initiators of modern painting:
Van Gogh, Gauguin and Cézanne.'[12] Whereas the
painting *Lise – La femme à l'ombrelle* (*Lise with
Parasol*, 1867; p. 209) by Pierre-Auguste Renoir
that entered the collection in 1901 was still a work
of early Impressionism, increasing acquisitions of
contemporary art reveal the overcoming of

haben sich drei Schwerpunkte herausgebildet:
Neben der Abteilung für naturkundliche Objekte gibt es eine Sammlung mit archäologischen
Stücken und internationalem Kunstgewerbe seit
dem Mittelalter sowie eine Galerie mit Kunst der
französischen und deutschen Moderne, welche
nach 1912 mit nichteuropäischen Artefakten in
Dialog tritt – ein grundlegender Unterschied zu
der Präsentationsform anderer deutscher Kunstmuseen.

1909 gründet Osthaus zudem das Deutsche
Museum für Kunst in Handel und Gewerbe mit
dem Ziel, die gesellschaftliche Relevanz von angewandter Kunst in Wanderausstellungen wieder
aufleben zu lassen. Darüber hinaus wirkt er unter
anderem im Städtebau-, Theater- und Verlagswe-
sen und setzt sich mit Fragen regionaler Kunst- und
Kulturpolitik auseinander. Auch im sogenannten
Hohenhof, dem von Henry van de Velde zwischen
1906 und 1908 erbauten Wohnhaus der Familie
Osthaus, finden Kunstwerke wie Ferdinand Hodlers
Gemälde *Der Auserwählte* (1903; Abb. 3) in auf sie
abgestimmten Raumensembles Platz.

Da beide Museen und Osthaus selbst während
der Kriegsjahre durch die Inflation und Kriegs-
anleihen verschuldet sind, verkauft Osthaus 1917
ausgewählte Werke aus seiner Sammlung privat
oder über Auktionen, unter anderem Gemälde von
Paul Gauguin und Vincent van Gogh. Die Nachkriegsjahre treffen das Museum Folkwang ebenfalls
schwer, sodass der von einer Rippenfellentzün-
dung stark angeschlagene Osthaus bis zu seinem
Tod im März 1921 mit finanziellen Problemen zu
kämpfen hat. Um die vorhandenen Bestände nach

dem Tod ihres Gründers möglichst geschlossen
und im Sinne des Sammlers zu bewahren, treten
seine Erben mit adäquaten Käufer:innen in der
deutschen Museumsszene in Kontakt; neben
Hagen und Essen besteht auch Interesse in München.[11] Zwischen Osthaus und Ernst Gosebruch
vom Kunstmuseum Essen hatte sich spätestens 1910
ein enger Austausch entwickelt. Nach zähen
Verhandlungen geht die Sammlung des Museum
Folkwang im Jahr 1922 an den zu diesem Zweck
gegründeten Folkwang-Museumsverein und die
Stadt Essen über. Die Bestände des Deutschen
Museum für Kunst in Handel und Gewerbe gelangen 1923 in den Besitz des Kaiser Wilhelm Museums in Krefeld, mit dessen erstem Direktor Friedrich Deneken Osthaus ebenfalls eng verbunden
war. Die für Osthaus konzipierten Gebäude wie das
ehemalige Museum oder der Hohenhof werden
weiterhin von der Stadt Hagen verwaltet. Heute
verwahrt das Osthaus Museum Hagen ebenfalls
den Großteil der Osthaus'schen Korrespondenz
sowie die Archivalien des Museum Folkwang aus
den Jahren bis zum Verkauf der Sammlung.

Im Vorwort des ersten und einzigen Bestands-
katalogs, der zu Lebzeiten von Osthaus erscheint,
ist im Jahr 1912 die Rede davon, dass das Museum
Folkwang ein neues Kunstverständnis angestoßen
habe: „Die wichtigsten Werke der Sammlung [...]
sind zu einer Zeit erworben worden, als ihre
Meister in Deutschland noch wenig oder gar nicht
bekannt waren. Sie haben dazu beigetragen,
das Verständnis für die großen Anreger moderner
Malkunst, van Gogh, Gauguin und Cézanne[,] in
Deutschland zu erschließen.“[12] Während mit dem

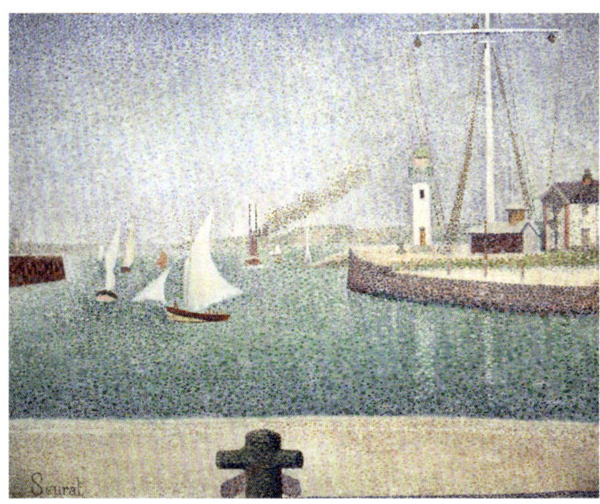

Abb. | Fig. 4
Georges Seurat, *Entrée du port d'Honfleur*,
1886, The Barnes Foundation, Philadelphia

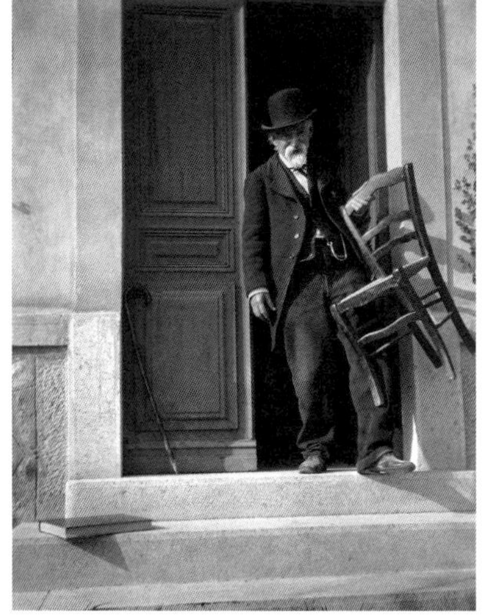

Abb. | Fig. 5
Gertrud Osthaus, Paul Cézanne
in Aix-en-Provence, 13. April 1906

Impressionism. These – mostly French – works include, for example, Van Gogh's painting *La moisson* (*The Wheatfield behind St Paul's Hospital with a Reaper*, 1889; p. 315), which Osthaus presented at the opening of the Museum Folkwang. It was the first work by Van Gogh to enter a German museum collection.[13]

The collection's profile, which was crucially shaped by Henry van de Velde as well, thanks to his numerous acquaintances in the art world, can be traced back in part to the means available to Osthaus, whose inherited wealth was modest compared to that of the collectors of the *grande bourgeoisie* or of an entrepreneur such as Kōjirō Matsukata. His acquisitions, made with the help of his advisors, therefore often concentrate on relatively affordable works of art: In the year the Folkwang opened, Osthaus purchased, among other works, *Entrée du port d'Honfleur (Entrance to the Port of Honfleur*, 1886; fig. 4) by Georges Seurat; *Saint Cloud (The Seine near St. Cloud*, 1900; p. 288) by Paul Signac; and *Coucher de soleil sur la mer (Sunset over the Sea*, 1896; S. 289) by Henri Edmond Cross.[14] Osthaus was also guided by his love of experiments and collected independent works 'that have not yet found any canonized position in the history of art and the museum business'.[15] As a 'promoter behind the establishment'[16] of French Post-Impressionism and German Expressionism, Osthaus did pioneering work, which – in keeping with his didactic project – aimed to aesthetically educate the viewer. By providing visitors with commentaries on the exhibi-

tion, he was both an imparter of and commentator on contemporaneous developments in art.

Osthaus showed enthusiasm for the simplification of the means of painting that he recognized in the work of Van Gogh, Gauguin and Cézanne and wrote of the last of these: 'His paintings are the first of our time that seem to exist only for the sake of colour.' (fig. 5)[17] More than that, he understood the French art of his day to be a stimulus for new artistic movements in Germany:

> Museums are higher schooling for artists as well, and it will depend on them whether our art will be worth something or not. […] That the acquisition of French paintings also has to be made from this point of view will be understood by everyone who knows what the French painter of the nineteenth century means for the history of that art's evolution.[18]

In 1903 and 1904, Osthaus became the first German collector to acquire works by Gauguin, including *Jeune fille à l'éventail* (*The Girl with a Fan*) and *Contes barbares* (both 1902; pp. 337, 339). In 1907, Osthaus purchased the painting *Maison de Bellevue et pigeonnier (House and Dovecote at Bellevue*, ca. 1890–92) and *La carrière de Bibémus (The Quarry at Bibémus*, ca. 1895; pp. 292, 293) by Cézanne. In 1911, Osthaus was offered a large set of twenty-seven works by the artist on the Dutch art market; the purchase was unsuccessful, however, because of a legal dispute that would continue until the First World War.

Gemälde *Lise – La femme à l'ombrelle (Lise
mit dem Sonnenschirm,* 1867; S. 209) von Pierre-
Auguste Renoir im Jahr 1901 noch ein Werk des
frühen Impressionismus Eingang in die Sammlung
findet, machen die zunehmenden Ankäufe zeitgenössischer Kunst die Überwindung des Impressionismus sichtbar. Zu diesen – meist französischen – Werken zählt beispielsweise Vincent van
Goghs Gemälde *La moisson (Die Ernte, Kornfeld
mit Schnitter,* 1889; S. 315), das Osthaus schon bei
der Eröffnung des Museum Folkwang präsentiert.
Es ist das erste Werk van Goghs, das in deutschen
Museumsbesitz übergeht.[13]

Das Profil der Sammlung, das auch Henry
van de Velde aufgrund seiner zahlreichen Be-
kanntschaften in der Kunstwelt maßgeblich prägt,
ist zum Teil auf die finanzielle Lage von Osthaus
zurückzuführen, dessen geerbtes Vermögen
im Vergleich zu großbürgerlichen Sammler:innen
oder einem Unternehmer wie Kōjirō Matsukata
eher bescheiden ausfällt. Die Ankäufe, die durch
Vermittlung seiner Berater:innen geschehen, konzentrieren sich daher oftmals auf vergleichsweise
erschwingliche Kunstwerke: Im Eröffnungsjahr
des Folkwang ersteht Osthaus unter anderem
Werke wie *Entrée du port d'Honfleur (Einfahrt
in den Hafen von Honfleur,* 1886; Abb. 4) von
Georges Seurat, *Saint-Cloud (Die Seine bei Saint-
Cloud,* 1900; S. 288) von Paul Signac und *Coucher
de soleil sur la mer (Sonnenuntergang über dem
Meer,* 1896; S. 289) von Henri Edmond Cross.[14]
Doch Osthaus wird auch von seiner Experimentier-
freude geleitet und erwirbt eigenständig Werke,
„die noch keinerlei kanonisierte Stellung in Kunst-

geschichte und Museumsbetrieb gefunden"[15]
haben. Als „Promoter bei der Etablierung"[16] des
französischen Post-Impressionismus und des
deutschen Expressionismus leistet Osthaus Pionier-
arbeit, die – dem erzieherischen Vorhaben des
Museumsgründers folgend – auf die ästhetische
Schulung der Rezipient:innen abzielt. Indem er
den Besucher:innen Ausstellungskommentare als
Anleitung an die Hand gibt, agiert er gleichsam
als Vermittler und Kommentator zeitgenössischer
Kunstentwicklungen.

Osthaus zeigt sich begeistert von der Vereinfa-
chung der malerischen Mittel, die er bei van Gogh,
Gauguin und Paul Cézanne erkennt, und schreibt
zu Letzterem: „Seine Bilder sind die ersten unserer
Zeit, die nur der Farbe wegen da zu sein scheinen."
(Abb. 5)[17] Mehr noch versteht er die französische
Kunst dieser Zeit als Stimulus für neue künstlerische Bewegungen in Deutschland: „Museen sind
auch für den Künstler eine hohe Schule, und es
wird von ihnen mit abhängen, ob unsere Kunst
etwas taugen wird oder nicht. [...] Daß von diesem
Standpunkt aus die Erwerbung französischer Bilder oft in Betracht gezogen werden mußte, wird
jeder verstehen, der weiß, was die französische
Malerei des 19. Jahrhunderts für die Entwicklungsgeschichte dieser Kunst bedeutet."[18] Als erster
deutscher Sammler ersteht Osthaus in den Jahren
1903 und 1904 Werke von Gauguin, darunter
Jeune fille à l'éventail (Mädchen mit Fächer) und
Contes barbares (beide 1902; S. 337, 339). Von
Cézanne erwirbt Osthaus 1907 die Gemälde
*Maison de Bellevue et pigeonnier (Haus auf be-
waldeter Anhöhe,* ca. 1890–1892) und *La carrière*

Abb. | Fig. 6
Emile Bernard, *L'africaine,* 1895,
Museum Folkwang, Essen

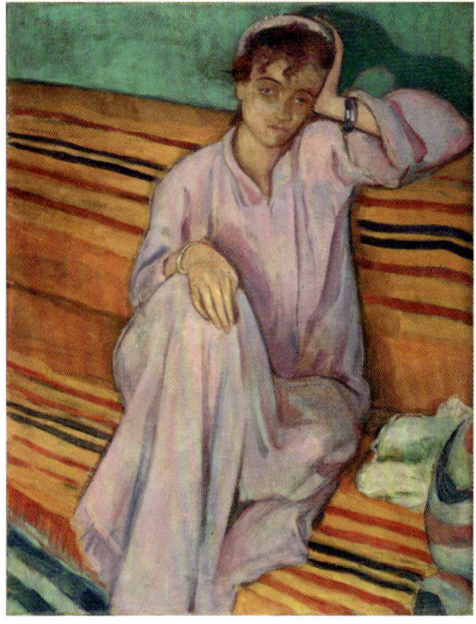

In the following years, works by, among others, Edouard Vuillard, Emile Bernard (fig. 6), Henri de Toulouse-Lautrec, Maurice Denis (p. 245), and Henri Matisse were added. In Amsterdam, Osthaus and his wife Gertrud sought out art dealers to acquire Asian art objects; in Domburg, they particular admired the artists' colony there with artists such as Piet Mondrian. Trips to Paris and the Netherlands in 1903 and 1904 were among Osthaus's most important efforts to expand his collection and network. Both Osthauses were in constant contact with artists, advisors and art dealers and visited studios and exhibitions. Osthaus continued to keep an eye on developments in contemporary art: acquisitions of works by artists such as Emil Nolde, Ernst Ludwig Kirchner, Franz Marc and Wassily Kandinsky soon testified to the museum director's commitment to Expressionism.

1   This text is based on earlier published descriptions of the life of Karl Ernst Osthaus in Herta Hesse-Frielinghaus et al., *Karl Ernst Osthaus: Leben und Werk* (Recklinghausen, 1971); Christoph Dorsz, 'Karl Ernst Osthaus und der Folkwang Impuls: Das Museum von 1902 bis heute', *Der Folkwang Impuls: Das Museum von 1902 bis heute*, ed. Tayfun Belgin and Christoph Dorsz, exh. cat. Osthaus Museum Hagen (Hagen, 2012), 10–129; and Uwe Fleckner, 'Karl Ernst Osthaus und die französische Moderne: Über das widersprüchliche Selbstverständnis eines Sammlers', in *'Das schönste Museum der Welt': Museum Folkwang bis 1933; Essays zur Geschichte des Museum Folkwang*, exh. cat. Museum Folkwang, Essen (Göttingen, 2010), 47–69. The following notes indicate only direct quotations from these publications with page references. Gloria Köpnick and Rainer Stamm are currently working on an updated biography of Karl Ernst and Gertrud Osthaus, to be published in 2022, which promises new insights.

2   See Nina Lawryniuk, 'Karl Ernst Osthaus und das Folkwang-Museum: Ein Wegbereiter zwischen Mythos und Moderne', in Fabian Fechner and Barbara Schneider (eds.), *Koloniale Vergangenheiten der Stadt Hagen*, 3rd ed. (Hagen, 2020), 35.

3   Sabine Riemer-Koeritz, 'Weltmachtpolitik und Hagen – der Alldeutsche Verband', in ibid., 115.

4   Karl Ernst Osthaus, 'Lebenslauf', quoted from idem, *Grundzüge der Stilentwicklung*, PhD diss. Hagen, 1918, in Rainer Stamm (ed.), *Reden und Schriften*, Kontext. Schriftenreihe für Kunst, Kunsterziehung und Kulturpädagogik 3 (Cologne, 2002), 23–24.

5   Herta Hesse-Frielinghaus, 'Folkwang 1. Teil', in Herta Hesse-Frielinghaus et al., *Karl Ernst Osthaus: Leben und Werk* (Recklinghausen, 1971), 123.

6   See Karl Ernst Osthaus, 'Lebenslauf', 23.

7   Ibid.

8   Ibid.

9   The role of Gertrud Osthaus in the genesis of the Folkwang collections is currently being researched by Gloria Köpnick and Rainer Stamm (see note 1).

10 See Karl Ernst Osthaus, 'Lebenslauf', 23.

11 Anonymous, 'Sammlungen', *Kunstchronik und Kunstmarkt* 57, N.S. XXXIII, nos. 6 and 4 (November 1921), 104.

12 Karl Ernst Osthaus, 'Vorwort', quoted from Kurt Freyer (ed.), *Moderne Kunst: Plastik, Malerei, Graphik*, Folkwang Museum (Hagen, 1912), in Osthaus, *Reden und Schriften*, 45.

13 See *Making van Gogh: Geschichte einer deutschen Liebe*, eds. Alexander Eiling and Felix Krämer, exh. cat. Städel Museum, Frankfurt am Main (Munich, 2019), 337.

14 On this, see the essay by Rainer Stamm in the present volume, pp. 92–105.

15 Uwe Fleckner, 'Karl Ernst Osthaus und die französische Moderne', 61.

16 Christoph Dorsz, 'Karl Ernst Osthaus und der Folkwang Impuls', 12.

17 Karl Ernst Osthaus, 'Cézanne', in *Feuer: Monatsschrift für Kunst und künstlerische Kultur* 2, nos. 2–3, (November–December 1920), in Osthaus, *Reden und Schriften*, 177.

18 Karl Ernst Osthaus, in *Im Kampf um die Kunst: Die Antwort auf den 'Protest deutscher Künstler'; Mit Beiträgen deutscher Künstler, Galerieleiter, Sammler und Schriftsteller* (Munich, 1911), in ibid., 43.

de Bibémus (Der Steinbruch Bibémus, ca. 1895; S. 292, 293). Im Jahr 1911 wird Osthaus ein großes Konvolut mit 27 Werken des Künstlers aus dem niederländischen Handel angeboten; der Ankauf scheitert jedoch aufgrund einer sich bis zum Ersten Weltkrieg hinziehenden gerichtlichen Auseinandersetzung.

In den nächsten Jahren kommen unter anderem Werke von Edouard Vuillard, Emile Bernard (Abb. 6), Henri de Toulouse-Lautrec, Maurice Denis (S. 245) oder Henri Matisse hinzu. In Amsterdam suchen Osthaus und seine Frau Gertrud Kunsthändler:innen auf, um Asiatika zu erstehen; in Domburg schätzen sie vor allem die dort ansässige Künstlerkolonie mit Künstler:innen wie Piet Mondrian. Die Reisen nach Paris und in die Niederlande während der Jahre 1903 und 1904 zählen zu den wichtigsten Unternehmungen von Osthaus, um Sammlung und Netzwerk zu erweitern. Gemeinsam steht das Ehepaar Osthaus in ständiger Verbindung zu Künstler:innen, Berater:innen und Kunsthändler:innen und besucht Ateliers und Ausstellungen. Nach wie vor behält Osthaus die Entwicklung der zeitgenössischen Kunst im Blick: So zeugen bald schon Erwerbungen von Künstler:innen wie Emil Nolde, Ernst Ludwig Kirchner, Franz Marc und Wassily Kandinsky vom Engagement des Museumsgründers für den Expressionismus.

1 Dieser Text basiert auf den bisher erschienenen Lebensbeschreibungen zu Karl Ernst Osthaus von Herta Hesse-Frielinghaus u. a., *Karl Ernst Osthaus. Leben und Werk,* Recklinghausen 1971; Christoph Dorsz, „Karl Ernst Osthaus und der Folkwang Impuls. Das Museum von 1902 bis heute", in: *Der Folkwang Impuls. Das Museum von 1902 bis heute,* hrsg. von Tayfun Belgin und Christoph Dorsz, Ausst.-Kat. Osthaus Museum Hagen, Hagen 2012, S. 10–129, sowie Uwe Fleckner, „Karl Ernst Osthaus und die französische Moderne. Über das widersprüchliche Selbstverständnis eines Sammlers", in: *„Das schönste Museum der Welt". Museum Folkwang bis 1933. Essays zur Geschichte des Museum Folkwang,* Ausst.-Kat. Museum Folkwang, Essen, Göttingen 2010, S. 47–69. Es werden im Folgenden nur direkte Zitate aus diesen Publikationen mit Seitenverweisen angegeben. Gloria Köpnick und Rainer Stamm arbeiten derzeit an einer aktualisierten Biografie zu Karl Ernst und Gertrud Osthaus, die 2022 erscheinen soll und neue Erkenntnisse verspricht.

2 Vgl. Nina Lawryniuk, „Karl Ernst Osthaus und das Folkwang-Museum. Ein Wegbereiter zwischen Mythos und Moderne", in: *Koloniale Vergangenheiten der Stadt Hagen,* hrsg. von Fabian Fechner und Barbara Schneider, 3. Aufl., Hagen 2020, S. 35.

3 Sabine Riemer-Koeritz, „Weltmachtpolitik und Hagen – der Alldeutsche Verband", in: ebd., S. 115.

4 Karl Ernst Osthaus, „Lebenslauf", in: ders., *Grundzüge der Stilentwicklung,* Diss. Hagen 1918, zit. nach: *Karl Ernst Osthaus. Reden und Schriften. Folkwang, Werkbund, Arbeitsrat (Kontext. Schriftenreihe für Kunst, Kunsterziehung und Kulturpädagogik,* 3), hrsg. und komm. von Rainer Stamm, Köln 2002, S. 23 f.

5 Herta Hesse-Frielinghaus, „Folkwang 1. Teil", in: dies. u. a., *Karl Ernst Osthaus. Leben und Werk,* Recklinghausen 1971, S. 123.

6 Vgl. Karl Ernst Osthaus, „Lebenslauf", S. 23.

7 Ebd.

8 Ebd.

9 Die Rolle von Gertrud Osthaus in der Genese der Folkwang-Sammlungen wird derzeit von Gloria Köpnick und Rainer Stamm erforscht (s. Anm. 1).

10 Vgl. Karl Ernst Osthaus, „Lebenslauf", S. 23.

11 Anonymer Autor, „Sammlungen", in: *Kunstchronik und Kunstmarkt,* 57, Neue Folge XXXIII, Nr. 6 und 4, November 1921, S. 104.

12 Karl Ernst Osthaus, „Vorwort", in: *Museum Folkwang,* Bd. 1, *Moderne Kunst. Plastik, Malerei, Graphik,* bearb. von Kurt Freyer, Hagen 1912 (Nachdruck 1983), zit. nach: *Karl Ernst Osthaus. Reden und Schriften,* S. 45.

13 Vgl. *Making van Gogh. Geschichte einer deutschen Liebe,* hrsg. von Alexander Eiling und Felix Krämer, Ausst.-Kat. Städel Museum, Frankfurt am Main, München 2019, S. 337.

14 Vgl. dazu den Beitrag von Rainer Stamm in diesem Band, S. 92–105.

15 Uwe Fleckner, „Karl Ernst Osthaus und die französische Moderne", S. 61.

16 Christoph Dorsz, „Karl Ernst Osthaus und der Folkwang Impuls", S. 12.

17 Karl Ernst Osthaus, „Cézanne", in: *Feuer. Monatsschrift für Kunst und künstlerische Kultur,* 2, 2/3, November/Dezember 1920, zit. nach: *Karl Ernst Osthaus. Reden und Schriften,* S. 177.

18 Karl Ernst Osthaus, in: *Im Kampf um die Kunst. Die Antwort auf den „Protest deutscher Künstler". Mit Beiträgen deutscher Künstler, Galerieleiter, Sammler und Schriftsteller,* München 1911, zit. nach: ebd., S. 43.

KŌJIRŌ MATSUKATA: COSMOPOLITE AND PHILANTHROPIST

Detmar Westhoff

Wearing a bright suit with white collar turned up and a tie, with a cigar in his hand, Kōjirō Matsukata is standing, smiling, next to Claude Monet (fig. 1). He does not look like a high-ranking Japanese business representative – serious and restrained – but rather cheerful and relaxed. His contemporaries were already impressed by the extraordinary cosmopolitanism and self-confidence with which Matsukata moved about in different cultures.[1] The entrepreneur and collector once described himself as a 'funny man',[2] which his grandson Ken Matsumoto understands as an allusion to his unusual personality and nonconformism: 'He did not mind being different from others. He tried to be a reformer or "game changer".'[3] How did Matsukata become the person who managed to build such an important art collection of European modernism, especially of Impressionism and Post-Impressionism?

Son of a Reformer:
Matsukata's Origins

Kōjirō Matsukata was born in 1866, as one of twenty-two children of Masayoshi Matsukata, who had contributed to the modernization of Japan as Minister of Finance and Prime Minister.[4] The reformation of the country had been actively pursued since the Meiji era (1868–1912) by an elite oriented around the United States and Europe in particular, because until it was forced to open in 1853, Japan had been isolated from the West for nearly two hundred years. Masayoshi Matsukata passed on to his sons his own decisive advocacy of modernization, of justice and humanity, even in the face of resistance, as well as his high esteem for art. He showed his important collection of Japanese painting from the Middle Ages to the

Im hellen Anzug mit hochgestelltem weißem
Hemdkragen, dazu eine Krawatte, steht Kōjirō
Matsukata mit einer Zigarre in der Hand lächelnd
neben Claude Monet (Abb. 1). Er wirkt nicht wie ein
hochrangiger japanischer Wirtschaftsvertreter –
ernst und zurückhaltend –, sondern heiter und
entspannt. Schon Zeitgenossen waren von der
außergewöhnlichen Weltgewandtheit und Souveränität beeindruckt, mit der Matsukata sich in
verschiedenen Kulturen bewegte.[1] Der Unternehmer und Sammler bezeichnete sich selbst einmal
als „seltsamen Mann"[2], was sein Enkel Ken Matsumoto als Anspielung auf seine außergewöhnliche
Persönlichkeit und Unangepasstheit versteht: „Es
machte ihm nichts aus, anders zu sein als die
anderen. Er versuchte, ein Reformer oder Game
Changer zu sein."[3] Wie wurde Matsukata zu dem
Menschen, dem es gelang, in Japan eine derart
bedeutende Sammlung von Kunst der europäischen Moderne, insbesondere des Impressionismus und Post-Impressionismus, aufzubauen?

<table>
<tr><td>351</td><td>Detmar Westhoff</td></tr>
</table>

Sohn eines Reformers –
Matsukatas Herkunft

Kōjirō Matsukata wurde 1866 als eines der 22
Kinder von Masayoshi Matsukata geboren, der sich
als Finanzminister und Ministerpräsident um die
Modernisierung Japans verdient gemacht hatte.[4]
Die Reformierung des Landes wurde seit der
Meiji-Zeit (1868–1912) aktiv von einer sich insbeson-
dere an den USA und Europa orientierenden Elite
verfolgt, denn bis zur erzwungenen Öffnung im
Jahr 1853 hatte sich Japan über fast 200 Jahre
weitgehend vom Westen isoliert. Masayoshi
Matsukatas entschiedenes Eintreten für die Moder-
nisierung seines Landes, für Gerechtigkeit und
Menschlichkeit auch gegen Widerstände gab er
seinen Kindern ebenso mit auf den Weg wie die

KŌJIRŌ MATSUKATA –
KOSMOPOLIT UND PHILANTHROP

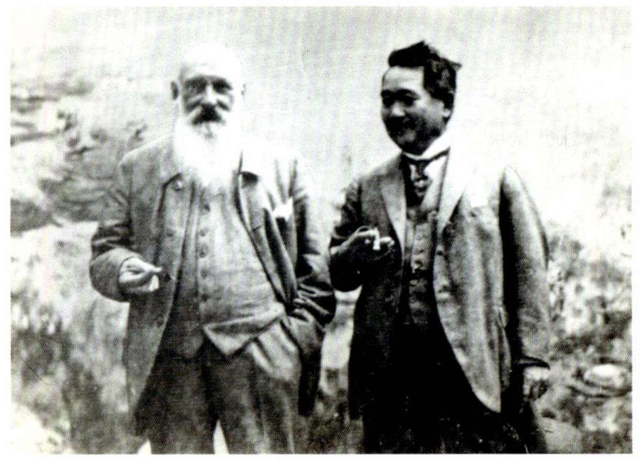

Abb. | Fig. 1
Claude Monet und | and Kōjirō Matsukata,
1921

eighteenth century in his Japanese house in
Tokyo, next to which he had built a residence in
the Victorian style by the British architect Josiah
Conder, for which he imported furniture from
England (fig. 2).[5] He expressed his admiration for
Western culture in Paris in 1878 by saying he
wanted to plant the seeds of this 'glorious civiliza-
tion'[6] in Japan, so that its greatness and beauty
would one day be achieved there too. His sons
Shōsaku and Kōjirō Matsukata did indeed become
passionate art collectors.[7]

Cosmopolite and Entrepreneur

Kōjirō Matsukata already demonstrated when
attending the preparatory school of University of
Tokyo that he was not always prepared to conform
to social expectations. After he had organized
a student strike, he had to leave school without a
Japanese degree. Following the model of his
brothers, he went to the United States and began
studying at Rutgers College in New Jersey in 1885
(fig. 3). The college had been an important arrival
point for Japanese moving to the United States
to support technical, social and cultural progress
in their country.[8] A photograph from this period
shows Matsukata standing upright and self-con-
fident in the middle of the freshmen class football
team, for which, characteristically, he played
forward (fig. 4).[9] In order to become a diplomat,
after a year Matsukata transferred to Yale to study
law, receiving his doctorate in 1890. During his
studies he was interested in political and social

theories, sympathizing with the socialist ideals of
older fellow student, Sen Katayama, who later
became the leader of the Communist movement in
Japan. In Paris at the Sorbonne in 1889 he became
fascinated with Jean-Jacques Rousseau and Social
Darwinism in particular.[10]

Matsukata loved to travel, in part because
it enabled him to escape the strict conventions of
Japan. He said of himself that he did not make
appointments because he would probably not
keep them anyway, often changing his plans and
sometimes even disappearing without explana-
tion: 'Why should I not live like a crook sometimes
if I want to?'[11] His independence did not help his
political career: after his studies Matsukata worked
only briefly as his father's secretary and also left
a job in the imperial household ministry because
as a reformer he met with stiff opposition.[12] In
private enterprise, by contrast, he was not only
able to implement his ideas for social reform and
modernization but also better able to express
his personality and love of freedom. Hence, from
1896 onward, he proved to be a successful president of the industrial corporation Kawasaki
Dockyard Ltd. In 1904, the first dry dock in Kobe's
port was completed under his direction. In 1907,
Kawasaki manufactured the first Japanese locomotive, and in the First World War Matsukata made
large profits with his bold 'stock boat' project,
which was harshly criticized in shareholders' meetings: at the beginning of the war, he had had a
reserve of numerous warships built, without having
been commissioned to do so, which then made

353

hohe Wertschätzung für Kunst. Er zeigte seine bedeutende Sammlung japanischer Malerei vom Mittelalter bis zum 18. Jahrhundert in seinem japanischen Haus in Tokio, neben dem er ein Wohnhaus im viktorianischen Stil durch den britischen Architekten Josiah Conder errichten ließ, für das er Mobiliar aus England importierte (Abb. 2).[5] Seine Bewunderung für die westliche Kultur formulierte er 1878 in Paris mit den Worten, er wolle die Saat dieser „glorreichen Zivilisation"[6] in Japan pflanzen, sodass auch hier eines Tages die Größe und Schönheit derselben erreicht werde. Tatsächlich wurden auch seine Söhne Shōsaku und Kōjirō Matsukata leidenschaftliche Kunstsammler.[7]

Kosmopolit und Unternehmer

Kōjirō Matsukata bewies bereits während seines Besuchs der Vorschule zur Kaiserlichen Universität in Tokio, dass er nicht bereit war, immer den gesellschaftlichen Erwartungen zu entsprechen. Nachdem er einen studentischen Streik organisiert hatte, musste er die Schule ohne japanischen Abschluss verlassen. Nach dem Vorbild seiner Brüder ging er in die USA und begann sein Studium 1885 am Rutgers College in New Jersey (Abb. 3). Die Hochschule war seit den 1860er-Jahren eine wichtige Anlaufstelle für Japaner:innen, die es in die USA zog, um technischen, gesellschaftlichen und kulturellen Fortschritt in ihrem Land zu fördern.[8] Ein Foto aus dieser Zeit zeigt Matsukata aufrecht und selbstbewusst inmitten des Freshmen Class Football Teams, wo er bezeichnenderweise als Angreifer spielte (Abb. 4).[9] Um Diplomat zu

werden, wechselte Matsukata nach einem Jahr zum Studium der Rechtswissenschaften in Yale, das er schon 1890 mit dem Doktorgrad abschloss. Er interessierte sich in seiner Studienzeit für politische und gesellschaftliche Theorien, sympathisierte mit den sozialistischen Ideen seines älteren Mitstudenten Sen Katayama, der später Führer der kommunistischen Bewegung in Japan wurde, und beschäftigte sich während eines Aufenthalts an der Pariser Sorbonne 1889 besonders mit Jean-Jacques Rousseau und dem Sozialdarwinismus.[10]

Matsukata liebte es zu reisen, auch weil er sich damit den strengen japanischen Konventionen entziehen konnte. Er sagte über sich, er mache keine Termine, da er sie wahrscheinlich ohnehin nicht einhalte, ändere oft seine Pläne und tauche auch mal unter, ohne eine Erklärung zu geben: „Warum soll ich nicht manchmal wie ein Gauner leben, wenn ich es möchte?"[11] Seine Unabhängigkeit war nicht förderlich für seine politische Laufbahn: Nach seinem Studium war Matsukata nur kurz Sekretär seines Vaters und verließ auch eine Stelle im Ministerium des kaiserlichen Haushalts, da er als Reformer auf zu starren Widerstand stieß.[12] In der freien Wirtschaft hingegen konnte er nicht nur seine sozialreformerischen Ideen und Modernisierungspläne realisieren, sondern auch seine Persönlichkeit und Freiheitsliebe besser entfalten. So erwies er sich ab 1896 als erfolgreicher Präsident des Industrieunternehmens Kawasaki Dockyard Ltd. 1904 wurde unter seiner Leitung das erste Trockendock im Hafen Kobes fertiggestellt, 1907 fertigte Kawasaki die erste japanische Lokomotive und im Ersten Weltkrieg machte Matsukata mit

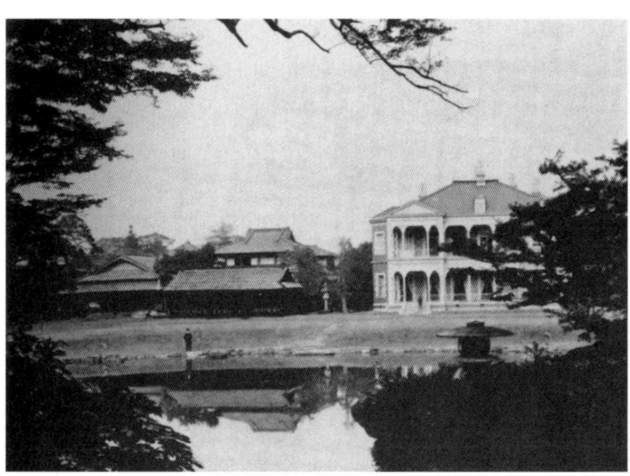

Abb. | Fig. 2
Die Residenz der Matsukata in Tokio,
vor März 1945 | The Matsukata residence
in Tokyo, before March 1945

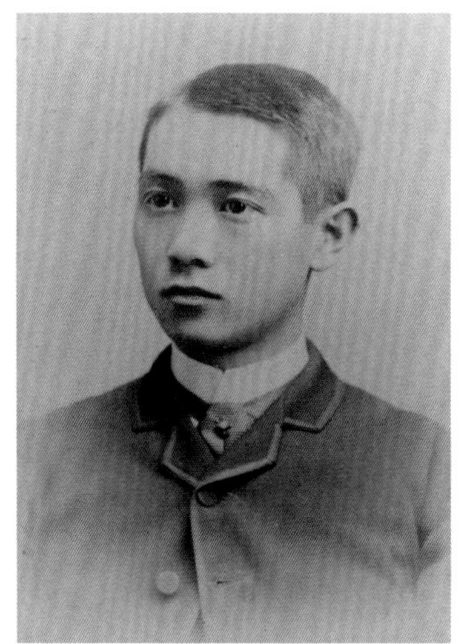

Abb. | Fig. 3
Kōjirō Matsukata, Rutgers College,
Klasse | class of 1889

a tidy profit in Europe during the war.[13] According to Ken Matsumoto, the profits from that practice, which was then a new one for the shipbuilding industry, were the cornerstone of the wealth that Matsukata would go on to invest in art.[14] Always looking out for his work force, he took their needs into consideration, offering employees rides to work with him in his carriage, for example, giving them training and educational opportunities in Europe and in 1919 by being the first businessman in Japan to introduce an eight-hour day instead of the then standard twelve hours.[15] He was accordingly popular. Beginning in 1916, Matsukata used his business trips abroad to visit galleries such as Georges Petit, Paul Durand-Ruel and Paul Rosenberg in Paris, others in London and New York and acquire art.

The idea of a collection of Western art may have preoccupied Matsukata even early on, but it was his great business success during the First World War that provided him with the necessary financial means to make his plan a reality.[16] For him, exemplary entrepreneurship meant taking responsibility for the society as a whole. That included his commitment to independent journalism with his contributions to the newspaper *Kobe Yu Shin Nippo* from 1895, and as president of the newspaper *Kobe Shimbun* from 1898.[17] He was, however, aware that a newspaper – unlike art – could lose importance after his death:[18] 'Art is the only enduring thing.'[19] Until the founding of what is now the Tokyo Metropolitan Art Museum in 1926, there were no art museums in Japan. Thanks to his

friendship with painters such as Kuroda Seiki, Matsukata was aware how much Japanese artists lacked opportunities to study works of Western art. He strove to create a museum on the model of a great encyclopaedic collection like that of the South Kensington Museum, now the Victoria and Albert Museum, in London, which would make it possible for the Japanese people to study the culture, art and essence of Western peoples but also their technologies and manufacturing methods.[20] By his own account, Matsukata viewed art as the 'expression of the soul of a people'.[21] At the same time, he knew how to use his plan for a museum to improve the international perception of Japan. By repeatedly reporting on it in the Western press and at receptions, Matsukata had journalists speculating whether his museum would even outdo the South Kensington Museum as the largest museum in the world.[22] In the process he was bringing to the West's attention the appreciation for art of the Japanese people, who should now be regarded as a peace-loving nation.[23] Matsukata met with politicians and important representatives of culture such as the Directeur des Beaux-Arts, Paul Léon, at a reception at the Musée Rodin in June 1921 (p. 144, fig. 1). In November 1921, he organized a banquet with a hundred guests at Claridge's in London and invited the Japanese ambassador as well as greats of the art world and the press. A year later he resumed his diplomatic efforts in Washington in 1937 and 1939 when he accompanied his younger brother Otohiko, who had been a friend of Franklin D. Roosevelt since they studied

seinem gewagten und auf Aktionärsversammlungen heftig kritisierten „Stock Boat"-Projekt große Gewinne: Zu Beginn des Krieges hatte er zahlreiche Kriegsschiffe ohne Auftrag auf Vorrat bauen lassen, die während des Krieges in Europa reißenden Absatz fanden.[13] Die Gewinne aus dieser damals für den Schiffbau neuen Praxis legten, so Ken Matsumoto, den Grundstein des Vermögens, das Matsukata in Kunst investierte.[14] Stets um seine Belegschaft bemüht, begegnete er ihr auf Augenhöhe, indem er seine Mitarbeiter:innen beispielsweise in seinem Wagen mit zur Arbeit nahm, ihnen Fortbildungen in Europa ermöglichte und 1919 als einer der ersten Unternehmer:innen in Japan statt des üblichen Zwölf- den Acht-Stunden-Tag einführte.[15] Dementsprechend beliebt war er. Seine Geschäftsreisen ins Ausland nutzte Matsukata ab 1916 dazu, in Paris, London oder New York Galerien wie Georges Petit, Paul Durand-Ruel oder Paul Rosenberg zu besuchen und Kunst zu erwerben.

Die Idee einer Sammlung westlicher Kunst mag Matsukata schon früher beschäftigt haben, aber erst der große wirtschaftliche Erfolg im Zuge des Ersten Weltkriegs brachte die notwendigen finanziellen Mittel, das Vorhaben umzusetzen.[16] Vorbildliches Unternehmertum bedeutete für ihn, Verantwortung für die gesamte Gesellschaft zu übernehmen. Dazu gehörte auch sein Engagement für den unabhängigen Journalismus mit seinen Beiträgen für die Zeitung *Kobe Yu Shin Nippo* ab 1895 sowie als Präsident der Zeitung *Kobe Shimbun* ab 1898.[17] Er war sich jedoch bewusst, dass die Zeitung – im Unterschied zur Kunst – nach seinem Tod an Bedeutung verlieren könnte[18]: „Kunst ist das

Einzige, was Bestand hat [...]."[19] Tatsächlich gab es bis zur Gründung des heutigen Tokyo Metropolitan Art Museum im Jahr 1926 keine Kunstmuseen in Japan. Aufgrund seiner Freundschaft mit Malern wie Kuroda Seiki wusste Matsukata, wie sehr japanischen Künstler:innen Werke westlicher Kunst zum Studium fehlten. Er strebte ein Museum nach dem Vorbild einer großen enzyklopädischen Sammlung wie jener des South Kensington Museum, des heutigen Victoria and Albert Museum in London, an, das es der japanischen Bevölkerung ermöglichen sollte, Kultur, Kunst und Wesen der westlichen Völker, aber auch Techniken und Fertigungsmethoden zu studieren.[20] Seinen eigenen Aussagen nach betrachtete Matsukata Kunst als „Ausdruck der Seele eines Volkes"[21]. Zugleich wusste er seinen Museumsplan für die internationale Wahrnehmung Japans einzusetzen. Indem Matsukata spätestens ab 1921 immer wieder darüber in der westlichen Presse und auf Empfängen berichtete und Journalist:innen zum Spekulieren brachte, ob sein Museum als größtes der Welt das South Kensington Museum noch übertreffen werde,[22] lenkte er die Aufmerksamkeit des Westens auf den Kunstsinn der japanischen Bevölkerung, die nun als friedliebendes Volk betrachtet werden sollte.[23] Matsukata begegnete dabei Politiker:innen und wichtigen Vertreter:innen aus der Kultur wie dem Directeur des Beaux-Arts Paul Léon auf einem Empfang im Juni 1921 im Musée Rodin (S. 144, Abb. 1). Im November 1921 lud er zu einem Bankett mit hundert Gästen im Londoner Claridge's Hotel neben dem japanischen Botschafter auch Größen aus Kunst und Presse ein. Jahre

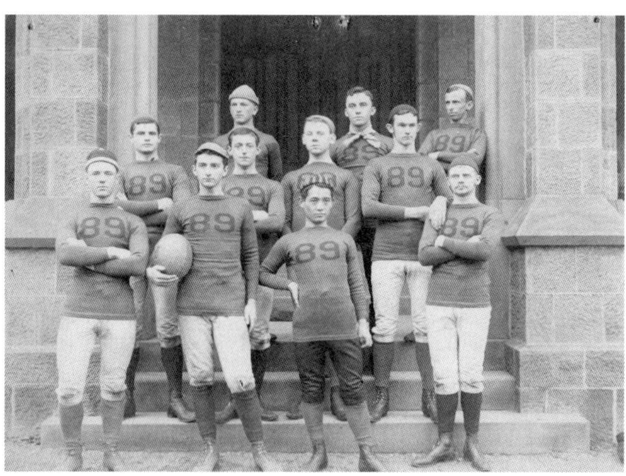

Abb. | Fig. 4
Kōjirō Matsukata mit dem | with Freshmen
Football Team, Rutgers College, 1885

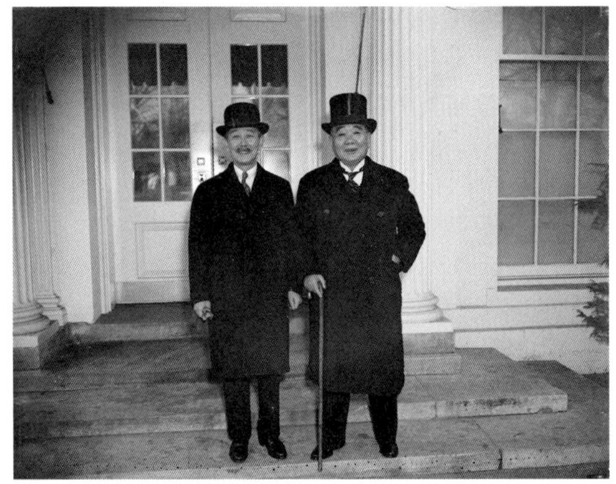

Abb. | Fig. 5
Kōjirō Matsukata (r.) und | and Otohiko Matsukata (l.)
vor dem Weißen Haus, 10. Dezember 1937 |
in front of the White House, 10 December 1937

at Harvard, to meet with the president to improve Japan's relationships with the United States (fig. 5).

Clever Businessman and Passionate Art Collector

Collecting art provided Matsukata with great satisfaction, because he was now able to apply his strategic thinking, diplomatic skill, tact and love of risk successfully in a new field and to plunge into another world. The art historian Yukio Yashiro accompanied Matsukata on his gallery tours in Paris in 1921 and observed how much Matsukata loved 'to negotiate a transaction [...]. With brio, he could turn away with laughter, a pirouette or playing the innocent when an art dealer adeptly urged him to purchase a work he did not want.'[24] Depending on the situation, he feigned interest or disinterest to lower prices, pretended not to understand[25] or employed his limited knowledge of French with gallerists either as a 'charming asset' or as camouflage – all with ease and grace.[26] According to Yashiro, 'he constantly varied his tricks, [...] so well that one did not see the thread of his well-calculated strategy: his natural instinct of a businessman or politician presumably guided him.'[27] Matsukata viewed the works deliberately with a cigar or pipe in his mouth and 'conveyed the image of a filthy rich magnate with elegant manners.'[28]

Although Matsukata rarely made appointments with galleries, art dealers were prepared for his visits, because the news spread quickly when the wealthy and ambitious collector was in town.

Matsukata appeared, as a rule, accompanied by his advisors, one of whom was the author and literary scholar Seiichi Naruse, and he enjoyed inviting them to dinner at the end of the day (fig. 6). That he sought expertise and denied being a connoisseur himself[29] does not at all mean that Matsukata did not continue to develop his sense for art. For example, Yashiro observed in Paris in 1921, compared to London in the 1910s, 'Matsukata as a totally transformed collector. [...] From then on, it was above all Impressionist paintings in bright and luminous colours that we admired every day: after the dominant bistre or purplish-grey shades of the English landscapes, the contrast was strikingly clear.'[30] Matsukata surely recognized the potential of these artists to point the way to the future for the artists in his homeland.

Like Karl Ernst Osthaus, Matsukata preferred to acquire works directly from the artist, firstly, because he very much appreciated direct contact and, secondly, could be sure of the authenticity of the works.[31] As an open, curious and humorous partner in conversation, he had the gift of quickly gaining sympathy and enthusiasm. On his stays in London between 1916 and 1918, he spent more time with the artists themselves than buying works,[32] and he won over Frank Brangwyn as a consultant.[33] The artist captured Matsukata, relaxed and effusive, in a drawing (fig. 7), probably made on one of the evenings in 1916 when he visited the artist in Chelsea, and they talked in good spirits well into the night.[34] Brangwyn then captured a different

später setzte er seine diplomatischen Bemühungen fort, als er 1937 und 1939 seinen jüngeren Bruder Otohiko, seit dem Studium in Harvard mit Franklin D. Roosevelt befreundet, nach Washington zu Treffen mit dem Präsidenten begleitete, um die Beziehungen Japans zu den USA zu verbessern (Abb. 5).

Kluger Geschäftsmann und leidenschaftlicher Kunstsammler

Das Sammeln von Kunst bereitete Matsukata großes Vergnügen, konnte er doch nun sein strategisches Denken, diplomatisches Geschick, Takt und Risikofreude mit Erfolg auf einem neuen Gebiet anwenden und in eine andere Welt eintauchen. Der Kunsthistoriker Yukio Yashiro begleitete Matsukata bei seinen Galerierundgängen in Paris 1921 und beobachtete, wie sehr Matsukata es liebte, „ein Geschäft auszuhandeln [...]. Mit Bravour wusste er sich mit Gelächter, einer Pirouette oder den Unschuldigen mimend abzuwenden, wenn ein Kunsthändler ihn geschickt bedrängte, ein Werk zu kaufen, das er nicht wollte.“[24] Je nach Situation täuschte er Interesse oder Desinteresse vor, um die Preise zu senken, kokettierte mit der Rolle des Unwissenden,[25] setzte gegenüber Galeristen seine begrenzten Französischkenntnisse entweder als „charmanten Trumpf“ oder zur Verschleierung ein, all dies mit Gewandtheit und Anmut.[26] Nach Yashiro „variierte er ständig die Tricks, [...] so sehr, dass man keine Spur einer hochkalkulierten Strategie sah: Sein natürlicher Instinkt des Geschäftsmanns oder Politikers leiteten ihn wahrscheinlich.“[27] Die Kunst-

werke betrachtete Matsukata bedächtig mit Zigarre oder Pfeife im Mund und „gab das Bild eines steinreichen Magnaten mit vornehmen Manieren ab.“[28]

Auch wenn Matsukata selten Termine mit Galerien vereinbarte, waren Kunsthandlungen auf seine Besuche vorbereitet, denn es sprach sich schnell herum, wenn der besonders finanzkräftige und ambitionierte Sammler wieder in der Stadt war. In der Regel erschien Matsukata in Begleitung seiner Berater:innen, zu denen auch der Autor und Literaturwissenschaftler Seiichi Naruse zählte und die er gerne am Ende des Tages zum Essen einlud (Abb. 6). Dass er sich Expertise einholte und abstritt, selbst Kunstkenner zu sein,[29] bedeutet keinesfalls, dass Matsukata seinen Kunstsinn nicht weiterentwickelte. So beobachtete Yashiro im Paris des Jahres 1921 einen im Vergleich zum London der 1910er-Jahre „vollständig verwandelten Sammler Matsukata. [...] Von nun an bewunderten wir jeden Tag vor allem impressionistische Gemälde in hellen und leuchtenden Farben. Nach den vorherrschenden schwarzbraunen oder graulila Tönen der englischen Landschaften war der Kontrast auffallend klar.“[30] Matsukata wird das in die Zukunft weisende Potenzial dieser Künstler:innen für seine Heimat erkannt haben.

Wie Karl Ernst Osthaus bevorzugte es Matsukata, Werke unmittelbar von Künstler:innen zu erwerben, da er zum einen die direkte Begegnung sehr schätzte und er sich zum anderen der Echtheit der Werke sicher sein konnte.[31] Als offener, neugieriger und humorvoller Gesprächspartner hatte er die Gabe, schnell Sympathien zu gewinnen und zu

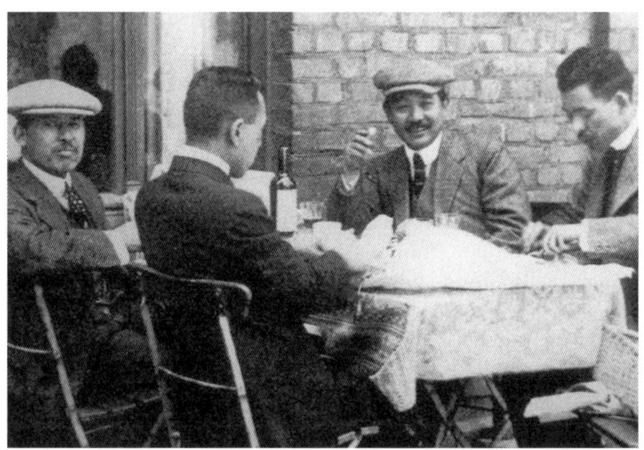

Abb. | Fig. 6
Kōjirō Matsukata mit Begleitern in Frankreich | with companions in France, 1921

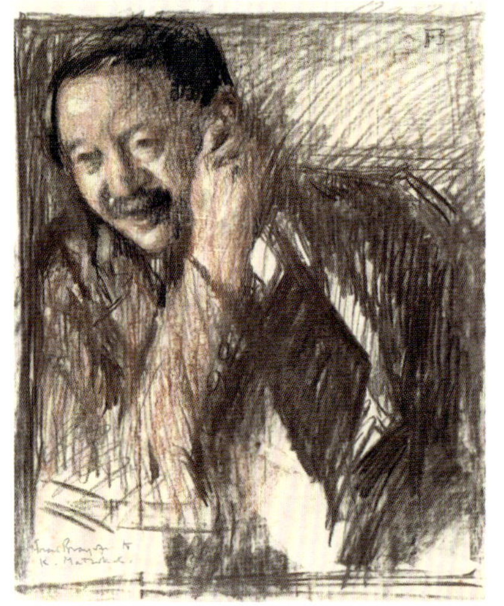

Abb. | Fig. 7
Frank Brangwyn, *Portrait of Mr Kōjirō Matsukata,*
ca. 1916, The National Museum of Western Art,
Tokyo. Ehemalige Sammlung Matsukata |
Ex-Matsukata Collection

facet of Matsukata's personality in a painting: his composure and serene energy (p. 197).

When visiting Monet in Giverny, too, Matsukata knew how to gain the artist's sympathy by mixing enthusiasm for his paintings, charm, and the gift of a cognac from 1808: 'Matsukata cried out during this visit "I like this painting"; "This landscape is superb"; and each time Monet replied: "I will give it to you, but only because it is you!"'[35] Although Matsukata's French was not perfect, he liked to speak to Monet in his native language in order to establish a personal relationship. In retrospect, his two visits to Monet proved to be the turning points for Matsukata's collection. For among the works of Western art that Matsukata acquired, Monet's works,[36] along with those of the Post-Impressionists, account for the high international rank and particular quality of his collection. Matsukata's personality, marked by humanity, commitment and tact, as well as his nose for politics, business and cultural diplomacy, seem crucial to his success in acquiring his collection. Even after his final return to Japan in 1922, Matsukata followed it feverishly[37] when his advisor Léonce Bénédite, then director of the Musée Rodin, acquired works on his behalf. As Matsukata wrote in a letter to

Bénédite, he missed 'the consolation in coming touch [*sic*] with the latest European fine arts these days'.[38]

Kōjirō Matsukata remained imperturbable through all the crises: as late as 1948–49, a photograph shows him happy in the circle of his grandchildren (fig. 8). Neither the Great Depression of 1927, in the wake of which he used his private fortune to cover Kawasaki's financial losses and ultimately retired from the firm,[39] nor the Second World War, with all its material and personal costs, left him embittered. He even preserved his independent opinions and openly criticized Japan in 1941 for attacking Pearl Harbor.[40] In the final months of the war in 1945, in the home of his oldest daughter in Karuizawa (in eastern Nagano Prefecture), he kept himself alive with squashes and potatoes he planted himself, without complaining, always very patient and very gentle with his grandchildren.[41] Collecting art had once, in Yashiro's words, 'swept [him] along the path of the beautiful',[42] since art has 'this incredible power to guide man towards nobility.'[43] As an 'authentic patron of the arts', with his collection he made not only himself but also others very happy.[44]

begeistern. So verbrachte er während seiner Aufenthalte in London zwischen 1916 und 1918 mehr Zeit mit Künstler:innen selbst als mit dem Kauf von Werken[32] und gewann Frank Brangwyn als Berater.[33] Gelöst und überschwänglich hält dieser Matsukata in einer Zeichnung fest (Abb. 7), wohl entstanden an einem jener Abende des Jahres 1916, als er den Künstler in Chelsea besuchte und sie sich bei guter Stimmung bis spät in die Nacht unterhielten.[34] In einem Gemälde zeigt Brangwyn dann eine andere Facette von Matsukatas Persönlichkeit, seine Unerschütterlichkeit und ruhige Kraft (S. 197).

Auch bei seinem Besuch bei Monet in Giverny wusste Matsukata, wie er die Sympathie des Künstlers mit einer Mischung aus Begeisterung für dessen Bilder, Charme und einem Cognac aus dem Jahr 1808 als Gastgeschenk gewinnen konnte. „Matsukata rief während dieses Besuchs ‚Ich mag dieses Gemälde‘; ‚Diese Landschaft ist großartig‘; und jedes Mal antwortete Monet: ‚Ich gebe es Ihnen, aber weil Sie es sind!‘"[35] Obwohl Matsukatas Französisch nicht perfekt war, redete er mit Monet in seiner Muttersprache, um eine persönliche Beziehung aufzubauen. Im Rückblick haben sich die beiden Besuche bei Monet als Sternstunden für Matsukatas Sammlung erwiesen. Denn unter den von Matsukata erworbenen Werken westlicher Kunst machen besonders die Werke Monets[36] neben denen des Post-Impressionismus den hohen internationalen Rang und die besondere Qualität seiner Sammlung aus. Matsukatas von Menschlichkeit, Engagement und Taktgefühl geprägte Persönlichkeit sowie sein Sinn für Politik, Geschäft und

Kulturdiplomatie scheinen entscheidend für seinen Erfolg beim Erwerb seiner Sammlung gewesen zu sein. Auch nach seiner endgültigen Rückkehr nach Japan im Jahr 1922 fieberte Matsukata mit,[37] wenn sein Berater Léonce Bénédite, der damalige Direktor des Musée Rodin, in seinem Auftrag Werke ankaufte. Wie Matsukata in einem Brief an Bénédite schrieb, vermisste er „den Trost, mit der aktuellen europäischen Kunst dieser Tage in Berührung zu kommen [...]."[38]

Kōjirō Matsukata blieb durch alle Krisen hindurch unerschütterlich; ein Foto zeigt ihn noch 1948/49 glücklich im Kreis seiner Enkel (Abb. 8): Weder die Finanzkrise 1927, im Zuge derer er auch mit seinem Privatvermögen für die wirtschaftlichen Verluste von Kawasaki einstand und sich endgültig aus der Firma zurückzog,[39] noch der Zweite Weltkrieg mit allen materiellen und persönlichen Verlusten ließen ihn verbittern. Auch seine unabhängige Meinung bewahrte er sich und kritisierte Japan 1941 offen für den Angriff auf Pearl Harbor.[40] In den letzten Kriegsmonaten des Jahres 1945 hielt er sich im Haus seiner ältesten Tochter in Karuizawa (im Osten der Präfektur Nagano) mit selbst angebauten Kürbissen und Kartoffeln am Leben, ohne je zu klagen, sondern er war stets sehr geduldig und zu seinen Enkeln sehr sanftmütig.[41] Einst war er, in Yashiros Worten, vom Kunstsammeln „auf dem Weg des Schönen mitgerissen"[42] worden, denn Kunst habe „die unglaubliche Macht, den Menschen zur Noblesse zu führen."[43] Als „authentischer Schutzherr der Künste" bereitete er mit seiner Sammlung nicht nur sich selbst, sondern auch anderen großes Glück.[44]

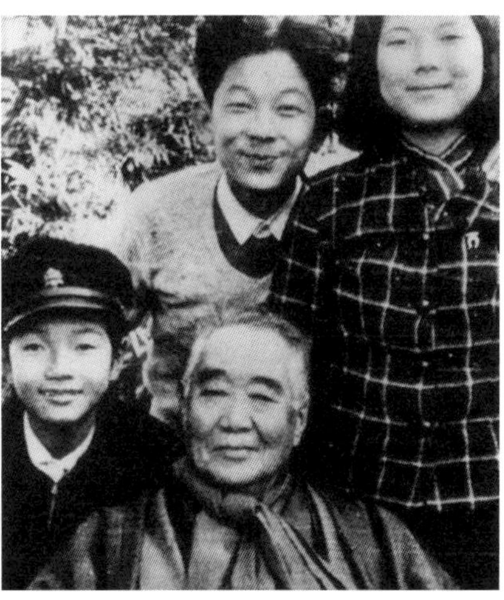

Abb. | Fig. 8
Kōjirō Matsukata im Kreis seiner Enkel, 1948/49, darunter Ken Matsumoto (1. v. l.) | with his grandchildren, 1948/49, including Ken Matsumoto (1st from left)

1 See, for example, Yukio Yashiro, 'Matsukata Kojiro (1866–1950)', in *L'ancienne Collection Matsukata: Réimaginer le rêve*, exh. cat. City Museum, Kobe, French insert in Japanese catalogue (Kobe, 2016), 18–35, esp. 23, 29.

2 Kōjirō Matsukata quoted in Anonymous, 'Matsukata Museum Largest in World' in *American Art News* 20, no. 15 (21 January 1922): 1–2, esp. 2.

3 Ken Matsumoto in an interview by the author, 15 April 2021. I am grateful to Ken Matsumoto for important references and his valuable memories of his grandfather. I also thank Megumi Jingaoka for putting me in contact with Ken Matsumoto and for suggesting important sources.

4 Haru Matsukata Reischauer, *Samurai and Silk: A Japanese and American Heritage* (Cambridge, MA, 1986), 21–152.

5 Ibid., 105–6, 108.

6 Masayoshi Matsukata quoted in Reischauer *Samurai and Silk*, 86. His son Kōjirō Matsukata will later write of 'glorious Paris'; see Bibliothèque de l'Institut national d'histoire de l'art (INHA), Paris, MS375 (6.5.1.), fol. 76., fol. 91.

7 On Shōsaku Matsukata's penchant for Peter Paul Rubens, see Reischauer *Samurai and Silk*, 266.

8 Fernanda Perrone, 'Japanese Students at Rutgers during the Early Meiji Period', in 近代日本研究 (*Bulletin of Modern Japanese Studies*) 34 (2017): 448(23)–68(3).

9 Information kindly provided by Fernanda Perrone, archivist, Rutgers University Libraries.

10 Reischauer *Samurai and Silk*, 277.

11 Kōjirō Matsukata quoted in Anonymous 'Matsukata Museum Largest in World', 2.

12 Reischauer *Samurai and Silk*, 278.

13 Ibid., 285–86.

14 Ken Matsumoto in an interview by the author, 15 April 2021.

15 Reischauer *Samurai and Silk*, 280, 288.

16 Yashiro 'Matsukata Kojiro (1866–1950)', 22.

17 Reischauer *Samurai and Silk*, 278.

18 Kōjirō Matsukata quoted in Anonymous 'Matsukata Museum Largest in World', 2.

19 Ibid.

20 Kōjirō Matsukata quoted in Anonymous 'Matsukata Museum Largest in World', 2.

21 Ibid.

22 See ibid., p.1, and Willard Slater, 'Why Japan Collects Western Art', in *International Studio*, LXXV, no. 300 (April 1922): 151–52.

23 Anonymous, 'Western Art for Japan: Treasure House in Tokyo', in *The Times* (6 October 1921).

24 '[…] adorait, "négocier une transaction […] Avec brio, il savait se détourner d'un éclat de rire, d'une pirouette, ou en faignant l'innocent, quand un marchand d'art le pressait habilement d'acheter une œuvre dont il ne voulait pas.' Yashiro 'Matsukata Kojiro (1866–1950)', 29.

25 Ibid., 34.

26 Ibid., 29.

27 '[…] il avait l'art de transformer ce handicap en charmant atout, ou d'en jouer tel un rideau de fumée en feignant de ne pas comprendre: […] il savait en user avec aisance et grâce.' Ibid.

28 'Il variait sans cesse les artifices, […] si bien qu'on n'y voyait nullement la trame d'une stratégie hautement calculée: son instinct naturel d'homme d'affaires ou d'homme politique devait probablement le guider.' Ibid., 24.

29 Kōjirō Matsukata quoted in Anonymous 1922, 2.

30 '[…] un collectionneur Matsukata totalement transformé. […] Désormais, ce furent surtout des tableaux impressionnistes aux couleurs vives et lumineuses que nous admirions tous les jours: après les dominantes bistre ou gris violacés des paysages anglais, le contraste était saisissant de claret.' Yashiro 'Matsukata Kojiro (1866–1950)', 24.

31 Anonymous 'Matsukata Museum Largest in World', 1.

32 Yashiro 'Matsukata Kojiro (1866–1950)', 23.

33 On the relationship between Brangwyn and Matsukata, see Megumi Jingaoka, 'The Matsukata Collection: A Century-Long Voyage', in *The Matsukata Collection: A One-Hundred-Year Odyssey*, exh. cat. National Museum of Western Art, Tokyo (Tokyo, 2019), 291–307, esp. 292–94, as well as Yashiro 'Matsukata Kojiro (1866–1950)', 23.

34 Yashiro 'Matsukata Kojiro (1866–1950)', 23.

35 Ibid., 31.

36 On the special appreciation of Impressionism in Japan, see Detmar Westhoff, 'Why the Japanese Love Impressionism', in *Japan's Love for Impressionism: From Monet to Renoir*, exh. cat. Bundeskunsthalle, Bonn (Munich 2015), 234–41.

37 See Kōjirō Matsukata to Léonce Bénédite, 1 September 1920, Bibliotheque de l'INHA, Paris, MS375 (6.5.1.), fol. 77.

38 Kōjirō Matsukata to Léonce Bénédite, 11 March 1923 (in English), Bibliothèque de l'INHA, Paris, MS375 (6.5.1.), fol. 202.

39 Reischauer *Samurai and Silk*, 289.

40 See https://global.kawasaki.com/en/stories/articles/vol31/business.html (accessed 27 May 2021).

41 Ken Matsumoto in an interview by the author, 15 April 2021.

42 Yashiro 'Matsukata Kojiro (1866–1950)', 35.

43 Ibid.

44 Ibid.

1 Vgl. etwa Yukio Yashiro, „Matsukata Kojiro (1866–1950)", in: *L'ancienne Collection Matsukata. Réimaginer le rêve,* Ausst.-Kat. Stadtmuseum Kobe, französische Beilage zum japanischen Katalog, Kobe 2016, S. 18–35, hier S. 23, 29.

2 Kōjirō Matsukata zit. nach: Anonym, „Matsukata Museum largest in world", in: *American Art News,* 20, 15, 21.1.1922, S. 1 f., hier S. 2 („funny man"; hier und im Weiteren Übers. des Autors).

3 Ken Matsumoto im Interview mit dem Verfasser, 15.4.2021, hier und im Weiteren Übers. des Autors. Die originalen Wortlaute werden in der englischen Fassung dieses Textes zitiert. Ken Matsumoto sei für seine wichtigen Hinweise und seine wertvollen Erinnerungen an seinen Großvater gedankt. Dank sei auch an Megumi Jingaoka gerichtet für die Herstellung des Kontakts zu Ken Matsumoto sowie bedeutende Quellenhinweise.

4 Haru Matsukata Reischauer, *Samurai and Silk. A Japanese and American Heritage,* Cambridge (MA) 1986, S. 21–152.

5 Ebd., S. 105 f., 108.

6 Masayoshi Matsukata zit. nach: Haru Matsukata Reischauer, *Samurai and Silk,* S. 86. Sein Sohn Kōjirō Matsukata wird später vom „glorreichen Paris" schreiben, vgl. Bibliothèque de l'Institut national d'histoire de l'art (INHA), Paris, MS375 (6.5.1.), fol. 76., fol. 91.

7 Zu Shōsaku Matsukatas Vorliebe für Peter Paul Rubens vgl. Haru Matsukata Reischauer, *Samurai and Silk,* S. 266.

8 Fernanda Perrone, „Japanese students at Rutgers during the early Meiji period", in: 近代日本研究 *(Bulletin of modern Japanese studies),* 34, 2017, S. 448(23)–468(3).

9 Freundlicher Hinweis von Fernanda Perrone, Archivarin, Rutgers University Libraries.

10 Haru Matsukata Reischauer, *Samurai and Silk,* S. 277.

11 Kōjirō Matsukata zit. nach: Anonym, „Matsukata Museum largest in world", S. 2.

12 Haru Matsukata Reischauer, *Samurai and Silk,* S. 278.

13 Ebd., S. 285 f.

14 Ken Matsumoto im Interview mit dem Verfasser, 15.4.2021.

15 Haru Matsukata Reischauer, *Samurai and Silk,* S. 280, 288.

16 Yukio Yashiro, „Matsukata Kojiro (1866–1950)", S. 22.

17 Haru Matsukata Reischauer, *Samurai and Silk,* S. 278.

18 Kōjirō Matsukata zit. nach: Anonym, „Matsukata Museum largest in world", S. 2.

19 Ebd.

20 Kōjirō Matsukata zit. nach: Anonym, „Matsukata Museum largest in world", S. 2.

21 Ebd.

22 Vgl. ebd., S. 1, sowie Willard Slater, „Why Japan Collects Western Art, in: *International Studio,* LXXV, 300, April 1922, S. 151 f.

23 Anonym, „Western Art for Japan. Treasure house in Tokyo", in: *The Times,* 6.10.1921.

24 Yukio Yashiro, „Matsukata Kojiro (1866–1950)", S. 29 (hier und im Weiteren Übers. des Autors).

25 Ebd., S. 34.

26 Ebd., S. 29.

27 Ebd.

28 Ebd., S. 24.

29 Kōjirō Matsukata zit. nach: Anonym, „Matsukata Museum largest in world", S. 2.

30 Yukio Yashiro, „Matsukata Kojiro (1866–1950)", S. 24.

31 Anonym, „Matsukata Museum largest in world", S. 1.

32 Yukio Yashiro, „Matsukata Kojiro (1866–1950)", S. 23.

33 Zur Beziehung von Brangwyn und Matsukata vgl. Megumi Jingaoka, „The Matsukata Collection – A Century-Long Voyage", in: *The Matsukata Collection. A One-Hundred-Year Odyssey,* Ausst.-Kat. The National Museum of Western Art, Tokio, Tokio 2019, S. 291–307, hier S. 292–294, sowie Yukio Yashiro, „Matsukata Kojiro (1866–1950)", S. 23.

34 Yukio Yashiro, „Matsukata Kojiro (1866–1950)", S. 23.

35 Ebd., S. 31.

36 Zur besonderen Wertschätzung des Impressionismus in Japan vgl. Detmar Westhoff, „Warum die Japaner den Impressionismus lieben", in: *Japans Liebe zum Impressionismus. Von Monet bis Renoir,* Ausst.-Kat. Bundeskunsthalle, Bonn, München 2015, S. 234–241.

37 Vgl. Kōjirō Matsukata an Léonce Bénédite, Brief vom 1.9.1920, Bibliothèque de l'INHA, Paris, MS375 (6.5.1.), fol. 77.

38 Kōjirō Matsukata an Léonce Bénédite, Brief vom 11.3.1923, Bibliothèque de l'INHA, Paris, MS375 (6.5.1.), fol. 202 (Übers. des Autors).

39 Haru Matsukata Reischauer, *Samurai and Silk,* S. 289.

40 Vgl. https://global.kawasaki .com/en/stories/articles/vol31 /business.html [zuletzt aufgerufen am 27.5.2021].

41 Ken Matsumoto im Interview mit dem Verfasser, 15.4.2021.

42 Yukio Yashiro, „Matsukata Kojiro (1866–1950)", S. 35.

43 Ebd.

44 Ebd.

Die Werktitel und ihre Übersetzungen richten sich nach den Vorgaben der jeweiligen Sammlungen, ihren Sammlungskatalogen sowie den Werkverzeichnissen der Künstler:innen. Bei fehlenden Angaben in den genannten Quellen ist die Sekundärliteratur zu Rate gezogen worden. Erst in einem letzten Schritt wurden Titel übersetzt. Diskriminierende und rassistische Begriffe, die heute politisch unkorrekt sind, wurden mit Stern (*) gekennzeichnet, die entsprechenden Originaltitel nicht in andere Sprachen übertragen, ebenso wenig wie Orts- und Eigennamen sowie die Titel der zeitgenössischen Werke.

Alle Werke des National Museum of Western Art mit der Erwerbsnotiz „Sammlung Matsukata" sind 1944 von der französischen Regierung beschlagnahmt und 1952 im Rahmen des Friedensvertrags von San Francisco der Autorität der französischen Regierung zuerkannt worden; seit 1959 befinden sie sich in der Sammlung des National Museum of Western Art in Tokio. Bei Arbeiten mit der Kennzeichnung „Ehemalige Sammlung Matsukata" handelt es sich um Ankäufe aus der Folgezeit. Soweit nicht anders angegeben, sind die Werke des Museum Folkwang zwischen 1901 und 1913 für Hagen erworben worden und gehören seit 1922 zum Essener Bestand.

Titles and their translations are based on the specifications of the respective collections, their inventory catalogues, as well as the artists' catalogues raisonnés. If information in these sources was missing, the secondary literature has been consulted. Only as a last resort were titles translated. Discriminatory and racist terms, which are politically incorrect today, have been marked with an asterisk (*), the corresponding original titles have not been translated, nor have place names, proper names, or the titles of contemporary works.

All works in the National Museum of Western Art marked with the purchase note 'Matsukata Collection' were sequestered by the French government in 1944 and vested to the authority of the French government under the San Francisco Peace Treaty in 1952; they entered the collection of the National Museum of Western Art in Tokyo in 1959. Works marked as 'Ex-Matsukata Collection' were purchased subsequently. Unless otherwise stated, all works from Museum Folkwang were acquired for Hagen between 1901 and 1913 and have been part of the holdings in Essen since 1922.

Anonymer Künstler im Stil des
Hokusai Katsushika | Anonymous
artist in the style of Hokusai Katsushika
kakemono (Hängerolle | hanging scroll),
19. Jh. | 19th century
   Tusche, Papier, Seide, Gewebeband,
   Holz | ink, paper, silk, fabric tape,
   wood, 223,5 × 37,3 cm
   Museum Folkwang, Essen
   S. | p. 255

Pierre Bonnard
L'oliveraie, 1912
Alpenlandschaft mit Ziegenherde |
Alpine Landscape with Goatherd
   Öl auf Leinwand | oil on canvas,
   94,5 × 71 cm
   Museum Folkwang, Essen
   S. | p. 291

Frank Brangwyn
Stormy Weather at Sea, 1889
Stürmisches Wetter auf See
   Öl auf Leinwand | oil on canvas,
   98 × 124 cm
   The National Museum of
   Western Art, Tokyo
   Ehemalige Sammlung Matsukata |
   Ex-Matsukata Collection
   S. | p. 201

Frank Brangwyn
Portrait of Mr. Kōjirō Matsukata, 1916
Porträt Kōjirō Matsukata
   Öl auf Leinwand | oil on canvas,
   73,8 × 84 cm
   The National Museum of
   Western Art, Tokyo
   Ehemalige Sammlung Matsukata,
   Schenkung der Erben von Kōjirō
   Matsukata 2017 | Ex-Matsukata
   Collection, donated by the heirs
   of Kōjirō Matsukata in 2017
   S. | p. 197

Frank Brangwyn
Aerial Perspective of Kyōraku Bijutsukan
(Sheer Pleasure Arts Pavilion), 1918–1922
Aufsicht des Kyōraku-Museums
   Bleistift und Lavierung auf Papier |
   pencil and wash on paper, 39 × 43 cm
   The National Museum of
   Western Art, Tokyo
   S. | p. 243

Frank Brangwyn
Aerial Perspective of Kyōraku Bijutsukan
(Sheer Pleasure Arts Pavilion),
Aufsicht des Kyōraku-Museums
   Aquarell und Bleistift auf Papier |
   watercolour and pencil on paper,
   39,5 × 53 cm
   The National Museum of
   Western Art, Tokyo
   S. | p. 20

Paul Cézanne
Maison de Bellevue et pigeonnier,
ca. 1890–1892
Haus auf bewaldeter Anhöhe |
House and Dovecote at Bellevue
   Öl auf Leinwand | oil on canvas,
   65 × 81,2 cm
   Museum Folkwang, Essen
   S. | p. 292

Paul Cézanne
La carrière de Bibémus, ca. 1895
Der Steinbruch Bibémus |
The Quarry at Bibémus
   Öl auf Leinwand | oil on canvas,
   65 × 81 cm
   Museum Folkwang, Essen
   Beschlagnahmt 1937, wiedererworben
   1964 mit Unterstützung des West-
   deutschen Rundfunks | confiscated in
   1937, reacquired in 1964 with the
   support of Westdeutscher Rundfunk
   S. | p. 293

Jean-Baptiste Camille Corot
Madeleine
Magdalena | Mary Magdalene
   Öl auf Leinwand | oil on canvas,
   74 × 59,5 cm
   Sumitomo Mitsui Banking
   Corporation, Tokyo
   Ehemals Sammlung Matsukata |
   formerly Matsukata Collection
   S. | p. 268

Gustave Courbet
La roche oraguay, Vallon de Maisières,
Doubs, 1860
Oraguay-Felsen, Maisières-Tal, Doubs |
Oraguay Rock, Maisières Valley, Doubs
   Öl auf Leinwand | oil on canvas,
   151,5 × 195 cm
   Museum Folkwang, Essen
   Erworben 1968 | acquired in 1968
   S. | p. 271

Gustave Courbet
*Rêverie tzigane**, 1869
   Öl auf Leinwand | oil on canvas,
   50,3 × 61 cm
   The National Museum of
   Western Art, Tokyo
   Sammlung Matsukata |
   Matsukata Collection
   S. | p. 269

Gustave Courbet
La vague, 1870
Die Woge | The Wave
   Öl auf Leinwand | oil on canvas,
   45 × 59 cm
   Museum Folkwang, Essen
   Erworben 1989 | acquired in 1989
   S. | p. 264

Gustave Courbet
La vague, ca. 1870
Die Wogen | Waves
   Öl auf Leinwand | oil on canvas,
   72,5 × 92,5 cm
   The National Museum of
   Western Art, Tokyo
   Sammlung Matsukata |
   Matsukata Collection
   S. | p. 265

Gustave Courbet
Le puits-noir, ca. 1872
Der Puits-Noir | The Shaded Stream
   Öl auf Leinwand | oil on canvas,
   65,2 × 95,2 cm
   Sumitomo Mitsui Banking
   Corporation, Tokyo
   Ehemals Sammlung Matsukata |
   formerly Matsukata Collection
   S. | p. 270

Henri Edmond Cross
Coucher de soleil sur la mer, 1896
Sonnenuntergang über dem Meer |
Sunset over the Sea
   Öl auf Leinwand | oil on canvas,
   52 × 59 cm
   Wallraf-Richartz-Museum & Fondation
   Corboud, Köln
   Ehemals Museum Folkwang, Hagen |
   formerly Museum Folkwang, Hagen
   S. | p. 289

Henri Edmond Cross
La promeneuse
Landschaft mit Baum | The Stroller
   Aquarell auf Papier | watercolour
   on paper, 16,9 × 24,5 cm
   Museum Folkwang, Essen
   S. | p. 305

Henri Edmond Cross
Les vagues (Le rocher)
Meeresküste | Waves
   Aquarell auf Papier | watercolour
   on paper, 17,2 × 24,5 cm
   Museum Folkwang, Essen
   S. | p. 304

Henri Edmond Cross
Paysage provençal
Provenzalische Landschaft |
Landscape Provençal
   Kreide auf Papier | chalk on paper,
   22,8 × 30 cm
   Museum Folkwang, Essen
   Ohne Abb. | without ill.

Charles-François Daubigny
*La plage de Villerville au soleil
couchant*, 1870
*Der Strand von Villerville bei
Sonnenuntergang* |
The Beach at Villerville at Sunset
  Öl auf Leinwand | oil on canvas,
  100 × 197 cm
  Sumitomo Mitsui Banking
  Corporation, Tokyo
  Ehemals Sammlung Matsukata |
  formerly Matsukata Collection
  S. | p. 267

Charles-François Daubigny
Les Sables-d'Olonne
  Öl auf Holz | oil on wood,
  39,1 × 67,1 cm
  Artizon Museum, Ishibashi
  Foundation, Tokyo
  Ehemals Sammlung Matsukata |
  formerly Matsukata Collection
  S. | p. 266

Maurice Denis
*Danse du génie. Statue grecque du
repos éternel,* zweite Hälfte des
19. Jh. | Second half of 19th century
*Tanz der Genie. Griechische Statue
der ewigen Ruhe* | *Greek Statue*
  Kohle und Pastell auf Papier | charcoal
  and pastel on paper, 75,5 × 50 cm
  The National Museum of
  Western Art, Tokyo
  Sammlung Matsukata |
  Matsukata Collection
  S. | p. 249 r.

Maurice Denis
Etude pour le théâtre, zweite Hälfte
des 19. Jh. | Second half of the
19th century
Tanzender (Studie für das Theater) |
Dancer
  Kohle auf Papier | charcoal on paper,
  91 × 44,5 cm
  The National Museum of
  Western Art, Tokyo
  Sammlung Matsukata |
  Matsukata Collection
  S. | p. 248

Maurice Denis
Vierge au baiser, 1902
Madonna mit Kind (Der Kuss) |
Madonna with Child (The Kiss)
  Öl auf Leinwand | oil on canvas,
  99 × 82 cm
  Museum Folkwang, Essen
  S. | p. 245

Maurice Denis
*L'éternel été. Le chant choral, l'orgue,
le quatuor, la danse*, 1905
*Der ewige Sommer. Der Choral, die
Orgel, das Quartett, der Tanz* (Paravent
mit Motiven des Gemäldezyklus für
das Musikzimmer von Kurt von Mutzen-
becher, Wiesbaden) | *Eternal Summer.
The Chorale, the Organ, the Quartet,
the Dance* (folding screen with motifs
for the decoration of Kurt von Mutzenbecher's music room, Wiesbaden)
  Tempera, Leimfarbe, Gouache (?),
  Bleistift, Kreide (?) auf Papier, die
  beiden zentralen Tafeln vollständig auf
  Holz geklebt, die beiden Seitentafeln
  aufgezogen | Tempera, glue-bound
  distemper, gouache (?), pencil,
  charcoal (?) on paper, the two central
  panels glued in full on wood, the
  two side panels mounted on chassis,
  179 × 78 cm (je Tafel | each panel)
  Musée d'Orsay, Paris
  Erworben 2015 | acquired in 2015
  S. | p. 246

Maurice Denis
L'éternel été. La danse, 1905
Der ewige Sommer. Der Tanz (Studie
oder Replik zum Gemäldezyklus für
das Musikzimmer von Kurt von Mutzen-
becher, Wiesbaden) | *Girls Dancing*
(study or replica for the decoration of
Kurt von Mutzenbecher's music room,
Wiesbaden)
  Öl auf Leinwand | oil on canvas,
  147,7 × 78,1 cm
  The National Museum of
  Western Art, Tokyo
  Sammlung Matsukata |
  Matsukata Collection
  S. | p. 247

Maurice Denis
*Etude pour la 9ème symphonie,
théâtre*, 1912
Studie zur „9. Symphonie" (Entwurf
für die Ausmalung des Théâtre des
Champs-Elysées) | *Study for "The Ninth
Simphony"* (Study for the Decoration
of Théâtre des Champs-Elysées)
  Kohle und Pastell auf Papier | charcoal
  and pastel on paper, 75 × 52,9 cm
  The National Museum of
  Western Art, Tokyo
  Sammlung Matsukata |
  Matsukata Collection
  S. | p. 249 l.

Maurice Denis
Rosmapamon, 1918
  Öl auf Karton | oil on cardboard,
  36,5 × 49,7 cm
  The National Museum of
  Western Art, Tokyo
  Sammlung Matsukata |
  Matsukata Collection
  S. | p. 332

Paul Gauguin
Baigneuses à Dieppe, 1885
Badende Frauen in Dieppe |
Women Bathing
  Öl auf Leinwand | oil on canvas,
  38,1 × 46,2 cm
  The National Museum of
  Western Art, Tokyo
  Sammlung Matsukata |
  Matsukata Collection
  S. | p. 325

Paul Gauguin
Paysage de Bretagne, 1888
Bretonische Landschaft |
Landscape of Brittany
  Öl auf Leinwand | oil on canvas,
  89,3 × 116,6 cm
  The National Museum of
  Western Art, Tokyo
  Sammlung Matsukata |
  Matsukata Collection
  S. | p. 327

Paul Gauguin
Baigneuses Bretonnes, 1889
Bretonische Badende |
Bathers in Brittany
  Zinkografie | zincography,
  23,5 × 20,1 cm
  Museum Folkwang, Essen
  Erworben spätestens 1929 |
  acquired in 1929 at the latest
  S. | p. 326 l.

Paul Gauguin
Les laveuses, 1889
Die Wäscherinnen |
Women Washing Clothes
  Zinkografie | zincography,
  21,5 × 26,4 cm
  Museum Folkwang, Essen
  Erworben spätestens 1929 |
  acquired in 1929 at the latest
  S. | p. 326 r.

Paul Gauguin
*Petites Bretonnes au bord de
la mer*, 1889
Kleine Bretoninnen vor dem Meer |
Two Breton Girls by the Sea
  Öl auf Leinwand | oil on canvas,
  92,5 × 73,6 cm
  The National Museum of
  Western Art, Tokyo
  Sammlung Matsukata |
  Matsukata Collection
  S. | p. 329

Paul Gauguin
Ramasseuses de varech (II), 1889
Die Tangsammlerinnen (II) |
The Kelp Gatherers (II)
  Öl auf Leinwand | oil on canvas,
  87 × 123,1 cm
  Museum Folkwang, Essen
  S. | p. 331

Paul Gauguin
Autoportrait Oviri, 1893
Selbstbildnis Oviri | *Self-Portrait Oviri*
  Bronze, 36,5 × 34,5 × 3 cm
  Museum Folkwang, Essen
  Erworben 1932 | acquired in 1932
  S. | p. 334

Paul Gauguin
*Paysage de Bretagne. Le moulin
de David*, 1894
*Bretonische Landschaft. Die David-
Mühle in Pont-Aven* | *Landscape in
Brittany, The David Mill*
  Öl auf Leinwand | oil on canvas,
  73 × 92,9 cm
  Musée d'Orsay, Paris
  1959 Zession der Rechtsansprüche
  an die Französischen Nationalmuseen
  in Anwendung des Friedensabkom-
  mens mit Japan | assigned to the
  French National Museums in application of the country's peace treaty
  with Japan in 1959
  S. | p. 333

Paul Gauguin
Deux femmes maories accroupies,
1894/95
Zwei kauernde Maori-Frauen |
Two Crouching Maori Women
  Zinkografie | zincography,
  16 × 20,9 cm
  Museum Folkwang, Essen
  S. | p. 335 l.

Paul Gauguin
La Orana Maria, 1894/95
Ich grüße Dich, Maria | *I Salute You Maria*
  Zinkografie | zincography,
  25,7 × 20,1 cm
  Museum Folkwang, Essen
  S. | p. 335 r.

Paul Gauguin
Cavaliers sur la plage (I), 1902
Reiter am Strand (I) |
Riders on the Beach (I)
  Öl auf Leinwand | oil on canvas,
  65,6 × 75,9 cm
  Museum Folkwang, Essen
  S. | p. 336

Paul Gauguin
Contes barbares, 1902
  Öl auf Leinwand | oil on canvas,
  131,5 × 90,5 cm
  Museum Folkwang, Essen
  S. | p. 339

Paul Gauguin
Jeune fille à l'éventail, 1902
Mädchen mit Fächer |
The Girl with a Fan
  Öl auf Leinwand | oil on canvas,
  91,9 × 72,9 cm
  Museum Folkwang, Essen
  S. | p. 337

Ida Gerhardi
Porträt Karl Ernst Osthaus, 1903
Portrait of Karl Ernst Osthaus
  Öl auf Leinwand | oil on canvas,
  110 × 76,5 cm
  Osthaus Museum, Hagen
  S. | p. 203

Vincent van Gogh
Paysanne arrachant de l'herbe, 1885
Ährenleserin | *Peasant Woman,
Stooping and Gleaning*
  Schwarze Kreide | black chalk,
  51,4 × 41,5 cm
  Museum Folkwang, Essen
  S. | p. 307

Vincent van Gogh
Les bateaux amarrés, 1888
Rhonebarken | *Quay with Men
Unloading Sand Barges*
  Öl auf Leinwand | oil on canvas,
  55,1 × 66,2 cm
  Museum Folkwang, Essen
  Erworben 1912 für das Kunstmuseum
  Essen, seit 1922 Museum Folkwang |
  acquired in 1912 for the Kunstmuseum
  Essen, since 1922 Museum Folkwang
  S. | p. 320

Vincent van Gogh
Portrait d'Armand Roulin, 1888
Porträt Armand Roulin |
Portrait of Armand Roulin
  Öl auf Leinwand | oil on canvas,
  65 × 54,1 cm
  Museum Folkwang, Essen
  S. | p. 321

Vincent van Gogh
Vue de la Crau, 1888
Ansicht der Crau | *The Plain of La Crau*
  Bleistift und Tusche | Indian ink
  with pencil, 27 × 49 cm
  Museum Folkwang, Essen
  S. | p. 316

Vincent van Gogh
La moisson, 1889
Die Ernte, Kornfeld mit Schnitter |
*The Wheatfield behind Saint Paul's
Hospital with a Reaper*
  Öl auf Leinwand | oil on canvas,
  59,5 × 72,5 cm
  Museum Folkwang, Essen
  S. | p. 315

Vincent van Gogh
Le parc de l'hôpital, à Saint-Rémy, 1889
*Der Garten des Hospitals von Saint-
Rémy* | *A Corner of the Asylum and the
Garden with a Heavy, Sawed-Off Tree*
  Öl auf Leinwand | oil on canvas,
  75 × 93,5 cm
  Museum Folkwang, Essen
  S. | p. 319

Vincent van Gogh
Paysage avec cyprès, 1889
*Landschaft mit Zypressen und vier
Landarbeitern* | *Cypresses with
Four People Working in the Field*
  Schwarze Kreide | black chalk,
  32 × 23,5 cm
  Museum Folkwang, Essen
  S. | p. 318

Vincent van Gogh
La pluie, 1890
Sämann im Regen | *Enclosed Field
with a Sower in the Rain*
  Bleistift und Kreide | pencil and chalk,
  23,3 × 31,6 cm
  Museum Folkwang, Essen
  S. | p. 317

Hokusai Katsushika
The Great Wave off Kanagawa
(Aus der Serie | from the series:
Thirty-Six Views of Mount Fuji), 1831
  Holzschnitt | woodblock print,
  25,5 × 38 cm
  Tokyo National Museum
  Ehemals Sammlung Matsukata |
  formerly Matsukata Collection
  Nicht in der Ausstellung |
  not in the exhibition
  S. | p. 261

Hokusai Katsushika
The Amida Waterfall on the Kisokaido
(Aus der Serie | from the series: *A
Journey to the Waterfalls of All the
Provinces*), 1833
　Holzschnitt | woodblock print,
　38 × 25,5 cm
　Tokyo National Museum
　Ehemals Sammlung Matsukata |
　formerly Matsukata Collection
　Nicht in der Ausstellung |
　not in the exhibition
　S. | p. 257

Georg Kolbe
Kopf Henry van de Velde, 1913
Portrait of Henry van de Velde
　Bronze, 54 × 16,5 × 20,5 cm
　Museum Folkwang, Essen
　S. | p. 210

Maximilien Luce
L'aciérie, 1900
Das Hüttenwerk | The Smeltery
　Öl auf Leinwand | oil on canvas,
　73,3 × 92,8 cm
　Museum Folkwang, Essen
　S. | p. 205

Edouard Manet
L'explosion, 1871
Die Granate | The Explosion
　Öl auf Leinwand | oil on canvas,
　37,5 × 45,5 cm
　Museum Folkwang, Essen
　S. | p. 222

Edouard Manet
Marine, temps d'orage, 1873
*Zwei Segelboote auf stürmischer
See | Sea in Stormy Weather*
　Öl auf Leinwand | oil on canvas,
　55 × 72,5 cm
　The National Museum of
　Western Art, Tokyo
　Ehemalige Sammlung Matsukata,
　erworben 2019 | Ex-Matsukata
　Collection, acquired in 2019
　S. | p. 199

Edouard Manet
*Portrait de Faure dans le rôle
d'Hamlet,* 1877
*Der Sänger Jean Baptiste Faure als
Hamlet | Portrait of Faure as Hamlet*
　Öl auf Leinwand | oil on canvas,
　194 × 131,5 cm
　Museum Folkwang, Essen
　Erworben 1927 | acquired in 1927
　S. | p. 223

Edouard Manet
La serveuse de bocks, 1878/79
Die Kellnerin | The Waitress
　Öl auf Leinwand | oil on canvas,
　77 × 64,5 cm
　Musée d'Orsay, Paris
　1959 Eingang in das Musée du Louvre
　in Anwendung des Friedensabkom-
　mens mit Japan | entered Musée du
　Louvre in 1959 in application of the
　peace treaty with Japan
　S. | p. 221

Edouard Manet
Portrait de Monsieur Brun, ca. 1879
*Porträt des Herrn Brun |
Portrait of Monsieur Brun*
　Öl auf Leinwand | oil on canvas,
　194,3 × 126 cm
　The National Museum of
　Western Art, Tokyo
　Ehemalige Sammlung Matsukata;
　Schenkung der Erben von Kōjirō
　Matsukata 1984 | Ex-Matsukata
　Collection; donated by the heirs
　of Kōjirō Matsukata in 1984
　S. | p. 220

Jean-François Millet
Spring (Daphnis and Chloë), 1865
Frühling (Daphnis und Chloë)
　Öl auf Leinwand | oil on canvas,
　235,5 × 134,5 cm
　The National Museum of
　Western Art, Tokyo
　Sammlung Matsukata |
　Matsukata Collection
　S. | p. 309

Jean-François Millet
Meules de foin
Heuhaufen | Haystacks
　Bleistift auf Papier | pencil on paper,
　40 × 60 cm
　The National Museum of
　Western Art, Tokyo
　Sammlung Matsukata |
　Matsukata Collection
　S. | p. 310

Claude Monet
La route de la ferme Saint-Siméon,
1861–1864
*Die Straße zum Hof Saint-Siméon |
Walk (Road of the Farm Saint-Siméon)*
　Öl auf Leinwand | oil on canvas,
　81,6 × 46,4 cm
　The National Museum of
　Western Art, Tokyo
　Sammlung Matsukata |
　Matsukata Collection
　S. | p. 275

Claude Monet
L'inondation, 1872/73
Die Überflutung | Flood at Argenteuil
　Öl auf Leinwand | oil on canvas,
　54,4 × 73,3 cm
　Artizon Museum, Ishibashi
　Foundation, Tokyo
　Ehemals Sammlung Matsukata |
　formerly Matsukata Collection
　S. | p. 276

Claude Monet
Neige à Argenteuil, 1875
*Schnee in Argenteuil |
Snow in Argenteuil*
　Öl auf Leinwand | oil on canvas,
　55,5 × 65 cm
　The National Museum of
　Western Art, Tokyo
　Sammlung Matsukata |
　Matsukata Collection
　S. | p. 277

Claude Monet
*Sur le bateau (Jeunes filles en
barque),* 1887
*Im Boot (Junge Mädchen in
Ruderboot) | On the Boat*
　Öl auf Leinwand | oil on canvas,
　145,5 × 133,5 cm
　The National Museum of
　Western Art, Tokyo
　Sammlung Matsukata |
　Matsukata Collection
　S. | p. 281

Claude Monet
Le portail, brouillard matinal, 1894
*Die Kathedrale von Rouen im Morgen-
nebel | The Portal (Morning Fog)*
　Öl auf Leinwand | oil on canvas,
　101 × 66 cm
　Museum Folkwang, Essen
　Erworben 1970 | acquired in 1970
　Gemälde derselben Serie ehemals
　in Sammlung Matsukata | Painting
　of the same series formerly in
　Matsukata Collection
　S. | p. 282

Claude Monet
Mer agitée à Pourville, 1897
*Stürmische See bei Pourville |
Heavy Sea at Pourville*
　Öl auf Leinwand | oil on canvas,
　73,5 × 101 cm
　The National Museum of
　Western Art, Tokyo
　Sammlung Matsukata |
　Matsukata Collection
　S. | p. 278

Claude Monet
Vétheuil, 1902
Blick auf Vétheuil | *View of Vétheuil*
 Öl auf Leinwand | oil on canvas,
 90 × 93 cm
 The National Museum of
 Western Art, Tokyo
 Sammlung Matsukata |
 Matsukata Collection
 S. | p. 279

Claude Monet
Le bassin aux nymphéas, ca. 1916
Der Seerosenteich |
The Water-Lily Pond
 Öl auf Leinwand | oil on canvas,
 131,2 × 201,3 cm
 Museum Folkwang, Essen
 Erworben 1965 | acquired in 1965
 S. | p. 283

Camille Pissarro
La conversation, ca. 1881
Die Unterhaltung | *The Conversation*
 Öl auf Leinwand | oil on canvas,
 65,3 × 54 cm
 The National Museum of
 Western Art, Tokyo
 Sammlung Matsukata |
 Matsukata Collection
 S. | p. 306

Camille Pissarro
La récolte, 1882
Die Ernte | *The Harvest*
 Tempera auf Leinwand | tempera
 on canvas, 70,3 × 126 cm
 The National Museum of
 Western Art, Tokyo
 Ehemalige Sammlung Matsukata;
 Schenkung der Erben von Kōjirō
 Matsukata 1984 | Ex-Matsukata
 Collection; donated by the heirs
 of Kōjirō Matsukata in 1984
 S. | p. 311

Camille Pissarro
*Les docks, Saint-Sever, Rouen,
fumées*, 1898
*Hafenanlagen, Saint-Sever, Rouen,
im Rauch* | *The Dockside Warehouses,
Saint-Sever, Rouen, Smoke*
 Öl auf Leinwand | oil on canvas,
 65 × 79 cm
 Sumitomo Mitsui Banking
 Corporation, Tokyo
 Ehemals Sammlung Matsukata |
 formerly Matsukata Collection
 S. | p. 198

Pierre-Auguste Renoir
Lise – La femme à l'ombrelle, 1867
Lise mit dem Sonnenschirm |
Lise with a Parasol
 Öl auf Leinwand | oil on canvas,
 184 × 115,5 cm
 Museum Folkwang, Essen
 S. | p. 209

Pierre-Auguste Renoir
*Parisiennes habillées en
Algériennes*, 1872
*Pariserinnen im algerischen Kostüm
(Der Harem)* | *Parisiennes in Algerian
Costume or Harem*
 Öl auf Leinwand | oil on canvas,
 156 × 128,8 cm
 The National Museum of
 Western Art, Tokyo
 Sammlung Matsukata |
 Matsukata Collection
 S. | p. 219

Pierre-Auguste Renoir
Bildnis Gertrud Osthaus, 1913
Portrait of Gertrud Osthaus
 Öl auf Leinwand | oil on canvas,
 55 × 46,5 cm
 Museum Folkwang, Essen
 S. | p. 202

Pierre-Auguste Renoir
La laveuse, 1916
Die Wäscherin | *Laundress*
 Bronze, 33,5 × 31 × 18,5 cm
 Museum Folkwang, Essen
 Erworben 1981 | acquired in 1981
 S. | p. 218

Auguste Rodin
Saint Jean Baptiste, 1880
(Guss | cast: 1944)
Johannes der Täufer | *Saint John
the Baptist Preaching*
 Bronze, 201 × 58 × 127 cm
 The National Museum of
 Western Art, Tokyo
 Ein weiteres Exemplar (Guss:
 spätestens 1921) ehemals in
 Sammlung Matsukata | another casting
 (cast: 1921 at the latest) formerly in
 Matsukata Collection
 S. | p. 239

Auguste Rodin
L'âge d'airain, ca. 1880 (Guss:
spätestens 1904 | cast: 1904 at the latest)
Das eherne Zeitalter |
The Age of Bronze
 Bronze, patiniert | patinated,
 180 × 72 × 52 cm
 Museum Folkwang, Essen
 Ein weiteres Exemplar (Guss: ca. 1919)
 in Sammlung Matsukata | another
 casting (cast: ca. 1919) in Matsukata
 Collection
 S. | p. 290

Auguste Rodin
Troisième maquette de *La porte de
l'enfer*, ca. 1881/82 (Guss: vor 1926 |
cast: before 1926)
Drittes Modell für *Das Höllentor* |
Third Architectural Model for
The Gates of Hell
 Gips, bemalt | plaster, painted,
 115 × 62 × 19 cm
 The National Museum of
 Western Art, Tokyo
 Sammlung Matsukata |
 Matsukata Collection
 S. | p. 228

Auguste Rodin
Ève, 1881 (Guss: spätestens 1904 |
cast: 1904 at the latest)
Eva | *Eve*
 Bronze, patiniert | patinated,
 174 × 38,5 × 64 cm
 Museum Folkwang, Essen
 Zwei weitere Exemplare (Guss:
 spätestens 1920 bzw. 1945) ehemals
 bzw. heute in Sammlung Matsukata |
 two other castings (cast: 1920 at
 the latest and 1945) formerly and
 currently in Matsukata Collection
 S. | p. 227

Auguste Rodin
Le penseur, 1881/82 (Guss:
spätestens 1919 | cast: 1919 at the latest)
Der Denker | *The Thinker*
 Bronze, 71,5 × 45 × 60 cm
 The National Museum of
 Western Art, Tokyo
 Sammlung Matsukata |
 Matsukata Collection
 S. | p. 229

Auguste Rodin
Cariatide tombée portant sa pierre,
ca. 1881/82 (Guss: spätestens 1919 |
cast: 1919 at the latest)
Karyatide mit dem Stein |
Fallen Caryatid Carrying Her Stone
 Bronze, 44 × 32 × 30 cm
 The National Museum of
 Western Art, Tokyo
 Sammlung Matsukata |
 Matsukata Collection
 S. | p. 233

Auguste Rodin
La femme accroupie, ca. 1882 (Guss:
spätestens 1913 | cast: 1913 at the latest)
Die Kauernde | *The Crouching Woman*
  Bronze, patiniert | patinated,
  84 × 61 × 54 cm
  Museum Folkwang, Essen
  Ein weiteres Exemplar (Guss:
  spätestens 1921) in Sammlung
  Matsukata | another casting (cast:
  1921 at the latest) in Matsukata
  Collection
  S. | p. 235

Auguste Rodin
Petite tête de damnée, 1885
Kleiner Kopf einer Verdammten
(Studie für *Das Höllentor*) |
Small Head of a Damned Woman
(Study for *The Gates of Hell*)
  Bronze, patiniert | patinated,
  9 × 9 × 5 cm
  Museum Folkwang, Essen
  Erworben 2009 | acquired in 2009
  S. | p. 230

Auguste Rodin
Je suis belle, ca. 1885 (Guss:
spätestens 1919 | cast: 1919 at the latest)
Ich bin schön | *I am Beautiful*
  Bronze, 70 × 32 × 33 cm
  The National Museum of
  Western Art, Tokyo
  Sammlung Matsukata |
  Matsukata Collection
  S. | p. 234

Auguste Rodin
Celle qui fut la belle heaulmière,
1885–1887 (Guss: spätestens 1919 |
cast: 1919 at the latest)
*Die einstmals schöne Helm-
schmiedin* | *Beautiful Heaulmière*
  Bronze, 50 × 31 × 24 cm
  The National Museum of
  Western Art, Tokyo
  Sammlung Matsukata |
  Matsukata Collection
  S. | p. 231

Auguste Rodin
Fugit Amor, vor | before 1887 (Guss:
spätestens 1919 | cast: 1919 at the latest)
Fliehende Liebe | *Fugitive Love*
  Bronze, 36 × 45 × 20 cm
  The National Museum of
  Western Art, Tokyo
  Sammlung Matsukata |
  Matsukata Collection
  S. | p. 236

Auguste Rodin
Le désespoir, vor | before 1890 (Guss:
spätestens 1937 | cast: 1937 at the latest)
Die Verzweiflung | *Despair*
  Bronze, 18 × 9 × 9 cm
  The National Museum of
  Western Art, Tokyo
  Sammlung Matsukata |
  Matsukata Collection
  S. | p. 232

Auguste Rodin
Méditation, nach | after 1900 (Guss:
spätestens 1921 | cast: 1921 at the latest)
Meditation
  Bronze, 155 × 72 × 65 cm
  The National Museum of
  Western Art, Tokyo
  Sammlung Matsukata |
  Matsukata Collection
  S. | p. 238

Auguste Rodin
Fauness debout (Guss: spätestens
1919 | cast: 1919 at the latest)
Stehende Faunin | *Standing Fauness*
  Bronze, 60 × 26 × 23 cm
  The National Museum of
  Western Art, Tokyo
  Sammlung Matsukata |
  Matsukata Collection
  S. | p. 237

Christian Rohlfs
Weiden, 1899
Willows
  Öl auf Leinwand | oil on canvas,
  58,7 × 75,5 cm
  Museum Folkwang, Essen
  Beschlagnahmt 1937, zurückgegeben
  frühestens 1938 | confiscated in 1937,
  returned in 1938 at the earliest
  S. | p. 212

Christian Rohlfs
Birkenwald, 1907
Birch Forest
  Öl auf Leinwand | oil on canvas,
  110 × 75 cm
  Museum Folkwang, Essen
  Beschlagnahmt 1937, wiedererworben 1958 mit Unterstützung der
  Stadt Essen | confiscated in 1937,
  reacquired in 1958 with the support
  of the City of Essen
  S. | p. 213

Dante Gabriel Rossetti
Risen at Dawn, 1877/78
Erwacht bei Morgengrauen
  Öl auf Leinwand | oil on canvas,
  108,4 × 53,1 cm
  The National Museum of
  Western Art, Tokyo
  Ehemalige Sammlung Matsukata;
  Schenkung der Erben von Katsumi
  Hachiya 2019 | Ex-Matsukata
  Collection; donated by the heirs
  of Mr Katsumi Hachiya in 2019
  S. | p. 217

Théo van Rysselberghe
Claire de lune à Boulogne-sur-Mer, 1900
*Mondnacht im Hafen von Boulogne-
sur-Mer* | *Moonlight in Boulogne-sur-Mer*
  Öl auf Leinwand | oil on canvas,
  65 × 80,6 cm
  Museum Folkwang, Essen
  S. | p. 303

Chiharu Shiota
I hope ..., 2021
  Installation: Seil, Papier, Stahl |
  installation: rope, paper, steel
  Courtesy of König Galerie, Berlin
  S. | p. 72/73

Soga Shōhaku
kakemono (Hängerolle | hanging scroll),
zweite Hälfte des 18. Jh. | second half
of the 18th century
  Tusche, Papier, Seide, Holz |
  ink, paper, silk, wood, 152 × 66,5 cm
  Museum Folkwang, Essen
  S. | p. 254

Paul Signac
Saint-Cloud, 1900
Die Seine bei Saint-Cloud |
The Seine near Saint-Cloud
  Öl auf Leinwand | oil on canvas,
  65 × 81,2 cm
  Museum Folkwang, Essen
  S. | p. 288

Paul Signac
Le port de Saint-Tropez, 1901/02
Der Hafen von St. Tropez |
The Port of Saint-Tropez
  Öl auf Leinwand | oil on canvas,
  131 × 161,5 cm
  The National Museum of
  Western Art, Tokyo
  Ehemals Museum Folkwang, Hagen |
  Essen | formerly Museum Folkwang,
  Hagen | Essen
  S. | p. 287

Paul Signac
Marseille, vieux port, 1907
Hafen von Marseille | Port of Marseille
Aquarell | watercolour, 29,6 × 43 cm
Museum Folkwang, Essen
Ohne Abb. | without ill.

Paul Signac
Segelschiffe bei Venedig, 1908
Sailing Boats near Venice
Aquarell | watercolour, 30,5 × 45,7 cm
Museum Folkwang, Essen
S. | p. 298 unten | bottom

Paul Signac
Venise. Quai à la Giudecca, 1908
Schiffe vor dem Canale Grande |
Venice, Quay
Aquarell | watercolour, 27,4 × 41,8 cm
Museum Folkwang, Essen
S. | p. 298 oben | top

Paul Signac
Kran an der Seine, 1910
Crane on the Seine
Aquarell | watercolour, 26,5 × 41 cm
Museum Folkwang, Essen
Ohne Abb. | without ill.

369

Paul Signac
Kathedrale von Albi, 1912
Albi Cathedral
Aquarell | watercolour, 46 × 59,8 cm
Museum Folkwang, Essen
Erworben zwischen 1914 und 1929
(vor 1922 für das Kunstmuseum
Essen, seit 1922 Museum Folkwang) |
acquired between 1914 and 1929
(before 1922 for the Kunstmuseum
Essen, since 1922 Museum Folkwang)
S. | p. 299

Paul Signac
Seinebrücke, 1912
Seine Bridge
Aquarell | watercolour, 22,7 × 30,7 cm
Museum Folkwang, Essen
S. | p. 297

Paul Signac
Le Pont des Arts, 1912/13
Der Pont des Arts | The Pont des Arts
Öl auf Leinwand | oil on canvas,
81 × 100,1 cm
Museum Folkwang, Essen
Erworben 1912 für das Kunstmuseum
Essen, seit 1922 Museum Folkwang |
acquired in 1912 for the Kunstmuseum
Essen, since 1922 Museum Folkwang
S. | p. 300

Paul Signac
La Tour Rose, Marseille, 1913
Hafen von Marseille | The Pink Tower,
Marseille
Öl auf Leinwand | oil on canvas,
72,9 × 91,8 cm
Museum Folkwang, Essen
Erworben 1912 für das Kunstmuseum
Essen, seit 1922 Museum Folkwang |
acquired in 1912 for the Kunstmuseum
Essen, since 1922 Museum Folkwang
S. | p. 301

Tabaimo
midnight sea, 2006
Videoinstallation | video installation,
Dauer | duration 4'00"
Courtesy of James Cohan Gallery,
New York, und | and Gallery Koyanagi,
Tokyo
S. | p. 262/263

Tabaimo
flower in the shadow, 2021
Einkanal-Videoinstallation |
one-channel video installation
Courtesy of James Cohan Gallery,
New York, und | and Gallery
Koyanagi, Tokyo
Ohne Abb. | without ill.

Hiroshige Utagawa
Mountains and Rivers Along the
Kisokaido Highway, 1857
Holzschnitt | woodblock print,
Triptychon, je | triptych,
each 38 × 25,5 cm
Tokyo National Museum
Ehemals Sammlung Matsukata |
formerly Matsukata Collection
Nicht in der Ausstellung |
not in the exhibition
S. | p. 258/259

Hiroshige Utagawa
One Hundred Thousand Tsubo
Plain at Susaki, Fukagawa
(Aus der Serie | from the series: *One*
Hundred Famous Views of Edo), 1857
Holzschnitt / woodblock print,
38 × 25,5 cm
Tokyo National Museum
Ehemals Sammlung Matsukata |
formerly Matsukata Collection
Nicht in der Ausstellung |
not in the exhibition
S. | p. 256

Henry van de Velde
Garten im Sommer (Wandgemälde
aus dem Esszimmer des Hauses
Wagemans, Antwerpen), ca. 1892
Garden in Summer (Wall painting from
the Dining Room of House Wagemans,
Antwerp)
Öl auf Leinwand | oil on canvas,
172 × 67,5 cm
Osthaus Museum, Hagen
S. | p. 211

Kanō Yōsen-in Korenobu
kakemono (Hängerolle | hanging scroll),
nach | after 1794
Seide, Papier, Holz, Elfenbein | silk,
paper, wood, ivory, 234,5 × 70,3 cm
Museum Folkwang, Essen
S. | p. 253

Nadine Engel ist seit 2018 Sammlungsleiterin für das 19. und 20. Jahrhundert am Museum Folkwang. Zusätzlich betreut sie den kunsthandwerklichen, archäologischen und ethnografischen Bestand. Nach dem Volontariat an der Neuen Sammlung und den Bayerischen Staatsgemäldesammlungen in München war sie von 2017 bis 2018 wissenschaftliche Mitarbeiterin an der dortigen Sammlung Moderne Kunst und co-kuratierte mit Oliver Kase die Ausstellung *Paul Klee. Konstruktion des Geheimnisses.* Am Museum Folkwang hat sie zuletzt die Reihe *Bauhaus am Folkwang* und eine Einzelausstellung der Keramikerin Young-Jae Lee organisiert.
Nadine Engel has been head of the 19th- and 20th-century collections since starting at the Museum Folkwang in 2018. She is also responsible for the museum's applied art, archaeological and ethnographic holdings. After a postdoctoral fellowship at the Neue Sammlung and the Bavarian State Painting Collections in Munich, between 2017 until 2018 she was an assistant curator at its Modern Art collection and co-curated the exhibition *Paul Klee: Construction of Mystery* with Oliver Kase. Most recently she has organized the *Bauhaus at Folkwang* series and a solo exhibition by the ceramicist Young-Jae Lee at the Museum Folkwang.

Frances Fowle hat den Lehrstuhl für die Kunst des 19. Jahrhunderts an der Universität von Edinburgh inne und ist Senior Curator für französische Kunst an den National Galleries of Scotland. Zu ihren Publikationen gehören: *Van Gogh's Twin. The Scottish Art Dealer Alexander Reid* (2010) und *Globalising Impressionism. Reception, Translation and Transnationalism* (2020). Sie hat unter anderem folgende Ausstellungen kuratiert: *Van Gogh and Britain. Pioneer Collectors* (2006), *Impressionism and Scotland* (2008), *Van Gogh to Kandinsky. Symbolist Landscape in Europe* (2012), *Inspiring Impressionism. Daubigny, Monet, Van Gogh* (2016) sowie *Toulouse-Lautrec and the Art of Celebrity* (2018).
Frances Fowle is chair of 19th-century Art at the University of Edinburgh and Senior Curator (French Art) at the National Galleries of Scotland. Her books include *Van Gogh's Twin: The Scottish Art Dealer Alexander Reid* (2010) and *Globalising Impressionism: Reception, Translation and Transnationalism* (2020). She has curated exhibitions such as *Van Gogh and Britain: Pioneer Collectors* (2006), *Impressionism and Scotland* (2008), *Van Gogh to Kandinsky: Symbolist Landscape in Europe* (2012), *Inspiring Impressionism: Daubigny, Monet, Van Gogh* (2016) and *Toulouse-Lautrec and the Art of Celebrity* (2018).

Peter Gorschlüter ist seit 2018 Direktor des Museum Folkwang. Nach mehrjähriger Tätigkeit als wissenschaftlicher Mitarbeiter und Kurator an der Kunsthalle Düsseldorf wirkte er von 2008 bis 2010 als Chefkurator an der Tate Liverpool und leitete dort die Abteilung Sammlung und Ausstellungen. Von 2010 bis 2018 war er stellvertretender Direktor am MMK Museum für Moderne Kunst Frankfurt am Main, wo er unter anderem Ausstellungen mit den Künstlerinnen Rineke Dijkstra, Jewyo Rhii, Fiona Tan, dem Modeschöpfer Kostas Murkudis sowie eine Retrospektive von Hélio Oiticica konzipierte.
Peter Gorschlüter has been the director of the Museum Folkwang since 2018. After working for several years as a research fellow and curator at the Kunsthalle Düsseldorf, between 2008 and 2010 he was chief curator at the Tate Liverpool, where he was head of exhibitions and displays. From 2010 until 2018 he was deputy director at the Museum für Moderne Kunst in Frankfurt, where he organized numerous exhibitions featuring the work of artists including Rineke Dijkstra, Jewyo Rhii, Fiona Tan, the fashion designer Kostas Murkudis and a retrospective of Hélio Oiticica.

Rebecca Herlemann ist als freie Mitarbeiterin für das Museum Folkwang tätig. Nach dem Studium der Kunstgeschichte an den Universitäten in Freiburg im Breisgau, Florenz und Leipzig arbeitete sie als Projektassistentin der Stiftung für Kunst und Kultur e. V. Bonn sowie drei Jahre lang als kuratorische Assistenz an der Schirn Kunsthalle in Frankfurt am Main. Dort war sie unter anderem an den Ausstellungen *Fantastische Frauen – Surreale Welten von Meret Oppenheim bis Frida Kahlo* und *Magnetic North – Mythos Kanada in der Malerei 1910–1940* beteiligt.
Junior curator **Rebecca Herlemann** is a freelancer with the Museum Folkwang. After studying Art History at universities in Freiburg im Breisgau, Florence and Leipzig she worked as a project assistant for the Stiftung für Kunst und Kultur, Bonn, and for three years as a curatorial assistant at the Schirn Kunsthalle in Frankfurt, where

she was involved with exhibitions including *Fantastic Women: Surreal Worlds from Meret Oppenheim to Frida Kahlo* and *Magnetic North: Imagining Canada in Painting 1910–1940*.

Megumi Jingaoka ist Kuratorin am National Museum of Western Art in Tokio. Ihr Spezialgebiet ist die französische Kunst der Moderne. In jüngster Zeit organisierte sie folgende Ausstellungen: *Bordeaux, Port de la Lune* (2015), *Théodore Chassériau. Parfum exotique* (2017) und *The Matsukata Collection. A One-Hundred-Year Odyssey* (2019). Zudem ist sie Mitverfasserin von *A History of Western Art 7: 19th Century, The Birth of Modern Art, From Romantic to Impressionism* (2017), und Mitherausgeberin von *The Matsukata Collection. Complete Catalogue of the European Art* (2 Bde., 2018/19). 2017 wurde sie zum Chevalier de l'Ordre des Arts et des Lettres ernannt.
Megumi Jingaoka is curator of the National Museum of Western Art in Tokyo. Specialist in Modern French Art, she organized the recent exhibitions, *Bordeaux, Port de la Lune* (2015), *Théodore Chassériau: Parfum exotique* (2017), and *The Matsukata Collection: A One-Hundred-Year Odyssey* (2019). She is co-author of *A History of Western Art 7: 19th Century, The Birth of Modern Art, From Romantic to Impressionism* (2017), and co-editor of *The Matsukata Collection: Complete Catalogue of the European Art* (2 vols, 2018–19). She was awarded the Chevalier de l'Ordre des Arts et des Lettres in 2017.

Michelle Latta hat die Entstehung der Ausstellung *Renoir, Monet, Gauguin – Bilder einer fließenden Welt* als Praktikantin am Museum Folkwang begleitet. Sie war bereits als Assistentin am Lehrstuhl für Neuere und Neueste Kunstgeschichte sowie als kunstwissenschaftliche Tutorin zum Thema *Geschichte und Zukunft des (Kunst-)Museums* an der Universität Duisburg-Essen tätig. Als wissenschaftliche Mitarbeiterin im Forschungsprojekt *diglcon. Digitale Bildkompetenz in der kunst- und bildwissenschaftlichen Lehre* beschäftigte sie sich mit Digitaler Kunstgeschichte. Nach ihren Praktika in Essen und im Kunstpalast Düsseldorf absolviert sie nun ihr Masterstudium der Kunstgeschichte in Berlin.
Michelle Latta helped to set up the exhibition *Renoir, Monet, Gauguin: Images of a Floating World* as an intern at the Museum Folkwang. Previously she had worked as an assistant at the department of New and Modern Art History and as a tutor of Art History specializing in *The History and Future of the (Art) Museum* at the University of Duisburg-Essen. As an academic contributor to the research project *diglcon: Digital Imaging Competence in the Theory of Art and Pictorial Science*, she has worked in digital Art History. After completing internships in Essen and at the Kunstpalast Düsseldorf she is now studying for a Masters in Art History in Berlin.

Maxime Georges Métraux arbeitet zur Zeit an seiner Dissertation zur Papillon-Dynastie und zum Holzstich. Zudem ist er als Experte für die Pariser Galerie Hubert Duchemin tätig und Gründungsmitglied des Forschungsnetzwerks Groupe de Recherche en Histoire de l'Art Moderne. Er lehrt an den Universitäten Gustave Eiffel und Paris I Panthéon-Sorbonne.
Maxime Georges Métraux is preparing a PhD thesis on the Papillon dynasty and wood engraving. He is also an expert for the Hubert Duchemin Gallery and a founding member of the Groupe de Recherche en Histoire de l'Art Moderne. He teaches at the universities of Gustave Eiffel and Paris 1 Panthéon-Sorbonne.

Die Schriftstellerin **Sayaka Murata** wurde 1979 in der Präfektur Chiba, Japan, geboren. Für ihre literarische Arbeit erhielt sie bereits mehrere Auszeichnungen. Ihr Roman *Die Ladenhüterin* gewann 2016 mit dem Akutagawa-Preis den renommiertesten Literaturpreis Japans und war in mehr als einem Dutzend Ländern ein großer Erfolg.
The author **Sayaka Murata** was born in 1979 in the prefecture of Chiba, Japan. She has already received several awards for her literary work. Her novel *Convenience Store Woman* won the 2016 Akutagawa Prize, Japan's most famous literary prize, and was a great success in over a dozen countries.

Léa Saint-Raymond schloss ihr Studium der Kunstgeschichte mit Promotion ab und dissertierte zum Thema der Einführung neuer Märkte bei den Pariser Auktionen (1830–1939), wofür sie 2019 mit dem Preis des Musée d'Orsay ausgezeichnet wurde. Nach Tätigkeiten als Gastwissenschaftlerin am Getty Research Institute und als Forschungsassistentin am Collège de France koordiniert sie das Observatory of Digital Humanities an der Ecole normale supérieure-PSI und das Studienprogramm zum Thema Kunstmarkt an der Ecole du Louvre in Paris. Ihr jüngster Essay, *Fragments d'une histoire globale de l'art*, erschien 2021 in den Editions Rue d'Ulm.
Léa Saint-Raymond holds a PhD in art history on the launch of new markets at Parisian auction sales (1830–1939) for which she was awarded the Musée d'Orsay prize in 2019. After having been a guest scholar at the Getty Research Institute and a research assistant at the Collège de France, she now coordinates the Observatory of Digital Humanities at the Ecole normale supérieure-PSL and the 'art market' programme at the Ecole du Louvre in Paris. Her new essay, *Fragments d'une histoire globale de l'art*, was published at the Editions Rue d'Ulm in 2021.

Shingo Shimada ist seit 2005 Professor für Modernes Japan mit sozialwissenschaftlichem Schwerpunkt an der Heinrich-Heine-Universität Düsseldorf; von 2002 bis 2005 lehrte er als Professor für Kulturvergleichende Soziologie an der Martin-Luther-Universität, Halle-Wittenberg. Seine Arbeitsschwerpunkte sind Theorien und Methoden des Kulturvergleichs, sozialer Wandel in der gegenwärtigen japanischen Gesellschaft und Kulturen des Alter(n)s.
Since 2005, **Shingo Shimada** has been Professor of Modern Japan at the Heinrich Heine University in Düsseldorf, with an emphasis on sociology; from 2002 until 2005 he taught as Professor of Comparative Cultural Sociology at Martin Luther University, Halle-Wittenberg. His work focuses on theories and methods of cultural comparison, social change in present-day Japanese society and cultures of age(ing).

Der Kunsthistoriker und Literaturwissenschaftler **Rainer Stamm** ist Direktor des Landesmuseums für Kunst und Kulturgeschichte Oldenburg. Er hat sich in zahlreichen Publikationen mit der Geschichte des Museum Folkwang auseinandergesetzt; seine Dissertation *Der Folkwang-Verlag. Auf dem Weg zu einem imaginären Museum* erschien 1999, 2002 gab er die gesammelten Reden und Schriften von Karl Ernst Osthaus heraus. 2022 erscheint die Biografie *Karl Ernst und Gertrud Osthaus. Die Gründer des Folkwang-Museums und ihre Welt* von Rainer Stamm und Gloria Köpnick im Verlag C.H. Beck, München.

Art historian and literary specialist, **Rainer Stamm** is director of the Oldenburg State Museum for Art and Cultural History. He has examined the history of the Museum Folkwang in numerous publications; his dissertation *Der Folkwang Verlag: Auf dem Weg zu einem imaginären Museum* was published in 1999, and in 2002 he published the collected speeches and writings of Karl Ernst Osthaus. His biography *Karl Ernst und Gertrud Osthaus: Die Gründer des Folkwang-Museums und ihre Welt* co-authored with Gloria Köpnick will be published by Verlag C.H. Beck, Munich in 2022.

Masayuki Tanaka ist Direktor des National Museum of Western Art in Tokio. 1987 schloss er sein Studium an der Universität von Tokyo ab. Nach weiteren Aufbaustudiengängen besuchte er von 1990 bis 1995 das Institute of Fine Arts der New York University. Von 1996 bis 2007 war er als Kurator am NMWA tätig und zwischen 2007 und 2021 war er Professor im Fachbereich Kunstgeschichte der Musashino Art University. Sein Spezialgebiet ist die Geschichte moderner und zeitgenössischer Kunst. Zu den von ihm kuratierten Ausstellungen am NMWA gehören *Picasso's World of Children* (2000), *Henri Matisse. Process / Variation* (2004) sowie *Munch. The Decorative Projects* (2007).

Masayuki Tanaka is director of the National Museum of Western Art in Tokyo. He graduated from the University of Tokyo in 1987. After completing further graduate studies, from 1990 to 1995 he attended the Institute of Fine Arts at New York University. He went on to work as curator at the NMWA from 1996 to 2007, and from 2007 to 2021 was professor of history of art at Musashino Art University. Specialized in the history of modern and contemporary art, exhibitions he has curated at the NMWA include *Picasso's World of Children* (2000), *Henri Matisse: Process / Variation* (2004), and *Munch: The Decorative Projects* (2007).

Detmar Westhoff ist Kunsthistoriker und Kurator. Nach Tätigkeiten für die Schirn Kunsthalle Frankfurt und die Kunstsammlung NRW konzentriert er sich seit 2006 auf die Vermittlung von Ausstellungen und Museumssammlungen (Kunsthaus Zürich, Städel Museum, Frankfurt am Main, Belvedere, Wien u. a.) zwischen Europa und Asien. Zu den von ihm initiierten und mitkuratierten Projekten zählen *Japans Liebe zum Impressionis-*

mus. Von Monet bis Renoir in der Bundeskunsthalle Bonn (2015/16) sowie *Die Wilden – der Expressionismus der Künstler von Brücke und der Blaue Reiter* im Museum de Fundatie in Zwolle.

Detmar Westhoff is an art historian and curator. After working for the Schirn Kunsthalle Frankfurt and the Kunstsammlung NRW in Düsseldorf, since 2006 he has worked on the mediation of exhibitions and museum collections (Kunsthaus Zürich, Städel Museum, Frankfurt, the Belvedere in Vienna and others) between Europe and Asia. Projects that he has initiated and co-curated include *Japan's Love of Impressionism: from Monet to Renoir* in the Bundeskunsthalle Bonn (2015/16) and *The Wild: Expressionism of 'Die Brücke' and 'Der Blaue Reiter'* at the Museum de Fundatie in Zwolle.

Robert Maximilian Woitschützke ist als Japan Foundation Fellow wissenschaftlicher Mitarbeiter am National Museum of Western Art in Tokio und *invited researcher* an der Tokyo University of Science. Er promovierte 2018 in Kunstgeschichte bei Anne-Marie Bonnet an der Universität Bonn zu Le Corbusiers *Museum of Knowledge*.

Robert Maximilian Woitschützke is research fellow at the National Museum of Western Art, Tokyo, and invited researcher at the Tokyo University of Science (Japan Foundation Fellowship). He holds a PhD in History of Art from Bonn University, 2018, with a thesis on Le Corbusier's *Museum of Knowledge*.

Yoshiyuki Yamana ist Professor für Architektur an der Tokyo University of Science. Er studierte an der Ecole Nationale Supérieure d'Architecture in Paris-Belleville und promovierte an der Universität Paris I Panthéon-Sorbonne. Yamana ist Dozent an verschiedenen Hochschulen in Frankreich, Präsident der DOCOMOMO Japan und kuratierte den japanischen Pavillon auf der Architekturbiennale Venedig 2016. Im Zuge seiner Bemühungen um die Eintragung des corbusierschen Werkes in den Katalog des Weltkulturerbes wurde er 2018 zum Chevalier de l'Ordre des Arts et des Lettres ernannt.

Yoshiyuki Yamana is Professor of Architecture at Tokyo University of Science. He studied at the Ecole Nationale Supérieure d'Architecture in Paris-Belleville and obtained his doctorate at the University of Paris I Panthéon-Sorbonne. Yamana is a lecturer at various universities in France, President of DOCOMOMO Japan and

curated the Japanese pavilion at the 2016 Venice Architecture Biennale. For his efforts to have the work of Corbusier entered in the UNESCO World Heritage List he was distinguished Chevalier de l'Ordre des Arts et des Lettres in 2018.

Marie Yasunaga ist Kunsthistorikerin mit dem Schwerpunkt auf interdisziplinären Kulturstudien und Museumsstudien. Nach ihrer Zeit als wissenschaftliche Mitarbeiterin am Getty Research Institute absolvierte sie ihre Promotion in Vergleichenden Literatur- und Kulturwissenschaften an der Universität Tokio zum Thema *Exhibiting the Un-Exhibitables. Art and Anthropology in the Asian Studies of Karl With*. Seit 2018 ist sie Mitglied des Forschungsprojekts *Freedom of the Streets; Gender and Urban Space in Europe and Asia* an der Amsterdam School of Historical Studies, wo sie zu visueller Geschichte und Digital Humanities forscht.

Marie Yasunaga is an art historian specialized in interdisciplinary cultural studies and museum studies. After being a research fellow at the Getty Research Institute, she obtained her PhD in comparative literature and culture at the University of Tokyo with her dissertation *Exhibiting the Un-Exhibitables: Art and Anthropology in the Asian Studies of Karl With*. Since 2018 she has been taking part in the research project *Freedom of the Streets: Gender and Urban Space in Europe and Asia* at the Amsterdam School of Historical Studies, where she works on visual history and digital humanities.

Impressum Imprint

Diese Publikation erscheint anlässlich
der Ausstellung

Renoir, Monet, Gauguin –
Bilder einer fließenden Welt.
Die Sammlungen von Kōjirō Matsukata
und Karl Ernst Osthaus

6. Februar – 15. Mai 2022
Museum Folkwang, Essen

This publication is released to
accompany the exhibition

Renoir, Monet, Gauguin:
Images of a Floating World.
The Collections of Kōjirō Matsukata
and Karl Ernst Osthaus

February 6 – May 15, 2022
Museum Folkwang, Essen

Unter der Schirmherrschaft von
Under the Patronage of
    Bundespräsident Frank-Walter Steinmeier

Eine Kooperation mit A Collaboration with

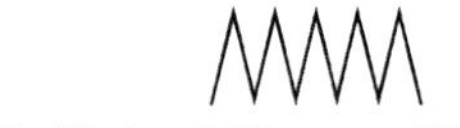
The National Museum of Western Art

Initiative und Vermittlung Initiative and Mediation
    Detmar Westhoff, Düsseldorf

Ausstellungsgestaltung und Szenografie
Exhibition Design and Scenography
    Antonia Gaida, Alicja Jelen, Clemens Müller,
    please don't touch GbR, Dortmund

Museum Folkwang
Museumsplatz 1
45128 Essen
Deutschland Germany
Tel + 49 201 88 45 000
Fax + 49 201 88 91 45 000
www.museum-folkwang.de

Ausstellung Exhibition

Direktor Director
    Peter Gorschlüter

Verwaltungsleiter Head of Museum Administration
    Thomas Grimm

Künstlerischer Koordinator und stellvertretender Direktor
Artistic Coordinator and Deputy Director
    Hans-Jürgen Lechtreck

Kuratorin Curator
    Nadine Engel

Kuratorische Assistenz Curatorial Assistance
    Rebecca Herlemann

Praktikantin Intern
    Michelle Latta

Restaurator:innen Conservators
    Marta Battista, Frederike Breder, Heike Koenitz,
    Peter Konarzewski, Céline Weyland, Silke Zeich

Registrarinnen Registrars
    Susanne Brüning, Lisa Rosche

Controlling und Buchhaltung Controlling and Accounting
    Deborah Herz, Fabian Klemt

Facility Management
    Stefan Hüller, Michael Peters, Christoph Weismüller

Produktionsmanager Production Manager
    Sandro di Sabatino

Museums- und Ausstellungstechnik
Museum and Exhibition Setup
    Reiner Baldau, Heiko Hönscher, Anatoli Marcin,
    Olaf Masuch, Klaus Schlüter, Susan Schmidt,
    Frank Sternberg, Susanne Vornweg-Bahrenberg,
    Till Wellner, Karin Weyers, Stephan Zmudzinski

Kommunikation und Marketing
Public Relations and Marketing
    Pia Beckmann, Yvonne Dänekamp, Anka Grosser,
    Sebastian Kapp

Datenbank und Webseite Database and Website
    Asja Kaspers

Bildung und Vermittlung Education and Information
    Peter Daners, Annika Schank

Forschung, Wissenschaftliche Kooperationen
und Provenienzforschung Research, Scientific
Cooperations, and Provenance Research
    Mathilde Heitmann-Taillefer

Besucherbüro Visitor's Office
    Stefanie Dixon, Petra Silberkuhl

Fotostudio Photo Studio
    Tanja Lamers, Jens Nober

Katalog Catalogue

Herausgeber Editor
    Museum Folkwang

Redaktion Editorial
    Nadine Engel, Rebecca Herlemann

Bildredaktion Photo editor
    Rebecca Herlemann

Projektmanagement Project management Hatje Cantz
    Richard Viktor Hagemann

Gestaltung Graphic design
    Martha Stutteregger, Wien

Lektorat Copyediting
    Annette Siegel (Deutsch German),
    Hannah Young (Englisch English)

Übersetzungen Translations
    Steven Lindberg, Shaun Whiteside (Deutsch-Englisch
    German-English), Alexandra Titze-Grabec
    (Englisch-Deutsch English-German), Sabine Mangold,
    Nanae Suzuki (Japanisch-Deutsch Japanese-German),
    Matt Treyvaud (Japanisch-Englisch Japanese-English)

Lithografie Lithography
    Longo AG, Bozen/Bolzano

Druckerei Printing Press
    Westermann Druck Zwickau GmbH

Papier Paper
    Magno Volume, 150 g/m2

Schrifttypen Fonts
    Basetica, Ogg

© 2022 Hatje Cantz Verlag, Berlin,
Museum Folkwang, Essen, und Autor:innen and authors

Erschienen im Published by
Hatje Cantz Verlag GmbH
Mommsenstraße 27
10629 Berlin
www.hatjecantz.de

Ein Unternehmen der Ganske Verlagsgruppe
A Ganske Publishing Group Company

ISBN: 978-3-7757-5127-8

Printed in Germany

Umschlagabbildung Cover illustration
Claude Monet, *Sur le bateau (Jeunes filles en barque)*, 1887,
The National Museum of Western Art, Tokyo

Bibliografische Information der Deutschen Nationalbibliothek
Die Deutsche Nationalbibliothek verzeichnet diese
Publikation in der Deutschen Nationalbibliografie;
detaillierte bibliografische Daten sind im Internet über
http://dnb.dnb.de abrufbar.
Bibliographic information published by the Deutsche
Nationalbibliothek
The Deutsche Nationalbibliothek lists this publication
in the Deutsche Nationalbibliografie; detailed bibliographic
data are available online at http://dnb.d-nb.de.

Im Anschluss an die Ausstellung im Museum Folkwang
setzt das National Museum of Western Art die Gegenüberstellung der Sammlungen Osthaus und Matsukata
mit einer Ausstellung zum Dialog zwischen Mensch
und Natur in Tokio fort, 4. Juni – 11. September 2022.
Following the exhibition at the Museum Folkwang,
the National Museum of Western Art will continue the
juxtaposition of the Osthaus and Matsukata collections
with an exhibition on the dialogue between People
and Nature in Tokyo, June 4 – September 11, 2022.

Hauptförderer Main Supporter

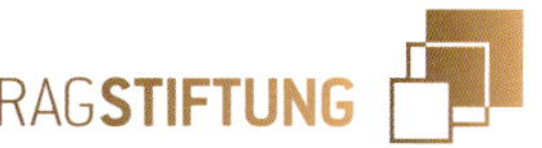

Hauptsponsoren Main Sponsors

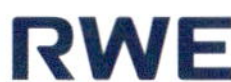 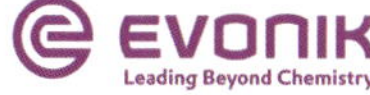

Förderer Supporter

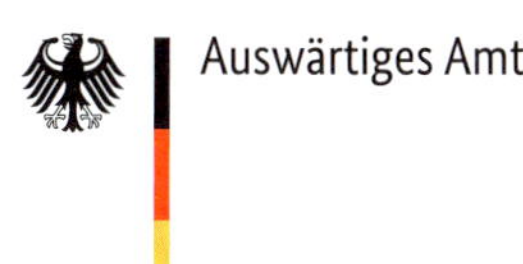

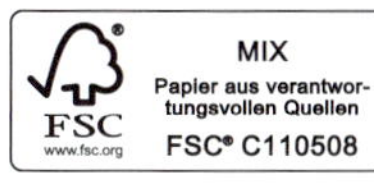